PSYCHOLOGY

The
Human
Science

Robert J. Trotter

James V. McConnell

HOLT, RINEHART AND WINSTON
New York Chicago San Francisco
Dallas Montreal Toronto London Sydney

PSYCHOLOGY

The Human Science

To my parents, with love.
R.J.T.

Developmental Editor Johnna Barto
Design Supervisor Robert Kopelman
Senior Project Editor Kathleen Nevils
Production Manager Annette Wentz

Library of Congress Cataloging in Publication Data
Trotter, Robert J.
      Psychology.
      Includes bibliographical references and index.
      1. Psychology.   I. McConnell, James V., joint
author.   II. Title.   [DNLM: 1. Psychology.   BF121
T858p]
BF121.T74   150   77-19200
ISBN 0-03-017401-5
Copyright © 1978 by Holt, Rinehart and Winston
All rights reserved
Printed in the United States of America
2 3 4   032   9 8 7 6 5 4

About the Authors

Born in 1943 in St. Louis, Robert J. Trotter attended St. Louis University and chose a career as a journalist specializing in science writing. Serving six years as Senior Editor/Behavioral Sciences Editor of *Science News,* Mr. Trotter contributed numerous articles to that magazine. He is currently Editor of *Science News.* With Boyd McCandless, Mr. Trotter is co-author of *Children: Behavior and Development* (Third Edition), published by Holt, Rinehart and Winston in 1977. Citing Mr. Trotter for honorable mention in its media awards, The American Psychological Association said of him, "Through your writing you have made a worthy contribution toward increasing the American public's knowledge and understanding of psychology."

James V. McConnell was born in Oklahoma, reared in Louisiana, and took his Ph.D. degree in psychology from The University of Texas in 1956. Accepting a position as instructor at The University of Michigan in 1956, he became professor of psychology in 1963 and has taught at Michigan ever since. In 1959 he founded the *Worm Runner's Digest,* an international scientific humor magazine. In 1964 he founded the *Journal of Biological Psychology* which, like the *Digest,* he still edits and publishes. Best-known for his early experiments on the biochemistry of memory, Dr. McConnell has in recent years been involved in the field of behavior modification. A consultant to many large industrial firms, he is also presently director of research at the Institute for Behavior Change, a private clinic in Ann Arbor, Michigan. Dr. McConnell has edited several books, published more than 100 articles, and is the author of *Understanding Human Behavior* (Second Edition), an introductory psychology text published by Holt, Rinehart and Winston. In 1976 he received the Distinguished Teaching Award from the American Psychological Foundation. The citation for this award describes him as "A distinguished scientist who loves to teach, an outstanding teacher who loves sciences, a scholar who learns with his students."

PREFACE

Comic strips, adventure books, mystery stories, science fiction, poems, plays, short stories, novels—reading has long been one of my favorite pastimes. It seems that as soon as I could, I started to read almost anything I could get my hands on. About the only things I didn't like to read were textbooks. As a student, I found most texts to be dull, boring, and even ugly. Therefore, in 1973, when I was asked if I would like to get involved in writing a textbook on psychology, my first thought was that I would do so only if I could work on a book that students would find interesting and enjoyable as well as informative. With that as a goal, work began on this book.

Five years and the efforts of numerous individuals have been devoted to achieving that goal and have resulted in the publication of *Psychology: The Human Science.* We all hope that the original goal (as well as many other objectives) have been met. The students and teachers who use this book will have to judge our success or failure, but I would like to explain some of the steps we took in attempting to achieve our goal.

First things first. This book was conceived in the mind of Ralph Protsik. It was Ralph who asked if I would be interested in writing or collaborating on a psychology text. The answer was "yes," but because I am a science writer, not a psychologist, it seemed only natural that I should work with a real psychologist. Again Ralph was instrumental. He arranged for James V. McConnell of The University of Michigan to join our team. The choice was excellent. Not only is Jim a well-known researcher and psychology teacher (for which he has since been recognized by the American Psychological Association), he was just completing work on the first edition of his own psychology textbook *Understanding Human Behavior.* This and his previous experience made him the perfect partner for someone like myself who had no experience with textbook writing and, as I said, no love for most such books.

Our first task was to decide on and define our intended audience. We agreed that the book would be directed at first- or second-year college and junior-college students who may or may not take another psychology course (though we all hoped that the book might be successful in encouraging students to continue their studies in psychology). With an audience in mind, it was Jim's task to come up with an organizational plan and an outline for the book. We eventually agreed on what we believe to be a most logical and straightforward organization. The five major units of the book deal with the body, the mind, personality, abnormal psychology (and therapy), and the social aspects of human behavior. An introductory chapter introduces the student to psychology and defines twentieth-century psychology. A concluding chapter looks forward to the future of psychology. These basic units are fleshed out in 17 chapters containing material intended to give readers an overview and understanding of the field of psychology, insights into how psychologists and social scientists go about their business, and indications of how psychology's data can be applied to everyday life.

With the audience and basic content pretty much agreed upon, we had to figure out how to package and deliver our material. At this point my personal interests came into play. Our original goal was to produce a book that was interesting, enjoyable, and informative, and some of the most interesting things I have ever read come under the heading of "literature." Not only is good literature interesting, I have often found it to be a valuable and valid description of human behavior and the human condition.

This being the case (at least in my mind), what better way to interest readers and capture their attention than with literary leads for each chapter. This we have done. Each literary episode points out some aspect of human behavior that is discussed in the chapter.

Once the first few chapters were written, we enlarged our team. Jim enlisted the aid of Bill Moy and his students at Washtenaw Community College near Ann Arbor. Jim asked them to help us by reading the chapters and making detailed comments on what they liked and didn't like, what they understood and didn't understand, what they found interesting and boring, and what they found useful and meaningless. At the same time, Jim was testing some of his ideas on students at The University of Michigan.

The comments from the students were interesting, useful, and sometimes funny—but not always easy to take. Some of the students seemed not to understand what we were trying to do. The fault, of course, was ours, not theirs. After rewrites and revisions, we tried again and finally got to a stage where most of the students not only understood where the book was going, some of them were actually interested enough to want to read more.

The final responses from the student reviewers were encouraging. Some of our goals had apparently been met. The proposed audience was interested in and perhaps even enjoying our work. We were getting the style and the reading level where we and the audience wanted them, but we still had to worry about content and accuracy. These were problems that could not have been solved without Jim McConnell. His comments and directions were heeded not only in the first but in the second, third, and following drafts of the manuscript. Fortunately, Jim McConnell is one of the most competent, industrious, and pleasant people I have ever had the pleasure of working with. If he hadn't been, revising, especially after the second time, could have been a miserable and boring job. Instead, because of Jim, my job was not only fulfilling and enjoyable, it was a learning experience throughout.

Students, as the audience, had to be consulted, but we realized that teachers also had to be considered. The third draft of the manuscript was sent to a score of reviewers across the country. Many of their comments and suggestions were incorporated into the fourth draft, and a dozen or more psychology teachers were asked for comments for the final version of the text.

At last we were getting close to a final manuscript, but we still had a long way to go. A textbook has to do more than tell the story of psychology. It has to be a teaching device. In an attempt to turn our book into a valuable teaching tool, several features (some of them unique) were added.

For one thing, there was the vocabulary we used. Teachers and writers tend to know and love words; students don't always have the word-knowledge that teachers expect of them. Yet students are eager to learn, if one takes the time to teach them in a rewarding manner. So we put vocabulary items in bold face in the text and gathered them together at the start of each chapter to alert the students to what words and terms they should master before beginning to read that chapter. (Putting vocabulary items in a glossary at the end of the book doesn't always help, since most students find it difficult to look up a word when they are engrossed in reading, and a few students never discover that the glossary "is there" until it's too late to do them much good.) Combined with the chapter overview, the glossary makes an excellent learning tool.

Psychology is a vital, living science that exists as much in the public press as it does in texts and journals. For some years—before becoming editor—I wrote most of the psychology items for *Science News*. I have added one such news story to each chapter of this book, both to bring it to the cutting edge of the field, and to give the students the flavor of an ongoing and exciting science.

Most introductory psychology texts have student guidebooks that are published separately for those individuals who need a bit more structure and regimentation than the text itself provides. We decided that it might be a good idea to combine the text with the study guide so that all students would benefit. Thus you will find a set of practice test items at the end of each chapter. We believe that the students who conscientiously attempt to answer all the questions will learn a great deal more about psychology than do those students who don't take the time to "cement" their learning as soon as they have finished a given chapter.

From the time of Ebbinghaus we've known that people tend to remember best what they like most. We know as well that students are frequently turned on (that is, motivated to learn) when the book they read is filled with exciting or dramatic pictures and illustrations. You'll find many such motivators in this book. But you'll find graphs and charts as well that will help lay out the material in easily memorable form.

So, there you are. We have written a book about psychology in which we use psychological technology (to the best of our ability) to enhance learning and comprehension. We hope you will like the book. More than this, we hope you will let us know your likes and dislikes, so that we too may learn how better to meet your needs in future editions.

Washington, D.C.   Robert J. Trotter
December 1977

ACKNOWLEDGMENTS

Although the authors of a book usually consider it "their baby," in fact there are always many other people involved both in the conception and in the delivery of the infant. Without these seminal donors and midwives, the whole project would surely be stillborn.

We acknowledge, first of all, Ralph Protsik, who thought up the idea and brought the two authors together. If the final product is close to his heart's desire, we are very pleased indeed. We thank Deborah Doty, our original acquisitions editor, at Holt, Rinehart and Winston. And most of all, we bless Johnna Barto who suffered through the birthing process with us, urging us on, supporting us psychologically, and correcting our mistakes, and who gave us the confidence necessary to finish. Johnna is a pearl without price.

We thank Robert D. Trotter for his superlative original art work, Esther Gilgoff for her help in the preparation of the manuscript, Jim Stacy for proofreading, and Margit Friedrich for preparing the index.

We thank Bill Moy for letting us try out the early drafts of the manuscript on his introductory students at Washtenaw Community College. We thank as well his students for their insights, comments, criticisms, and suggestions.

Many of our colleagues were kind enough to read and criticize the manuscript. We thank them all, including

Joyce Allen, Alan Berkey, Cecil Cheek, Betty Conover, David Feinberg, Bess Fleckman, Franz A. Fredenburgh, Edward J. Gunderson, Ilona Henderson, Sidney Hochman, Robert Hoeppner, James Howell, William L. Jackson, Edward E. Kennedy, Georgia Witkin Lanoil, Glen Mapes, Eydie McCrary, Carston S. McKay, Henry Paar, Dan G. Perkins, John C. Reibsamen, Vinita M. Ricks, Martin A. Schulman, Max Sheanin, Jane Y. Stormer, George M. Strong, Jeffrey S. Turner, Charles G. Verschoor, Alice W. Wilson, and Michael Wertheimer.

We wish to acknowledge the considerable assistance of Joshua R. Gerow of Indiana University—Purdue University at Fort Wayne who prepared the study guide material that appears at the end of each chapter. We thank as well the many people at Holt, Rinehart and Winston who aided in the production of the book, including

James Mirrielees, General Manager; Harry McQuillen, Editor-in-Chief; David P. Boynton, Publisher; Roger L. Williams, Associate Publisher and Psychology Editor; Jeanette Ninas Johnson, Managing Editor; Patrick Powers, Marketing Manager; Johnna Barto, Developmental Editor; Annette Wentz, Production Manager; Robert Kopelman, Design Supervisor; Kathleen Nevils, Senior Project Editor; Robin Moses, Project Assistant; and Norma Scheck, Nancy Wildermuth, and Roseanne Jensen, Secretaries.

Last, but surely not least, we wish to thank all the psychologists, past and present, whose research studies and field observations, whose theories and insights, have made psychology such an interesting science to write about. Without their work, there would be no science, and no book at all.

Robert J. Trotter
James V. McConnell

CONTENTS

INTRODUCTION

UNIT ONE: BIOLOGY AND BEHAVIOR

UNIT FIVE: SOCIAL PSYCHOLOGY

CONCLUSION

APPENDIX *581*

Statistics *582*

PSYCHOLOGY

The
Human
Science

INTRODUCTION

Helen of Troy, a character in *The Iliad*.

Humans have always been fascinated by the complexity of their own behavior, and for centuries people have been asking questions about human nature. Today, many of the answers come from the study of psychology. By examining how questions about human behavior were answered in the past and by looking at what psychologists do today it is possible to gain a better understanding of ourselves and of psychology, the human science.

What Is Psychology?

chapter 1

When you have completed your study of this chapter, you should be able to:

► Define psychology and provide reasons why we study it
► Trace the development of psychology as a science
► Compare and contrast the basic ideas of functionalism and structuralism
► List and describe the five steps of the scientific method
► Describe the basic features of behaviorism, Gestalt psychology, psychoanalysis, and cognitive psychology
► Explain how to do an experiment, referring to independent, dependent, and intervening variables

Anatomy (ann-ATT-oh-mee). From the Greek word meaning "to dissect or cut apart." The scientific study of the structure of living tissue, usually made by cutting the tissue apart. The word also means "structure of anything."

Aptitude test (APP-ta-tude). From the Latin word *aptus*, meaning "readiness to learn." If you have an aptitude for something, you have the natural tendency to learn or perform that thing readily. An aptitude test thus measures ability to learn a given task or skill.

Assumption (a-SUM-shun). If you assume that something is true, you are taking it for granted, even if you don't have proof that the thing is true. Thus, an assumption is a guess or belief about something.

Attribute (ATT-tra-bute). From the Latin word meaning "to give." If you assume that most college students are brighter than average, then intelligence is an "attribute" that you have given to or perceive in college students.

Behaviorism. A branch or school of psychology founded in the early 1900s by John B. Watson. Behaviorists believe that it is impossible to study the mind directly, since you cannot see or measure the workings of the mind. But you can see and measure a person's behavior directly.

Blind experiment. A method of controlling for people's expectations by not telling the subjects of an experiment what the experiment is all about, or what type of treatment the subjects are really receiving. In other words, the subjects would be "blind" to which treatment they received in the experiment.

Cognitive (COG-nuh-tiv). From the Latin word meaning "to know." In psychology, the word means "of the mind," or "having to do with intellectual or mental processes."

Conditioning (kon-DISH-un-ning). When an organism is trained to give a particular response to a specific stimulus, we say that it has been conditioned to respond to that stimulus.

Consciousness (KON-shuss-nuss). The act or process of being aware, particularly of one's surroundings and bodily condition. Being alert, understanding what is happening.

Control group. In an experiment, the subjects receiving no treatment act as a "control" whose performance is measured against that of the "experimental group subjects" who receive treatment.

Dependent variable. The response of the subjects to the experimental conditions.

Double-blind experiment. An experiment in which neither the subjects nor the scientists are told what the experiment is all about, or which group of patients is being given which treatment.

Eclectic (ek-KLEK-tick). From the Greek word meaning "to pick out." In science, to be eclectic means to pick or choose what seems best from various scientific viewpoints.

Empiricism (em-PEER-uh-sizz-um). From the Greek word meaning "to experience" or "to experiment." Empiricism is the pursuit of knowledge by observation and experience.

Ethics (ETH-icks). From the Greek word meaning "custom or character." Ethics relates to moral actions or motives.

Experimental group. That group of subjects on which a scientist "experiments." That group of subjects which receives the "experimental treatment," such as a new drug that might cure headaches.

Experimenter bias. The subjects in an experiment are often biased in favor of doing what is expected of them. Subjects are also very sensitive to the behavior of the experimenter. Thus, in some experiments, the scientists might unconsciously prejudice or "bias" the results by behaving differently toward the subjects given the "real drug" than toward the subjects given the sugar pill.

Functionalism. A school of psychology founded by William James. Functionalists believed it was possible to understand human behavior by considering the on-going processes of the mind and body.

Gestalt (guess-TALT). A German word that literally means "good form" or "good figure." Also means the tendency to see things as "wholes" rather than as jumbled bits and pieces.

Hypothesis (high-POTH-uh-sis). From the Greek word meaning "to put under." An hypothesis is an assumption one makes in order to explain something. A tentative explanation or hunch not yet supported by data.

Independent variable. Those aspects of an experiment under the control of the experimenter.

Instinct. Inherited desire, goal, or behavior pattern.

Intelligence test. Also called IQ test. A test that presumably measures a person's ability to reason, to problem-solve, or to survive in a given environment.

Intervening variable (in-turr-VEE-ning). The assumptions that scientists often make to explain why their experiments turned out as they did.

Introspection (inn-troh-SPECK-shun). The act of looking within one's mind to see what is happening.

Mores (MOR-ays). From the Latin word meaning "customs" or "conventional behaviors."

Motivation. From the Latin word meaning "to move." Whatever motivates you typically "moves you to act or respond" in a particular way. When you get hungry, you are motivated to seek food.

Mythology (mith-OLL-a-gee). From the Greek word meaning "fable" or "folk tale." A mythology is a collection of myths or ancient stories or beliefs.

Organism (ORR-gan-ism). Literally, a collection of organs, More practically, an organism is any individual life-form.

Perception (purr-SEPT-shun). The process of matching sensations with images. "To perceive" usually means "to recognize" or "to be aware of."

Physiology (fizz-ee-OLL-a-gee). From the Greek words meaning "the study of nature." Today, physiology means the scientific study of bodily processes.

Psychoanalysis (SIGH-ko-an-AL-uh-sis). A theory of personality involving psychosexual development and a form of psychotherapy developed by Sigmund Freud.

Psychology. From the Greek word meaning "soul" or "mind." The scientific study of human activities, mental and behavioral.

Sample. All the people in the U.S. make up the "total population" of this country. If you randomly selected 2000 of these people to interview, you would have selected a small "sample" of the total population.

Scientific method. Combination of theorizing and testing of the theory; practiced by both scientists and people in everyday life.

Sensation. Any information input message coming from a sensory receptor, such as the eye, the ear, the tongue, the nose, or the skin.

Stimuli (STIM-you-lie). Incoming sensory messages that cause either a mental or physical reaction. The singular is "stimulus," the plural is "stimuli."

Structuralism. A school of psychology founded by Wilhelm Wundt that looked inward to one's own experiences to discover the simplest structures of the mind.

Symptom (SIMP-tum). The visible evidence of a disease or disturbance. Headache, running nose, and sore throat are often symptoms of a cold.

Trait. A distinguishing quality of character or particular mental ability or skill; anything characteristic of a given individual or group of individuals.

Validity (va-LID-a-tee). A psychological test is valid if it really measured what it is supposed to measure.

INTRODUCTION: THE ILIAD

The war began when Helen, a queen of Greece, left her husband and ran off with a young man named Paris. The lovers fled across the sea to Troy, a walled city on the coast of Asia Minor (now Turkey), but they did not live happily ever after. Helen's husband reacted quickly. He called together the armies of Greece and set sail for Troy, determined to bring his wife home. The Trojans, unwilling to give Helen back, called out their soldiers, and for ten years the mighty armies clashed on the plains of Troy.

The Trojan war took place more than 3000 years ago, but it remains one of the most well-known events in the history of western civilization. It was described by the Greek poet Homer in *The Iliad* twenty-five centuries ago. Since then, *The Iliad* has been read and reread by countless generations of students and scholars. Homer's poem has retained its popularity because it faithfully describes human nature in all of its mysterious complexity.

Life and death, love and hate, joy and sorrow, bravery and cowardice, war and peace — these are matters that concern us all. They are also the subject matter of *The Iliad* and of much of the world's greatest literature. Whenever a piece of literature accurately describes human thoughts, feelings, and behaviors, that piece of literature becomes valuable as a tool for learning about ourselves as well as about others. Good literature, in other words, offers us a reliable picture of the world and allows us to sit back and watch the people of that world. And watching people, whether fictional or real, is one of the most important methods we have of learning about people.

PSYCHOLOGY AS PEOPLE-WATCHING

From time to time, we all enjoy watching the people around us. But there is more to people-watching than merely observing the actions of others. Part of the time, you may wish to lean back and watch yourself — that is, look at your own actions, your own feelings, your own mental and emotional experiences. You may then compare yourself to others, or even wonder if the person sitting next to you is having the same sort of inner experience that you are having.

Although these two different types of people-watching may seem much the same to you at first glance, there is a very important difference between the two. When you look at someone else, all you can see is the other person's actions. You may occasionally believe that you can "read somebody's mind," but in

People-watching is a universal pastime. We all enjoy observing, in an informal way, the people around us. We try to understand why people behave as they do and try to guess what they will do next.

fact, you cannot do so directly because other people's thoughts and feelings are invisible to you. You *can,* however, look directly at your own mental activities — but these inner experiences of yours are so intensely private that you are the only individual who can witness directly what goes on inside your mind.

After giving close attention to your own mental processes, and after you have studied the actions of other individuals as well, you may *assume* that the people you have watched experience the world and themselves much as you do. But this is an **assumption** you have made, and it is a most difficult thing indeed to prove.

Similarly, another person may observe your actions and reactions, and then assume that you must have the same sort of inner experiences that almost everyone else has. But again, does anyone else *really* know what goes on inside your head?

Inside-out, or Outside-in?

This, then, is the first problem you must face when studying psychology — or when doing serious people-watching. Do you want to understand why you think and feel as you do? If so, you may end up defining psychology in purely subjective, almost mystical terms, since you will be dealing with inner events that only you can be sure of. Furthermore, you will soon discover that much of what goes on inside your mind is strongly influenced by the people around you, past and present. Therefore, you will probably develop a psychology that goes from the inside out — from your own subjective experiences to the actions of others.

If you are more interested in others than in yourself, you might begin by making a list or catalogue of all the things that one other person did during a brief period of time. But when you then tried to explain *why* the individual acted as he or she did, you might end up making assumptions about what went on inside

One way to make people-watching a more exact science is the objective, or outside-in, approach. Photographers provide objective evidence of human behavior.

that person's mind. In this case, your psychology or people-watching would be from the outside in.

As we will soon see, people-watchers have for centuries been arguing about which type of activity to engage in—looking at individuals from the outside in, or from the inside out.

The subjective, inside-out approach is often a warmly satisfying technique that can tell you a lot about yourself but precious little about others (and hence very little about how you got to be the way you are).

The objective, outside-in approach is a much more scientific way of dealing with people, for it focuses on their actions first, and then makes guesses about their inner experiences. And actions can readily be measured (that's often what we mean when we use the term *objective*). But the outside-in sort of people-watching often leaves us feeling cold and dissatisfied, as if we've somehow missed the real essence of being human.

Should our people-watching be objective or subjective? Warm or cold? Outside-in, or inside-out? Do we want to understand ourselves? Or is our goal that of explaining and predicting the actions and reactions of others?

It was not until the twentieth century that we were able to state these questions precisely, and thus it was not until fairly recently that the casual art of people-watching turned into psychology, the human science. To understand why it took so long for this change to occur, we must go back many hundreds of years to see how people viewed themselves (and others) in those days.

EARLY APPROACHES

The Gods

To explain the whys and wherefores of human existence, people-watchers in many ancient civilizations invented gods and goddesses. These supernatural beings were said to be responsible for many otherwise unexplainable human actions. Because the sun, the moon, the planets, and the stars moved about the skies with what appeared to be a mysterious power of their own, these heavenly objects were often worshipped as gods and goddesses. The movements of the heavenly bodies were carefully charted, and complicated systems of **astrology** were developed and used to explain how the heavens influenced the course of human affairs.

For every unexplained human thought or action, some mysterious and powerful force—in heaven or in hell—was often blamed. By Homer's time there were gods of love, war, fertility, and even of drunkenness. A great many human thoughts and actions are described in *The Iliad,* but in almost every case the behavior is said to have been caused by one or more of the gods. It was a goddess who told Paris to steal Helen away from her husband. It was the gods who gave the soldiers their courage and helped them fight their battles.

As civilizations became more **sophisticated,** human activities became more complex. Cities, nations, and empires grew up and sometimes vanished. People went to school, they worked, they wrote poetry and sang songs. More and more gods were used to explain all of these behaviors. **Mythology**—the collected stories of a people and their gods—became increasingly complicated. As the heavens became more crowded with the mythical gods that people used to explain their own behavior, some individuals began to realize that they were not really answering questions about human behavior. You can blame a good act or a bad act on the heavens or on the gods, but in doing so you have not really *explained* the act itself. To say that the gods made you fall in love does not tell you very much about the process of love, why the gods wanted you to fall in love; what biological or psychological changes occurred inside you, much less what mechanisms the gods employed to cause these changes. Better answers had to be found if people were to understand their own behavior.

The Greeks

Aristotle, the Greek philospher, was interested in the causes of human behavior. He knew the stories of the ancient gods and goddesses, but he understood that these tales were only myths. The gods were not real, and their actions could not really explain human behaviors such as thinking and loving. There must be, Aristotle decided, something inside each person that does the thinking, makes the decisions, produces emotions, and controls behavior. Something inside each person, rather than a god of love, for instance, might explain why and how people fall in love. This unseen, internal thing Aristotle called the *soul*.

It is from Aristotle's concept of the soul—and from mythology—that psychology takes its name and its original definition. According to classical mythology, Psyche was a beautiful young woman who fell in love with Cupid, the god of love. Unfortunately, Cupid's mother Venus, the goddess of love, did not like Psyche and did not think that her immortal son should marry a mere human. Venus separated the lovers and kept them separated by imposing numerous hardships on Psyche. But Psyche's love was strong, and her determination to get back to Cupid impressed the other gods and goddesses. According to the myth, these gods decided to help Psyche perform her tasks, and eventually Cupid persuaded the king of the gods to turn Psyche into a goddess and make her immortal too. Cupid's pleading did the trick, and the lovers were reunited for eternity.

Psyche and Cupid's story was the classical description of true love. And to the Greeks, true love was the highest achievement of the human soul. Psyche, therefore, became the symbol of the human soul. The original definition given by Aristotle was that **psychology** is *the study of Psyche, or the study of the human soul.*

Down through the Ages

Aristotle's definition of psychology as "the study of the soul" was useful for many centuries, but eventually it failed to satisfy people because the definition really did little more than put the ancient gods and goddesses inside the human body. The soul was still invisible, still untouchable; all one could do was to make educated guesses about the soul's actions and **attributes.** So, during the Middle Ages, the philosophers would sit around and speculate on, or make guesses about, the nature of the soul.

The philosophers were the forefathers of all the modern sciences, including psychology. They would argue their opinions and beliefs and would attempt to explain how the soul influenced human behavior. The philosophers, however, could not really prove anything they said because, after centuries of arguing and searching, they had still failed to find the soul. Aristotle believed that it ran through the blood vessels. Others believed that the heart was the seat of the soul, and still others stated that the soul had no physical existence at all since it was immortal and the body wasn't. But no one was really sure. For without getting a good look at the soul—that is, without finding some way of *measuring* either the soul or its activities—not even the most persuasive philosopher could come up with a description of the soul that would please everyone.

WHY PSYCHOLOGY?

As we trace the historical roots of psychology, we must keep one very important point in mind. Casual people-watching is fun, but the scientific study of human behavior can be very demanding and a great deal of work. Therefore, why should you take the time and effort to try to learn about the thoughts, feelings, and actions of others? What need does this knowledge satisfy, or what good does all this information do you?

You may well find these questions a little surprising, because it may seem to you that the need for understanding yourself and others is "fairly obvious." After all, you have to live with other people, you have to get along with them and they with you. The more you know about human behavior, including your own, the more likely it is that you will succeed in life, right?

But asking the question, "Why should anybody bother trying to learn about thoughts, feelings, and human behavior" is rather like asking, "Why do people breathe?" Such questions are at once too simple and yet too complex for quick-and-easy answers. A thousand years ago, people thought they breathed because the gods made them do so. Later on people decided that they breathed because of a "life **instinct**" that forced them to take air into their lungs and then breathe it out. Now we realize that there are certain parts of the nervous system that control breathing. These "breathing control centers" inside you respond to various **stimuli**—such as the amount of oxygen and of carbon dioxide in your blood—by increasing or decreasing the amount of air you take into your lungs. But your breathing is also influenced by psychological stimuli—when you are shocked or surprised, you take a sudden gasp of air. You breathe deeply as well when you walk outdoors for the first time on a warm and glorious spring day. You breathe in quite a different way when you are excited or extremely anxious than when you are calm or very depressed. The more that we learn about our bodies, minds, and social environments, the more we realize how complex a behavior *breathing* really is.

The same may be said of psychology. People study other people for many reasons, some of which we still understand only vaguely. However, we do know that people seem to act as if they had an instinctual need to comprehend, predict, and sometimes even to control their own behaviors as well as the actions of others. Such knowledge not only helps us, it often allows us to help other individuals as well. Thus, like breathing, serious people-watching is probably necessary for our very survival.

Why psychology? To help us survive! Little wonder, then, that the history of psychology can be seen as a movement away from magical explanations (such as "the devil made me hit my little brother") toward more testable and proveable ideas (such as "my parents used to hit me when I annoyed them, so probably I imitate their behaviors when somebody like my little brother frustrates me").

As we will see, however, attempts to be more objective or scientific about human conduct were not always easy for many people to make.

EIGHTEENTH-CENTURY PSYCHOLOGY

By the 1700s, some individuals interested in understanding human behavior stopped studying the soul and began studying the body and the environment. These early psychologists left spiritual matters to religion and began instead to look for more concrete, measurable ways to explain human actions. Since they no longer had to relate all thoughts and movements to the soul, these early psychologists were free to investigate behavior in a number of new ways. They looked at the senses (sight, hearing, touch, and so forth) and tried to figure out how information about the world got inside the body. Next, they measured human responses such as the length of time it took different people to react to informational inputs. Some people reacted quickly to stimuli, others more slowly. Why? And why did the same person respond rapidly to a warning signal one day, but much more slowly on another day?

Since psychologists could no longer blame such individual differences on the gods, or on the soul, they had to find a new way of explaining the relationship between stimulus inputs and responses, or outputs. When earlier psychologists asked someone, "Why did you respond more slowly today than yesterday?" the person may have answered, "Because I wasn't paying much attention to things today, and I just wasn't conscious that the signal had appeared." Thus the concept of **consciousness** became part of psychology, and with it the concepts of the mind and mental activities. In the eighteenth century, then, psychology became *the study of mental actions and consciousness.*

It had been Aristotle's opinion that the soul was immortal and had no real physical existence. The soul could exist without the body. The mind was different from the soul because it was tied directly to the body; the mind lived and died with the body. Psychologists could hope to measure what went on inside the mind because it was a part of or extension of the body. That is, mental activities were presumably those internal processes that determined what response or output a given person would make to a particular stimulus or input. But this approach to human behavior also had serious drawbacks. It was the mind and consciousness that intrigued early psychologists, not the description of inputs and outputs. And while "mental activities" may be easier to talk about than gods or the soul, they aren't much easier to see—and seeing is believing.

THE SCIENTIFIC METHOD

For centuries, philosophers presumed that they could best solve problems and answer questions by thinking and arguing about them logically. Arguing or debating can be great fun and often is a useful part of science, but "pure logic" does have its limitations. For example, it is said that before Aristotle's time, philosophers argued at great length about how many teeth a horse *should* have. Some ancient philosophers assumed that since horses were larger than humans, they ought to have more teeth than we do. Other philosophers believed that since horses were obviously inferior and mentally less developed than humans, they should have fewer teeth than we do. Both points of view have a certain "logic" to them, but eventually it dawned on people like Aristotle—as it probably has on you too—that a better way of solving such problems would be to open a horse's mouth and count its teeth. Better yet, you could inspect the teeth of many different horses and "take an average." Why argue about what *should* be when you can measure what actually *is?*

Psychology became a real science when people stopped using philosophical arguments as their only intellectual tool and began as well to make precise observations of and experiments on human behavior.

Observation and experimentation were soon found to be good methods for getting satisfactory answers to many questions that logic or common sense alone couldn't handle. Reliance on observation and experimentation is known as **empiricism.** As empirical methods became popular, a new breed of thinker—the scientist—was born. Not that scientists ignore philosophy, logic, reason, or common sense. Scientists still make educated guesses about things, and they often argue violently about many matters. But empiricists call their guesses **hypotheses**—that is, empiricists use whatever facts they already have on hand to make guesses or hypotheses about the way the world is. Then they go out into the world and test their theories by performing experiments or making controlled observations that yield new facts. If the new facts don't fit the old theory, then the theory must be changed or abandoned. It is this combination of theorizing *plus testing the theory in the real world* that we now call the **scientific method.**

FIG. 1–1.
Before the scientific method came into use, philosophers tried to answer questions with pure logic. They would argue about how many teeth a horse *should* have rather than going to the horse's mouth and counting the teeth, which would have been the scientific method.

Five Steps

The scientific method can be applied to almost any problem, and it is not the private property of scientists. Most people use it, or a variation of it, *every day* without even thinking about it. For example, suppose you turn on the television and nothing happens. *Step one* of the scientific method is recognizing and defining the problem. In this case, the problem is that the television used to work but now it doesn't.

Step two of the scientific method usually consists of developing an hypothesis or making an intelligent guess about why the problem exists. The television set might not be working for one of several reasons. The set isn't plugged in, the picture tube is burned out, there's an electrical short in the set somewhere, a fuse has blown, or perhaps the whole city is in a blackout because of an energy crisis. Each of these possible causes is an hypothesis that can be tested in two important ways—first, to see how accurately the hypothesis explains why the set isn't working; and second, to see how well the hypothesis predicts what you must do to get the TV functioning once more.

Steps three, four, and *five* of the scientific method consist of checking out the various hypotheses, finding out which one gives the best explanation, and then finding out how to get the set working again. A philosopher might list all the possible reasons why the TV isn't functioning and then spend hours arguing which reason *should* be the correct one. An empiricist gets up and checks out the possibilities—and keeps on checking until the set is working again.

NINETEENTH-CENTURY PSYCHOLOGY

Although physics, chemistry, astronomy, and biology became empirical sciences during the 1700s and 1800s, empiricism came late to psychology because many people still thought about human behavior in terms of the soul. It was not until 1879 that the first psychological laboratory was founded—by Wilhelm Wundt at the University of Leipzig in Germany. At about the same time in the United States, William James set up the first laboratory for psychological experimentation at Harvard University. By applying the scientific method to the study of human conduct, these two men produced two of the first major psychological theories or schools of thought: **structuralism** and **functionalism.**

Structuralism

Physicists and chemists made their sciences work, in part, by trying to break matter down into its simplest elements or structures. The closer the scientists got to the basic structure of matter, the easier it became for them to understand how the physical and chemical worlds are put together—and the easier it became for these scientists to predict the results of new experiments.

Wilhelm Wundt and his associates at Leipzig attempted to use this same approach in their analysis of what they called *mental matter.* These psychologists are known as the founders of *the structural school of psychology* because they tried to discover the simplest structures or "atoms" of the human mind. The most basic mental elements, they decided, were the **sensations** or sensory inputs (sights, smells, sounds, and so forth) that influenced consciousness.

William James was the founder of functionalism, the school of psychology that attempted to explain human behavior by investigating the ongoing functions of the body and the mind.

To describe the contents of the mind, the structuralists used a method known as **introspection,** or *looking inward on one's own experiences.* Subjects in Wundt's laboratory would be exposed to a particular stimulus input such as the ticking of a mechanical clock. The subject would then "introspect" about the experience — that is, the subject would try to describe his or her feelings or conscious awareness of the ticking in the simplest or most basic of terms. These *introspective* descriptions might include terms such as loud, noisy, fast, pleasant, and so on. Wundt and his associates would then compare the reports of the subjects and try to arrive at a set of basic sensations or elements that would adequately describe the mental experience they all encountered while listening to the ticking sound.

Structuralism has two serious problems. First, it is a very subjective way of examining human behavior. That is, each subject in Wundt's experiments reported his or her own personal experiences, and the subjects seldom came up with the same descriptions. What was loud to one person was only medium-loud to another. What was pleasant to one individual was unpleasant to another.

Second, and perhaps even worse from Wundt's point of view, the subjective experiences of his subjects changed noticeably from one day to the next. What was a pleasing sound on Monday sometimes turned out to be rather blah on Tuesday and downright annoying on Wednesday. The atoms in a lump of iron don't change much from day to day. The "atoms of the mind" that Wundt was looking for appeared to be constantly changing. Wundt's structural psychology had its moment of glory, and then faded when psychologists began to realize that consciousness is a process of continual growth and change, not a set of mental atoms bound rigidly in place forever and ever.

Functionalism

William James and his followers in the United States attempted to avoid the faults of structuralism by taking a broader view of human consciousness and mental life. Instead of structure, James and his colleagues emphasized the functions or processes of the mind. They called themselves *functionalists,* and James is usually considered to be the founder of the *functional school of psychology.*

James defined the mind as "the sum total of a person's experiences." He realized that the human mind, like the human body, functions in various ways to enable people to change or adapt to different situations. You get up in the morning, for instance, and decide to have a glass of orange juice. If you find there is no orange juice in the refrigerator, you must make a decision about what to drink. It is the function of your mind to make such decisions, and so you might decide to adapt by having tomato juice instead. From morning to night, from cradle to grave, your mind must make such decisions and adapt to the changing situations you find yourself in. It is this adaptive *functioning,* James said, that is responsible for the vast number of different human behaviors — not the "basic structures" of the mind itself.

Structuralism and Functionalism Compared

In a sense, the arguments that occurred between the structuralists and the functionalists can be compared to the arguments that occasionally take place between anatomists and physiologists. **Anatomy** is the study of the body's basic physical structures; **physiology** is the study of how the parts of the body function or relate to each other under varying circumstances. Like the structuralists, anatomists tend to study the body at one frozen moment in time, usually after death. Like the functionalists, the physiologists tend to investigate ongoing activities in living **organisms.**

Those psychologists who create personality and intelligence tests owe a debt to the structuralists, for these sorts of tests are usually aimed at discovering the anatomy or basic elements of the mind at the specific moment that the person takes the test. Those psychologists who do therapy, or who help people learn new skills, owe a debt to the functionalists, who insisted that life is a process of change, adaptation, and growth.

TWENTIETH-CENTURY PSYCHOLOGY

The functionalists emphasized the observation of external behavior rather than the description of internal feelings or sensations, because James and his colleagues believed that behavior was little more than a **symptom** or signal of what was going on inside the mind. However, early in this century, a few empirical psychologists began to disagree with James. Mental life, the empiricists said, cannot be observed directly and therefore (like the soul) cannot be accurately described. All that we can describe is *behavior*—the actions and reactions that we all make. We cannot see your thoughts, but we can measure how quickly you solve a problem; we cannot measure your emotions directly, but we can notice your physical reactions when you encounter an emotional stimulus (such as someone you love or hate). The mind may exist, just as the soul may exist; but since we can't hold a measuring stick up to the mind—while we can measure behavior—some psychologists have concluded that we should build the science of psychology only on what is observable and stop guessing about what we can't see or touch or feel.

This emphasis on empirical evidence led to the theory of **behaviorism,** one of the first major schools of psychology to emerge during the early years of this century.

Behaviorism

John B. Watson was the founder of the behaviorist movement. He began by ignoring everything in psychology that was not directly observable or countable. Drinking a glass of tomato juice is observable; you can see it, and so can everybody else. Your hand grasps the glass. Your arm brings the glass to your mouth.

You swallow the juice—rapidly or slowly, loudly or quietly. We can put a measuring stick up to your actions if we so desire; therefore, your drinking behaviors can be part of the science of psychology. Your *decision* to drink tomato juice rather than orange juice, however, cannot be seen. Whatever mental processes went on inside your head that led you to drink the tomato juice cannot be measured; therefore, these processes cannot be a part of empirical psychology.

As you might imagine, Watson's behaviorism infuriated both the structuralists and the functionalists. After all, it must be quite clear to you that you *do* make decisions, that you *do* have things going on all the time inside your mind. How could behaviorists simply ignore that fertile field of existence we call *mental activities?*

The answer is, the behaviorists didn't really ignore such processes as decision making. Rather, they explained these inner processes in terms of prior experiences or behaviors, all of which could be measured. Why did you "decide" to drink tomato juice on a particular morning? In behaviorist terms, you drank the tomato juice because you had been trained or **conditioned** to do so in the past. Most of the time in the past you drank orange juice because you had been rewarded for doing just that. You liked the orange juice, and drinking it was a pleasant or rewarding experience. But at times you had also been conditioned or rewarded when you drank tomato juice as a substitute for orange juice. Therefore, when there was no orange juice present, you drank the (less-often-rewarded) tomato juice instead. Even more complicated behaviors—such as driving a car, working an algebra problem, or falling in love—could be broken down into a series of learned behaviors. According to Watson, no matter how complex your actions might be, you do what you have learned to do. And learning or conditioning is always based on *observable behaviors and their consequences.* Watson and the behaviorists therefore called psychology *the scientific study of behavior.*

Watson's empirical approach to human behavior was born at a time when many psychologists were beginning to feel that their science was getting them nowhere. Physicists and chemists were making great strides because they had observable, physical objects and events to work with. Before Watson, psychologists were mainly arguing about what they were *supposed* to be working with. Because Watson gave psychologists something they could study empirically—observable behaviors—he became one of the most prominent scientists of his time, and with him psychology entered the twentieth century as a full-fledged (if very young) science.

Other Answers

A great many people believe that there is more to human experience than behavior. What, for instance, is love? Depending on one's viewpoint, love can be defined as an internal state or condition, a process or function, an emotion, a type of motivation, or a blissful feeling that "makes the world go 'round." However one defines it, love is often credited with making people behave in certain ways that can be counted, measured, and tested.

Some experiences can only be described through introspection or looking inward. Scientific study probably could not adequately describe the feelings this couple have for each other.

The loving behavior that one person shows toward another can be measured, but the love itself cannot. From a purely objective or empirical point of view, love does not exist as an object. Instead, love is an explanation that we sometimes use to explain why people behave as they do. Hate, goodness, evil, dignity, honor, and many similar qualities that are said to elevate humans above the level of animal existence are also invisible and can't be readily explained in terms of "pure behavior." In an attempt to account for some of these invisible human qualities, several schools of psychology have grown up outside the behaviorist tradition.

Gestalt Psychology

Gestalt is the German word for "form," "organization," or "configuration." Gestalt psychologists believe that experiences cannot be broken down to basic "atoms" or elements (as in structuralism) or explained in terms of simple behaviors and conditioning (as in behaviorism). Instead, Gestalt psychologists say that each experience has a particular form, organization, and configuration that determines the characteristics of all the various parts of that experience. The *whole*

TABLE 1-1   **The Major Schools of Psychology**

	School	Founders	Main Goal	Method
Nineteenth Century	Structuralism	Wilhelm Wundt	To understand human behavior by looking inward to one's own experiences; to discover simplest structures or elements of mind	Subjective introspection; mental testing
	Functionalism	William James	To understand human behavior by considering functions or ongoing processes of the mind and body	Objective measures of thoughts and actions
Twentieth Century	Behaviorism	Ivan Pavlov John B. Watson	To learn about the mind by observing and describing behavior	Empirical evidence
	Psychoanalysis	Sigmund Freud	To learn about the unconscious forces that affect behavior	"Free association"
	Gestalt	Wolfgang Köhler Kurt Koffka	To learn about the mind by discovering how people perceive the world	Perceptual test

Sigmund Freud is known as the father of psychoanalysis. Freud attempted to explain how unconscious forces influence human behavior.

of an experience, they say, is not the same as the *sum of its parts*. Gestalt psychology was developed early in this century by several German psychologists who were primarily interested in **perception** — that is, in our recognition of the world around us. Many illustrations of Gestalt psychology have to do with those forms of *perception* we call seeing, hearing, touching, and so forth (see Chapter 3). For example, consider a motion picture. It is made up of many single, still pictures, but looking at each picture singly does not result in the same experience as seeing the movie "whole," as it was meant to be seen. Looking at single aspects of human behavior, the Gestalt psychologists say, is not the same as viewing the behavior in its totality.

Psychoanalysis

At about the same time as Gestalt psychologists were studying perception, Sigmund Freud developed a theory of psychology which says that structures, functions, and previous conditioning are not enough to explain why we do the things that we do. After analyzing the thoughts, emotions, and behaviors of his

(*Above left*) The Swiss psychologist Jean Piaget is associated with cognitive psychology, which is concerned with how the human mind processes information. He has made extensive investigations of the mental development of children. (*Above right*) Cognitive psychology helps us to understand how children learn. A child's mind must reach a certain stage of development before it can perform certain tasks.

patients, Freud concluded that some human actions are the results of unconscious forces hidden within each person. In his many works, Freud gave names to these forces and attempted to explain how they influence human behavior. He called the process of discovering these forces **psychoanalysis.** Freud's theories, which revolutionized thinking about human behavior, will be more fully discussed in later chapters.

Cognitive Psychology

Cognitive comes from the Latin word that means "to know." Cognitive psychologists say that people are not just machines—that is, we are not just robots who react blindly and mechanically to events in the external world. From the cognitive point of view, the human mind knows more than the information that it gets from the environment. The mind "processes" or acts upon incoming information, makes comparisons and decisions, and produces new thoughts and ideas that are more than just combinations of past experiences.

Jean Piaget, the Swiss psychologist, is well known for his cognitive approach to human behavior, and especially for his investigations of the mental development of children. Piaget's experiments with children have helped demonstrate that the mind develops—at least in part—by going through various stages that don't appear to be totally dependent on past experiences. Until a child's mind has reached a certain point in its development, says Piaget, that child will be unable to understand certain things—such as how to do algebra problems. The child must reach a particular point in its cognitive growth before it can handle such complex ideas as mathematical relationships. Once it has reached the appropriate stage, however, it can learn mathematics with little difficulty. Before it has reached that stage, no amount of training will be sufficient to teach the child how to handle complex math. (Piaget will be covered more fully in Chapter 7.)

Piaget's viewpoint differs considerably from behaviorist theory, which says that even a very young child should be able to master algebra if it is given enough training and conditioning. While neither Piaget's nor Watson's theory has been accepted by all psychologists, we might note that very few children actually do learn algebra until they have reached a stage of development similar to that which Piaget says is necessary.

The Eclectic Approach

Each of the theories of human behavior we've described so far gives us a different view of people and a different definition of what psychology is all about. And there are many more such theories and definitions that can be used by a twentieth-century psychologist. Increasingly, however, psychologists are getting away from the idea of sticking to only one school of thought. Psychologists are becoming more **eclectic** — which is to say that they tend to select and use what they consider to be the best from each of the many theories available. By becoming more eclectic and broad-minded, psychologists can apply behaviorist theory when it seems to fit the situation, and apply cognitive or Freudian theory when they seem to apply. Therefore, a complete definition of psychology must make some reference to mental or cognitive processes as well as to behavior. Psychology, as we define it in this textbook, is the *scientific study of mental processes and of behavior.*

PUTTING PSYCHOLOGY TO WORK

Not only do psychologists have different theories with which to work, they also have different approaches within the scientific method with which to answer questions about mental processes and behaviors. Among the most-often-used approaches are tests, surveys, questionnaires, interviews, naturalistic observation, and experimentation.

Tests

Almost everyone in the United States has been exposed at one time or another to psychological tests. Schools give **intelligence tests** in an attempt to measure a student's mental abilities. Employers give **aptitude** and **achievement tests** whose scores can indicate the type of job for which someone might best be suited. Aptitude tests are supposed to measure a person's ability to learn or perform a particular job or task. Achievement tests are designed to measure the

FIG. 1–2.
Different tests attempt to measure various human abilities. The results can sometimes help us to predict human behavior.

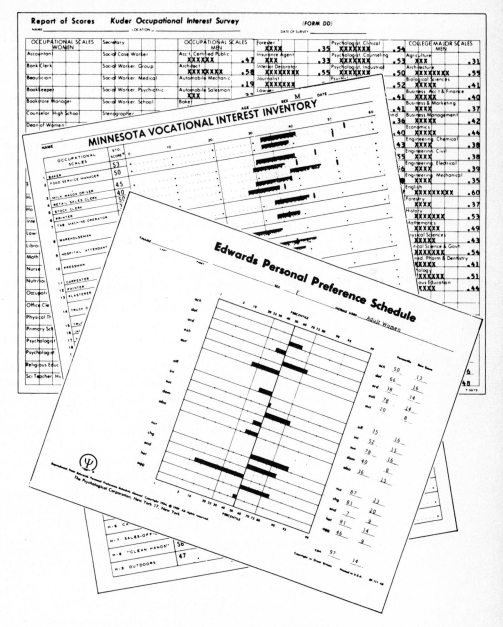

knowledge or skill that an individual has already gained through training in a specific area.

Interest tests do just what their name implies. They indicate what your interests are and try to predict what type of work you might enjoy most. If you are interested in becoming a lawyer, your scores on the interest test will probably indicate this fact. However, if you are considering the law as a profession, and your aptitude and achievement test scores indicate that you might be better suited for teaching, you might wish to reconsider your career choice or talk matters over with a counselor. You must realize, though, that these tests are far from being completely accurate indicators of what job you'd be best at. Aptitude and interest tests are designed to be given to thousands of people, and job satisfaction is determined by a great many factors other than your own personal skills and interests. Your own **motivations** and your ability to adapt to changing circumstances are at least as important as your test scores. If you are relatively undecided about what you want to make of your life, however, these tests might give you some very valuable insights.

Personality tests are another tool used by many psychologists in an attempt to describe or characterize an individual. These tests, however, are usually a good deal less accurate than are aptitude and interest tests. As we will see in later chapters, there are many different theories of personality, and each theoretical approach has its own way of testing "what makes you tick." Even so, when personality tests are properly used, they can give a trained psychologist important knowledge about some of your **traits** or personal characteristics.

Surveys, Questionnaires, and Interviews

Tests ask questions and are used to gather information about whoever is taking the test. Surveys and questionnaires have a similar form — they ask questions — but their results are used to gain information about whole groups or populations of people.

In 1936 the Gallup Poll correctly predicted that President Franklin D. Roosevelt would be re-elected. Since that time, polls or surveys have become a major part of the political picture in most western countries. The word *poll* refers to people, and polls are supposed to give an indication of the opinions, thoughts, or attitudes of "the people" on a specific topic. But in order for anyone to find out what *all* the people in the United States really think, every living human being would have to be questioned in detail. But such an undertaking would be very expensive and would take months or even years. By the time the results were in, many people would have changed their minds — and the poll might be worthless. Before a presidential election, for instance, polls are updated almost weekly. A political poll taken six months ago would be useless, especially in times when public opinion changes almost as rapidly as the weather.

In order to make public opinion surveys timely, useful, and as **valid** as possible, pollsters attempt to select a **sample** of the population that accurately represents the views of people throughout the country. This cross-section of the population can be polled very quickly; and if the sample is truly representative, the results of the poll can be very accurate. But because public opinion is a very difficult thing to pin down, even the best-designed of polls can be wrong at times. In 1948 all the polls predicted that Thomas E. Dewey would defeat Harry

S. Truman in the presidential election. A few newspapers, believing the polls, even printed headlines ("Dewey Defeats Truman") before the votes were counted. But the pollsters stopped asking questions long before the election, public opinion changed in the meantime, and Truman was elected rather than Dewey.

Surveys of Sexual Behavior

Political opinion is only one small area of human behavior that can be investigated by surveys. Beginning in the 1940s, Alfred Kinsey and his colleagues began using the survey and interview methods to find out about the sexual experiences of people in the United States. Psychologists, like everybody else, had many theories and ideas about sexual practices. They had not, however, been able to test these theories on a large scale, and in 1940 they had no real knowledge of what most people were actually doing in private. The only way to find out, Kinsey decided, was to interview as many people as possible and ask them to explain their sex-lives in detail. Sex might seem like a subject that people would be reluctant to talk about with a stranger — and in some cases it is. But when Kinsey promised not to use any names in his report, he found most people would talk quite openly about many aspects of their private lives.

Kinsey's first report (on the sexual behavior of men) was published in 1948. When this report first appeared, it shocked many people — to say the least. Even psychologists were unprepared for some of the findings that Kinsey published. He found, among other things, that young, unmarried males from the lower educational and occupational levels were more likely to find sexual release in actual intercourse than were similar males from higher educational and social levels, who were more likely to find sexual release in masturbation and petting. Another of Kinsey's surprising findings was that homosexual acts occurred much more frequently than most people had realized. Up to 20 percent of the females and 40 percent of the males in the Kinsey surveys stated that they had had some homosexual experience.

Since the 1940s, when Kinsey's group first began its work, the sexual **mores** of people in the United States have changed somewhat. However, more recent surveys by such magazines as *Playboy* and *Psychology Today*, and interviews conducted on large samples of people by many other scientific groups, all suggest that Kinsey's original findings were fairly accurate.

Naturalistic Observation

In many instances it is not possible to test or question people. For instance, very young children cannot take written tests and cannot answer difficult questions about their personalities, feelings, or their sexual attitudes (if any). And in some cases, people are simply unwilling to answer questions or may give misleading answers. When psychologists suspect that this will be the case, they sometimes resort to scientific people-watching. That is, the psychologists observe people in their natural settings and record as objectively as possible the behaviors the people engage in. Piaget, the cognitive psychologist, spent many years just watching young children's behaviors before he began developing his theories of how children's minds grow.

Experiments

Sometimes it is necessary for scientists to study people in their natural habitats, to see how people act in the "real world." The woman above, who stopped to aid a man having an epileptic seizure, might have responded differently in the artificial conditions of the laboratory.

There is one basic problem with most forms of people-watching and people-questioning. When you ask people whom they are going to vote for in the next election, and they say "Candidate X," you have no real way of knowing that they won't change their minds before the election. In fact, you don't really know for sure that they will vote at all. The attitudes or opinions that people express are not always directly related to what they will do when the real situation comes along. And if you are interested in how people will react to an unusual situation—such as what they would do if they saw their families being attacked—you may never find out how they would actually respond because it is unlikely that their families will ever experience such an attack.

When psychologists don't have the opportunity to test or question people, or have reason to distrust their answers, and whenever the psychologists don't want to wait for a particular set of circumstances to occur in real life, they often make use of another method of people-watching. That is, the psychologists will conduct an experiment that attempts to duplicate the situation they are interested in studying.

Whenever possible, psychologists use experiments to test their theories. These experiments don't really prove that a particular theory is *right,* but a well-designed experiment can demonstrate that one theory gives a more accurate explanation of human behavior than does a second theory. To put it differently, an experiment can occasionally prove that a specific theory is *wrong* (if the theory doesn't predict the results of the experiment). But experiments can't prove that a theory is absolutely correct, because all that one can show by experimentation is that one theory does a better job of predicting and explaining the experimental results than does any other theory. Even if one theory seems to be correct, the possibility still exists that an as-yet-undreamed-of theory could explain the experimental findings with even greater accuracy.

Objective Measurements

Experiments are more valuable for testing theories than are arguments for many reasons, not the least of which is that an experiment is really a type of *controlled observation* that involves *objective measurements.* Generally speaking, the more control the scientists can exercise over the factors that influence a particular behavior, the more reliable the results of their studies will be. Since laboratories are highly controlled environments, many psychologists prefer to observe human behavior in their labs whenever possible.

Most of us are biased in our people-watching. That is to say, we often tend to see what we want to see in people rather than what is really there. To remove as much of this subjective bias as they can from their observations, psychologists utilize a variety of mechanical and electronic devices to record the behavior of their subjects. For instance, in an experiment designed to study mother–child interactions, a psychologist might use a movie camera to film the number of times that a mother actually touches, looks at, or talks to her infant. The filmed record of the mother's behavior would be objective because anyone who watched the film afterwards could count exactly how many times the mother did interact with her child. Neither the woman's personal memory of how she played with the child — nor the psychologist's, for that matter — would be as accurate a record of what really happened as the film would be. Furthermore, the film could be replayed again and again, while real-life events not recorded on film or tape seldom can be repeated exactly as they originally happened.

Experimental and Control Groups

To make their objective measures of behavior even more reliable, psychologists often use several groups of subjects in an experiment. Each of the groups is subjected to somewhat different experiences. Comparing the data from the various groups often tells a psychologist more than would the data from an experiment employing just one group of subjects.

Suppose that you wanted to study the effects of smoking marijuana on people's pulse rates. You might begin by asking volunteer subjects to smoke marijuana while you used an electronic sensor to record their heartbeats. Probably you would compare their pulse rates before, during, and after they had smoked the marijuana cigarette. If your subjects' pulses increase significantly while they are smoking, you might conclude that marijuana speeds up the action of the heart. And because these would be the most important subjects in your experimental study, they would be called the members of the **experimental group.**

If you were to study informally the effects of marijuana on pulse rate, it would be important to control other, outside influences. In this picture, what factors do you see that may influence the study?

But stop and think about your study for a moment. Could the reactions of your experimental group be due to factors other than the marijuana itself? Perhaps the *act of smoking* anything at all, or even just the *thought* that they were inhaling marijuana, would be enough to increase the pulse rate in your subjects. So, if you wanted to be more careful with your experiment, you would probably use additional groups of subjects to *control* for these possibilities. One such **control group** might be given cigarettes that looked, smelled, and tasted like they contained marijuana, but actually contained some other substance instead. Another group of control subjects might be told to *imagine* that they were smoking marijuana while the sensor recorded their heartbeats. Still another control group might be made up of subjects asked to watch someone else while that person smoked marijuana.

As you might imagine, if the increase in pulse rate you found in your experimental group did not show up in your control group subjects, you could be reasonably confident that marijuana does act to speed up the action of the heart.

In the language of scientists, smoking the marijuana is called an **independent variable** since it is something that you (the experimenter) control. The increased pulse rate (the subjects' response) is called the **dependent variable** because it depends on your experimental manipulations. Any other factors (such as thinking about inhaling marijuana) are called **intervening variables.** Independent, dependent, and intervening variables are the basic factors in any experiment.

Experimenter Bias

Since psychologists were people before they became scientists, they are just as likely to be biased in some of their observations as anybody else. And sometimes the scientist's preconceived notions about what the results of a study *ought to be* can strongly influence what the outcome *will* be. For example, if you were absolutely convinced before you conducted the experiment that marijuana would increase the pulse rate, might you not communicate your expectations to your experimental subjects in a variety of subtle ways? Might not the subjects be affected by what you communicate to them?

To guard against this sort of **experimenter bias,** scientists often resort to what are called **blind experiments.** That is, the people who actually talk to the subjects and record their data are "kept in the blind" as to the experimental conditions until after the experiment is completed. (For instance, in your marijuana study, you might have someone else prepare the two types of cigarettes used and not tell you which was which until after your subjects had finished smoking.)

Subjects, too, will occasionally try to perform the way that they think the scientist wants them to perform, rather than acting the way they normally would. For this reason, subjects are often "kept in the blind" as to what's actually happening in a study. Those subjects given cigarettes to smoke that looked, smelled, and tasted as if they contained marijuana are a good example of a *blind* control group.

If both subjects and experimenters are "blind" as to the purpose or conditions of the experiment, the study is said to be a **double-blind experiment.** In general, data from "double-blind" studies are more trustworthy than are data from studies in which these controls for bias are not utilized.

Animal Experiments

Some behavioral experiments must be conducted on animals. These infant monkeys have been separated from their mothers for an extended period of time. An ethical psychologist would never conduct such an experiment with human infants.

For various reasons, many of them obvious, psychologists cannot always use human subjects in their experiments. It would not be very wise, for instance, to test the effects of a new drug on humans. It is even illegal to do so, for it is a question of **ethics.** The government has set up strict conditions that must be followed before any new drug can be administered to human beings. As part of these conditions, the particular drug must first be given to animals, usually in very large doses. The researchers must then wait for a given amount of time to see how the animals fare. Only if the experimental animals show no ill effects can such a new drug be given to humans. Even then, the drug is usually given in small doses and only to a few people until its safety is proved.

Some behavioral experiments must also be conducted on animals. A psychologist who wants to learn the effects of complete social isolation cannot very well lock up someone in a dark room for six months. Animals (rats, pigeons, and monkeys are among the most often used) are often the subjects in studies that might prove harmful to humans. For example, psychologists have long suspected that if an infant is removed from its mother for a period of time, the child will show unusual behavior patterns both during the separation and for some time afterwards. But how can you prove such a suspicion? You can hardly isolate a bunch of infants from their parents, rear the infants in solitary confinement, and then release them into the world as adults to see how they react. Instead, isolation experiments have been done with infant monkeys.

In one such experiment, when the monkeys were between 21- and 32-weeks old, they were separated from their mothers for varying lengths of time, one of the variables being tested. (Remember that a variable in an experiment is something that can be varied or changed. In this experiment some of the infants were separated for six days, some for 13 days. In this manner the researchers were able to test the effects of different lengths of separation.) The infant monkeys were observed both during the separation and after they were returned to their mothers.

The results of the experiment seem to support the researchers' original theory. They found that when the mother is removed for a few days, the infants become very upset at first and scream a great deal. Later the infants stop crying but show a decrease in normal movement and play activity. Follow-up tests given six months and two years later strongly suggest that the ill effects of infant–mother separation are long lasting. The young monkeys appeared to be mentally disturbed and seemed to stay that way. Control group monkeys, who had undergone no separation, did not display any of these unusual behaviors.

Of course, monkeys are not humans, and we must be cautious about concluding that infant humans separated from their mothers would react the same way. However, monkey behavior develops in much the same way that human behavior does, so the monkey experiment does strongly suggest that it is unwise to take a human infant from its mother unless there is some terribly good reason for doing so—and even then, we would want to employ a "mother substitute" if we possibly could. We will not know *exactly* how human infants respond to separation, however, until someone actually undertakes a study with human infants similar to that performed on the young monkeys.

By using all these techniques—experiments, tests, surveys, questionnaires, interviews, and observations—psychologists no longer have to speculate or guess about human behavior as much as they did a hundred years ago. By applying the scientific method, by being objective, and by controlling for bias and subjectivity, psychologists have learned more about human existence in the last hundred years than their forerunners learned in the previous hundred centuries.

Experimental Psychology

Experimental psychologists are typically more interested in using the scientific method to discover new facts about behavior than they are in applying these facts to the solution of real-life problems. Some experimentalists are interested in the biological underpinnings of behavior—that is, they attempt to find out what physiological and chemical changes occur in the body when people learn new tasks, experience new emotions, or develop new perceptions of the world. Other experimentalists are interested primarily in the psychological or cognitive experiences people have during their lives. These scientists attempt to work out the "laws of learning," or study such mental processes as feelings, motives, sensory inputs, and problem solving. Many experimental psychologists make extensive use of animal subjects; others work entirely with humans.

Industrial and Engineering Psychology

Industrial psychologists use tests and interviews to help people decide what sort of work they should be doing. They help in the training and supervision of personnel. They counsel employers and employees and are sometimes called upon to help settle disputes between labor and management.

Engineering psychologists use their knowledge of human behavior to help design the equipment and machinery that people must use. They take part in deciding such things as what would be the most convenient and useful placement of knobs and dials on airplane and automobile dashboards in terms of reaction time, frequency of reaction, and so on.

School and Educational Psychology

In addition to giving psychological tests and working with the individual problems of students, school psychologists help design intelligence tests and school entrance exams. Educational psychologists are concerned with increasing the efficiency of learning in school. They do this by applying their knowledge about one particular human behavior, learning. More recently, many educational psychologists have begun specializing in "classroom management" — that is, they train teachers in those social and psychological skills needed to make classrooms happy and productive environments.

Social Psychology

Most psychologists focus on the behavior of individuals. Social psychologists, however, focus on the actions of groups or organizations of people. A biological psychologist studies how the *interactions* between a person's heart, brain, stomach, and lungs produce particular reactions. The social psychologist studies interactions or relationships among people, and theorizes on how these relationships help determine the actions of groups of individuals working or living together.

After gathering information, making hypotheses, and conducting experiments on the behavior of groups, social psychologists often take part in the development of social action programs — such as drug abuse programs — that attempt to deal with the many problems of modern society.

THE LAST WORD

The Iliad has fascinated millions of readers because its objective description of human thoughts, feelings, and actions reveals something of human nature. But literature is only one of the methods we have of finding out more about ourselves and others. As we have seen throughout this chapter, people have been questioning the whys and wherefores of human behavior for thousands of years. At first the answers were slow in coming and many of them were fairly useless. Before Aristotle, the heavens were thought to contain the answers to human behavior, but blaming what people did on gods, goddesses, and the stars didn't help anyone to understand human behavior. No one knew what the heavens had in store and, like the weather, not much could be done about the stars (or the gods).

Studies of the soul, mind, and consciousness were not much better. These things couldn't be seen and therefore couldn't be completely understood. Without sufficient or usable answers, questions continued to be asked. Inquiring minds wanted to understand the actions and behaviors of their neighbors. They wanted to understand their own actions and behaviors as well.

It was the decision to study behavior itself that finally began to pay off for psychology. Behavior is not like the weather, because something can usually be done about changing behavior. And that is the goal of most sciences, to understand a particular behavior (whether it be the actions of clouds or of people) and, by understanding it, to be able to predict and possibly even control future behaviors. Weather scientists study cloud patterns in an attempt to understand them and predict and sometimes control future weather. Psychologists study human behavior patterns in an attempt to understand them and predict and sometimes control future behavior (including their own actions).

Did it ever rain on your parade? Even the best weather forecaster can make a mistake. The clouds, the wind, and the temperature might seem to predict a sunny day, but then it rains because there was some unforeseen factor that the forecaster overlooked. Human behavior is much more complicated than the weather and the possibilities for unforeseen factors are endless. So psychologists too can make mistakes.

As a science, psychology is relatively young. It is at least a hundred years behind the hard sciences like physics and chemistry. Therefore, it has much more testing and experimentation to do before it even begins to become an exact science. In the meantime, if psychology's predictions are correct more often than they are wrong, these predictions can be used to answer questions and to solve human problems. Psychology's findings can, in other words, be applied to human problems. Abnormal psychology can be applied to the problems of abnormal behavior. Social psychology can be applied to the problems of society.

Psychologists don't have all the answers, but they have come up with and will continue to come up with answers that are applicable to some of the questions of human behavior. Psychologists continue to test, experiment, hypothesize, and predict in the hope of developing scientific principles that can be applied usefully by everyone in every situation.

So the last word is "application." That completes the definition of twentieth-century psychology.

Psychology is the scientific study of mental processes and behavior and the application of knowledge gained through that study.

► *SUMMARY*

1. *The Iliad,* like most of the great literature of the world, has for centuries offered us one method of examining human behavior. While Homer and other poets and writers may have turned people-watching into art, modern psychologists have attempted to turn people-watching into an objective science—psychology, the people science.

2. Questions about human behavior have been asked and answered in many ways. The first answers suggested that the gods controlled all human actions, but such answers told us little about ourselves. Greek philosophers like Aristotle searched for more meaningful answers and decided that the soul was responsible for human thoughts, feelings, and actions. When attempts to study the soul proved to be fruitless, people interested in understanding human behavior looked elsewhere and eventually turned to science.

3. "Why Psychology?" is a question whose answers involve the human instinct to comprehend, predict, and sometimes control—survival in other words.

4. In the eighteenth century, psychology evolved to become the study of mental actions and consciousness, a scientific advance that was still limited in its methods of investigation.

5. It wasn't until the nineteenth century that the **scientific method,** relying on observation and experimentation, came into use. Facts are gathered and hypotheses, or educated guesses, are made about the facts. Experiments are conducted in order to test or disprove the hypotheses.

6. Using the scientific method, psychologists of the nineteenth century produced two major theories of human behavior. **Structuralism** attempted to describe the basic structures of the mind. **Functionalism** emphasized the adaptive functioning of the mind. Both approaches proved to be inadequate because the mind and mental processes have yet to be observed, measured, or clearly defined.

7. In the twentieth century **behaviorism** became one of the most popular approaches to understanding human behavior. Behaviorism says that psychology, if it is to be truly scientific, must concentrate only on objective, observable behaviors.

8. Behaviorism gave psychology a solid scientific footing, but in doing so it had to ignore many aspects of human behavior that seem to exist, even if they can't be seen. Love, hate, good, evil, dignity, and honor are among these unseen human qualities. **Gestalt psychology, psychoanalytic theory,** and **cognitive theory** are among the schools of psychological thought that attempt to explain mental processes and some of the unseen aspects of human nature.

9. The most frequently used tools of psychology are tests, surveys, questionnaires, interviews, naturalistic observation, and experimentation. These tools provide psychologists with basic information about human behavior.

10. To obtain empirical evidence, scientists divide subjects into **experimental and control groups.** By manipulating the **independent variable,** the experimenter can study the **dependent variable** and any **intervening variables.** Objectivity can often be ensured by running **blind and double-blind experiments.**

11. Because no psychologist can explain all human behavior, a number of specialized schools of psychology have grown up. They include such things as industrial and engineering psychology, school and educational psychology, and social psychology. Information gathered from these fields of study helps us to better understand ourselves and can be applied in attempts to solve some of the problems of human behavior.

12. By examining how questions about human behavior have been answered in the past and by looking at what psychologists do and how they do it, we can gain an understanding of what psychology is. *Psychology is the scientific study of mental processes and behavior and the application of knowledge gained through that study.*

Suggested Readings

American Psychological Association. *A career in psychology.* 1200 17th St., N.W., Wash., D.C., 20036.

Blatty, William Peter. *The exorcist.* New York: Bantam, 1972.

Cohen, David. *Psychologists on psychology.* New York: Taplinger, 1976.

Homer, *The Iliad.* (Richmond Lattimore, Jr.) Chicago: University of Chicago Press, 1961.

Malnig, Lawrence. What can I do with a major in? St. Peter's College Press, Kennedy Blvd., Jersey City, N.J., 07306.

► STUDY GUIDE*

A.   RECALL

Sentence Completion

1. In *The Iliad,* Homer wrote convincingly about a war that took place

[p. 8]   _____ years ago.

2. When you observe other people, all you can see are their _____, not

[p. 8]   what goes on in their _____.

3. The outside-in approach to people-watching is more scientific and

[p. 11]   _____ than the inside-out approach.

4. Ancient civilizations devised systems of _____ to explain how the heav-

[p. 11]   ens influenced the course of human affairs.

5. Giving a god blame or credit for a behavior does little to actually _____

[p. 12]   that behavior.

6. Aristotle replaced the earlier myths about the gods with the concept of

[p. 12]   _____.

7. We eventually have to abandon the idea of psyche or soul in science because we

[p. 13]   find that we cannot _____ it.

8. During the eighteenth century the concept of _____ became a central

[p. 14]   part of an emerging psychology.

[p. 15]   9. The reliance on observation and experimentation is known as _____.

[p. 15]   10. _____ is another term for "educated guess" that is used in science.

[p. 17]   11. The very first step in the scientific method is to _____ the problem.

12. The first psychological laboratory was founded by _____ in 1879 at the

[p. 17]   University of Leipzig.

13. William James is credited with beginning the school of thought in psychology known

[p. 17]   as _____.

14. The structuralists in Wundt's laboratory tried to analyze _____

_____ using the same sort of methods as those used by physicists and chem-

[p. 17]   ists.

* At the end of the book you will find an answer key for all study guide questions follow-ing the indexes. Numbers in brackets indicate the text pages on which answers may be found.

[p. 18] 15. The primary method of the structuralist school was _____.

[p. 18] 16. The large differences among behaviors are due to _____ functioning, according to William James and the functionalists.

[p. 19] 17. That we should build a science of psychology only on what is observable is the key to the school of _____, founded by _____.

[p. 22] 18. For Gestalt psychologists, the whole is _____ the sum of its parts.

[p. 22] 19. Gestalt psychologists were primarily interested in the principles underlying _____.

[p. 23] 20. Freud called the process of discovering the unconscious forces that affect human actions _____.

[p. 23] 21. Information processing, making comparisons, and decision making are part of what _____ psychologists study.

[p. 24] 22. To pick and choose that which you prefer from a number of different theories is to be _____.

[p. 26] 23. While tests may give us information about an individual, _____ and _____ give us information about whole groups or populations of people.

[p. 27] 24. In the 1940s Kinsey did a now-famous study on _____, using the survey and interview methods.

[pp. 27–28] 25. Piaget is a cognitive psychologist who used the method of _____ _____ extensively.

[p. 28] 26. Experiments are best suited when one wishes to prove that any given theory is _____.

[p. 30] 27. The subjects in an experiment who do *not* receive the experimental treatment are members of the _____ group.

[p. 30] 28. In an experiment, the response that the subjects make and that the experimenter records are called the _____ variables.

[p. 30] 29. To guard against experimenter bias, scientists often use what are called _____ experiments.

[p. 32] 30. Psychologists who help design the equipment and machinery that people have to work with are _____ psychologists.

B.   REVIEW

Multiple Choice: Circle the letter identifying the alternative that most correctly completes the statement or answers the question.

   1. In *The Iliad,* Homer explained the behavior of the people he wrote about by attributing their behavior to:
   A. the whim of the gods.
   B. the workings of the psyche.
   C. how the fluids of the blood went through the body.
   D. the soul.

   2. Philosophers:
   A. were not at all active during the Middle Ages.
   B. could not prove what they said about the soul.

    C. seldom have to rely on logic or reasoning.

    D. have had little to say about behavior since the early seventeenth century.

3. By the eighteenth century, psychologists, freed from worrying about the soul or psyche, began to study:

    A. the senses.

    B. consciousness.

    C. mental actions.

    D. all of the above.

4. To actually find out something by measuring and observing is to use:

    A. the scientific method.

    B. hypothesis testing.

    C. empiricism.

    D. all of the above.

5. Developing an hypothesis is:

    A. the first step in the scientific method.

    B. a technique of modern philosophy.

    C. not a part of psychology, but only the "old" sciences like physics.

    D. about the same thing as making a guess.

6. Introspection was a method common in the _____ school of psychology.

    A. structuralist

    B. behavioristic

    C. functionalist

    D. Gestalt

7. Referring to "conditioned responses" is something you might expect from which type of psychologist?

    A. Gestalt

    B. behavioristic

    C. cognitive

    D. psychoanalytic

8. To be "eclectic" is to be:

    A. subjective.

    B. scientific.

    C. selective.

    D. old-fashioned.

9. In an experiment, that which the experimenter manipulates is called the _____ variable.

    A. independent

    B. intervening

C. control
D. dependent

10. According to your text, a definition of psychology should include:
    A. mention of the fact that psychology is a science.
    B. the fact that psychology studies behavior and mental processes.
    C. the application of knowledge of psychology.
    D. all of the above.

unit ONE

BIOLOGY AND BEHAVIOR

Movie still from *Lord of the Flies*.

Why do human beings sometimes act aggressively toward others? Do they learn violent behavior or is it a trait they are born with? Before we can begin to answer these questions, we must look at the human brain and nervous system—how they developed during millions of years of evolution and how they function. We must also consider how social order evolved.

Evolution, the Brain, and Behavior

chapter 2

When you have completed your study of this chapter, you should be able to:

► Discuss the nature-nurture controversy.
► Relate Darwin's theory of evolution to behavior, the development of language, and aggression
► Compare and contrast reflexes and instincts
► Explain how imprinting and innate releasing mechanisms work
► Describe the structure and function of the neurons, nerve nets, and primitive brains
► Summarize the functions of the human cerebral cortex, referring to the two hemispheres and split-brain experiments

Aggression. From the Latin term meaning "to approach." An unprovoked or hostile attack, or an encroachment on someone else's territory or life-space.

Agonistic behavior (agg-oh-NISS-tic). From the Greek term referring to athletic contests, most of which involved physical aggression. Agonistic behavior is aggressive behavior.

Assassination (ass-sass-a-NAY-shun). An assassin (ass-SASS-sin) is a hired killer. About 1000 years ago, a famous Mohammedan leader hired men to kill his enemies. To "psych up the killers," the leader got them "stoned" on hashish or marijuana, then supposedly showed them a beautiful garden that represented the heaven they would go to if they obeyed his orders. These groups of killers were called *hashshashin*, from which our word "assassin" comes.

Axon (AX-onn). The "tail end" of the nerve cell. When the nerve impulse reaches the axon, the axon releases certain chemicals that stimulate other nerve cells.

Bilateral symmetry (buy-LATT-terr-al SIMM-ett-tree). "Bi-" means "two," and "lateral" means "sides." Anything that is bilateral (such as your body) has two sides to it, a left and a right. Symmetrical means "having balanced or equal proportions." Since the left side of your body is a mirror image of the right side, your body has bilateral symmetry.

Brainstem. The bottom or "stem" of the brain that sits atop the spinal cord. The various parts of the brainstem have considerable control over such involuntary behaviors as breathing, heart rate, and so forth.

Cell body. The center part of the neuron.

Cerebrum (sa-REE-brum). From the Latin word meaning "brain." The largest part of the human brain. The cerebrum, which is divided into two hemispheres, sits atop the brainstem and center brain.

Cilia (SILL-ee-uh). In biological terms, cilia are hairlike "feelers" that are found on the surface of many cells. When the cilia "beat" or thrash around, the cell moves. The dendrites and axons on your own nerve cells may have evolved from the cilia on primitive, nervetype cells.

Corpus callosum (KOR-pus kah-LOW-sum). The bridge of nervous tissue that connects the major and the minor hemispheres. The Latin word *corpus* means "body," from which we get our word "corpse."

Cortex (KOR-tex). The thin outer layer of the brain, about ¼ inch (0.64 centimeters) thick. The millions of nerve cells in your cortex influence most of what you think, feel, and do.

Dendrites (DEN-drights). The feelers that extend from the cell body of a neuron—the "front end" of the nerve cell.

Electroencephalogram (ee-LEK-tro en-SEF-uh-low-gram). Also called EEG. A graphic record of your brain waves, or of the electrical activity in your brain. The Greek word *cephalo* means "head."

Epilepsy (EP-a-LEP-see). From the Greek word meaning "to seize" or "to attack." When the neurons in the brain are overstimulated (usually because of sickness or damage), they may become overburdened and respond in a very abnormal way. After any epileptic attack, the person typically is normal for a period of days or weeks.

Ethology (ee-THOL-a-gee). The scientific study of animal behavior. Usually refers to scientific observations made in natural surroundings rather in a laboratory.

Excretion (ex-KREE-shun). From the Latin word meaning "to discharge." Literally, excretion is releasing wastes from the body.

Feedback. Literally, giving information back to the original source of the information. In psychological terms, information about performance; inputs that tell a system how close it is coming to the desired output.

Hemisphere (HEMM-ess-fear). *Hemi* means "half." Your cerebrum is roughly round or spherical. Thus, each of your two hemispheres is half of your cerebrum.

Imprinting. To *imprint* means to "stamp in." When baby ducks, geese, and other birds first hatch, they tend to follow the first object that moves. The image of this object seems to be "imprinted" on their brains, and becomes a "mother object" to them under most circumstances.

Innate (inn-EIGHT). The Latin word *natus* means "born." Anything in your mind or body that was present on the day you were born is "innate" to you.

Innate releasing mechanisms. Abbreviated IRM. Ethologists believe that there are certain innate behavioral patterns that are common to any species of animals. These behaviors are usually "released" by stimuli in the animal's environment. Roughly speaking, these stimuli can be considered "innate releasing mechanisms."

Instinct. Inherited desire, goal, or behavior pattern. Instincts are usually fairly broad and lengthy behavior patterns that may be made up of many different innate responses that are "released" in sequence.

Living system. A set of related components or subsystems which has a common goal, which is self-motivated, and which is controlled by feedback.

Mirror focus. Your brain is bilaterally symmetrical, which means that for each spot in your left hemisphere, there is a similar spot or "mirror focus" in your right hemisphere.

Natural selection. Darwin's theory that the environment "selects out" those plants and animals that are best-suited for survival in that particular environment.

Nature. Realm of the innate and instinctive, as opposed to "nurture," through which behavior is learned.

Neuron (NEW-ron). A single nerve cell.

Nurture. From the Latin word "to nurse." To nurture is to take care of, or to cause to grow healthy. In psychology, the "nature–nurture" problem has to do with the question of which characteristics are innate ("nature") and which are learned or acquired through experience ("nurture").

Paramecium (PAIR-uh-MEE-see-um). A tiny but highly complex single-celled organism.

Planarian (pla-NAIR-ee-an). From the Latin word meaning "flat or planelike." An inch-long flatworm that lives in water. The simplest animal alive with humanlike neurons, a true brain, and bilateral symmetry.

Reflexes. Automatic or involuntary responses. May be learned or innate.

Social learning theory. The belief or theory that almost all human behaviors are learned or acquired through experience (chiefly with other humans). According to most social learning theorists, the two major ways we learn to act, feel, and think as we do are from imitating the actions of others, and from being rewarded or punished.

Species (SPEE-sees). From the Latin term meaning "outward appearance or shape." A group of animals or plants which possess in common one or more distinctive physical or psychological characteristics.

Spinal cord. The nerve tracts that lie inside the bones of the spine. Messages from the nerve cells in your body flow up your spinal cord to your brain. Messages from the nerve cells in your brain flow down your spinal cord to the rest of your body.

Split brain. When the two hemispheres of the brain are isolated (by cutting the corpus callosum), each half of the brain is free to operate more or less independently.

Stroke. A form of brain damage usually caused by destruction of the blood vessels that "feed" some portion of the brain.

Theory of evolution. The theory, first made by Charles Darwin, that complex animals (such as humans) evolved or developed from very simple organisms through the process of natural selection.

"Kill the pig. Cut her throat. Spill her blood . . . Kill the pig. Cut her throat. Bash her in."

A group of long-haired, painted savages chanted these words over and over as they danced wildly in a circle around a freshly killed pig they were about to cook and eat. A few short months earlier these same blood-soaked young savages would have taken their meals quietly with napkins and silverware like proper young gentlemen. They were, in fact, a group of British schoolboys.

William Golding's novel *Lord of the Flies* tells the frightening story of how a group of grade-school boys, stranded on a deserted tropical island, turns into a pack of wild savages. At first, following the example of their parents and civilization, the lost boys set up an orderly society on the island. They elect leaders, draw up rules, and send out groups to gather food. Within a very short time, however, the society breaks down. The boys quit following the rules and begin to fight among themselves. Their hunger for meat eventually forces them to make spears and hunt the wild pigs on the island. At first this all seems like good sport, but the boys gradually become less and less civilized, especially while hunting. The thrill of the first kill makes them even wilder and more savage. The fighting and hunting are no longer games but have become a necessary way of life.

"Kill the beast! Cut his throat! Spill his blood! . . . Kill the beast! Spill his blood! Do him in!"

The wildness of the young hunters becomes even worse one night when they begin chanting and working themselves into a frenzy. They attack one of their own group as he crawls out of the jungle. The hunters scream and dance. The spears fly. The blood flows. The boy is killed.

Could this tragedy really happen? Is the human race nothing more than a pack of bloodthirsty savages? Are the laws of society the only things that keep people from brutally murdering each other? Is there a defect in human nature, as Golding's book seems to suggest? Are we born with a killer instinct?

Most people would answer, "No. Humans are humane. They respect life and each other." History, however, seems to support the idea that humans are little more than violent, aggressive savages. Some of the earliest literature of western civilization, like the Greek classic *The Iliad*, tells of bloodshed and brutal warfare. In the Middle Ages the Crusaders plundered, raped, and murdered their way across Europe, Africa, and the Middle East. During World War II, Hitler

Violence and aggression are very evident in team sports. Spectators at hockey games usually expect to see brutal confrontations.

and the Nazis cold-bloodedly tortured and murdered millions of Jews. The Atomic Age opened when one bomb with the power of 20,000 tons of TNT killed almost 200,000 people in Hiroshima, Japan. John Kennedy, Robert Kennedy, Martin Luther King, and Malcolm X were all **assassinated** within a few short years.

But these, it is argued, are special cases. People don't really go around killing each other all the time. Some people manage to avoid almost all violent and aggressive situations. Even so, as much as we may dislike admitting it, humans can be destructively aggressive. According to government statistics, there are as many as 15,000 murders, 30,000 rapes, and more than 300,000 cases of violent assault in the United States every year.

Everyone—from a small child receiving a spanking, to college students watching a football game, to an elderly couple enjoying a typically violent television program—knows what human violence and **aggression** are. With violence so evident in human behavior, perhaps Golding was right. Perhaps humans are born with a tendency to be aggressive, and perhaps it is only the rules of society that keep us from being more aggressive than we are.

Not everyone is willing to accept such a warlike picture of the human race. Most people say they dislike violence. No child wants to get a beating, most people dread getting into fights, and certainly no one really wants to get raped, mugged, or murdered. These facts, as well as the existence of human qualities like kindness and cooperation, suggest that aggression may not be something we are born with. Those scientists who believe that violence and aggression are not inborn human characteristics have a problem, though. If we don't inherit our violent tendencies, where do they come from? According to **social learning theorists,** aggressive behaviors are *learned*—that is, violence is a habit that we all may pick up from our parents, teachers, friends, from watching television, and from our society in general.

Learned or innate? If aggressive tendencies are inherited or built into each individual, then we probably cannot eliminate such behaviors entirely. Rather, we must find ways to reduce the frequency and strength of our violent outbursts. On the other hand, if aggressive tendencies are mostly acquired habits, then perhaps we can reduce violence by discovering the various ways in which our society "shapes" or trains us into being overly aggressive. For example, in 1972, the Surgeon General of the United States reported that some 75 percent of the prime-time programs on television contain at least one episode of violence. Psychologists estimate the average child in the United States witnesses nearly 1000 murders or violent deaths on television each year. Social learning theorists maintain that we might go a long way toward reducing murder and **mayhem** in our society if we could somehow reduce or even ban the showing of violent aggression on TV.

THE NATURE–NURTURE QUESTION

The basic causes of human aggression are yet to be determined, but as important as this subject is, it is only part of a much larger problem — the nature–nurture question. Which aspects of human nature are a direct result of nature or biological inheritance, and which are learned as a result of **nurture** or rearing? We will focus in this chapter on human aggression, but intelligence, creativity, and many other human characteristics have been attributed either to nature or nurture by different theories.

Actually, nature and nurture are probably both involved in most aspects of human behavior. Without nature (the body and brain we inherit) there would be no behavior. Without nurture (the care and information we receive from our parents and society) infants would not survive. Therefore, in order to understand aggression or almost any other human behavior, it is necessary to have some understanding of the effect of both nature and nurture. It is necessary to understand which behavior patterns are primarily innate or inherited, and which are primarily the result of learning or experience. In this chapter we will take a close look at how nature (through our bodies, nervous systems, and brains) contributes to our behavior.

A child who watches television may be influenced by the excessive violence he or she views on the screen.

THE THEORY OF EVOLUTION

Nature provides each human being with a physical body, and every human behavior is in some way a result of the workings of the body and its brain. One method of better understanding the complexities of human behavior and the workings of the body is to study the development and behaviors of less complex organisms (living systems). It was the British scientist Charles Darwin who first proposed a theory to help us understand the development or **evolution** of the world's many different organisms, including plants, animals, and humans.

In 1831, Darwin took a job as a naturalist aboard a ship called the *Beagle,* which was setting out on a five-year voyage to map the coast of South America. Darwin was amazed at the enormous variety of plants and animals he saw in South America. He began to wonder how so many **species** or variations came to be. Traditional thinking in the nineteenth century held that the world, with all of its plants and animals, including humans, had been created at one time — perhaps in six days, as the Bible says. But seeing such a variety of life, Darwin soon became convinced that the world could not have been created with a single set of unchanging species. Instead, he reasoned, plant and animal species might develop or *evolve* differently when they are isolated from each other. A specific type of plant growing in England, for instance, might inherit certain characteristics and evolve into a very different type of plant after many generations. An identical plant growing in a different environment, such as South America, might inherit a different set of characteristics and evolve into a type of plant completely different from the one growing in England.

But why would one plant evolve in one direction while another evolved in a different direction? Darwin worked out an answer to this question after reading an essay on population by the famous English economist, Thomas Malthus. Malthus had said that populations usually grow faster than their food supplies; because of this overpopulation, people must compete for food. Darwin applied a similar line of thought to populations of plants and animals. In a very crowded forest, trees throw a lot of shade and cut each other off from one of their basic energy supplies (sunlight). But if, perhaps through a lucky accident of nature, one particular tree inherits the characteristic of tallness, that tree will grow above the others and get more sunlight. It will have inherited a characteristic that helps it *survive* more efficiently in its particular environment. If this tree survives, it will be likely to reproduce and hence pass on its characteristics and produce more tall trees. Eventually, the shorter trees will be starved out, and the taller species will be all that is left.

The search for food has influenced the evolutionary development of both the plant and animal kingdoms. Why do you think giraffes have such long necks?

For trees growing in a different environment, such as in parts of South America where the sun shines more often than it does in England, evolution may take another direction. The characteristic of tallness may not be as important as it is in the English forests, and trees that inherit such a characteristic may not have a particular advantage in the competition for survival. Trees with broader branches or a different type of root system, however, may survive better in South America. The environment will "select out" these surviving trees, and their characteristic types of branches or roots will be the ones most likely to be passed along to future generations of trees.

The same is true for animal species. In a situation where there are too many animals and not enough food, the animals must compete for food. Those that may have inherited characteristics that help them in the competition for energy are most likely to survive. They will pass on their characteristics to their offspring. In this way nature acts as a *selective force* to kill off the weakest and produce new species from the survivors. (Because aggressiveness and competitiveness are characteristics that can be helpful to survival, Darwin's theory can be used to explain how such characteristics may have been inherited by the human species.)

In the 1840s Darwin wrote out a complete explanation of his theory but did not publish it. It seems that he did not want to become involved in the controversy and argument he knew his theory would produce. Darwin's theory not only goes against the biblical account of creation by suggesting that every plant and animal that ever existed could have evolved during billions of years from only one life form, it suggests as well that humans might have evolved from lower forms of life—from monkeys and apes. Darwin realized that many people would be unwilling to accept such a suggestion.

Darwin could not avoid the controversy he knew his theory would produce. When another naturalist, Henry Wallace, came up with the identical theory, Darwin decided not to let someone else take all the credit (or blame) for something to which he had devoted 20 years. In 1859, when Darwin published his now famous book, *The Origin of Species,* the expected controversy arose—and it hasn't completely died down yet.

Regardless of the controversy, Darwin's theory of evolution has survived. It has survived because it has been extremely useful in explaining not only the origin of plants and animals, but also the development of the human species. The theory of evolution explains how both physical and behavioral characteristics may have evolved.

THE EVOLUTION OF BEHAVIOR

According to the **theory of evolution,** the most successful animal species are those that can adapt or change in ways that would help them survive in whatever environment they found themselves. Physical changes (such as growing thicker fur in winter) are important, but *behavioral changes* (such as learning to migrate to warmer climates during cold weather) are just as necessary to animal survival.

Generally speaking, the simplest or most basic forms of life have the least complicated types of behavior patterns. Even those very simple *living systems* we call plants have a limited type of behavior. The sunflower, for instance, turns its head to follow the sun and extends its roots toward sources of water.

One-celled animals have slightly more complex behaviors. Consider the

paramecium, a slipper-shaped little animal found in ponds and puddles all around the world. The paramecium is so small that you would need a magnifying glass to inspect it closely. Yet small as it is, the paramecium has many complicated behavior patterns. Without ever having been trained to do so, paramecia will move away from danger, but will move toward food. Put another way, paramecia are innately "programmed" to approach some stimuli and to avoid others. But before we can discuss how this **innate** programming comes about, we must first take a look at some general properties of several types of living systems.

Living Systems

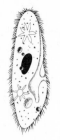

FIG. 2-1.
A paramecium is a one-celled animal. It takes in food, digests it, and moves on to find more food.

Plants, paramecia, and people are all **living systems.** In other words, you, a sunflower, and a paramecium all have certain characteristics in common. For instance, all living systems are made up of parts that must work together in a coordinated fashion if the system is to survive. The paramecium is a single cell, but it has a surface covered with hairlike bits of flesh called **cilia,** which it waves back and forth when it wants to move. Paramecia also have a mouth, a primitive digestive system, and spots on their surface that are sensitive to light, heat, touch, and to various chemicals. Some parts of the paramecium body detect changes in its environment; other parts "process" this incoming information by transmitting commands to the animal's cilia and muscles, which move the animal around. Thus, like all living systems, the paramecium's behavior is determined by its inputs, its internal processes, its outputs—and by the **feedback** that the environment gives it on its behavior.

Paramecia eat bacteria. Once the animal has eaten its meal, various digestive processes inside the animal's body extract the edible parts of the bacteria and **excrete** the rest back into the water. These excretions irritate the cilia, so the paramecium soon swims away in search of food elsewhere.

Living organisms, then, have various types of *internal processes* that allow the animals to respond appropriately to various types of stimulus inputs. Some of these inputs have to do mostly with the *energy* the organism needs to survive—the bacteria themselves are an input once they have reached the paramecium's mouth. Other inputs have to do with *information* the organism needs in order to approach food and to avoid unpleasant things like heat and cold.

Reflexes

Reflexes are simple, automatic behavior patterns in which a specific stimulus input is always followed by a specific response output. *Innate reflexes* are those internal processes that organisms inherit from their parents. For example, if you had a shallow bowl of water full of paramecia, and you applied heat to one side of the bowl, practically all of the little animals would immediately begin a twisting, spiraling sort of dance that would soon get them away from the hot stimulus. Those animals that didn't move away quickly would tend to get "cooked" and die, and wouldn't be around to pass along their weaker heat-avoidance reflexes to any offspring. The paramecia's environment tends to *select* out those animals best suited to survive in that environment by killing off animals with unsuitable internal processes. If for some reason the environment changed radically, it might "select" for survival paramecia with quite different reflexes. This process of **natural selection,** which is sometimes called the "survival of the fittest," lies at the heart of Darwin's theory of evolution.

Although innate reflex patterns are inherited, they usually can be modified by experience. Biologist Philip Applewhite is one of several scientists who have demonstrated recently that even single-celled organisms are capable of learning. Most such learning involves changing the animal's internal processes so that it gives a new response output to a familiar stimulus input.

For instance, many paramecia tend to avoid bright light. But if you shine a light into their bowl just before dumping some bacteria into the light beam, the paramecia might eventually learn to respond to the light by approaching it rather than avoiding it. This type of training presumably "reprograms" the paramecia's innate reflexes.

Humans are born with a few rather mechanical innate reflexes. If you blow a puff of cold air toward an infant's eyes, it will blink reflexively. The infant doesn't need to be trained to do so. However, if you now sound a bell just before blowing the puff of air at the child, and you do so several times, the infant will soon begin blinking at the sound of the bell.

Instincts

Reflexes are simple, automatic behavior patterns in which a specific stimulus input is always followed by a specific response output. Single-celled animals seldom show much more than basic, innate reflexes. More advanced species are capable of showing quite complicated behavior patterns, presumably because there is a very strong relationship between the size and complexity of an organism's nervous system and the complexity of its behavioral outputs. Generally speaking, the bigger an animal's brain (or the more nerve cells that it has), the more the animal can learn, and the less dependent it is for survival on its innate reflexes.

All living systems behave as if they had goals, their major goal being that of survival. When you watch a paramecium approach and devour a clump of bacteria, you can often pick out each individual reflex that brings the paramecium to its dinner. But how would you describe the lioness in an African jungle who scents a zebra, stalks it for miles, lies quietly in wait until it is near, runs the zebra down, kills it, eats part of the flesh, and then takes some of the rest back to her den to give to her cubs? Is this whole, complicated sequence of feeding behaviors nothing more than a set of innate reflexes?

The answer must be *no,* because not all of the lioness's responses are "simple and automatic." Yet these responses serve much the same goal or purpose as do the feeding reflexes of the paramecia.

When describing the highly complex but goal-oriented reactions of higher animals, psychologists often use the term **instincts.** Instincts are fairly complicated behaviors in which the *goal* seems to be inherited, but in which the manner of *achieving* the goal may change considerably — depending on the environment the animal finds itself in, its past experience, and the size of its brain.

One of the best-known examples of instinctive behavior is the maternal behavior of some animals, such as the urge of certain female animals to build nests and care for their young. Web-spinning in spiders, swimming in most fish, and mating responses in most higher animals are all believed to be instinctive behaviors. But even behavioral outputs that appear to be inherited may be highly dependent on learning. When female rats are not allowed to work with or handle any kind of nesting material in their early lives, they often fail to build nests or adequately care for their young. These animals may have a so-called maternal instinct, but instincts are always expressed as a complex sequence or chain of simple reflexes — some learned, some innate, but all dependent upon the present environment and on past experience. Without the opportunity to acquire simple, reflexive skills in handling nesting materials, the female rats apparently are unable to satisfy their "maternal instinct." The *urge* may be there—

Both hereditary and environmental factors contributed to the maternal instinct that this rodent exhibits by building a nest for her young.

but the learned internal programs needed for the animal to reach the instinctual goal are not present.

Many human behaviors have been called instinctive. It has been said, for instance, that children instinctively know their own mothers, or that humans have a "killer instinct" (as William Golding suggests in *Lord of the Flies*). We do have simple reflexes that are inherited — almost all newborn infants gasp and cry when spanked. But as the child grows older, it cries in Spanish, Chinese, Portuguese, or English. Its initial gasping reflex (provided by nature) is rapidly modified into an incredibly complex response we call *language behavior* (provided by nurture). Your urge to talk may be innate (instinctual), but the language you speak was determined by the environment that nurtured you.

The behavior patterns of paramecia are almost entirely innate reactions; the behavior patterns of adult human beings are almost entirely learned responses. The behavioral outputs of the other animal species lie between these two extremes on the nature–nurture pole. Thus we may say that paramecia are little more than a bundle of automatic reflexes; that fish and birds and cats have increasingly complex instinctual responses; but that humans are so complicated that we cannot easily determine what reflexes and instincts we really have.

Imprinting

By careful observation of animals, we may sometimes be able to figure out which of their behaviors are innately determined and which are primarily acquired or learned. **Ethology** is the scientific study of animal traits and behaviors. By observing animals in their natural environments, ethologists attempt to understand the built-in behavior patterns that evolution has produced.

The first moving object these geese saw after hatching was Konrad Lorenz. The young geese imprinted on Dr. Lorenz and behave as if he were their real mother.

The work of a German ethologist, Konrad Lorenz, has helped explain some of the relationships between innate and acquired behaviors. In one series of experiments, Lorenz reared geese that had been hatched in an incubator. The first moving object these geese saw after they hatched was not their mother, but Lorenz. Instinctively, the young geese began to follow the scientist around. They behaved as if he were their real mother. Later, when the geese were placed with their mother, they ignored her and ran back to Lorenz for protection. Lorenz found that young geese instinctively follow the first moving object they see after they are hatched, no matter what it is. They attach themselves to an object, and (according to Lorenz's theory) the image of that object is stamped or **imprinted** on their brains. Lorenz experimented with the *imprinting* process and found that he could even imprint geese to such things as balloons simply by moving a balloon around in front of the geese shortly after they hatched.

The imprinting process is obviously related to survival. Young geese must have a *model* to learn appropriate goose behavior from. Since the first moving object young geese would normally see is their mother, she usually becomes the imprinted model. The young geese who became attached to Lorenz or to balloons did not learn the gooselike behaviors that would prepare them for life as adult geese.

FIG. 2–2.
As this diagram
suggests, the innate
releasing mechanism
liberates or releases
stored-up energy in
response to either a
single specific stimu-
lus, or to a series of
related stimuli.

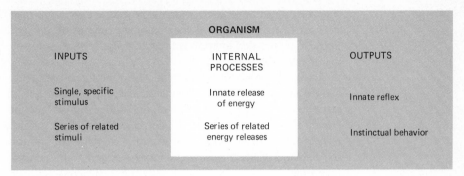

ORGANISM

INPUTS	INTERNAL PROCESSES	OUTPUTS
Single, specific stimulus	Innate release of energy	Innate reflex
Series of related stimuli	Series of related energy releases	Instinctual behavior

FIG. 2–2. As this diagram suggests, the innate releasing mechanism liberates or releases stored-up energy in response to either a single specific stimulus, or to a series of related stimuli.

Innate Releasing Mechanisms

The ethologists and other scientists who have studied animal behavior have taught us many important lessons, not the least of which is this: Animals are not mere blobs of motionless flesh that must be poked or stimulated into action by the environment. Rather, all living organisms store energy that is *released* by environmental inputs. The external cues that trigger mating behavior in geese, for example, do not *stimulate* or push the male goose into courting and mating with a receptive female. Instead, the sights and sounds of the receptive female release (and perhaps guide) the complex dance that the male goose typically performs in the presence of a sexually active female. Some aspects of the dance pattern are **innate** reflexes; other parts of the dance are strongly influenced by past learning. These innate and learned reflexes are like *programs* that you might store in a computer so that the machine would be ready to respond appropriately when you gave it a problem to solve. In the case of the male goose, the mating response is already present (pre-programmed) long before the response is needed.

Ethologists have given the name **innate releasing mechanisms** to those stimulus inputs that evoke or release instinctual behavior patterns.

To put the matter in scientific terms, all living systems need two types of inputs from their environments: (1) Energy inputs, which provide the "fuel" to keep the system going (e.g., the goose's readiness to mate); and (2) informational inputs, which release this energy while guiding the system toward its goals (e.g., the receptive stance of the female goose). Innate releasing mechanisms are stimulus inputs that release instinctual goal responses that have already been pre-programmed into the organism's nervous system and brain.

THE NERVOUS SYSTEM

Life first appeared on earth more than a billion years ago. Judging from all the scientific evidence presently available to us, the first living systems were single-celled organisms not too different from the paramecium. The evidence also suggests that many-celled animals did not appear until millions of years later. Charles Darwin suggested that complex organisms *evolved* from single cells because multicelled animals often had a better chance of surviving their changing environment.

For just a moment, you might wish to compare yourself to a paramecium. Your body is made up of trillions of cells; the paramecium must make do with just one cell. You have a stomach and other organs to convert food into tiny, energy-rich particles; lungs to take in oxygen and help get rid of carbon dioxide; a heart to pump the food particles and oxygen throughout your body; eyes to see with and ears to hear with; a nervous system to transmit sights and sounds to your brain; a "central computer" (your brain) to process and store incoming information and decide on appropriate responses; you have legs to move your body about, hands with which you manipulate or change your environment, and a tongue to help you communicate with other people. Little wonder that the paramecium has many fewer and much more simple response patterns than you do. Little wonder too that you can survive and prosper in thousands of environments that would kill a paramecium instantly.

The Neuron

As the original single-celled organisms evolved into more complex life forms, the cells themselves began to specialize. A paramecium has to take care of itself, but each nerve cell in your brain does not have to go out and hunt for food, or get oxygen, or protect itself, or hunt for a mate. Because other cells or groups of cells (organs) take care of its basic needs, the nerve cell (or **neuron**) is free to "do its own thing"—that is, to transmit messages from one part of your body to another.

Each neuron in your body has three main parts—the **dendrites,** the **cell body,** and the **axon.** The *dendrites* are cilialike feelers that reach out to receive informational inputs from other cells and from the environment. This incoming information is *processed* by various parts of the neuron, including the cell body.

FIG. 2–3.
The neuron or nerve cell is made up of three main parts: (a) the dendrites, which receive information from other cells or the environment; (b) the cell body, which helps process the information, and (c) the axon, which reaches out to make contact with the dendrites of other cells.

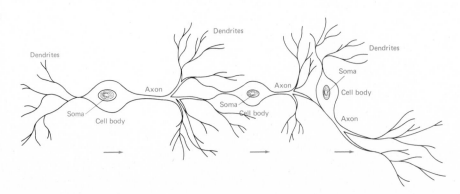

FIG. 2-4.
The jellyfish is one of the lowest order of animals to possess a nerve net; it does not have a brain.

Then the information is sent out along the "tail" of the neuron, which we call the *axon*. The axon of each neuron reaches out to make contact with the dendrites (and sometimes with the cell bodies) of other cells.

When somebody hits you on the arm in anger, the pressure of the blow excites the dendrites of various neurons buried in the skin of your arm. The neurons respond in alarm and send a message along their axons to a group of nerve cells in your **spinal cord.** These spinal neurons relay the alarm to your brain, where a whole host of neurons receives the message and tries to figure out (very quickly indeed) what to do about the fact that you have just been attacked. Depending on the situation and your own past experience, your brain may react in a number of different ways. The nerve cells in your brain may send urgent signals down to the muscles in your legs ordering them to run away. Your brain might signal the muscles in your arms to hit the person back. Or the muscles in your tongue might be ordered to say a few kind or unkind words to whoever hit you.

No matter what the stimulus, and no matter how you respond, the messages to and from your brain will travel over nerve pathways made up of thousands of individual neurons, each connected to the other in "head-to-tail" fashion. And because neurons typically transmit messages only in one direction (dendrite to axon), your body has one set of nerve pathways for handling stimuli, and another set of pathways for responses.

Nerve Nets

As we said, the first living systems to appear on earth probably were single-celled organisms. The next step upward in evolution probably was a multicelled animal much like the jellyfish you might encounter when swimming in the ocean. The jellyfish has neurons, but it does not have a brain. Rather, the neurons in the jellyfish are connected much like the strings in a fishnet. If you stimulated one neuron in the net, the message would rapidly spread out to almost all the other neurons in the animal's body. If a crab grabbed at a jellyfish with its claws, the jellyfish might respond to this painful input by rapidly contracting most of the muscles in its body and swimming away. Because the jellyfish has no central mass of nerve cells to "process" or evaluate incoming information, its whole body usually responds to almost any kind of painful stimulation.

Primitive Brains

The simplest animal alive today with a true brain is the planarian flatworm, found in ponds and rivers throughout the world. We assume that many millions of years ago a wormlike animal with a brain evolved from a jellyfishlike animal that didn't have a brain. What we know for certain is that all present-day animals more complex than the jellyfish do have brains.

The importance of the brain has to do with how it aids survival. The jellyfish

The simplest animal to possess a real brain is the planarian, or flatworm.

cannot readily tell the difference between friend and foe because it lacks a brain to help it make important decisions. Its neurons do contain simple pre-programmed (innate) reflexes, but it cannot learn very much because it has no brain capable of changing (re-programming) these response patterns. On the other hand, as dozens of scientists have demonstrated in recent years, flatworms can be taught many fairly complex new habits.

The nervous system of the flatworm differs from that of the jellyfish in two important ways. First, the worm has a brain made up of two lumps or groups of nerve cells. Although the two lumps are connected to each other and pass messages back and forth, each lump seems to control just half of the animal's body. (The importance of having two separate halves to one's brain will become clear later in this chapter.)

Second, the worm brain has input pathways, processing areas where "programs" presumably are stored, and output pathways. Different parts of its brain have different capabilities, and different tasks to perform. The jellyfish nerve net is limited in its usefulness because almost all of its neurons respond if any one or two nerve cells respond. The jellyfish tends to run away from any unusual stimulus (other than food). The flatworm can react to a stimulus input either by running away, by attacking, or by simply ignoring the stimulus if the worm has learned the stimulus is not threatening.

Generally speaking, the more complicated an animal's nervous system is, the more complex its internal programs are, and the more complex its behavior becomes. And the more neural tissue the animal has, the more it can learn, adapt, and survive in various types of environments. It probably took a billion years for the simplest flatworm-type brain (which has about 3000 neurons) to evolve into the human brain (which has more than 10,000,000,000 neurons). One of the major reasons why you can study a flatworm, but a flatworm can't study you, is the fact that the flatworm's brain has 3000 neurons while your brain has 10,000,000,000 neurons.

THE HUMAN BRAIN

Your brain sits atop your spinal column. If you could look at your own brain in a mirror, it would look much like the cap on a large, gray mushroom sitting atop a skinny stem (the spinal cord). Since there are no muscles in your brain, it wouldn't move about as you inspected it. Despite its lack of muscles, your brain uses up about 25 percent of the "fuel" your body takes in. This is such a high percentage because your brain is really a "battery" of stored-up energy used by its 10 billion or so nerve cells as they flash messages back and forth to coordinate all your thoughts and movements.

Your spinal cord contains millions of nerve pathways that route incoming stimuli from your body up to the brain. The spinal cord also carries "command messages" back from the brain to your muscles, ordering them to respond appropriately to whatever environment you find yourself in.

FIG. 2–5.
The basic structure of the human brain includes: (a) spinal cord, which routes messages from the nerves to the brain and sends commands back to the muscles; (b) brainstem, which coordinates blood circulation, breathing, reflexes; (c) middle brain, or cerebellum, which sorts out sensory messages and influences emotional responses; and (d) cerebrum, which is the largest and thickest part of the brain. The cortex, or the surface of the cerebrum, is involved in speech, intelligence, learning, and decision making.

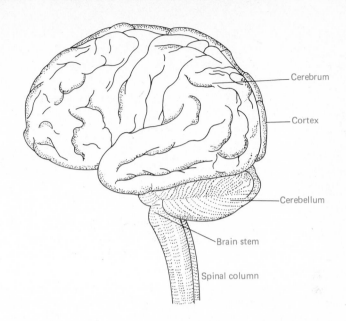

Cerebrum

Cortex

Cerebellum

Brain stem

Spinal column

The top of your spinal cord widens out slightly to become your **brainstem.** The brainstem influences some of the most essential activities of your body, such as circulation of your blood, breathing, and certain reflex actions.

Above the brainstem, your brain continues to widen into the middle brain, which acts as a sort of "central switchboard" for most of the sensory messages coming into your brain. The middle brain is also involved in many types of emotional responses.

Above your brainstem and your middle brain lies the "cap of the mushroom," which is your **cerebrum,** by far the largest and thickest part of your brain. If you looked at your brain from the top, about all you would see would be the cerebrum.

The outer surface of your cerebrum contains a layer of cells about 1 centimeter thick (.25 inches thick) that is called the **cortex.** If you cut through a human brain, the cortex would look much like the outer skin on a piece of sliced mushroom.

Most psychologists consider the cortex to be the most important part of the brain, because research suggests that speech, intelligence, learning, perception, and decision making are primarily functions of the cortex. The lower centers of your brain are greatly involved in emotional responses, in consciousness, in motivation, and in some movements of your body; but your cortex adds the "fine tuning" to almost everything you do. If we could somehow peel away this thin outer layer of your brain, you would still be a human being—but you would be unable to talk, to see or hear very well, to learn, to remember, or to make fine movements with your hands, fingers, feet, and tongue.

In evolutionary terms, the cerebrum was the last part of the brain to develop.

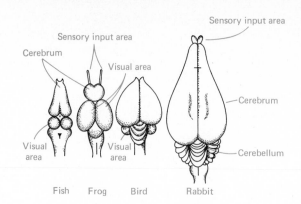

FIG. 2–6.
The brains of lower animals are made up chiefly of sensory-input areas and motor-output areas (such as the cerebellum). The larger the cerebrum is in relation to the rest of the brain, the more complex the behavior the organism is typically capable of. Your cerebrum makes up the major part of your brain and is more than 100 times larger than the cerebrum of the rabbit.

To give you an idea: Humans have a much better-developed cerebrum than do monkeys; monkeys have more cerebral tissue than do dogs; dogs have more than rats; rats more than pigeons; pigeons more than goldfish; and flatworms don't really have a cerebrum at all. Humans also have a more highly developed cortex than do any other animal species. Generally speaking, the larger and more complex an animal's cerebrum and cortex, the more complex that animal's behavior patterns are likely to be.

The Dominant Hemisphere

If you were to cut a flatworm in half—from the tip of its snout to the end of its tail—the left half of the animal's body would be a mirror image of the right. The flatworm is the simplest living animal to possess this **bilateral symmetry.** All animal species more advanced than the flatworm have *bilateral symmetry,* including humans. If you were to draw an imaginary line through the middle of your own body, you would see this same bilateral symmetry. The left half of your body is very nearly a mirror-image of the right half.

Your cerebrum, which is as roundish or spherical as the cap of a mushroom, also has two halves—the left hemisphere and the right hemisphere.

Your left hemisphere directly controls the muscles in the right side of your body, while the right hemisphere controls the left side of your body. Such a situation might be awkward if one side of your brain did not have overall control over what you do. Imagine what might happen if your right hemisphere ordered your left leg to sit down, while your left hemisphere ordered your right leg to run. But such things do not usually happen because one side of your brain is *dominant*—that is, it generally makes the major decisions about what your body is going to do, while the other side of your brain obeys rather passively.

If you are right-handed, your left hemisphere probably controls your body movements (including your speech). If you are left-handed, the right half of your brain may be the dominant side. However, the left hemisphere is probably dominant in some left-handers, and in a few "lefties" neither side of the brain really dominates the other. (For your own information, about 90 percent of the people on earth are right-handed.)

If your left or dominant hemisphere decides that your body should run, it tells the muscles in your right leg to start moving. At the same time, your left hemisphere orders your right hemisphere to make the left side of your body run. Your right hemisphere will ordinarily obey and then signal back that it has carried out the order.

Even though the two halves of your brain are mirror images, and each controls the muscles for half your body, each hemisphere has certain abilities that the other lacks. Your left hemisphere is (usually) dominant; it also contains the brain centers that enable you to speak. Proof for this statement can sometimes be seen in people who have suffered a **stroke.** Particularly in elderly people, a blood clot in the arteries can sometimes cut off the blood supply to the neurons in certain areas of the brain. These neurons soon starve to death, and those parts of the body that were formerly controlled by the dead neurons become paralyzed.

With time and training, the stroke victim may recover at least partially from the paralysis because other (undamaged) parts of the brain may take over control of the lost functions. However, if the stroke hits that area of the left hemisphere just in front of and above the left ear, right-handed people may permanently lose their ability to speak, to read, or to make sense out of words. This language ability seldom returns despite treatment.

But if the stroke hits the same area near the ear in the right hemisphere, right-handed people usually suffer only a temporary problem with speech and reading—or the person's language ability may not be affected at all. Since speech is one of the few behaviors that the right hemisphere cannot take over from the left after a stroke, we are reasonably confident that the "speech center" in your brain is located only in your left hemisphere (if you are right-handed). To put the matter another way, whenever you say something out loud, it is your

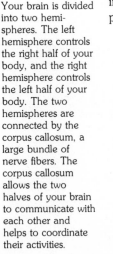

FIG. 2-7.
Your brain is divided into two hemispheres. The left hemisphere controls the right half of your body, and the right hemisphere controls the left half of your body. The two hemispheres are connected by the corpus callosum, a large bundle of nerve fibers. The corpus callosum allows the two halves of your brain to communicate with each other and helps to coordinate their activities.

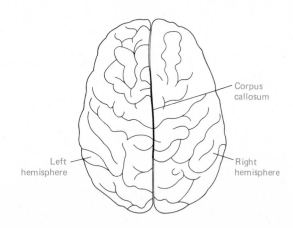

dominant hemisphere that is talking. Your other hemisphere can express itself with bodily movements, and it has a few special tricks of its own, but it cannot speak.

The Corpus Callosum

Bilateral symmetry has tremendous survival value. The fact that there are two halves to your brain gives you a certain amount of "insurance" against strokes, head wounds, and certain types of disease that destroy neural tissue. An undamaged hemisphere can take over many of the activities previously performed by the damaged side because it has been closely connected with all of these actions. Your right hemisphere seldom controls the right side of your body, but it can learn to do so (except for speech). The reason one hemisphere can learn the functions of the other is that the two hemispheres are connected to each other by a large bundle of nerve fibers called the **corpus callosum.**

If your left hand is wounded, this painful information is first registered in your right hemisphere. The information is then immediately sent via the corpus callosum to the left side of your brain. If your left hemisphere orders your left leg to move, the message goes first across the corpus callosum to your right hemisphere, which moves your leg (and sends a "mission accomplished" feedback signal across the corpus callosum to the left hemisphere).

The corpus callosum thus allows the two halves of your brain to coordinate their activities, and allows your dominant hemisphere to have control over your entire body. If somebody destroyed your corpus callosum, your hemispheres would have to find new and unusual ways of communicating with each other — and for a time, at least, you would have difficulty performing even such simple acts as walking or clapping your hands.

THE SPLIT BRAIN

Psychologists Roger Sperry and R. E. Meyers uncovered much of the first information about what happens when the corpus callosum is destroyed when they performed a series of experiments on what we now call **split-brain** cats. First Sperry and Meyers sliced the corpus callosum of a living cat's brain and thus prevented the two hemispheres of the animal's cerebrum from communicating with each other. This operation allowed each hemisphere to act on its own. Next the scientists performed a rather special operation on the nerves leading from the cat's eyes. Although you might not realize it, information from your left eye goes to both hemispheres of your brain, and stimulus inputs from your right eye also go to both of your hemispheres. The same sort of arrangement holds in cats, but after the operation performed by Sperry and Meyers, inputs from the left eye were fed just to the cat's left hemisphere, while information from the right eye went just to the right hemisphere.

After the operation, the animal had some difficulty in coordinating its movements, since the left half of its body didn't always "want" to do the things that the right half of its body was doing. However, the cat eventually got over this problem. Either the separate sides of the animal's brain learned to cooperate with each other, or they took turns controlling the entire body.

Once the cat was able to move around fairly normally, Sperry and Meyers taught it to solve a series of visual problems. In some of the experiments, the cat could use both its eyes; in other experiments, either the left or the right eye was blindfolded. The results of these early studies were most surprising.

If you taught a normal cat to approach a black square to get food with both its eyes open, and then you blindfolded one of its eyes, do you think the cat could still perform the task? (Can you recognize a good friend of yours when one of your eyes is blindfolded?) In fact, both normal and split-brain cats can do this sort of task rather well — if they learn with both eyes open, they can perform with either eye blindfolded.

But what would happen if you taught a cat to approach a black square with its right eye covered, then *tested* the animal's memory with the right eye open but the left (trained) eye blindfolded? A normal cat can perform such tasks easily, since during the learning, the information about the black square is stored in both hemispheres. Thus it doesn't matter which eye is used for training, or for the memory test.

But the split-brain cat is a different beast entirely. When Sperry and Meyers trained their split-brain cat with only its left eye uncovered, then blindfolded the "trained" left eye and tested the animal with its "untrained" right eye open, the cat simply had no idea what to do. It seems that the memory was stored only in the "trained" left hemisphere, which couldn't communicate directly with the right hemisphere. Therefore, when the right eye was tested, the right hemisphere was almost totally ignorant of what the left hemisphere had learned. The "memory" simply didn't transfer from one hemisphere to the other, as it would in cats with a normal corpus callosum.

Summing up their extensive research program on split-brain animals, Sperry and Meyers concluded that cutting the corpus callosum seemed to leave the animals with *two separate minds* that learned and operated independently.

Humans with Split Brains

If, for some terrible reason, your own corpus callosum were cut or damaged, would you end up with "two separate minds"? The answer seems to be *yes,* you would. But before we talk about what your two minds might be like, let's first discuss some unfortunate humans suffering from **epilepsy** who had their corpus callosums cut (in order to save their lives).

An **electroencephalogram** or EEG is an instrument for monitoring electrical activity in various parts of the brain. A small sensor is attached to the person's scalp and a fairly accurate reading of electrical activity can be taken from the area of the brain under the sensor. In a person with brain damage, abnormal EEG readings usually come from the damaged area.

Epilepsy is a brain condition that usually produces periodic fits or seizures and muscle convulsions. EEG readings have shown that epilepsy is the result of brain damage, often on only one side of the brain. Just before an epileptic attack or seizure begins, the damaged area starts to send out abnormal impulses. These impulses are flashed across the corpus callosum and they begin to excite the nerve cells in the **mirror focus** in the opposite hemisphere. The neurons at the mirror focus immediately feed back messages to the damaged area in the other hemisphere. Since the damaged tissue is on the warpath anyhow, these "feed-back messages" excite the damaged tissue more than they usually would. The damaged area then sends even stronger signals to the mirror focus in the other hemisphere, which feeds the signal right back—and soon the whole brain is "on fire" and a seizure occurs.

In a sense, an epileptic's brain responds much the same way that the boys in Golding's *Lord of the Flies* responded when they danced around the fire, psyching themselves up to attack and kill one of their group. When the first boy began dancing and jeering, his behavior excited a second boy to do the same. When the second boy started chanting, his behavior encouraged the first boy to shout a little louder and to become a little more vicious. Eventually, this emotional feedback from one boy to another reached the crisis point, and the murderous attack occurred.

Epileptic attacks usually occur because of the feedback that each hemisphere sends to the other. And because all of these abnormal feedback messages travel across the corpus callosum, surgeons have in some very extreme cases split the brains of epileptics for whom there was no other type of treatment possible. Cutting the corpus callosum prevents the undamaged cells at the mirror focus from feeding back strong signals to the damaged tissue. But while the operation reduces the frequency and severity of the seizures, cutting the corpus callosum does have unfortunate side effects. The speaking side of the brain loses control over the other hemisphere, which may then begin to act as if it "had a mind of its own." Some patients have reported that their left hand and leg do not always do what they are supposed to do. In some cases, the left (speaking) hemisphere actually has to talk out loud to the right hemisphere and tell it what to do. If the

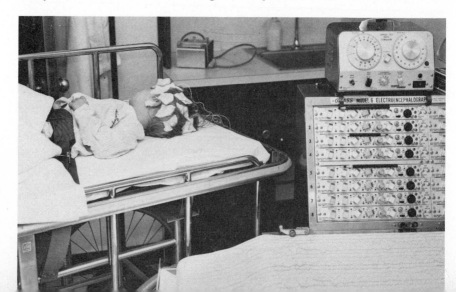

This person is hooked to an electroencephalograph or EEG machine. The sensors attached to the head record the electrical activity of the brain.

right hemisphere disagrees, however, it cannot talk back. All it can do is act. These actions sometimes lead to awkward, embarrassing, or even dangerous situations for split-brained people (which is why the operation is seldom performed).

Two Minds in the Same Body

By working closely with split-brained patients, psychologists have learned much about the differences between the two halves of the cerebrum. The right hemisphere used to be called the *minor* hemisphere (in right-handed people) because it did not have the speech areas, and because the left hemisphere seemed to be dominant or in control. However, much recent research suggests that even though the right hemisphere is silent, it is not inferior or minor. The speaking half of the brain seems to be the logical side and is concerned primarily with "running" the body in an orderly and coordinated matter. The right, nonspeaking hemisphere has other, very important abilities. It understands speech, although it cannot talk. It deals with images rather than with logic, and it may be involved in artistic and creative thinking. The nonspeaking hemisphere also seems to "monitor" or keep track of what the speaking hemisphere is doing—and it apparently can feed back this information to the speaking hemisphere.

SOCIAL EVOLUTION

When some of the boys in *Lord of the Flies* began to go wild, it was not because their brains or nervous systems were malfunctioning. Golding suggests that the boys' behavior was out of control because they no longer had their parents, teachers, or the laws of society to guide them. It is true that the beautiful complexity of the human brain is responsible for coordinating and controlling our behavior. But as we said at the outset of this chapter, both nature (the brain) and nurture (what the brain learns) are involved in most aspects of human behavior. And much of what we learn comes to us as a result of generations of social evolution.

It may seem hard to believe after studying the complexities of the brain, but life seemingly began on earth as a single cell. After a time, these simple, one-celled organisms probably learned to clump together and to cooperate with each other. Eventually these clumps of cells evolved into multicelled organisms like the jellyfish.

Cells that have "clumped together" have great survival value. They can protect each other, help each other obtain food, and defend each other from hungry rivals. But to cooperate with each other—and hence to survive—the cells had to work out various ways of communicating with one another. It was from this need, we assume, that the nervous system came into being. The purpose of the nervous system is to pass messages back and forth among cells. Some of

Your distant ancestors began to gain some control over their environment when they learned to make simple tools and to use them to hunt animals for food and clothing.

these messages have to do with information about what's going on in the outside environment, so that the organism may feed or flee as the need arises. But other messages have to do with *internal control*. The various parts of your body speak to each other in part by way of your nervous system. When your stomach is empty and dinnertime is at hand, your stomach sends neural signals to your brain that begin to disrupt your chain of thought and encourage you to think about hamburgers and pizzas instead of studying psychology. But if you are in the middle of an important examination, your brain can send messages back to your stomach telling it to quiet down for awhile. If the parts of your body could not communicate with each other, this sort of *mutual control* would be impossible—and you would have a great deal of trouble "getting yourself together."

According to the best scientific evidence we presently have, human beings first appeared on earth several million years ago. We know vaguely what these first humans looked like, because we have discovered their bones. But we have no real way of knowing what early human *behavior* was like, because people didn't get around to inventing written language until some 10,000 years or so ago. However, we can make some fairly good guesses about how language, customs, and social behaviors evolved over the years.

The first humans were primarily hunters, but in the beginning they probably had to catch and kill their dinners with their hands and teeth—just as lions and tigers do today. Later on, they apparently learned to use simple tools—stone knives and spears and wooden clubs. They began using animal skins to keep themselves warm, and fire to cook their food and frighten away dangerous animals. These new-found skills apparently allowed them to kill larger and larger animals, including other humans.

At some point in the distant past, humans also discovered that living together in families, tribes, or hunting teams provided the same sort of advantage that the first cells got by "clumping together." One member of the group could stand watch at night while the other members slept. If danger appeared, the lookout could give the alarm and arouse the sleepers.

Furthermore, forming themselves into groups increased the odds that their infants would grow into adults. A newborn horse can run about after its mother within an hour or so after birth. But human infants don't even crawl for many months after they are born. Somebody has to take care of the infant for many years before it can fend for itself.

We presume that *social evolution* occurred much as did the physical evolution of the various parts and organs of your body. Your hands and legs and teeth and brain protect your stomach and get food for it; your stomach digests the food and thereby keeps your hands, legs, teeth, and brain alive. In early social groups, it seems likely that the younger men and women did the hunting and fighting, while the oldest members of the family or tribe cooked, cared for the children, and gathered fruits and berries.

The Evolution of Language

Your body survives because the messages carried by your nervous system allow one part of your body to influence what the other parts are doing. The more accurate these "internal messages" are, the better you get along. Thus the more complex your nervous system is, the better your chances of living to a ripe, old age.

For a group to survive, its members must have some way of communicating with each other, some way of monitoring and influencing each other's activities. The dominant male or "boss" of a troop of baboons controls his group members by communicating with them. He excites them by signaling danger or by showing them where food is. He calms them down by letting them know when danger has passed. He pulls the stragglers back into the troop, and he defends his position against young males who occasionally challenge him. A few grunts, some facial expressions, and arm waving are all the signals the boss baboon needs to keep his troop functioning fairly smoothly.

(Your brain is the "boss" organ of your body. With just a few neural signals, it can speed up the action of your heart when danger is imminent, or slow down your heart rate when the threat is over. But your brain could not exercise this control if it did not know what the other organs of your body were up to. Thus all the parts of your body send messages to your brain letting it know how they are functioning, and how they are responding to the command signals your brain sends them.)

Many animals communicate with each other in simple ways. Birds have danger signals and love calls. Bees do a dance that may be a way of signaling to other bees where honey is to be found. Some monkey troops have 20 or more special "signal sounds." They use one warning cry to signal danger from the air — such as a bird of prey. They scream a different way to warn of danger from the ground—such as a snake. All these signals aid the animals in their continuing battle to survive.

For the most part, the sounds that animals make serve as stimulus inputs that release innately determined responses. These instinctual cries and grunts deal with the *here and now*. Wild animals seem to have no way to communicate with

TABLE 2-1   **Rhesus Calls**[1]

Sound	Description	Significance
Roar	Long, fairly loud noise	Made by a very confident animal when threatening another of inferior rank
Pant-threat	Like a roar, but divided into "syllables"	Made by a less confident animal who wants support in making an attack
Bark	Like the single bark of a dog	Made by a threatening animal who is insufficiently aggressive to move forward
Growl	Like a bark, but quieter, shriller, and and broken in short sound units	Given by a mildly alarmed animal
Shrill-bark	Not described	Alarm call, probably given to predators in the wild
Screech	An abrupt pitch change; up then down	Made when threatening a higher-ranked animal, and when excited and slightly alarmed
Geekering screech	Like a screech, but broken into syllables	Made when threatened by another animal
Scream	Shorter than the screech and without a rise and fall	Made when losing a fight while being bitten
Squeak	Short, very high pitched noises	Made by a defeated and exhausted animal at the end of a fight

[1] *Adapted from Figure 2, Rowell, T. E. Agonistic noises of the Rhesus monkey* (Macaca mulatta). *Symp. Zool. Soc. Lond. No. 8 (1962): 91-96 by permission of the Zoological Society of London.*

each other about the past and the future. Only human beings have taken the next step upward—our language allows us to describe past events in detail, and to plan for the future in carefully considered steps. Language gives us a sense of history in that we can monitor or mentally experience things that happened centuries ago if someone describes the events clearly. Language also gives us a command of the future in that by speaking to each other (or to ourselves), we can often predict what *might happen if* we did certain things next week or next year. Most scientists agree that it is our ability to communicate in a spoken and written language that finally sets us completely above all other animals.

Once we had acquired the ability to talk, our survival rate began to skyrocket. This is because language gives us the opportunity to pass knowledge along from generation to generation. Baboon troops today are probably not much different than they were thousands of years ago, but human society has evolved tremendously in the same period of time. Five hundred years ago, the average life expectancy was not much more than 30 years. Now most of us can expect to live well into our seventies. We are bigger and stronger and better educated than ever before—primarily because our culture has learned how to store information now and make use of it later, when the need arises.

In most animal species (including monkeys and baboons), verbal cries and grunts are controlled by tissue buried deep in the brain. In human beings, speech is controlled by certain specialized areas of the cortex. Children born without cortexes never develop real speech. Adults who lose the functions of their cortical speech centers no longer can use or understand language as you do. In a very real sense, then, it is the complexities of our cortexes that led to our developing meaningful communications, and hence to our developing the marvelously complex cultures that we presently live in.

AGGRESSION

During the millions of years of human development—as our brains became increasingly larger and as our cortexes evolved in greater and greater complexity —aggression seems to have been an essential part of life. The first human hunters surely had to be violent and sometimes brutal in their fight for survival. They had to kill animals and even other human beings who were competing for the same food, mates, and territories. Because aggression was necessary for our early survival, some present-day theorists suggest that violence is an instinctive or built-in part of human nature.

You don't need to slap someone's face or stomp on a person's toes to know that such actions often cause an equally aggressive and sometimes violent response. This violent output in response to a violent input is what Golding implies is "innate" in his novel *Lord of the Flies*. In animals, aggression often does lead to counteraggression. Psychologist Nathan Azrin and his colleagues found out how easy it is to bring out aggression in rats while they were trying to train two animals to be more social. The rats were put in a box with a metal grid on the floor. A painful electric shock could be passed through the grid. The experimenters planned to reward the rats every time they moved close to each other by turning off the shock. But the experiment backfired. As soon as the shock was turned on, the animals instantly became aggressive and began to fight with each other. Azrin and his crew—realizing that they had released an innate form of aggression—changed the objective of their experiment. Instead of studying social responses, they went on to perform a brilliant series of studies on **agonistic** or aggressive reactions.

Azrin and his co-workers learned several things about aggression in animals. They found that the stronger the shock, the longer the aggression lasted. The more often the shock was given, the more violent and vicious the attacks became. They also determined that this agonistic behavior seemed to be instinctive. Even animals that had been reared in isolation from other rats—and hence never had the chance to *learn* to be aggressive—would attack each other when they were given electric shock in the confines of a small, escape-proof box. The shock was indeed an innate releasing mechanism.

When animals receive a painful shock, they may become aggressive. After this raccoon and rat were shocked, they responded aggressively by attacking each other.

The researchers also found that frustration could lead to the same sort of aggression as did pain. Azrin and his associates taught pigeons how to peck at a button to get a piece of grain. Once the birds knew how to get food this way, the scientists stopped feeding the birds when they hit the button. The pigeons pecked and pecked but got no food. As their frustration apparently increased, the birds began attacking the button. Then they would attack anything else that was near, including another bird. The other bird, feeling the painful attack, would fight back. This agonistic or aggressive feedback, of course, added to the pain and frustration of the first bird, and soon a battle royal was in progress.

Next, Azrin and his colleagues studied ways to reduce or prevent the occurrence of this innately determined violence. They found that if the animal were allowed to escape from the shock box, it would often run away instead of fight. Furthermore, if they rewarded the animal for making nonaggressive responses, it could often take the pain and frustration in stride. Thus even animals with strong aggressive instincts can learn through experience to avoid or prevent violent reactions against other animals.

Are Wars Inevitable?

What about human aggression? Most of us have, at one time or another, responded to pain and frustration by attacking people near us. Do Azrin's studies —and Darwin's theory of evolution—suggest that war, murder, rape, and assault are "instinctual" in humans? Are we doomed by our animal heritage to go on killing each other forever? Or have our brains now evolved sufficiently that we can use language to build cultures that are peaceful and productive, rather than being warlike and hostile? In fact, there are many examples of people who have learned to be cooperative and nonaggressive.

In 1971, on the island of Mindanao in the Philippines, a tribe of very primitive people was discovered. This tribe, known as the Tasaday, had been almost completely isolated from the rest of the world for at least 600 years. When they were found, the Tasaday were living much as our ancestors had lived thousands of years ago. One outstanding characteristic of the Tasaday is that they are completely lacking in aggression. Their language has no words for "weapon," "hostility," "anger," or "war." When Tasaday children become aggressive, they are either ignored or mildly reproved. When they play together cooperatively, they earn the approval and love of the adults around them. The Tasaday, unlike the boys in the novel *Lord of the Flies,* are a good indication that human nature is not necessarily aggressive.

Taking all these facts into consideration, can we now say that human aggression is learned? Or is it instinctual? Actually, it is a bit of both—just as all human responses are influenced by innate reflexes (nature) and by past experience (nurture). But the most important point of all is this one: Although we may inherit aggressive tendencies or reflexes, we also have inherited a brain capable of learning other ways of handling pain and frustration. We continuously monitor the behaviors of people around us and give them verbal and nonverbal feedback to let them know whether we approve or disapprove of what they are doing. Using language, we have built a culture that includes certain social roles and behavioral expectancies. If we *expect* people to be innately violent—as Golding surely does in his novel—then we are likely to get what we expect. But if we use our monitoring and language abilities to let people know that nonviolent solutions to human problems are best, then we are likely to become less hostile and agonistic in the future. Once we realize that culture is represented by "neural programs" in our cortexes, and once we recognize that these programs

The Tasaday, a tribe of primitive people, were recently discovered in the Philippines. Isolated from the rest of the world for at least 600 years, the Tasaday remained a gentle people, completely lacking aggressive behavior.

are capable of being changed, we can use both nature and nurture to help us build a society with even greater chances of survival than societies had in the past.

All other animal species have evolved blindly — in response to random changes in their environments. Using the blessing of language, and the complexities of our brains, humans have begun to take charge of their own evolution. We should never be ashamed of our animal heritage, but we should take much greater pride in knowing that we have brains enough to remake this heritage in the future.

► SUMMARY

1. Is human **aggression** an inborn tendency or is it a learned behavior pattern? This question, which can be asked about many aspects of human behavior, is usually called the **nature–nurture question.** In this chapter we examine nature's contribution (the nervous system and the brain) to our behavior.

2. Darwin's **theory of evolution** helps explain how the forces of nature may have worked to provide us with a body, a brain, and certain behavior patterns. In short, the theory of evolution says that those plants and animals that have acquired characteristics that help them to survive more successfully in a particular environment will not only be more likely to survive but will be more likely to pass on their characteristics to their offspring, eventually resulting in a new species.

3. The behavior patterns of all living systems are determined by inputs, internal processes, and outputs. **Reflexes** are among the most basic of behaviors. They are mostly unlearned, automatic responses to changes in the environment. In other words, reflexes are the internal processes that connect specific inputs to specific outputs.

4. Instincts are highly complex behavior patterns in which the goal of the behavior seems to be inherited, but in which the means of achieving the goal may change. This will depend on the environment an animal finds itself in, the animal's past experience, and the size of its brain.

5. Imprinting, first demonstrated in geese, is another example of how inherited behavior patterns and learning work together to produce useful behaviors in some species. **Innate releasing mechanisms** are those stimulus inputs that evoke or release instinctive behavior patterns.

6. The nervous system produces behavior by transmitting inputs to and outputs from the brain. The **neuron,** or nerve cell, is the basic unit of the nervous system. Each neuron has three main parts — **dendrites, the cell body, and the axon.** Messages travel in one direction, from dendrite to axon.

7. The more complex an animal's nervous system is, the more complex its internal programs are, and the more complex its behavior can be. Simple living systems, like the jellyfish, have nets of nerves. More complex animals, like the flatworm, have a central mass of nerve cells (a brain) with which to process and evaluate incoming information. The human brain has more than 10 billion nerve cells.

8. The major structures of the brain are the **brainstem,** the middle brain, the **cerebrum,** and the **cortex,** in which intellectual functioning takes place. The brain is divided into two almost identical halves, with each half or **hemisphere** controlling the opposite side of the body. The halves of the brain are connected by a bundle of nerve fibers called the **corpus callosum.**

9. In most individuals, the speech centers of the brain are located in the left hemisphere. The left brain is also believed to be associated with logical and orderly thinking and with such things as time. The right brain deals mainly with images and may be involved in artistic and creative thinking.

10. The human brain evolved during millions of years of physical and social evolution. The early humans probably survived because they learned to live and hunt in groups. The necessity of group living led to the evolution of social behavior, and cooperation and communication became important aspects of human behavior.

11. Aggression, which is seen in most humans, can be explained as an innate characteristic. But the fact that some humans seem to live without aggression suggests that aggression is learned rather than innate. It is probable that aggression, like many other human traits, is a result of both nature and nurture. In either case, whether aggression is inborn or learned, all humans have a brain capable of much learning . . . and of learning to control aggression.

Suggested Readings

Darwin, Charles. *Origin of species.* New York: Macmillan, 1962.
Golding, William. *Lord of the flies.* New York: Putnam, 1959.
Lorenz, Konrad. *On aggression.* New York: Harcourt Brace, 1966.
Morris, Desmond. *Naked ape.* New York: Dell, 1969.

► STUDY GUIDE

A.   RECALL

Sentence Completion

1. If violent behavior tendencies are not inherited, it must be that they are

[p. 47]   _____ .

2. The controversy over whether or not parts of human nature are learned or inherited

[p. 48]   is most often referred to as the _____–_____ question.

3. Darwin suggests that characteristics that help a plant or animal to _____

[p. 49]   will be those characteristics passed on to future generations.

4. Although he had written it years earlier, Darwin did not publish his *Origin of Species*

[p. 50]   until the year _____ .

5. Living organisms have different types of _____ _____ that

[p. 51]   allow them to respond appropriately to various types of stimulus inputs.

6. At the heart of Darwin's theory of evolution is the notion of _____

[p. 52]   _____, which is often referred to as the "survival of the fittest."

7. _____ are simple, automatic behavior patterns in which a specific stimu-

[p. 51]   lus input is always followed by a specific response output.

8. The term _____ can be used for fairly complicated behaviors where the
goal of the behavior seems to be inherited, but where the manner of achieving the goal is

[p. 53]   not inherited.

[p. 54]   9. _____ is the scientific study of animal traits and behaviors.

10. The process of _____ is exemplified by Lorenz's finding that young

[p. 54]   geese instinctively follow the first moving object that they see after they are hatched.

11. Stimulus inputs that evoke or release instinctual behavior patterns are called

[p. 55]   _____ _____ _____ by ethologists.

12. The single nerve cell, or _____, has as its major function the transmission

[p. 56]   of impulses from one part of the body to another.

13. Within a nerve cell, messages travel from the _____ to the

[p. 56]   _____ _____ to the _____ .

14. The jellyfish does not have a real brain, but has a system of nerve cells connected in a

[p. 57]   pattern called a _____ _____ .

15. The neurons in the simple brain of the flatworm number only _____,

[p. 58]   while there are as many as _____ neurons in the human brain.

16. At the base of the brain, or top of the spinal cord, is the _____, which in-

[p. 59]   fluences circulation, breathing, and other basic reflex actions.

17. Generally speaking, the larger and more complex the _____ of the

[p. 60]   animal's brain, the more complex that animal's behavior patterns are likely to be.

18. The muscles in the right side of your body are controlled by centers in the

[p. 60]   _____ side of your brain.

19. The _____ half of the brain is the dominant side for nearly 95 percent of

[p. 60]   all people.

20. For most people, speech centers are located in the _____ hemisphere of

[p. 61]   the brain.

[p. 62]

21. Information from one side of the brain can be passed through the _____ _____ to the other side.

[p. 63]

22. The _____ is an instrument for monitoring the electrical activity in various parts of the brain.

[p. 64]

23. In epilepsy attacks, damaged cells in one hemisphere strongly excite cells at the _____ _____ in the opposite hemisphere.

[p. 66]

24. The process whereby one part of your body uses the nervous system to communicate with other parts of the body is called _____ control.

[p. 68]

25. As opposed to wild animals, humans have evolved a language for communicating not only about the here and now, but also about the _____ and the _____.

[p. 68]

26. In human beings, speech is controlled by specialized areas of the _____.

[p. 69]

27. In Azrin's experiments on agonistic or aggressive reactions, it was determined that the electric shock acted as an _____ _____ _____.

[p. 69]

28. Azrin and his colleagues discovered that aggressive behavior can be manipulated by changes in amounts of _____ or _____.

[p. 70]

29. The _____ tribe in the Philippines seem to be a tribe of people completely lacking in any signs of aggression.

B.   REVIEW

Multiple Choice: Circle the letter identifying the alternative that most correctly completes the statements or answers the question.

1. Darwin got his ideas for his theory of evolution:
   A. after contemplating all of the violence and aggression in the world.
   B. after reading Henry Wallace's book on the subject.
   C. in order to account for all the variability in plant and animal life that he observed.
   D. in order to disprove the writings of the social learning theorists.

2. The theory of evolution:
   A. can be applied to physical changes but not to behavioral changes.
   B. suggests that the environment has nothing to do with natural selection.
   C. was first proposed early in the twentieth century (around 1908).
   D. was almost immediately a source of controversy.

3. Simple internal processes that connect specific stimulus inputs to specific response outputs are known as:
   A. reflexes.
   B. instincts.
   C. imprinted responses.
   D. innate releasing mechanisms.

4. The most basic building block of the nervous system is the:
   A. nerve net.
   B. neuron.

C. spinal cord.

D. brainstem.

5. A nerve cell:

    A. transmits energy.

    B. may be connected to many other nerve cells.

    C. is located only in the spinal cord or brain.

    D. can carry information from dendrite to axon or from axon to dendrite.

6. One side of the brain is connected to the other side of the brain by:

    A. bilateral symmetry.

    B. nerve nets.

    C. the corpus callosum.

    D. the cerebral cortex.

7. In most right-handed people, behavior is controlled by:

    A. the left hemisphere of the brain.

    B. the right hemisphere of the brain.

    C. the corpus callosum.

    D. both hemispheres of the brain.

8. The minor hemisphere of the brain:

    A. controls speech.

    B. is usually the left hemisphere.

    C. deals with images and creative thinking.

    D. does not know what the major hemisphere is doing.

9. Ethologists call stimulus inputs that evoke behavior patterns:

    A. innate releasing mechanisms.

    B. instinctual stimuli.

    C. imprinted responses.

    D. reflex inputs.

10. The _____ influences circulation, breathing, and other basic reflex actions.

    A. corpus callosum.

    B. brainstem.

    C. spinal cord.

    D. nerve net.

EMOTIONS HEAD TO THE RIGHT

The brain of Phineas T. Gage represents a sort of landmark in medical history. In 1848 at a construction site, a poorly timed excavation blast sent a crowbar exploding upward through the left side of Gage's head. Surprisingly, the wounded man was sitting up and talking within several minutes. The fact that Gage survived at all is amazing. But an even more important aspect of the case is the information it provided about the functioning of the brain. After the accident Gage was a changed man. The formerly quiet and well-liked man had become a highly emotional, irreverent, profane, and stubborn individual, according to the doctor who treated him.

Gage's case, like other incidents of brain damage, suggests that the left and right hemispheres of the brain may have different functions, and researchers are continuing to find specific differences between the hemispheres. Gary Schwartz and his co-workers at Harvard University have conducted experiments which indicate that the right hemisphere may have a special role in emotional behavior.

One relatively simple method of measuring hemispheric activity has to do with side-to-side lateral eye movements. When a question is asked, a person will often glance slightly to the left or to the right before answering. Looking to the right is thought to indicate left hemisphere activity, while looking to the left indicates right hemisphere activity. Research has shown that right-looking (left hemisphere) is usually associated with verbal questions (such as, What is the difference between the words "recognize" and "remember"?). Looking to the left is usually associated with spatial questions (On the face of a quarter, does the face of George Washington look to the right or to the left?). Schwartz and his co-workers now suggest that the right hemisphere also plays a role in emotional processes. This could explain why Phineas Gage became so emotional after the loss of part of his left hemisphere.

What the researchers did was ask a number of people various types of questions (verbal, spatial, emotional, and nonemotional). The subjects, who did not know that the experiment had to do with eye movements, were watched closely as they answered each question. All eye movements were recorded. As expected, right eye movements were most often seen in association with verbal questions, while left eye movements were associated with spatial questions. Nonemotional questions were associated with right eye movements, and emotional questions (When you visualize your father, what emotion strikes you?) were most often associated with left eye movements. The results of these experiments, say the researchers, provide support for the hypothesis that the right hemisphere has a role in the regulation of emotional processes.

C. NEWS STORY QUESTIONS

1. What were the most noticeable changes that occured in Phineas Gage's behavior after his accident? _____

_____

2. In what way does lateral eye movement relate to brain function? _____

_____

3. If the right hemisphere of the brain is associated with emotionality and spatial relations, what is associated with the left hemisphere? _____

_____

_____

Movie still from *Dr. Jekyll and Mr. Hyde*.

The brain controls much of human behavior, but it cannot do so without information about the world. This information comes through the senses. Therefore, in order to understand human behavior it is necessary to understand the senses—taste, smell, touch, hearing, and vision. One method of studying the senses is to observe what happens when information from the senses is interfered with by drugs or by more natural circumstances.

Sensation and Perception, Sleep and Drugs

chapter

When you have completed your study of this chapter, you should be able to:

▶ Define and give examples of different altered states of consciousness, including the effects of various drugs
▶ Summarize the McGill experiments on sensory deprivation
▶ Describe the workings of the reticular activating system
▶ Diagram the structures and functions of the chemical senses and the skin senses, the eye, and the ear
▶ Differentiate between sensation and perception
▶ List the stages of sleep and discuss the importance of dreaming and/or REM sleep.

Albino (al-BY-noh). From the latin word meaning "white." Any organism lacking the normal skin coloration at birth, hence having pinkish eyes and a dead-white skin.

Altered state of consciousness. When you are asleep, unconscious, dreaming, intoxicated or drugged, hypnotized, or wildly euphoric, your state of consciousness is "altered" or different from the normal, waking state.

Amphetamines (am-FET-uh-meens). A type of stimulant or "upper." Also called "speed."

Anal stage. The second of Freud's four stages of psychosexual development, during which the toilet-training takes place.

Analgesics (an-al-GEE-sicks). From Greek words meaning "no pain." Technically speaking, any drug that reduces pain without causing a loss of consciousness.

Aqueous humor (AK-we-us). The watery substance between the iris and the cornea that keeps the front of the eyeball inflated to its proper size and shape.

Auditory (AW-dih-torr-ee). From the Latin word meaning "to hear." Anything "auditory" has to do with the sense of hearing.

Barbiturates (bar-BITT-your-ats). Neural inhibitors that come from barbituric acid; often used as sleeping pills.

Bone conduction deafness. A type of deafness that occurs when the three little bones in the middle ear no longer function properly.

Chemical senses. Taste and smell are called chemical senses because the stimulus inputs that trigger off these senses are usually chemical molecules.

Color blindness. The inability to see one or more colors at all. Only a few individuals (such as albinos) are totally color-blind. Red and/or green partial color blindness is the most common type.

Coma (KOH-mah). From the Greek word meaning "sleepy." A state of profound insensibility or unconsciousness, usually brought on by injury, disease, drugs, or poisons.

Cones. The color receptor cells in the retina of the eye.

Consciousness. The state of being awake, alert, and aware of one's surroundings.

Cornea (KORN-knee-uh). From the Latin word meaning "hornlike." The tough, transparent, outer covering of the eyeball.

Depressant. A drug or chemical that inhibits, slows down, or depresses neural activity. Also called a "downer."

Depth perception. The ability to see the world in three dimensions.

Dilates (DIE-lates). From the Latin word meaning "to widen." The opposite of "contracts." When you enter a dark room, the pupils in your eyes dilate to let in more light.

Electromagnetic (ee-LEK-tro-mag-NET-ic). A type of energy or wave produced by the vibration of electrical current.

Enkephalin (enn-KEFF-uh-linn). A natural pain-killer discovered in the brain by scientists in the United States and Great Britain.

Euphorics (you-FOR-icks). From the Greek words meaning "good feelings." Euphorics are drugs that arouse you and make you feel good.

Fovea (FOE-vee-uh). A small pit in the center of the retina of the eye where vision is at its clearest in daylight. Contains several million cones, but no rods.

Genetic. Anything having to do with the genes or with inherited traits or characteristics.

Genital stage (JENN-uh-tull). The fourth and final of Freud's stages of psychosexual development. Occurs during puberty, when young men and women reach sexual maturity.

Hallucinate (ha-LU-sin-ate). To see or hear things that are not really there.

Hallucinogens (ha-LU-sin-o-gens). Drugs

that disrupt the brain's ability to process incoming messages.

Hypnosis (hip-NO-sis). From the Greek word meaning "sleep." Altered state of consciousness characterized by suggestibility and deep relaxation.

Iris (EYE-rus). The colored part of the eye that contracts or dilates to let in as much light as possible.

Lens. The part of the eye, just behind the pupil, which focuses the visual image on the retina.

Maturation. The act of developing, either physically or psychologically.

Modeling. In social learning theory (see Chapter 2), the act of showing someone how to perform or behave.

Nerve deafness. A type of deafness caused by damage to or destruction of the neurons in the inner ear, or in the auditory nerve running from the ear to the brain.

Neurotransmitters. Chemicals that help transmit messages from one neuron to another.

Night blindness. The inability to see well in dim illumination, usually because of some problem with the rods in the eye.

Olfactory (all-FACK-torr-ree). From the Latin word meaning "to smell." Anything having to do with the nose, or with the act of smelling.

Optic nerve. Once light has struck either a rod or a cone, the light causes the receptor neuron to send a message to your brain via the optic nerve.

Oral stage. The first of Freud's four stages of psychosexual development, during which the infant gains most of its pleasurable inputs through its mouth.

Psychedelic drugs (sigh-kah-DELL-ick). Drugs that promote an altered state of consciousness, or that create changes in mood that are often accompanied by hallucinations. LSD is a psychedelic drug.

Pupil. The opening in the iris through which light passes.

Receptors. Nerve cells that receive stimulus inputs from the environment, or from the ac-

tions of the person's body. The rods and cones in your eyes are receptor neurons.

Reflexes. Automatic or involuntary responses. See Chapter 2.

REM sleep. Toward the end of each 90-minute sleep cycle, the eyes move about rapidly for 8 to 15 minutes. It is during this period that most dreaming seems to occur.

Repress. To push down or to hide from consciousness.

Reticular activating system (ra-TICK-you-lar). Also called RAS. That part of the brain stem that "alerts" your cortex that a signal is coming through from your sense receptors. Keeps your cortex awake and alert.

Retina (RETT-tih-nuh). From the Latin word meaning "network." The retina is a vast network of cells that covers the inner surface of the eyeball. Contains the visual receptors — the rods and cones.

Rods. The black-white receptor neurons in the retina of the eye.

Sensory deprivation. To be deprived of most or all incoming sensory inputs or messages.

Stereoscopic (stair-ee-oh-SKOP-pick). From the Latin words meaning "three-dimensional vision." Depth perception means seeing things in "3-D," or stereoscopically.

Stimulants (STIMM-you-lants). Drugs that increase or stimulate bodily activities, particularly in the nervous system. "Uppers."

Tranquilizers. Drugs that slow down or reduce bodily activities, or that reduce stressful feelings.

Ulcers. An open wound or sore of any kind is called an ulcer. Stomach ulcers may be caused by stress, which causes the release of too much acid into the stomach.

Visual cliff. An apparatus used for testing depth perception in infants.

Visual spectrum (SPEC-trum). The rainbow of colors that make up visible light.

Vitreous humor (VITT-tree-us). From the Latin word meaning "glass." The vitreous humor is a clear, glass-like substance in the center of the eyeball that keeps the eye in its proper rounded shape.

INTRODUCTION: JEKYLL AND HYDE

The doctor reached into the drawer and withdrew several strange-looking jars that contained liquid and powdered chemicals. He measured out some red liquid and added to it one of the powders. The mixture, which at first was of a reddish color, began to brighten as the powder dissolved. It began to bubble noisily and to give off colored fumes. Suddenly, the bubbling and smoking stopped and the mixture turned a dark purple, which faded again to a watery green.

The doctor put the glass to his lips and drank off its contents at one gulp. A cry followed; he reeled, staggered, clutched the table and held on, staring with wild eyes, gasping with open mouth. Then there came a change. The respected Dr. Henry Jekyll turned into the evil and hated Edward Hyde.

Robert Louis Stevenson's famous short novel *The Strange Case of Dr. Jekyll and Mr. Hyde* tells the story of a man who uses a secret drug to change his behavior. Dr. Jekyll, a well-known London physician, is famous for his hard work and good deeds. After he takes the drug, his thoughts and behavior patterns change for a brief period of time during which he calls himself Mr. Hyde. Hyde is a repulsive and evil man who has no respect for other people. On one occasion, for no apparent reason, Hyde brutally beats a defenseless old man to death. This act eventually leads to Hyde's (and Jekyll's) downfall and death.

ALTERED STATES OF CONSCIOUSNESS

The complete and total change that overcame Dr. Jekyll when he used his drug can be called an **altered state of consciousness.** In other words, the drug altered or changed the doctor's conscious understanding of himself and his world. Whenever someone experiences the world in a manner that is different from the normal waking state, that person is said to be in an altered state of consciousness.

Drug use is probably one of the best-known ways of altering consciousness, but long before humans learned to use alcohol or other drugs, they were probably getting high on a variety of experiences that had nothing to do with drugs. Many religious ceremonies, for example, contain rituals that can actually produce altered states of consciousness. Prolonged dancing and chanting are among the religious customs of some primitive tribes and some modern churches. If the chanting and dancing are done in a certain manner, they can

Members of the
Yanomamö tribe of
South America alter
their consciousness
by blowing ebene,
a hallucinogenic
drug, into each
other's nostrils
through a hollow
tube.

sometimes produce highs very similar to those produced by alcohol, marijuana, or LSD.

Chanting and dancing are only two of the many ways of altering consciousness. In *The Book of Highs* (Quadrangle, 1973), Edward Rosenfeld lists 250 ways of altering consciousness without drugs. He mentions such things as meditation, long periods in the desert, self-hypnosis, spinning, voluntary silence, pain, floating on water, prolonged sex, jumping up and down, massage, Yoga, metronome watching, and automobile destruction. These and all of the methods mentioned by Rosenfeld have one thing in common — *they alter consciousness by drastically changing the inputs to the senses.* That is, they either *overload* or *deprive* one or more of the body's senses. Chanting is an example. Concentrating on and repeating a chant over and over tends to focus awareness or consciousness on the chant and shuts out most other sensory stimulation (sights, sounds, smells, and so on). In this way, chanting produces a sort of **sensory deprivation** that has been found to lead to altered states of consciousness.

Sensory Deprivation

Some of the first experiments on altered states of consciousness were conducted at McGill University in Canada in the 1950s by psychologists W. Heron, W. H. Bexton, T. H. Scott, and B. K. Doane. In an attempt to study the effects of isolation on humans, these psychologists paid student volunteers $20 a day to spend

FIG. 3–1.
This is a sensory
deprivation chamber
similar to that used
in the McGill experi-
ments. Visual and
auditory stimulation
were blocked out by
such things as spe-
cial goggles and an
air conditioner.

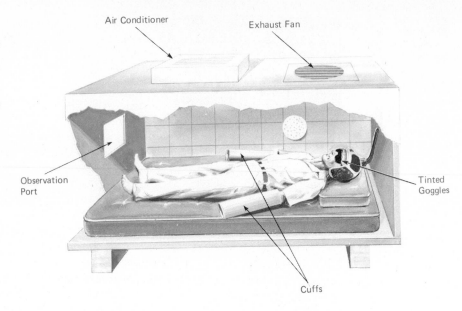

Air Conditioner

Exhaust Fan

Observation
Port

Tinted
Goggles

Cuffs

as many days as they could alone in a specially designed sensory deprivation chamber. All the students had to do to earn the money was to remain in the small experimental room. Even food and drink were supplied.

The experiment did more than isolate the students from other people, however. It cut them off from almost all sensory input. The students were told to lie on a small cot so they got little stimulation from moving around. They had to keep their arms in long cardboard tubes so they got very little stimulation from feeling things with their hands. Visual stimulation was reduced by special goggles that let in some light but no clear images. **Auditory** stimulation (sound) was blocked by the constant noise of an air conditioner.

It would seem that this kind of an experiment would be a good way for students not only to earn some extra money, but to get a good, long rest as well. Surprisingly, however, most of the subjects quit the experiment during the first two days. What the students (and the psychologists) thought was going to be a relaxing experiment turned out to be a stressful and even frightening experience.

The first thing most of the students did in the sensory deprivation chamber was pass the time by getting some sleep. Once their bodies had all the sleep they needed, the students turned to such things as concentration and work on mental problems. But this, they reported, didn't last very long. Soon their minds began to drift. They began to lose track of time and to have long mental blackouts. They were conscious or awake but they didn't seem to be able to control their flow of consciousness. Almost 80 percent of those who took part in the experiment reported that they began to **hallucinate** — to see and hear things that weren't really there.

Your brain — like all the organs in your body — needs information to process if it is to function properly. When your stomach is deprived of food for a long time, and when you are put under extraordinary stress, your stomach may actually begin to "digest" its own tissues — a condition that may lead to **ulcers.** When your brain is cut off from its normal sensory inputs, it often turns on itself and begins to process or digest its own internal activities — a condition that often leads to hallucinations.

If you are to survive, you must be able to adjust to your environment. Your brain must somehow produce the behavioral outputs that will help you recognize and approach such rewarding inputs as food and shelter — and help you avoid such dangerous elements as extreme temperatures and angry enemies. Much of what we call "thinking" and "conscious awareness" is just our brain's attempts to match our behaviors to our present environments. And when the environment is severely narrowed or closed off — as in the sensory deprivation experiments — the brain simply doesn't function as it should.

For example, the McGill students were given mental tests before, during, and after their stays in the sensory deprivation chambers. Almost all of the students performed poorly while undergoing deprivation. Many of them could not remember things very well, and they had difficulty solving simple math and reasoning problems. This loss of mental ability was temporary, however. When the students were retested a short while after leaving the isolation chambers, they were mostly back to normal.

The results of the McGill studies suggest that your thought processes are to a surprising extent dependent on and controlled by stimuli from your environment. When these inputs are greatly reduced, your ability to think logically is also reduced. When you are isolated from your environment, your brain can no longer make much sense out of what's happening to you. You begin to hallucinate, and you often misinterpret what little input does come into your brain.

According to McGill students, the most frightening aspect of sensory deprivation was what they called "loss of control": They couldn't control their thinking processes, and they often misunderstood what their bodies were trying to tell them. Some of the students reported that their minds seemed to be floating in air, suspended several feet above their bodies. Other students insisted that they had somehow acquired a second body, a twin of some sort that was lying in bed with them. Since their perceptions of their bodies returned to normal after the students left the chamber, we may assume that without normal environmental stimulation, the students' brains simply couldn't process or control the messages coming fom various parts of their bodies.

The Reticular Activating System

The sensory deprivation experiments suggest that one of the prime functions of your nervous system is to predict and control your sensory inputs. Much of what we call **maturation** or growing up is learning how to change your thoughts and behaviors so that you can get the things you want out of life. To put the matter more precisely, you learn to control your mental processes and behaviors in order to gain control over your environment. What we experience as "con-

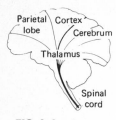

FIG. 3–2.
The reticular activating system is a network of neurons that acts as an alarm system to help your cortex select the most important incoming stimulus messages.

sciousness" is to a great extent the result of our brains' attempts to match inputs with outputs.

Your own *flow of conscious experiences,* then, is highly dependent upon a continuing flow of sensory inputs from the world around you.

Further evidence of the relationship between stimulus inputs and consciousness comes from a series of experiments performed by H. W. Magoun and his associates at UCLA. They discovered a network of neurons—called the **reticular activating system**—that runs from the top of the spinal cord up through the brainstem to the lower parts of the cerebrum. Magoun and his group proved that the job of the reticular activating system is to keep your cortex alert and "conscious."

Your reticular activating system receives stimulus inputs from almost all your senses. Whenever a message comes in to your nervous system from the outside world, the message passes through the reticular activating system. If the message is painful or important to you in some way, your reticular activating system rings a neural "alarm" and your cortex pays attention to the incoming stimulus. If the message is unimportant, your cortex tends to ignore it because your reticular activating system won't sound an alarm.

During all your conscious life, sensory messages from your eyes, ears, tongue, nose, and muscles bombard your cortex. Your brain could not possibly pay attention to all of them. Indeed, at any one given instant in time, your cortex probably is conscious of just one or two of the dozens of sensory inputs that it is receiving at that instant. One of the main functions of the reticular activating system, then, is to help your cortex select those stimulus messages your cortex should attend to and to help your cortex **repress** or ignore those messages of little or no importance.

Your reticular system also works with your cortex to keep you awake. Magoun and his colleagues found that if they destroyed a cat's reticular activating system, the animal lapsed into a **coma** from which it never recovered. The animal remained alive—as long as its biological needs were taken care of—but it remained in a deep sleep. Stimulus inputs still got through to the cat's cortex, but the cortex was unconscious because it wasn't being *activated* by the damaged reticular system.

The UCLA scientists also discovered that they could wake up a sleeping, normal cat by giving its reticular system just the briefest of electrical stimulation. The animal became conscious immediately. It jumped to its feet, its eyes open and its teeth bared, just as if somebody had stuck it with a pin or stepped on its tail. When Magoun and his group applied the same brief electrical stimulation to almost any other part of the brain, the cat merely slept on as if nothing had happened.

Under normal circumstances, the continual flow of stimuli from the environment keeps your reticular system alert, and your reticular system keeps your cortex conscious so that it can process the incoming signals. When you are deprived of sensory stimulation—as the McGill students were—your reticular system slows down its activity, your cortex cannot predict and control its inputs, and you experience an altered state of consciousness that can be terrifying. No wonder so few of the McGill students chose to remain in the isolation chamber for more than a day or two.

It is a psychological truism that whoever controls your sensory inputs, controls to a great extent the workings of your mind. Given the importance of these sensory stimuli to the shaping of your thoughts, feelings, and behaviors, perhaps it will pay us to look in some detail at the marvelous receptors your body has for "sensing" what is going on in the world around you.

THE SENSES

Imagine a very small chamber. It has no light and very little sound. The chamber is too small to move around in. The temperature remains almost constant and for all practical purposes there is no sensory stimulation. Is this another sensory deprivation experiment? No. The chamber is the womb, and for everyone life begins in the womb in a state of almost total sensory deprivation.

The students in the McGill experiments were subject to several days of isolation that resulted in a temporary lessening of their mental ability. It took them several days to get their brains back in shape. But this short period is nothing compared to what newborn infants must go through to get their brains in shape to make sense of the world. For infants everything is new, and nothing makes sense. Hundreds of colors, shapes, sounds, smells, and bodily sensations strike them all at once in what must be the most confusing bombardment of sensory stimulation that they will ever experience.

This sudden explosion of sensory experience is probably fairly meaningless to human infants. Only gradually does the world begin to fall into place and to make sense. Gradually each individual begins to develop a **consciousness** or personal way of experiencing the world. How does this consciousness grow? Unfortunately, infants cannot explain exactly what they go through. The only information available about the development of human consciousness comes from observations of how infants respond to their environment and to sensory stimulation.

When touched softly on the lips, babies exhibit the innate reflex of sucking. This inborn response enables an infant to receive food without having to learn the response first.

At first, young children do little more than eat and sleep—that is, they take in, process, and store energy. They are able to do this and little else because this is what their brains are prewired to do. In other words, there are certain groups of nerve cells in the brain that are connected in specific ways that allow infants to perform those actions that are necessary to life. These brain connections provide everyone with innate **reflexes,** which are made in response to the environment. The eyes of a newborn infant will reflexively follow moving objects. A soft touch on its cheek will cause the child to turn its head in the direction of the touch. A soft touch on the lips will "release" sucking motions. These and other innate reflexes are enough to help an infant find its mother's breast for feeding. Such inborn responses are necessary at birth because an infant does not have time to learn how to find food.

As the child's life becomes more complicated, however, it must learn other reactions. You can't always get food just by turning your head and starting to suck on the nearest object. Although newborn infants will innately accept and swallow sweet-tasting fluids, and will spit out sour liquids, each growing child must eventually learn what foods are good for it and which are not. And as each child learns to adjust to its environment, it gradually builds up new sets of neural connections in its brain. And all of this learning and adjustment is dependent upon information provided by the child's senses.

How is this information supplied? The environment gives off various forms of energy that can be detected by specific human sense organs or **receptors.** For newborn infants, much of this information is meaningless at first. Infants can hear, but what they hear makes little sense to them because they do not yet have any language. They can see, but it takes a while before they begin to understand what it is they are looking at. Surprising as it may seem, much of the most important information newborn children need for survival comes not through vision and hearing, but rather through their senses of smell, taste, and touch.

The Chemical Senses

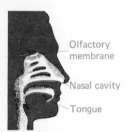

Olfactory membrane

Nasal cavity

Tongue

FIG. 3-3
Chemical stimuli enter the nasal cavity through the nose. The olfactory receptors code these messages and send them to the brain, where they are interpreted as odors. The taste buds on the tongue function in a similar way to help us identify various tastes.

Smell and taste are the **chemical senses.** They respond to chemical inputs from the environment. The nose, for instance, has millions of **olfactory** or odor receptor cells. These receptors are tiny nerve endings that are sensitive to and stimulated by specific chemicals. Each stimulus is coded by the receptors in the same way that a telegraph operator codes the words and letters into dots and dashes. The code is then sent to the brain where the dots and dashes are decoded in the form of a message that the brain "reads" as an odor. The brain cannot smell. It can only decode messages from the nose. In a similar manner the brain decodes messages from all of the body's sense organs.

Taste is another chemical sense that is very important to infants. Your taste or gustatory receptors are located in your taste buds—those tiny bumps on the surface of your tongue. Hundreds of these receptors in each of your taste buds respond specifically to the chemicals contained in the food you eat.

Scientists believe that there are four basic types of taste receptors in your tongue. One type of receptor codes or responds to sugars and other "sweet" chemicals. A second type responds to sour or acidic foods, a third type responds to salty chemicals, while the fourth type of taste receptor reacts to bitter chemical inputs. These four basic taste qualities—sweet, sour, salty, and bitter—account for most of the complicated flavors that foods have.

Most of what we typically call the flavor or taste of food, however, actually comes from our noses and not our tongues. Whenever you chew food, chemical molecules are released and carried up to the olfactory receptors in your nose. These smell inputs greatly enhance the pleasures most of us get from eating, and without these smells, most food tastes flat or uninteresting. When you have a cold, for instance, and your nose is stopped up, food often loses it flavor. But it is your olfactory receptors that are not responding properly, not the taste buds in your tongue. The next time your nose is badly clogged from a cold, you might wish to pay particular attention to what you eat. Under these circumstances, you have an excellent opportunity to learn the difference between the *taste* and the *smell* of different foods.

The chemical senses are sometimes regarded as minor senses because in the adult world they do not seem as necessary to life as do vision and hearing. To infants, however, the chemical senses are extremely important. Along with the sense of touch, the chemical senses are the most meaningful contact that infants have with the world. The chemical senses provide most of the inputs that infants use to learn about their environment, and to develop a conscious awareness of what that world is like.

The mouth (oral cavity) and the chemical senses are so important to infants that Sigmund Freud described the first stage of human development as the **oral stage.** During the first eight months, life revolves around the mouth. Children receive their first sensations of pleasure through their mouths, and they learn to love with their mouths. Freud believed strongly that the learning experiences of the oral stage are very important in adult life. If children are not satisfied during the oral stage or if they are frustrated by not getting enough food or love, said Freud, they sometimes continue to concentrate much of their adult life on seeking oral pleasure. All adults, of course, seek pleasure with their mouths. Some, however, overdo it. According to Freud's theory, some cases of overeating, excessive drinking, smoking, and fingernail biting are the result of frustrations during the oral stage.

The Skin Senses

The second stage in human development, according to Freudian theory, is the **anal stage,** and it is associated with another set of bodily senses — the skin senses. This period lasts from approximately one year or 18 months to about four years.

Like the chemical senses, the skin senses consist of a number of different types of receptors that, when stimulated, send input messages to the brain. The touch receptors, located all over the body, respond to various physical, rather than chemical, energies. Like the chemical senses, the skin senses are very important to newborn infants. Infants do not need to learn a language, for instance, to be able to interpret the sensation produced by the prick of a pin. The brain usually has no trouble at all decoding such messages. Combinations of skin sensations can yield pleasant feelings such as soft and warm, or unpleasant and painful sensations like damp and itchy.

Children learn to control their bowels and their bladders in order to avoid pain and get pleasure.

With information from the skin senses, infants begin to learn that their mouth is not the most important thing in the world. A few sensations — a warm bath, a soft blanket, a wet diaper — begin to give children an awareness of the rest of their bodies and to teach them that the mouth is not the only provider of pleasant and frustrating sensations.

It is during the anal stage that children are typically forced by their parents to gain some measure of control over their bodies. In addition to feeling the movement and the pressure of muscles in the their mouths, arms, and legs, infants become aware of their internal organs. Infants gradually gain enough muscle coordination to control their bladders and their bowels. As children learn to control their bodies, they also learn that their bodies can have an effect on other people. Young children get pleasure or avoid pain by releasing their bowels or bladders whenever they feel the urge. During toilet training, which usually takes place during the anal stage, children learn that it is sometimes necessary to please other people by developing voluntary control over their biological outputs.

In the **phallic** or **genital stage** of development, according to Freud, the sensual awareness of the body shifts from the anal area to the genital areas. As the sense receptors in the genital areas mature, children begin to become more aware of their own sexuality. The male's penis and the female's vagina and clitoris become objects of sensual pleasure. Sexual differences gradually become apparent and children become aware of the fact that there are other people and other sexes in the world. This discovery reinforces the idea that there is more to life than the child's own self, that there are many people in the world. More and more, the other senses — hearing and vision — become important to the child for finding out about and communicating with these other people.

Hearing

At first, sound performs a one-way function. Infants cry when they are hungry or in pain. They learn to call attention to themselves by making noise. Eventually, they come to realize that other people are also making noise. As some sounds — such as the names of people and objects — are repeated or **modeled** over and over, children learn to associate the sounds with the people or objects. By listening to and imitating the sounds other people make, children begin to build up a vocabulary and to learn a language. The result is two-way communication.

For a child to learn to speak a language, three conditions must usually be met. First the child must be given a model to follow or a goal to achieve. Second, someone (usually the parents) must give the child **feedback** or some kind of evaluation of how it is performing. Third, the child must be motivated to learn, usually by being encouraged to imitate the model provided by the parents and by receiving praise for its accomplishments.

If you think for a moment about these three conditions for learning to speak, you will soon see why deaf children seldom learn to talk. First, they cannot hear the model words spoken by their parents. Second, they cannot hear the sounds they themselves produce, and, therefore, they cannot easily adjust their voices to match the model. Luckily, deaf children are now generally taught to use their eyes instead of their ears; that is, the children are taught to communicate using sign language. They can see their own finger movements and those of the person whom they imitate. However, deaf children still miss much of the thrill of the world around them, for they cannot hear music, listen to the news on the radio,

Even children with hearing problems can be taught to speak by imitating the lip movements of a teacher.

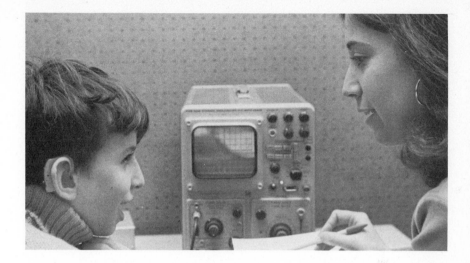

or talk to people on the telephone. More than this, deaf children cannot "talk" to most people, since few of us bother to learn sign language if our hearing is normal.

People who lose their hearing as adults also face special problems. Although most of these individuals can still talk, they cannot control their voices very well and tend to speak in a flat monotone. Since most "normals" don't know sign language, deaf individuals must read lips in order to understand what the normal person is saying to them. If the normal person turns away while speaking, or accidentally covers his or her mouth, or speaks too fast, even the most talented lip-reader rapidly loses the thread of the conversation. People with normal hearing often find it boring or difficult to communicate under these circumstances, and, hence, tend to avoid individuals with hearing problems. Employers frequently discriminate against anyone with a physical handicap, so the deaf person is not only cut off from much social contact, but may also find financial security hard to come by.

There are two main types of deafness, and to understand the differences between them, you must first understand how your ear works. Whenever you talk, your lips, tongue, and vocal cords make sounds by causing air molecules to vibrate—much as the string on a guitar vibrates when you pluck it. The air around you carries these mechanical vibrations or sounds to someone else's ear. When sounds arrive at the ear, they hit the eardrum and set it in motion—in the same pattern of vibration that you made when you spoke out loud. Your eardrum is connected to three small bones (the incus, malleus, and stapes) in your middle ear. These bones transmit the vibrations to your inner ear, where the vibrations are coded by special neural receptors. These nerve cells translate "sounds" into "neural messages" and send them to your reticular formation and to your cortex. Your brain then decodes the messages, and you "hear" what someone said to you.

FIG. 3-4.
Vibrations enter the
ear and hit the ear-
drum, which sets in
motion the bones in
the middle ear. In
the inner ear, these
vibrations are coded
into messages and
sent by the auditory
nerve to the brain,
where they are de-
coded as sounds.

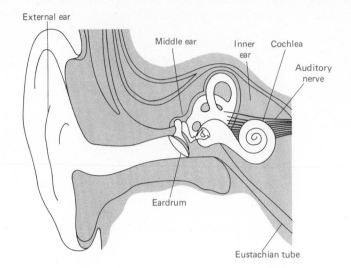

As people grow older, the three bones in their middle ears often get stiff and don't work very well. This condition—technically called **bone conduction deafness**—can often be helped if the person will wear a hearing aid.

The second type of deafness is called **nerve deafness.** This condition occurs when disease or accident destroys some or all of the neural receptor cells in the inner ear. Unfortunately, hearing aids don't generally help someone whose nerve cells have been damaged. The person with nerve deafness must usually learn to use vision as the main way of communicating with other people.

Vision

Vision is probably the most obvious and important of the human senses. Not only do your eyes gather a variety of informational inputs, but they often work with and reinforce your other senses. You see a fire and know that it will feel hot. You see an apple and can almost taste it. But your vision does much more than merely help your other senses. It is probably the best aid you have in getting around in the world. You can feel your way across a dark room like a blind person, but only with the sense of vision can you move through the world with ease and get an understanding of such things as color, depth, distance, and space.

The Eye

The stimulus input for vision is *light.* Under normal circumstances, light enters your eye through your **cornea,** which is the clear, outer "skin" of the eyeball. The light then passes through the **aqueous humor,** the **pupil,** the **lens,** and the **vitreous humor.** *Humor* is actually a Latin word that means "fluid" or "moisture." The aqueous and vitreous humors act primarily to keep your eyeball in its normal, round shape—just as water inside a balloon keeps it from collapsing.

FIG. 3–5
Light enters the eye through the cornea. It then passes through the aqueous humor, pupil, lens, and vitreous humor. When light reaches the retina, the visual receptors send messages to the brain by the optic nerve.

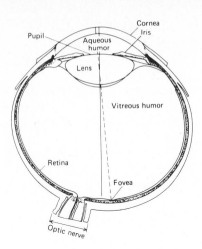

The pupil is the opening in the **iris** that acts like the opening in a camera. When you are outdoors in bright sunlight, the iris in each of your eyes contracts to shut out much of the brightness. At night, or in dim light, the iris expands or **dilates** to let in as much light as possible. Whenever the iris expands, the pupil gets larger; whenever the iris contracts, the pupil gets much smaller.

The lens in your eye acts much like the lens in a camera. That is, the lens "adjusts" the light rays entering your pupil so that whatever you are looking at is sharply focused on the **retina.** The retina is the inner surface of the eye that contains the visual receptors that allow you to see. As you look about you— focusing now on something near you, then on something far away—the lens changes shape so that the visual image of what you're looking at is focused sharply on the retina.

The visual receptors are the **rods** and **cones.** These tiny nerve cells are contained within the retina and thus are spread all across the inside surface of the eye. There are about 100 million rods and about 6 million cones in each eye. To reach the rods and cones, the light that you see must first travel through the cornea, the aqueous humor, the pupil, the lens, and the vitreous humor. When a ray of light strikes either a rod or cone, the light sets up a chemical reaction that causes the receptor neuron to send a message to your brain via the **optic nerve.**

Color Vision

Your rods see the world in black and white, which is to say that your rods are *color-blind.* Your rods are more sensitive to light than are your cones. At night, when there isn't much light present, your rods help you see things that your cones would miss.

Your cones see the world not only in black and white, but also in all the colors of the rainbow or **visual spectrum,** as it is called. Light is actually a form of **electromagnetic** energy much like radio waves and X-rays. The visual spectrum of colors runs from deep violet through blue, green, yellow, and orange to deep red. And just as each radio station on the dial has its own unique wavelength (radio frequency), so does each color have its own specific frequency or wavelength. (See Color Plate 1.)

Even though your cones are less sensitive than your rods, most of your visual experiences in normal or bright light are processed by your cones. Your cones are located primarily at the center of your retina, where your vision is at its sharpest. Your rods, on the other hand, are most numerous at the far edges of your retina.

When you look at something closely under normal illumination, your lens will focus the visual image so that it is sharpest at the **fovea,** which is a tiny spot at the very center of the retina. Although the fovea is no larger than the head of a pin, it contains several million cones — *and no rods at all*. So, under normal circumstances, when you look closely at something, you will see it in full color since you see it with your cones.

At night, however, your rods see better than your cones. Thus, when you stare at something under very dim light, you may not see it very well because your lens will try to focus the visual image on your fovea. Since your fovea contains no rods, the object you're looking at may appear dim and fuzzy — or it may disappear entirely if you stare at it directly! If you want to see something in faint light, try focusing on some object to the side of what you really want to see. When you look at something this way — "out of the corner of your eye" — the visual image of what you really want to see will fall on the edges of your retina, where your rods are. Thus, at night you will see dimly illuminated objects much more clearly if you don't try to look at them directly!

Night Blindness and Color Blindness

Some people see perfectly well during the day or in bright light, but see poorly at night when the light is very dim. Most of the time, these people have rods that aren't working very well. **Night blindness** has many causes, but a lack of Vitamin A is perhaps the most common one. The rods use up Vitamin A when they react to light. If your rods don't have enough Vitamin A available to them, then you won't be able to see things well at night. Since yellow vegetables such as carrots often contain large amounts of Vitamin A, physicians often recommend these vegetables to night-blind persons.

About one person in 40,000 suffers from **color blindness.** Most of these people are **albinos,** who suffer from a **genetic** problem that gives them colorless hair, a dead-white skin, and pink eyes. Albinos seem to have no functional cones at all in their eyes, and, therefore, their foveas are completely blind. When they look at an object directly, they cannot see it since their lenses tend to focus the image on their nonfunctional foveas. Albinos can usually see objects clearly only when focusing on the objects "out of the corners of their eyes."

Some 5 percent of the people in the world are almost totally blind to one or two of the colors on the color spectrum, but can see the others perfectly well. For this reason, the person is said to be *partially color-blind*. The most common form of partial color blindness is the inability to see either red or green. A red-blind individual would see a bright red rose as being black in color, and wouldn't be able to see a pure red light at all. The red-blind person might also have some trouble with various shades of green, but usually can see yellows and blues perfectly well.

Another 10 percent or so of the people in the world are color-weak. That is, they can see all the colors of the rainbow, but one or more of these colors appears weaker to them than would normally be the case. A man who is "red weak" (the most common type of problem) would see a red rose as being dull pink in color, and would see a bright red light as being faint or dim pink.

Color blindness is usually inherited and affects men much more than women. Some 90 percent or more of the partially color-blind or color-weak people are males.

Visual Perception

When light strikes your retina, your rods and cones send "visual input" messages to your brain by way of the optic nerve. Your brain receives these messages and knows that your eyes are looking at something. But seeing — or visual perception — is a great deal more complex than "just looking at something." For your brain must process or make sense out of the visual inputs, or most of the time you won't know what it is that your eyes are focusing on. (See Chapter 4 for a more detailed discussion.)

Perception is the process by which your brain decodes all the inputs it receives at any given time and converts these inputs into a meaningful psychological experience. This "**decoding**" typically involves memory and past experience. Thus, you are born to see, but you must learn to perceive most of the things you see. A newborn infant stares at its mother's face and doesn't recognize who or what she is. You look at your mother's face and perceive not only that it is a face, but a human face, and the face of someone you have known and loved for a long time.

When we look at another person, we can see what color the person's eyes and hair and skin and clothes are. But we perceive that the person has a particular shape and size and how far the person is from us. We may also perceive that the person is standing behind a chair, but in front of a cabinet. For the most part, this perception of space or depth appears to be acquired through experience.

Depth Perception. The world exists in three dimensions. It has height, width, and depth. The surface of a movie screen has only height and width. Even so, the action on the screen seems to be taking place in all three dimensions. If there are mountains in the background of a movie scene, the mountains really appear to be in the background. People's faces don't look flat on the screen. They appear to have contours, are rounded, and have depth. In the process of **depth perception** the human brain, making use of previous experiences and what it has learned about the visual world, adds the third dimension (depth) to the movie screen.

There are a number of visual cues or clues that your brain uses to achieve the effect of depth. If the image of a person cuts off the view of a large rock, your brain assumes that the person is standing in front of the rock. If two similar people are pictured but one appears to be much larger than the other, your brain assumes that the smaller person is farther away. Lights and shadows also add to the illusion of depth. A perfectly round, white circle will appear as a flat disk. If that same circle is partially shaded on one side, it will appear as a ball or as a round, solid object.

All of these and other cues are at work to make photographs, paintings, and movies appear to be three-dimensional to your brain, even though all these images are only two-dimensional. But the real world is not flat, and a person with a good pair of eyes does not see it as flat.

Stereoscopic Vision. The retina of the eye—the area where light reaches the rods and cones—is two-dimensional, like a movie screen. People with only one good eye see the world in the same manner that people with two eyes see a movie. Everything is first registered on the two-dimensional surface of the retina, then the brain makes use of all the visual cues available to construct a mental image of the world with depth. People with two good eyes have an advantage— **stereoscopic vision.** Just as a stereophonic record player produces sounds that reach the listener from two directions, stereoscopic vision gives people two slightly different views of the world. Different sounds reaching the ears of a listener from different directions give stereophonic music an impression of depth. Stereoscopic vision does the same thing. It produces an image that appears to be solid or three-dimensional.

The human eyes and ears are set slightly apart to produce the stereo effect. Each of your eyes gets a slightly different view of the world. The brain puts the two flat images together to produce one three-dimensional image. Frogs and other animals whose eyes are on different sides of their head, instead of in front, do not get this effect. Each of their eyes sees something completely different, and the images cannot be fused or put together to make the third dimension—depth.

In the 1950s, movie makers decided that the world was ready for three-dimensional films. A three-dimensional effect was produced by showing two slightly different images on the screen at the same time. Viewers had to wear special glasses that allowed the right eye to see one image while the left eye saw the other image, which had been filmed from a slightly different angle. The result was surprising. Animals on the screen seemed to jump right off the screen. Things seemed to be happening right in the middle of the theater. But apparently the effect was not worth all the trouble, and three-dimensional movies never caught on. The human brain, it seems, does a good enough job of constructing three-dimensional images without the bother of specially made glasses and films.

The Visual Cliff. The visual perception of depth is important in many ways. If infants did not have depth perception, they would not be able to manage the reaching, grasping, and manipulation of objects that is necessary if they are to learn about the world around them. An experiment reported by Eleanore Gibson in 1960 made it quite obvious that by at least six months of age infants have an understanding of depth. Gibson's experiment used what is known as a **visual**

Studies show that infants have depth perception. This baby will not crawl out on the glass surface of the cliff side because it perceives the drop to the checked surface below.

cliff. It consists of a flat center board with a solid surface extending outward on one side and a drop-off or "cliff" on the other side. Infants old enough to crawl (six months and older) were placed on the center board and then called by their mothers from different sides of the board. The infants could see over the cliff, but they could not fall because a flat sheet of glass extended out from the center board and protected them.

When mothers called from the solid side of the center board, the infants crawled toward them. When the mothers called from the cliff side, the infants would not move out on the glass surface. The children could feel the solid glass surface, but they could also see the drop-off. Apparently they could understand or perceive the height and would not crawl over the edge.

Scientists are not entirely sure whether the response that infants make to the visual cliff is learned, innate, or a combination of the two. When newborn animals have been tested on the visual cliff, many of them have refused to move out onto the glass. Some animals—kittens, for instance—do not avoid the cliff when they first begin walking, but usually will do so after they have had some experience moving around. Although the visual cliff experiments suggest that depth perception is innate in newborn humans, it remains likely that nurture or experience is as responsible for cliff-avoidance as is nature.

NORMAL AND ABNORMAL PERCEPTIONS

A camera can "see" or record a visual cliff, but only the brain is capable of perceiving the danger that could come from falling off the edge. Perception is therefore an inner, psychological experience that under normal circumstances is strongly influenced by sensory inputs.

But once you have learned to perceive the world around you, you can add up memories of past experience "in your mind's eye." You can daydream about things that you would like to happen. That is, you can "perceive mentally" experiences you've never had. And at night, when you are asleep, you may sometimes have horrible nightmares about monsters that don't exist and, therefore, have no stimuli associated with them.

If you take certain types of drugs, you may misperceive or misunderstand those inputs that your senses do send to your brain.

Perception is thus dependent not only upon present inputs and past experiences, but also on the present state of your own consciousness.

By the time you are an adult, you will have experienced billions of sensory inputs, and you will have used these inputs to develop a normal, conscious awareness or perception of the world, and of yourself. But you will also have experienced several types of altered states of consciousness. Some of these altered states of awareness occur naturally to everyone; other altered states—such as the personality change experienced by Dr. Jekyll when he took the drug and turned into Mr. Hyde—are abnormal and are perceived or experienced by few individuals.

Sleep and Dreams

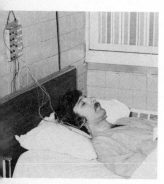

Attaching a sleeping subject to an EEG machine allows scientists to record the brain activity during five stages of sleep. It is believed that most dreams occur when rapid eye movement (REM) is detected.

Of the naturally occurring altered states of consciousness, the most widespread is sleep. Since five different stages of sleep have been identified, we assume that sleep consists of at least five different types of awareness or consciousness. A scientist can detect these stages by using EEG equipment to monitor the sleeper's brain activity. The five stages represent the increasingly deeper levels of sleep that come about as the brain and the body become relaxed. In one of these stages, however, the body stays relaxed while the brain shows suddenly increased activity. This stage of sleep is accompanied by jerky movements of the sleeper's eyes; it is known as rapid eye movement or **REM sleep.** It is during REM sleep that most dreaming takes place. In fact, some researchers have suggested that the rapid eye movements are the result of the dreamer's looking at whatever is occuring in the dream.

Everyone needs sleep, although a few individuals have been identified who can get by on very little if any sleep. For most people, however, lack of sleep produces not only fatigue but also disruptions of mental processes, hallucinations, and many of the same symptoms brought about by sensory deprivation. Sleep is necessary, but REM sleep and dreaming seem to be especially important. In several studies, scientists have monitored sleepers' brain waves and roused them each time they began to dream. Although the subjects in these experiments were allowed as much total sleep as they normally would get, they did little or no dreaming at all. After going several nights without dreaming, many of these subjects reported various forms of mental and emotional distress. Some subjects complained that they were beginning to hallucinate. They also found it difficult to concentrate, and to remember things that had happened to them during this dream deprivation.

No one knows for sure why people dream, or why dreams seem to be so necessary to our good health. But Sigmund Freud — one of the first modern scientists to pay attention to the matter — had some very definite ideas about dreams. Noting that about 80 percent of the contents of our dreams have to do with the day's activities, Freud stated that we use dreams as a way of working through the day's activities and storing these events away in perceptual memory. He called this memory storage "dream work." Freud believed that the other 20 percent of our dreams have to do with acting out in fantasy many of our unfulfilled desires.

For more than 50 years, few scientists believed that Freud's ideas had a sound basis in fact. However, in the past decade, several scientists have performed experiments that tend to support Freud's position. For instance, Ramon Greenberg, Director of Sleep Research at the Boston Veterans Hospital, reports several studies in which animals and humans were deprived of REM sleep after being given various tasks to learn. In almost all cases, the subjects of these studies could not remember the tasks as well the next day as did control subjects allowed to dream to their mind's content. Greenberg believes that dreams may be the brain's way of transferring memories of the events of the day from the input areas of the brain to the parts of the cerebrum that are involved in long-term memory storage.

And as support for Freud's notion that some dreams are wish-fulfilling, we need look no farther than Robert Louis Stevenson. He actually dreamed the story of Dr. Jekyll and Mr. Hyde one night—and then got up in the morning and started putting it down on paper.

Hypnosis

The hypnotized patient in this photograph is wearing special glasses that allow him to see only the disk. By concentrating on the disk and listening to the suggestions of the hypnotist, the subject may be able to shut out distracting sensory inputs.

Sleeping and dreaming are common altered states of consciousness that everyone experiences. A less common altered state is the one produced by **hypnosis.** The hypnotic state is similar in some ways to sleep, and the word hypnosis actually comes from the Greek word for sleep. But anyone who has seen television or stage hypnotists at work knows that hypnosis is not like any ordinary sleep.

Some strange tales have been told about hypnotism and the power of suggestion—tales of people performing unnatural acts while hypnotized or people becoming slaves to a master hypnotist. While people have been known to do some odd things while hypnotized, they usually won't do anything they couldn't be talked into doing under normal circumstances. Someone who believes that murder is morally wrong would not under hypnosis murder another person without a good reason. Such a person might be talked into killing if the hypnotist could make the person perceive it as a matter of self-defense, but not into killing for no reason.

The hypnotic state, like any state of consciousness, has to do with messages from the senses and how these messages are perceived in the brain. Sleep is like a light form of sensory deprivation. The senses become less active, fewer messages are sent to the brain, and the sleeper is able to relax. Hypnosis is similar in some ways. The hypnotic subject is asked to concentrate on specific sensory stimuli ("Look into my eyes") and to ignore or shut out the others, as in sleep. This narrowing or focusing of attention allows the subject to relax and to pay particular attention to the suggestions of the hypnotist. If the suggestions from the hypnotist contain orders or commands that are possible and that the subject might normally act on, they are carried out.

Hypnotic **suggestibility** is much harder to achieve when the hypnotist does not have the confidence of the subject because the hypnotist does not merely make suggestions, but must talk the subject into acting. If the subject does not trust the hypnotist, nothing may happen. Hypnotic suggestibility also depends on the type of person being hypnotized. People who are used to following instructions and taking orders, such as grade-school children, are usually the best subjects for hypnosis.

Researchers have yet to explain hypnosis adequately, and some have tried to explain it away by saying that hypnotic subjects are fooling themselves and the hypnotists. Whatever hypnosis is, a real phenomenon or an unconscious trick, doctors and therapists have found it to be a useful tool. It has been used instead of pain-killing drugs by dentists, and during some types of surgery, and even during childbirth. The subject is just told to feel no pain, and the brain does the rest.

Self-hypnosis is much the same as hypnosis. Once someone has learned to get into a light hypnotic trance, that person can usually do it again without the help of the hypnotist. By learning to concentrate and to shut out sensory stimuli, people can hypnotize themselves and give themselves useful suggestions. Some programs designed to help people stop smoking or to control other habits teach self-hypnosis. People learn to how to hypnotize themselves and then do it two or three times a day for 10- to 15-minute periods. While in the altered state they make suggestions to themselves about the dangers of smoking or overeating and their reasons for quitting. The technique has had some limited success—but even if the patients don't always manage to give up their problem habit, they do learn a pleasant way of relaxing.

Meditation

Many people alter their state of consciousness by practicing meditation. The meditation helps a person to learn control of breathing and body posture; it will be discussed in greater detail in Chapter 11.

Drugs

The most publicized altered states of consciousness are probably those produced by drugs. Everyone has heard stories of the horrors of heroin addiction, the dangers of overdose, the drunken driver, and the people who have lost their minds after taking **psychedelic drugs.** Most of these stories are true to some extent, but people continue to take drugs. And all of this drug taking, whether on doctor's orders or not, is usually an attempt to achieve an altered state of consciousness. People who are sick or in pain take drugs in order to feel better. Sleep, hypnosis, or some other altered state of consciousness can sometimes relieve pain, but drugs are usually a faster and more effective method.

Because drugs can be so effective at making people feel better, millions of people take them when they are not sick or in pain. Cigarettes, coffee, and alcohol are probably the most commonly used drugs in the United States. Heroin, cocaine, LSD, mescaline, marijuana, and amphetamines are less common and often illegal—but still widely used. But no matter what drugs a person takes to alter consciousness, the drugs all work either by changing sensory inputs, or by altering the way the brain handles such information.

Energy from the environment stimulates your sense receptors to send inputs to your brain, which processes or "makes sense out of" the inputs. But before a message from your environment can be processed or decoded by your cortex, the message must travel along various nerve pathways and through various parts of the brain. Since neurons, or nerve cells, cannot physically move around to deliver these messages, the neurons must relay the signals by other means.

Nerve cells throughout the body communicate with each other by releasing very small amounts of chemicals that stimulate other neurons. These chemicals are called **neurotransmitters,** because they serve to help transmit messages from one neuron to another. Various drugs that people take can affect nerve cells just like the neurotransmitters released by the neurons. Some drugs can make the brain and the nervous system operate at high speed; other drugs can slow the brain down or block out certain types of sensory messages. Still other drugs can so jumble the brain's normal activities that it can't make much sense out of anything. (See Table 3-1.)

TABLE 3–1   **Common Drugs and How They Work**

	Effects	Examples
Depressants (Downers)	Affect sensory input by slowing down brain and blocking out certain messages; most are highly addictive	Alcohol Barbiturates Sleeping pills Tranquilizers Analgesics (pain-killers) Aspirin, opium, morphine
Uppers	Affect sensory input by making brain and nervous system operate at high speed; may be addictive	Caffeine Coffee, tea, cola Amphetamines
Hallucinogens	Affect normal impressions by disrupting brain's ability to process incoming messages	d-lysergic acid diethylamide (LSD) Mescaline
Euphorics	Affect normal impressions by producing "good feelings" high; may also cause mild hallucinations and "loss of control"	Heroin Cocaine Marijuana

Alcohol

Alcohol is usually classified as a mild **depressant** — a drug that slows down or depresses neural activity. When alcohol affects that part of the brain which controls bodily functions, the drinker's breathing and other physical activities slow down. When alcohol acts on other parts of the brain, the drinker's ability to think logically and make good decisions is retarded. Most drinkers do not notice that their thoughts and behaviors are affected because alcohol also slows down the functioning of that part of the brain that monitors the person's own activities. Because they cannot always appreciate how poorly they are performing, people drunk on alcohol often insist that they still can perform adequately a complex task like driving an automobile. As an unfortunate consequence, some 25,000 people in the United States alone are killed on the highway each year by drunk drivers.

Many people do not realize that alcohol is primarily a depressant because its first effect sometimes seems to be the opposite. A drink or two will usually loosen people up and make them seem livelier and quicker than usual. However, this loosening up seems to occur because alcohol first of all affects those parts of the brain that normally inhibit or hold back certain behaviors. Individuals whose social inhibitions have been relaxed by alcohol get high, noisy, excited — and frequently do things they probably wouldn't do if sober. But as a person drinks more and more, the alcohol begins to affect the rest of the brain, the body slows down, and the depressant effects show up in the person's speech and other behaviors.

Uppers and Downers

As we noted, alcohol makes a person high by slowing down the inhibiting parts of the person's brain. Other drugs cause a person to become high because the drugs speed up most types of brain functions. These chemicals — called **uppers** — increase the rate at which the brain processes incoming messages and the speed with which the muscles in the body react. The most common upper is the caffeine found in coffee, tea, and cola drinks. A person who feels slow and sluggish in the morning may drink coffee in order to get his or her bodily processes in high gear. The more powerful uppers or **stimulants** are often called **speed.** Such drugs — mostly various types of **amphetamines** — are sometimes prescribed for medical reasons, but occasionally are misused by people who just want to get high. This type of high may be momentarily exciting, but the body can be speeded up for only so long before some very unpleasant side effects begin to show up.

Downers — such as the **barbiturates,** sleeping pills, and the **tranquilizers** — are the opposite of uppers. Downers retard or slow down brain and body functions. These drugs can yield a relaxed sort of experience but, like uppers, they can be misused. Downers are especially dangerous when used with alcohol, which we have already noted is a depressant.

Analgesics

Many of the messages that our brains receive are painful or unpleasant, but there are a number of drugs that can block out such messages. The most common of these pain-killing or **analgesic** drugs is aspirin. The strongest of the pain-killers are the drugs derived from the opium poppy.

For centuries opium, the gummy substance that comes from the poppy, was used in the Orient. This substance can be dried, hardened, and then smoked in a pipe. Opium was used not only as a physical pain-killer, but as a way of escaping the psychological pains and frustrations of life. In the nineteenth century, Western medicine discovered that opium could be refined and made into morphine, a more powerful drug. Morphine does not actually keep pain signals from reaching the brain, but it does keep such sensations from being interpreted as they normally would.

Morphine was found to be such a powerful pain-killer that it was given to a

Injecting oneself with heroin may block out pain and discomfort and produce a temporary "high." However, it stops the body from producing its natural pain reducer enkephalin.

great number of patients before doctors found out that it had a serious side effect: Morphine is addicting. The patient's body gets so used to the drug (and to the lack of pain) that the person cannot do without the drug after awhile.

Until fairly recently, no one was quite sure why morphine was so addicting. However, in the mid-1970s, scientists in the United States and in England discovered that the body itself manufactures a morphinelike drug, called **enkephalin.** Under normal conditions, your body keeps a small supply of enkephalin on hand to help soothe its pains and aches. When your body is badly damaged or wounded, your supply of enkephalin is not big enough to block out all the pain. But morphine seems to affect your perception of pain just as does enkephalin—and the usual medical dose of morphine contains more pain-killer than your entire supply of enkephalin. But while the morphine is reducing your discomfort, it also stops your body from producing the usual amount of enkephalin. If you take morphine regularly and then stop, your body is left defenseless—it takes you several days to build up your normal supply of enkephalin. During this period of withdrawal from the morphine, each little cut or scratch may be as painful to the addict as major surgery would be to a normal person.

Late in the 1800s, scientists looking for a way to help morphine addicts discovered heroin—a stronger pain-killer that is also derived from opium. Heroin cured the pains suffered by morphine addicts, but turned out to be even more addicting than morphine. When artificial enkephalin was first manufactured in a laboratory, scientists hoped it would help cure heroin addiction. But, to their dismay, they soon found that synthetic enkephalin is even worse at causing addiction than is heroin. So far, the only "cure" that seems even partially effective with opium addiction is psychological therapy—treatment in which the individual learns sufficient self-control to withstand pain during withdrawal, and acquires sufficient skills to be able to overcome the painful obstacles in the person's life.

Hallucinogens

While some drugs prevent certain sensory messages from reaching the brain, other drugs act primarily to mix up or disrupt the brain's normal ability to handle or process incoming messages. Those drugs that cause the brain to misperceive reality, or to hallucinate, are called the **hallucinogens**—the best-known of which are LSD and mescaline.

LSD and acid are the common or street names for d-lysergic acid diethylamide. This drug was first made or synthesized in Switzerland in 1938; it did not become popular in the United States until the 1960s. Because it expands or distorts all incoming sensory messages, LSD often produces very strange hallucinations. The smallest sensory details become enlarged, and the drug-taker sees and hears things that aren't really there. By distorting most of the person's sensory inputs, LSD forces people to experience reality or consciousness in a totally different or distorted manner. This altered state of consciousness can sometimes be a pleasant experience — particularly if the dose taken is small — but it can also be a frightening one. Perhaps the most terrifying aspect of a bad trip is that the drug-taker loses control of his or her flow of consciousness. The larger the dose of LSD that a person takes — and the more impure it is — the greater the chances are that the person will have a bad trip.

Mescaline, the drug made from the buttons of the peyote cactus, is also an hallucinogen. Less powerful than LSD, it has been used for many years by American Indians as part of their religious ceremonies.

Euphorics

In addition to affecting a person's physical experience of the world, drugs can change a person's psychological impressions of the world. Alcohol does this. It can put people in a good mood or in a bad mood. Heroin (also used as an analgesic), cocaine, and marijuana can also help people get high by getting them into a good mood. These drugs are called **euphorics** from the Greek word that means "good feelings."

Cocaine, like many drugs, has had a long and interesting history. It is made from the leaves of the coca plant. South American Indians have long used it for religious purposes and to help them work longer. Western medicine discovered cocaine in 1859, and it soon became a popular medicine. Medical papers of the day called it a "miracle drug." They claimed it could be used to cure such things as gonorrhea, morning sickness, sea sickness, hay fever, opium addiction, sore nipples, whooping cough, asthma, syphilis, and even the common cold.

Freud was an early user of cocaine. He took it himself and gave it to his patients as a pain-killer. But soon, he found out that cocaine can be psychologically addictive, and so he quit using and prescribing it. Robert Louis Stevenson, who was ill with a lung disease, may have been taking cocaine as a medicine at the time he wrote Jekyll and Hyde. This could account for the amazing speed at which he wrote and then completely rewrote the story (60,000 words in six days). Today cocaine is used in powder form by many people who sniff or snort it through the nose. It produces a pleasant rush or high feeling.

In 1977 the National Institute on Drug Abuse issued a report summarizing cocaine use in the United States. While the report emphasized that overuse of cocaine could be dangerous, it stated that there is little concrete evidence to suggest that cocaine is dangerous when taken infrequently and in moderate doses.

In the United States today, marijuana is probably the most popular of all the illegal drugs used to alter consciousness. Marijuana comes from the hemp or cannabis plant, a weed that can be grown almost anywhere. Because marijuana is so popular and easy to get, much research has been conducted on its effects. One of the most thorough reports on marijuana has been published by the United States government's Department of Health, Education, and Welfare. Based on more than 100 studies, the report concludes that there are probably no unhealthy physical effects from the moderate use of marijuana. The report states that marijuana use does not lead to the use of other drugs and is not asso-

There are hundreds of ways of altering your state of consciousness. The Macumba tribe in Brazil get high by spinning.

ciated with the commission of crimes. Animal research conducted for the report established that the margin of safety with THC (delta-9-tetrahydrocannabinal), the active ingredient in marijuana, is very high. In other words, there is not much chance that anyone could die of an overdose of marijuana. The report did warn, however, that marijuana can have a deteriorating effect on mental and physical performance, and that people should not drive while under the influence of marijuana.

The final chapters of the government report discussed the therapeutic or medical uses of the drug. There are indications that marijuana can be useful in the treatment of depression, alcoholism, and epilepsy. It may be useful in the treatment of some skin diseases and, because marijuana lowers the pressure inside a person's eyeballs, it has been prescribed as a treatment for glaucoma, a blinding disease caused by pressure in the eyes.

GETTING HIGH

A dope-fiend's paradise—that's what the United States was a hundred years ago. Marijuana was legal and widely used as a medicine. Opium sold for only $10 and $12 per pound and was available in a variety of medicines that could be purchased at any grocery or general store. Ayer's Cherry Pectoral, Mrs. Winslow's Soothing Syrup, Darby's Carminative, Godfrey's Cordial, McMann's Elixer of Opium, and Dover's Powder were only a few of the patent medicines containing narcotics, according to Edward Breecher and the editors of Consumer Reports. They discuss the interesting history and current state of drug use in their book *Licit and Illicit Drugs* (Little, Brown, 1972).

The Consumer Reports book makes the point that drug taking is extremely common in today's society, but also points out that taking drugs to get high is not a totally modern-day pastime (or problem). People have been using and abusing various drugs for thousands of years. Getting high is just a new name for an old game. The Old Testament notes that even Noah got a little tipsy at times. And for centuries people have been searching for ways to get high and to find better and more exciting ways of experiencing life or perceiving the world. They have been trying to get into altered states of consciousness that make life more pleasant or more fun, and they continue to do so today with the literally hundreds of drugs that are available.

Up in the morning with coffee and a cigarette, a beer or two at lunch, a martini before dinner, a joint or a snort at a party, back to bed with sleeping pills—drug-taking has become a way that many Dr. Jekylls use to make themselves over into various types of personalities. And the indications are that, if anything, drug use will become even more popular in the future. But whenever we reach for a chemical to alter our consciousness and change our perceptions of things, we might remember that the simplest and most effective way of getting high is to sense and experience the world fully. Or as Rosenfeld puts it in his *Book of Highs,* the 250th way of getting high is living.

► *SUMMARY*

1. Dr. Jekyll and Mr. Hyde were the same person. However, the chemical taken by Dr. Jekyll altered the way he normally perceived the world. As a result his behavior was so changed that he became in effect a different person—the hideous Mr. Hyde.

2. The senses are all-important to human behavior. Everything we do is related in some way to information received through the senses. In addition to studying the senses themselves, it is possible to get an understanding of the importance of sensory stimulation by observing what happens when the normal operation of the senses is interfered with. Sensory overload, sensory deprivation, and drug use all interfere with the senses and can produce **altered states of consciousness.**

3. Whenever someone experiences the world in a manner that is different from the normal waking state, that person is said to be in an altered state of consciousness. The altered state of consciousness produced by sensory deprivation points out the importance of sensory stimulation. Even temporary sensory deprivation can cause **hallucinations** and strange bodily sensations as well as interfere with mental performance.

4. The **reticular activating system** (RAS) is your brain's alarm system. Consisting of a network of nerves that identifies important sensory inputs, the RAS makes sure that important messages to the brain are not shut out. Without your reticular activating system you would respond to no messages at all. You would fall into a deep coma and would not recover.

5. The senses work by responding to different types of energy in the environment. The chemical senses, taste and smell, respond to various chemicals in different ways. The responses are interpreted in your brain as different flavors and odors.

6. The skin senses respond primarily to physical, rather than chemcial, stimulation. The chemical and skin senses are especially important to infants because it is through these senses that infants begin to learn about the environment. An infant's first experiences with the world are so important that Freud described the first two stages of human development (**the oral and anal stages**) in terms of sensory stimulation. Unpleasant stimulation and harsh treatment during these early stages, he believed, can lead to later behavior problems.

7. In the later stages of human development, social contact becomes increasingly important. According to Freud, the **phallic** or **genital stage** follows the anal stage, and the child becomes aware of other people. The senses of hearing and vision are especially helpful in making social contact and in learning from and dealing with other people. The faculty of hearing, hand in hand with speech, makes two-way communication possible between people. To learn speech, the child, ideally, must be given a model, feedback, and motivation. Where speech is physically impossible, however, sign language has been developed. The fact remains that the hearing-, speech,-, and sight-impaired have learning and communication problems that point out the importance of these faculties in everyday functioning.

8. Vision is especially important in helping you move through and experience the world. Through your eyes you pick up messages or sensations from the things around you. The various parts of the eye (**lens, retina, fovea, rods, and cones**) receive the messages and then send them to the brain by the optic nerve. Perception is the process of decoding all of these inputs or messages.

9. The **cones** allow us to see colors. People with poorly functioning cones may experience **night blindness** or **color blindness.**

10. Because you have two eyes (**stereoscopic vision**), neural pathways to and from your brain, and past experience, you are able to perceive a solid and three-dimensional world through **depth perception.** This is important for survival. Studies have been done with a **visual cliff** to investigate the nature of depth perception in newborns and animals.

11. The senses help people achieve a normal conscious awareness of the world, but there are levels of awareness or states of consciousness that are different from the normal waking state. Sleeping, dreaming, and the hypnotic state are among them. These states are all influenced by inputs from the senses.

12. Sleep is necessary, but rapid eye movement or REM sleep, the state in which most dreaming occurs, seems to be especially important. People deprived of REM sleep and dreams show signs of fatigue and irritability and may even have hallucinations. Freud suggested that dreams are the key to understanding our unconscoius desires. It is also possible that dreams play a role in helping us remember the events of the day.

13. Hypnosis is a little-understood phenomenon. It appears to be related to a reduction in sensory awareness, with attention focused on the hypnotist. In the hypnotic state the suggestions of the hypnotist can be especially powerful. Hypnosis has proved to be a useful medical tool, especially in the control of pain. Self-hypnosis allows the individual some independence from a therapist as well as ease in making suggestions to the self as needed.

14. The most talked-about altered states of consciousness are those produced by drugs. Drugs affect the way messages from the senses are interpreted in the brain. Drugs can speed up, slow down, and even completely distort messages from the senses.

15. Alcohol, the number-one problem drug in the United States, is a **depressant** that, in limited quantities, pleasantly loosens up the individual; with added quantities, judgment and coordination become impaired. **Amphetamines (uppers), barbiturates (downers), analgesics** (pain-killers), and **euphorics** (pleasure-inducing drugs) when prescribed are medically valuable, but when abused can be illegal and destructive, both mentally and physically. Still being investigated is marijuana, a euphoric popularly used in this country. Results seem to indicate that it can be medically beneficial, is not lethal, but can have a deteriorating effect on mental and physical performance.

16. Drug use has been around for a long time and will probably become even more popular in the future. Drugs are helpful in fighting illness, controling pain, and in producing sometimes pleasant or exciting altered states of consciousness. Drugs, however, do this by interfering with our awareness of the world, an awareness that is necessary if we are to deal effectively with our environment.

Suggested Readings

Brecher, Edward and the Editors of *Consumer Reports*. *Licit and illicit drugs*. Boston: Little, Brown, 1972.

Gibson, James J. *The senses considered as perceptual systems*. Boston: Houghton Mifflin, 1966.

McCord, William and Joan McCord. *The origins of alcoholism*. Stanford, Ca.: Stanford University Press, 1960.

Rosenfeld, Edward. *The book of highs*. New York: Quadrangle, 1973.

Stevenson, Robert Louis. *The strange case of Dr. Jekyll and Mr. Hyde*. New York: Dodd, 1961.

► STUDY GUIDE

A.   RECALL

Sentence Completion

1. The "conversion" of Dr. Jekyll to Mr. Hyde was accomplished by the use of

[p. 82]   _____.

2. A group of psychologists at _____ University conducted the first experi-

[p. 83]   ments on sensory deprivation.

3. When someone _____, they report seeing and hearing things that are

[p. 84]   not really there to be seen or heard.

4. One of the prime functions of the nervous system is to predict and control

[p. 85]   _____ _____.

5. The network of neurons in the brain that controls our arousal, alertness, or con-

[p. 86]   sciousness is the _____ _____ _____.

6. If an organism's reticular activating system is destroyed, the organism will lapse into a

[p. 86]   _____.

7. The womb can be thought of as a chamber in which an animal experiences almost

[p. 87]   total sensory _____.

8. Even at birth the brain contains prewired connections that provide everyone with in-

[p. 87]   nate _____ which are made in response to the environment.

9. The chemical senses are more commonly called _____ and

[p. 88]   _____.

[p. 88]   10. _____ _____ are your receptors for taste.

11. The primary qualities of taste are _____, _____,

[p. 88]   _____, and _____.

[p. 89]   12. The _____ senses include such sensations as pressure, warmth, and cold.

13. There are two general types of hearing loss: _____ deafness, and

[p. 92]   _____ deafness.

14. Light enters the eye by passing first through the _____, and ends up at

[pp. 92–93]   the _____.

15. The actual visual receptors in the retina of the eye are the _____ and the

[p. 93]   _____.

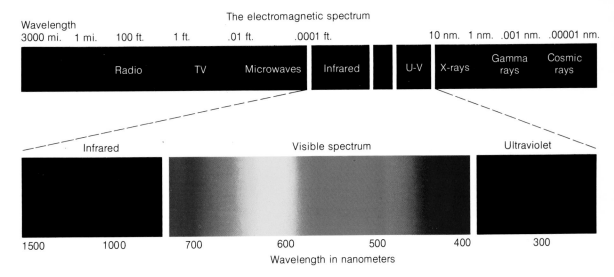

The electromagnetic spectrum

Plate 1   How acute is human vision? This diagram shows the full spectrum of electromagnetic energy from radio waves through cosmic rays. The human eye can see only the narrow band from 400 to 700 nanometers in wavelengths, that is, the colors from deep violet to deep red. (A nanometer is equivalent to one-billionth of a meter; a meter is 39.37 inches.)

Plate 2   Different wavelengths of light result in the perception of different colors. The color names and their corresponding wavelengths are given along the outside of the circle. Complementary colors are those colors opposite each other on the circle; they result in gray when mixed. The mixing of other wavelengths gives us an intermediate color. Some colors such as purple cannot be produced by a single wavelength, or monochromatic light. We can produce all colors on the wheel by proper mixing of three wavelengths equidistant in the circle.

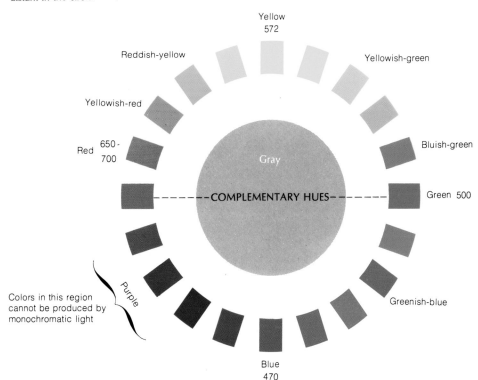

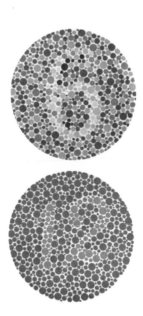

Plate 3 What number do you see in the top plate? the bottom plate? People with normal vision see a number 6 in the top plate while people with red-green color blindness do not. Those with normal vision see a number 12 in the bottom plate; color-blind individuals may see one number or none. These two illustrations are representative of a series of charts used to test color blindness. (American Optical Corporation from their AO Pseudo-Isochromatic Color Tests.)

Plate 4 This water color is similar to the colorful inkblots used in the Rorschach test. A psychologist can gather data about an individual's personality by asking the person to report what he or she sees in the inkblots.

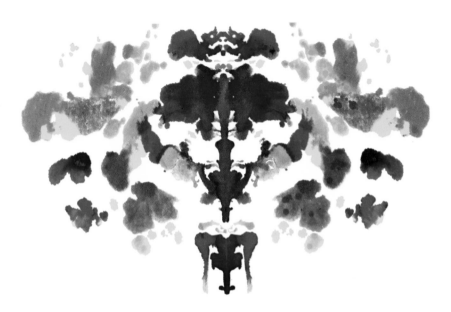

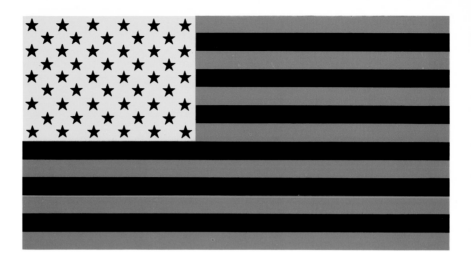

Plate 5 The red, white, and blue? Stare at the center of this flag for about 30 seconds. Then look at a white wall or sheet of paper. You will see a negative after-image in colors complementary to those shown here.

Plate 6 The painter Georges Seurat used the technique known as pointillism to create *Port-en-Bessin, Entrance to the Harbor.* Your perceptual abilities allow you to look at this painting, which is really a series of points or dots, and see a complete scene. (Collection, The Museum of Modern Art, New York. Lillie P. Bliss Collection.)

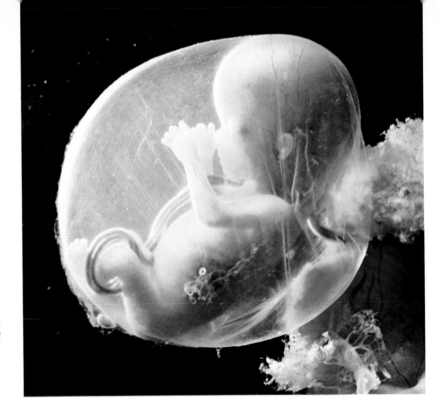

Plate 7 From the warmth and safety of a nurturing womb, each of us grows and develops into a unique individual. This three-month-old fetus is about three inches (7.5 centimeters) long and weighs about one ounce (28 grams). (Photograph by Lennart Nilsson from *Behold Man.* © 1973 by Albert Bonniers Förlag, Stockholm, published by Little, Brown & Company, Boston, 1974.)

Plate 8 Watching people and interacting with them makes life interesting and worthwhile. A variety of environments and experiences combine to produce the diversity of personalities that we meet and observe during our lives. (Photo copyright © Arthur Sirdofsky.)

[p. 94]   16. The _____ of the eye contains several million cones and no rods at all.

17. Dimly illuminated objects are seen best by areas of the retina containing
[p. 94]   _____.

[p. 94]   18. The most common cause of night blindness is a lack of _____.

19. Total color blindness is typically an _____ disorder, and is most com-
[pp. 94–95] monly found in _____.

20. The fact that each eye receives a slightly different view of the world than does the
[p. 96]   other helps to account for the effects of _____ vision.

21. A device used for the testing of depth perception in the very young is the
[p. 96]   _____ _____.

[p. 98]   22. We monitor a sleeper's brain activity by using the _____.

23. When we dream, we do so during a phase of sleep referred to as _____
[p. 98]   sleep.

24. The most common (legal) drugs in wide use in this country are _____,
[p. 100]   _____, and _____.

25. Chemicals released by one nerve cell in order to stimulate other nerve cells are called
[p. 101]   _____.

[p. 101]   26. Alcohol is a drug classified as a mild _____.

27. Drugs called _____ cause a person to get "high" by speeding up most
[p. 102]   types of brain functions.

28. _____, _____, and _____ are examples of
[p. 102]   depressants, or "downers."

[p. 102]   29. Pain-killing drugs are called _____.

[p. 103]   30. Mescaline and LSD are examples of _____.

[p. 104]   31. No doubt, _____ is the most commonly used (illegal) euphoric drug.

[p. 105]   32. The active ingredient in marijuana is _____.

B.   REVIEW

Multiple Choice: Circle the letter identifying the alternative that most correctly completes the statement or answers the question.

   1. The McGill experiments:
      A. involved studies of sensory deprivation.
      B. altered states of consciousness through hypnosis.
      C. were conducted at UCLA during the 1950s.
      D. compared states of meditation with drug-induced states.

   2. The reticular activating system:
      A. runs from the top of the spinal cord up to the cerebrum.
      B. controls levels of arousal.
      C. helps you to pay attention to some stimuli while ignoring others.
      D. all of these.

   3. During the _____ stage of development, the organism is concerned with the skin senses.
      A. oral

B. anal

C. sexual

D. genital

4. Which of the following is *NOT* a primary quality of taste?

A. sweet

B. sour

C. sharp

D. salt

5. Sound waves become transformed into neural messages in the:

A. eardrum.

B. inner ear.

C. bony middle ear.

D. outer ear.

6. Light travels through the eye in which sequence?

A. lens, pupil, aqueous humor, retina

B. pupil, cornea, lens, retina

C. cornea, pupil, lens, retina

D. lens, pupil, cornea, retina

7. Dreams:

A. may be interesting, but are probably not necessary.

B. occur during the deepest, most quiet stage of sleep.

C. can be disrupted or interfered with for months on end, and little change in the person's behavior will result.

D. may be important for getting new learning stored in our long-term memories.

8. Which of the following drugs may be classified as an hallucinogen?

A. mescaline

B. cocaine

C. any analgesic

D. any amphetamine

9. When a person hears or sees things that are not really there, he or she is probably:

A. extremely creative.

B. retarded.

C. hallucinating.

D. taking analgesic drugs.

10. Alcohol may be classified as a mild:

A. hallucinogen.

B. depressant.

C. upper.

D. euphoric.

LEBOYER'S BABIES: PROTECTING THE SENSES AT BIRTH

Imagine stepping out of a warm, dark movie theater into a cold, glaring sunny afternoon.

Imagine being wakened from a quiet, restful sleep by the blaring noise of a brass band.

If your reflexes and senses are normal, these drastic changes would not only be shocking, they might be extremely painful.

Now imagine what it would be like to experience all of these sensory changes if you were a naked, newborn infant. Such shock is what greets most infants at the moment of birth. They are faced with blinding lights, noise, cold air, and fabrics that might feel harsh against their tender skin. The infants are held aloft by their feet and snapped into an erect position. They are slapped on the rear and made to cry. These are part of what French physician Frederick Leboyer calls the violence of birth as it takes place in many of the clean, efficient delivery rooms of Europe and the United States.

There may be a more soothing way of being born. In *Birth Without Violence* (Alfred A. Knopf, 1975) Leboyer describes what he believes to be the pain infants suffer being born. "What more proof do we need?" he asks. "That tragic expression, those tight-shut eyes, those twitching eyebrows . . . that howling mouth, that squirming head trying desperately to shield the face—that gesture of dread. Those furiously kicking feet, those arms that suddenly pull downward to protect the stomach. The flesh is one great shudder . . . Every inch of the body is crying out: 'Don't touch me!' And at the same time pleading: 'Don't leave me! Help me!' Has there ever been a more heartrending appeal?"

In answer to this appeal, Leboyer offers a method of making birth less painful and shocking to the infant. It is a slow, quiet birth in which everything is done to protect the infant's delicate senses from shock. The infant's sensitive eyes are spared the glare of delivery room lights and flood lamps. "Of course," admits Leboyer, "some light is necessary to watch over the mother, so that she will not be injured when the child's head emerges." But then, he says, extinguish all light, except a small night light. "And this is all to the good, since newborn infants are almost always ugly . . . It is better that the mother discover her child by touching it."

Unnecessary noise is also avoided. The Leboyer method calls for complete silence in the delivery room, instead of the loud commands, such as "Push, push," that might possibly upset the mother and that might be painful to the infant.

Once the child's head appears, the birth can be eased along by the doctor's fingers under each of the infant's armpits. Supported so, the infant is gently settled onto the mother's abdomen. There, for several minutes the child is allowed to adjust slowly to its new environment while it continues to receive warmth and comfort from its mother (as it did before birth).

The Leboyer method eliminates the traditional holding up of the child. The infant's spinal column, while in the mother's womb, has never been completely straight. Holding the infant up by the feet snaps the spine into a straight position. This, says Leboyer, may be as shocking and painful to the infant as the slap on the rear that usually follows.

The traditional slap on the rear is meant to make the infant cry and thus take its first breath and begin using its lungs for breathing. A shortage of oxygen at this time could result in serious brain damage. The Leboyer method does not use the slap, but instead allows the infant to lie quietly on its mother's abdomen with the umbilical cord still attached. Through this cord the infant continues to receive blood and oxygen from its mother as it did before birth. Gradually, after several minutes, the child's lungs and breathing system begin to function on their own and the umbilical cord stops operating. The child will have been continually been fed oxygen but will not have been slapped.

Next, instead of placing the infant on a cold scale for weighing, it is gently lowered into water that has been warmed to near body temperature. Here the infant is rinsed and will eventually open its eyes and begin to move its limbs freely. The result of such a nonviolent birth, concludes Leboyer, is not a screaming, kicking, terrified infant but a relaxed and even smiling child.

Although there is not a great deal of evidence to suggest that the Le-

boyer method has any beneficial effects on development, a study of infants born the Leboyer way has found some promising results. The study was conducted by Danièle Rapoport of the French National Center for Scientific Research.

At a hospital in a middle-class neighborhood in Paris 120 women were randomly assigned to Leboyer-type delivery rooms. During the next three years the children of these women were given standardized physical coordination exams and were observed on various occasions by a team of researchers. The parents were also interviewed. Tests indicate that the physical development of these children is slightly advanced over that of children born the usual delivery room way. Observations of the children show that they are exceptionally clever with both hands. The children also began walking at an earlier age (13 months on the average, instead of the usual 14 or 15 months). They also showed less than the usual amount of difficulty in toilet training and in learning to feed themselves. They also seem to be protected from colic and shortness of breath, which is often seen during the first months of life.

The parents too seem to have been affected by the delivery process. The mothers spoke of it as being a profound experience, extraordinary, moving, remarkable, and said they felt privileged. They liked all aspects of the delivery and expressed a desire to have any future children in the same way.

Interestingly, the fathers seemed to take an exceptional interest in their children, especially the fathers who came into the delivery room (after the child had been put into the bath). "You get more interested in a baby when you have to deal with it so soon," said one father. So, in addition to helping physical develop- ment, the Leboyer method may strengthen the attachment between parents and children. This, in turn, can have lasting positive effects on parents' relationships with their children.

C. NEWS STORY QUESTIONS

1. Compared to today's delivery room procedures, what must the birth process have been like back, say, in pioneer days? _____

_____

2. What is the basic idea behind the Leboyer method? _____

_____

3. Is there any evidence that the Leboyer method has any effects on behavior after the delivery itself? _____

_____

Movie still from *Man of La Mancha*.

The senses enable us to reach out and make contact with the world. It is only with learning and experience, however, that the brain is able to interpret and make sense of the information the senses provide.

Perceptual Development

chapter 4

When you have completed your study of this chapter, you should be able to:
- ► Define perception
- ► Define and give examples of sensory overload and sensory limitations
- ► Explain sensory adaptation and give examples
- ► Describe how our personal needs and values and our past experiences affect our perceptions, and sometimes create psychological blind spots
- ► Summarize the methods and results of Skeels's work
- ► State the significance of illusions, and cite some problems created by restoring sight to the blind

Dilates (DIE-lates). From the Latin word meaning "to widen." The opposite of "contracts." When you enter a dark room, the pupils in your eyes dilate to let in more light.

Habituation (habb-bit-you-A-shun). From the Latin word meaning "to dwell in or become accustomed to." When your environment stays the same for a period of time, your nervous system has two major ways of keeping you alert. One is sensory adaptation; the other is habituation. Adaptation takes place at the level of the sensory receptors themselves. If you sat in a tub of hot water for a while, your skin receptors would eventually adapt to the constant "warm" stimulus and stop sending messages to your brain. Thus, you would perceive the water as growing colder—even if it stayed at the same temperature. Habituation occurs in your brain. If you lived next to a stockyard, you would eventually habituate to the smell. That is, your brain would stop paying attention to the smell, even though the receptors in your nose might continue to send messages to your brain each time you came home.

Illusions. Misperceptions caused by the way that your receptors respond to a stimulus input. The cause of the illusion usually is in the stimulus itself, or in the structure of the receptor organ. Hallucinations, on the other hand, are caused by incorrect processing of normal incoming sensations, and hence are a fault of the cortex and not of the receptors of the external stimulus. If you look at an oddly shaped cat and "see" it as a dog, that is an illusion. If you look at empty space (perhaps when you're drunk or "high") and think you see a dog, that is an hallucination.

Input overload; input underload. Your brain needs an optimum amount of stimulation in order to function properly. If your brain has to pay attention to too many stimulus inputs all arriving at the same time, you

may become confused and unable to think clearly and precisely. We refer to this stressful condition as input overload. If you are experiencing sensory deprivation (see Chapter 3), your brain will have too few sensory inputs, and you may begin to hallucinate. We refer to this type of stress as input underload. Pilots of jet airplanes often suffer from input overload when they are landing or taking off because they have too many dials, radio signals, and visual inputs to handle in a very brief period of time. When the plane is flying smoothly at 33,000 feet (about 10,000 meters) and is on automatic control, the pilot often has nothing to do for long periods of time. Under such conditions, pilots flying jet fighters often report seeing very vivid hallucinations.

Inaudible. The word audition means "to hear." A sound is inaudible if you can't consciously hear it. You may occasionally respond to a noise that is just barely inaudible (by turning your head toward the source of the sound) even though you are not aware of why you turned your head in that direction. Your body responds to many sensory inputs that are not strong or important enough to reach the level of conscious awareness.

IQ. Intelligence quotient (KWO–shunt). Mental age divided by chronological age times 100. The average IQ is arbitrarily assumed to be 100.

Optic nerve. The tract of nerve tissue (chiefly axons) that runs from the eyeball to the back of the brain. Visual input messages from your eyes travel along the optic nerve to your brain before you "see" them or are conscious of them.

Perception (per-SEP-shun). The process of matching sensations with images. "To perceive" usually means "to recognize."

Prejudice. To pre-judge. To make up your mind about something before experiencing it. To be biased for or against something or someone for emotional or social reasons, rather than dealing with the person or thing logically.

Sensory adaptation. See "Habituation."

Sensory deprivation. To be deprived of most or all incoming sensory inputs or messages. Without sensory inputs, the reticular activating system often "turns off" the cortex so that thinking and/or consciousness drop to near zero. See *"Input underload."*

Sensory limitation. Your sense organs are marvelously sensitive, but they are not perfect. You cannot "see" radio waves, and you cannot "hear" musical tones with a frequency of much more than 20,000 Hertz (cycles per second). To survive in your environment, you should probably learn as much about your sensory limitations as about your sensory capabilities.

Sensory stimulation. Necessary for the development of perceptual abilities. Infants must experience such stimulation if they are to attain normal intelligence and adjustment.

INTRODUCTION: DON QUIXOTE

She was a simple country girl. He was an educated, middle-aged gentleman. She didn't know or care that he was alive. He was madly in love with her.

This situation contains all of the elements of a typical love story. But in this particular case, there is much more to the story than meets the eye. Even though the woman in the story was poor, homely, and dressed in rags, her lover saw her as the most beautiful woman in the world. He saw her as a royal princess whose wealth, beauty, breeding, and charm were beyond compare.

Beauty, it is often said, is in the eye of the beholder. Actually, it is in the brain of the beholder. In this case, the beauty's name was Aldonza Lorenzo. Her lover called her Dulcinea. The strange beholder was a man named Quixano. He called himself Don Quixote, the Knight of La Mancha. The story of these two was written almost 400 years ago by the Spanish writer Miguel de Cervantes Saavedra.

Don Quixote's love-life was not his only problem. Just as he saw Dulcinea as a beautiful princess, he saw other women — even barmaids and prostitutes — as royal ladies. He saw taverns and roadside inns as castles and fortresses. He saw his broken-down, old horse as a powerful charger. But even more importantly, he saw himself as a knight in shining armor, and he believed that it was his duty to right the wrongs of the world.

Don Quixote's peculiar way of seeing the world can obviously lead to trouble, and it often did. In one of his most famous adventures Don Quixote and his faithful companion Sancho Panza came upon a field of windmills. As soon as he saw them, Don Quixote said, "Look Sancho, there stand more than 30 monstrous giants whom I intend to slay! I will do a good deed and remove those wretched monsters from the face of the earth."

Sancho saw things differently. "What giants?" he asked. "Those are just windmills and what seem to be arms are the sails being moved by the wind."

Don Quixote was not a man to be argued with. Here was a field of evil giants, and with great courage he charged into them with his lance. At that precise moment, just as the Spanish knight ran his lance into the sail of one of the wind-mills, the wind picked up and whirled the sail around. Don Quixote, his lance, and his skinny horse were sent flying. They tumbled over and over across the rocky field. Covered with bruises and badly shaken, the knight pulled himself to-gether and claimed that an evil magician must have turned the giants into wind-mills just as he attacked. Proudly, Don Quixote picked himself up, and he and Sancho rode off to even greater misadventures.

Another time, again while riding across the plains of Spain, the knight and Sancho saw two clouds of dust in the distance. Don Quixote immediately an-nounced that he and Sancho were about to be attacked by two vast armies. When he looked out across the field, Don Quixote saw golden armor, shields, emblems, and soldiers of many nations approaching. Sancho looked out and saw two flocks of sheep and some shepherds. Don Quixote heard the sound of battle charges, trumpets, and drums. Sancho heard only the sound of bleating sheep. Again Sancho tried to explain the situation to his master, but he was un-successful. Don Quixote charged into battle with the poor, scared sheep. He courageously killed seven enemy knights (sheep) with his lance. The sight of a skinny, old knight attacking helpless sheep was probably quite funny to anyone watching, but the shepherds were not amused. They pelted the knight with stones, threw him from his horse, and knocked out a few of his teeth. As on many previous occasions, Don Quixote was left sitting in the dust, battered and bruised.

THE PERCEPTION PROCESS

Don Quixote had a problem. He didn't see things the way everyone else saw them. His eyes, ears, and other senses worked well enough, but still he insisted that prostitutes were princesses, windmills were giants, and sheep were soldiers.

The problem was not Don Quixote's ability to sense the world. The problem had to do with the way impressions from the senses were handled after they got to his brain. The senses don't actually pick up an image or a sound from the en-vironment and pass that sensation directly to the brain. The senses only pass *coded messages* to the brain. Such messages are not always complete, and they are not always handled or processed in the same manner. Each person's brain processes information from the senses in a slightly different manner. (Don Quixote's brain processed the information in a drastically different manner.) This phenomenon, known as **perception,** was defined in Chapter 3 as the process by which your brain decodes all the inputs it receives at any given time and con-verts these inputs into a meaningful psychological experience. Perception can differ from individual to individual because it is influenced by many things—sen-sory inputs, innate reflexes, past experiences, and personal needs.

What do you perceive in this picture? A UFO? Actually, the light on the right is the moon. The other light is a plate illuminated by a flashlight and blurred by hand motion.

Sensory Inputs

When Don Quixote saw giants, it was not because his eyes were sending the wrong messages to his brain. After the battle was over, he saw the windmills just as clearly as his friend Sancho saw them. The problem wasn't in the knight's senses, but in his brain where he *perceived* the windmills as giants. Perception does, however, start in the senses. And everyone, from time to time, perceives things that are not quite the same as physical reality.

One of the most obvious examples of perceiving something that isn't real takes place at the movies. The images on the screen appear to move, but a motion picture is nothing more than a series of slightly different still pictures being flashed on the screen one after another in rapid succession—more than 1000 per minute. The human eye sees all of these pictures, but the brain perceives a moving picture with smoothly flowing action. And, as we learned in Chapter 3, our brains add depth to moving pictures.

Going to the movies is a typical sensory experience. In a theater people watch the movie, but they do much more than watch. They use all of their senses to gather information from the screen and from the world around them. Moviegoers see the film, but if they take time to look they can also see the other people around them. They hear the music and voices that go with the film, and if they listen they can also hear the people around them whispering and rustling candy wrappers. They can taste and smell popcorn, and they can feel the comfortable or uncomfortable chairs in which they are seated. There are many other stimuli present that the moviegoers could also sense—including those bodily sensations that tell people where their arms and legs are, how tight their clothing is, and rumbles and upsets from their stomachs, bladders, and bowels. But if the people in the movie were totally aware of *every* stimulus input that reached their brains at any one instant, they would have considerable trouble paying attention to the plot of the movie.

Your brain was designed to receive, process, and react to stimuli—and one form of "processing" is recognizing and understanding the meaning of those inputs. But your brain works best when it has a relatively constant supply of input messages to deal with. In Chapter 3, we pointed out some of the problems you might face if someone deprived you of most environmental stimulation.

FIG. 4–1.
When you go to the movies you are usually able to ignore distracting influences around you and concentrate on the film. You usually perceive the series of still pictures as smoothly flowing action; the motion picture becomes reality for you.

Under these conditions, you have nothing but the workings of your body to attend to, and your brain begins to search desperately for something to perceive or pay attention to.

Your brain has just as much difficulty when it is overloaded with work—that is, when it is forced to process or perceive too many important inputs at once. Your reticular activating system cannot screen out or suppress very many of these messages, because they all demand your attention. Your body becomes tense, and you often feel the same sort of stress that people feel when they've taken too many uppers. Psychologists often refer to this situation as **input overload.**

Your reticular activating system helps determine which incoming sensory signals your cortex pays attention to, or consciously perceives. Under some conditions, your cortex and your reticular system can actually block out some inputs—not merely by blocking them out when they reach your brain, but by "turning off" your sense receptors themselves so that the receptors don't respond to your environment as they normally would. When you want to listen to a favorite piece of music on the radio or stereo, you may either turn down the lights or shut your eyes so that you are not distracted by visual stimuli while the music is playing. Your reticular system can achieve a similar result by blocking out visual messages even before they leave your eyes.

Sensory Limitations

The perceptual process involves experiencing, understanding, and giving personal meaning to those stimulus messages that you attend to or that you are consciously aware of. Sensing is the first step in the perceptual process, because you cannot pay attention to a sensory input that just doesn't exist, or that never reaches your brain. But your environment is full of millions of different stimuli, and your senses are really fairly limited in the types of stimuli to which they respond. In other words, everyone is blind and deaf to some extent. Even the

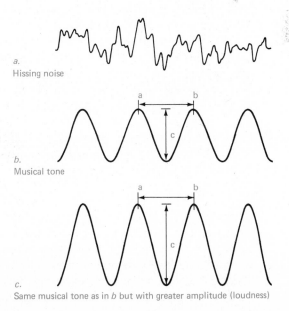

a.
Hissing noise

b.
Musical tone

c.
Same musical tone as in *b* but with greater amplitude (loudness)

FIG. 4–2.
Sound waves can be recorded and interpreted. A sound wave is measured from peak to peak. The closer together the waves are, the higher will be the pitch of the sounds they produce.

FIG. 4–3.
Electromagnetic
waves from the sun
contain high- and
low-frequency en-
ergies, some of
which stimulate our
visual receptors.
Many of these
waves may be too
low (cosmic) or too
high (short-wave) to
be perceived by hu-
mans.

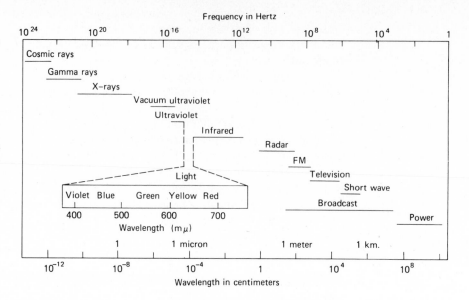

best of sense organs, working with the best of brains, cannot detect all of the stimulus energies in the world. Sound, for instance, travels through the air in the form of a wave of energy. The closer together the waves are, or the higher in frequency the waves are, the higher will be the pitch of the sounds they produce. Chalk screeching on a blackboard and the wail of a police siren are the result of high-frequency sound waves. The very low sounds of bass guitars and bullfrogs are the result of low-frequency sound waves. The human ear can detect these sounds, but there are many higher and lower frequency sounds that go undetected. There is a type of dog whistle, for example, that produces a very high frequency wave that humans cannot hear. Dogs can hear such high-pitched sounds and will come running at the sound of the "silent" whistle.

Vision is much the same. There are high- and low-frequency energies that do not stimulate the visual receptors of the eyes and that cannot be seen. Cosmic rays, gamma rays, X-rays, ultraviolet light, radar, radio, and television waves are all forms of energy similar to visible light energy. These waves are not seen because they are either too high or too low to be detected by the human visual receptors.

It might be interesting to see radio waves or to be able to detect some of the other forms of energy that exist, but considering the number of messages that are flying back and forth through the air, it would be very confusing if you were aware of everything. The human senses are designed to respond to certain energies that must be sensed in order to make the world understandable. Additional sensory information might overload the brain. In effect, the limitations of the senses protect your brain and allow it to interpret the information it does receive.

Sensory Adapation

The senses have other characteristics that protect the brain from overload. If you leave a dark theater in the middle of the day, you might be faced with the light of a very bright sun. This experience can be painful and temporarily blinding, but within a very short time your eyes will adjust or adapt to the bright sunlight. Stepping out of the hot, bright sunlight back into the cool, dark theater calls for another form of adaptation. At first the theater seems almost totally dark and as cold as a freezer. This change may be painful or annoying at first, but your eyes and your body's temperature sensors gradually grow used to or adapt to the new situation.

All of the senses have the ability to adapt within limits. A traveler might notice that the water tastes strange in some cities, but after several days the nervous system adapts to the strange taste. The water will seem to taste normal again. A traveler passing through Omaha, Nebraska, might notice the strong smell of the stockyards, where animals are being butchered. People who live near the stockyard may hardly notice the smell. They will have had plenty of time to get used to it. Pressure sensations are the same. After a while, people no longer feel the pressure of their eye glasses, hats, watches, rings, and clothes—until they take off any of these items. Then, rather quickly, people will notice the change.

Your senses work primarily by detecting *changes in your environment.* Once you have detected a change (entering Omaha, leaving a theater, putting on a hat), your sense receptors gradually quit sending messages to your brain. And your brain is likely to ignore those weak messages that do get through. Whenever a stimulus input remains constant for a period of time, both your receptors and your brain will adjust and will then be better able to detect any future changes in your environment.

Sensory adaptation is a form of protection that allows your brain to ignore many unnecessary sensory messages and to concentrate on more important information. The weaker a message is, the easier it typically is for the brain to ignore it. If a sensory message is too strong, however, it is not easily adapted to. Too bright a light, extreme cold or heat—all of these things can be extremely painful and dangerous. Anyone exposed to such strong stimulus inputs will probably not adapt to them entirely, but will have to take other steps to avoid what might be a dangerous situation.

An extreme change in sensory input requires some time for adaptation. Moving from a dark interior to bright sunlight may momentarily blind you.

PERSONAL NEEDS

When your recticular activating system is in good working order, it is constantly on guard for important or out-of-the-ordinary messages from the environment. But your brain itself cannot reach out into the world for the information it needs. Your senses have to reach out. They are your brain's only link with reality. Your senses cannot just sit back and hope that the important messages will be detected. They must work for the information that is needed.

Your eyes are a good example. They are constantly searching the environment for clues that might be important to you. A hungry person driving through a city will almost always be aware of advertisements for restaurants or food. A person who has just eaten and is driving past the same signs will be able to see the advertisement but probably will not be as aware of them as the hungry person. In brief, your senses actually search for information that will help fulfill your specific needs

This selective filtering action of the brain works for all of the senses. Two people standing on a busy street corner can carry on a serious conversation and hardly notice the many sights, sounds, and odors around them. This ability to concentrate on selected portions of incoming information is helpful and necessary to perception. But shutting out information can be dangerous if it is carried too far. People concentrating on a movie or listening to a friend on a noisy street corner might filter out the word "fire." This could be dangerous if there really is a fire, but the brain usually knows not to filter out important messages. People almost always hear the word "fire," even if they aren't paying attention to the person who says it. Even people who often sleep through the noise of their alarm clock will usually respond to messages they have learned are important ("fire!") and wake up. Don Quixote would probably have responded to the word "giant" no matter how soundly asleep he was.

Pupil Reactions

The pupils of the eyes are especially important in this search for information. The pupils, the small black spots in the center of the eyes, are the openings through which light enters. Just as the lenses of some cameras can be adjusted to let in more or less light for correct exposure, your pupils adjust to let in more or less light. When you walk out into the bright sunlight, your pupils contact. That is, they get smaller and let in only the amount of light that is necessary for vision. When you enter a dark room, your pupils **dilate** (get larger) so that as much light as is available can enter your eyes.

Contraction and dilation are methods the eyes have of adapting to the environment, but the pupils do more than react to light. The pupils sometimes dilate in an active search for more information. The more intently people stare at an object, the wider their pupils open. Experiments conducted by Eckhard Hess show how the pupils of different individuals respond differently to the same information. While a group of college students was being shown various photographs, their pupils were measured. The pupils of the females became much larger when pictures of infants and of nude males were shown. The pupils of these women did not dilate as much at the sight of landscapes or of nude females. The males in the experiment reacted differently. Their pupils became dilated at the sight of nude females, but not so much at the sight of infants, landscapes, or nude males. Hess's experiments suggest that the personal interests

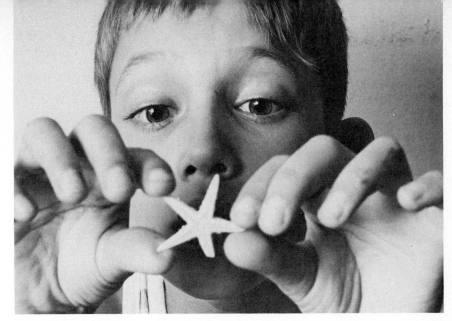

When you look at something extremely interesting to you, the pupils of your eyes become dilated, or get larger, and allow more light to enter your eyes.

(such as sexual needs and maternal feelings) of people can affect the way their sense organs operate. Don Quixote wanted to see a world full of knights and beautiful ladies. His sense organs may have been on the lookout for clues to such a world.

"Dirty Word" Experiments

Experiments conducted by Elliott McGinnies and others suggest that our personal needs do more than influence the sense organs. An individual's personal needs also seem to have some control in deciding which information should be perceived or interpreted by the brain. In McGinnies's "dirty word" experiments, words were flashed on a screen for a very brief time. McGinnies measured exactly how long it took for people to recognize or perceive the words. If an ordinary word, such as "table" or "chair," was flashed on the screen for one-tenth of a second, most people were able to recognize it at least half the time. If an emotional word, such as "whore," was used, some of the subjects in the experiment seemed to need almost twice as much time as the others to recognize it. The results of these experiments suggest that the brain is sometimes capable of filtering out information that it does not want to deal with. The dirty words used in the experiment were words that some people would rather not see or have to deal with. When the words were flashed for only a brief period, these people could ignore them. Only when the words were left on the screen for a longer time did these subjects recognize them. Some people, of course, found the dirty words interesting and recognized them quite easily. This type of reaction might explain some of the behavior of Don Quixote. He wanted to believe that his beloved Dulcinea was a wealthy, refined woman. He did not want to see her ragged clothes or hear her coarse language. He may have been able to ignore such facts.

Values and Perceptions

Another set of experiments suggests that our personal needs control not only what information is perceived but influence how that information is interpreted. In these perception experiments young children were asked to judge the size of a poker chip. They did this by adjusting the size of a spot of light on a screen until it appeared to be the same size as the chip. Most of the children were pretty accurate in judging the size of the chips. They overestimated by only about 5 percent. Half of the children in the experiment were then told that they could trade in their chips for candy. The other children, the control subjects, did not get candy for their chips. For the children who did get the candy, the chips had an increased personal value.

The object of this experiment was to determine if the perceived size of the chips would increase as the value of the chips increased. When all of the children were retested with the spot of light, those who had received candy overestimated the size of the chips by 13 percent. Those subjects whose chips had not increased in value performed the same as on the first test. The increased value of the chips had influenced the children's perception of the size of the chips.

PAST EXPERIENCES

Reactions such as pupil dilation are involuntary. They are mechanisms of the brain and the senses that help people gather necessary information from the environment. There are, however, other ways of gathering information. People can voluntarily direct or focus their attention on specific aspects of the environment. People in a movie theater do not watch the screen because their reticular activating systems make them do so. They focus on the screen or direct their attention on the movie because that is what they want to do. Students in a classroom do the same thing when they decide to listen to the teacher rather than look out the window.

In a theater or in a classroom, sensory messages are always pouring into your brain from more than one sense. But your cortex cannot possibly attend to all of these incoming messages—any more than you can watch a dozen different television channels all at the same time. Your cortex (with help from your reticular activating system) usually picks just one sensory "channel" to pay attention to at any one instant in time, just as you will usually pick just one TV channel to watch for a while. The messages coming in on this one channel are the ones that your brain decodes or processes, and you perceive and understand the messages. This process of perceiving is not the same as sensing, and it is not the same as focusing attention—though both activities are involved in perception. Infants see, but they do not fully perceive or understand what it is they are sensing. Infants can focus their attention on objects for short periods of time, but this fact does not mean that they appreciate what it is they are focusing on. The senses send messages to the brains of infants, but these messages are usually meaningless because infants have not yet learned how to decode them. Looking at the words in a book is seeing, but reading and perceiving what the words mean requires much learning and experience. Listening to a foreign language is hearing, but understanding the language takes practice and learning from experience. Only with such experience can messages from the senses be recognized and fully interpreted.

Why is experience necessary? Because the senses do not always represent the world the way it really is. The movie screen is nothing but a flat reflective surface. Yet, at times, this screen can reflect whole worlds of experience. Animals or racing cars might seem to jump from the screen. Don Quixote and Sancho might ride into a filmed battle with sheep. People talk and make love on the screen. Armies clash, cities burn, monsters crawl out of the black lagoon, and sometimes it all seems as real as anything outside the theater. Then the house lights come up, and there is nothing there but a big, flat screen. And there wasn't anything there but a series of lights and shadows of different shapes and colors. It is the human brain with its experience at interpreting such stimuli that really created the almost lifelike situations on the screen. Outside the theater it is much the same. The brain makes use of all its past experiences in order to perceive and "make sense" of the sensory inputs from the world.

Inborn Perceptual Abilities

Does the brain actually have to learn to perceive such things as motion, or are humans born with this ability? People born blind who have their sight returned as adults provide some answers. When such people are first able to see, they can usually pick out objects in the environment and focus their attention on them. That is, they can distinguish an object from its background. They can also follow moving objects with their eyes, and they can usually tell one color from another. They cannot, however, identify specific objects (faces, cubes, triangles, and other common shapes), and they cannot connect the different colors they see with the names of those colors. All of these perceptions take time, training, practice, and experience.

Work with formerly blind individuals suggests that some of the elements of perception (the ability to distinguish colors or to distinguish a figure from its background) may be present at birth. But this evidence is not conclusive because it is possible that some of these processes may have matured even without practice during the years of blindness. The visual cliff experiments (see Chapter 3) do suggest that the ability to perceive heights is present shortly after birth. Even so, perception takes practice, experience, and learning. If people did not learn, they would always perceive the world as infants do, and they would remain perceptual infants.

Sensory Stimulation and Development

From the moment of birth, what people see and experience with all of their senses helps them build up the connections in the brain that are necessary in their developing an accurate understanding and awareness of the world. **Sensory deprivation** experiments show how this awareness can be disturbed by even short periods of lack of stimulation. Such experiments suggest that a certain amount of **sensory stimulation** is necessary for everyone. The work of H. M. Skeels demonstrates just how important sensory stimulation is to both physical and mental development.

In the 1930s, Skeels shocked a good many people by claiming that he had been able to increase the intelligence test scores of apparently mentally retarded children by placing them in an unusual environment. This finding was especially surprising to the many people who believed that human intelligence is entirely inherited and hence determined at birth. If this were true, then it would be impossible to increase the intelligence of children who are born retarded. Making Skeels's findings even harder to believe was the fact that the special environment in which he placed the children was an institution where they were cared for by retarded women.

Skeels had been working at an orphanage in Iowa. The buildings used to house the children were old, some dating back to the Civil War. Inside the buildings, conditions were dreary. The infants were kept in cribs with sheets draped over the sides. They couldn't see each other and received little social stimulation. They had few toys, and their only human contact was with busy nurses who did little more than feed and change them on schedule. At the age of two, the children were moved to cottages, where they ate and slept according to rigid schedules. At the age of six, the orphans received some small amount of schooling on the orphanage grounds. In every respect, their environment was dull and unstimulating.

One day Skeels took special note of two young girls. He described these infants as "pitiful little creatures" who were undersized, sad, and inactive. They spent most of their time rocking back and forth on their beds. Intelligence tests available at the time suggested that these girls were far below average in intelligence. They had **IQ** scores of 50 or less (an IQ score of 100 is considered normal or average). Because of their extremely poor mental and physical condition, it was not likely that these girls would be adopted. They were, therefore, transferred to a home for the mentally retarded.

Some time later, Skeels began to work at the home for the retarded. There he was surprised to find "two outstanding little girls. They were alert, smiling, running about, responding to the playful attention of adults and generally behaving and looking like any other toddlers." They were the same two girls who had previously been considered to be mentally retarded. Skeels tested them and found their IQ scores to be normal. He didn't believe his findings at first, so he waited a year and retested the girls. They scored in the normal range again.

What had happened to these children who had been placed with groups of

Sensory stimulation is important to both physical and mental development. The baby in the above picture is receiving stimulation from toys and family members.

retarded women? Skeels found that each child had been "adopted" by a woman who had had plenty of time to devote to a child. Other women in the home began to consider themselves as "aunts" of the girls and shared in caretaking responsibilities. Even the nurses and attendants (unlike those in the orphanage) devoted time to the children—who no longer spent time rocking back and forth on their beds.

Skeels was convinced that moving the girls into a more stimulating and exciting environment where they were given more attention was responsible for their improvement. In an attempt to prove this, he set up an experiment. During the next several years, 13 more infants were removed from the orphanage and placed in an institution for the mentally retarded. All the children showed signs of improvement. Marie Skodak Crissey, who worked with Skeels, has kept in touch with many of these individuals for 40 years. Of this group who had experienced a highly stimulating environment for some part of their early lives, none is retarded. All are living on their own and none are in institutions. The same is not true for another group who had been normal at infancy, but who for one reason or another were not adopted and remained in the orphanage. Of this group of 12, 10 ended up spending nearly all of their lives in institutions for the retarded.

More recently, psychologist Rick Heber and his colleagues at the University of Wisconsin have confirmed Skeels's findings about the importance of the child's early environment. Heber and his group selected 40 infants from a slum in Milwaukee. A group of children given special training and a highly stimulating environment scored an average of 20 points higher on IQ tests than did the control group (see Chapter 8).

Perceiving the Familiar

Experiments conducted by Jerome Frank have shown how important a person's previous experiences are in perception. Frank used a device that allowed his subjects to see a different picture with each eye. Both eyes received the visual stimulation at the same time, but the brain had difficulty interpreting two completely different visual inputs at the same time. When pictures are shown in this manner for a short time, only one of the pictures is usually perceived. The two pictures shown in Frank's experiment were of a baseball player and a bullfighter. Grade-school children from two different backgrounds took part in the experiment. Students from North America tended to see only the baseball player. Students from Mexico almost always saw the bullfighter. In each case, the students perceived the object with which they were most familiar from their own experience.

Changing Perceptions

Frank's experiments are another indication that perception is a personal experience and that perception can differ from person to person. Even for an individual, perceptions can change from time to time. In order to show this, Frank

Propaganda aims to influence people's perceptions of groups or ideas. This World War II poster depicts Germans, Japanese, and Italians in a negative way. These Axis Powers were the enemies of the Allied Forces. Our perceptions of these nationalities have changed during the past 30 years. We no longer identify Germans with Hitler, Japanese with Tojo, or Italians with Mussolini.

analyzed polls taken in the United States in 1942. He found that at that time most people perceived or thought of the Germans and Japanese as warlike, treacherous, and cruel. In 1966 the polls showed that the Russians and Chinese Communists, not the Germans or Japanese, were seen as warlike, treacherous, and cruel. People's perceptions had changed with time and experience.

Don Quixote's perceptual problems can be explained in terms of his personal needs and his past experiences. Something in his personal experience influenced him in such a way that he saw windmills as warlike, treacherous, and cruel. This confused Spanish knight did not have trouble with his senses or with sensory adaptation. Even his reticular activating system was probably in good working order. It was Don Quixote's personal needs and past experiences that produced his peculiar perceptions of the world. For years Don Quixote had lived a quiet, dull life. His only excitement came through the many books he read about the days of knighthood and chivalry. He learned to like this fictitious world of knights and ladies, dragons and giants much more than he liked his own world. In the make-believe world of these books there was always a happy ending, good always triumphed over evil, and the world was a just and beautiful place. Eventually Don Quixote's boredom and dissatisfaction with his own imperfect world got to him. He began to see things the way he wanted them to be, instead of the way everyone else saw them.

THE BLIND SPOT

While Don Quixote's confused perceptions blinded him to many fac[...] each one of you also has blind spots. The retina, the area in the re[...] eyeball where the light receptors are located, has a small hole in it. At the [...] where the **optic nerve** (the nerve that leads from the eye to the brain) meets [...] retina there are no light receptors. Any light that falls on this spot is not sensed. The result is a blind spot in each eye. The brain, with practice and experience, learns to fill this visual gap so well that most people are not even aware of the hole in their visual world.

Your brain goes through life filling in many blind spots in your sensory inputs. When only the bottom half of a line of type is visible, you can still sometimes read the words because your brain fills in the missing tops of the letters. When a noisy airplane flies over as you are watching a television talk show and some of the words become **inaudible,** your brain does its best to fill in the missing words. If the lights go out in your room during a storm, your brain usually attempts to construct a mental image of the room, making it possible for you to feel your way across in the dark. But your brain's attempts to aid your senses are not always perfect. Whenever your brain must work with partial or incorrect information, you may make perceptual mistakes. You might "hear" words on the TV show that were never said, or you might trip and fall over a chair in a dark room.

Illusions

Learning to fill in sensory blind spots is a necessary and helpful ability, but it does have its drawbacks. A plate sitting on a table, for instance, looks flat and round to a person looking down on it from above. If the person sees the same plate from across the table, it looks oval. When the person holds the plate up flat and level with his or her eyes, the plate appears to have no curvature at all. Most people have seen many plates, and plates usually have the same general shape—they are flat and round. The brain, therefore, learns to generalize about plates. In other words, your brain has a general memory image that applies to plates, no matter how they are viewed. So when someone is asked about the shape of a plate sitting on the other side of the table, the answer will usually be, "Flat and round." But what if there is an oval plate sitting there? The person answering, "Flat and round," will have been fooled by a false perception or an **illusion.**

The world is full of illusions. A door, when viewed from straight on, casts a rectangular image of the retina. As the door is opened, the viewing angle changes and a different image hits the retina. Even so, anyone looking at a partially open door will perceive the door as rectangular. Similarly, most adults are perceived as being about the same height. Even when you see someone from a great distance, and hence a very small image hits your retina, you will usually perceive that person as being of normal height. Generalizations (about doors,

A   B

C. Do you see
   an old lady? Or a
   young lady?
D. Do you see two
   profile faces? Or
   a wine glass?

C   D

height, or anything else) come in handy, but they are not always correct. There
are oddly shaped doors (but not many) and different-sized people. Sometimes
we must go out into the world and test the reality of our perceptions.

Psychological Blind Spots

Illusions and perceptual judgments based on generalizations or on personal values can all lead to perceptual errors. Some people go through life with psychological blind spots that never get filled in, or that get filled in incorrectly. These
people may make false judgments about reality based on their illusions or generalizations. They may prejudge aspects of the world without testing their perceptions against reality. Such prejudgments or **prejudices** do not always hold up in
the light of reality. Many people, for instance, are taught that their race, their
religion, or their sex is superior to another race, religion, or sex. These people
may go through life with a prejudice about other people's beliefs because they
do not take the time to test their generalizations and learn more about reality.

Much of reality cannot and need not be tested. And no one can learn all
there is to know about the world. Therefore, much of our lives must be based on
generalizations and prejudgments. But the more that we know about ourselves

Is one of these men a midget and one a giant? Actually, the man on the left is the same height as the man on the right. These men are standing in the Ames "distorted room."

and the world around us, the more likely it is that our perceptions will be based on facts and not merely on socially acceptable fictions. And the more that we subject our perceptions to reality-testing, the more likely it is that we will survive in our complex environments.

Psychologist Roger Sperry, whom we met before in Chapter 2, has pointed out that our nervous systems are built to produce behavioral outputs — our perceptions of reality are just one important step in the process of sensing and responding to our worlds. Indeed, most of our perceptions carry with them some hint of possible action on our parts: Shoes are made to be worn on the feet, music is made to be listened to and enjoyed, and people exist to be loved or related to in some way. We perceive things and people because we must react to most of them at one time or another, and things and people are likely to react to or affect us in return. Part of what your brain does when it perceives the world, then, is to generate mental predictions of how your reactions will influence the behaviors of others, and how their reactions will influence you. Thus, when you go out into the world to test reality, you often generate important sensory feedback on the adequacy or truthfulness of your perceptions. If it turns out that people don't respond to you as you think they ought to, then it is likely that you are perceiving them (and yourself) in a prejudiced or biased fashion.

Most people do use their senses to learn about, experience, and test reality. Most people do learn to perceive the world in an adequate manner. Few individuals actually have the perceptual difficulties and psychological blind spots that Don Quixote had. But then, few individuals pay as little attention to real-life feedback — such as the remarks of his friends — as Don Quixote did. Because he ignored the information his senses gave him, things did not work out so well for him. He saw only what he wanted to see, and when he was finally forced to test reality and to face the facts of life as other people saw them, he did not like and could not accept what he saw. To him, the real world was ugly and senseless — a place he didn't want to live in.

FIG. 4–5.
Could a modern
psychoanalyst con-
vince Don Quixote
that his giants were
really windmills?
Could Don Quixote
survive in a realistic
world deprived of
his illusions?

Most of us would disagree with Don Quixote. Illusions can be comforting for a while, but in the long run they don't help us survive very well. Reality—stripped of prejudice and blind spots—has a beauty to it that few illusions can match. But to experience reality, we must be willing to test our perceptions constantly, and to change our perceptions and our behavioral outputs according to the inputs that our senses give us.

▶ SUMMARY

1. Don Quixote's sensory abilities worked as well as Sancho Panza's. They both could look at windmills. Sancho saw windmills but his master perceived them as giants. It was Don Quixote's perception that caused him problems.

2. The senses provide us with information about the world, but the brain must interpret this information before we can make sense of the world. The processing and interpretation of information from the senses is known as **perception.** Perceptions may differ from person to person and from time to time because they are based on factors that change — **sensory inputs,** personal needs, and past experiences.

3. The human senses respond to different types of stimuli in the environment, but **sensory limitation** protects the brain by screening incoming sensations. If the senses detected all levels of environmental energy, the brain would be overwhelmed with sensory information and would experience **input overload.**

4. Sensory adaptation protects the brain from overloading and from irrelevant information. The senses can adapt or grow used to many environmental stimuli. If a stimulus does not change, the senses may quit sending messages about it to the brain. This keeps the brain from having to deal with unnecessary information, leaving it free to concentrate on more important messages.

5. The brain, like the senses, has the ability to adjust to sensory inputs. After much training and experience, the brain learns to shut out some information and pay attention to only the information that is necessary in a particular situation.

6. Our personal needs affect our senses and our perceptions. The eyes, for instance, constantly search the environment for information that might be important to their owner. A hungry person will be more likely than a full one to spot a restaurant. Similarly the eyes contract and dilate in response to the environment and the individual's needs, as **pupil reaction** reflects personal interests.

7. Experiments have shown that people may sometimes avoid perceiving sensory inputs (such as "dirty words") with which they would rather not deal. Experiments have also shown that our personal values can affect our perceptions of reality.

8. Some perceptual abilities may be inborn, but most perceptions are the result of learning and experience. Infants can sense the world, but they have little perception (or understanding) of much of what they experience. If we were unable to learn, we would always perceive the world as infants do and would remain infants.

9. Perceptions are learned through experience, but experiences differ from time to time and from person to person. The fact that experiences differ helps explain why people of different backgrounds may perceive some aspects of reality differently. It also explains why one person's perceptions may change with time and experience.

10. Sensory stimulation is necessary to help infants and children develop perceptual abilities. Studies have demonstrated that stimulation of the senses is very important in both psychological and mental development.

11. With experience, people begin to make **generalizations** about reality; for example, plates are generally round. Generalizations can be useful, but they can sometimes be mistaken and can lead to false perceptions. Perceptions that do not match reality are called **illusions.**

12. People sometimes make judgments based on generalizations or on illusions. Because generalizations and illusions do not always give accurate representations of the world, judgments (**prejudices**) based on them are sometimes faulty. In such cases reality must be tested if we are to experience the world as it really is.

Suggested Readings

Cervantes-Saavedra, Miguel De. *Two Cervantes short novels*. (F. F. Pierce, Ed.) New York: Pergamon, 1970.

Gregory, Richard L. *The intelligent eye*. New York: McGraw-Hill, 1970.

Locher, J. L. (Ed.) *The world of M. C. Escher*. New York: Harry N. Abrams, 1971.

► STUDY GUIDE

A. RECALL

Sentence Completion

1. The distortion of perception that Don Quixote had was really in his
[p. 118]   _____, not in his senses.

[p. 118]   2. The senses only pass _____ _____ to the brain.

3. _____ is defined as the processing and interpretation of sensory infor-
[p. 118]   mation.

[p. 118]   4. Perception starts in the _____.

5. Your brain works best when it has a relatively _____ supply of messages
[p. 119]   to deal with.

6. _____ _____ is the term used to describe the situation in
[p. 121]   which your brain is stimulated by more information than it can cope with.

7. _____ _____ _____ is the brain structure that
[p. 121]   helps to block out extra, or unwanted, sensory inputs.

[p. 121]   8. Our senses are _____ in the range of stimuli that they can respond to.

9. Becoming used to, or accustomed to, changes in levels of stimulation is called
[p. 123]   _____.

[p. 123]   10. Your senses work primarily by detecting _____ in your environment.

11. Studies on pupil size demonstrate that _____ _____ of
[p. 124]   people can affect the way their sense organs operate.

[p. 125]   12. The "dirty word" experiments were conducted by Elliott _____.

13. When children thought that poker chips could be used to buy candy, they
[p. 126]   _____ their size.

14. To appreciate or understand what we see or hear necessarily requires our
[p. 127]   _____ _____.

15. Two perceptual abilities that may be present at birth are our abilities to distinguish
[p. 127]   _____ and to distinguish _____.

16. Skeels claimed he could raise children's IQs by placing them in _____
[p. 128]   environments.

[p. 128]   17. The subjects in Skeels's "experiment" were _____.

18. When each of our eyes is shown a different picture, we will tend to perceive just one,
[p. 129]   the one that is more _____ to us.

19. The point in each retina of the eye where the optic nerve begins, and where there are
[p. 131]   no light receptors is called the _____ _____.

[p. 131]   20. An _____ may be defined as a false perception.

21. Prejudices or prejudgments may affect our perceptions, and may be referred to as
[p. 132]   psychological _____ _____.

22. To really experience reality we must be willing to _____ our perceptions
[p. 134]   against the real world.

B.   REVIEW

Multiple Choice: Circle the letter identifying the alternative that most correctly completes the statement or answers the question.

1. Don Quixote's problem was that:
   A. his sensory receptors did not function properly.
   B. he was simply just not very intelligent.
   C. no one would help him do what he wanted to do.
   D. he perceived the world differently from everyone else.

2. Our senses:
   A. pass coded information directly to the brain.
   B. interpret the information that they receive.
   C. act selectively on the information that they receive.
   D. process information and organize it at the receptor site.

3. When your brain is forced to process too much information:
   A. you are in a condition of input overload.
   B. your reticular activating system stops working.
   C. you will probably not perceive any of it.
   D. you are apt to lapse into a coma.

4. Which of the following types of energy is *NOT* a form similar to visible light energy?
   A. X-rays.
   B. radar.
   C. high-frequency sound waves.
   D. radio and television broadcast energy.

5. _____ is a form of protection that allows your brain to ignore many unnecessary sensory messages and to concentrate on more important ones.
   A. pupil dilation.
   B. sensory adaptation.
   C. sensory deprivation.
   D. input overload.

6. When judging the size of objects in our environment, we may tend to overestimate the size of stimuli that:

    A. we value.

    B. are moving.

    C. we are very familiar with.

    D. all of the above.

7. Skeels found IQ scores of orphaned children were raised dramatically after the children were given to _____ to raise them.

    A. psychologists.

    B. retarded women in an institution.

    C. their real mothers.

    D. a nursery school for orphans.

8. Illusions:

    A. may be psychological as well as visual.

    B. do help with survival in the long run.

    C. are often based on generalizations and prejudgments.

    D. all of the above.

9. The pitch of a sound is determined primarily by the:

    A. size of the sound waves.

    B. frequency of the sound waves.

    C. sensitivity of the ear.

    D. size of the bones in the middle ear.

10. When a picture of a bullfigher is presented to one eye at the same time that a picture of a baseball player is being presented to the other eye:

    A. children see the pictures before adults do.

    B. Mexican children almost always see the bullfighter.

    C. we tend not to be able to make out what either picture is.

    D. all of the above.

THE CASE OF S. B.

The trip from the darkness of the womb to the brightness of the world must be a shocking one, but no one can remember enough about it to really describe it. Some of the effects of such a shocking sensory change, however, can be examined in special cases. British psychologist Richard L. Gregory has reported the case of a man who was born blind. In a manner of speaking, this man had to live his life in a dark cave. Everything he knew of the world came through his other senses. This man, known as S. B., could feel, taste, smell, and hear the world. He could not see it. From his other senses he got impressions of the world, but he could not get a look at it.

The cornea is the thick, transparent, outer part of the eye that covers and protects the lens of the eye. In a normal eye, light enters through the cornea and travels to the light receptors in the retina at the back of the eye. In the case described by Gregory, the blind man's corneas were badly damaged and scarred. No light could get through them and S. B. was totally blind, When he was 52 years old, however, it became medically possible to remove his damaged corneas and replace them with clear ones. The operation, a cornea transplant, was performed, and S. B. was able to see for the first time in his life. He was able to step out of the cave of blindness and face the sun.

At first the light was too bright. It took S. B. several days to get used to it and to adapt to his new way of experiencing the world. He could, for instance, recognize people by their voices, but he had to learn what they looked like. He had to feel some objects with his hands before he could tell what they were. He had to learn to judge distances and heights. But gradually, with practice, S. B. learned to feel at home in the world of color and light. He learned a whole new way of experiencing reality and life.

But learning and facing reality are not always pleasant. S. B. had opened his eyes to the beauty of the world as he expected, but at the same time he opened his eyes to some of the ugly sights of life. A person with a beautiful voice and soft hands might have a badly deformed face or body. A comfortable room in a warm house might be part of an ugly slum. For years S. B. had been thinking about all the beauty he was missing. He had not considered the fact that he might open his eyes to ugliness. In many instances his incomplete shadow reality had been more pleasant than the real thing. S. B. became depressed, and Gregory reports that S. B. would sometimes withdraw from the world and spend hours alone in a dark room. He would, in effect, return to his blindness.

C. NEWS STORY QUESTIONS

1. In the story, what was S. B.'s problem, and how was it solved? _____
   _____

2. With his sight restored, was S. B.'s reaction in all ways a positive one? How so? ___
   _____

   _____

Movie still from *The Diary of Anne Frank*.

Why do we do what we do? Why do we feel what we feel? These are questions that most of us probably ask ourselves from time to time. Many of the answers to these questions can be found in the study of the various theories of human motivation.

Motivation and Emotion

chapter

When you have completed your study of this chapter, you should be able to:
- ►Define "motivation"
- ►Summarize the major components of the drive theory of motivation and distinguish between primary needs and drives, and secondary needs and drives
- ►Summarize the major components of the arousal theory of motivation and relate it to the concept of homeostasis
- ►Define "emotion" and list its five subparts, relating them to the autonomic nervous system
- ►Compare and contrast counterconditioning and desensitization
- ►Describe Maslow's theory of human motivation

Adrenal gland (uh-DREE-nal). You have two adrenal glands, one sitting atop each of your kidneys. The adrenals secrete (release into the bloodstream) hormones that influence sexual development, urine production, and physiological arousal.

Adrenalin (uh-DREN-uh-lin). One of the two "arousal" hormones released by the adrenal glands. Also called epinephrine (EP-pih-NEFF-rin).

Affect (AFF-fect). From the Latin word meaning "desire" or "emotion." A person who lacks affect is someone who is extremely calm, cool, collected, unemotional. A person with too much affect might be overexcited and wild, or severely depressed or sad.

Arousal hormones. Complex chemicals released by the adrenal glands which stimulate the autonomic nervous system and hence lead to arousal.

Arousal theory. An alternative theory to drive theory; states that the homeostasis in the organism is the point of optimum stimulation, which varies according to situation.

Autonomic nervous system (OUGHT-toe-NOM-ick). "Autonomic" means automatic or reflexive, involuntary. The autonomic nervous system is a collection of neural centers which takes care of most of your normal body functions that take place automatically—without having to think about them.

Conditioning. A type of learning. The two main types of conditioning are respondent (Pavlovian) and operant (Skinnerian).

Counterconditioning. Pavlov conditioned his dogs to salivate when he rang a bell. If you took one of Pavlov's trained dogs and reconditioned it to bark and become excited when you rang the bell, you would find that it would no longer salivate to the bell. Since the dog could not be excited and salivate at the same time, your training would be a type of counterconditioning. Counterconditioning always involves teaching the organism a new response that is incompatible with its prior training.

Desensitization (DEE-sen-sit-tie-ZEY-shun). A type of counterconditioning developed by psychiatrist Joseph Wolpe (WOHL-pee). The patient is typically trained to relax in the presence of a feared stimulus such as a snake. Once the counterconditioning has taken place, the patient is no longer "sensitive" to or aroused by the feared stimulus.

Drive theory. An early psychological theory of motivation in which the lack or need of something necessary for life presumably creates within the organism a strong drive to satisfy the need and hence reduce the drive.

Emotions. From the Latin word meaning "agitated motion or movement toward a goal."

Estrogens (ESS-troh-jens). Female hormones.

Feeling tone. That part of the emotional experience perceived as pleasant or unpleasant.

Free-floating anxiety. A type of broad or generalized fear that is not focused on any particular stimulus object.

Gonads (GO-nads). The primary sex glands; the ovaries in the female and the testes in the male. The ovaries produce the egg cells, which may be fertilized by the sperm secreted by the testes.

Hierarchy of fears (HIGH-er-ark-kee). As used in desensitization therapy, a hierarchy of fears is a list of dreaded stimuli running from the most feared to the least feared.

Homeostasis (home-ee-oh-STAY-sis). The tendency to move toward a need-free or drive-free condition. Any action that an organism makes to reduce its drives is called a "homeostatic behavior."

Inanimate (in-ANN-uh-mutt). From the Latin word meaning "having no spirit" or "having no soul." The early Greeks and Romans believed that every living (animate) thing had a spirit or soul that gave it life and motivated it to satisfy its needs.

Motivation. Like the word "emotion," comes from the Latin words meaning "to move." Motivation is the "explanation" we give for why we do what we do.

Need achievement. Abbreviated n-ach. According to psychologist David McClelland, the "need to achieve" is as basic (but not necessarily as strong) in most of us as is the need to eat. Also called "the achievement motive."

Noradrenalin. One of the two "arousal" hormones released by the adrenal glands.

Orgasm (ORR-gazz-um). A sudden release of tension or excitement, as in sexual climax.

Palpitations (pal-puh-TAY-shuns). From the Latin word meaning "to feel or stroke." A series of rapid pulsations, or an unusually rapid beating of the pulse or heart.

Parasympathethetic nervous system (PAIR-uh-sim-puh-THET-tick). That half of the autonomic nervous system which is "beyond" or opposed to the sympathetic system. The parasympathetic system "turns off" or slows down most emotional activity.

Physiologist (fizz-ee-OLL-oh-gist). Anatomy is the study of the structure of the body. Physiology is the study of the functioning of the parts of the body.

Polygraph (POLL-ee-graf). A polygraph is a machine that makes a graph of many different physiological responses simultaneously. While it is sometimes called a "lie-detector," it records emotional responses, not "lies."

Primary drive. According to drive theory, an innately determined drive such as the need for food, air, or water.

Primary need. The body "needs" certain things in order to live. The lack of any such substance leads to the creation of a primary drive.

Projective tests. The test materials are so vague or indefinite that the subject is expected to "project" his or her personality onto the test materials in order to make sense out of them.

Progesterone. A female sex hormone.

Relaxation training. A technique, used in counterconditioning or desensitization therapy, in which the subject is trained to relax his or her muscles "on command."

Secondary needs. According to drive theory, all needs other than primary physiological needs are learned. The need for food is a primary need that creates a primary drive (hunger). The need for a hamburger (rather than a bowl of soup) is a secondary need acquired because hamburgers have often satisfied hunger in the past.

Self-actualization. Abraham Maslow's term for "achieving one's highest potential."

Social motives. Motivations or needs concerned with social behaviors, such as the need for companionship, love, achievement, or belonging to a group.

Stress. To feel stress, one must usually be under pressure or must feel intense strain.

Sympathetic nervous system (sim-puh-THET-tick). The sympathetic nervous system is that half of the autonomic nervous system responsible for "turning on" your emotional reactions.

Thematic Apperception Test (thuh-MATT-tick app-purr-CEPP-shun). Abbreviated as TAT. A projective test developed by psychologist Henry Murray. Consists of a set of 20 rather vague stimulus pictures. The subject responds to each picture by making up a story about what the subject believes is happening to the people shown in the picture.

Theory. A "guess" or set of assumptions used to explain any facts of nature or of life. In science, theories are never "proven" no matter how sensible they may seem to be, but are accepted only until they can be disproven by further research.

Thermostatic process (thur-moh-STAT-tick). The process by which the temperature of a machine, place, or living organism is controlled. Certain neural centers in your brain monitor your temperature and motivate you to help keep your temperature at 98.6° F. (37° C.).

INTRODUCTION: THE DIARY OF A YOUNG GIRL

On her thirteenth birthday Anne Frank received a diary which she used to record the events of her life as well as her thoughts, feelings, and emotions.

On her fourteenth birthday Anne celebrated in a secret apartment at the rear of a warehouse, where she and her family were living in hiding — afraid that they might be captured and sent to their deaths at any moment.

On her fifteenth birthday Anne was still in hiding, but she looked forward eagerly to freedom and was excited about life. She had received her first truly romantic kiss and was falling in love with Peter Van Daan, the only son of the family that shared the Franks' hiding place.

Anne didn't have a sixteenth birthday. She died in a German concentration camp two months before she would have been 16, and two months before she and her family would have been free to leave their secret hiding place.

Anne Frank, the second daughter of a well-to-do Jewish family, was born in Germany in 1929. Four years later Otto Frank, Anne's father, decided that life in Germany was no longer safe for Jews. Adolf Hitler, an extremely dangerous man who hated Jews, had taken control of the German government and was planning to rid the country of all Jewish people — by murder if necessary. In order to escape from Hitler, Otto Frank and his family moved to Amsterdam, the capital of Holland (now known as the Netherlands). The Franks lived in comfort and safety among the Dutch people (the people of Holland) for several years — until the German army took control of Holland. Again the Jews were persecuted.

Eventually the Franks were forced into hiding. For more than two years they lived a secret life in a hidden apartment. The four Franks and the four others who shared the apartment did not once step outside. A few friends brought them what food could be obtained (food was scarce for almost everyone in Holland during the war). The diary Anne received for her thirteenth birthday tells how the Franks and their friends survived for these two years. Then, shortly after Anne's fifteenth birthday, the diary stops.

Anne Frank did not live to regain her freedom, but her diary lives on as one of the most moving documents of World War II. When Otto Frank returned to Amsterdam after the war, he was told that some friends had found his daughter's diary in the apartment after the Germans left. The diary was published in 1947. Since then millions of people around the world have read it or seen it produced as a movie, on television, or as a play.

The diary of Anne Frank became and remains popular for a number of reasons. Not only is it a rare, first-hand account of what life was like for Jews under Hitler, it is also an intelligent description of the thoughts and feelings of a young girl nearing maturity. But perhaps more important than what the diary tells us about Anne and her situation are the questions it raises. First and most obvious are the questions about war. "What, oh, what," asks Anne, "is the use of war? Why can't people live peacefully together? Why all this destruction?"

The question of human violence and aggression is a complex one (see Chapter 2), and Anne Frank does not have the answers. Her diary, however, is much more than a war story. It is a highly personal and private account of two years in a young girl's life, and it raises some very personal questions about human behavior. Why, for instance, did Anne even keep a diary? Why did she bother to keep a careful record of her thoughts, feelings, and behaviors? Anne explains at the beginning of her diary: "It's an odd idea," she says, "for someone like me to keep a diary; not only because I have never done so before, but because it seems to me that neither I—nor for that matter anyone else—will be interested in the unbosomings of a thirteen-year-old schoolgirl. Still, what does that matter? I want to write, but more than that, I want to bring out all kinds of things that lie buried deep in my heart." In other words, Anne's writing was sort of a process of self-discovery. In order to write seriously and truthfully about herself, Anne had to examine and question her behavior. She had to ask why she did what she did and why she felt what she felt. And for any of us, examining and questioning our behavior and feelings can be a process of self-discovery (whether we write the questions and answers in a diary or not).

MOTIVATION

Humans satisfy their hunger drive in many ways. These nomads from Mali are searching for food in the drought-stricken Upper Volta region of Africa.

Why do we do what we do? Why do others do what they do? These are questions that Anne asked and that all of us probably ask ourselves from time to time. They are also among the questions that psychologists ask, and many of the answers can be found in the study of human motivation.

The word **motivation** comes from the Latin term meaning "to move." Ancient scholars were fascinated by the fact that some objects in the world seem to be self-movers, while other objects remain stationary unless acted on by some outside force. The ancients assumed that self-initiated motion was caused by an inner spirit that pushed the object into action. Not only plants, animals, and people but rivers, clouds, and other moving objects were thought to be inhabited by some inner spirit or force that caused them to move.

Nowadays we assume that only living organisms are capable of self-determined movement, but it was not until the seventeenth century that Western scientists learned enough about the laws of physics to explain the movement of **inanimate** (nonliving) objects, such as rivers and clouds. With a growing knowledge of the laws of physics, scientists began to explain the movements of inanimate objects in purely physcial or nonspiritual terms. The law of gravity, for instance, rather than a "river spirit," explains the downhill movement of rivers. Other physical laws explain the movement of clouds, the wind, the stars. Once scientists had made these intellectual discoveries in the area of physical movement, they began to wonder if the activities of living organisms (people, plants, and animals) could also be explained in purely physical, mechanical, or nonspiritual terms. Attempts to come up with such explanations have led to several theories of motivation based on the belief that all human activities are just about as mechanical as the movements of rivers or clouds. Two of the best known mechanistic approaches to human motivation are **drive theory** and **arousal theory.**

DRIVE THEORY

Physics became a science when physicists began to explain the movements of inanimate objects in terms of fairly simple physical laws. During the past century many psychologists have attempted to imitate the physicists by reducing the complexities of human behavior to a set of fairly uncomplicated biological laws. Instead of explaining human motivation in terms of inner spirits or forces, these psychologists tried to explain all human movement and behavior in terms of physiological or biological processes. Rather than assuming that people (or animals) are capable of self-determined actions, these psychologists suggested that living organisms are driven or pushed into action by external forces, similar to the way in which rivers and clouds are moved by natural physical forces, or to the way an automobile engine is cranked into motion when someone turns the ignition key. At its simplest, this physiological or biological approach to motivation is known as *drive theory*. Drive theory says that all human behavior is motivated by the need to reduce certain biological drives.

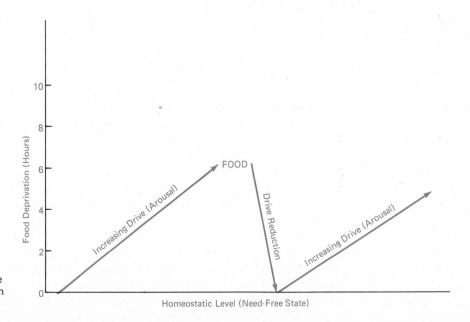

FIG. 5–1.
This diagram illustrates how the drive theory of motivation operates.

Primary Needs and Drives

What are biological needs and how do they motivate or cause human behavior? One of the most obvious examples of a biological need is the need for food. Without food, biological survival is not possible. Those things that we absolutely must have in order to stay alive are called **primary needs** (meaning primary or first in importance). Primary needs include food, water, air, and a proper temperature range.

Each of the primary needs is associated with a **primary drive.** The need for food, for instance, is associated with the primary drive known as hunger. When you go without food for a certain amount of time, a hunger drive is said to build up within you. The longer you go without food, the stronger the drive will become. When this primary drive becomes strong enough, it tends to motivate you or move you to satisfy your need for food.

The need for food, or the drive to satisfy one's hunger, results in numerous human activities, from farming and grocery shopping to cooking and eating. Anne Frank and her family devoted a good deal of their time and energy to relieving their hunger. They and their friends would spend hours just trying to figure out how to get enough food into the secret apartment to feed them all. Even when they did get food, it was often nothing more than boiled lettuce or rotten potatoes. But whether it be rotten potatoes, fancy French food, or a Big Mac, hundreds of people and thousands of human behaviors are usually involved in helping us satisfy our hunger drive. According to drive theory, all of these behaviors are motivated by the hunger drive.

Considering the importance of our primary biological drives and the amount of time we spend responding to them, it is not surprising that some drive theorists have assumed that biological needs and drives are what rule our lives, motivate us, and determine our behavior.

Drive States and Homeostasis

As long as all of your primary needs are being met, your body presumably ticks along smoothly in a quiet state of balance. When your body begins to run low on something required for survival, the balance is upset. According to drive theory, when your biological balance is upset you become aroused and enter what is known as a primary drive state. Generally speaking, the longer you are deprived of a primary need, the greater your drive state will be and the more aroused or motivated you will be. Eventually, the arousal or movement produced by the drive state usually brings you into a position to satisfy your need. (A hungry person will usually become aroused enough to get up and look for something to eat.) Once your biological need has been met, the original balance is restored, your drive state is greatly reduced, and your arousal (motivation) disappears. In other words, immediately after you have eaten a big meal you are not likely to feel aroused or motivated to eat again.

The biological process involved in turning drive states on and off is known as the *homeostatic process* (from the Greek words meaning "home state" or "natural condition"). The balanced state this process brings about is known as **homeostasis,** and any action that an organism takes to reduce a drive state is known as a homeostatic behavior.

One easy way of understanding the homeostatic process of our bodies is to look at the **thermostatic process** of an air conditioner. Suppose that on the morning of a pleasant summer day you set the thermostatic control of a room air conditioner at 75 degrees F. (23.9 degrees C.). For a while the machine stays quiet because the room is still cooler than the temperature for which you set the control. But as the day wears on, things begin to warm up. When the temperature of the room goes above 75 degrees, the thermostat inside the machine detects this fact and puts the machine into a drive state. In other words, the machine's fan and motor begin operating to cool the room. Cool air blows into the room, and the temperature begins falling. This cool air reduces the machine's "drive state." Once the room is again at 75 degrees (the normal or balanced state), the thermostat detects this, and the machine's drive state or arousal is turned off until the temperature goes above 75 degrees again.

Physiologists — the scientists who study the physical workings of the body — suggest that many of our biologically determined behaviors are turned on and off by internal thermostats that detect our needs and help make sure that we try to keep our bodies in a need-free, unexcited condition. The concept of homeostasis — the return to the normal or unexcited state — plays an important role in drive theory. Figure 5-1 is a diagram illustrating drive theory.

Secondary Needs and Drives

During two years of hiding, Anne Frank and her family fulfilled their **primary needs** by whatever means were available. If they had nothing to eat but rotten potatoes, that's what they ate. Their homeostatic processes told them when a need existed, and (according to drive theory) they were then motivated to meet that need. Human motivation, however, is far too complex to be explained in terms of rather simple biological needs. Why, for instance, do some people go to a restaurant and order a hamburger while others order fish? If we were motivated only by our primary needs, we probably wouldn't care what we ate as long as it reduced our hunger drive. But we do care. We all have likes and dislikes, favorite foods and drinks. These likes and dislikes (which are supposedly directly related to our primary needs) are called **secondary needs.**

Secondary needs are believed to be acquired or learned, rather than built in. According to drive theory, the reinforcing pleasure that comes from satisfying a primary need is very strong. This pleasure *generalizes* to any input that is present when a primary drive is reduced. If a young girl is very hungry and her mother gives her a hamburger, the girl's hunger drive is reduced and she feels pleasure. She then associates the pleasure with the hamburger and, when she is hungry again, she may ask for a hamburger in preference to some food she's never

Secondary needs are learned likes and dislikes that often vary from culture to culture. Crisp vegetables and raw fish may satisfy the needs of Orientals, while Americans would prefer a hamburger and soda.

tasted before. And if the girl's mother is always the one who helps the girl satisfy her primary needs, some of the reinforcing pleasure associated with need reduction will generalize to the mother as well. Thus, according to drive theorists, we tend to love those people and things that have become associated with satisfying our primary drives, and to hate those people and things that have become associated with deprivation, pain, or an increase in our primary drives.

Because secondary needs are learned from past experience, they vary greatly from person to person and from culture to culture.

In summary, the drive approach to motivation is a straightforward theory based on our biological needs. According to drive theory, all human motivation and behavior results from attempts to fulfill our primary needs. Individual differences in motivation result from attempts to fulfill our learned or secondary needs.

There is little doubt that humans are strongly influenced by their biological needs, but as we shall see, there are human motives, needs, and drives that are not completely explained by drive theory.

AROUSAL THEORY

Imagine spending two years locked in a small apartment with seven other people the way Anne Frank did. No matter how interesting the people were, you would probably get tired of them, grow bored, and feel the need for a change. You would probably be motivated not only to seek out different people but to experience different sights, sounds, and sensations. How is this sort of motivation explained?

In the late 1950s, Elizabeth Duffy (and others) began to realize that drive theory did not fully explain all types of human motivation. Duffy pointed out that our drives are not always related to needs for such things as food, air, or water. It appears that we have *informational needs* as well (see stimulus input needs,

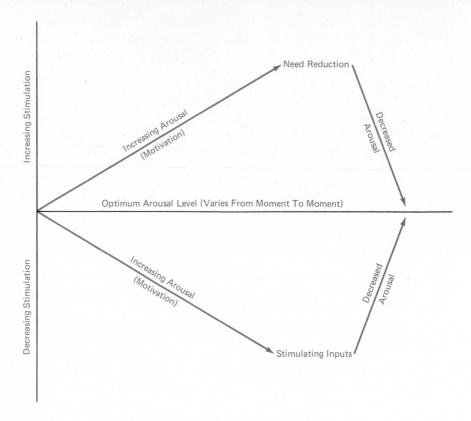

FIG. 5–2.
The arousal theory
of motivation is
shown in this dia-
gram.

Chapter 3). These informational or stimulus needs are as innate and as highly motivating as the drive associated with the lack of food.

The human need for arousal or stimulation led Duffy and other scientists to propose a new approach to motivation. This approach is sometimes called **arousal theory.** It can be summarized as follows:

1. The homeostatic "home base" is not a state of *zero* excitation but rather a point of **optimum** or best stimulation.
2. This optimum point may change from time to time, depending on our biological condition.
3. A decrease in optimum stimulation may be as arousing or motivating as an increase.

Arousal and Homeostasis

Arousal theory had its beginnings in the sensory deprivation experiments performed in Canada and in the discovery of the reticular activating system by Magoun and his associates (see Chapter 3). Consider the sensory deprivation experiments for just a moment. You will recall that the subjects in these experiments apparently had all of their biological needs met all the time, yet most of them could not endure the deprivation for more than a day or so. They all seemed to need more stimulation than they were getting. But this "need for stimulation" is not explained by the simple homeostatic model of drive theory, which says we are motivated by the need to *reduce* stimulation, such as the stimulation associated with hunger. Arousal theory suggests, instead, that we need a certain amount of stimulation, and that we are sometimes motivated by the need to *increase* stimulation.

Duffy also pointed out that we do not have a single "homeostatic level" that is set at birth and never varies thereafter. Rather, our need for stimulation changes according to our past experiences and present conditions. As explained in previous chapters, your sensory receptors are designed to detect environmental *change*. For the first few moments that you turn on a fan in an otherwise quiet room, the fan may seem particularly noisy. After a while, however, your nervous system stops responding to the sound of the fan. Similarly, if you had to eat steak at every meal, you might eventually find that it didn't taste as good as it once did. These examples (as well as the results of the sensory deprivation experiments) make it quite clear that we do need a certain amount of stimulation. But because our bodies adjust to almost any constant sensory input, the optimum level of stimulation that we need varies from moment to moment. We need a certain amount of stability in the world around us — just as the homeostatic model predicts. But we also need a certain amount of variety in stimulation — as arousal theory predicts — or our sense receptor system will turn off and leave us without any input at all. The reticular activating system seems designed to stir us into activity whenever our input becomes either too different or too much the same. Figure 5-2 is a diagram illustrating the arousal theory of motivation.

MENTAL EXPERIENCES AND MOTIVATION

Why do you sometimes eat when you aren't hungry? Why did Hitler order the murder of millions of people? Why did Anne Frank spend hours sitting alone with her friend Peter? A great deal of human behavior can be explained in terms of primary and secondary needs and drives, but there are many activities that just do not seem to be adequately explained by either the drive or arousal theory of motivation. A freshly baked pie, for instance, may look and smell so good that you are tempted to eat it even if you have just eaten a large meal and have no real biological need for food. Hitler did not have a biological need to have people murdered. Instead, he appears to have been motivated by (among other things) his strong feelings about Jews — he hated them. Anne Frank was motivated at times by her strong feelings for Peter — she loved him. In these instances, as well as in many more throughout our lives, it is thoughts, feelings, and emotions rather than biological needs that seem to move us to action.

TABLE 5-1   **Approaches to Motivation**

Drive Theory	All human behavior is motivated by needs to reduce certain biological drives and to maintain a fixed homeostatic point	*Primary Needs* 1. Food 2. Water 3. Air 4. Proper temperature *Secondary Needs* 1. Likes 2. Dislikes	*Primary Drives* 1. Hunger 2. Thirst 3. Breathing 4. Warmth/coolness *Secondary Drives* 1. Approach 2. Avoidance
Arousal Theory	Human drives are not always related to needs for food, water, air. We also have need for stimulation and information inputs	Needs for stimulating inputs	Increase or decrease stimulation to reach point of optimum stimulation

EMOTIONS

Love, hate, joy, anger, fear, rage—these are among the words that come to mind when we think of human **emotions.** And we all probably learn from experience that these and other emotions can have a powerful influence on our lives, powerful enough to be at the root of much human behavior. You may love learning, for instance, and try to do well in school because of your strong feelings. You may hate certain types of foods or activities and do all you can to avoid them. In fact, the powerful thoughts and feelings we call emotions are among the most important factors in human motivation. The word "emotion" even comes from the same Latin word as does the word "motivation." "Emotion" actually means "to move, to respond," or "to be stirred up."

How do our emotions stir us up or move us to action? First of all, it must be understood that emotions are much more than thoughts or subjective feelings. Emotions are complex reactions that consist of at least five different parts:

1. *Physiological arousal.* The physiological "stirring up" that accompanies emotion tends to involve arousal and sometimes depression. When you become frightened, for instance, your pulse rate increases as your heart begins to pound rapidly. Your stomach muscles may clamp down or tighten up, your breathing rate usually speeds up, you may perspire, your mouth may go dry, and you may feel tension in your neck and the small of your back. All of these physiological changes can be seen or measured objectively.

2. *Cognitive awareness.* As your body becomes aroused (or depressed), your mind usually becomes aware that something has happened to you. When you experience a mildly threatening situation, for instance, you may note that you are suddenly more aware of your environment and your bodily reactions. If you have been trained to do so, you may notice tension in various

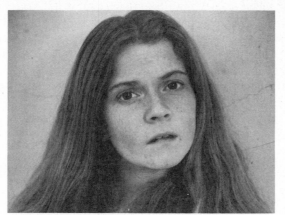

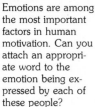

Emotions are among the most important factors in human motivation. Can you attach an appropriate word to the emotion being expressed by each of these people?

parts of your body. You may also notice that you perceive the threatening object or situation more clearly and in greater detail.

Cognitive awareness of an emotional state cannot really be measured objectively. If a psychologist asked you to describe what your mind was experiencing when you felt threatened, you could perhaps talk about your perceptions rather well. But you might notice—as most people do—that the mere act of describing what was happening to you changed much of the emotion you were experiencing.

3. *Feeling tone.* Emotions are seldom neutral. Rather, they are almost always pleasant or unpleasant. You may enjoy and seek out certain types of emotional experiences, but others may be so painful to you that you go out of your way to avoid them. The **feeling tone,** or affect, of an emotion is usually a separate or distinct part of the experience. If you are walking through a swamp and see a coral snake, you may become very aroused because you perceive the snake as an unpleasant danger you must avoid. If, on the other hand, you are a zoologist on a snake-collecting expedition, you may become pleasantly aroused because you perceive the animal as a valuable addition to your collection.

153

4. *Emotional behaviors.* We seldom experience an emotion that does not cause us to react in some way. Aggressive acts—running from or approaching a snake, violent fits of crying or laughing, screaming, sexual responses of various kinds—all these are the *behavioral* components of various emotions.

5. *Feedback.* Emotions are usually not experiences that happen and are over and done with in a second or two. Rather, our emotions tend to increase and decrease over a period of time. The actual *course* that one of your emotions runs is frequently influenced by the type of feedback that you experience. Some of this feedback comes from your own body; some from the world around you.

Fear is an example. When you see a snake, you may catch your breath. As you perceive the danger, your heart begins to pound, your breathing quickens, your hair may stand on end and you may start to tremble. You do all these things—and you often notice almost unconsciously what your physiological reactions are. The fact that you perceive that your heart is beating faster may actually make your heart rate increase even more. So you begin to run away, and the act of running makes demands on your body that cause your heart to pump blood even more vigorously.

But suppose a zoologist friend of yours is with you when you cry, "Snake!" And this friend immediately reminds you that the animal is harmless and picks it up and begins playing with it. Most probably you will begin to relax, you won't run away, and your pulse rate will decrease. You may *perceive* that you are relaxing and hence relax even more, and your pulse rate will drop back to near normal. In this case, feedback from your friend—and from your own body— prevented you from experiencing a full-fledged attack of fear.

Analyzing Emotions

Anne Frank and her family knew fear. They lived in silence during the daytime, afraid that someone in the warehouse would hear them and report them. At night, when the warehouse was empty, they were free to talk and move around, but they still had to be careful. On several occasions, for instance, they heard strange noises outside their secret door. Anne wrote after one of these frightening experiences: "I turned white at once, got a tummy-ache and heart **palpitations,** all from fear."

Anne was in the "grip of fear." Her physiological reactions, thoughts, and behaviors were being influenced and controlled by her fear. One of the reasons that many of us become "prisoners of our emotions" is that emotions are terribly complex experiences. Most of the words we use to describe emotions—such as fear, love, hate, jealously, anxiety, joy, lust, and anger—do not take into account the five different aspects of the emotional experience. Is love a biological response? Those individuals who consider love and sex to be the same thing might argue yes. Those people who consider love to be a state of inner awareness, or a strongly pleasant feeling tone, might argue otherwise. But love is also a behavior pattern, and it is almost always strongly affected by the actions (feed-back) of the person we have fallen in love with.

Words like "love" and "hate" are so imprecise that they often confuse us, leaving us thinking that we understand them when we don't. If someone says I love Beethoven, hate scrambled eggs, love my mother, hate spiders, love my country, hate violence, love playing ball, hate studying — what has that person told you about the emotions of love and hate? Is loving your mother or Beethoven the same psychological experience as loving to play ball or loving your country? Would you be willing to bet that hating violence is the same experience as hating scrambled eggs?

We cannot begin to understand our emotions or how they motivate us until we can define them fairly precisely. And any reasonably precise definition of emotional reactions will include the five aspects of emotionality already mentioned — physiological arousal, cognitive awareness, feeling tone, emotional behaviors, and feedback.

Physiological Arousal

As the physical scientists found out centuries ago, the more accurately you can measure something, the more likely it is you can control or change it. The biological aspects of emotional experiences are (in some ways) the easiest to measure precisely. Because we can look at our physiological responses accurately and objectively, we know a fair amount about them, about how they influence and motivate us, and how we can sometimes influence and control them.

Your biological reactions to emotional situations are primarily under the control of your **autonomic nervous system.** The word *autonomic* means "automatic," and most of the time your body does respond to emotional challenges automatically. You don't have to tell your heart to beat faster when you see someone you love — your autonomic nervous system takes care of the situation for you automatically. When you become frightened, your lungs inhale more frequently whether or not you remember to tell them to do so.

The autonomic nervous system has two parts — the **sympathetic nervous system** and the **parasympathetic nervous system.** See Figure 5-3 for a diagram of both systems.

When your *sympathetic* nervous system becomes more excited than usual, your pulse rate goes up, your blood pressure increases, your breathing speeds up, your digestion slows down, your pupils open to let in more light, you perspire more, and your hair may stand on end. The sympathetic nervous system is associated with physiological arousal.

When your *parasympathetic* nervous system is stimulated, your pulse rate and blood pressure decrease, your breathing rate slows, your pupils contract or close a bit, your stomach begins digesting food (if you have just eaten), and you perspire less. The parasympathetic nervous system is associated with physiological relaxation or depression.

Generally speaking, the sympathetic and parasympathetic nervous systems

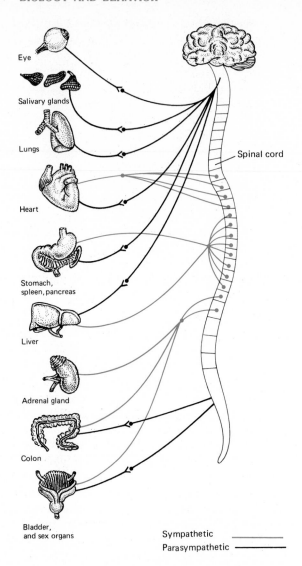

Eye

Salivary glands

Lungs

Spinal cord

Heart

Stomach,
spleen, pancreas

Liver

Adrenal gland

Colon

Bladder,
and sex organs

Sympathetic ————
Parasympathetic ————

FIG. 5–3.
The sympathetic
nervous system
(brown line) is asso-
ciated with physio-
logical arousal. The
parasympathetic ner-
vous system (black
line) is associated
with physiological
relaxation or depres-
sion. These two sys-
tems work together
to balance your
physiological state of
arousal.

work hand-in-hand—when activity increases in one system, activity usually
decreases in the other. Your physiological state of arousal at any given moment
is primarily a result of the *balance* of activity in the two halves of your autonomic
nervous system.

Hormones and Emotions

Your body creates its own natural "uppers," which are called **arousal hormones.** Hormones are complex chemicals secreted or manufactured in many
different glands inside your body. The arousal hormones are secreted primarily

TABLE 5-2   **Physiological and Psychological Responses to Stress**

Stage	Physiological Response	Physiological Response Costs	Psychological Response	Psychological Response Costs
1. Alarm Reaction	Sympathetic arousal Parasympathetic depression Arousal hormones released	Energy used	Perception of threat Fear Coping and planning May be mildly pleasurable	Interferes with normal activities
2. Resistance	Sympathetic overarousal Parasympathetic arousal Hypertension	Energy resources near depletion Body has difficulties repairing itself Body has difficulties defending against new threats and disease	Unpleasant anxiety Fear of failure "Mental handwringing" and hyperemotionality Beginning of depression	Occasional perceptual distortions Regression to less mature thought and behavior patterns
3. Exhaustion	Sympathetic collapse (Depression) Exhaustion of arousal hormones Parasympathetic overarousal (Depression)	Physiological resources exhausted Body cannot defend itself at all Disease and death possible	Massive depression Withdraw into self Feelings of utter failure Unresponsive to most external stimuli	Learned helplessness Learned passivity Mind no longer can control or direct voluntary movements

by the two **adrenal glands,** one of which sits atop each of your kidneys. The two main arousal hormones are **adrenalin** and **noradrenalin.**

Any time that you become excited or aroused, your sympathetic nervous system swings into gear almost instantaneously in response to this **stress.** As part of its normal functioning, the sympathetic nervous system stimulates your adrenal glands. The adrenals quickly begin pumping adrenalin and noradrenalin into the blood stream. These hormones affect your body in much the same way as does activity in your sympathetic nervous system—but the effects of the hormones are usually longer lasting. If you are startled by a loud explosion, your sympathetic nervous system will arouse your body almost immediately and will also cause the release of adrenalin and noradrenalin. If you then discover that the explosion was only a firecracker, your sympathetic system may drop back to near-normal within a few seconds—but the hormones may keep you "hyped up" or aroused for several minutes more.

The human body also creates its own natural "downers," which work with the parasympathetic system, just as adrenalin and noradrenalin work with the sympathetic system. The "downer" hormones act in much the same way that tranquilizing or depressant drugs do (see Chapter 3). Perhaps because the effects that these "downer" hormones have on us are less dramatic than the effects of adrenalin and noradrenalin, the "downer" hormones have been studied less, and we know less about them. Table 5-2 details the body's physiological and psychological responses to stress.

Many other chemicals secreted by your body can affect the course of emo-

FIG. 5–4.
This graph shows the percentage of married women in the Udry and Morris experiment who reported having intercourse and orgasm. Hormone levels are lowest about day 4 in the menstrual cycle and highest about day 15. As you can see, the high and low points in intercourse and orgasm follow a similar pattern.

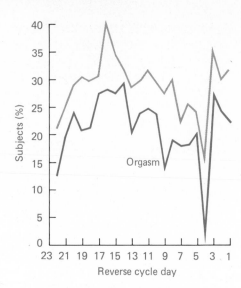

tional experience. Your adrenal glands and **gonads** produce sex hormones. Whether you are a man or woman, your body manufactures both male hormones, or **androgens,** and female hormones, the **estrogens** and **progesterone.** The relative balance of these types of hormones makes your body take on the physical and behavioral characteristics that we associate with maleness and femaleness.

Hormones also influence sexual pleasure. For example, female rats and mice are physically more active when "in heat" than when they are not. J. R. Udry and N. M. Morris reported in 1968 that married women are more likely to engage in sexual intercourse, and to achieve **orgasm,** during the middle of their menstrual cycle (when their hormone levels are highest) than at any other time during the cycle (see Fig. 5-4). Human males are more likely to seek out and participate in sexual experiences when given an injection of male sex hormone than they are a few days before or after the injection.

For the most part, then, hormones and other body chemicals influence emotional experiences by arousing or depressing a person's general activity level.

Cognitive Awareness of Emotions

Arousal and physiological activity have a strong influence on your emotions, but we cannot explain all of your emotional experiences in terms of your hormones and your autonomic nervous system. In a number of studies, volunteer subjects have been injected with adrenalin or noradrenalin when the subjects were in a calm and peaceful state. Some of the subjects reported no effects at all. Others reported that they felt aroused, even emotional — but the emotion was somehow "cold" or "empty." Many of the subjects stated that they felt they ought to be angry about something, or afraid of something, but they couldn't figure out what it was that they were supposed to be upset over.

In almost all cases, your perception of what is happening to you when you become emotional *directs* or *guides* the flow of your emotional experiences. The one possible exception to this statement is **free-floating anxiety,** which is a mild state of fear or apprehension in which people can't always consciously perceive what it is that is bothering or frightening them. However, even highly anxious people can perceive that there definitely is something in their environment (or their unconscious minds) that is causing the experience.

We may love our mothers, and we may also love good music. But we behave differently toward our mothers than toward a stereo because we perceive them as being different objects. The perception of what we love (or hate or fear), then, strongly influences both our internal experiences of emotion and our emotional behaviors.

In 1884, Harvard psychologist William James suggested that the cognitive or mental aspect of emotionality was determined almost completely by our bodily reactions. According to James, if we are walking in the woods and encounter a huge and hungry bear, we run from it. We run because our autonomic nervous system — through past learning — goes into action immediately and gets us away from the bear. Minutes later, when we are safe, we notice that we have run from something and that our bodies are still physiologically aroused. So we assume we must have been frightened because we acted that way. As James put it, "We are afraid because we run; we do not run because we are afraid."

Most theorists disagree with James. The general viewpoint in psychology today is that our biological reactions to emotional situations have but one main effect — to change the way our brains process or handle various inputs. According to Robert Leeper, for instance, perception is the most important aspect of any emotional experience. Without perception, Leeper points out, our physical reactions would lack direction and thus be as meaningless as the "cold fear and anger" experienced by the subjects injected with adrenalin. Our body arouses us — but our perceptions and past experiences guide us in our emotional reactions to this arousal.

Feeling Tone

Arousal and perception are important aspects of emotion, but the most overwhelming part of an emotional experience is often the **affect,** or feeling tone, that accompanies the emotion. Some emotions are very arousing but gloriously pleasant; others are just as arousing but unbelievably painful. To many of us, the feelings that we have about our experiences are more important than our bodily reactions and our cognitive awareness of what's happening to us. However, if we are clever enough to analyze our emotional experiences, we can usually see that our feelings — good or bad — are often closely connected to our state of arousal and our perceptions.

For example, when you have gone without food for a while, the amount of sugar present in your blood drops considerably. This decrease in your blood-sugar level stimulates certain neural centers in your brain, and you become physically aroused. If at this moment someone offered you an ice cream sundae, you probably would accept the gift joyously and devour the good-tasting dessert in a hurry. But after you have eaten two or three huge sundaes, your blood-sugar level rises to normal, and your arousal level falls. If you were forced to eat a fourth or fifth huge sundae, the ice cream might taste the same (sweet), but it simply wouldn't "taste as good." And no matter how hungrily aroused you were, if someone offered you a dish of raw human flesh to eat, your *perception* of the flesh might well push you more toward painful vomiting than toward eager eating.

Your autonomic nervous system and your hormones prepare your body to respond. Your perceptions determine the direction the response will take. But the pleasant or unpleasant feeling tones you experience typically determine the *strength* of your emotional reactions—and whether or not you will approach or avoid similar situations in the future.

Emotional Behaviors

The list of emotional behaviors is almost endless. Sometimes our whole bodies are involved—we run away from a bear, we dance or jump for joy, we embrace someone we love. Sometimes we express our emotions subtly—by smiling or frowning, by sweating or trembling. Sometimes we scream in pain, sometimes we merely whisper, "I love you."

Emotional behaviors can be measured objectively, but most of us are better at seeing how other people respond than we are at seeing our own reactions. If

Some emotions are gloriously pleasant.

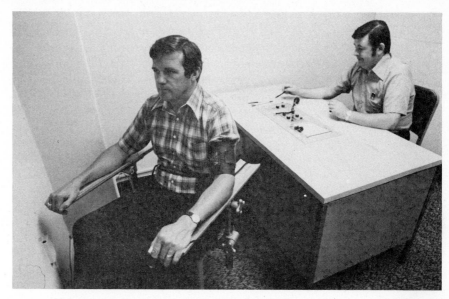

The polygraph, or lie detector, measures your body's emotional responses such as breathing, blood pressure, muscle tension, and perspiration. The polygraph can detect lies only when the subject responds emotionally while lying.

you have ever watched a film or videotape of yourself, or heard a tape recording of your voice made when you were in a state of high emotion, you probably were shocked or surprised at how you behaved and sounded.

There are various scientific devices for measuring the body's emotional responses, the best-known of which is probably the **polygraph,** or lie detector. The polygraph consists of several instruments that measure your breathing, your blood pressure, the tension in some of your muscles, and how much you are sweating.

The polygraph is considered by many experts to be an accurate lie detector because it indicates when many people are having an emotional reaction. The majority of people sweat more, breathe differently, have higher blood pressure, and tense their muscles when they feel guilty about telling a lie. Since the polygraph measures emotional responses, it can often detect when a person *responds emotionally* while lying. But polygraphs are less than 100 percent accurate in detecting lies. Some people are overemotional and may react strongly to almost *every* question they are asked during a lie detector test. The polygraph will often indicate that these people are lying when they are telling the truth. Other people may feel no guilt at all about lying. The polygraph will not usually be able to detect these people's lies. Because the polygraph detects *emotional reactions*, not *lies*, it is still not acceptable as evidence of guilt in many courts of law.

The majority of our emotional reactions are not as subtle as those detected by the polygraph. Indeed, most emotional behaviors are fairly easy to measure, because they involve approaching a goal or avoiding something unpleasant. Most emotional behaviors, then, are related to what we want out of life, and what our past rewards and punishments have been.

Feedback and Emotional Adjustment

Arousal, perception, feeling tone, and behavior are the critical elements in *experiencing* an emotion. But feedback is the most important element in *adjusting* or changing our emotional reactions. When we see a bear and run from it, most of us are not aware of all the physiological changes that occur inside our bodies. We generally do not perceive that our hearts are pumping faster, that our pupils have widened, that our muscles have grown tense, that we are sweating profusely, or that our adrenal glands are pumping adrenalin into our blood stream. We do not perceive these physiological reactions because, generally speaking, we are seldom taught to pay attention to them. Thus we have no *direct* way of getting feedback about what our bodies are doing during periods of high emotionality. However, if we do get adequate feedback, about how our bodies and minds are actually responding, it is sometimes possible for us to learn to control these responses and thereby to control our emotions.

Many students "clutch" when they are faced with taking an important examination. As the day of the exam approaches, they begin to feel increasing anxiety that interferes with their studying. The night before the test, they are often so tense they have trouble sleeping. The next morning they find themselves sweating profusely, their stomachs upset, their blood pressure increased. As they walk toward the exam hall, they may begin to tremble and shake. Finally, to avoid the overwhelming unpleasantness of the situation, they may turn and flee before entering the building. If they do attend the exam, they may find themselves unable to think clearly because they simply are too aroused for clear and logical thought.

Since students are not born with an innate fear of examinations, the "clutching" emotional response to tests *must be learned* — probably because the students have had one or two exceptionally negative experiences involving exams in the past. This type of learning is known as **conditioning** (see Chapter 6). The student has learned to perceive certain conditions (exams) as unpleasant. The student's conditioned reaction to exams is fear. Conditioned reactions can be helpful, such as when we automatically run from a snake. But in some cases, a conditioned reaction can be troublesome, such as when a student "clutches" at exam time. Fortunately we need not always be controlled or motivated by our emotions. It is sometimes possible to unlearn a conditioned response. The most successful ways of unlearning the fear reaction involve feedback of one kind or another. Unlearning a conditioned response is known as **counterconditioning** (meaning "against conditioning").

Counterconditioning and Desensitization

Consider a young man named Joe who "clutches" when he must take a math exam. The conditioning stimulus is the mathematics test. The conditioned response involves sympathetic nervous system arousal—including sweating, muscle tension, and increased pulse rate. Joe knows that he hates math tests and that he, therefore, tries to avoid them. But he doesn't know what to do about adjusting to or changing this self-defeating pattern of emotional responses.

More than 20 years ago, psychiatrist Joseph Wolpe pointed out that one way of treating Joe would be to condition a *new* response to the old stimulus (the exam). It should be obvious that Joe cannot be aroused and upset if he is also cool, calm, and collected. Being calm is just as much a learned response as is being excited and "clutching." Therefore, said Wolpe, perhaps we can **countercondition** Joe so that, when he is faced with a math exam, his conditioned response is to become relaxed rather than tense.

Wolpe often begins treating someone like Joe by training him to notice the *feedback* that comes from his muscles when he is relaxed—and how different that feedback is from the muscular sensations associated with tension and anxiety. At the start of **relaxation training,** Wolpe would ask Joe to tense the muscles in his body deliberately—and to pay attention to the feedback his muscles send to his brain. Then Joe would be told to relax deliberately, and again "listen" to what his muscles tell him when they are relaxed. Very soon Joe will learn to perceive the difference between muscular tension and relaxation. He will also learn that he can make himself relax merely by "willing" his muscles to go limp, and by continuing to do so until muscular feedback from his body tells him that he is really relaxed.

Next Wolpe has Joe describe his perceptions of the examination situation. What frightens or arouses him most? Perhaps it is the moment Joe sits down in his seat and the teacher passes out the test. What arouses Joe the least? Perhaps it is momentarily thinking about a math test coming up in three weeks. Between these two extremes are hundreds of other exam-related stimulus situations that arouse more anxiety than "thinking about the test three weeks beforehand," but less fear and trembling than "getting the test from the teacher while seated in class."

Wolpe then has Joe make a list of all the fear-inducing stimuli, starting with the weakest and working up to the strongest. Wolpe calls this list a **hierarchy of fears.**

Once Joe has decided on his own particular hierarchy of fears, Wolpe begins the counterconditioning procedure. Wolpe asks Joe to think of the weakest fear-inducing stimulus ("momentarily thinking about a math test coming up in three weeks") and then tells Joe to order his muscles to go limp and to think of pleasant, relaxing things. Joe repeats this procedure again and again, until after a while the stimulus ("thinking about an exam three weeks away") becomes associated with relaxation rather than with arousal and fear. As soon as this counterconditioning of the weakest stimulus has taken place, Joe is encouraged to tackle the next-strongest stimulus on his hierarchy. Perhaps this stimulus is picking up his math book two weeks before the exam. Again, Joe learns to relax when he faces this stimulus situation, and soon it too has become a conditioned stimulus

NOVEMBER

SUN.	MON.	TUES.	WED.	THURS.	FRI.	SAT.
		1	2	3	4	5
6	7	8	9	10	11	12
13	14	15	16	17	18	19
20	21	(22)	23	24	25	26
27	28	29	30			

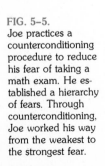

FIG. 5–5.
Joe practices a counterconditioning procedure to reduce his fear of taking a math exam. He established a hierarchy of fears. Through counterconditioning, Joe worked his way from the weakest to the strongest fear.

for relaxation rather than a stimulus that automatically calls forth the arousal response.

According to Wolpe, most people work their way from the bottom of the fear hierarchy up to the top in about 10 to 20 hours of treatment. At the end of the training, most of the subjects are able to control their emotional responses well enough so that they seldom if ever "clutch" during future examinations. Wolpe calls his treatment **desensitization,** because it appears to reduce greatly the emotional sensitivity that many people experience when faced with fear-inducing stimuli. Since Wolpe's technique actually involves the use of conditioning and voluntary control over the muscles using feedback, many psychologists prefer the term *counterconditioning.* (Conditioning will be discussed in greater detail in Chapter 6.)

SOCIAL/BEHAVIORAL INFLUENCES ON MOTIVATION

Anne Frank was not the type of person to "clutch" at exam time. Before she was forced to go into hiding, Anne had been an excellent student who loved learning. Even though she sometimes talked too much and joked around in school, she was almost always at the top of her class. While in hiding, the thing Anne missed most about the outside world was school.

Why was learning such a motivating force in Anne's life? Biological needs provide only part of the answer. Success in school can lead to success in the working world — and with a highly paid job you can usually afford to take care of your primary needs. According to drive theory, then, you work and learn in order to be able to eat and protect yourself from the environment. Arousal theory would predict that there is more to working and learning than satisfying one's basic urges, however. Often we learn for the joy of stimulating our minds. The perceptual theorists would also insist that learning allows us to perceive and understand the world better; therefore learning would satisfy a "basic perceptual need."

Many of us are motivated to earn diplomas in order to obtain highly paid jobs that help us take care of our primary needs.

As important as biological, arousal, and perceptual needs are, however, most of us have other very important reasons for going to school that have to do with our *social* needs. Some students enter college because their parents want them to get a good education. Anne Frank had always been told by her parents that learning was a pleasant and valuable experience. She found this to be true and grew to love school and all its challenges. Other people attend a university because their friends are going, because they want to meet new and interesting people, or because they hope to make contacts that will be of value to them in their later lives. Still others go to college because it gives them a chance to *achieve* social goals such as recognition, prestige, or the esteem of other individuals. From a psychological standpoint, these **social motives** are just as strong and as important as motivations stemming from biological, arousal, or perceptual needs.

Achievement Motivation

Social motives influence our behavior by guiding our perceptions. Societies set up certain goals, tell us those goals are valuable, and motivate us toward those goals. One of the most powerful social goals or motives in the United States is **need achievement,** the need to strive for higher standards of performance in school, on the job, in social groups, and in a wide range of situations. The need for achievement (unlike the need for food or for water) differs from person to person, from time to time, and from one society to another. While some people appear to be highly motivated by the need for achievement, others seem to be less interested in success. No matter what type of success a person is interested in, however, the need for achievement can be one of the most powerful and important motivating forces in anyone's life. Because achievement appears to be such an important motivating force in our society, psychologists have taken a close look at it and have attempted to determine why achievement motivation differs so much from one individual to another.

One of the methods used to investigate the motivating forces in an individual's life is the **Thematic Apperception Test (TAT).** This test consists of a number of pictures of people doing various things. The person being tested is asked to make up a story to go along with each picture. The person being tested is told that the story should explain the events leading up to the scene shown in the picture, explain what is happening in the scene, and predict how things will turn out for the people in the picture. Scoring the Thematic Apperception Test depends on the fact that people sometimes reveal something of themselves in the themes of the stories they make up. They project some of their own motives into the stories (tests such as this are known as **projective tests**). A simple scene showing two people talking, for instance, might prompt a hungry person to say that the people in the picture are discussing what to have for dinner.

Psychologist David McClelland and his associates have found the Thematic Apperception Test to be helpful in evaluating an individual's need for achieve-

A picture similar to this may be used in a Thematic Apperception Test (TAT). What is happening here? What led up to this scene? What will happen next?

ment. People who score high in achievement on the test (perhaps by telling stories whose themes revolve around success and achievement) have usually been found to be hard workers who have been very successful in school and at whatever job they have chosen. Investigations of the backgrounds of high achievers suggest that achievement motivation is usually learned very early in life. The people who turn out to be high achievers were more likely than low achievers to have been very independent as children. Their parents allowed or even insisted that they tie their own shoes, take care of their belongings, and learn to feed themselves at a very early age. Early independence in the children who later became high achievers was often encouraged and rewarded by smiles and by physical affection from the parents. The people who score lower in achievement on the Thematic Apperception Test were often overprotected as children, were not allowed to be independent, and had everything done for them. They may even have been scolded or punished for independent acts.

Studies of achievement motivation among women have revealed some interesting findings. Women often face a conflict between a high need for achievement and a fear of success because society does not expect women to be highly successful. However, current research indicates that some men may experience a similar conflict. As the results of McClelland's research on achievement suggest, not all families provide their members with the same goals and motives. Different social inputs lead to different goals and help account for the individual differences seen in the need for achievement.

SELF-ACTUALIZATION

Why do we do what we do? Why do others do what they do? As we have seen throughout this chapter, human motivation is a complex subject, and we have at least three different motivational processes. We have biological motives, psychological motives, and social/behavioral motives. These three separate types of motivation interact with and influence each other. In some situations a social input (somebody criticizing you) may trigger strong emotional and bodily reactions; in other situations, a biological input (a drug) may affect your perceptions and your social behaviors. In most situations, the three systems operate simultaneously and in parallel fashion in a kind of mutual interdependence. To overemphasize the importance of any one of the systems is to prevent us from appreciating the marvelous complexities buried in the simple question: Why do we do what we do?

Psychologist Abraham Maslow has developed a theory of human motivation that helps us to see how the three basic motivational systems build upon each other and work together to influence human behavior. Maslow's theory is often pictured as a pyramid (see Figure 5-6). At the bottom of the pyramid are the biological needs seen in drive theory. Once you have satisfied these needs, according to Maslow, you will want and be able to fulfill the needs of the second level of the pyramid. This second level consists of your needs for sensory stimulation, physical activity, and sex—the type of needs covered by arousal

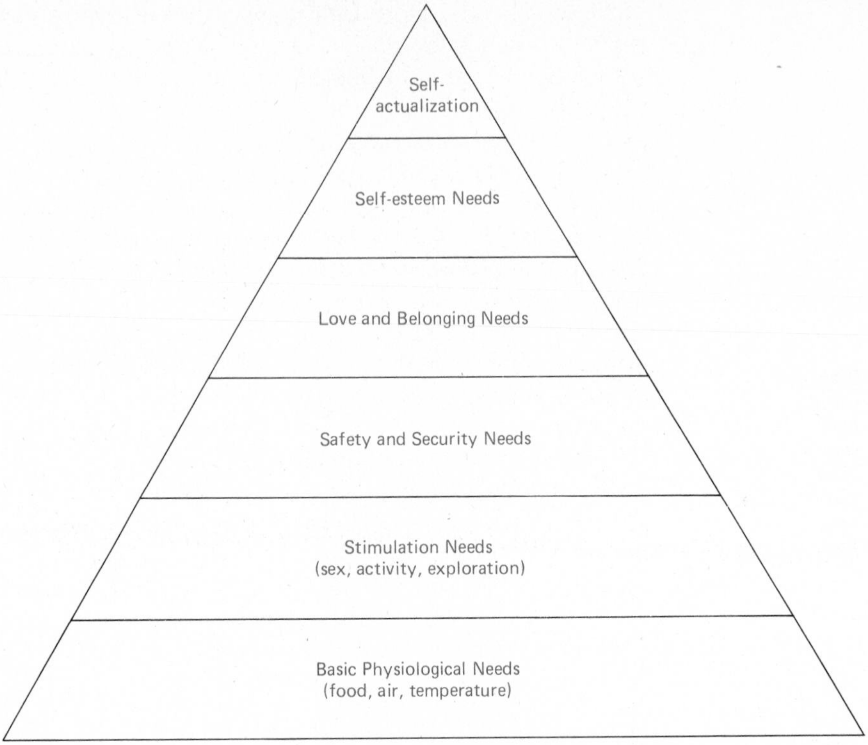
Self-
actualization
Self-esteem Needs
Love and Belonging Needs
Safety and Security Needs
Stimulation Needs
(sex, activity, exploration)
Basic Physiological Needs
(food, air, temperature)

FIG. 5-6.
Abraham Maslow developed this pyramid theory of human needs. Which level have you reached?

theory. When these arousal needs are met, you will be motivated to fulfill the needs of the third level: safety, security, and protection. This third level includes many of your emotional needs, such as the need to be out of danger and free of fear.

The fourth level of Maslow's pyramid represents the human needs for love, belonging, and closeness. These are among the most basic of our social needs. A person who has reached this level wants to love and be loved, to have close friends, and to be wanted as part of a group. Unpublished research from Ohio State suggests that about 90 percent of college students operate at the third level—that of security needs. However, some students have achieved the fourth level and use college as a stepping stone to level five—the esteem needs. Achievement, competence, independence, freedom, and prestige are among the esteem needs. Success at school or on a job—and recognition for a job well done—help fulfill the needs of the fifth level and put people in a position to move upwards toward the final goal—**self-actualization.**

According to Maslow, self-actualization involves achieving the highest possible level of fulfillment or human potential in every area of life. Maslow even suggests that humans have an inborn drive to better themselves continually, to move from one level of the pyramid to the next until they reach the level of self-actualization.

Although the need to achieve self-actualization cannot be measured or even

Eleanor Roosevelt was instrumental in drafting the United Nations' Universal Declaration of Human Rights. According to Maslow's criteria she achieved self-actualization.

adequately defined, Maslow has offered examples of famous individuals who seem to have achieved a high degree of self-actualization. They include Eleanor Roosevelt, Abraham Lincoln, Einstein, and Beethoven.

Anne Frank can also be seen as a person who achieved a high degree of self-actualization. Although she had great difficulty fulfilling even her most basic needs while in hiding, Anne seems never to have lost sight of her long-term goals. She wanted to be a good writer, she wanted to learn about the world, and most of all she wanted to understand herself. Anne Frank was not allowed to live a long life, but her diary shows that she was well on the way to fulfilling her highest goals. She was doing all she could under the most difficult circumstances to understand herself, her motives, and her goals. In Maslow's terms, she was attempting to fulfill her potential as a human being and to achieve self-actualization. As Eleanor Roosevelt says in her introduction to *The Diary of a Young Girl,* "Anne's diary makes poignantly clear the ultimate shining nobility of [the human] spirit. Despite the horror and humiliation of their daily lives, these people never gave up."

▶ *SUMMARY*

1. Why do we do what we do? Why do others do what they do? Anne Frank asked similar questions as she attempted to examine her own thoughts, feelings, and behaviors in her diary. Psychologists also question the whys of human behavior, and many of their answers can be found in the study of human **motivation.**

2. Attempts to explain human behavior in purely physical terms have led to

169

two mechanistic approaches to human motivation—**drive theory** and **arousal theory.**

3. In order for humans to stay alive there are certain biological needs that they must meet. The primary or most important of these needs include such things as food, water, air, and temperature control. Associated with each **primary need** is a **primary drive,** such as hunger, thirst, breathing, and warmth or coolness. According to drive theory, all human behavior is motivated by the need to reduce our biological drives. In addition to the primary needs there are numerous **secondary needs** that are presumably associated with primary needs. Secondary needs are usually learned rather than innate.

4. The biological processes involved in turning **drive states** on and off are known as **homeostatic processes.** These processes help detect our needs and make sure that we try to keep our bodies in a need-free unexcited state.

5. Drive theory does not fully explain human motivation. In addition to our primary needs, it appears that we have informational needs or stimulus needs. The need for arousal or stimulation has led to the development of an arousal theory of motivation, which says that we are sometimes motivated by the need to increase stimulation (rather than always decrease stimulation, as drive theory says).

6. In addition to our biological needs, there are certain mental or cognitive experiences that motivate us. Among the most powerful of these are our **emotions.** In order to understand how emotions motivate us, we must examine the five aspects of emotionality—physiological arousal, cognitive awareness, feeling tone, emotional behaviors, and feedback.

7. Many emotional reactions are influenced by the activity of the nervous system and by hormones that either arouse or depress us. Our perceptions and our past experiences guide us in our emotional reactions to the body's arousal or depression.

8. Many of our emotional reactions, such as fear, are learned rather than innate. The type of learning involved is known as **conditioning. Counterconditioning** or **desensitization** is a process by which some learned emotional responses can be unlearned.

9. In addition to physiological and cognitive needs, we are also motivated by numerous social needs and drives. The need for achievement is an example.

10. As we have seen in this chapter, human motivation is a complex subject with at least three motivational systems—physiological, cognitive, and social. Maslow's theory of motivation helps illustrate how these three systems build on and interact with each other to influence human behavior. The highest human need, according to Maslow, is the need for **self-actualization.**

SUGGESTED READINGS

Carnegie, Dale. *How to stop worrying and start living.* New York: Pocket Books, 1974.
Frank, Anne. *Anne Frank: The diary of a young girl.* New York: Pocket Books, 1972.
Read, Piers P. *Alive!* New York: Avon, 1975.

► STUDY GUIDE

A.   RECALL

Sentence Completion

[p. 144]   1. Anne Frank was a German Jew who escaped with her family to _____ to hide out from the Nazis.

[p. 145]   2. The word "motivation" derives from the Latin term meaning "to _____."

[p. 145]   3. The ancients assumed that self-initiated motion was caused by an _____.

[p. 146]   4. The _____ theory of motivation suggests that all human behavior is motivated by the need to reduce certain biological deficits.

[p. 147]   5. The satisfaction of _____ or biological needs is necessary for the organism's survival.

[p. 147]   6. A need for food may give rise to a hunger _____.

[p. 147]   7. When your biological balance is upset, you become aroused and enter what is known as a primary _____ _____.

[p. 148]   8. When your biological functions, needs, and drives are in a state of balance, or equilibrium, you are in a state of _____.

[p. 148]   9. _____ needs are said to be typified by our likes and dislikes.

[p. 148]   10. According to drive theory, secondary needs are _____ rather than built in.

[p. 149]   11. According to drive theorists, we would tend to like those people and things associated with satisfying our _____ _____.

[p. 149]   12. That we have needs for stimulation and "informational inputs" as well as biological needs is central to the _____ of motivation.

[p. 150]   13. Arousal theory got its start from experiments in _____ _____ performed in Canada.

[p. 151]   14. Sometimes we are motivated by our thoughts, feelings, and _____ rather than just our biological needs.

[p. 152]   15. To be sure, one thing that happens when we become emotional is that we experience changes in our _____ processes.

[p. 152]   16. To say that you know what is going on when you are emotional is to say that you have a _____ _____ of how you are affected by the emotion.

[p. 154]   17. When our own responses act as stimuli, we are providing ourselves with _____.

[p. 155]   18. Your biological reactions to emotional situations are primarily under the control of your _____ _____ _____.

[p. 155]   19. The _____ part of the autonomic nervous system is associated with physiological arousal, while the _____ part is associated with relaxation or depression.

[p. 156]   20. _____ are complex chemicals secreted or released by many different glands in your body.

[p. 157]   21. The arousal hormones are secreted by the _____ glands.

[p. 159]
22. _____ anxiety is a mild state of apprehension in which people cannot consciously perceive what it is that is bothering them.

[p. 159]
23. William James might have said that when we run from a bear, "we are afraid because we _____."

[p. 160]
24. The pleasant or unpleasant feeling tone of an emotion typically determines its _____.

[p. 161]
25. A lie detector is also known as a _____.

[p. 161]
26. The lie detector detects _____ _____, not lies.

27. _____ is the most important element in adjusting or changing our emo-

[p. 162]
tional reactions.

28. Learning to respond emotionally to certain stimuli is referred to as

[p. 162]
_____ _____.

29. The psychiatrist Joseph _____ was perhaps the first to suggest the possi-

[p. 163]
ble advantages of counterconditioning.

30. Social motives or needs may be measured by the _____

[p. 166]
_____ _____.

31. Abraham _____ suggests that our needs can be placed in a hierarchy

[p. 168]
with the need to _____ _____ on the very top.

B.   REVIEW

Multiple Choice: Circle the letter identifying the alternative that most correctly completes the statement or answers the question.

1. Anne Frank:
    A. kept an important personal diary for two years.
    B. died in a Nazi concentration camp.
    C. was a German-born Jew.
    D. all of the above.

2. The drive theory of motivation:
    A. is no longer at all popular in psychology.
    B. is the same as the arousal theory of motivation.
    C. relies heavily on the notion of homeostasis.
    D. denies the importance of physiology for behavior.

3. Which of the following is *not* a primary drive?
    A. approach/avoidance
    B. hunger
    C. thirst
    D. warmth/coolness

4. According to drive theory, secondary needs are:
    A. biological.
    B. learned.

C. not important.

D. more common in nonhumans than in humans.

5. When your sympathetic nervous system becomes active:
    A. you are lying.
    B. your heart rate increases.
    C. your stomach begins to digest food.
    D. you perspire less.

6. "We are afraid because we run; we do not run because we are afraid" is a view held
by:
    A. virtually all psychologists.
    B. Robert Leeper.
    C. Williams James.
    D. the arousal/cognitive theorists.

7. According to Maslow, the lowest or first needs to be attended to are the
   _____ needs.
    A. safety and security
    B. love and belonging
    C. physiological
    D. self-actualization

8. The arousal theory of motivation:
    A. is an older point of view than the drive theory.
    B. relates human drives to the needs for food, water, and the like.
    C. does not deal with homeostasis.
    D. suggests that there is a need for informational inputs.

9. Relaxation training is an important component of:
    A. feeling tone.
    B. desensitization training.
    C. self-actualization experiences.
    D. the need to achieve.

MEASURING EMOTIONS ELECTRONICALLY

Most people know when they are happy or sad, but researchers and therapists can't always be sure that the people with whom they are working are accurately reporting their feelings. Now researchers report that by monitoring facial muscles they can detect even subtle emotional states. The research was done by Gary E. Schwartz of Harvard University and a group at Massachusetts General Hospital.

At least six distinct emotions can be recognized in the human face: happiness, sadness, anger, fear, surprise, and disgust. But these feelings are not always shown by a big grin or an obvious frown. And the speed and sensitivity of facial muscle activity is sometimes too rapid or subtle to be detected by the average observer. Discrete patterns of low-level muscle activity can, however, be detected electronically. The researchers recorded electromyographic (EMG) activity as a measure of facial muscle activity.

In an experiment, the EMG activity, facial expressions, and emotions of 24 women were monitored. The women were first rated on a scale of depression — 12 scored in the normal range, 6 were classified as depressed, and the remaining 6 were even more depressed and were about to begin drug therapy. With electrodes placed over specific muscles, each woman was asked to imagine happy, sad, and angry situations that had evoked strong emotions in the past. The EMG patterns were distinct enough to distinguish depressed from nondepressed women. As would be expected, the nondepressed subjects generated more happy and less sad patterns even when they were imagining neutral situations. Video tapes of the womens' faces showed that what the EMG picked up would not always have been detected visually. The researchers suggest that "facial EMG can provide a sensitive and objective procedure for indexing normal and clinical mood states."

EMOTION AT THE FINGERTIP

Human emotions have two components: an internal or subjective state and an external or physical expression. Because of the complexity of this dual system, measuring and comparing emotions is a tricky business. But Manfred Clynes of Rockland State Hospital in Orangeburg, N.Y., has developed a testing device that simplifies and standardizes the measurement of emotions.

Anger, for instance, is expressed in many ways, but it is not practical to compare one person's hit to another person's kick. To get around this problem, Clynes measures emotion in only one finger. A person is told to think about a specific emotion and express the feeling by pushing a button. The vertical and horizontal components of the finger pressure are fed into a computer. What comes out is a curve that

Clynes calls the essentic form of a particular emotion. He has found that every emotion (anger, hate, love, grief, sex, joy, etc.) has a specific essentic form that is the same in cultures around the world. Clynes has tested people in Bali, Japan, and Mexico. In addition to measuring the depth of an emotion, Clynes feels certain forms can be used in a psychoanalytic context to measure personal relationships. "How do you feel about your mother," for instance, produces a different form than, "How do you feel about your father."

C. NEWS STORY QUESTIONS

1. Researchers at Harvard claim that they can reliably detect six distinct emotional reactions that are not obvious from just looking at the subjects. What instrumentation did they use, and what emotions can they detect? _____

_____

2. Manfred Clynes of Rockland State Hospital in New York claims to be able to detect different emotional states. By what method? _____

_____

_____

unit TWO

COGNITION

Movie still from *A Clockwork Orange*.

Learning is one of the most important aspects of human behavior. If we could not learn (acquire new behaviors), we would not even survive. By examining the processes involved in learning we gain an understanding of this important ability and discover effective methods of modifying our own behavior.

Learning

6 chapter

When you have completed your study of this chapter, you should be able to:

▶ Define "learning" and state the "law of association"
▶ Diagram the important stimuli and responses involved in classical and operant conditioning and provide examples
▶ Describe the process of extinction as it occurs in both classical and operant conditioning
▶ Compare and contrast positive reinforcement, negative reinforcement, and punishment
▶ Discuss different forms of behavior therapy
▶ Compare and contrast generalization and discrimination, providing examples of both

Alcoholism. A psychological or physiological addiction to a drug called alcohol. Most physicians and social scientists consider alcoholism the major drug problem in the United States today, for alcoholism costs us several billion dollars each year in medical bills, lost wages, and social services.

Behavior modification. Therapy that aims at changing the behaviors of the patient rather than the person's feelings, thoughts, or perceptions.

Behavior therapies. Psychological treatment based primarily on the principles of operant or respondent conditioning. Generally speaking, behavior therapy involves rewarding or reinforcing the patient for changing his or her actions.

Behavioral engineering. Systematic attempts to shape or "engineer" new responses using rewards and punishments.

Classical conditioning. Also called "respondent" or "Pavlovian" conditioning. When Pavlov first began training his dogs, he found that they salivated naturally when given food. He called the food an "unconditioned" stimulus (**UCS**) because it innately called forth (elicited) the "unconditioned" response (**UCR**) of salivation. By pairing the sound of the bell (a "conditioned" stimulus, or **CS**) with the food, Pavlov taught his animals to salivate to the musical tone. Once the animals had been trained, the salivation became a "conditioned" response (**CR**)—in that sounding the bell was the "condition" under which the salivation occurred.

Elicit. From the Latin word meaning "to draw out." In classical conditioning, the conditioned stimulus elicits or draws out the conditioned response once learning has occurred. The response is not voluntary, but is automatic or involuntary.

Extinction (ex-TINK-shun). The loss of a learned response. In classical conditioning, extinction occurs primarily when the conditioned stimulus is repeated without presentation of the unconditioned stimulus. In operant conditioning, extinction occurs primarily when the response the animal makes is no longer rewarded or reinforced.

Extinction training. The act of training an organism not to give a conditioned response. Repeating the CS without the UCS, or refusing to reinforce a previously rewarded response.

Generalization. In one of his experiments, Pavlov showed a dog a circle, then gave it food. After several trials, the animal began salivating at the first sight of the circle. Pavlov then showed it an ellipse (oval-shaped figure). When the dog salivated, Pavlov assumed that the response had "generalized" to a stimulus similar to the circle. But when Pavlov continued to present the circle with food, and to present the ellipse without the food, the dog soon came to "discriminate" between the two stimuli and salivated only when shown the circle. This procedure is now called "discrimination training."

Impulses. From the Latin word meaning "to impel or drive." Sudden or spontaneous actions. When a nerve cell becomes excited, it responds with brief impulses of electrical current.

Law of association. The first "law" of behavioral psychology. Any two events or stimulus inputs which occur at the same time or in the same place tend to become associated. In Pavlovian conditioning, the conditioned stimulus gains its power to elicit the conditioned response because the CS occurs at the same time as the UCS (unconditioned stimulus).

Learning. The act of acquiring a new response, insight, emotion, perception, or understanding.

Modeling. Providing someone with a set of actions or behaviors to be imitated. Since most children grow up to act pretty much like their parents, we assume that children often imitate or model their behaviors after their parents' actions.

Negative reinforcement. Rewarding someone by removing an unpleasant or painful stimulus from the person's environment. If someone were to subject you to electric shock until you smiled, that person would be "negatively reinforcing" you for smiling.

Operant behaviors (OPP-ur-rant). Those actions that an organism gives freely or voluntarily in a given environment. A conditioned response (such as salivation) is *not* an operant behavior since it would be an involuntary response. Asking someone out to dinner just because you wanted the pleasure of their company would be an operant response.

Operant conditioning. A type of training developed by B. F. Skinner which involves strengthening operant behaviors by rewarding them. If the person you asked out to dinner was exceptionally nice to you, that person would have increased the probability that you would ask the person out again.

Personalized system of instruction. A type of teaching, growing out of Skinner's research, in which each student proceeds at his or her own given pace. When the student has mastered a certain amount of the material, the student takes a standard examination. If the student passes the exam, he or she is given the next batch of material. If the student fails the exam, the student must reread the material and retake the test later.

Positive reinforcement. Giving an organism something it wants when the organism makes a desired response. Positive reinforcement always increases the probability that a response will occur again.

Punishment. In extinction training, an experimenter usually "removes" an undesirable response by no longer reinforcing it. In punishment training, an experimenter usually tries to remove an undesirable response by giving the organism a painful stimulus whenever the response occurs. Punishment typically *suppresses* the desired response temporarily, but seldom leads to real extinction. Punishment also often has unfortunate side effects not associated with extinction training.

Reinforcement. The act of strengthening a response by giving the organism a reward immediately after the response occurs, or by removing a painful stimulus immediately after the response occurs. The former is called positive reinforcement; the latter is called negative reinforcement. Both types of reinforcement increase the likelihood that the organism will repeat the response later on.

Salivary glands (SALL-ih-verr-ee). Small glands that secrete saliva into the mouth. This saliva contains chemicals that begin digesting your food even before you swallow it.

Salivation (sall-ih-VAY-shun). When your mouth "waters" at the sight or taste of food, you have salivated. Salivation to the taste of food is an unconditioned (unlearned) response; salivation to the sight of food is a conditioned (learned) response.

Successive approximations. The act of progressing toward a goal in small, rewarded steps. In behavior modification, once the goal has been set or agreed upon, the organism is usually reinforced for each action that approximates or is a movement toward that goal.

INTRODUCTION: A CLOCKWORK ORANGE AND WALDEN TWO

The place: London
The time: The Twenty-first Century

Alex loved Beethoven. He could sit for hours listening to the stirring music of the great German composer. But Alex liked something else even better than Beethoven. He enjoyed what he called "a bit of ultraviolence." The 15-year-old Alex and his friends would roam the streets of London and amuse themselves by committing random acts of violence. Mugging, rape, destruction of property, gang fights, and even murder were among the activities that Alex and his friends enjoyed most.

Alex is the disgusting but pitiable hero of Anthony Burgess's book, *A Clockwork Orange,* one of the many novels that attempt to predict and warn about what the future may be like. Burgess's novel and the movie based on it are full of gruesome violence. But Burgess is not warning his readers about violence. He is concerned with the possible ways in which violence may be treated. A very special treatment was devised for young Alex.

After a particularly brutal murder of an elderly woman, Alex was captured, convicted, and sentenced to 14 years in prison. After only two years of prison life, Alex had had enough. In prison he was beaten, kicked, and bullied by the warders, leered at and bothered by the other inmates. Prison was a hellhole and a human zoo, said Alex, so he took the first available opportunity of getting out. He volunteered to take part in an experimental treatment program. Alex was told that if the treatments were successful he would be free to leave in two weeks. Naturally, he agreed to cooperate.

As part of the experimental treatment, Alex was strapped to a chair with his head held forward and his eyes kept open by metal clamps. The experimenters then began to show Alex a variety of movies — most of them having to do with sex or violence or both. This is fine, thought Alex, just what I would have selected. But watching the movies didn't remain pleasant for very long. The experimenters had given Alex a drug that would make him painfully and violently ill while the films were being shown. Alex couldn't move his head or close his eyes. All he could do was sit and watch violence and be terribly sick.

Day after day, as the experiment continued, Alex was exposed to movies of sex and violence and made violently sick at the same time. It didn't take Alex long to make the connection between the movies and the sickness. He learned that every time he was confronted with sex or violence he would become ill. By the end of only two weeks of treatment, Alex had learned the lesson so well that he would double up in pain at the mere thought of anything to do with either sex or violence. The prison experimenters concluded that the experiment had been a success. They believed that Alex would do his best to avoid even thinking about raping, mugging, or murdering. And even if he did think of such things, he would become too sick to commit any acts of violence.

The experts were right. Alex reacted just like clockwork. Just like a mechanical toy, he performed exactly as the experimenters had programmed him to perform.

Almost immediately after his release, Alex got into a fight with his friends who had betrayed him to the police in the first place. But Alex could no longer fight. He got so sick that he could not even defend himself. After a couple of similar painful experiences with violence, Alex realized that he would have to be very careful about his behavior. But no matter how hard he tried, Alex could not avoid the excessive amounts of violence that were everywhere in his society. He was almost always getting sick, no matter what he did. And the prison experiment had another terrible side effect. While Alex was being shown the violent films, music was played in the background. The music was Beethoven, and after the experiment poor Alex could never again listen to his beloved Beethoven without getting sick.

A Clockwork Orange paints a dreary, frightening picture of life in the future. It expresses the fear that psychology is too strong a force—that someday psychology might be used to create and control us and deprive us of our personal freedom.

There is, however, another novel about the future which suggests that psychological knowledge and technology can be used not to control people but to make them happy in a more efficiently operated world.

Walden Two, a novel by Harvard psychologist B. F. Skinner, is the story of a group of people who use the principles of psychology to set up and control a perfect society. The **behavioral engineering** methods used in *Walden Two* are based completely on a system of rewards. Punishment is outlawed. All property is shared. No one is overworked, and everyone is happy.

Who is right? Will the future be like *A Clockwork Orange* or like *Walden Two?* Probably neither. Psychology is a powerful tool, but no one has yet devised a way to control all of the people all of the time—nor is it ever likely to happen. Both Burgess and Skinner would admit that in order to control a person's behavioral outputs, you must have complete control over the person's genetic inheritance, past experience, and present environmental stimuli. No psychologist—and more important, no politician—ever has had that sort of control. Even Alex's newly learned behavior wore off, presumably because he left the prison environment.

People can be trained to do many things—but once they are away from the

In many cases an Israeli kibbutz is like Skinner's Walden Two. Everyone shares the work and is rewarded by the bounty of the harvest.

training situation, their new behaviors may begin to disappear. At best, psychology can suggest ways by which *some* of the behavior of individuals (and perhaps groups of people) can be controlled *some* of the time. And of all the psychological processes involved in controlling or changing a person's behavior, surely the most important is that of **learning,** the process by which new information, habits, or behaviors are acquired.

SIMPLE LEARNING

"A blooming, buzzing confusion" greets us upon our entry into the world, said William James, one of the first psychologists in the United States (see Chapter 1). What James meant was that infants are faced with millions of sights, sounds, tastes, and other environmental stimuli that are completely new and meaningless to them. How do these infants learn to make sense of this confusion?

Infants begin by responding to the world in a reflexive manner (see Chapter 2). They blink at bright lights and withdraw from pain. Reflexive behaviors are the result of pre-existing connections in the nervous system and brain. These connections are part of the genetic blueprint each individual is born with.

In many lower species, such as paramecia, simple reflexes and instincts are about all that are necessary for survival. Paramecia are born with a set of behaviors that do not change much throughout their lives. Paramecia behave like paramecia and remain paramecia. If human infants continued to rely only on their innately determined reflexive behaviors, they would remain infants forever. But infants are capable of a tremendous amount of learning. The "pre-wired" neural connections in their brains can be readily changed, and when the connections are changed, the infants behave in new ways. The new connections and the new behaviors are the result of learning.

So-called educational toys help a child to make associations between colors, shapes, and sounds.

Associations

The first rule of learning is often called the **law of association.** If two inputs arrive at the brain at the same time, they often become linked or associated with each other. Alex learned to associate sex and violence with pain. In other words, associative learning took place. We all learn to make millions of associations between different aspects of the environment because we see or hear or taste or experience these aspects at the same time. Those aspects of the environment that become paired, consistently, with observable responses or changes in behavior in us are instances of associative learning.

Classical Conditioning

The formation of associations is an important part of any type of learning, but there is much more to learning than forming associations between different environmental stimuli and responses. One of the most basic or classic types of learning is called classical conditioning (having to do with the conditions under which associations are made).

The Russian physiologist Ivan Pavlov was one of the first scientists to describe **classical conditioning.** Pavlov was investigating the process of digestion in dogs when he first became aware of conditioning. Digestion begins in the mouth with the production of saliva. As a physiologist interested in the digestive system, Pavlov attempted to measure the amount of saliva produced by his laboratory animals. Usually, as soon as a dog sees its food, saliva is produced. Similarly, hungry people's mouths begin to water at the sight of food. But Pavlov ran into a problem with his experiments. The dogs sometimes began salivating before they even saw the food. If the dogs heard their keepers rattling the food dishes, they would begin to salivate. At first this response bothered Pavlov because he was interested in studying **salivation** in connection with digestion, not in connection with the sounds of dishes rattling. But eventually, Pavlov came to realize that something interesting was happening.

In dogs and in humans, food usually stimulates or activates the **salivary glands.** But in Pavlov's experiments, the dogs were reacting to a type of stimulation that should not normally cause salivation. Pavlov called this "psychic stimulation," and he designed experiments to study it. He used a musical note as a stimulus and played it just before the dogs were given a bit of food. The food naturally caused salivation, but before long the dogs began to salivate at the sound of the musical note (before they had received any food). The animals had apparently learned that the sound meant food was on the way. They had made an association between the sound and the food.

Under normal conditions, food is a stimulus that causes salivation as a response. Because food will cause salivation unconditionally (under almost any conditions), the food in Pavlov's experiment is called an unconditional or unconditioned stimulus (UCS). The salivation response is called an uncondi-

FIG. 6-1.
In his classical conditioning experiments, Pavlov used an apparatus similar to this one to measure the salivation of the dog. The dog learned to associate the sound of rattling dishes with food and salivated before the actual food was presented.

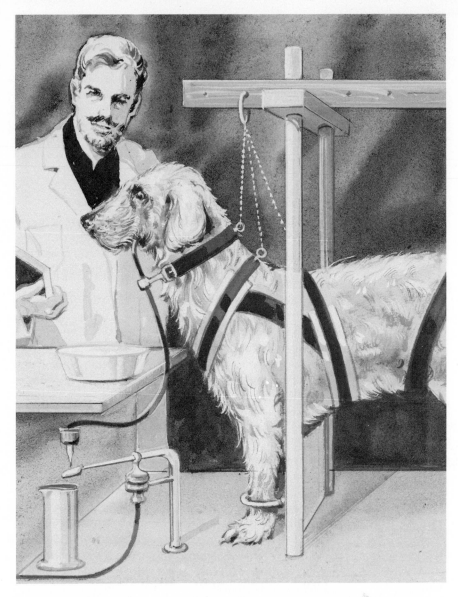

tioned response (UCR) for the same reason. The unconditioned response occurs under almost any conditions when food is presented. When Pavlov introduced a special condition, the musical note, it was called a conditional or conditioned stimulus (CS). Usually a conditioned stimulus is neutral. That is, musical notes do not normally cause salivation. With training, however, Pavlov's dogs learned to associate the conditioned stimulus (music) with the unconditioned stimulus (food). These conditioned dogs eventually got to the point

Classical Conditioning:

1. The connection between the UCS and the UCR is innate or has been learned previously:

$$\textbf{UCS} \xrightarrow{\text{(Innate S-R connection)}} \textbf{UCR}$$
(Food)   (Salivation)

2. Learning occurs when a neutral CS is paired repeatedly with the UCS:

$$\textbf{CS} \xrightarrow{\text{(Learned through association)}} \textbf{UCS} \xrightarrow{\text{(Innate)}} \textbf{UCR}$$
(Musical tone)   (Food)   (Salivation)

3. When conditioning occurs, the CS can elicit or call forth the UCR even if the UCS is occasionally omitted. Since the CS is physically different from the UCS, the response it elicits when the UCS is omitted is slightly different from the usual UCR. This slightly different UCR is called the *conditioned response,* or CR.

(Learned S–R connection)

$$\textbf{CS} \longrightarrow \textbf{UCS} \longrightarrow \textbf{UCR} \longrightarrow \textbf{CR}$$
(Tone)   (Food)   (Salivation)   (Slightly less salivation)

4. In classical conditioning, the most important association is that which takes place between the CS and the UCS. Thus, if the UCS is omitted for several trials, the learning disappears or "extinguishes."

Operant Conditioning

1. Various internal and external stimuli (most of which are unknown or unspecified) lead the animal to emit or give forth a response, such as pressing on a lever:

$$\textbf{S} \xrightarrow{\text{(Innate)}} \textbf{R}$$
(Internal and external stimuli)   (Pressing lever)

2. As a consequence of pressing the lever, the animal is rewarded (G) with food:

(Previously learned or innate)

$$\textbf{S} \longrightarrow \textbf{R} \longrightarrow \textbf{G}$$
(Stimuli)   (Pressing lever)   (Food reinforcement)

3. After several trials, the animal learns to associate pressing the lever with food reinforcement:

$$\textbf{S} \xrightarrow{\text{(Innate)}} \textbf{R} \xrightarrow{\text{(Learned through association)}} \textbf{G}$$
(Stimuli)   (Pressing lever)   (Food reinforcement)

4. In operant conditioning, the most important association is that between the response of pressing the lever and the consequence of getting food reinforcement. If the reinforcer is omitted for several trials, the learning disappears or "extinguishes."

FIG. 6–2.
This diagram compares Pavlovian (classical) conditioning and operant conditioning.

where the conditioned stimulus (music) almost always produced the unconditioned response (salivation). When this happens, the unconditioned response
can be called a conditioned response (CR). In classical conditioning, a conditioned stimulus (such as music) always results in a conditioned response (such as
salivation).

Classical conditioning, of course, is not restricted to dogs and to salivation.
Alex, in *A Clockwork Orange,* was being subjected to a form of classical conditioning. The pain inflicted on him was an unconditioned stimulus that almost
always causes fear (an unconditioned response) in humans in the same way that
food causes salivation in dogs. A conditioned stimulus — films of sex and violence
— was then introduced and associated with the unconditioned response (fear) in
the same way that musical notes were associated with the dogs' salivation. After
a certain amount of time and a number of exposures to the conditioning treatment, fear became a conditioned response in Alex every time he saw scenes of
sex and violence.

Classical conditioning is a simple, straightforward learning process that everyone experiences from the time of birth. Infants learn to associate their
mothers with food. Schoolchildren learn to associate the sound of the lunch bell
with food and the sound of a fire alarm with danger. Much of this conditioning
occurs without our really being aware that it is taking place. We learn to eat some
foods because our parents and friends do, and to reject other foods as "unsuitable" or "immoral" because our families reject them. Jews and Arabs often reject
pork as being "unclean," but accept beef. Some people in India accept pork but
reject beef because to them cows are sacred animals. Most individuals in the
United States enjoy both pork and beef, but we might grow sick if someone offered us roast puppy. Yet in many cultures, dog meat is considered a delicacy.

For the most part, our tastes are conditioned. But can you remember being
taught not to eat roast poodle? What then are the factors that influence this type
of learning?

Making Classical Conditioning Work

Pavlov and many other researchers discovered that there are situations in which
conditioning works best. The most important factor in conditioning seems to be
the strength of the conditioned stimulus. Pavlov's dogs would not have learned
very easily to respond to a specific sound if that sound had not been strong
enough or loud enough for them to hear — or distinct enough to be separated
from the other sounds in the laboratory. Alex was subjected to especially strong
stimuli.

The order in which a conditioned stimulus and an unconditioned stimulus
are presented is also important. Conditioning works best if the conditioned stimulus (musical note, sex and violence) comes *before* the unconditioned stimulus
(food, pain). If the dogs are fed before the musical note is sounded, they will
have trouble making the association and will probably not learn to associate the
sound with the food. The amount of time between the conditioned stimulus and
the unconditioned stimulus is also important. If the bell rings 20 minutes before

the food is presented, the association between the two will probably not be made. The dog will probably not learn that the sound has anything to do with the food. For the best results, the conditioning stimulus (sound) should be presented a second or two before the unconditioned stimulus (food).

Another important factor in conditioning is repetition. Under normal circumstances, a musical note means nothing to a dog. The first time the dog hears the sound just before being fed, the musical note still has no meaning, and the dog does not salivate. But after the sound is presented in connection with the food several times, the animal begins to make an association between the two. By the time the conditioned stimulus (sound) has been presented with the unconditioned stimulus (food) on a dozen or more occasions, the association between the two stimuli will be quite strong. Sound the musical tone, and the dog will salivate (conditioned response) whether or not you give the animal food. After a certain number of pairings of the conditioned and the unconditioned stimuli, however, not much more learning will take place and continued training would be a waste of time.

Extinction

Conditioning is not always permanent, and what is learned through conditioning can usually be unlearned. Alex was taught to get sick every time he came in contact with violence. The prison experimenters used a drug to make Alex sick, but once out of prison Alex was no longer given the drug. He continued to get sick, however, because the associations produced by the conditioning were strong enough to last for quite a while. But eventually, after some time without the drugs, Alex reached a point where violence only made him slightly ill. Finally he got to the point where violence had very little effect on him at all. The process by which the effects of conditioning wear off is known as **extinction.** The training Pavlov gave his dogs could be extinguished by presenting the conditioned sitmulus (sound) over and over again without presenting the unconditioned stimulus (food).

Operant Conditioning

Pavlov's experiments explained a very simple type of learning that goes on in everyone's life. For every action there is a reaction, the physicists say. For every stimulus there is a response, Pavlov said. And with the proper kind of conditioning, people and animals can learn to respond to different stimuli. With the millions of stimuli in the world and the millions of responses that people are capable of, stimulus–response (S–R) learning or classical conditioning can account for many of the behaviors of humans. But classical conditioning does not explain all human behavior.

A hungry dog does not sit in the back yard and wait for someone to ring a bell. People do not just sit and wait for some stimulus in the environment to cause them to react. Dogs will beg for food, and people will operate on their environment to get what they want. In other words, people stimulate their environment—including the other people in the environment. Stimulating or operating on the environment then causes the environment to react. Actions that stimulate or operate on the environment are called **operant behaviors.**

Just as S-R behaviors can be learned by classical conditioning, operant behaviors can be learned by **operant conditioning.** B. F. Skinner, the author of *Walden II,* is the psychologist who developed many of the theories that explain how operant conditioning works.

Classical conditioning can be used to get animals or people to respond with involuntary and unlearned responses. Salivation, for instance, is not a learned behavior. It is a behavior that occurs naturally. Classical conditioning does not change involuntary behaviors (such as salivation). It only changes the stimuli that cause the behaviors. Operant conditioning, on the other hand, works on voluntary behaviors. Operant conditioning changes or modifies voluntary behaviors and is sometimes known as **behavior modification.**

A rat in a cage with no food has certain voluntary behaviors. It will explore, sniff around, stand up, sit down, and perform other natural acts. If there is a button or lever in the cage that can be pushed, the rat will probably hit that lever sooner or later. Up to this point, the rat has performed a number of voluntary actions. If, immediately after the lever is pushed, a piece of food rolls down a chute into the cage, the rat will eat the food and then go back to exploring. After a while, the rat will probably hit the lever again. If food drops into the cage again, the rat may begin to make an association between the lever and the food. If food pops into the cage every time the rat hits the lever, the rat will eventually learn a new voluntary behavior and will push the lever whenever it wants food. In a similar manner, thirsty people learn to put money in soda machines and press buttons.

In Pavlovian or classical conditioning, a set of stimulus inputs (sound and food) is used to **elicit** or bring forth a response output (salivation). In operant conditioning the response (the rat pushing the lever) is voluntary and not elicited or brought forth by a particular stimulus. Whether or not the animal repeats the response, however, is influenced by any rewarding stimuli (food) that appear immediately after the response is made.

According to the principles of operant conditioning, the rat will learn that if it pushes the lever, food will drop down the chute and into the cage.

Making Operant Conditioning Work

The special cage with the lever and the feeding machine was designed by B. F. Skinner for use in operant conditioning experiments. By watching rats, pigeons, and other animals in such cages—now known as Skinner boxes—the Harvard psychologist developed a set of principles to explain how operant behaviors are learned.

If the rat in Skinner's box had never hit the lever, it would never have learned how to use the lever to get food. Someone who has never seen a soda machine might never put a coin in the slot. So the first thing a hungry rat or a thirsty person must do is find out that a certain behavior—pushing a lever, putting money in a soda machine—can produce the desired results. Skinner allowed the rat to work by trial and error. The rat just roamed around the cage until it accidentally hit the lever. When this response occurred, the rat got food and began to learn the relationship between the lever and the food. Young children use a similar type of hit-or-miss technique as they acquire a language. An infant who knows only a few words, for instance, may try each word in an attempt to get someone to give it a toy. When the child hits on the right word, the parents know what the child wants and respond (sometimes) by giving the child the toy. The child begins to learn that one specific word will produce a desired result.

The hit-or-miss approach works, but it is sometimes very slow. The rat might not get around to pushing the lever for a long time. It might be hours before a child comes out with the right word—or before a student comes up with the proper solution to a problem in mathematics. Experimenters and teachers, therefore, have ways of speeding up learning or the acquisition of proper responses. A child or a student can be told how to behave or what the proper response should be. Parents say words over and over to young children in the hope that the infants will learn the words and learn how to use them. Teachers spend hours explaining a subject to students in the hope that the students will be able to come up with the proper response at test time.

Modeling

It is impossible to explain the process of lever pushing to a rat. It is difficult to tell children how to ride a bike. And it is sometimes difficult to solve a particular type of problem by explaining the solution. When verbal instruction doesn't seem to work, **modeling** is often used. A teacher or instructor models or acts out the behavior.

A rat in a Skinner box may play around for hours before hitting the lever. If a second rat who has already learned how to push the lever is put into the box, learning is speeded up. The first rat watches the second rat push the lever and receive food. Before long the first rat will probably catch on and begin pushing the lever. Parents speed up a child's learning by showing the child how to get on and ride a bike. Teachers use a blackboard to show students how to do long

Parents serve as models for their children. When these children reach the proper stage of development, they will probably learn to ride a bike by observing the behavior of their parents.

division. Demonstrating, or modeling a behavior, is one of the most common and effective methods of teaching. Children are great imitators, and much of what they learn during the first years of life is a direct result of their imitating the actions of parents and others who serve as models. We are all capable of learning by imitation, and much of what we learn throughout life is a result of modeling. (Modeling will be discussed more fully in Chapter 9.)

Reinforcement

Teaching a rat to push a lever or a student to do long division requires more than sitting back and waiting for the correct response. The most important step in operant conditioning is getting the subject to perform the desired behavior. Getting such a response from a subject is the first step in "shaping" or forming a specific behavior. Modeling, for instance, is one way in which a behavior can be shaped or encouraged. Once a behavior has been brought about, the next step in operant conditioning is getting the rat, the student, or whoever is doing the learning to repeat the desired behavior. A rat cannot be said to have learned a new behavior if it only pushes the lever once and never does so again. Solving one long-division problem does not mean that a student has mastered long division. Learning has taken place only if the desired behavior can be repeated.

There is one very important way to help make sure that a behavior will be repeated. The behavior must be **reinforced.** This is often done by means of reward. The rat gets a reward when food drops into the cage. The student is rewarded when the teacher passes out gold stars, good grades, or an encouraging word and a pat on the back. The student is also rewarded by the knowledge that a problem has been solved and a skill has been mastered. These rewards serve to reinforce the particular behavior and, therefore, increase the chances of its reoccurring.

When rats and people are not reinforced or rewarded for a particular behavior, they are not likely to learn or to repeat the behavior. When people are rewarded, the reinforcement strengthens the behavior and increases the chances that the behavior will be repeated.

Rewarding or pleasant reinforcement is called **positive reinforcement.**

FIG. 6–3.
When a rat pushes a lever, the electricity is turned off. The act of pushing the lever is rewarded by removal of the painful stimulus (electricity). The reward increases the probability that the rat will repeat the act of pressing the lever. This process is known as negative reinforcement.

Dogs are rewarded by bones. Workers are rewarded by paychecks. Students are rewarded by good grades and the knowledge that they have learned something. And almost everyone is rewarded by praise.

Another important type of reinforcement is called **negative reinforcement.** Instead of performing behaviors that lead to a pleasing reward, people and animals sometimes have to behave in a way that will remove an unpleasant stimulus. And removing an unpleasant stimulus can be a very nice reward. A rat in a cage with a painful electric current running through the floor will try to escape or avoid the pain by any means possible. If there is a lever in the cage that turns off the electricity, the rat will learn to push the lever every time the current is turned on.

In some cases alcoholics seem to be reacting to a kind of negative reinforcement. If they are not pleased with their life, they may drink to forget their troubles so that **alcoholism** becomes an escape. People take medicine to reduce pain, study to avoid getting poor grades and, in general, avoid situations that they know will be unpleasant.

Punishment

Negative reinforcement is not punishment. Reinforcement, positive or negative, is used to *increase* the probability that a behavior or an action will be repeated. **Punishment,** on the other hand, is used to *decrease* the probability that a behavior will be repeated. Who ever heard, for instance, of spanking a child for getting good grades?

Spankings and other forms of punishment are very often used, however, in an attempt to get people to change their behavior. Children are spanked for not eating their vegetables or for getting poor grades. Criminals are punished and put behind bars for antisocial acts or crimes.

Punishment may be used a lot in our society, but that does not mean that punishment is the best way to change someone's behavior. Some children get hundreds of spankings and still never learn to eat their spinach or to do well in school. Hundreds of thousands of criminals are put in prison every year and many of them come out of prison and go right back to a life of crime.

There are several reasons why punishment does not always work. Punishment often comes too late for the child to learn what its parents want it to learn. A child who does not study for a test in school may flunk an examination. Two weeks later, when the child's parents get the report card, they may spank the child. But the spanking does not occur at the time that it should if the law of association is to work—that is, the punishment does not happen at the moment the child decides not to study for the test. Punishment coming so long after the misbehavior will usually have little effect on when and how the child studies. Instead, the punishment may become associated with what was happening at the time the spanking occurred—and the child may grow up to hate its parents.

Skinner's rats were rewarded immediately. If they hadn't been reinforced immediately, they might not have been able to make the correct associations between the response and the reward. The same time sequence holds true for

FIG. 6-4.
Punishment is any act that decreases the probability that a behavior will be repeated. If this child makes an association between being spanked and getting poor grades, he will probably study harder to achieve better grades and avoid punishment. Punishment usually works best when coupled with a reward for the desired behavior.

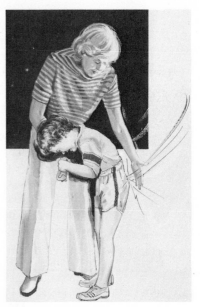

punishment. If a child gets a spanking two weeks late, the child simply may not make the connection between the punishment and its failure to study for the examination.

Even when punishment is administered at the time of the poor behavior, the punishment may not be effective. If a child is trying to go through the various steps of a long-division problem, for example, and the teacher continually interrupts and scolds the child for mistakes, the child may become so nervous and overanxious that the problem never gets solved. Even if the problem does get solved, there is a chance that the child may forever associate long division with punishment. That child may never be comfortable doing long division or any other type of mathematical problem.

Since the idea of conditioning and teaching is to get people to acquire new behaviors, punishment should very rarely be needed. If and when punishment does seem to be called for in order to get rid of an undesired behavior, the punishment should probably be paired with a reward. If children are to be taught to eat their spinach, for instance, they might be given a choice. "Eat your spinach and then you will be given your dessert. If you don't want any dessert, don't eat the spinach." When children are confronted with either reward or punishment (the loss of dessert), the chances are that they will prefer the action that leads to the reward rather than the action that offers punishment or no reward. Prisoners, too, can be given a choice. Many people get out of prison and get in trouble again because they don't have much of a choice. The most rewarding behavior they know is usually the criminal behavior that will earn them some money—and lead back to prison. If such people are given a choice, however, such as job training, or education, they may find out that crime and punishment are not the best and most rewarding alternative. In fact, Skinner pointed out in *Walden Two* that if proper reinforcements are made available, punishment almost never need be used.

Feedback

Skinner's and many subsequent experiments have pointed out some of the important factors in reinforcement. For one thing, a reinforcer must be something that the rat or person is aware of (sometimes only unconsciously). Rats will not push levers if they are not rewarded, and people will not work if they are not paid in some way. Both rats and people must also know that they are being rewarded. Rats and people must get information fed back to them that lets them know that their behavior is producing the desired results. Positive information or feedback, such as rat food or good test grades, increases the possibility that a voluntary or operant behavior will be repeated.

For feedback to be effective, it should always let the rat or person know that a behavior has caused some effect. Feedback need not, however, always come in the form of a direct reward. Food is a direct reward for hungry animals, but chimpanzees have been trained to work for chips or tokens that could later be traded for bananas. People work for money that can later be traded for bananas, among other things.

FIG. 6-5.
(A) Patti's inappropriate behavior had been reinforced unknowingly. When she raided the refrigerator, she got a lot of attention. (B) Then Patti's parents made her leave the kitchen when she behaved in an unacceptable way such as making a mess when she ate. (C) Finally, when Patti learned to control her impulses and ask for the food she wanted, she was rewarded.

A

B

C

BEHAVIOR THERAPY

What good is all of this information about operant conditioning? For one thing, the principles of operant conditioning explain one of the most important ways in which we learn. For another thing, knowledge of the processes involved in conditioning has led to the development of therapies, or treatments, for some types of learning and behavior problems. These treatments are called **behavior therapies,** and they have been found to be especially effective with children who have learning problems. The case of Patti K., a 4-year-old girl who was born with brain damage, is a good example.

In addition to brain damage, Patti had numerous physical problems during infancy and early childhood. At about 18 months of age she became seriously ill and lost almost a quarter of her body weight. For a while the left side of her body seemed to be partially paralyzed, and she had trouble learning to walk and run. Because of these physical problems Patti's early behavior patterns were never normal. A family physician attempted to treat the child's physical problems, but because of her behavior problems, including her inability to communicate effectively and to adjust to nursery school, she was put in the care of two behavior therapists, Donald E. P. Smith and Timothy Walter.

Patti had a number of bad habits. First of all, she was something of an impulsive and compulsive eater. At various times during the day she would open the refrigerator, take out several dishes of food, and eat as much as she could. Nothing her parents did, including appeals to reason and spankings, had much effect on this behavior.

A second set of unacceptable behaviors involved screaming. When Patti failed to get what she wanted, she would let out a series of sharp, loud cries that would usually convince people around her to give her what she wanted.

A third problem involved toilet training. Often when Patti did not get her way, especially at nursery school, she would say, "Oh! Oh! B. M." (meaning bowel movement). Then she would soil her pants. By the time her clothes were changed and she was cleaned up, the argument had usually been resolved in Patti's favor.

After observing Patti for some time, as well as talking to her parents and teachers, the therapists decided that Patti's major problem was that she somehow had learned many inappropriate ways of getting what she wanted. The screaming and the soiling of pants were **operant behaviors** that she had learned to use because they helped her get her way. Because these behaviors were successful once or twice, Patti used them over and over again. Each time the screaming and soiling produced the desired reaction, the more likely it became that Patti would use those behaviors again. Patti's overeating was a little more difficult to analyze, but Smith and Walter decided that it occurred because Patti had never learned to talk very well. She couldn't communicate the fact that she was hungry, nor could she explain what kind of food she was hungry for. She simply took whatever she could get whenever it was handy.

In order to help Patti and her parents get along better, and to make it more likely that Patti would succeed in school, Smith and Walter decided to help the child learn more appropriate and socially pleasing ways of getting what she wanted. This treatment involved, first of all, helping Patti unlearn some of her unpleasant habits.

Extinction Training

As mentioned earlier, conditioned behaviors and habits need not be permanent. They can be unlearned through a process known as extinction. If a habit or behavior is never rewarded or reinforced, it will usually disappear or be extinguished. Smith and Walter used **extinction training** as part of their therapy for Patti by trying to make sure that her inappropriate behaviors were never reinforced. The therapists' observations of Patti had convinced them that her parents, teachers, and the other schoolchildren were actually helping maintain Patti's bad habits by unknowingly rewarding her whenever she misbehaved. Her teachers insisted that they had punished Patti when she screamed. The punishment, however, was usually very mild and probably not strong enough to outweigh the rewarding aspects of getting what she wanted. When Patti screamed, she got a lot of attention, which was rewarding. In addition, Patti usually got the toy that she wanted or got out of doing something she didn't want to do. When Patti raided the refrigerator, her parents would get upset and spank her, but she usually got the food she wanted as well as the undivided attention of her parents for a significant period of time.

The therapists decided to attempt to extinguish Patti's unpleasant behaviors as well as teach her more acceptable ways of getting what she wanted. The extinction training consisted of ignoring all of Patti's antisocial behaviors. The teaching of new behaviors was somewhat more complex. Part of Patti's problem was the fact that she didn't know the names of most of the foods she wanted to eat. Another part of her problem was that she had difficulty keeping her **impulses** under control. When she saw something she wanted, she did not want to wait for it. She wanted it immediately. Smith and Walter set up a training program to help Patti increase her vocabulary and help her learn to accept delays in getting the rewards she wanted.

Successive Approximations

The therapists knew they couldn't expect Patti to change overnight. But they hoped to make a little progress each day by teaching her a few words at a time and by teaching her to wait a few seconds longer for her rewards. This technique is called **successive approximations** toward a goal. The process consists of moving in very small steps from the behavior a person exhibits at the beginning of therapy toward the new behaviors that are considered to be the goal of the therapy. Each movement, no matter how small, that the person makes toward the goal is rewarded. Each incorrect response that is not aimed in the right direction is ignored.

Since not all people are rewarded by the same things, Smith and Walter had to find out what Patti wanted as a reward for the progress she made. The therapists found that Patti was fond of sweet cereals and cookies, and they made use of these items in Patti's training. They began by pointing to an object and saying its name: "Milk, Patti, this is milk. Can you say 'milk'?" She couldn't, but if she muttered any sound at all the therapists would give her a piece of sweet cereal or a bite of cookie. After Patti had learned to make a noise whenever the therapists asked her to, the therapists began selectively rewarding noises that sounded like "milk," such as "meek" or "mik." They ignored any sounds that were not close to "milk." Soon Patti began to make "milk" sounds more and more often, and the therapists could get her to come closer and closer in her approximations of the word before they rewarded her. Using the successive approximations technique, Smith and Walter were able to teach Patti new words in only a few minutes. They began taking her on walks and got her to name many of the things she saw. Eventually they took her to supermarkets and taught her to name most of the foods she saw there.

Impulse Control

While the verbal training was going on, the therapists also worked on Patti's impulse control. Patti's parents agreed to stop giving her attention when she overate. If they caught her at the refrigerator, they would take the food away without saying anything to her and would make her sit in a corner for five minutes. Once Patti's vocabulary had increased, Smith and Walter taught her to ask for the foods she wanted and to say "please." Patti was rewarded for these behaviors with a piece of whatever food she had asked for. If Patti opened the refrigerator door without saying "please," her parents would shut the door until she did say "please." After Patti had learned to say "please," she was taught to wait longer between the time she first asked for something and the time she received it. And because Patti knew that if she waited she would be rewarded, she learned to control her impulses. Still using the technique of successive approximations, the researchers taught Patti to wait before eating her reward until she was told she could eat it.

At the start of the therapy, if Patti had seen a cookie she would not have waited more than a few seconds before screaming that she wanted it. After only a few weeks of training Patti could hold a cookie in her hand for several minutes and not eat it until told to do so. After six months of training Patti's parents took her to a party where the success of the training was proved. Instead of heading to the refreshment table and stuffing herself, Patti, at her parents' suggestion, passed around plates of food to the other guests and waited until everyone had been served.

COMPLEX LEARNING

Classical and operant conditioning are the basic mechanisms by which behaviors are changed and by which new behaviors are learned. But even with the ad-

FIG. 6–6.
(A) By pairing a white rat with a loud noise, experimenters taught Little Albert to fear the white rat. (B) Then Little Albert generalized his fear of the white rat to fear of all white, furry objects. (C) Little Albert even came to fear Santa Claus.

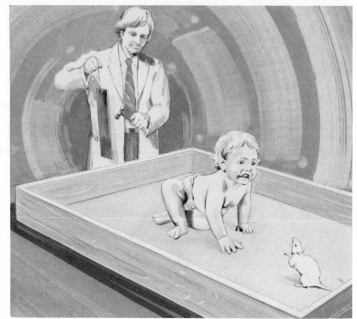

A

B

C

dition of modeling, or imitation, conditioning does not fully explain human learning. There are more complex forms of learning. Two of these are generalization and discrimination.

Generalization

A psychological study that may have been the basis for the conditioning treatment in *A Clockwork Orange* was published in 1920 by John B. Watson and R. Raynor. An 11-month-old child known as Little Albert was shown a white rat. Albert seemed interested in the furry, white animal and attempted to play with it. But every time Albert crawled toward the animal, the experimenters made a loud noise that frightened the child. The experimenters were using classical conditioning. After several attempts to reach the rat, Little Albert began to associate the rat with the frightening noise. Eventually Albert learned to fear the rat, but something else happened. When Little Albert was shown a white rabbit he reacted to it in the same manner that he had learned to react to the rat. In other words, Albert's conditioning was not restricted to rats. Albert had learned to fear all white, furry objects. A fur coat and a Santa Claus mask could make Little Albert cry as easily as a rat could make him cry.

In Albert's case we can see the phenomenon of **generalization** at work — the conditioned response had become generalized from a specific fear of white rats to a general fear of all white, furry objects. Alex was shown only a limited number of films of violence, but his conditioning was supposed to bring about a generalized response that would make him fear all forms of violence.

Discrimination

The opposite of generalization is discrimination. Pavlov conditioned a dog to salivate at the sight of a drawing of a circle. After the conditioning was strong enough, Pavlov showed the dog a variety of drawings of different shapes — squares, stars, rectangles, and triangles. The dog generalized from the original drawing of the circle and salivated at the sight of some of the other figures. The more like the circle a figure was, however, the more likely the dog was to salivate. Pavlov then trained the dog to tell the difference, or to discriminate, between the various figures. The dog was shown a circle and then fed. When an ellipse was shown the animal was not fed. After a while the dog could discriminate between the circle and the ellipse, and would only salivate when the circle was shown. In fact, the dog eventually became very good at discriminating between circles and even those elipses that were almost perfectly round.

Generalization and discrimination come in handy in everyday life. A person who has learned to be careful with one gun will probably (through generalization) be careful with firearms in general. A person who has learned to get ready to eat when the lunch bell rings will probably be discriminating enough not to salivate when a church bell rings.

MODIFYING YOUR OWN BEHAVIOR

When behavior therapy first became prominent some twenty years ago, many people rejected this type of treatment because it seemed highly manipulative. That is, both Pavlov and Skinner saw learning as something that was typically *forced* on a person or animal by someone else (as it was forced on Alex). Pavlov did not ask his dogs if they wanted to learn to salivate when he sounded a musical tone, nor did Skinner ask his rats if they wished to learn to press a lever to get food. The early behaviorists countered this objection by pointing out that, for the most part, they worked only with human volunteers who decided on their own goals. Nevertheless, not all of the patients were happy about having someone else reinforce them for improvement. These patients often complained that the treatment was too "mechanical." After all, the therapists were still the ones who "shaped" the new responses.

Other patients did well while the therapists were around to reward the patients, but lost much of what they had learned when the therapists were not present. And since the therapists usually saw these patients only an hour or so a week, the patients never did make much progress.

Benefits of "Self-Change"

You can learn to modify your own behavior. By practicing self-relaxation, this woman has learned to calm herself in the midst of a hectic world.

In the past decade, behavior therapists have, to a great extent, changed their approach to treatment. Rather than shaping the patients themselves, the therapists teach the patients how to modify their own behaviors. The patients learn how to set their own personal goals for change, how to measure or monitor their own behavioral outputs, and how to reward themselves for successive approximations to these goals.

By teaching their patients the techniques of self-control, the behavioral therapists overcame many of the problems associated with this type of treatment. First, no one manipulates or forces the patients to change — so fewer people object that the therapy is "mechanical."

Second, after the patients have learned how to change themselves, they no longer need to have someone else around to reinforce their actions. The patients reinforce themselves. No one is around you 24 hours a day — except you, yourself. Therefore, you are by far the best "therapist" for yourself if you really want to make some basic changes in the way you think and feel and act.

Third, when most of the patients began monitoring their own reinforcements, they often became aware of something surprising — their friends and families were often rewarding the patients for very inappropriate behaviors. Usually their friends and families were not consciously aware of giving the patients these reinforcements — but then, were Skinner's rats aware of who he was and what he was doing? Once the patients understood what was happening to them, though, they could often get their friends and families to help the patients — rather than unconsciously hinder their progress.

The behavioral approach to weight loss involves making a record of everything you eat. The chart provides immediate feedback of your progress.

Fat Wives and Insecure Husbands

Whether you realize it or not, the people around you do reinforce certain of the things you say and do. But the fact that you aren't consciously aware of this reinforcement doesn't make the rewards any less effective in influencing your behaviors.

The importance of this point was made dramatically clear several years ago by behaviorist Richard B. Stuart, who was at the time performing research at the University of Michigan. Stuart was working with married women who seemed to be unable to lose weight. He suspected that the husbands might be at least partially responsible for the overeating, so he asked the couples to make tape recordings of their dinner conversations. Stuart found, among other things, that the husbands were four times more likely to offer food to their wives than the other way around—even though the husbands knew that their wives were on a diet.

Stuart then interviewed 55 men who were married to women who were trying to lose weight. He found that many husbands seem to enjoy demonstrating what they consider to be their masculine power by coaxing or forcing their wives to become fat. In addition, Stuart found out that some husbands used their wives' fatness to win arguments. A husband can usually get the final word in an argument by calling his wife a "fat slob." If the wives were successful in losing weight, the husbands felt (perhaps unconsciously) that they would not win as many arguments.

In addition to using fatness to win arguments and to keep wives faithful, Stuart found that some husbands who were no longer sexually attracted to their wives used fatness as an excuse for lack of sexual desire. In most cases, the husbands lost their desire first and then started to fatten up their wives.

Weight Loss—The Behavioral Approach

People eat for many reasons, not just because they have been without food for a while. People eat because their blood-sugar level has fallen, because brain mechanisms urge them to eat, because their stomachs are contracting, because their dinner time is approaching, or because they have just seen or smelled or heard about something good to eat. And there are other reasons. People eat because their parents thought that fat babies are healthy babies, and because food and eating have a variety of symbolic and social values. Obviously, any dieting program must take into account not just calories and exercise. Motives, mannerisms, and environmental factors must be considered as well.

While most purely medical approaches to weight loss yield a success rate of about 10 percent, many behaviorists claim a success rate of better than 70 percent. For people who do not have a severe weight problem, the behaviorists suggest the following:

1. Begin by recording everything you eat for a week or two. Take note of where you eat, the events (and thoughts) that occur just before and after you eat, and record who is around you when you eat and what their response is to your food intake.
2. Write down all of the rewards and punishments that will come to you if you gain better control over your eating behavior.
3. Break your eating habits by changing mealtimes to a very irregular schedule several weeks before you go on a diet.
4. Any weight-control program will probably be more efficient if you increase your physical activity to burn off excess fat. If you are not particularly athletic, think about what forms of physical activity you like best and try to arrange to get more of this kind of exercise.
5. Involve as many people as possible in your program. If someone close to you consciously or unconsciously wants you to remain fat, think of substitute rewards that will encourage that person to help you lose weight. You may even have to offer people money or services for every pound they help you lose.
6. When you start the program, make a chart or graph on which you record your daily weight and each aspect of your daily routine, including the amount of food eaten and exercise taken. Post the graph in a prominent place so that everyone can see your progress and comment on it. Arrange to have someone give you regular rewards (money, privileges, a verbal pat on the back) each time you meet your daily goal. Such a graph may be the most important part of any weight-control program because it provides you with immediate feedback.
7. Don't expect too much too soon or set unrealistic goals. The average weight loss is about a pound per week. Long-term weight loss is difficult for most people to achieve because so many factors are involved. But success is encouraging, so make sure that the first goals—the first few days' changes in behavior—are easy to achieve.

Not everyone, of course, can lose weight without professional help. Some people may have to seek the assistance of a psychologist and a physician to make sure that their symbolic as well as their physical needs are accounted for in their weight-loss programs. And since about 5 percent of all weight problems are the result of physical ailments, any weight-control program should probably begin with a physical check-up.

Anyone who has tried to lose weight or change a habit knows how hard such a task can sometimes be. But if the behavioral approach can help people learn new ways of responding 70 percent of the time, then behavior modification is indeed a powerful tool—perhaps as powerful as the writers of *A Clockwork Orange* and *Walden Two* said it is. But these novels were visions of a future in which psychologists conditioned or manipulated other people whether the people liked it or not. Judging from the results of recent studies, it would seem that the future of behavior modification lies not in pushing people around by reinforcing or punishing them—rather the future lies in helping people learn the techniques of self-control so that they can become what they want to be rather than what psychologists think they ought to be.

▶ *SUMMARY*

1. By applying psychological procedures, we can change a person's behavior. We can use psychology to control personal freedom as the doctors did with Alex in *A Clockwork Orange*. Or we can use the knowledge of psychology to help people learn new and rewarding behaviors and build a better society as envisioned by B. F. Skinner in *Walden Two*. Significant issues are being raised and wonders are possible, but there may be a price in the form of side effects or loss of personal freedom.

2. **Learning,** The process by which new information, habits, and behaviors are acquired, is one of the most important aspects of human behavior. If we were not able to learn, we would have to rely on instinctive and reflexive behavior patterns, and our behaviors would remain much as they were at the time of birth.

3. The first rule of learning is often called the **law of association.** If two inputs arrive at the brain at the same time, they often become associated with each other. We all learn to make millions of associations between different aspects of the environment because we see or hear or taste or experience them at the same time.

4. One of the most basic types of learning common to everyday living is **conditioning.** In **classical** or **Pavlovian conditioning** an association is made between a stimulus and a response. In **operant conditioning** an association is made between one's own behavior and its effect on the environment.

5. In classical conditioning the strength and timing of the stimulus as well as the order in which the stimulus and response occur help determine whether or not an association will be made. In operant conditioning it is the type and timing of the response that strengthens or reinforces the stimulus (one's own initial behavior). In operant conditioning reinforcement is sometimes called feedback.

6. By manipulating the timing of feedback and the type of **reinforcement** it is sometimes possible to strengthen associations and to modify behavior. Behav-

iors that have been learned through conditioning can usually be unlearned through the process known as **extinction.**

7. Conditioning accounts for much but not all learning. **Modeling** or **imitation** is another important process by which new behaviors are acquired.

8. Learning can be said to have taken place if a newly acquired behavior can be repeated. Reinforcement is one method of helping make sure that a behavior is repeated. Rewarding or pleasant reinforcement is called **positive reinforcement.** A second type of reinforcement is **negative reinforcement.** Instead of behaving in a way that will lead to a pleasing reward, we sometimes have to behave in a way that will remove an unpleasant stimulus. Reinforcement that removes an unpleasant stimulus is called negative reinforcement.

9. Reinforcement (positive or negative) is used to increase the probability that a behavior or an action will be repeated. **Punishment** is a type of stimulus used to decrease the probability that a behavior will be repeated.

10. Behavior therapists can help people to learn more acceptable and rewarding behaviors. They do this by providing feedback that reinforces desirable behavior and ignores unacceptable behavior. **Extinction training** may be used, as well as the technique of **successive approximations,** whereby the individual progresses gradually toward new desirable behaviors. Behavior therapists also try to teach impulse control.

11. **Generalization** and **discrimination** are examples of more complex types of learning. Generalization allows for the transfer of learned behaviors from one situation to another. Discrimination is the process that helps prevent incorrect responses to similar stimuli.

12. Knowledge of the processes involved in learning not only helps us to understand what we mean by "learning," but also has led to the development of therapies that have proved to be effective in treating some types of learning and behavior problems. In the last 10 years, many behaviorists have sought not so much to use this knowledge to shape behavior themselves, but rather to train the patient in self-change. Each of us is the best "therapist" for ourselves.

Suggested Readings

Bandura, Albert. *Principles of behavior modification.* New York: Holt, Rinehart and Winston, 1969.

Burgess, Anthony. *A clockwork orange.* New York: Norton, 1963.

Lazarus, Arnold A. *Behavior therapy and beyond.* New York: McGraw-Hill, 1971.

Liberman, R. P. Learning interpersonal skills in groups: Harnessing the behaviorist horse to the humanistic wagon. In P. Houts and M. Berber (Eds.), *After the turn-on, what?* Champaign, Ill.: Research Press, 1972.

Skinner, B. F. *Walden Two.* New York: Macmillan, 1948.

Thoresen, Carl E. and Michael J. Mahoney. *Behavioral self-control.* New York: Holt, Rinehart and Winston, 1974.

► STUDY GUIDE

A.   RECALL

Sentence Completion

[p. 182]
1. Alex's problem in *A Clockwork Orange* was his extreme enjoyment of _____ behaviors.

[p. 183]
2. The behavioral engineers in Skinner's *Walden Two* modified behavior by using a system of _____.

[p. 184]
3. _____ may be defined as the process by which new information, habits, or behaviors are acquired.

[p. 184]
4. Human infants must be able to _____ in order to survive.

[p. 185]
5. The so-called law of _____ suggests that two inputs arriving at the brain at the same time may become "linked" together.

[p. 185]
6. _____ _____ was first described in detail by the Russian physiologist Ivan _____.

[p. 185]
7. In Pavlov's experiments, _____ acted as the unconditioned stimulus, while _____ was the unconditioned response.

[p. 185]
8. When a dog learns to salivate to a tone, as in classical conditioning, that salivation is know as a _____ _____.

[p. 188]
9. Perhaps the most important factor in classical conditioning is the _____ of the conditioned stimulus.

[p. 189]
10. For classical conditioning to work best, the _____ stimulus should come before the _____ stimulus.

[p. 189]
11. _____ is the process by which the effects of conditioning decrease in strength or wear off.

[p. 190]
12. Actions that stimulate or act on the environment in which they are produced are called _____ behaviors.

[p. 190]
13. The psychologist _____ is credited with developing most of the theories that explain how operant conditioning works.

[p. 190]
14. In operant conditioning the response that the learner makes is thought to be _____ as opposed to being elicited.

[p. 191]
15. An effective method of teaching involves demonstrating or _____ the behavior to be learned.

[p. 192]
[p. 193]
16. Rewards serve to _____ behavior and increase the chances of the behavior's recurring.

17. _____ reinforcement involves the removal of an unpleasant stimulus.

[p. 193]
18. Punishment is used in an attempt to _____ the probability that a behavior will be repeated.

[p. 193]
19. To be effective, punishment, like reward, should be administered _____ after the response to be modified.

[p. 195]
20. Reinforcements are useful when they provide _____ or information to the learner about his or her progress.

21. The application of learning theory to solving behavioral problems is called

[p. 197]
_____ _____

[p. 198]
22. If a behavior is never reinforced, it will probably disappear or be _____

[p. 198]
23. For Patti K. _____ probably acted like a strong reward.

24. By the method of _____ _____ one moves in small steps

[p. 198]
toward a goal.

25. When Little Albert demonstrated that he was afraid of all white, furry objects, not just

[p. 201]
the CS, he showed _____

26. Learning to "undo" generalization and to respond only to some stimuli and not other

[p. 201]
similar ones shows _____

27. Stuart studied wives who were _____ and found that their

[p. 203]
_____ helped to continue their condition.

28. Behaviorists claim a success rate as high as _____ percent for bringing

[p. 204]
about weight loss.

B.   REVIEW

Multiple Choice: Circle the letter identifying the alternative that most correctly completes the statement or answers the question.

1. In *Walden II,* Skinner suggests that _____ can be used to control _____ behaviors.
   A. punishment; violent
   B. psychology; only unimportant
   C. reward; all
   D. hypnosis; unpleasant

2. In Pavlov's original classical conditioning demonstration the _____ was a musical tone.
   A. CS
   B. UCS
   C. CR
   D. UCR

3. In the Little Albert experiment, the unconditioned stimulus was:
   A. fear.
   B. a white, furry animal.
   C. a loud noise.
   D. crying.

4. Extinction occurs by:
   A. reinforcing a given response.
   B. letting the effects of conditioning wear off.
   C. successive approximations.
   D. presenting the CS and the UCS together.

5. Allowing a rat to turn off an electric shock to the floor of its cage by pressing a lever is an example of:
  A. punishment.
  B. negative reinforcement.
  C. extinction.
  D. positive reinforcement.

6. As a means of changing behavior, punishment:
  A. is the same as negative reinforcement.
  B. needs to be immediate to be truly effective.
  C. cannot really control behavior.
  D. is generally preferred over reward.

7. Behavior therapy uses:
  A. principles of operant and respondent conditioning.
  B. impulse control.
  C. extinction training.
  D. all of the above.

8. In *A Clockwork Orange*, Alex's behaviors were changed by:
  A. making him more violent.
  B. rewarding positive changes in his behavior.
  C. making him sick whenever he saw violence.
  D. assertiveness training.

9. Operant behaviors:
  A. have some effect on the environment.
  B. cannot be changed.
  C. are the same as UCRs and CRs.
  D. include being afraid of loud noises.

10. Losing weight through behavior modification techniques:
  A. doesn't work as well as medical approaches.
  B. requires well-trained therapists to act as modifiers.
  C. may be successful as much as 70 percent of the time.
  D. all of the above.

ACHIEVEMENT PLACE: A BEHAVIORALLY ORIENTED TREATMENT PROGRAM FOR JUVENILE DELINQUENTS

In the 1950's juvenile delinquents had greasy ducktails, black leather jackets, bicycle chains and zip guns. In the 1970's this particular stereotype is seen more often on the stage than on the street, but juvenile delinquency still exists and is a problem. It is characterized by antisocial behavior (truancy, waywardness or incorrigibility) that is considered to be beyond parental control and therefore subject to legal action. For many such youthful offenders (usually between the ages of 11 and 18) legal action means confinement in a state institution. This keeps them off the streets but does little to correct delinquent behavior or teach socially acceptable behavior. Researchers in Lawrence, Kan., are attempting to change this situation by reeducating delinquents in a controlled environment designed specifically to overcome behavioral difficulties.

The model environment they are using is called Achievement Place. It consists of a residential home, two teaching-parents, and seven or eight boys or girls (11 to 16 years of age) who have been sent there by the Juvenile Court or the Department of Social Welfare in the community. The home is run according to the principles of behavior modification, and its goals are to educate youths in academic, social, and self-care or vocational skills.

Most youths sent to Achievement Place are having trouble in school. Truancy, tardiness and disruptive behavior have usually led to suspension or dropping out. A great many factors are involved in producing such behavior but lack of motivation is often the major problem. These students don't care about getting an education and see no connection between doing well in school and success in later life. One way to change the situation is to make the rewards of doing well in school more immediate and more tangible. Students at Achievement Place go back to or remain in their community school, but immediate feedback and positive reinforcement are provided by a token or point system. Each student has a daily report card. Teachers in each class sign the card and note whether or not the student has behaved in class, completed homework or other assignments and performed adequately on tests or exams. Back at Achievement Place the student is given points for all desired behaviors. Points, in turn, can be used to purchase a variety of privileges (free time, trips, spending money).

Elery L. Phillips, Dean L. Fixsen and Montrose M. Wolf of the University of Kansas in Lawrence helped design and put Achievement Place into operation. They report that before using the daily report card, students spent about 25 percent of their time in appropriate study behavior. Using the card and token system increased the figure to almost 90 percent. An average of one letter grade increase was common for most students after a nine-week period. Gradually, as appropriate behavior is learned, the supportive system is removed and students are returned to the normal feedback system.

School, however, is only part of the problem for many delinquents. In the Achievement Place home, teaching-parents (trained in human development at the University of Kansas) instruct their wards in such things as proper social interaction, personal cleanliness and community involvement. Specific behavior goals for each youth are based on behavior that members of the family, school, community and teaching-parents believe should be changed. Desired behavior earns points while speaking aggressively, arguing, disobeying, being late, stealing, lying and cheating lose points.

The immediate feedback provided by the point system helps the youths learn to respond to more natural rewards. When self-control, responsibility and the ability to work productively at home and school are demonstrated, the individual is ready to return to the community.

Youths spend up to one year at Achievement Place.

Follow-up data indicate that the effects are long-lasting. The results can be seen in comparisons between Achievement Place delinquents, similar youths sent to a state institution and youths put on probation by the Juvenile Courts:

	AP	Inst.	Prob.
Offenses per year			
prior	3.8	3.6	2.6
during	0.4	0.5	1.3
1 year	0.7	2.4	2.5
2 year	0.0	1.4	0.8
Recidivism (%)			
1 year	6	13	31
2 year	19	53	54
School attendance (%)			
prior	75	75	77
during	100	100	84
1 semester after	84	58	69
2 semester after	90	9	37

C.   NEWS STORY QUESTIONS

1. What is the rationale for putting juvenile delinquents in institutions in the first place? ___

2. How does Achievement Place attempt to modify its students' school behavior? ___

3. Is there evidence that Achievement Place has any impact beyond school behavior? Summarize. ___

Movie still from *Sherlock Holmes in Washington*.

Most of our behaviors are aimed at solving one type of problem or another. In this chapter we will examine three aspects of human behavior that are necessary in most forms of problem solving, and are essential to survival. These three important behaviors are talking, thinking, and remembering.

Talking, Thinking, and Remembering

When you have completed your study of this chapter, you should be able to:

- ►Define "language" and summarize two theories of language development
- ►Define "adaptation," "assimilation," and "accommodation"
- ►Review Piaget's four stages of intellectual development
- ►Define what is meant by "sensory-information storage" and "eidetic imagery"
- ►Review the structure and functions of short-term memory and long-term memory
- ►Summarize the flatworm experiments that show the importance of RNA and protein in memory
- ►Outline the steps in proper problem solving

Abstract. From the Latin term meaning "to draw from or to separate." As used in psychology, the word usually means an idea or principle that does not refer to something concrete, or to an object in everyday life. According to Piaget, abstract thinking involves the ability to manipulate symbols in one's mind.

Accommodation (ack-kom-moh-DAY-shun). From the Latin word meaning "to adapt." People who accommodate us are people who try to satisfy our needs or adjust to our desires. In Piaget's terms, children accommodate when they learn to adjust their actions to the requirements of their environments.

Acronym (ACK-roh-nim). A fancy Greek term meaning "a word made from the first letters of other words." For example, NASA is an acronym for the National Aeronautics and Space Administration.

Adaptation. To adapt means to adjust or to change something for some purpose. The movie script for "Jaws" was an *adaptation* made from a novel by Peter Benchley.

Amnesia (am-KNEE-zha). From the Greek word meaning "forgetful." A person with amnesia cannot remember certain things that happened to the person earlier.

Anthropology (ann-throw-PAHL-oh-gee). From the Greek words meaning "the study of man." Anthropology is a social science that deals primarily with the evolution of cultures and of the human body.

Anxiety. A type of free-floating fear or nervousness.

Archeology (ar-key-AHL-oh-gee). A branch of anthropology dealing with the study of the physical remains of past human life and activities. Those scientists who dig up and study ancient cities or burial sites are archeologists.

Assimilation (uh-simm-uh-LAY-shun). From the Latin word meaning "to make similar." According to Piaget, children assimilate the cultures into which they are born by learning the rules and regulations of society and then by working out their own moral or behavioral standards.

Calculator (KALL-cue-lay-terr). From the Latin word meaning "to count using stones." In ancient days, people would often figure out sums by using small piles of limestones to keep track of their additions and subtractions. Nowadays we use electrical impulses instead of limestones, but the principle is the same as using stones.

Cannibal. A word taken from a Caribbean language meaning "someone who eats human flesh." Hence, any animal that eats its own kind.

Chunking. Your short-term memory is limited to about seven items at once. But you can remember more than seven things if you group them together into chunks of information.

Concrete operational stage. The third of Piaget's developmental stages, during which the child begins to visualize series of operations independent of its own actions.

Eidetic imagery (eye-DETT-tick). From the Greek word meaning "images." If you have a photographic memory, you can form "in you mind's eye" an exact photograph (eidetic image) of what you have seen before.

Formal operational stage. The final stage of intellectual development, which is reached around the age of 12. According to Piaget, it is at this stage that the child can handle such abstract concepts as truth, honor, and personality.

Functional fixedness. The inability to shift to a new way of thinking, feeling, or behaving. If you have learned to solve a problem a particular way, you may attempt to apply this solution to every problem you encounter in the future. Even if the old way of problem solving doesn't work, you will continue doggedly to use it because your mind is "fixed" on this way of proceeding.

Linguistics (ling-GWISS-ticks). From the Latin word *lingua,* meaning "tongue." Linguistics is the scientific study of languages and language behaviors.

Maturation. From the Latin word meaning "to become ripe." To mature is to grow up, to become adult both physically and mentally.

Memory molecule. Whenever you learn something, or change your behavior, there must be some physical change within your body that allows you to remember, or to behave in a new way. Some scientists believe that learning is associated with changes in specific chemical molecules in your nerve cells. While many laboratory experiments offer support for this viewpoint, many psychologists prefer alternate explanations of how memory works.

Mental set. A tendency to experience the world in a pre-determined way. Put another way, we tend to see what we expect or want to see.

Mnemonics (na-MAHN-icks). From the Greek word meaning "memory." Mnemonics are devices that are intended to help you remember something.

Originality. The ability to create new things, or to arrange old things so that they appear new and different. A psychological trait often praised in the abstract, but punished in real-life situations.

Pre-operational stage. The second of Piaget's developmental stages, during which a child learns to speak and to manipulate its world symbolically.

RNA. Literally, ribonucleic acid (RYE-bo-new-CLAY-ick). Complex genetic molecules usually produced by DNA, or deoxyribonucleic acid, which contains the genetic material. In some exceedingly small organisms, such as viruses that cause colds or flu, the genes may be made of RNA rather than DNA.

Regenerate. To regrow, or to replace missing parts. Very simple animals—such as flatworms—do not die when cut in half. Rather, each piece regenerates all the pieces that it

needs to become a complete animal again. In human beings, some tissue (such as the skin) regenerates, but most tissue (such as brain cells) does not regenerate.

Repression. The act of putting down, or intentionally forgetting. This repression of unpleasant memories may occur consciously or unconsciously but, according to Freud, is almost always a deliberate act by your Ego to protect your self-image.

Scotophobin (sko-toe-FOE-bin). From the Greek word meaning "fear of the dark." A "memory molecule" synthesized or made by Georges Ungar and his associates that supposedly causes animals to fear the dark when it is injected into the animals' bodies.

Senility. A set of psychological and biological problems associated with old age.

Sensory-information storage (SIS). The first stage of memory storage. The ability of your sense receptors to "hold" incoming stimuli for brief periods of time even after the stimuli have disappeared.

Sensory-motor stage. The first of Piaget's developmental stages, during which the infant tries to correlate its sensory inputs with its motor outputs.

Short-term memory (STM). You experience millions of different sensory inputs every day. As these incoming stimulus messages are passed to your brain from sensory information storage, some part of the brain interprets them and "remembers" them for a few brief seconds. If the inputs are not important, they are soon forgotten.

Syntax (SIN-tax). From the Latin word meaning "to put in order." The syntax of a sentence is the order in which the parts of the sentence appear. In English sentences, the subject usually appears first, then the verb, then the object.

Transformation. To transform something is to change if from one state or condition into another. The rods and cones in your eye transform light energy into chemical energy. Maturation is the process by which a helpless infant is transformed into a self-actualized adult.

INTRODUCTION: A SCANDAL IN BOHEMIA

"Elementary, my dear Watson," Holmes would say to his confused companion, and then go on to explain the reasoning process he had used in solving some particularly difficult problem. Dr. Watson would listen with amazement at how Holmes had spotted all the clues and made sense of them, while he had either missed them or misinterpreted them.

Sherlock Holmes, the master detective, was known and respected for his cold, calculating, precise mind. Holmes usually accepted only those cases that others had failed to solve, but no matter how difficult the problem he always came up with the correct solution. Therefore, it came as quite a surprise when Irene Adler outwitted Holmes, as she did in a story called *A Scandal in Bohemia*.

One evening in 1888 while Watson was visiting Holmes's Baker Street flat, a tall, distinguished-looking visitor arrived wearing a mask. Within seconds Holmes had gathered enough information to figure out that the disguised visitor was none other than the young king of Bohemia (now part of Czechoslovakia). The king admitted his identity and went on to explain the need for secrecy. It seems that five years earlier the king had fallen in love with an actress named Irene Adler. The king loved and respected this woman, but neither his family nor his position would allow him to marry someone not of royal blood. Irene Adler, however, wanted to marry the king and was determined that if she couldn't have him no one else would. She let the king know that if he ever attempted to marry she would tell the world of their affair. As proof, she could show a large photograph of the two of them together. This, of course, would create a scandal.

The king of Bohemia was planning to marry a Scandinavian princess. He didn't want any scandal, and he didn't want his future wife to find out about his previous affair with Irene. His agents had tried and failed in their attempts to recover the photograph, but Irene was well aware of its value and kept it hidden in a safe place. With his marriage announcement only three days off, the king had finally decided to seek the help of Sherlock Holmes.

Holmes was fascinated by the challenge—just as millions of readers have been fascinated by the fictional adventures of Sherlock Holmes and his friend Dr. Watson. These adventures, which were written by Sir Arthur Conan Doyle, all involve intricate problems that the master detective solves with amazing powers of observation and reasoning.

One of the reasons that the Sherlock Holmes stories have remained popular for the past 75 years is that they deal with problem solving—something that we are all concerned with, in one way or another, from the moment we are born. As infants we are quite helpless, but we will usually let out a yell if we are hungry, or in pain, or bored. We soon learn to solve our problems by attracting the attention of those who will help us. By the time we enter school, we will have learned more direct ways of attacking our problems and will be preparing ourselves (through education) to solve many more problems. In fact, if you think about it, a great many of our human behaviors can be seen as an attempt to solve some kind of problem. Not only are we faced with millions of problems, most of us go out of our way to solve more problems. Some of us, for instance, work crossword puzzles. Others read detective stories and try to figure out "who done it" before the detective does. It seems that problem solving is a necessary and important part of our lives. So the more we learn about problem solving, the better equipped we will be to solve our own problems.

Sherlock Holmes, the scientific detective, was described by Dr. Watson as having extraordinary mental powers. The mind, of course, is all important in problem solving, but "mental powers" consist of several abilities that must be considered if we are to understand how Holmes, or we ourselves, solve problems. First of all, there is language. We use language to communicate and to gain information. And except for those unfortunate individuals who have severe language problems, most of us use language in our thought processes. In addition to language and thought processes, another aspect of mental behavior especially important to problem solving is our ability to remember. If we couldn't remember, or hold in our minds the clues we have collected, we would have little success in solving most of our problems. These then are the aspects of human behavior we will examine in this chapter—*language, thinking,* and *remembering.* They are essential not only to problem solving but to survival.

LANGUAGE

Sherlock Holmes would not attempt to solve his problems until he had gathered enough information to make a reasonable guess. "It is a capital mistake," he would say, "to theorize before one has data." But how does one gather data?

All information comes into your brain through your senses, but you don't have to experience something directly to know that it exists. You can learn that fire is hot by sticking your hand in the flames, or you can learn more comfortably by having someone warn you that you might get burned. Once a small child has learned the meaning of the word "hot," often by painful experience, that child usually will not touch things its parents say are hot. The child gets the message— it learns that certain things are too hot to handle from its parents or other teachers. And in most cases, such messages are passed along by language.

A language is a system of signs and symbols that one person can use to communicate with another. In a very simple way, the musical note used by Pavlov in his experiments was part of a language that the dogs learned to respond to. The music was a warning sign or signal that gave information to the dogs that they were about to be fed. Lower animals, such as planaria, can learn

FIG. 7–1.
Musicians can communicate with abstract symbols.

only a few such signs. Dogs can learn more, and animals with complex brains can learn a great many signs or signals. Chimpanzees, for instance, have been taught to use 100 or more signals with which to communicate.

A symbol is qualitatively different from a sign or a signal. A symbol is an abstraction—a word or number or drawing that stands for a complex idea or experience of some kind. A stop sign is just that—a signal that you must bring your car to a complete stop. The traffic ticket that you might get for not stopping is also a signal—a signal that you must appear in court and pay a fine. But words like *speed, law, justice, guilt, mercy, hope, hate,* and *love* are abstract terms that don't really stand for any specific action or thing; such words are merely symbols for complex ideas. Mathematics is difficult for many people because numbers don't really represent real-world objects, but are only symbolic. The number *9* doesn't stand for nine children, or nine hamburgers, or nine Supreme Court justices. Rather, the number *9* represents the concept of "nine-ness."

There is considerable argument among scientists as to whether animals are intelligent enough to use symbols as well as signs when they communicate with each other (and with us). There is no argument about our ability to use symbols. Our language is full of them. There are almost 200 major languages that are spoken in the world today. Some of these languages (such as English) contain at least a quarter of a million words. And each of these words, in each of these languages, is a sign or symbol that humans have learned to use. How have such complex systems of communication come to be?

The Origins of Language

We cannot see our minds, but an understanding of the human language ability and its origins will give us some idea of how our minds work. Throughout history, great thinkers have often found the question of the origin of language to be central to any understanding of the human species. The chief characteristic that distinguishes humans from all other animals has always been considered to be the possession of language and speech. In fact, language has been associated closely with basic human traits such as learning, thinking, social behavior, and the possibility of possessing and passing on information.

The lack of solid evidence has prevented a clear understanding of the origin and evolution of language. Since we can't go back a million years or so and watch our ancestors evolving, a certain amount of guesswork will probably always be involved in our understanding of language. Even so, there is a long history of attempts to study the origin of language.

Nearly 2500 years ago, the Greek historian Herodotus described one of the first known experiments with language. An Egyptian king wanted to find out which was the oldest nation on earth. So he took two infants at birth and isolated them from all human speech to find out which language they would speak if left to their own devices. It was thought that the infants' language would be the "true" or "natural" language of the human race. The first word uttered by the isolated children was not Egyptian but something that sounded like part of the Phrygian language (Phrygia was a country in Asia Minor). The Egyptian king was disappointed because to him it meant that Phrygia, not Egypt, was the oldest nation on earth. Since that time, similar experiments have been recorded, with the result that the first word spoken often sounded like a word from the Hebrew language. The same experiment was still being tried as late as the eighteenth century, but by then it was generally realized that such experiments should not be undertaken because of the harm the isolation can do to the children (see Chapter 3).

In the search for an original or natural language, attention next focused on children who for some reason had been abandoned and had grown up with animals (see the so-called wolf children, Chapter 14). Such cases were rare, and even when they did turn up they offered few clues to a natural language. Eventually, the search for a natural language was abandoned when it was realized that unless children learn to use language during their early years, they will probably never be capable of more than the crudest forms of communication. In recent years it has been discovered that the babbling of infants during the first months of life contains all the sounds necessary for the development of any language, including ancient Phrygian, Egyptian, Hebrew, and English.

A different approach to the study of the origins of language was made by Condillac, an eighteenth-century psychologist who was interested in the philosophy of language. Condillac believed that language began with natural cries that expressed some inner passion — screams of fear, sighs of pleasure, and so on. He called these vocal gestures the "language of action." After these involuntary sounds occurred many times, early humans were able to recall them and use them at will. For example, they could warn other people of an approaching danger such as a ferocious animal. Condillac thought that continued use of these natural cries led to deliberately created verbal symbols or language.

With Condillac the tradition of a philosophy of language came to a temporary halt. During the nineteenth century, the study of the origin of language was at times even prohibited for religious reasons. Language was thought to be a gift from God, so it was considered a sin to talk of the evolution, rather than the divine origin, of language.

Scientific Approaches to Language

By the twentieth century Darwin had published his theory of the evolution of the species, and the study of the origin of language was reestablished — this time as a science, rather than a philosophy. The scientific study of the nature and structure of language is know as **linguistics,** but many other areas of research are currently adding to our understanding of language; they include **archeology, anthropology,** biology, animal behavior, brain research, and psychology.

Montagu's Theory

Where, when, and how did the human language ability originate? Anthropologist Ashley Montagu has one answer. He suggests that a detailed study of early human tool making may give us some clues to the thought processes of early humans and to the origin and evolution of language and speech. Montagu believes that speech originated in the process of tool making; he says that the variety of tools made by our ancestors indicates an ability to communicate on a symbolic level that would have required speech. Big-game hunting, as well as tool making, says Montagu, was probably related to the development of speech. If the hunters can verbally signal to each other about changes in plans or strategies, hunting is much more successful. Montagu thinks that tool making, big-game hunting, and spoken language probably all evolved together with a sort of three-way feedback relationship leading to the further development of each. If Montagu's tool-making theory is correct, some form of human speech may have been in use one or two million years ago, the age of some of the oldest human stone tools.

FIG. 7–2.
Montagu believes that language evolved when our distant ancestors began to make tools. He thinks the variety of tools made by early humans required an ability to communicate on a symbolic level.

Jaynes's Theory

Psychologist Julian Jaynes of Princeton University disagrees with Montagu. Jaynes says that speech was not necessary for teaching such simple skills as tool use and tool making. Such teaching, he says, was done solely by imitation in exactly the same way chimpanzees teach their young the trick of inserting a vine stem into an ant hill to get ants. In our own culture, he says, it is doubtful if language is at all necessary in the transmission of such skills as swimming or riding a bicycle.

Therefore, it is probable, Jaynes feels, that speech and language evolved much more recently than one or two million years ago. He says they must have developed during a time when some portion of the human population was being forced into a new environment to which it was not fully adapted. Any ability as universal in a species as language is, Jaynes says, must have developed during an age when it would have had a great survival value or problem-solving value.

Probably the most dramatic environmental changes to which the human species has been subjected were the great ice ages. The severe changes in living conditions caused by the advancing ice could have resulted in sufficient pressures to make language necessary for survival. Jaynes suggests that language probably developed during the most recent ice age, which lasted from 70,000 to 10,000 years ago. Prior to that, he says, members of the human species probably communicated as present-day monkeys and apes do, with visual, vocal, and tactile (touch) signals. Most likely their language was without **syntax,** the meaningful arrangement of words in phrases or sentences.

How did language begin? Like Condillac, Jaynes believes that language may have begun with the "language of action." This type of communication ability is seen in many species, and it often consists of visual–gestural (sign language) communication. But visual signals became less effective as early human populations moved into the darker northern climates and as tool use made it important to free the hands for other activities. Under such pressures, it is possible that vocal signals took on the function that was formerly performed by visual signals alone.

The first real elements of speech, suggests Jaynes, were the variations in the endings of intentional cries and their association with different meanings. This was a step toward syntactic language. Jaynes goes on to explain how the different parts of speech and syntax were developed during the relatively short span of 70,000 years.

Jaynes's theory of the evolution of language is based on a mixture of available information and guesswork about the past. Like any theory, it should not be considered the final word. As new evidence is gathered, the theory may have to be modified. However, such a theory is valuable because it offers a framework within which to think about the nature of language and all that it implies about the nature of humanity.

LEARNING A LANGUAGE

No one is born speaking a particular language. Everyone has to learn to use words and sentences. And anyone who has ever tried to learn a foreign language knows how difficult such a task can be. A child usually needs four years to master its native language. During its first few months of life, an infant does little more than make meaningless sounds. As the infant's speech equipment and brain develop, the sounds become more complex. By the time most children are six months old, they can make a variety of sounds and they even seem to enjoy hearing the sounds they can make.

The infantile cooing and babbling sounds that children make are the same around the world. Humans seem to be pre-wired to make such sounds. The more complex sounds that six-month-old children begin to make are the beginnings of a language. But a particular language is not pre-wired into each individual child, so language must be learned. No one is quite sure of all the processes that are involved in learning a language, but one factor seems to be of primary importance — *imitation.* At a very early age, children begin to imitate the sounds that the people around them make. As infants attempt to imitate speech, they eventually begin to produce sounds that resemble words. And when a child

FIG. 7–3.
Imitation is of primary importance in learning a language. Infants imitate the sounds that are made by people around them, whether it be English or Spanish.

(usually by its first birthday) manages to come out with something like "mama" or "papa," the parents usually encourage the child to say that word over and over.

By the time a child reaches its second birthday, it has usually learned the names of many objects in its environment. A small child will point to a ball and say "ball." (In a Spanish-speaking home, the child will say "pelota.") The parents smile and reward the child for such an achievement and encourage it to go on to name other objects. One-word utterances gradually become two-word and three-word sentences. As a child continues to imitate its parents or other teachers and as the parents continue to reward and encourage correct responses, the child begins to build up a large vocabulary and to use words in a grammatically proper manner. With continued imitation, practice, and encouragement, a child usually learns to use its native language effectively by about its fourth birthday. By the time most people get to college, they are familiar with at least 15,000 words. And with this language the young child and the college student gain information, communicate, think, and solve problems.

Is Language Learning Innate?

Some scientists believe that our brains are innately wired so that all humans learn to talk in more or less the same way. These scientists note that most languages have a fairly similar structure — that we all tend to speak in sentences in which there is a subject, a verb, and one or more objects. According to this viewpoint, if all our languages have a similar grammar or underlying structure, then it is likely that our brains have imposed this structure on the languages. Thus, some aspects of language learning are surely innately determined.

Other scientists disagree. They believe that our brains can be taught to process informational inputs in millions of different ways, and that humans are quite capable of learning languages that don't have the same underlying logic or structure as their native language does.

As is typically the case in these nature–nurture battles, the truth seems to be somewhere in the middle. Most human brains do tend to process incoming informaion in rather standard ways—that is, we associate two events because they occurred at the same time, and we need environmental feedback in order to learn new words and new ways of behaving. But there is no evidence presently available proving that we couldn't learn a language with a different basic structure from English—provided, of course, that someone could dream up such a language. It seems more likely that our ability to learn to communicate is inherited, but that the signs and symbols we use in talking with each other are determined more by our environments and our past history than by the structures of our brains.

THINKING

Psychologist John B. Watson once described thinking as nothing more than a very quiet type of talking. And at times thought does seem to be a sort of "mental speech," because all the thinking that we are conscious of involves the internal manipulation of words and sentences—or at least ideas and concepts that are consciously expressed in words. But we should remember that conscious thought occurs primarily in the "speaking hemisphere" of the brain. The nonspeaking hemisphere may have its own nonverbal way of processing incoming information.

Surely we have ample evidence that thinking is possible without language in many instances. Some people, for example, can think in images. Other people, such as musicians, can sometimes think in sounds. Most often, however, language is our tool of thought. And as we learn to speak, our ability to think develops.

Jean Piaget, the Swiss child psychologist, has spent many years studying the cognitive or mental development of children. From these studies and observations of children, Piaget has constructed a theory that traces the intellectual development of children and the mental stages that children seem to go through.

Adaptation, says Piaget, is the most important process in intellectual functioning. If it is cold outside, people adapt to the weather by putting on a coat. If it is hot outside, people adapt by taking off some clothes. The weather, however, is only one environmental condition that people learn to adapt to. There are millions of sensations and experiences that people must learn to live with.

There are many specific ways of adapting to the environment but, explains Piaget, there are only two basic ways of adapting. One form of adaptation is **assimilation;** the other is **accommodation.** Assimilation means to take in, which is what an infant does as it listens to people around it talking. The child as-

similates or takes in the various sounds and parts of a language and gradually builds up its own language.

Accommodation is an outgoing process by which people adjust or adapt to the environment. After a child has assimilated some words, it will begin to use them. The outgoing words are usually meaningless at first. In order to speak properly and communicate efficiently, the child must learn to change the sounds it makes. The child must learn to accommodate its speech to conform to the speech of the people around it, or no one will know what it wants. By assimilation and accommodation, therefore, the child learns to adapt to the particular language of its environment. And each assimilation and each accommodation leads to mental growth and development.

With experience and a parent's help, a child will learn not to touch hot objects. After touching something hot and hearing the word "hot" several times, most children will assimilate the meaning of the word "hot" and accommodate by not touching certain objects. The result is a useful adaptation that keeps the child from getting burned. To the child, the word "hot" is no longer a meaningless sound. The child learns that the word "hot" applies to more than one object. The world is full of things that are hot and that should not be touched. The child begins to build up a mental concept or category of things that are hot. Similar concepts for such things as food, water, toys, and people soon develop. See the diagram below.

FIG. 7-4.
Children learn by assimilating, or taking in, various sounds and actions around them. Then children accommodate their speech and action to their environment.

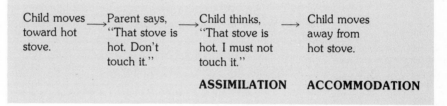

Child moves toward hot stove.	→	Parent says, "That stove is hot. Don't touch it."	→	Child thinks, "That stove is hot. I must not touch it."	→	Child moves away from hot stove.
				ASSIMILATION		**ACCOMMODATION**

In order to form concepts or ideas about the world, says Piaget, three things are necessary. The first is *experience* — touching something hot. The second thing necessary in concept formation is *social transmission,* or the passing along of information by parents or teachers — "Don't touch that, it's hot!" The third necessary factor in concept formation and mental development is *maturation* — a one-month-old child is just not ready to understand the word "hot," or to form a mental category of hot objects.

Piaget's Four Stages

The **maturation** of mental development, says Piaget, is divided into four stages or periods: (1) the sensory-motor stage, (2) the pre-operational stage, (3) the concrete operational stage, and (4) the stage of formal operations. Piaget believes that each child must go through each of these stages in the same order, no matter what culture the child is reared in or how much experience and training a child receives. Various parts of the stages may overlap, and some children may go faster than others (especially with more experiences and teaching), but the steps must always be taken in the same order.

Not all research supports Piaget's theory, and some children do seem to be able to handle certain mental problems before Piaget's theory predicts that they should. What probably happens is that maturation and intellectual development are continuous. There may be no specific stages. The process of mental development is easier to understand, however, if it is broken down into major stages.

The Sensory-Motor Stage

During the sensory-motor stage (from birth to about the second birthday) the first noticeable signs of intelligence seem to be related to a child's sensory perceptions and motor activities. A child in the sensory-motor stage can follow a moving object with its eyes, turn its head in response to a noise, and begin to reach out and touch and grasp things. At first a child is only conscious of itself; but gradually as the child reaches out to the objects and people in its world, it begins to build up a mental picture that contains more than just itself. By the age of two, with the beginnings of language and the ability to communicate and use symbolism, children have usually had enough sensory-motor experience to realize that they are not the center of the universe.

The Pre-operational Period

During the pre-operational stage (from about two to seven years) a child begins to acquire the ability to perform internal mental activities or operations—as opposed to purely physical operations. During the sensory-motor stage, for instance, a child will reach for a toy or object that it wants. In the pre-operational stage the child learns to think about and ask for toys. With this ability to imagine and symbolize the world, pre-operational children begin to play at "make-

A child can follow a moving object with its eyes and can reach out and grasp things during the sensory-motor stage.

Pre-operational stage children play "make-believe" and pretend they are someone else.

believe." In pretending or making believe that they are someone else (a parent, a teacher, or a doctor), young children assimilate and begin to learn the customs and manners of the people around them. By imitating teachers, doctors, and other people with whom they come in contact, young children accommodate to new and strange experiences.

No one can see the mind or its mental developments, but some of Piaget's experiments with young children demonstrate rather vividly the mental changes that a child seems to go through. Piaget, for instance, shows a child two balls of soft clay of equal size. Once the child agrees that the balls are the same size, Piaget rolls one of the balls into a long sausage shape. He then asks the child if the two pieces of clay are still the same size and if they still contain the same amount of clay. The pre-operational child will usually say that the sausage contains more clay because it is longer. If the sausage is then rolled back into a ball, the child will once again agree that both balls contain the same amount of clay. A pre-operational child's mind, says Piaget, has not developed to the stage where it can grasp **transformations,** or changes in shape.

By the time a child reaches the age of six or seven (sometime called the age of reason), transformations do not seem as hard for the child to understand. If the sausage is rolled out very thin and long, the child may still say that it is bigger than the ball. But if the sausage is short and fat (closer to the shape of the ball) the child will realize that the sausage and the ball contain the same amount of clay. The child may even wonder why anyone would ask such a stupid question.

The Concrete Operations Stage

FIG. 7–5.
Although both pieces contain the same amount of clay, children in the pre-operational stage often say that the rolled-out piece is bigger because it is longer.

During the next stage of development, the period of concrete operations (from about seven to 11 years of age), a child's thinking begins to speed up. The child can look at a ball of clay and realize that it will contain the same amount of clay, no matter what shape it is in. The child gradually begins to understand other types of changes. A cup of milk in a bowl, for instance, is the same amount of milk as a cup of milk in a tall thin glass—even though the containers have different shapes. During the stage of concrete operations, a child will use its mental ability to think about what happens to concrete or solid objects without having to actually experiment with the objects. Because the child can mentally skip over the physical or sensory-motor parts of an experience, its mental operations can be greatly speeded up. A pre-operational child might search through every room in a house for a lost toy, but a child in the concrete operations stage can sit back and think about where the toy might be without having to go through all the motions of a physical search. A child in the concrete operations stage can usually think about any concrete or physical object that it has had some experience with. The same child cannot usually extend such thinking to cover nonconcrete or **abstract** objects.

The Period of Formal Operations

Abstract thinking comes during the final stage of mental development, the period of formal operations (after the age of 11 or 12). Piaget calls this final period the stage of formal operations because during this stage adolescents learn to follow the form of thinking or reasoning. In the formal operations stage a child can think about thoughts or operate on operations. Piaget explains much of this stage in terms of mathematics. Someone in the formal operations stage can understand terms like "a billion years," which must be thought of in abstract rather than concrete terms. People in the formal operations stage can generalize and form hypotheses about such things as justice, truth, honor, and personality. It is people thinking at the level of formal operations who read Sherlock Holmes mysteries and solve difficult intellectual problems.

According to Piaget, our mental development is complete by the time we are 14 or 15 years of age—just as our physical development is typically complete by the time we are17 or 18 years of age. In our later years, we may grow fatter or thinner, we may develop our muscles or let them gradually weaken—but after we are 18 or so, we don't really "grow" any more. In similar fashion, Piaget's stage of formal operations marks the end of the growth of our basic mental processes. We may learn (and forget) a great deal after that age, but in Piaget's terms this type of learning is comparable to adding fat or exercising one's muscles.

MEMORY

By the time we reach the stage of formal operations, we are quite familiar with solving problems. Anyone who has gone through the school system in the United States, for instance, is familiar with one particular type of problem solving. It is taking tests. Most of us realize that our ability to pass an exam depends on several important abilities. We must (1) obtain informational inputs, (2) hold or store them until we need them, and (3) then recall these specific inputs in order to answer the questions on the test.

All this information comes to us through our senses. Our receptors code incoming messages and then send them onto our brains where the information can be interpreted or made sense of. But information comes in so fast from so many sources that even the best brain cannot process or interpret all the inputs our bodies receive. With the help of our reticular activating system (see Chapter 3), we screen out many incoming stimuli and focus on the ones that are most important to us. Generally speaking, any information that we don't pay attention to doesn't get filed away in our memories for very long.

Sensory-Information Storage

Sometimes your brain needs a second or more to decide whether or not a given input is important enough for you to pay attention to. Because there is this short delay, your senses have a mechanism for holding onto some stimulus inputs. Your senses, in other words, have a primitive sort of memory. When a flash bulb goes off in front of you, the image receptors in your eyes hold or store the image

FIG. 7–6.
Some sensory stimuli
are held in your brain
only a few seconds;
they become part of
your short-term
memory, or STM,
and are then forgot-
ten. But if the infor-
mation is important
enough, it will be
processed and held
by the brain for
longer periods of
time; it becomes part
of your long-term
memory, or LTM.

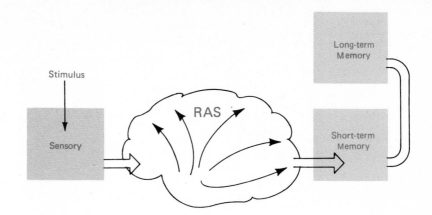

of that flash for several seconds or longer—which is one reason why a flash bulb "blinds" you for a few seconds. Even less intense stimuli are also held in your senses for very brief periods of time. This type of memory is called **sensory-information storage (SIS)**.

Under normal circumstances, your senses do not hold onto informational inputs for very long, but research has shown that SIS can last for up to several minutes. In one experiment, subjects in a dark room were shown a bright color slide for only 1/50 of a second. The room remained dark and some of the subjects were able to hold the image of the slide and actually see it in front of their eyes for several minutes. By pressing slightly on their eyeballs, a few subjects were able to bring the image back as long as 30 minutes after the slide had first been shown.

Whenever you look at something, the sense receptors in your eyes continue to send the picture or image of this object to your brain for a brief period of time. However, as soon as you look at something new, the inputs from this new object "erase" from your visual SIS the image of the previous object and send a new message to your brain. But as long as the SIS in your eyes holds onto an image, your brain can extract information from that image and decide if you ought to pay more attention to the input. Once the input has been erased from your visual SIS, your brain can no longer retrieve any information about the object directly from your eyes.

Short-Term Memory

Once a stimulus input reaches your brain, the input is typically held in your **short-term memory (STM)** while your brain makes a more thorough interpretation of the input. But your short-term memory can hold information for only a few seconds longer than your SIS usually does. Those few seconds, however, are usually enough for your brain to decide what to make of the input and—just

FIG. 7–7.
Information runs out
of your short-term
memory like water
from a leaky bucket.

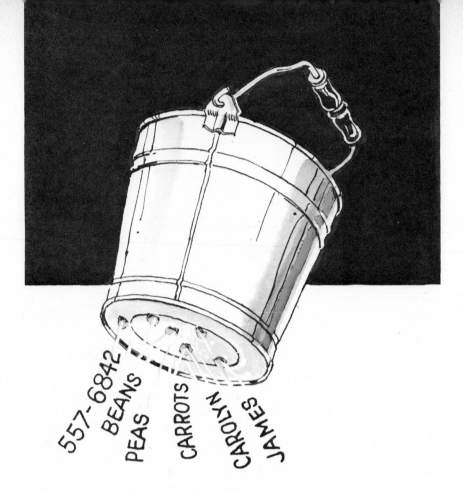

as important — whether or not you should file the input away in more permanent memory storage.

Your STM is like a bucket with a hole in it. Information that pours into the top of this bucket constantly leaks out the bottom within a few seconds. In addition, your STM "bucket" is very small. It can hold only about five to nine items of information at one time. But as long as an item is in your STM, you can pull it out for inspection or remember it in fairly precise detail.

Most people are familiar with the workings of the STM. You are reading a book, for instance, when someone walks in and asks you a question. You look up and say, "What?" But before the question is repeated, your brain has fished the question out of the STM bucket and is already preparing an answer. If six questions are asked, however, you probably won't be able to remember or to answer all of them. Some will have leaked out of the bucket in the length of time it takes you to answer the others.

Your STM is almost always in use. In many cases — such as the immediately recalled question — your STM works on its own without any conscious help. There are many instances, however, when you must remember something for longer than a few seconds. In these instances, there are a few ways of getting around the shortcomings of your STM. You need a phone number, so you look the number up, dial it, and wait for an answer. In most cases the number will leak out of your STM bucket before the person you are calling answers. But what if the phone is busy? Then you have to look up the number again and redial. After you have done this several times, you may decide to memorize the number or consciously hold it in your memory. Usually you can hold a phone number in your STM for quite a while by simply blocking out further inputs to your STM bucket—that is, by concentrating on the number and screening out other distracting stimuli. But if you are trying to concentrate when someone comes up and asks you a question, you may forget the number while answering the question. In such cases, you may wish to *rehearse* the number by repeating it over and over to yourself. This rehearsal reinserts the number into your STM over and over again, and is a very effective way to keep information in your STM for brief periods of time.

Most likely you can hold at least five items in your STM at any given time. But if you must remember a grocery list that contains 15 items, you may have a problem recalling everything on the list. One method of solving this problem and remembering more than five or six items is called **chunking.** By dividing the 15-item list into three 5-item chunks, you can often insert the entire list into your STM bucket. For instance, you might divide the grocery list into three or more major categories—perhaps fruits, vegetables, and meats. Then you can organize the entire list by putting several items under each category. Once you have done this, you need remember only the three major categories. When you recall these categories, you will usually be able to remember the items you have filed under each category.

Mnemonics

Some lists cannot be organized into categories or "chunks" as easily as groceries. However, there are a number of other "memory tricks" that you can use to help you remember things. **Mnemonics**—from the Greek word for "memory"—is the name given to devices or tricks that aid the memory. One type of mnemonic or memory trick is called an **acronym.** An acronym is a word that is made up of the first letters of several other words. For example, USSR is an acronym that stands for "Union of Soviet Socialist Republics," while NASA is an acronym that stands for "National Aeronautics and Space Administration." If you have a long list of unrelated words to memorize, you might wish to make up your own acronym. SIS and STM are both acronyms that should help you remember Sensory-Information Storage and Short-Term Memory.

Abbreviations are another mnemonic that most of us use. Yet another type of mnemonic is the jingle that many people memorize to help them remember how many days are in the months of the year: "Thirty days hath September, April, June, and November. . . ." The rhythm and rhymes of the jingle help us recall the entire sequence of months and days.

Could you remember all the items on this shopping list?
Hamburger
Carrots
Potatoes
Oranges
Beans
Pork chops
Apples
Lettuce
Bananas
Peas
Chicken
Grapes
Veal cutlets
Peaches
Steak

You could probably remember many more items if you "chunked" them in categories:

Fruit	Vegetables	Meat
Peaches	Carrots	Hamburger
Apples	Potatoes	Veal cutlets
Bananas	Peas	Pork chops
Grapes	Beans	Steak
Oranges	Lettuce	Chicken

A fourth type of mnemonic involves deliberately using the law of association. Most of us have trouble remembering names—but not faces. When you meet someone new, you might try associating the person's name with how the person looks. Thus, if you are introduced to a big, muscular man named Smith, you can associate his name with the fact that blacksmiths have to be big and strong in order to put shoes on horses.

Long-Term Memory

By organizing information into chunks, and by using mnemonics, we can often extend the life of information in our memories for minutes or hours or even years. But these tricks do not really explain how we can recall some events for decades without ever really trying to. Names, faces, songs, mathematical formulas, historical facts—we store all of these and millions of other informational inputs in our brains and then recall them whenever we wish. The portion of your memory that is able to hold so much information for so long is called the long-term memory (LTM).

Your long-term memory or LTM seems to be practically limitless. That is,

FIG. 7–8.
For short-term memory, your brain categorizes information much the same way magazines are arranged temporarily on a drug store rack. For long-term memory, your brain classifies and files information more carefully much the same way that books are stored in a library.

your LTM is large enough to contain as much information as you can put into it. Unlike your STM, your LTM does not really have a leak in it.

No one is quite sure how the long-term memory works, but it seems to be dependent on a special type of organization. The LTM is organized like a large library. Compared to this library of the brain, the STM is only a drugstore magazine rack. Magazines and books come and go from the rack but none stay forever. Some items, however, are taken off the rack or out of the STM and placed in the library of the LTM. The transfer to the LTM is not done in a random fashion, however. Before an item can be stored in the brain's LTM library, the item must be properly coded. That is, the item must be identified in some way and then put on the correct shelf in a certain section of the brain's library. Information about trombones, for instance, generally does not belong in the history section of the brain's library. If it did, no one would ever be able to find the information on trombones. In other words, a bit of information about trombones must be stored in the LTM in a certain way or that information will not be remembered or recalled when it is needed. Trombone information should properly be stored in the musical instrument section.

Trombones do, however, have a history. Therefore, when the trombone information is brought to the library of the brain and placed on the correct shelf, an index card is filled out for the history section. Similar cards are filled out for color, shape, use, and sound of trombones. Other index cards might have information on people who play trombones. Each of the index cards is filled out and filed in its proper place in the LTM, and each of the cards is cross-indexed to refer to all of the other cards on trombones. In this way, when the librarian wants information on trombones, there are many index cards that can be checked. And each card should contain information that will send the librarian not only to the musical instrument section but to all of the other sections where information on trombones can be found. Getting all of the coding and cross–referencing done

FIG. 7–9.
In long-term memory, your brain categorizes information and stores it in your brain so that it is ready for quick retrieval — somewhat like the index cards found in the library.

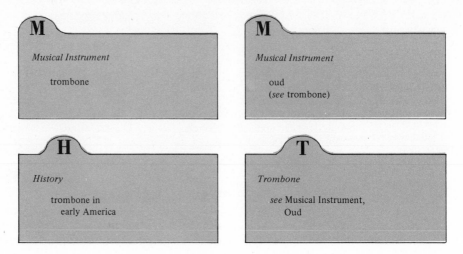

takes time, but it is the most important factor involved in placing new books or information in the brain's LTM library. Information that is inadequately coded is difficult to retrieve and is sometimes lost to conscious recall — rather like a library book that somebody has filed away on the wrong shelf.

Information that has many associations or many index cards is most easily found or remembered. The word trombone, for instance, has many associations for some people. As soon as these people hear the word trombone, they can remember what a trombone is, and they can remember much of the other information that they have stored away on trombones.

The word "oud" does not have very many associations for most people in the United States. In fact, most people have probably never even heard of an oud. And if they haven't heard the word, they certainly don't remember what it means. In parts of North Africa, however, almost everyone knows what an oud is. It is a guitar- or mandolin-like instrument that is more popular in North Africa than the trombone is in the United States. As soon as people in North Africa hear the word "oud" they immediately make many associations (they have seen and heard ouds many times in many places, and they or their friends may play the oud), and they remember exactly what an oud is. Many of these same North Africans, however, would not know what a trombone is. Even if they have heard of a trombone, they probably have few associations or mental index cards on trombones.

The general rule applying to your LTM seems to be this one: The more associations you have about a given item, the easier it is for you to pull that item out of LTM. Thus, any time you want to be able to recall an item at a later date — such as the name of someone interesting you've just met — you should make a strong effort to link that item (name) with as many familiar experiences as you can. For the more associations or linkages you can create between the new items and things already stored away in LTM, the more readily you will be able to pluck that name out of long-term storage later on.

REMEMBERING AND FORGETTING

If the word "oud" is on a test tomorrow, will you remember it? Probably. Will you remember it next year? Only if you take oud lessons, or make a conscious effort to form some other strong associations with the instrument. But there are some memories that are stored away in your LTM that you can retrieve only with the greatest of difficulty. Under normal conditions, for instance, most people can't recall much about their early childhood. This inability to remember one's very early years probably comes from the fact that most of our index cards for the LTM are filled out with words and language. A young child who does not hear or speak a language may not be able to properly code an event for its memory. Also, young children have had very little experience and, therefore, cannot usually make enough associations for proper coding. Some psychologists, however, have reported that drugs can be used to help people recall early life experiences sometimes. And hypnotists, too, have seemingly been able to get people to recall events from their early life. It is likely that the most that drugs and hypnotism do is help people to concentrate and search through their index cards very thoroughly. In general, however, it seems that it is much easier to get information *into* than *out* of the LTM.

Eidetic Imagery

One type of memory that many people have heard of but that few people have experienced is called **eidetic imagery,** or a photographic memory. Some people, usually children, are able to look at a page of type or a picture for a few seconds and then recall everything on the page or in the picture. Either these people can hold a complex image for a very long time or their brains are able to make an incredible amount of associations in a very short time. Eidetic imagery

FIG. 7–10.
The ability to recall everything on a page or in a picture is called eidetic imagery. Popularly known as photographic memory, this ability can prove very useful when taking a test.

has not been fully explained, but those few people who seem to have a photographic memory do not seem to be any better off than people with a normal memory. On regular school tests, children with eidetic imagery don't usually perform any better than anyone else.

Forgetting

Forgetting occurs for several reasons. Items from the SIS are forgotten as soon as new sensory information replaces and erases them. Items from the STM are forgotten after a short time or when too many new items are added. Items from the LTM are forgotten for several other reasons. Some types of brain damage, including the gradual loss of brain tissue that comes with old age or with **senility,** can cause loss of memory. A severe shock or a bump on the head can sometimes make a person forget things that happened just prior to the misfortune. We call this type of memory loss **amnesia.** Scientists believe that amnesia occurs because the shock or accident prevents the brain from transferring items from STM to LTM. Your brain needs about 30 minutes to store items away in LTM; any event that disrupts the normal chemical functioning of your brain is likely to erase or wipe out your memory of what happened to you for about 30 minutes prior to the disruption.

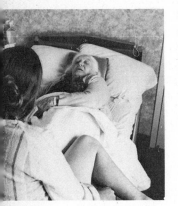

Sometimes senile people do not recognize their own relatives. The loss of brain tissue that comes with old age often causes people to lose their memory.

Because some part of LTM storage does seem to involve biochemical processes, there are many drugs that will cause amnesia or forgetting. Alcohol, marijuana, and some types of antibiotics can apparently interfere with and prevent your brain from coding items for storage in your LTM.

Amnesia can also occur because people want to forget. Freud explained some types of amnesia or forgetting as a sort of unconscious defense mechanism. This type of motivated forgetting is called **repression.** One of Freud's patients, for instance, could never seem to recall the name of one particular business associate. Freud found out that the business associate had married the woman that the patient was in love with. After the marriage, every time the patient thought about his business associate, the memory of the entire affair came back and caused the patient pain. In order to avoid this pain, some part of the patient's unconscious mind blocked out all memories of the business associate, including his name.

Since Freud's time, experiments have shown that pain can cause people to forget or repress certain memories. In one experiment, for instance, subjects were shown a list of nonsense syllables (usually three letters that don't make any sense such as "xod" or "acz"). Each nonsense syllable was paired with a normal word, and the subjects in the experiment were supposed to remember which words were associated with which nonsense syllables. During the training or learning part of the experiment, the subjects were given a slightly painful electric shock when some of the nonsense syllables were presented. The subjects were later tested to see which of the associations they remembered. The nonsense syllables were shown, and the subjects tried to remember the words that went with them. In many instances, these people could not recall the words that were supposed to be paired with the nonsense syllables that had been accompanied by the painful shock.

MEMORY RESEARCH

Today many people, including school children, use pocket calculators to help solve problems.

Scientists may have discovered ways of interfering with our memories, but they are also hard at work on research projects that may eventually help us improve our memories and make our problem solving easier. The electronic computer, for instance, is one of the greatest technical advances of the twentieth century. Fifty years ago such computers didn't even exist. Thirty years ago most computers were gigantic, expensive, complicated machines that few people had access to and even fewer people knew how to use. Today, most hospitals, universities, and big businesses have or share computers. There are also pocket-sized **calculators** that most people can afford to own and learn to use. In the near future, people will have more than midget mathematical calculators. The day will come, experts predict, when everyone, even young schoolchildren, will have their own personal minicomputers that could solve many of their daily problems and, properly used, could help answer test questions for them.

Memories in a Molecule?

Another line of research that could be promising for us problem solvers is an attempt by scientists to isolate what has been called a **memory molecule** — a chemical substance or molecule that actually contains one or more memories. If such molecules do exist, and if they could be manufactured in large numbers, presumably people could get an injection of algebra, history, or even Chinese. Getting an injection of the proper memory molecules would obviously make studying, test taking, and problem solving a lot easier for us.

The electronic computer can be used to categorize and process vast amounts of information to be retrieved when needed. It has become the memory machine for big business.

The memory molecule research sounds like science fiction, but many scientists have found evidence that such chemicals might really exist. This line of research began in the early 1960s, when psycholgists at the University of Michigan began performing experiments with planarian flatworms. Planarians are very simple animals but they do have brains that are capable of learning. More than this, flatworms have a very unique talent—they can **regenerate.** If you cut a flatworm in half, the head-end would soon regenerate or regrow a new tail, while the tail-end would regenerate a new head complete with brain, eyes, and sense receptors. If you cut a large planarian in five pieces, all the pieces would soon regrow their missing parts and become flatworms again. If you split the head-end with a razor blade, each piece would regenerate, and you would end up with a two-headed worm. Each head would have its own working brain, and the heads would compete or "argue" about which one was going to control the worm's body.

The Michigan psychologists used Pavlovian methods (discussed in Chapter 6) to condition their flatworms to respond to light as a conditioning stimulus. The scientists used electric shock as the unconditional stimulus. If you pass a mild electric shock through a trough of water containing an untrained planarian, the worm will always contract or curl up as soon as the shock hits it. The shock is an unconditioned stimulus since you don't have to teach the planarian to curl up when it is shocked—the flatworm will do so the first time you stimulate it electrically. The scientists used the light as a conditioned stimulus because they had found that planarians seldom respond to the onset of a light by curling up. So the Michigan group began pairing the light with the shock—that is, they would turn on the light for two seconds just prior to shocking them. At first, the planarians curled up only when the shock came on. But after 150 trials, they regularly responded to the onset of the light by contracting. At this point, the "curling up" had become a conditioned response that the flatworms made as soon as the conditioned stimulus (light) was presented to them.

Once the planarians had been conditioned, the psychologists cut the animals in half and allowed them to regenerate. A month later, the flatworms were tested to see which half remembered the original conditioning. Surprisingly, both the tails with new heads and the heads with new tails remembered the conditioning.

Next the Michigan scientists cut trained flatworms into three or four parts and let them regenerate. A month later, when the regenerated pieces had replaced all their missing parts, the animals were tested. All the regenerated animals seemed to remember the training given to the original planarians.

When the head of a planarian is split, each piece will regenerate a head with a working brain.

The Cannibal Worm Studies

How can the tail or the middle section of a trained flatworm remember as much as the head (which keeps the brain of the original planarian)? The Michigan psychologists concluded that when a worm learns, the memory is stored not just in the animal's brain, but throughout the animal's body. The only way that such memory storage could take place would be if the flatworms' memories were

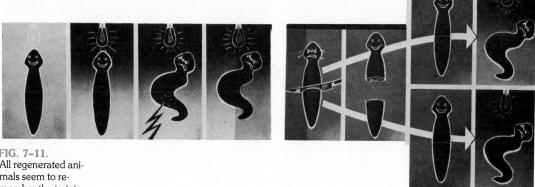

FIG. 7–11.
All regenerated animals seem to remember the training given the original planarians.

somehow stored in a chemical molecule. In other words, the Michigan scientists assumed that when a flatworm was conditioned, some kind of unique chemical change took place throughout its body.

These psychologists made one additional assumption. They guessed that if two worms learned the same task, the chemical changes inside both their bodies would be almost identical. If two worms with the same training had similar chemicals inside their bodies, then it ought to be possible to transfer the "memory" of the task to an untrained planarian if the chemicals inside a trained animal could somehow be gotten inside the body of the untrained worm. In an attempt to test this rather wild idea, the Michigan group took advantage of the fact that many planarians are **cannibals.**

The cannibals used in this experiment were all untrained. Half of the cannibals were fed "victims" that had been given light-shock training; the other half were fed "victims" that were completely untrained. Two days later—after the cannibals had presumbly "digested" their meals—both groups of cannibals were tested with the light. Those cannibal planarians that had devoured "educated" victims responded to the light as if they "remembered" the training given to their victims. Those cannibals that had eaten untrained victims responded to the light as if they had never seen it before. These experiments—presuming their results are valid—suggested not only that memory storage is in part chemical, but also that memories can be transferred from one organism to another.

But what chemicals are involved in memory storage? In yet another experiment, the Michigan psychologists trained large numbers of flatworms using the light-shock conditioning technique. The scientists then ground up the worms and extracted a complex chemical called **RNA** from the "worm soup." They then injected this RNA directly into the bodies of untrained planarians. A second group of animals was injected with RNA extracted from the bodies of untrained worms. Both groups were then tested with the light. The worms that received RNA from untrained planarians seemed to "remember" what the light meant;

the worms that received RNA from untrained planarians showed no evidence of "remembering" that the light meant shock was coming. These results suggest that RNA may be one chemical involved in memory storage.

Memory Transfer in Rats and Goldfish

In more recent experiments, Georges Ungar has reported a similar type of *memory transfer* in rats and in goldfish. Ungar trained rats to fear the dark. He then ground up their brains and extracted various chemicals from the "brain soup." When one of these brain chemicals was injected into untrained rats, the animals reacted as if they too had been trained to fear the dark.

The chemical Ungar isolated is a protein that he called **scotophobin,** from the Greek words meaning "fear of the dark." Similar but slightly different proteins have been extracted from the brains of rats trained to ignore the sound of a loud bell, and from the brains of goldfish trained to avoid certain colors. Ungar claimed that these chemicals are also memory molecules and that when they are injected into untrained animals, these chemicals help the animals "remember" the training they have not received.

The memory molecule research is fascinating, but it is far from being conclusive. Although scientists in more than 100 different laboratories have successfully repeated the flatworm and rat studies, many other scientists have failed to get good results. Many researchers claim that scotophobin and the other so-called memory molecules have nothing to do with memory. Such chemicals, some scientists say, merely change an animal's behavior (as many drugs do), but do not contain any memories. Thus, the issue is still in doubt and still hotly contested among scientists.

Even if there is such a thing as a memory molecule, it will probably be quite some time before you can study for a test by taking an injection of a teacher's memory. Until memory molecules are developed for humans—if they ever are—people will have to rely on more conventional methods of solving their problems. Like Sherlock Holmes, we will have to work with the "computers" we were born with—our brains—and with the information and memories that are fed into those computers. But with this equipment we can solve most of our problems.

PROBLEM SOLVING

How do we go about solving our problems? There is no single method of solving all problems, but there is a general method of attacking problems. The *first step* in solving any problem is realizing that a problem exists. Take three examples—a student, an artist, and Sherlock Holmes. A student knows that at test time the correct answers must be filled in on a blank test paper. A painter knows that a blank canvas has to be filled. Sherlock Holmes knew that he had three days to find a well-hidden photograph. In each case the problem is easily recognizable.

The *second step* in problem solving calls for thinking and memory. The student looks at the test questions and tries to think about and remember all of the information that will go into the answers. The painter remembers various paintings and painting techniques, and thinks about how those techniques can be applied in a new painting. Sherlock Holmes gathered as much information as he could about Irene Adler and tried to figure out where she would keep a valuable photograph.

The *third step* in problem solving consists of trying out the solution you have decided upon. Once someone confronted with a problem has all the available information, that person will usually try out various solutions in his or her head and then decide on one of these solutions. The student recalls as many facts as possible and writes out the answers to the test questions. The painter decides on subject matter and style and gets to work. Holmes decided that Irene Adler would probably keep the photograph hidden in her home. He disguised himself as a priest and used a trick to get himself admitted to Irene's home.

The *final step* in problem solving calls for an evaluation of the solution that has been tried. The student taking the test remembers some of the facts and forgets others. A teacher makes the final evaluation. The painter comes up with a highly original and abstract painting that is evaluated in several ways. Some people see the painting as a creative work of art that represents the world in a beautiful and radically different manner. Others see the painting and say it is nothing but a meaningless jumble of wild colors and strange shapes. Holmes evaluated his theory about where the photo was hidden in a rather clever way. Dr. Watson was hiding outside Irene Adler's home waiting for a signal from Holmes. When the signal was given, Watson threw a smoke bomb through the window. Holmes immediately began to yell, "Fire! Fire!" When Irene heard the alarm, she ran immediately to where her most prized possession was hidden. Holmes had his eye on her every minute, and he soon knew exactly where the picture was hidden. Before Irene could take the photo out of its hiding place, Holmes yelled, "False alarm," and got rid of the smoke bomb. Irene relaxed and left the photo hidden, but Holmes already knew where it was. His plan was to return later that evening with the king and retrieve the scandalous picture. Unfortunately for Holmes and the king, this solution was not quite good enough.

FIG. 7–12.
The steps in problem solving are: (1) realizing the problem exists; (2) thinking how the problem can be solved; (3) trying out the solution; and (4) evaluating the solution.

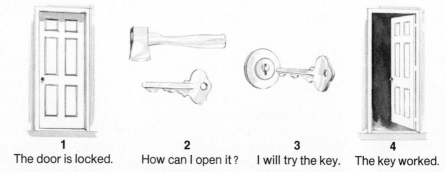

| 1 | 2 | 3 | 4 |
| The door is locked. | How can I open it? | I will try the key. | The key worked. |

Motivation

Why do some solutions fail and others succeed? There are several important factors involved in problem solving that can affect the outcome of any solution. One of these is motivation (see Chapter 5).

Motivation almost always has something to do with problem solving. Students who are highly motivated to get good grades—to please their parents, teachers, friends, or themselves—usually spend an adequate amount of time studying. If they study properly, they can make the correct associations and fit new information properly into the LTM. At test time, a highly motivated student will usually remember more information and perform better than a student who does not particularly care about getting good grades and who has not studied properly.

Motivation can sometimes have an adverse effect on problem solving, however. High levels of motivation can cause **anxiety.** A student who fears punishment or embarassment due to poor grades, for instance, might be highly motivated to perform well. But the anxiety that is sometimes associated with such motivation can cause people to "block" and perform poorly. The psychological pain that is associated with failure is like the electric shock that caused the subjects in the memory experiment to forget which words were associated with

Sometimes high levels of motivation can cause anxiety. A student who wants to achieve high grades may also fear failure so much that it interferes with his or her performance.

which nonsense syllables. A person who continually experiences failure may become even more anxious about future tests and do even worse.

Sherlock Holmes was highly motivated. He wanted to solve the king's problem so he worked hard to find the photograph. Holmes had his reputation to think about, but he did not become overanxious. He had rarely failed at anything, and he felt sure that he would come up with a good solution if he just used his brain. He did and he almost succeeded. The artist who did the abstract painting was motivated to do a beautiful and original interpretation of the world. All of the painter's skill, talent, and previous experience went into the painting, which many people judged to be a success.

Mental Set

Previous experience has a lot to do with problem solving. People tend to search for types of solutions that have been successful in the past. A person who has learned to use mnemonics, for instance, will tend to use such devices over and over whenever material has to be memorized, especially if the mnemonics have worked in the past. Much of our education system is based on teaching and developing types of solutions that are called **mental sets.** Mathematics courses teach a set of principles that can be applied to mathematical problems. When we apply the same principles over and over, we usually build up a set or habitual way of approaching a problem. Once a set has been developed, it is usually very useful in solving new problems. With a set way of attacking certain types of problems, people can go right to a solution without taking time to search for possible ways of solving the problem. A painter may study perspective and develop a set way of painting pictures with depth. Holmes had a set way of finding hidden objects.

Mental sets are useful but they can also cause problems. When a problem requires a new kind of solution, the old set may interfere with the search for a new solution. A detective with only one set way of finding hidden objects will fail whenever the object is not hidden in a place where the detective can watch the owner try to protect it. The best problem solvers are those who have a variety of mental sets that can be applied to their problems.

Functional Fixedness

Another mental factor influencing problem solving is the fact that people tend to use certain objects in set ways to solve certain problems. A pliers, for instance, is for grasping objects. The function of a pliers is fixed in the minds of most people, and people tend to forget that pliers can be used for different functions than grasping objects. N. R. F. Maier of the University of Michigan has devised a problem that demonstrates **functional fixedness.**

Problem: Two ropes are hanging from the ceiling, 15 feet apart. The solution to the problem requires that the ends of the ropes be tied together. The set way of approaching this problem would be to take the end of one rope, walk with it to the other hanging rope and then tie the two together. In this partular case,

FIG. 7–13.
People tend to use
certain objects in set
ways to solve prob-
lems. This drawing
illustrates how a cre-
ative person uses the
pliers in an original
way to solve the
problem of tying to-
gether two ropes
which are hanging 15
feet apart.

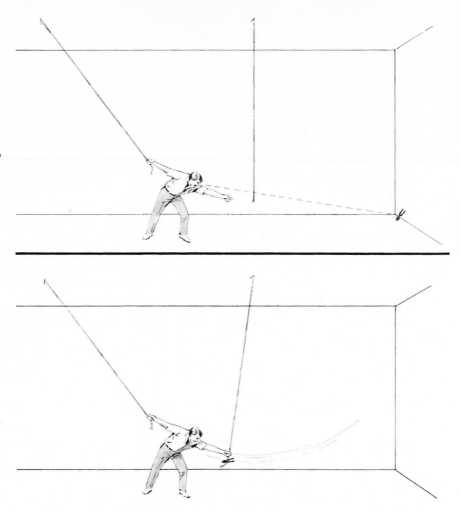

however, the ropes are too far apart. A person holding onto one rope cannot
stretch far enough to reach the second rope without letting go of the first rope.
The set solution does not work.

In the corner of the room with the hanging ropes there is a pliers. A person with a fixed idea about the function of a pliers might not see any way to
use the pliers to tie the two ropes together. A person with a more flexible
mind might have different ideas about pliers. The pliers can be picked up
and tied to the end of one of the ropes. The rope with the pliers can then be
set swinging in a wide arc. While this rope is swinging back and forth, it will be
possible to walk over to the other rope and wait for the weighted rope to come
close enough to be grabbed. With the two ropes in hand, there is no trick to tying
them together.

Originality and Creativity

Most problems are solved by directed thinking. That is, most people follow specific direct steps in thinking about and attacking their problems. Sometimes, however, directed thinking is not enough. New and different ways of responding must be tried. Sherlock Holmes used **originality** in trying to find the photograph. By thinking creatively he was almost able to solve his problem. While creativity and originality are often helpful, they do not always work, however. Holmes's originality did not work in this case because Irene Adler was also creative. She had all the mental equipment necessary to solve her own problems and to outwit Sherlock Holmes. Irene rushed to where her valuable photo was hidden when Holmes yelled, "Fire!" But as soon as she did so, she realized what was happening and figured out the detective's plan. When Holmes returned several hours later with the king, he expected to walk right to where the picture was hidden. Instead, he found an empty house. Both Irene and the photo were gone. Holmes was amazed. From that moment on, Irene Adler was one of the few people he truly respected. She had earned this respect by solving her problem. And she did it without the help of injections of memory molecules — she used only her personal computer — her brain.

► *SUMMARY*

1. Sherlock Holmes, one of fiction's best known detectives, has remained a popular character because of his fascinating ability to solve almost any problem that came his way. As we have seen in this chapter, the use of language, thinking, and memory is an important factor in problem solving.

2. Problem solving begins with the gathering of information, and **language** is one of the most important methods we have for collecting information. A language is a system of signs and symbols that one person uses to communicate with another.

3. The question of whether the human language ability is innate or learned has not yet been answered, but it appears that both processes are involved and necessary. The human brain is prewired with the ability to learn a language, but learning, especially in the form of **imitation,** is probably a necessary part of acquiring a language.

4. Thinking is one of the most important of all human abilities. Piaget's description of the intellectual development of children helps us to better understand our own intellectual functioning.

5. Adaptation, according to Piaget, is the most important process in intellectual functioning. Two forms of adaptation are **assimilation** and **accommodation.** Assimilation means to take in, as in listening or gathering information. Accommodation is an outgoing process by which we adapt or adjust to our environment.

6. The maturation of mental development, says Piaget, takes place in four

stages: the **sensory-motor stage,** the **pre-operational stage,** the **concrete operations stage,** and the **period of formal operations.** Piaget believes that each child must go through these stages in the same order. He also believes that we complete our intellectual development by the time we are 14 or 15 years old.

7. Our ability to solve problems depends on obtaining information, holding or storing that information, and then recalling or remembering the information when it is needed. **Sensory-information storage (SIS)**, **short-term memory (STM)**, and **long-term memory (LTM)** are the names of the major memory processes that we use to store and retrieve information.

8. **Mnemonics** is the name given to devices or tricks that aid the memory. **Eidetic imagery** is the name given to the type of memory known as photographic memory.

9. Forgetting occurs for several reasons. Brain damage, senility, drugs, hypnotism, and severe shocks can all result in **amnesia** or loss of memory. Amnesia can also occur because people want to forget. This type of motivated forgetting is called **repression.**

10. Memory research, which may eventually help us in problem solving and remembering, suggests that memories may be stored in chemical molecules. Memory molecule research, however, is not conclusive, and it may be years, if ever, before any of us receive an injection of memory molecules.

11. Even without injections of memory molecules, most humans are expert at problem solving. The most important steps in problem solving (similar to the steps of the scientific method; see Chapter 1) are: (1) realizing that a problem exists, (2) thinking about the problem, (3) trying out various solutions, and (4) evaluating the solution.

12. Although motivation can sometimes lead to anxiety, motivation is always important in problem solving. **Mental set** and **functional fixedness** also aid in problem solving but can hinder us if they prevent us from being flexible and original in our thinking.

Suggested Readings

Gordon, William J. *Synectics*. New York: Harper & Row, 1961.
Lorayne, Harry. *Good memory — good student*. New York: Stein and Day, 1976.
Luria, A. R. *The mind of a mnemonist*. New York: Basic Books, 1968.
Wickelgren, W. A. *How to solve problems*. San Francisco: Freeman, 1974.

► STUDY GUIDE

A.   RECALL

Sentence Completion

1. _____, _____, and _____ are essential to

[p. 217]   both problem solving and survival.

2. A language is a system of _____ and _____ that one per-

[p. 217]   son can use to communicate with another.

3. A _____ is an abstraction — something that stands for a complex idea or
[p. 218]   experience of some kind.

4. About 2500 years ago the Greek historian _____ described one of the
[p. 219]   first known experiments with language.

5. The _____ of infants during the first months of life contains all the
[p. 220]   sounds necessary for the development of almost any language.

6. Condillac called the natural vocal gestures or cries of the beginning stages of lan-
[p. 220]   guage the "language of _____."

[p. 220]   7. _____ is the scientific study of the nature and structure of language.

8. Ashley Montagu believes that speech originated in the process of _____
[p. 220]   _____.

9. Jaynes believes that the earliest languages were forms of _____–
[p. 222]   _____ communication.

[p. 222]   10. A child usually requires _____ years to master its native language.

11. As infants attempt to _____ speech, they eventually begin to produce
[p. 222]   sounds that resemble words.

12. If all languages were found to have similar components (such as grammatical similari-
             ties), there would be some evidence that part of language acquisition is
[p. 223]   _____.

[p. 224]   13. _____ described thinking as little more than talking to one's self.

14. The Swiss psychologist, Jean Piaget, has been studying the _____ or
[p. 224]   mental development of children.

15. For Piaget, _____ is the most important process in intellectual function-
[p. 224]   ing.

[p. 224]   16. _____ and _____ are two basic ways of adapting.

17. The _____-_____ stage is the first of Piaget's four stages of
[p. 226]   intellectual development and includes the first two years of life.

18. When a child is able to perform internal mental activities, as opposed to purely physi-
[p. 226]   cal ones, it is in the _____ stage of development.

19. Abstract thinking ability comes about during Piaget's final stage of development,
[p. 227]   called the period of _____ _____.

20. Your senses have a mechanism for holding onto some stimulus inputs for a brief
[p. 228]   period, called _____-_____ storage.

21. Your short-term memory can hold only about _____ to
[p. 230]   _____ items of information at one time.

[p. 231]   22. In order to hold information longer than usual in our STM, we _____ it.

23. Grouping or categorizing items together so as to store more information in STM is
[p. 231]   called _____.

[p. 231]   24. _____ are tricks or rhymes we use to help us to remember things.

[p. 232]   25. The capacity of our _____ memory seems to be limitless.

26. When information is stored in our LTM in an organized, logical way, we can say that
[p. 233]   it is properly _____.

27. Something that seems to help the retrieval of an item from LTM is the number of
[p. 234]   _____ given to that item.

28. It seems that it is much easier to get information _____ our LTM than it
[p. 235]   is to get it _____ our LTM.

29. Psychologists refer to a truly photographic memory as _____

[p. 235] _____.

[p. 236] 30. The shock or accident that causes retrograde amnesia prevents the brain from transferring information from the _____ to the _____.

[p. 236] 31. The Freudian mechanism of _____ is essentially a form of motivated forgetting.

[p. 240] 32. As demonstrated by the flatworm studies, _____ is an important chemical in the study of memory.

[p. 241] 33. The third stage in the process of problem solving is to _____ the solutions that have been decided upon.

[p. 242] 34. Motivation can have an adverse effect on problem solving when it becomes so high as to create _____.

[p. 243] 35. Developing a habitual pattern or way of solving the same kind of problems may give rise to a _____ _____.

[p. 243] 36. The tendency to see objects as having only one or two specific functions is _____ _____.

B.   REVIEW

Multiple Choice: Circle the letter identifying the alternative that most correctly completes the statement or answers the question.

1. Language:
   A. should not be allowed to interfere with problem solving.
   B. is a system of signs and symbols.
   C. has been found to exist in dolphins and chimpanzees.
   D. has been found in as many as 60 percent of all human cultures.

2. The origin of language:
   A. is still a debatable issue.
   B. can be traced directly to the use of tools.
   C. occurred about 2500 years ago in Greece.
   D. is a matter of only recent concern to linguists and psychologists.

3. Which of the following is important to the development of language?
   A. babbling
   B. imitation
   C. innate predispositions
   D. all of the above

4. A child will develop its native language in about _____ years.
   A. one
   B. two
   C. three
   D. four

5. According to Piaget, which of the following is not necessary for the formation of a concept?
   A. experience
   B. language
   C. social transmission
   D. maturation

6. Which of the following is the sequence of cognitive development proposed by Piaget?
   A. sensory-motor, pre-operational, concrete operations, formal operations
   B. formal operations, concrete operations, pre-operational, sensory-motor
   C. sensory-motor, formal operations, pre-operational, concrete operations
   D. concrete operations, formal operations, sensory-motor, preoperational

7. When we look up a phone number and go to dial it, the number is probably stored in our:
   A. sensory-information storage
   B. very short memory
   C. short-term memory
   D. long-term memory

8. Which of the following stages of memory seems to have an unlimited capacity?
   A. SIS
   B. STM
   C. LTM
   D. none of the above

9. Making up a little jingle like "Thirty days hath September, April, June, and November . . ." is an example of the use of:
   A. mnemonics
   B. acronyms
   C. assimilation
   D. chunking

10. To be able to store a complete and detailed picture in your "mind" would be to demonstrate:
   A. amnesia
   B. eidetic imagery
   C. mental set
   D. repression

THE TRUTH THE WHOLE TRUTH
& NOTHING BUT . . .

Screech. Thump. Scream. Thud! A pedestrian has just been hit by a car and you are an eye witness. You saw exactly what happened and will probably be called upon to testify in court. But did you really see everything that took place? And even if you did, will you remember the events accurately?

Many people would give an unqualified "yes" to those questions and be prepared to swear to the truth of what they remember. People tend to put great faith in the memory as an objective recorder of the facts, and the memory is usually thought of as a fairly stable and reliable instrument. An "eyewitness" account is often the deciding factor in a court case.

But can eye witnesses be wrong? Does the memory sometimes err in recording information from the senses? Does the memory sometimes confuse sensation with imagination? Do people unconsciously fabricate or elaborate on incoming information? The answer is "yes" on all counts. Many times eye witnesses tell different stories about the same event. Why and how does this happen? Research conducted by Elizabeth Loftus of the University of Washington in Seattle suggests some answers.

Loftus's research begins at the scene of the accident. She uses film of an accident, for experimental purposes. Her thesis is that "questions asked about an event shortly after it occurs may affect, in terms of alteration or distortion, the development of a witness's memory for that event." The questions asked of a witness are important for several reasons. Studies have shown that the wording of a question can have a substantial effect on the answers given. In one experiment Loftus and her colleagues showed films of auto accidents and then immediately asked the viewers questions about what they had seen. Some subjects were asked, "How fast were the cars going when they smashed into each other?" Others were asked, "How fast were the cars going when they bumped into each other?" The word "smashed" in the question consistently elicited higher estimates of speed than did "bumped," "collided," "contacted" or "hit."

In another experiment, 100 students viewed a short film segment showing a multiple-car accident. They then filled out a 22-item questionnaire that contained six critical questions; three about items that appeared in the film and three about items not present in the film. For half of the subjects the critical questions began with the words, "Did you see a . . .," as in, "Did you see a broken headlight?" For the other half, the critical question began with the words, "Did you see the . . .," as in, "Did you see the broken headlight?" Witnesses who were asked "the" questions were more likely than the others to report having seen what was asked about—even if that object did not appear in the film. So the wording of a question, even the changing of an article, can have a measurable effect on answers given.

But the main concern of Loftus "is not on the effect of the wording of a question on its answer, but rather on the answers to other questions subsequently asked, often considerably later." In other words, she is studying memory and what she calls a "memorial phenomenon of some importance." She has explored this phenomenon through a number of experiments.

In one study, 150 students were shown a film of a multiple-car accident in which one car (Car A), after failing to stop at a stop sign, makes a right turn into the main stream of traffic. The cars in the oncoming traffic lane stop suddenly and a five-car collision results. At the end of the film a 10-item questionnaire was administered. For half of the subjects the first question was, "How fast was Car A going when it ran the stop sign?" For the other half the first question was, "How fast was Car A going when it turned right?" The last question was the same for all subjects: "Did you see a stop sign for Car A?"

More than 50 percent of those in the "stop sign" group reported that they saw the stop sign. Only 35 percent of those in the "turn right" group reported seeing the stop sign. "Thus," says Loftus, "the wording of a presumption into a question asked immediately after a recently witnessed event can affect the answer to a question about that pre-supposition asked a very short time later."

One possible explanation of this effect is the "construction hypothesis." In answering the initial stop sign question, subjects may visualize or mentally reconstruct that portion of the incident needed to answer the question. If the presupposition is accepted, then a stop sign may be introduced into the visualization whether or not it was truly in the memory. When asked later about the stop sign, subjects may respond on the basis of the visualized or constructed stop sign rather than on what was remembered from the actual incident. If this is what is happening, then parts of the memory might be constructs of the mind, rather than objective representations based on fact. But the stop sign did exist.

Loftus' work raises some interesting questions for memory theorists, but it also has some important practical implications for everyone. If a nonexistent stop sign can be remembered, it is quite possible that a nonexistent gun, knife, word or almost anything else can be remembered. Memories like that can be extremely important, especially in the legal system. Loftus's work tells judges, lawyers, police interrogators, accident investigators and all potential witnesses to anything to be aware of the malleability of the memory.

C. NEWS STORY QUESTIONS

1. What does Loftus's research suggest may influence our eyewitness report of an accident scene? _____

2. What is Loftus's example of what she calls the "construction hypothesis"? _____
_____

Movie still from *Pygmalion*.

Most people will agree that intelligence is one of the more important of all human characteristics. If we look at how psychologists attempt to measure intelligence we begin to understand how complex and changeable human intelligence is. What has been learned about intelligence suggests that intelligence can sometimes be increased.

Intelligence

8 chapter

When you have completed your study of this chapter, you should be able to:

- ▶ Define "intelligence"
- ▶ Describe the Binet-Simon test of intelligence and compute an IQ score
- ▶ Summarize Spearman's and Thurstone's views of the nature of intelligence
- ▶ List the characteristics of good psychological tests
- ▶ Summarize the nature–nurture controversy as applied to intelligence
- ▶ List and describe at least five causes of mental retardation
- ▶ Describe and evaluate the Milwaukee Project

Bell-shaped curve. The curve generated by the distribution of IQ scores taken from a large sample of people. Also called the "normal distribution"; since most of the students should be "average," their scores should bunch up in the middle of the distribution.

Binet-Simon test. (bee-NAY see-MOAN). First well-known intelligence test; constructed in the early 1900s for use with French schoolchildren by Alfred Binet and Théophile Simon.

Chitling test. The IQ tests most used in U.S. schools today were constructed by middle-class whites, and thus may be biased against blacks (or white or other children who grew up in deprived circumstances). The "Chitling Test" was devised with a deliberate black bias to it, because to score well on the test, one must have intimate knowledge of black culture. Sometimes eaten by Southern blacks, chitlings — or chitterlings — are a type of "soul food" that consists of the smaller intestines of pigs, usually served boiled or fried.

Chromosomes (KRO-moh-sohms). From the Greek words meaning "colored bodies." The genes of a cell are strung together like strands of colored beads; these "strands" are the chromosomes. Each chromosome may be made up of several thousand genes.

Chronological age (kron-oh-LODGE-ih-cal). Chronos was the Greek god of time. Your chronological age is the length of time you have lived since birth.

Cognitive. Having to do with mental events or activities.

Correlation (KOR-re-lay-shun, or KO-re-LAY-shun). Things that "go together or that are "co-related" or related to each other in some way. Most blondes have blue eyes, so eye color and hair color are correlated. However, blue eyes don't *cause* light-colored hair; rather, both traits are determined by related genetic factors.

Down's syndrome (SIN-drome). Also called "mongolism" and "trisomy-21" (TRY-some). A relatively common form of birth defect in which the facial features of the person somewhat resemble Oriental or Mongolian characteristics. Some form of mental retardation is often associated with Down's syndrome, although the person's intellectual development is often as "retarded" by poor teaching techniques as by physiological fault.

Enzyme (EN-zime). Proteins found in most living tissue that speed up chemical reactions. Without the enzymes found in your saliva and stomach, you could not digest your food very well.

General intelligence (g factor). Some psychologists — most notably Charles Spearman — believe that intelligence is of two main types: (1) a general trait (called the "g factor") that is common to all people; and (2) special abilities (called "s's") that were only loosely related to "general intelligence." Other psychologists — most notably J. P. Guilford — deny that there is any real evidence to establish the existence of a "g factor."

Genes. The basic unit of heredity. Complex chemical molecules (made up primarily of DNA) found in almost all cells that control the activities within the cells and that provide the mechanism by which cells reproduce.

Intelligence. Although there are many different definitions of intelligence, most of them boil down to one basic thought. People who survive and thrive in a particular environment are usually considered "intelligent," while people who have problems surviving in that same environment are usually considered "not so intelligent."

Intelligence quotient (KWO-shunt). Also called "IQ." In most intelligence tests, the IQ is figured by dividing the person's mental age (MA) by the person's chronological age (CA), and multiplying by 100. However, a person's IQ test score may vary by 20 or more points depending on the person's age, experience, motivation, general state of health, and the test used.

Mental age (MA). According to Simon and Binet, the average 7-year-old child should have an average mental development. Hence the child should have a mental age of 7. Your mental age is thus a measure of your mental maturity.

Mental retardation. According to Webster's, "a failure in intellectual development resulting in social incompetence that is considered to be the result of a defect in the central nervous system and (hence) incurable." However, we now suspect that many forms of mental retardation are "helpable," if not yet entirely curable.

Milwaukee Project. A study by University of Wisconsin psychologist Rick Heber and his colleagues which suggests that early experience has a profound influence on IQ scores.

Montessori method (monn-tess-SOAR-ee). An educational method developed by Italian educator Maria Montessori in which children are encouraged to develop at their own speeds in a richly stimulating and warmly accepting environment.

Phenylketonuria (fee-null-key-toe-NURR-ee-uh). A rare but curable type of disability found in newborn infants. If not treated at once, the infant may become mentally retarded. Also called PKU.

Phonetics (foe-NETT-icks). From the Greek word meaning "to produce a sound." The scientific study of speech sounds in various languages.

Psychometrician (sigh-ko-muh-TRISH-shun). From the Greek word meaning "to measure the mind." A psychometrician is someone who gives mental tests to people.

Reliability. Reliable friends are those people you can count on when the going gets tough — whose behavior toward you seldom varies. Reliable mental tests are those that yield the same test scores again and again.

Standardized test. A test in which the procedures for administering and scoring the test have been made uniform or standard.

Stanford-Binet test. The first U.S. version of the Binet-Simon IQ test, developed by psychologist L. M. Terman at Stanford University.

Trait. A talent, skill, or way of performing. Intelligence is assumed to be a personality trait.

Validity (va-LIDD-ih-tee). Anything that is valid is believable or accurate. A valid IQ test is one that really measures intelligence, rather than some other trait.

Wechsler Adult Intelligence Scale (WAIS). A widely used, standardized IQ test for adults developed by U. S. psychologist David Wechsler.

INTRODUCTION: PYGMALION

Pygmalion hated women. He had been unlucky in love. Because Pygmalion could find no female that suited him, he decided to give up women altogether. He hid himself away on the island of Cyprus and devoted himself to his work as a sculptor. But Pygmalion could not get women completely out of his mind. He soon began to create a statue of a beautiful young maiden. The more he worked, the more beautiful and lifelike the statue became.

To Pygmalion, his statue was more than a piece of stone or even a work of art. It was what he considered to be the physical representation of the perfect woman. The statue was so perfect, in fact, that the young sculptor fell in love with it. He would talk to the statue, touch it, kiss it — even bring gifts to it.

Poor Pygmalion — he was hopelessly in love with a lifeless piece of stone. Fortunately for the lovesick sculptor, the gods, as they usually do in Greek myths, decided to take a hand in human affairs. Venus, the goddess of love, used her powers to make Pygmalion's statue come to life.

It is a tempting thought to be able to create the perfect mate from stone or from some other material. But there is much more to humanity than physical form. Pygmalion's story is incomplete because his beloved statue had only one thing — beauty. A complete person must have a whole pattern of individual psychological traits and characteristics. In other words, every person must have a personality.

George Bernard Shaw, the famous British playwright and intellectual, took Pygmalion's story and gave it a realistic twist. In 1913, Shaw wrote a play about a woman named Eliza Doolittle and a man named Henry Higgins. (More recently, Shaw's play has been made into the Broadway musical and movie *My Fair Lady*.) In Shaw's *Pygmalion*, Higgins is not a sculptor of statues but he is, in some ways, a molder of minds. Higgins is an expert in **phonetics,** or the sounds of words, and he teaches people how to speak and pronounce the English language. Eliza is not a piece of clay or stone but, like all humans, she has the ability to learn and to grow and change or be molded.

Eliza is a poor flower girl from the slums of London, and her pronunciation of the English language is almost unintelligible. Very near the opening of the play Eliza talks like this:

Ow, eez ye-ooa san, is e? Wal, fewd dan y' de-ooty bawmz a mather should, eed now bettern to spawl a pore gel's flahrzn than ran awy athaht pyin.

Upon hearing Eliza's language, Higgins brags to a friend:

You see this creature with her kerbstone English: the English that will keep her in the gutter to the end of her days. Well, sir, in three months I could pass that girl off as a duchess at an ambassador's garden party.

Three months was not quite long enough, but within six months Higgins had done what he said he could do. He took Eliza into his home, gave her her first bath, some new clothes, and an entirely different language. In effect, Higgins turned Eliza into a different human being. He not only taught her how to speak, he also gave her a changed personality and a different outlook on life.

Eliza's story is somewhat exceptional. There are no courses with teachers like Henry Higgins that can create totally new or different individuals within six months. But people do change as they grow and as they learn. Each individual's unique set of physical, **cognitive,** and social **traits** develops during years of growth, training, and education. Because of different genes, different forms of education — and an endless variety of biological, psychological, and social experiences — each individual is different from every other individual.

Because people must deal with each other and with each other's differences, it is necessary for us to have an understanding of what the differences may be and of the causes of individual differences. Each human being, however, is a complex combination of a great many traits that must be examined one at a time.

One important factor in a person's individuality is intelligence — that is, the ability to solve life's problems and to achieve success. This "practical intelligence," however, is not always the sort that shows up in IQ tests. Let us first look at some definitions of intelligence, and then see why the whole concept is caught up in controversy these days.

INTELLIGENCE

The most intelligent people have yet to decide exactly what intelligence is. And almost everyone who has ever studied intelligence has come up with a different definition of what it is. In general, however, **intelligence** can be said to be a combination of those mental traits or characteristics that enables anyone to survive in a particular environment.

At one time, perhaps 50,000 years ago, intelligence consisted of knowing how to build fires, hunt for food, and survive the hardships of the elements. Eliza Doolittle had a certain type of intelligence that allowed her to behave in a certain manner and survive quite well as a flower seller in London. Henry Higgins had a different set of mental traits that allowed him to survive in a different segment of London society. A somewhat different set of mental abilities is necessary for survival in the United States today.

Among the most important aspects of intelligence is the ability to make good use of the powers of memory and reasoning in order to learn and adapt to new situations. Infants use their mental powers to survive in a nursery, but they must develop the powers of memory and reasoning in order to acquire the skills necessary to survival in the adult world. It was by using such general mental abilities that Eliza was able to learn those behaviors that were necessary for survival in a society different from the one in which she was born and reared.

MEASURING INTELLIGENCE

Eliza showed herself to be a very clever and intelligent pupil. Even Henry Higgins, a rather selfish and thoughtless teacher, had to admit that Eliza had intelligence. But intelligence, itself, cannot be seen. Only the results of intelligence — that is, intelligent and unintelligent behaviors — can be seen. Therefore, any discussion or even definition of intelligence must deal with behavioral outputs that are either more or less intelligent than other behavioral outputs. Thus, it is *behavior* that people have been trying to measure for many years in order to better understand exactly what intelligence is.

Rightly or wrongly, some psychologists have long been convinced that intelligence is somehow related to the speed of one's reactions, or the quickness with which one solves mental problems. The first scientific attempts to understand mental abilities came from an early attempt to measure the amount of time it takes the human brain to react to the onset of a light. In 1816, F. W. Bessel — a German astronomer — noted that it took some of his assistants a fraction of a second longer than others to respond to the onset of a light. Bessel believed that those assistants with quicker reaction times might be smarter than those who reacted more slowly. In 1883, Sir Francis Galton, the British scientist and inventor, suggested that perhaps many other types of mental and physical reaction times were related to intelligence. He even invented machines to test various types of sensory responses that he thought important. By 1890, James McKeen Cattell, an experimental psychologist in the United States, had followed Galton's notions by developing a "mental test" for measuring such simple abilities as a person's reactions to sensory experiences. Even today, many IQ tests give extra points to subjects who answer difficult questions quickly.

The Binet-Simon Test

The first important studies and measures of intelligence began in France in 1905. Alfred Binet observed the intellectual reactions of his children and came to the conclusion that the physical reactions Cattell and many others were studying were not enough to explain such complex mental powers as imagination, memory, and comprehension. Binet began to work on a variety of methods that could possibly test or measure some of the higher functions of the intellect.

While Binet was involved in these studies, he was asked by the French government to develop a test that could discriminate between children who were mentally deficient and children who had normal mental abilities but were not studying hard enough.

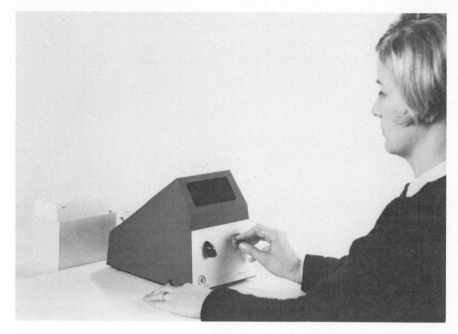

The quickness of reactions to sensory stimuli is often thought to be related to intelligence. This woman is being tested for reaction time. She is asked to move a switch as soon as she detects a signal stimulus.

Binet began with the assumption that retarded children learn very slowly and, therefore, would not know as much as normal children of the same age. If this were true, then what was needed was a test that most French schoolchildren of a certain age could pass. Any child of the age group being examined who could not pass the test might possibly be mentally defective. Working with Théophile Simon, Binet developed a set of tests that could discriminate between children of various ages. One set of tests, for instance, contained a group of simple questions that most normal five-year-old French schoolchildren should be able to answer. Another set of questions was developed for six-year-olds, another for seven-year-olds. A five-year-old should be able to count to four and be able to draw a square. An eight-year-old should be able to count backwards from 20 to 0. All of the tests were given to a great many children until Binet and Simon knew exactly which questions should normally be answered by the children of each age group. (See Figure 8-1.)

With the **Binet-Simon test,** French teachers were able to tell a child's **mental age.** If a five-year-old could answer all of the questions on the test for six-year-olds, that five-year-old child would be considered to have a mental age of six (as compared to an actual **chronological age** of five). But if a 10-year-old child could only answer the questions on the test for five-year-olds, the teacher could assume that the 10-year-old had a mental age of five and thus was mentally defective in some way or had some other problem.

These first intelligence tests worked so well that teachers could use them to do more than test for **mental retardation.** Teachers began to use the tests to tell how poorly or how well normal children were doing. If a seven-year-old

FIG. 8–1.
The chronological age of each child is indicated on his or her back; the mental age is given directly above the head of each. Using the Terman formula, can you calculate each child's IQ? (Answers: 85.7, 116.6, 100)

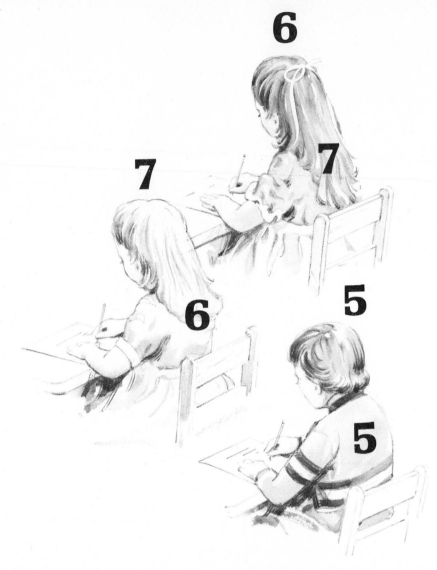

passed the test for seven-year-olds, that child was considered to be normal. If the same child could only pass the test for six-year-olds, then that child might need extra help. And if the seven-year-old could pass the test for eight-year olds, that child was considered to be doing better than average work.

IQ

The Binet-Simon tests were so successful and useful to French teachers that L. M. Terman and a group of psychologists at Stanford University decided to develop a version of the tests for use in the United States. Their test, the **Stan-**

ford-Binet, has become one of the most widely used intelligence tests in the United States.

In addition to translating the tests into English and otherwise strengthening them, Terman introduced the term IQ, or **intelligence quotient.** By developing a numerical indication of intelligence, Terman hoped to be able to tell how poorly or well a child was doing. Terman calculated IQ by a simple formula:

$$\frac{\text{Mental age}}{\text{Chronological age}} \times 100 = IQ$$

A seven-year-old child who can pass the test for seven-year-olds, therefore, has an IQ of 100, a score that is considered to be normal or average because almost all seven-year-olds are supposed to be able to pass the seven-year-old's test. A seven-year-old who can pass the test designed for nine-year-olds has a very good IQ of 128. A nine-year-old who can only pass the test for seven-year-olds has a rather low IQ of 77. (Multiplying by 100 gets rid of the decimals.)

Standardization

If, as young students, both Eliza and Higgins had taken IQ tests that were designed for upper-class British schoolchildren, Eliza would probably have shown a very low IQ, while Higgins might have scored well above average. But regardless of IQ, both Eliza and Higgins were intelligent people, and they were both good survivors in their particular environments. Eliza would probably have done poorly only because she had not been exposed to the same schools, learning situations, and environment that Higgins had grown up in. Eliza's vocabulary, for instance, would have limited her greatly not only in answering questions and making herself understood to the tester but even in understanding the test instructions. None of these problems would have bothered Higgins. On the other hand, if the test had been designed to accurately judge the intelligence of Eliza and the street people like her, Higgins might have scored below average. Even if he could understand the language, there were many things about Eliza's way of life that Higgins would not have been able to react to correctly without experience and training.

In order to accurately test the intelligence of anyone, a test must take into account that particular person's background. But no two people are ever exposed to identical experiences and environments. Therefore, to allow for all individual differences, a different test would have to be designed for each person. Making up a new test for each person to be tested, however, would be an impractical task. Therefore, **standardized tests** are designed that can be given to large groups of people. Binet's tests, for instance, were designed for all French schoolchildren. For use in the United States, the test had to be slightly altered to fit the background and experiences of children who had grown up and gone to school in the United States.

In order to come up with a test that was actually suited to French schoolchildren, Binet had to test many French children. If the test was to be an accurate in-

FIG. 8–2.
This bell-shaped curve shows the normal distribution of IQ scores. As you can see, 68 percent of all scores range from 84 to 116, resulting in a bell-shaped curve.

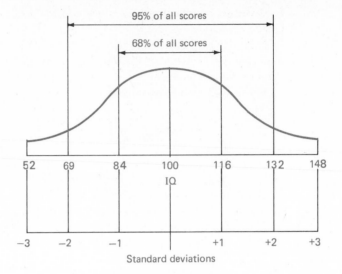

strument for a particular age group, many people in that age group had to be tested, and most of them had to score in the 100 IQ or normal range. For a test to yield a normal distribution, only a few people should score very much above or below the average norm. When the results of a test with normal distribution are plotted on a graph, the result is a curve that is shaped like a bell (see Figure 8-2 and the Statistical Appendix).

Many psychologists believe that any IQ test that does not yield a **bell-shaped curve** when given to a large group of people is probably not a valid indicator of intelligence for the people of that group. If a large percentage of people score well above 100, the test is probably too easy. If a large percentage of people score well below 100, the test is too difficult.

Since the introduction of the Stanford-Binet, scientists have learned much about intelligence. At one time, for instance, general intelligence was considered to be a special type of energy or force that each person had more or less of. In 1904, British psychologist Charles Spearman called this force g. In 1938, L. L. Thurstone expanded Spearman's theory and said that g, or **general intelligence,** was not a single force but was made up of seven primary mental abilities. They are:

N — Numerical ability
W — Word fluency
V — Verbal meaning
M — Memory
R — Reasoning
S — Spatial relations
P — Perceptual speed

FIG. 8–3.
Various tests are
used to measure IQ.
This test is part
of a mini-test from
the American Mensa
Society. The sole
qualification for
membership in this
organization is place-
ment at the 98th
percentile or higher
on a validated IQ
test. How did you
score on their mini-
test? (Answers: 1. d;
2. c; 3. e, code: A =
1, B = 2, C = 3, D
= 4, etc.; 4. d; 5. b;
6. a; 7. c)

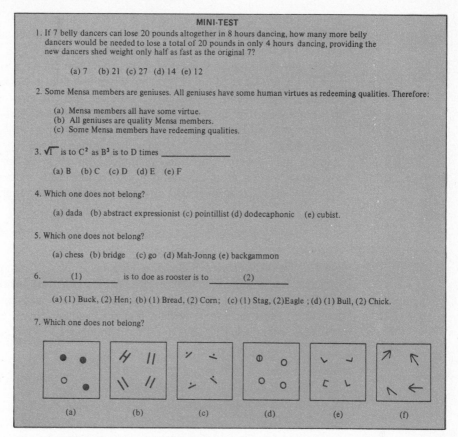

MINI-TEST

1. If 7 belly dancers can lose 20 pounds altogether in 8 hours dancing, how many more belly dancers would be needed to lose a total of 20 pounds in only 4 hours dancing, providing the new dancers shed weight only half as fast as the original 7?

  (a) 7   (b) 21   (c) 27   (d) 14   (e) 12

2. Some Mensa members are geniuses. All geniuses have some human virtues as redeeming qualities. Therefore:

  (a) Mensa members all have some virtue.
  (b) All geniuses are quality Mensa members.
  (c) Some Mensa members have redeeming qualities.

3. $\sqrt{1}$ is to C^2 as B^3 is to D times _____

  (a) B   (b) C   (c) D   (d) E   (e) F

4. Which one does not belong?

  (a) dada   (b) abstract expressionist (c) pointillist (d) dodecaphonic   (e) cubist.

5. Which one does not belong?

  (a) chess   (b) bridge   (c) go   (d) Mah-Jonng (e) backgammon

6. _____(1)_____ is to doe as rooster is to _____(2)_____

  (a) (1) Buck, (2) Hen;   (b) (1) Bread, (2) Corn;   (c) (1) Stag, (2)Eagle ; (d) (1) Bull, (2) Chick.

7. Which one does not belong?

    (a)   (b)   (c)   (d)   (e)   (f)

But even these seven abilities are not enough to fully explain intelligence. In the 1960s, J. P. Guilford suggested that there are as many as 120 separate intellectual abilities. No matter what true intelligence is, however, it is a person's ability to use mental abilities that IQ tests attempt to measure.

IQ and Age

Many mental testers assume that IQ is primarily determined by one's genes. One's IQ scores, therefore, shouldn't change very much as one grows older. Unfortunately, the cold, hard facts don't support this belief very strongly. If you tested a thousand people when they were two years old, and gave them IQ tests again when they were 22, you'd find that there really wasn't too great a connection or **correlation** between the two sets of scores. True, many of the subjects with high scores at age two would also have high IQs 20 years later — but at least as many of them would have shown a noticeable drop in their scores. Likewise, many of the two-year-olds who did poorly at first would, when tested as adults, show a remarkable increase in their IQs. Thus, at least part of one's intelligence —as measured by an IQ test—is determined by how much one learns when growing up.

It is also true that the score you get on an IQ test depends to some extent on what test you take and how old you are when you take it. If a psychologist gave you the Stanford-Binet test when you were 10, and you answered all the questions correctly and promptly, you could get an IQ score of more than 200. If you took the Stanford-Binet when you were 20, and again performed perfectly, your score would only be about 150. Since the Stanford-Binet is primarily a test for children, the "ceiling" (top score possible) is much lower for adults than for youngsters. However, a 20-year-old who scored 150 on the Stanford-Binet might well score more than 200 on a test constructed for adults.

The WAIS

In 1939, David Wechsler of Bellevue Hospital in New York introduced an intelligence test designed for adults. The **Wechsler Adult Intelligence Scale (WAIS)** was designed not to test for abilities that are necessary for schoolchildren, but to test for mental abilities that are necessary in an adult world. The WAIS and other adult IQ tests are often administered to job applicants.

Group Tests

Psychological testing, especially intelligence testing, has become very popular during the past 50 years. But tests like the Stanford-Binet and the WAIS are designed to be administered on an individual basis. An examiner usually tests only one person at a time. To speed up the testing process, the United States Army came up with the idea of giving tests to whole groups of people at the same time. Group tests are the tests that students in the United States are probably most familiar with. With such tests the Army decides who should become an officer, who should be a private, and who should not even by in the Army. Group tests are also used to decide who gets into college and who gets into graduate school. The School and College Ability Tests (SCAT), the Scholastic Aptitude Test (SAT), and the Graduate Record Exam (GRE) are among the most popular of the group tests given in the school systems.

Group tests save a lot of time and energy on the part of the examiners, but group tests have some special drawbacks. Individual tests allow for close contact and communication between the examiner and the person being tested. Group tests, which are often scored by machine, do not offer such personal contact. People who don't understand the instructions or who have some other difficulty often have trouble getting their problems taken care of in a group setting. Test administrators often don't have time or the ability to deal with the problems of every individual taking a test.

RELIABILITY AND VALIDITY

Eliza Doolittle, her family, and friends were poor. Because they were poor they were often looked down on by people like Henry Higgins. In many societies, wealth has always been one of the most often-used measures of superiority and even of intelligence. Rich people often feel that they are better and more intelligent than poor people simply because of their money. But Eliza proved that she was as good as anyone else. She not only passed herself off as royalty but married someone from the upper class and eventually became a prosperous businesswoman.

Wealth and social class are still sometimes used as a measure of superiority and intelligence, but most people realize that money has little to do with brains. A person born into a wealthy family has certain advantages, but that does not mean that that person has more intelligence than someone born in the ghetto. Children from rich and poor families often end up on the same college campus —and the poor students often get better grades.

Today, instead of money and social class, another measure of superiority is often used—the IQ test. People with lower IQs are sometimes discriminated against, and people with high IQs are given superior postions in school and in life in general. Because IQ tests are often used to make decisions that can influence a person's entire life, the **psychometricians** (the experts who design and administer psychological tests) take special care to construct tests that will be fair and accurate for anyone who takes them.

TABLE 8-1   **Intelligence Tests**

Individual Tests	Subjects	Description
Binet-Simon	Children	Developed in France to discriminate between children of normal mental abilities and mentally deficient children; determines mental age
Stanford-Binet	Children	Translated the Binet-Simon test into English for use in the United States; introduced the term "intelligence quotient" or IQ
Wechsler Intelligence Scale for Children (WISC)	Children	One of the most widely used IQ tests for children
Wechsler Adult Intelligence Scale (WAIS)	Adults	Designed to test mental abilities necessary in the adult world; often administered to job applicants

Group Tests	Subjects	Description
School and College Ability Tests (SCAT) Scholastic Aptitude Tests (SAT) Graduate Record Exam (GRE)	Adults	Used to test scholastic ability and to determine who gets into college and graduate school

First of all, IQ tests should be standardized on the group of people who will be using them. That is, a test must be designed so that it gives standard or truly representative results and is fair for everyone using it. The bell-shaped curve of normal distribution is one of the methods of ensuring that a test is adequately standardized.

Standardization, however, is only one check on the accuracy of a psychological test. There are two other factors that must always be taken into account when psychological tests are being designed. IQ tests must be both reliable and valid.

Test Reliability

A ruler is a reliable measure of distance. A meter-stick is always 100 cm. (about 39.37 in.) long—and every meter is exactly the same length. If a track is 100 m. long the first time it is measured, it will still be 100 m. long the second, third, and fourth time it is measured. Similarly, an IQ test should be *reliable* enough to give the same results time after time. Someone who has an IQ of 110 on Monday should be able to take the same test on Tuesday, Wednesday, and Thursday and still score 110. A test that repeatedly gives the same results would presumably be reliable.

Unfortunately, IQ tests are not as reliable as are rulers. You may have scored 110 on Monday, but you might have a headache or some personal problems on Tuesday. Such problems might interfere with your concentration and cause you to score only 100 on Tuesday. There is also the chance that you might be highly motivated and feel much better and score 120 on Wednesday. By Thursday you might score even higher after having practiced with and gotten used to the test. Or, you might be bored with the same test and do worse than on Monday.

A metric ruler is always one meter (100 centimeters or 39.37 inches). No matter how many times you use the metric ruler, you will get the same result. Therefore, a metric ruler is a reliable instrument of measurement.

One way psychometricians try to achieve **reliability** is by having people take the same test two or more times. Even so, a completely reliable IQ test has not yet been designed. There are just too many factors involved—such as motivation, health, and experience—that can affect the reliability of a test. Unlike rulers, IQ tests almost never give exactly the same results twice.

Test Validity

Validity is as difficult to achieve as reliability as far as IQ tests are concerned. A *valid* test is one that accurately measures what it says it will measure. IQ tests should measure intelligence. But intelligence means different things to different people. Primitive tribes in the African desert, slum-dwellers in London or New York, middle-class children in suburban America, executives in the world of big business—for each of these groups of people, intelligence has a different meaning. And because intelligence can mean so many things to so many people, no truly valid measure of intelligence has yet been created.

If IQ tests are neither reliable nor valid, why is almost every schoolchild in the United States made to take IQ tests? IQ tests, like the Stanford-Binet, are useful because they can sometimes indicate a child's potential to achieve a certain type of success—success in the present school system.

Most IQ tests are designed by and for people who have gone through the school system, and IQ tests are usually standardized on the intellectual norms of white, middle-class children, who are a major part of the school system in the United States. Being designed by people who are products of a certain system and constructed for people in that system, IQ tests reflect the values of that system. In other words, most IQ tests measure those mental abilities that are especially valuable or useful for success in the middle-class schools of the United States.

Being designed for a particular group—white, middle-class students—IQ tests are most reliable and valid when applied to that group. IQ tests are less useful when applied to minority groups—blacks, Spanish-speaking people, Orientals, and lower-class children of all races and ethnic backgrounds. Blacks, for instance, as a group usually score lower on IQ tests than do middle-class whites. Orientals usually perform better than whites.

The fact that white, middle-class children usually outperform black, lower-class children does not mean that any one white child is more intelligent than every black child or that all whites are more intelligent than all blacks. It does mean, however, that most middle-class and upper-class whites are better prepared to succeed in white, middle-class schools than are most lower-class, black children. If blacks had designed the test for blacks, or if American Indians had created the tests for Indians, whites would probably not do as well.

IQ tests have their greatest validity in predicting how some children will perform in school, but these tests do very poorly in predicting how anybody will do outside of the school environment. The mere fact that you have a high IQ does not mean that you will do well in the business world. In fact, many people with

FIG. 8–4.
IQ tests, which are used to evaluate people of many cultures, attempt to avoid questions that are dependent on specific cultural knowledge. Unfortunately, few IQ tests are totally free of cultural influences. Since most IQ tests are based on white, middle-class culture, such tests are generally unfair to the people of other cultures. During the 1960s, Adrian Dove, a sociologist, used his knowledge of the culture of the Watts ghetto in Los Angeles to design a test that would be culturally unfair to middle-class whites. Most whites would agree that "the chitling test" is culturally unfair to them. In the same way, many blacks and other minority groups have a valid argument when they complain that white-based IQ tests are culturally unfair to minorities. (Answers: C is the answer to all the questions.)

THE CHITLING TEST

1. A "handkerchief head" is:
    (A) a cool cat
    (B) a porter
    (C) an Uncle Tom
    (D) a hoddi
    (E) a preacher

2. Which word is most out of place here?
    (A) splib
    (B) blood
    (C) gray
    (D) spook
    (E) black

3. A "gas head" is a person who has a:
    (A) fast-moving car
    (B) stable of "lace"
    (C) "process"
    (D) habit of stealing cars
    (E) long jail record for arson

4. "Bo Diddley" is a:
    (A) game for children
    (B) down-home cheap wine
    (C) down-home singer
    (D) new dance
    (E) Moejoe call

5. If a man is called a "blood," then he is a:
    (A) fighter
    (B) Mexican-American
    (C) Negro
    (D) hungry hemophile
    (E) Redman or Indian

6. Cheap chitlings (not the kind you buy at a frozen-food counter) will taste rubbery unless they are cooked long enough. How soon can you quit cooking them to eat and enjoy them?
    (A) 45 minutes
    (B) two hours
    (C) 24 hours
    (D) one week (on a low flame)
    (E) one hour

high IQ scores never meet success once they leave the academic world. Others, with low IQ scores, turn out to be quite successful in the world of business and industry. An IQ test, for instance, would probably not have indicated how successful Eliza Doolittle would be in life.

THE ROOTS OF INTELLIGENCE

For many years, intelligence was considered to be a static quality. You either had it, or you didn't. Whatever amount of it you had as a child, that was what you'd have when you grew up. Slaves were supposed to remain slaves because they didn't have the intelligence to be anything else. People like Eliza were supposed to stay in the slums because that kind of life was all they had brains for. But recent studies have shown that intelligence—or at least the cognitive side of human life—is not completely determined by one's genes. Biological factors interact with environmental and social factors to produce what we now call human intelligence.

Biological Influences

We cannot as yet define intelligence precisely nor measure it as accurately as we might wish. But thanks to many recent scientific experiments, we do have a clearer understanding now of the biological factors affecting intelligence than we did 20 years ago.

At least one type of mental retardation is thought to be inherited or due to genetic causes. **Phenylketonuria (PKU)** is a biological disorder caused by the lack of a specific body chemical or **enzyme.** Without the enzyme, the body cannot break down another chemical—phenylalanine—found in many foods. In people who inherit PKU, phenylalanine builds up in the blood and eventually damages the brain. Most children who are born in the United States are checked for PKU. If the condition is spotted within the first 10 to 20 days of a child's life, the missing chemical can be replaced, and brain damage can often be avoided. By maintaining a special diet, people with PKU can usually develop normal intellectual functioning.

Another type of retardation—**Down's syndrome,** or mongolism—can sometimes be present at birth but probably is not an inherited disorder. Down's syndrome is the result of a genetic abnormality. Most people with Down's syndrome have 47, instead of the normal 46, **chromosomes.** The cause of the abnormality is not known. It could be due to defective genes or to a malfunction of the growth process. Because women in their 40s are more likely than younger women to give birth to a child with Down's syndrome, some experts have suggested that the disorder may be due to genetic damage caused by exposure to certain types of radiation. The older a woman is, the greater chance there is that she may have been exposed to harmful radiation. With modern technology, however, chromosomes can be examined, and women can be told whether or not they are likely to give birth to a child with Down's syndrome.

While some types of mental retardation (and therefore much of the human intellect) may be due to genetic or chromosomal causes, much of what we call mental retardation is probably due to other types of biological inputs. Physical damage to the infant's brain before, during, or after birth can sometimes result in mental retardation. If a pregnant woman gets German measles during the first three months of pregnancy, for instance, she might give birth to a brain-damaged or retarded child. Malnutrition as well as the excessive use of certain drugs like alcohol have also been known to cause pregnant women to give birth to retarded children. Severe physical shocks to a pregnant woman, such as a car accident or a fall, can possibly result in mental retardation for an unborn child.

During birth, especially during a difficult birth, a child is also in danger of brain damage. Lack of oxygen during birth can destroy brain cells in an infant. Brain damage is also caused sometimes when mechancial instruments, such as forceps, are used to assist in the birth.

Environmental Influences

Physical damage is not the only thing that can cause retardation. People can learn to be retarded. Experiments with monkeys and rats show that isolation can result in retardation, and the same thing can happen with humans. Some children who are unwanted or unloved by their parents learn to psychologically isolate themselves from the world. Such isolation may protect a child from the world, but psychological isolation — like true physcial isolation — can eventually result in retardation.

No matter what the causes of retardation, there is now evidence that most retarded individuals can be helped and can be taught. Retarded people usually have difficulty learning because they have slightly different motivations and slightly different ways of learning than do normal individuals. We call a child "bright" if it learns to read and write rapidly, even if we don't bother to give it

When given constant positive feedback, retarded people can learn surprisingly well. These youngsters are receiving special training in gardening skills.

TABLE 8–2   **Mental Retardation**

Biological Influences	
1. Chemical imbalance	PKU
2. Genetic abnormality	Down's syndrome or mongolism
3. Physical damage	Brain damage caused by mother suffering from malnutrition, German measles, drugs, or physical shock during pregnancy; lack of oxygen during birth

Environmental Influences
1. Isolation (physical and psychological)
2. Lack of intellectual stimuli

much attention or much schooling. We would call the same child "retarded" if it failed to learn under the same set of circumstances. But recent studies by behavioral psychologists suggest that this "retarded" child might do surprisingly well if we give it a different sort of training.

If we show the average young child the letter "C" and ask the child to copy it, the child is likely to pick up a pencil and, after making a few mistakes, copy the letter fairly accurately. The child obviously perceives the letter "C" as a unit and knows what we mean when we ask, "Please copy this letter." But the retarded child may not perceive the letter "C" as a single unit at all. It may not know how to pick up and hold a pencil correctly, and it may not understand the command, "Please copy this letter." However, if we first give the child two weeks of training in how to pick up and hold a pencil, and how to make marks on a piece of paper, the child may be able to do so. If we break the letter "C" down into small units, and if we demonstrate to the child again and again what we mean when we say, "Please copy this letter," the child may in fact be able to do so. Particularly if we give the child constant positive feedback on its accomplishments and reward the child consistently for paying attention to and following our instructions.

Children who do not learn rapidly and with little instruction soon realize that they are somehow different from normal. Many parents and teachers grow impatient with these children and excuse their slow learning by letting the child know that it is retarded. Thus, the child never learns to pay attention to intellectual stimuli because no one ever taught it how to pay attention to such things. In fact, retarded children can learn a great deal—if we take the time and effort to adapt our teaching methods to their own unique abilities, and if we convince them that they are capable of learning.

At one time, retarded people were sent to institutions where they were often left to sit in a corner and vegetate for the rest of their lives. Those individuals who are so *physically* handicapped that they cannot take care of themselves will always need help from others. But by using recently developed training techniques, we can often help mentally retarded individuals to feed and dress themselves. In many cases, we can use these same methods to teach retarded people useful occupations that enable them to become valuable members of society.

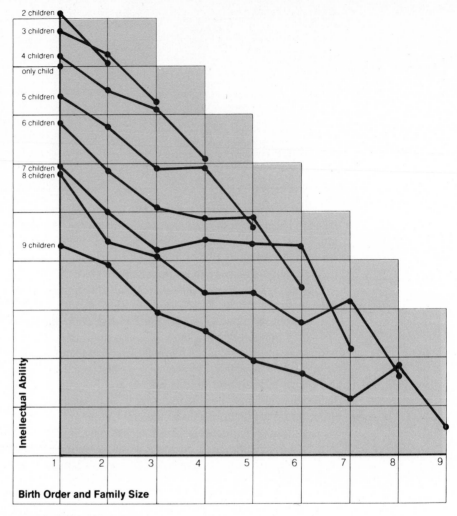

FIG. 8–5.
According to studies by Robert Zajonc, intellectual ability decreases as size of family grows. The brightest children come from the smallest families, and are born first. The estimated difference between the highest score, for the older of two, and lowest, for the last of nine, is ten IQ points.

Intellectual Ability

2 children
3 children
4 children
only child
5 children
6 children
7 children
8 children
9 children

Birth Order and Family Size

Intelligence and Birth Order

Studies of birth order and family size have almost always shown that firstborn children tend to be more intelligent than later-born children. And children from smaller families tend to be more intelligent than those from large families. Various explanations have been offered for such differences. Parents with only one child will have a certain amount of time, attention, and even money to spend on that child. When the second child comes along, the parents will have to divide their time and resources between the two children. With each additional child, parents have less and less time and energy to devote to individual children. But the time and energy parents spend on creating an intellectual environment for their children is not the only factor involved in intellectual development. Individuals in a social unit are affected by all of the other individuals in their environment. The outputs of all members of a family (not just of the parents) can become the inputs of all other members of a family. Therefore, children are affected by the intellectual outputs of their parents as well as of their brothers and sisters.

Robert B. Zajonc of the University of Michigan has examined the IQ test results of a great many children from different-sized families. He found that within a particular family, intellectual ability usually declines with birth order. This decline in IQ occurs, says Zajonc, because a child's intellectual growth is partly determined by the overall intellectual climate of the household. Children from large families, who spend more time in a world of child-sized minds, will probably develop more slowly and attain lower IQs than children from small families, who have more contacts with grown-up minds.

Increasing Intelligence

Many studies have shown that intelligence is not set at birth. Skeels, for instance, took young, seemingly retarded girls out of a dreary orphanage and introduced them into a more stimulating environment, where they made great gains in IQ and eventually proved to have at least normal intelligence (see Chapter 4). Kagan noted the same ability to make great intellectual changes in young Guatemalan children whom he studied. In both cases, it was the environment that changed the intellectual lives of the children. Because such studies have shown that retardation need not always be permanent, attempts have been made to increase the intelligence of normal as well as of retarded individuals.

If special education can bring retarded children up to almost normal levels, what can special education do for normal children? One of the most famous educators of the twentieth century asked this question, and she set out to find the answer.

The Montessori Method

Maria Montessori (1870–1952) was the first woman ever to graduate from medical school in Italy. As a young doctor, she began to spend much of her time working with young retarded children in the slum neighborhoods of Rome. By paying special attention to the needs and learning problems of the retarded, Montessori was able to bring many such children up to the levels of normal children. Her success prompted Montessori to try out some of her teaching methods on normal children.

When Maria Montessori began her work, a well-disciplined classroom was thought to be a classroom in which a group of students sat perfectly still and listened to the words of a sometimes uninteresting teacher. Montessori had a different idea about learning. People do not live their lives sitting still, she said. The real world is full of movement and activity and interesting things to do. If a child

Early in this century, discipline was the key word in the classroom. The teacher often drilled her students in reciting lessons and gave no thought to providing a stimulating environment.

is supposed to learn how to survive in the real world, then a child should be exposed to a normally active environment in school.

Maria Montessori did not force her students to sit still in class. She allowed them a certain amount of freedom to move around the classroom and to play and interact with each other. Most European and American educators were shocked by Montessori's methods. Most teachers thought that children would play instead of learn in such an undisciplined atmosphere. But Montessori introduced another important factor into her classrooms. The students were given a variety of interesting and stimulating educational toys and materials that would hold their interest. Montessori found that most children would sit down with their educational materials and work and concentrate much harder than they would in a normal classroom. By doing instead of listening, the children learned much more than they did in some normal classrooms.

The Montessori system worked. Maria Montessori was able to teach normal children to read, write, count, and add before they were six years old.

The Milwaukee Project

Almost all of our current definitions of intelligence—as well as the test we use to measure intelligence—are culturally biased. As an example of how important this sort of cultural bias is—and how one can sometimes overcome it with special training—consider the research of Rick Heber and his colleagues at the University of Wisconsin (see Chapter 4). In 1967, Heber and his associates selected for study 40 infants who were born to black parents living in one of the worst sections of Milwaukee. Although many parts of Milwaukee are delightful

In today's open classrooms, students are free to move about and join activities that they find interesting.

places in which to live, people in this particular section of town have the lowest average family income and education level found in Milwaukee; they also have the highest rate of unemployment and the highest population density. Although less than 3 percent of the city's people live in this area, it accounts for about 33 percent of the total number of children classified as mentally retarded. The mothers of the 40 infants in this Milwaukee Project all had IQ scores below 75 and, in many cases, the fathers were not living with the families.

Of these 40 infants, 20 were randomly selected to be in what Heber considered the "experimental" group, while the other 20 were placed in an untreated "control" group. The families of the experimental-group infants were given intensive vocational help and training in homemaking and childcare skills as soon as the children were born. When these "experimental" infants were 30 months old, they were put into a special education center for 35 hours a week. The training at this center focused on the development of language and cognitive skills. The experimental-group children remained in this center year-round until they were six years old and could enter school. The families and children in the control group received none of these benefits.

The children in both groups were given IQ tests frequently. In the summer of 1976, when the youngsters were all about nine years of age, the experimentally treated children averaged 110, while the children in the control group averaged below 80 on the tests. During the nine-year period they were tested, the groups' differences were never less than 20 IQ points and frequently were as high as 30 points. Dr. Heber believes that this superiority was due to the special training which the children in the experimental group (and their families) were given—most of which was aimed at teaching them the same sorts of mental skills that middle-class, white children typically acquire as part of their normal cultural tradition.

THE IQ CONTROVERSY: NURTURE VS. NATURE

The Milwaukee Project and other similar special education programs—such as Project Head Start—are based on the theory that intelligence is largely a product of the environment (nurture). Children reared in impoverished circumstances—such as Skeels's orphans—usually have lower IQ scores than do children reared in stimulating environments. Rats raised from birth in bare wire cages learn slower than do rats raised in cages full of exciting rat "playtoys." A stimulating environment is exactly what Henry Higgins provided for Eliza Doolittle.

But what about heredity (nature)? Certainly, it must play some part in determining a person's intelligence. There are, in fact, many studies suggesting that *certain aspects* of intelligence are strongly influenced by an organism's genes. Tall parents tend to have tall children, while short parents tend to have short children. Shouldn't bright parents, therefore, tend to have bright children, and duller parents tend to have duller offspring?

As we have noted before in discussing the nature–nurture controversy, the truth usually lies somewhere between the two extreme positions. Intelligence is related to how well you detect, perceive, remember, and respond to stimulus inputs. Intelligence is therefore a matter of how well your brain can process incoming information and react to whatever environment you find yourself in. Some people are surely born with better brains than others. If your genes — or an accident of birth — gave you a badly damaged brain, you will probably never be able to understand physics as well as Albert Einstein did. But the brain that you are born with is not quite the same organ as the brain you are using as you read these words. Your brain — damaged or normal — had to grow and mature; it had to learn signs and symbols and useful ways of solving problems. Rats raised from birth in bare wire cages not only learn slowly, they also have smaller brains than do rats raised in stimulating environments. A starved child does not grow to be as tall as its parents (if they were well-fed); a child deprived of knowledge and stimulation does not score as high on an IQ test as does its parents (if they were reared in an enriched environment).

Einstein is said to have had an IQ score of about 185. But even Einstein's marvelous brain had to grow and mature, as did his mind. Had Einstein been brought up on a desert island by savages, he never would have known as much about modern physics as you do right now. And his IQ score (as tested in the U.S.) would surely have been closer to 85 than to 185.

Your **genes** are the architect who provides the basic physical blueprint for the brain-house your mind lives in, and some people are surely born with better

Even Albert Einstein experienced learning difficulties as a young child. However, hereditary and environmental factors helped him to grow up to become a great physicist.

blueprints and, hence, greater mental potential than others. But your environment is the builder who puts the house together and who determines how great your mental life will finally be. The architect sets the limits; the builder constructs the best house possible within these limilts—by using whatever materials are available.

How much of your intelligence is determined by your genes, and how much by your environment? We cannot answer that question, because it has no meaning. Your intelligence is not a *thing* that is fixed or shaped forever at birth. Rather, your intelligence is an ever-changing *process* that results from the *interaction* between your heredity and your environment—between nature and nurture.

Each of us is born with somewhat different genes, and it is likely that each of us would reach our greatest potential in somewhat different environments. Once we are conceived, there is little we can do to change our genes. But there is a great deal we can all do to make sure that our environments are as well furnished intellectually and as enriching as possible for ourselves and for all other members of our society.

Eliza Doolittle's parents gave her good genes, but little training or stimulation when she was young. Henry Higgins provided a different sort of environment for her, and she blossomed like a flower that had been starved for water. Once she understood what mental growth was all about, she had the inherited capability of seeking out her own best environment and becoming whatever she wanted to become.

► SUMMARY

1. Intelligence is that combination of mental traits or characteristics that enables an individual to survive in a particular environment. In *Pygmalion*, Eliza Doolittle, the flower girl, was not necessarily any less intelligent than Henry Higgins, the phonetics expert. Before they met, each was able to function quite well in her or his own environment.

2. Intelligence itself cannot be seen. Only the results of intelligence—intelligent or unintelligent behaviors—can be seen. It is these behaviors that intelligence tests attempt to measure.

3. Early attempts to measure intelligence involved tests of mental quickness. Measures of reaction time, however, give information on only one aspect of intelligence. It was Alfred Binet who first developed methods for testing or measuring some of the higher functions of the human intellect.

4. The Binet-Simon tests were designed to measure a child's **mental age.** With such information, it was possible to tell how well or how poorly a child was doing, compared with other children of the same age.

5. The Stanford-Binet is used in the United States. It yields a numerical score called an **intelligence quotient** or IQ (**mental age** divided by **chronological age** times 100).

6. IQ tests are designed to yield a normal distribution, which will appear as a **bell-shaped curve** in graph form. That is, most of the individuals in a particular age group should score near 100 or in the "normal" range. If a test is **standardized** in this way, very few individuals will score much higher or much lower than 100 (see Statistical Appendix for a more complete discussion of the mathematics involved in **standardization**).

7. The **Stanford-Binet** and **Wechsler Adult Intelligence Scale (WAIS)** are individual tests. Specially trained examiners administer these tests to individuals on a one-to-one basis. There are, however, a number of commonly used intelligence tests that are designed to be administered to large groups of people at the same time. Examples are the Scholastic Aptitude Test (SAT) and the Graduate Record Exam (GRE).

8. **Reliability** and **validity** are two important qualities that psychometricians try to build into their tests. A test that gives the same results day in and day out would presumably be reliable. A test that accurately measures what it says it will measure (intelligence) would be considered valid. Both qualities, reliability and validity, are difficult to achieve in intelligence tests because human intelligence is an extremely complex and changeable trait.

9. Biological, environmental, and social factors all combine to produce the complex human characteristic we call intelligence. There is usually little we can do about our biological inheritance, but our environments and stimulus inputs can be manipulated.

10. Cultural bias is a problem that faces all tests that try to measure intelligence scores of people from diverse backgrounds. In the past, IQ tests tended to favor individuals of white, middle-class background, but newer tests are seeking to resolve this problem. **The Chitling Test** was created to show the white, middle-class individual what a culturally unfair test is like.

11. Biological influences on intelligence include two forms of mental retardation: **phenylketonuria (PKU)** and **Down's syndrome** (mongolism). Other factors include prenatal brain damage, certain childbirth difficulties, or mother's malnutrition, German measles, or physical shock.

12. Environmental influences on intelligence include psychological and physical isolation in childhood and lack of intellectual stimulation in the home. Newly developed training techniques give us increased optimism that more and more of the mentally retarded can be helped to function as valuable members of society.

13. Recent studies, such as the **Milwaukee Project,** suggest that manipulating the environment (increasing the type and number of stimulus inputs) can foster intellectual growth. **The Montessori method,** developed by Maria Montessori, has helped not only mentally retarded children but normal children. The method stresses the variety of stimulating educational materials and freedom of interaction and movement in classroom.

14. The IQ controversy is based on disagreement on whether the origins of intelligence are primarily nature or nurture. The truth probably lies between the two, and it is important to remember that intelligence is not fixed. It is a process undergoing constant change.

Suggested Readings

Rosenthal, Robert and Lenore Jacobson. *Pygmalion in the classroom.* New York: Holt, Rinehart and Winston, 1968.

Shaw, G. B. *Pygmalion.* New York: Penguin, 1961.

Terman, Lewis M. and Melita Oden. *The gifted group at midlife.* Stanford, California: Stanford University Press, 1959.

► # STUDY GUIDE

A.   RECALL

Sentence Completion

[p. 256]   1. In Shaw's *Pygmalion*, Henry Higgins is an expert in _____.

[p. 257]   2. The point of *Pygmalion* is that Higgins not only gives Eliza a new way to speak, but he also changes her _____.

[p. 257]   3. Of all _____ traits, one of the most important is the one we call intelligence.

[p. 257]   4. Intelligence may be defined as a combination of mental characteristics that enable anyone to _____ in a particular environment.

[p. 258]   5. When we try to measure intelligence, we are restricted to measuring _____.

[p. 258]   6. The earliest measures of intelligence were concerned primarily with assessing a person's _____ _____.

[p. 259]   7. In constructing his intelligence test, Binet assumed that retarded children learn more _____ than do normal children.

[p. 259]   8. If a six-year-old child behaves like a normal five-year-old child, we can say that the child's _____ _____ is five.

[p. 261]   9. The IQ of an eight-year-old child with a mental age of six is _____.

[p. 260]   10. A psychologist at Stanford University, _____, brought the Binet-Simon tests to the United States and revised them.

[p. 262]   11. The normal distribution describes the scores earned by many people who have taken an IQ test; it is shaped like a _____.

[p. 262]   12. Thurstone claimed that intelligence is made up of seven _____ _____ _____.

[p.263]   13. If IQ is determined by a person's _____, it should not change as the person grows older.

[p. 264]   14. The _____ is an intelligence test designed expressly for adults.

[p. 264]   15. The first intelligence tests that could be administered to groups of subjects all at the same time were devised by the _____.

[p. 265]   16. _____ are the experts who design and administer psychological tests.

[p. 266]   17. If a test measures something consistently over time, it is said to be _____.

[p. 267]   18. If a test measures what it says it is measuring, the test is said to be
_____.

[p. 267]   19. Most intelligence tests are designed to be particularly useful for _____
_____ students.

[p. 267]   20. IQ tests do _____ in predicting academic success, but do
_____ in predicting success in the business world.

[p. 269]   21. Phenylketonuria (PKU) is caused by the lack of a specific _____, or
body chemical.

[p. 269]   22. Most people with Down's syndrome have _____ chromosomes.

[p. 270]   23. Psychological isolation during infancy and early childhood can eventually result in
_____.

[p. 273]   24. The _____ method of education plays down the importance of discipline in the classroom.

[p. 275]   25. The Milwaukee Project that enriched environmental experiences of children demonstrated that IQs of children reared in enriched environments could be raised by
_____ to _____ points.

[p. 275]   26. Whether intelligence is primarily inherited or is a function of experience is seen as
one aspect of the larger _____–_____ controversy.

[p. 277]   27. Your intelligence is an ever-changing _____ that results from the
_____ between your heredity and your environment.

B.   REVIEW

Multiple Choice: Circle the letter identifying the alternative that most correctly completes the statement or answers the question.

1. Personality emerges from the development of:
   A. physical traits.
   B. cognitive traits.
   C. social traits.
   D. all of the above.

2. Intelligence is the ability to:
   A. solve mathematical problems.
   B. survive in one's environment.
   C. learn lists of verbal material.
   D. use a large vocabulary.

3. One reason Alfred Binet devised his test of intelligence was to:
   A. see which of his three children was the brightest.
   B. determine the intellectual differences between mentally deficient and normal
      children.
   C. prove James McKeen Cattell was wrong in his theory of intelligence.
   D. assess the correlation between reaction times and higher cognitive abilities.

4. The IQ of a six-year-old child who has a mental age of eight is:
   A. 75.
   B. 100.
   C. 133.
   D. 150.

5. _____ believed that intelligence consisted of seven primary mental abilities.
   A. J. P. Guilford
   B. L. L. Thurstone
   C. Alfred Binet
   D. Louis Terman

6. Who devised the first group tests of intelligence?
   A. Alfred Binet
   B. the French government
   C. Stanford University
   D. the U. S. Army

7. If a test measures what it says it is supposed to measure, it is then:
   A. valid.
   B. reliable.
   C. standardized.
   D. none of the above.

8. The mentally retarded:
   A. are so because of inherited causes only.
   B. may learn to be retarded.
   C. cannot truly benefit from training or education.
   D. should be institutionalized for their own good.

9. The Milwaukee Project:
   A. studied the intellectual growth of 40 poor black children.
   B. involved the training of different kinds of rats at the University of Wisconsin.
   C. tested the intelligence of everyone in the city and determined that whites scored higher than blacks.
   D. confirmed the notion that most of what we call intelligence is inherited.

10. The WAIS test of intelligence:
   A. was written before the Binet-Simon test.
   B. is used by the U. S. Army to test IQ.
   C. is more appropriate for adults than is the Binet-Simon test.
   D. was designed to assess children's abilities to do well in school.

ARTIFICIAL INTELLIGENCE

Robots and mechanical monsters lumbered across the pages of science fiction novels for years before technological advances such as transistors, television, and computers made it possible for these mechanical marvels actually to step into the world of scientific reality. Even when they did, in the 1950s and 1960s many people considered them nothing more than expensive toys. But this didn't discourage the inventors of such toys. The field of **artificial,** or machine **intelligence** has grown steadily during the past 20 years, and attempts to design a "thinking" machine have continued. Mathematicians and engineers at the Massachusetts Institute of Technology's Artificial Intelligence Laboratory, for example, have combined a computer, a television camera, and a mechanical arm into a system with enough artificial intelligence to recognize blocks of various sizes, colors, and shapes and to assemble them into structures without step-by-step instructions from an operator. For more complex tasks an advanced arm has been developed with eight movable joints that can reach around obstacles. A similar mechanical arm at Stanford University has been programmed to pick up the pieces of a water pump, assemble them, and screw them together. Such machines will eventually be able to perform mechanical tasks too minute or too delicate for human hands. But so far these machines don't do much of what would be called thinking. Other machines, however, do seem to have a basic sort of intelligence.

Checker- and chess-playing machines even have the ability to learn from their mistakes. One at MIT has been rated as a better-than-average chess player in tournament chess. Such research has been attacked as a useless and frivolous waste of time because machines will probably never be able to really think. But artificial intelligence researchers say robots are only tools for the study of intelligence. Getting a machine to learn English, for example, demonstrates the problems and methods humans have in learning a language. Such problems don't always show up in a language laboratory. Seymour Papert, co-director with Marvin Minsky of the Artificial Intelligence Laboratory at MIT compares the study of intelligence to the study of flight. He points out that just as flight couldn't be analyzed until the principles of aerodynamics were worked out, human intelligence can't be thoroughly studied until the basic prinicples of intelligence are formulated. Jean Piaget (see Chapter 7) is investigating principles of intelligence by observing the mental development of children. Papert and his co-workers are doing the same thing by finding out how machines learn. The end result, Papert says, will be theories of intelligence that apply to humans and machines.

Papert and Minsky believe that enough is already known about machine intelligence to use it as a basis for planning new learning environments for children. One of their projects demonstrates how artificial intelligence technology can be used in education. The idea is not to use machines as teachers; instead, computers are being used to give children practice in thinking. To do this it is not sufficient merely to have a computer. It is necessary to develop situations in which the computer can be used by a child to solve real problems. Several computer-controlled devices have been designed to do this. One is a music generator that enables a child to produce songs and to experiment in music composition. Another is a graphic system with the ability to produce animated cartoons. The computer can be programmed to compose stories or poems. There is also a mechanical animal called "the turtle" that can be programmed to do a number of things, including move around a classroom and leave a track or draw a picture on the floor. By learning to program the computer to generate music, pictures, or physical activities, the student is supposed to develop the mental tools to think about such things as time, space, sound, and physical matters.

This approach can be seen in many projects as the children program machines to imitate some aspects of their own behavior. To understand how to make the turtle move, for example, the children look at their own motions. To make the computer produce grammatical English, they look at their own sentences. By programming a computer to play games of skill, children begin to understand the processes involved in improving their own mental skills. Work with music may lead to a child's being able to think clearly about time as it applies to things other than music. Eventually, Papert and his co-workers hope to use computer technology and what they have learned about intelligence to develop methods of helping children learn in such areas as physics, linguistics, biology, and psychology.

C.   NEWS STORY QUESTIONS

1. Whether or not machines can be developed that truly show a capacity for "thinking," what are two good reasons (applications) for continuing to try? (a) _____

(b) _____

unit THREE

PERSONALITY

Movie still from *Portnoy's Complaint.*

Each human being is a unique, complex individual. Theories of personal development attempt to explain how we achieve our individual personalities by examining the biological, cognitive, and social or environmental influences on our lives. In this chapter we will look at different theories of personal development, and we will see that when our basic needs are being met we each have the ability to direct our own mental, moral, and behavioral development.

Personal Development

chapter

When you have completed your study of this chapter, you should be able to:

- ▶ List and describe Freud's five stages of psychosexual development and his three components of personality
- ▶ List and summarize Erikson's eight stages of psychosocial development
- ▶ Discuss the relationships between Piaget's and Kohlberg's schemes of moral development
- ▶ Summarize the social learning theorists' view of personal development
- ▶ Describe Bandura's view of learning through modeling and imitation
- ▶ Characterize the humanistic psychologists, focussing on self-actualization.

Anal stage (AY-null). The second of Freud's psychosexual stages, during which the infant presumably gains pleasure primarily both from expelling and from retaining urine and feces. Lasts from the end of the child's first year of life to the third or fourth year.

Autonomy (aw-TAHN-oh-me). The Latin word *auto* means "self." Thus an automobile is a self-moving machine. In psychological terms, autonomy is the freedom to direct one's own movements, to make one's own decisions and choices without outside interference.

Conscious self. In Freud's terms, the *Ego* Those thoughts, behaviors, feelings, and attitudes that you have about yourself are part of your own individual conscious self.

Ego (EE-go). The conscious self. Obeys what Freud called "the reality principle" and tries to keep the Id under control. From the Latin word meaning "I."

Ego integrity (EE-go in-TEGG-ritt-tee). Our word "integrity" comes from a Latin word meaning "whole" or "untouched." According to Freud, your Ego has various defense mechanisms it uses in order to keep itself intact or undamaged from impulses or commands from the Id and the Superego.

Fixated. Fixation is a Freudian defense mechanism involving an interruption of normal psychosexual development. If an infant's oral needs are not satisfied, its maturation may be disrupted and its personality may remain stopped or fixed at the oral level.

Generativity (jen-ur-uh-TIV-uh-tee). To generate is to produce. Generativity is having the power of producing or originating things.

Genital stage. The last of the Freudian stages of psychosexual development, during which a person learns that giving pleasure to a sexual partner is as satisfying as receiving genital stimulation oneself.

Humanistic psychology. Humanists such as Carl Rogers and Abraham Maslow believe that each person instinctively becomes better and grows into a mature and happy human being if given the chance. This development process is often called self-actualization.

Id. The primitive, instinctual, childish, unconscious portion of the personality that obeys the pleasure principle, thus constantly warring with the Ego.

Identity crisis. One of the eight crises that Erikson says each person must face during personality development. During puberty, the crisis is that of finding one's identity. The adolescent must decide what the future will hold and who he or she will become.

Latent period. According to Freud, the sexual fantasies that children experience during the phallic stage raise so much guilt and anxiety that the child enters into a period of sexual repression called the latent period. This developmental stage begins at age 5 or 6, and ends at puberty.

Level of conventional morality. The second of Kohlberg's stages of moral development, during which the child conforms to the moral principles of society.

Level of preconventional morality. The first of Kohlberg's stages of moral development, during which the child "behaves" merely to avoid punishment or to gain selfish rewards. Called "premoral stage" by Piaget.

Level of postconventional morality. Last of Kohlberg's three stages of moral development, during which the individual behaves according to his or her conscience, or according to what the person sees as being abstract ethical principles.

Lewdly (LOOD-lee). From an old English word meaning "vile" or "evil." Most openly erotic or sexual forms of behavior are likely to be considered lewd.

Masturbation. Sexual self-stimulation.

Model. From the French word "mode," meaning a manner of doing something. We learn ways of behaving by imitating the actions of others, particularly those of our parents.

Modeling therapy. A type of behavioral treatment developed by Albert Bandura in which the client is encouraged to act in a manner similar to that of the therapist. If the client fears handling snakes, the therapist "shows the client how" by handling snakes in a calm, relaxed, and rewarding manner.

Moral development. According to Lawrence Kohlberg, each person passes through three levels of moral development, each level having two stages.

Oral stage. The first stage in psychosexual development in which—according to Freud—the child's satisfactions come chiefly from the mouth.

Phallic stage (FAL-ick; rhymes with "PAL sick"). The Greek word for "penis" is *phallos*. Freud called the third stage of psychosexual development the phallic stage, during which the child gains pleasure from genital stimulation.

Phobias (FOE-bee-uz). From the Greek word meaning "fears." Phobias are strong and often unusual fears of something.

Premoral stage. Piaget's first level of moral development. Similar to Kohlberg's level of preconventional morality.

Psychosocial stages. According to Erik Erikson, each human being must pass through eight developmental stages on his or her way to complete maturity.

Puberty (PYU-burr-tee). The onset of sexual maturity, when the person becomes physically capable of sexual reproduction.

Self-actualization. Maslow's term for the highest type of meta-need. Self-actualization typically involves gaining enough insight and self-control to become what one wishes to become.

Sex roles. A *social role* is a set of standard responses to certain social situations—a set of behavior patterns appropriate to a given culture or environment. Sex roles are cultural expectations governing how a man or a woman should behave in most social situations.

Social learning theorists. Behaviorally oriented psychologists who theorize that most forms of behavior are learned or acquired—usually through imitation and reinforcement.

Stage of autonomous morality. According to Piaget, the final stage of moral development during which one follows the promptings of one's conscience.

Stage of moral realism. According to Piaget, the second stage during which the child behaves in a way to please others.

Superego. That part of the human psyche that—according to Freud—is concerned with the moral laws of the society the individual grows up in. The conscience.

Tabula rasa (TABB-you-lah RAH-sah). Literally, "a blank slate" or "blank tablet." The belief—according to John Locke—that the human mind is a "blank tablet on which experience writes." Locke denied that we are born with any instinctual ideas or beliefs. Rather we learn everything that we know.

Trauma (TRAW-muh). From the Greek word meaning "wound." A physical or psychological injury, or a terribly wounding experience.

INTRODUCTION: PORTNOY'S COMPLAINT

Portnoy had a problem. He didn't like himself, and he didn't like what he was becoming. To the world, Alexander Portnoy was a highly successful and intelligent social worker. To himself, Portnoy was a disappointment. He lived alone but didn't want to be alone. He had lovers but could not find any woman who satisfied him. Portnoy was full of doubts and fears and guilts, and he totally disapproved of himself. In the hope of getting to the causes of his condition and of perhaps finding a solution to his problem, Portnoy took his complaint to a psychiatrist.

Portnoy's Complaint is a novel by Philip Roth. It consists of a long discussion by Portnoy of his past and present problems. The result is a **lewdly** sexual but sometimes funny satire of family life and adolescence in the 1940s.

Portnoy believed that what made him what he was was his family and in particular his overpowering mother. From the moment Alex Portnoy was born, he was the apple of his mother's eye. She constantly told him that he was a perfect prince, a unique and brilliant genius. At first Alex enjoyed being the center of his family's attention and the object of his mother's worship. He tried to live up to everyone's expectations by doing exactly what he was told. When he got all As in his classes, his mother called him "Einstein the second."

But even while Alex was being called a genius, his mother was making him feel incompetent and helpless. He was fed and watched over and pampered constantly. He never had a moment to himself. Everything he did his mother knew about. Portnoy complained that his mother was like a big bird hovering over and smothering him. Even when he became an adult, his mother would call him her "lover" and say, "To us you're still a baby, darling."

As Alex neared adolescence he came to resent the way his mother treated him. Coming out of a restaurant, for instance, she would go on and on about what a good boy he had been. He used his little napkin and his silverware, and he didn't spill any of his potatoes. A perfect little gentleman, she would say. "*Fruitcake*, Mother," Alex thought to himself. "A little *fruitcake* is what you saw —and exactly what the training program was designed to produce."

Alex didn't want to turn into a fruitcake. His resentment soon turned into rebellion, and he quit being an obedient and helpless little boy. He began to fight with his parents. He wouldn't eat what he was supposed to eat. He wouldn't go to the synagogue. He took up a new hobby—**masturbation.** It was the only thing he had to himself, he would say.

Masturbation wasn't the answer to Portnoy's problems. In fact, it only made matters worse. After years of doing only what he was supposed to do, he was now doing something he felt guilty about. Alex was in constant fear of getting caught, and he was terrified that he was going to give himself cancer. Even so, he continued to masturbate—with a passion. His sexual urges were so strong that they were in constant battle with his desire to be a good little boy.

As an adult, Portnoy had similar problems. On the one hand, he had done everything his mother wanted him to do. He got straight As in college, graduated at the top of his law-school class, and he was a highly respected member of the community who worked to solve other people's problems. On the other hand, he had not solved his own personal problems. That was his complaint. His sexual desires were still in conflict with his other personal needs and the needs of his family and society. Portnoy wanted to be a father and a husband. His parents wanted him to remain their perfect little boy. Society wanted Portnoy to be a hard-working and productive citizen, but still he went from woman to woman, from affair to affair, in search of more and more sexual adventures. He felt guilty about his sex-life. He hated living alone and hurting his parents. But still, he would not settle down and change his ways. Portnoy could not find a middle ground between what his sexuality wanted him to be, what his parents and society wanted him to be, and what he wanted himself to be. In all of this confusion he could not really find himself. Why? That's the question Portnoy asked his psychiatrist.

Portnoy's Complaint, like all good fiction, contains much that is true about the human condition. Portnoy's search for himself, although somewhat exaggerated, is similar to what many of us in the United States go through trying to find an acceptable identity for ourselves.

We all have biological needs, cognitive or intellectual needs, and social needs. Some of these needs are determined by our genetic blueprints, some by the social environment we grew up in, and some by our present real-life situation. Each person's pattern of needs differs somewhat from everyone else's. For the most part, however, we all tend to satisfy our needs by seeking out biological, cognitive, and social inputs from our environments. But in satisfying one set of needs, we may end up having to deny others. For example, in order to achieve spiritual satisfaction (cognitive), we may have to give up eating certain types of food or starve ourselves for a period of time (biological), or even isolate ourselves from our friends for brief periods (social).

The way that each person achieves a balance of some kind between the biological, cognitive, and social inputs that he or she desires has a great deal to do with determining that person's individuality. And because there are so many possible needs and inputs to satisfy them, and so many possible conflicts, it is almost impossible for anyone to keep a perfectly balanced identity at all times.

DEVELOPING INDIVIDUALITY

There are many well-known theories of personality—that is, theories of how people develop their own unique ways of dealing with their needs and their problems. Some theories emphasize biological or inherited influences on personality, some emphasize cognitive or intellectual influences, and others emphasize social learning and environmental factors. Most of the older theories assume that personality development is pretty well complete by the time a person goes through adolescence. Many of the newer theories assume that we continue to grow and adjust all our lives.

Of all the theoretical approaches, perhaps the best-known is that of Sigmund Freud. Freud was a physiologist who assumed that our personalities are determined primarily by genes. Perhaps for this reason, Freud placed primary importance on our biological or emotional needs, and believed that our individuality is pretty well set or fixed by the time we reach 15 years of age.

According to Freud, we pass through five major stages of personality development (also discussed in Chapter 3). The first is the **oral stage.** During this time, Freud says, a child's personality is almost completely related to its mouth or its biological need for oral inputs (food and water). The second period is called the **anal stage.** As a child learns to control its own biological functions or outputs, it becomes cognitively aware of itself as an individual. During the third or **phallic stage,** which begins when the child is about three, the child learns that other people have an existence independent of its own perceptions. The child becomes aware of sex differences, and builds up a warm relationship with whichever parent is of the opposite sex — the boy with his mother, the girl with her father. During the phallic stage, the child also learns that its sexual organs can give it sensual pleasures. But its pleasure needs come into conflict with parental or social demands. According to Freud, most children solve this conflict by giving up self-stimulation (masturbation) during the **latent period.** During this period, children solve their problems of relationships with opposite-sex parents by forming close ties with same-sex agemates. When the child reaches **puberty,** the fifth or **genital stage** begins. During the genital stage, the young person begins to seek pleasure from contacts with the opposite sex.

At each of these four stages, the child's biological, cognitive, and social needs may be in great upheaval and conflict. The well-adjusted child solves the conflicts and enters into adulthood during the genital stage. The child who cannot adjust may become **fixated** at one of the earlier stages and may carry some childish habits and problems into his or her adult years. We will discuss fixations more fully in Chapter 10.

We do not live by bread, book, or friends alone. In order to develop a mature personality, we must learn to meet our biological, cognitive, and social needs.

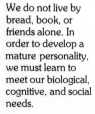

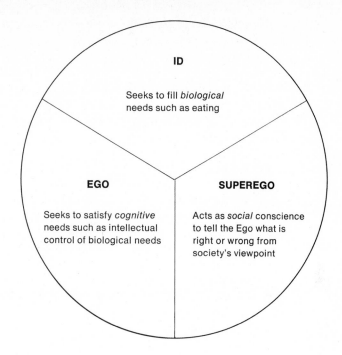

FIG. 9–1.
According to Freud, a well-rounded person is able to balance the biological, cognitive, and social needs.

Id, Ego, and Superego

Freud divided the human personality into three components. The **Id** is Freud's term for the unconscious part of the personality that is constantly and selfishly seeking biological pleasure and gratification. During the oral stage, children are presumably almost all Id. Most of their time is spent in eating and sleeping. As the child matures, its Id is said to be responsible for other biological drives, such as sex. Portnoy's Id controlled much of his life.

The cognitive or conscious part of the personality Freud called the **Ego.** The Ego begins to develop during the anal stage as children are forced to learn control over their own biological functions. The Ego, like the Id, seeks pleasure—but not always biological pleasure. Portnoy's Ego, for instance, wanted many things, including an understanding of who he was and why he had such a strong Id. Portnoy's Ego spent much of its time trying to keep his Id under control.

Freud called the social part of the personality the **Superego,** which comes into play during the phallic stage as the child begins to identify with a parent or older person of the same sex. Thus, as their Superegos develop, boys begin imitating and identifying with men, and girls begin imitating and identifying with women. The Superego is a sort of "social conscience" that tells the Ego which things are right or wrong according to the society it developed in—that is, according to the men or women it identified with. It was Portnoy's Superego that gave him constant guilt feelings and made him dissatisfied with his accomplishments in life.

Freud developed his theory of personality after spending many years working with and studying people who had mental problems. Since many of the people whom he treated had sexual hangups, Freud tended to emphasize the biological influences on human growth and development. Some of Freud's followers, therefore, have taken his theories and expanded on them in an attempt to account for some of the other important factors in becoming an individual. One of the best known of these theories is the one proposed by Erik H. Erikson.

Erikson's Psychosocial Stages

Before coming to the United States, Erik H. Erikson studied in Vienna with Freud and his daughter Anna. Erikson agrees with much of Freud's thinking about the importance of sexuality, but he does not agree that personality development stops at adolescence. The Ego, says Erikson, is much more important than the Id or the Superego. And the Ego's interactions with the environment and society are much more important than the Ego's interactions with some unconscious sexual desires (the Id). It is a particular society and the environment that shape the Ego and the personality, according to Erikson. And because people deal with society throughout their lives, individual Egos are constantly being shaped by society.

Erikson suggests that there are eight stages of personality development. Each stage is directly related to forces in society so Erikson calls them the **psychosocial stages.** During each stage, individuals are faced with a particular crisis or conflict. These conflicts are like tests that have to be passed. As each conflict is resolved or each test of personality is passed, individuals move up to the next stage of development. People may fail to pass one or more of the tests, but this failure does not mean that personality development must stop. The test materials are always available (the society and the conflicts that it presents). At any time, individuals may develop the personality skills necessary to resolve a past crisis or pass a past test.

1. Trust vs. Mistrust *(From Birth to the First Year)*

The first of Erikson's psychosocial stages is similar to Freud's oral stage and is called the sensory stage. It is the time during which infants must rely on other people in their social environment to help meet almost all their needs. If children receive loving care during this stage, they will learn to trust and rely on their caretakers. The crisis in this stage comes when children get poor or inconsistent care. Then they may learn to mistrust others rather than trust them.

2. Autonomy vs. Shame and Doubt *(Second Year)*

Erikson's second stage of psychosocial development is called the muscular or anal stage. During this period children learn to control their own muscular movements. They learn to crawl and then to walk and to make use of the independence their movements give them. This awareness of physical freedom results in a feeling of **autonomy,** or independence. The crisis during the muscular stage occurs if parents are afraid to let their children show any independence. According to Erikson, if children are not allowed to gain some autonomy at an early age, they may begin to doubt their abilities or to feel ashamed of themselves.

3. Initiative vs. Guilt *(Third to Fifth Year)*

Erikson's third stage, that of locomotor control, is similar to Freud's phallic stage. During this period the child becomes more assertive and outgoing. If the child is encouraged to explore its world, the child gains initiative. If the child is overly punished by the parents (or other people), the child experiences a crisis and may develop feelings of guilt about expressing itself.

4. Industry vs. Inferiority *(Sixth Year to Puberty)*

The fourth stage is one of latent development. Its early sexual conflicts resolved, the child is ready to learn social and intellectual skills. If the child is rewarded for its achievements, it becomes industrious. If it fails at everything it tries, it experiences a crisis that may lead it to feel inferior about its talents for the rest of its life.

5. Identity vs. Role Confusion *(Adolescence)*

One of the strengths of Erikson's theory is that he recognized the problems that people face during adolescence when they are trying to find themselves. Erikson states that most of us go through an **identity crisis** at this time. At this point in our lives, we must discover not only our sexual identities and preferences, but decide on our life's occupation. We must also settle on the social and economic values that will influence much of what we do the rest of our lives. If we are encouraged to "pull it all together and become ourselves," we create a unique identity—what Freud called a healthy Ego. But if we experience social conflict, if the people around us punish us for being ourselves or try to make us follow unworkable social models, we may experience a severe crisis about what our role in life should be.

6. Intimacy vs. Isolation *(Young Adulthood)*

Unlike Freud (and Piaget), Erikson believed that personality development continues after adolescence. If the individual has established a firm identity by early adulthood, the person is able to share life's intimacies with another individual. If the person fails to resolve the identity crisis, however, the person will remain isolated from the closest forms of psychological "sharing" with others. Few people are ever completely successful at getting through the first six stages of development. Most individuals have some successes and some failures at each stage. Therefore, according to Erikson, the search for intimacy is not always entirely successful. Almost four of every 10 marriages in the United States, for instance, end in divorce.

1

2

3

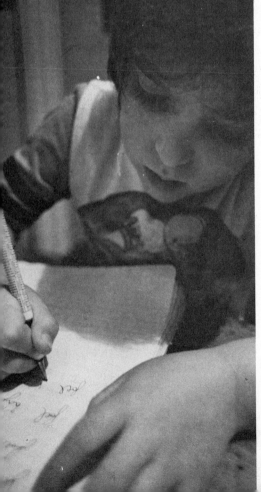

I AM
A HUMAN BEING:
DO NOT FOLD,
SPINDLE OR
MUTILATE

ANARCHISTS
UNITE!

YOU FIGHT & DIE
BUT CAN'T
VOTE
AT
18

BLACK
POWER

MAKE LOVE
NOT WAR

DON'T TRUST ANYONE
OVER
30

BURN
POT
NOT
PEOPLE

MOBILIZATION TO
end
the war
now
APRIL 15, 1967

YOU FIGHT &
BUT CAN'T
DRINK
AT
18

4

5

According to Erikson, there are eight stages of psychosocial development: (1) During the first year of life, an infant must rely on other people. (2) During the second year, the child must learn to control its own muscular movements. (3) During the third stage, the child gains locomotor control and becomes more outgoing. (4) During the fourth stage, the child learns social and intellectual skills. (5) During adolescence, most of us experience an identity crisis. (6) After the individual has established a firm identity, he or she is ready to share life's intimacies with another person. (7) Successful adults are productive and continue to grow. (8) With maturity comes the ability to integrate all stages of development and to look back with a sense of achievement.

6

7

8

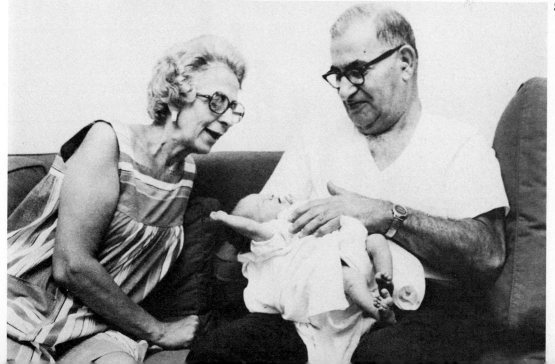

7. Generativity vs. Stagnation *(Adulthood)*

The crisis in middle age comes about when people sit back and do not continue to grow and develop socially and intellectually. **Generativity** means the ability to reproduce, generate, or be productive. Successful adults do more than produce children. They should be able to generate work and ideas. People who continue to be productive show concern for themselves, their family, and for society in general. People who do not continue to produce or who produce only what they themselves need are usually self-centered. They are often complacent and do not continue to grow and develop in a social or intellectual sense. Such people become stale or stagnant.

8. Integrity vs. Despair *(Late Adulthood)*

Maturity comes with the pulling together or integration of the first seven stages of development. Those few people who have been successful in solving all of life's crises or conflicts reach what Erikson calls **Ego integrity.** They can look back with a sense of achievement on their lives. Those people who have not been so successful often look back and feel that their life has had no meaning or was useless and wasted. Those people who look back on an incomplete life often look ahead to death with a feeling of despair.

Considering the number of conflicts and crises that we must face during the various stages of development, it seems almost impossible for anyone ever to achieve maturity or what Erikson calls Ego integrity. But most people do reach

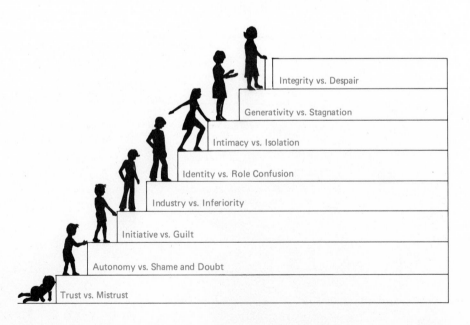

FIG. 9–2.
Erikson's eight stages of personality development can be viewed as steps that lead us through life.

Integrity vs. Despair

Generativity vs. Stagnation

Intimacy vs. Isolation

Identity vs. Role Confusion

Industry vs. Inferiority

Initiative vs. Guilt

Autonomy vs. Shame and Doubt

Trust vs. Mistrust

some degree of maturity. And at any stage, people can go back and work on past failures—as Alexander Portnoy did in his mature years. It is only perfection that is really difficult to achieve.

MORAL DEVELOPMENT

Freud was interested primarily in emotional and biological development; he saw the growth of the Ego as being the body's way of defending itself against the emotional impulsiveness of the Id. Thus, to Freud the thinking or cognitive side of maturation was little more than an outgrowth of the development of one's biological heritage. Erikson made many changes in the Freudian view. First, he noted that one's personality continues to grow throughout one's life; therefore, he increased Freud's five stages of development to eight. Second, Erikson believed that social factors are much more influential in shaping our adult destinies than are our genes. As far as Erikson was concerned, our minds could (with the help of other people) work through and hence overcome whatever problems occurred during our early development.

Piaget's Position

Like Freud, Swiss scientist Jean Piaget sees mental growth as being completed by the time the person is 15 or so (see Chapter 7). And also like Freud, Piaget believes that all human beings must pass through four stages of development that are rigidly determined by our genetic blueprints. Social influences may speed up or retard cognitive growth, Piaget says, but the basic pattern of development is fixed by our biological inheritance.

In recent years, Harvard psychologist Lawrence Kohlberg has attempted to extend part of Piaget's theory in much the same way that Erikson extended Freud's. Piaget states that part of mental development concerns the perception of right and wrong, of what is ethical or moral and what is not. Very young children behave in an orderly fashion only because they are forced to do so by their parents and other adults. In the first, **premoral stage,** children are still in the sensory-motor and pre-operational stages. They follow rules—but they do so only to escape punishment or to gain rewards. Once the child reaches the stage of concrete operations, however, it typically becomes interested in rules and regulations for their own sake. During this **stage of moral realism,** the child conforms to societal rules and often regards such rules as being sacred and unchangeable.

Once the child reaches the stage of formal operations, however, it is mature enough to realize that rules are made by humans and hence are subject to change. The child has reached Piaget's **stage of autonomous morality,** in which it is capable of dealing with such abstract concepts as *social justice.* In this final stage, Piaget says, the child appreciates the fact that rules are made to help people get along with each other in a fair and equitable way. The young person in this stage can appreciate the wisdom of the Golden Rule, "Do unto others as you would have them do unto you."

Kohlberg's Moral Levels

Lawrence Kohlberg has expanded Piaget's theory in several ways, mostly by taking into account (as Erikson did) the strong influence of social factors on human development. Kohlberg describes three levels of moral development that are similar to Piaget's, but Kohlberg believes that each level has two rather specific stages to it.

1. Level of Preconventional Morality
Stage 1. The child obeys parental rules in order to escape punishment.

Stage 2. The child becomes mature enough to realize that it can also gain rewards by following rules. But the child still has no true moral understanding of right and wrong and does what it is told to do only to satisfy its own self-centered need for pleasure.

2. Level of Conventional Morality
Stage 1. "Good girl"/"good boy" stage. The child's rewards are no longer exclusively biological, but are partially social. The child behaves in order to gain approval or to avoid disapproval of others.

Stage 2. "Law and order" stage. The child is now mature enough to have developed a sense of personal guilt or shame. It begins to perceive the necessity for "authority," and follows rules rather rigidly in order to satify its own need for order and to avoid feeling guilty.

3. Level of Postconventional Morality
Stage 1. Contract or individual rights stage. According to Kohlberg, only those people who have reached Piaget's stage of formal operations are likely to achieve the third level of moral development. The first stage at this level is a sort of "democracy in action" position in which the person considers contracts made with others as being morally binding. Actions are "right" or "wrong" because they have been judged so by the people in a given society. The individual at this level obeys laws both to gain the respect of other people and to avoid being thought immoral by society.

Stage 2. Stage of personal conscience. Few individuals ever reach this final peak of moral development, according to Kohlberg. Someone who has achieved this stage has the ability to think of right and wrong in purely abstract terms, and behaves according to his or her own standards of ethics or justice — even if these personal standards may occasionally go against society's rules. At this stage, moral principles come from within, and the individual acts to avoid self-condemnation.

Both Piaget and Kohlberg believe that moral development—like perceptual

TABLE 9–1   Stages in Personal Development

Psychosexual (Freud)	1. Oral	2. Anal	3. Phallic	4. Latent	5. Genital		
Psychosocial (Erikson)	1. Trust vs. Mistrust	2. Autonomy vs. Shame and Doubt	3. Initiative vs. Guilt	4. Indus-try vs. Inferior-ity	5. Identity vs. Role Confusion	6. Inti-macy vs. Iso-lation	7. Gen-era-tiv-ity vs. Stag-nation	8. Integ-rity vs. Des-pair
Cognitive Development (Piaget)	1. Premoral during sensory-motor and preopera-tional stages of cognitive development		2. Moral Realism during concrete operations stage of cognitive development		3. Autonomous Morality during formal operations stage of cognitive development		
Moral Development (Kohlberg)	1. Preconventional A. Obeys parental rules to escape punish-ment B. Follows rules to gain rewards		2. Conven-tional Morality A. "Good girl"/ "good boy" stage B. Law-and-order stage		3. Post-conventional Morality A. Contract or indi-vidual rights stage B. Stage of personal conscience		

development—is primarily determined by one's genetic inheritance. Thus, all people in all societies should go through the stages in the same order (although at different speeds). Not all the evidence supports this view, however. Indeed, many psychologists believe that moral and perceptual development will differ radically depending on the person's individual experiences and the culture in which the person grows up.

SOCIAL LEARNING THEORY

Alexander Portnoy began life as a single cell. His genetic blueprint was created the moment his father's sperm fertilized the egg lying inside his mother's body. That single cell divided millions and millions of times—without needing any guidance from his mother while doing so. Nine months later, Alex was born as a white male with a large nose (which he didn't like), black, curly hair (which he didn't mind), and possessed of genes that determined he would grow up to be a medium-sized man with a well-developed body.

Portnoy's genes also determined the general course his body would take while growing into manhood. Muscular coordination in a child occurs in a "head to foot" direction. The child gains control over its head and neck muscles in the first month or so after birth, but it cannot grasp and hold onto things with its hands until about the third or fourth month. As the connections between its brain and its muscles continue to grow and develop according to the plan laid

FIG. 9–3.
Muscular coordination develops gradually in a head-to-foot direction.

0 months
Fetal posture

1 month
Chin up

2 months
Chest up

3 months
Reach and miss

4 months
Sit with support

5 months
Sit on lap, grasp object

6 months
Sit on high chair, grasp dangling object

7 months
Sit alone

8 months
Stand with help

9 months
Stand holding furniture

10 months
Creep

11 months
Walk when led

12 months
Pull to stand by furniture

13 months
Climb stair steps

14 months
Stand alone

15 months
Walk alone

down in its genetic blueprint, the child gains the ability to sit (sixth or seventh month) and then to stand with help and to creep (seventh through tenth month).

Most children begin to walk between the twelfth and eighteenth month after birth, and so did Alex. Because his physical maturation could not be changed very much by his parents, it wouldn't have mattered had they encouraged him to walk or not. Alex still would have begun to move about when his body was ready and not before.

But what about his mental and moral development? Freud and Erikson would have said that Alex had a naturally strong Id that was hard to control, a confused Ego, and a Superego that continually made him feel guilty. Piaget would have noted that Alex went through the four stages of cognitive development found in most of the middle-class European children Piaget studied. Kohlberg might have noticed that Alex Portnoy reached at least the first stage of the level of postconventional morality typical of the educated, middle-class young adults that Kohlberg studied in the United States.

But the important question to many psychologists is this: Would Alex have had the same sort of mental and moral development had he been born to a working-class family in China or to an upper-class family in Africa? No matter where his parents had lived and no matter what their station in life, Alex Portnoy would have walked when he was about a year old. But would his Id have been as strong had he grown up on a Pacific island where children are encouraged to engage in sexual activities while quite young? And would he have achieved the same level of moral development in the same way had his parents been members of the ruling class in a country where people were casually shot to death for the least of crimes?

Alex was a white male of average size with black hair and a large nose. These physical characteristics were not under his control, but they did influence the way his mind grew and the way he perceived himself. However, many psychologists would claim that his nose and hair and skin color were not important in and of themselves. Rather, they affected him because of the way that people around Alex reacted to how he looked. In some cultures, a large nose is considered handsome; in other cultures, a white skin is a mark of inferiority. How much of what Alexander Portnoy became was determined by the way he was *taught* to react to himself and others?

The *Tabula Rasa*

The great English philosopher John Locke (1632–1704) believed that all people are born good, independent, and equal. He further believed that each human being is born with a mind that is like a **tabula rasa** — two Latin words meaning a blank tablet on which the pencil of experience writes. To put Locke's belief another way, he said that our minds are blank at birth, and that all that we think and believe, all of our moral and perceptual development, is taught to us by the people around us as we grow up.

Freud, Erikson, Piaget, and Kohlberg (and maybe even Alexander Portnoy) might not agree with Locke's viewpoint. However, many modern psychologists do accept the *tabula rasa* theory at least in part. Despite the fact that a person's biological development cannot generally be speeded up very much, the way that a person's mind grows is tremendously influenced by the social setting into

The social setting in which a child lives has a very important influence on his or her development. Surrounded by a loving family, this baby has a good chance to learn and develop into a healthy and mature individual.

which the person is born. Infants begin to learn from the moment they are born. They eat instinctively—but what they eat, and when and how they eat, are behaviors that are determined to a great extent by the attitudes and actions of the people who feed them. Children learn in many ways—by imitating others, by being rewarded or punished for acting or talking in certain ways, and by experiencing certain events that happen to occur at the same time (see the law of association, Chapter 6). Some of this learning is concrete and specific—infants are conditioned to like orange juice or to hate pain and violence. Some of this learning is abstract and general. For example, when little boys are told to "act like a man," they begin to acquire a general notion of what maleness or masculinity is all about in their particular culture.

Theorists such as Freud and Piaget noted how *similar* people are (particularly if they have grown up in similar environments). We all begin to walk and talk at about the same age; we all experience sexual puberty at about the same time. Therefore, reasoned Freud and Piaget, our mental development too should be about the same no matter where or how we are reared. John Locke—and modern psychologists who call themselves **social learning theorists**—note how *different* people are (even if they have grown up in similar environments). People with fairly similar bodies often have wildly different attitudes and actions. Furthermore, some individuals show radical changes in their values and behaviors in very short periods of time. According to the Bible, Saul of Tarsus was a man who spent years hating the Christians and trying to put them in jail. Then, on a trip to Damascus (a city in the middle-eastern country of Syria), Saul underwent a great mystical experience. Three days later he became a Christian himself, and spent the rest of his life helping the very people he had previously persecuted. We know him today as St. Paul, one of the founders of the Christian church. How would Freud and Piaget have explained the dramatic mental and spiritual changes that occurred to St. Paul on that dusty road to Damascus nearly 2000 years ago?

Like many biologically oriented scientists, Freud and Piaget were primarily interested in the influences of physical growth on mental development. The social learning theorists are primarily interested in the effects of family and cultural influences on personal change and adjustment.

Modeling

How do people learn? Stanford psychologist Albert Bandura is one of the best-known of modern social learning theorists. According to Bandura, one of the major reasons we become who and what we are is that we tend to imitate the behaviors of the people we live with. For example, our parents often serve as **models** whose actions and beliefs we tend to adopt without realizing that we are doing so. A young boy may prefer a certain breakfast food because a famous male rock star has endorsed it. A young girl may select a certain type of tennis racket because she associates it with a famous female tennis champion.

The developmental theorists all admit that modeling does occur, and that we learn many things by imitating or identifying with others. But to Freud and Piaget, modeling is less important than, and is always limited by, one's genetic inheritance. Therefore, if an adult experiences irrational fears (called **phobias**), the cause of the fear is probably due to some **trauma,** or emotional upheaval, that occurred when the person was young. This traumatic event would surely interrupt the person's normal development. To cure the fear, therefore, one would have to help the person work through his or her memories of the emotional event.

Bandura would not agree. To a social learning theorist, phobias are acquired because the feared object is somehow associated with an unpleasant or punishing stimulus input. Therefore, phobias are learned reaction patterns that can best be cured by encouraging the person to model, or behave like a person who is not afraid. In a research study reported in 1969, Bandura and his colleagues seem to have proved their point.

Modeling Therapy

Many people are afraid of snakes. To Freud, this fear was natural and somewhat innate since he believed the snake was an unconscious symbol of the penis, or male sex organ. If, during a person's mental development, an individual had a traumatic sexual experience, that person might end up fearing snakes as a symbolic way of expressing a fear of sex or sex organs. However, attempts to cure people of snake phobias using Freudian techniques take a long time indeed, and are not always successful.

Bandura and his colleagues used **modeling therapy** to help 32 people learn to overcome their irrational fear of reptiles. They began by advertising in a newspaper for subjects who wished help in getting rid of their snake phobias. Thirty-two people answered the ad. One was a museum official who was afraid to enter the snake exhibit in his own museum. Several were individuals who feared going hunting, fishing, or hiking because they might encounter a reptile. Others were schoolteachers whose young students often brought snakes to class for "show and tell." One woman had a neighbor who kept a boa constrictor as a pet; thinking about the closeness of the snake had nearly given the woman a heart attack.

Modeling can be used in therapy situations. This series of photographs shows how a girl learned to overcome her fear of dogs first by watching another child safely play with a dog, then by imitating his behavior.

Bandura and his associates compared several different types of treatment. Some of the subjects were randomly selected to receive no therapy at all during the first part of the experiment. These people made up the no-treatment "control group." Other subjects were merely shown movies of adults and children playing with snakes, or were asked to talk over their fears in a very relaxed manner.

A fourth group was given modeling therapy. At the beginning of treatment this fourth group watched through a glass partition while the therapist played with a snake to show that it wasn't dangerous. The therapist tried to model all of the snake-handling behaviors he wished the subjects to learn. Then the subjects entered the room where the therapist was, but all stayed some distance away from the dreaded reptile. Next, gradually, they were encouraged to approach the snake and touch it, just as the therapist had modeled doing. As the subjects gained confidence in playing with the snake, the therapist faded out of the picture.

The "final exam" for the effectiveness of the therapy was somewhat dramatic. The subject was asked to sit in a chair for 30 seconds, hands at side, while a snake was placed on the subject's lap and allowed to crawl all over his or her body. Every member of the modeling therapy group passed the test with ease. A few of the members of the film and the "talk" treatment groups passed, but almost no one in the no-treatment control group could tolerate touching the snakes.

At the close of their study, Bandura and his colleagues did something unusual—they gave modeling therapy to the members of the other groups who hadn't shown improvement. The psychologists report "cures" in 100 percent of these subjects.

As Bandura points out, modeling (learning by imitation) occurs whether or not we know that it is taking place. Social learning theorists have shown that young children become more aggressive after watching movies in which aggression is featured. Furthermore, more than half of the parents arrested in any given year for battering or abusing their children were abused or badly beaten themselves when they were young. A battered child may not like being harmed by its parents, but they are usually the only "model" that the child has. So when the child grows up, it acts like its parents and abuses its own offspring. Very few children who come from loving homes grow up to be child-abusers. Alexander Portnoy grew up sexually confused in no small part because his parents were themselves confused.

Learning Sex Roles

We learn to think of ourselves as men and women—and to behave in what our society thinks of as masculine or feminine ways—in part through modeling. But we maintain these **roles** throughout our lives because the people around us reward us for complying with cultural expectations.

Traditionally, little girls have been encouraged to imitate the "feminine" roles of their mothers. In many cultures, they are given dolls and tea sets to play with. In social situations, girls are usually rewarded for passive, dependent behavior. Historically, society has expected women to become wives and mothers and not to consider a career outside the home.

On the other hand, the "masculine" traits of independence and leadership have traditionally been fostered in little boys. In Western cultures, boys are given toy guns and taught to participate in rough contact sports. They are expected to be assertive leaders in pursuing a career in order to support a wife and family.

Each person—whether male or female—is a unique individual who can learn

From same-sex parents, children learn roles that society considers appropriately masculine or feminine. Often these roles have been stereotypes. However, children can learn positive roles from opposite-sex parents.

to develop fully his or her potential abilities and perform any social role he or she desires. An infant girl can grow up to be an independent woman who is a successful and influential business executive. And a baby boy can develop into a supportive and loving father who spends the majority of his time in the home.

Social Rewards and Punishments

Although some aspects of social roles may be genetically determined, many behaviors are learned. Almost all of our actions are strongly influenced by past rewards and punishments, or by our attempts to gain rewards and punishments in the near or distant future. Alexander Portnoy had problems relating to other people, particularly women who attracted him sexually. It took him a long time to see how subtly if unconsciously his parents and his friends had trained him to feel confused and to have difficulties in getting along with others.

But as social learning theorists like to point out, whether a behavior (or a social role) is learned or innately determined, it can usually be changed through training—that is, through the wise application of rewards and punishments. In a study reported by K. E. Allen and other behaviorists in 1964, a four-year-old girl named Ann was taught to get along better with other children her age. Ann's nursery school teachers became worried that she seemed to prefer interacting with adults to playing with the other children. The teachers asked the behavioral psychologists for help. These psychologists began by making careful observations of what Ann did, and how the people around her responded to her actions. Ann was a bright and outgoing child whom the teachers liked. Whenever she went over to talk to the teachers, they responded in a friendly way—that is, they rewarded Ann for approaching them. The other children were not as rewarding. Therefore, Ann spent close to 50 percent of her time interacting with the teachers, and less than 20 percent of her time playing with the other children. Although they were not aware of doing so, the teachers were actually maintaining Ann's "problem" by giving her attention and praise for approaching them, and punishing her by ignoring her whenever she did happen to interact with a child her own age.

The psychologists suggested to the teachers that they reverse their rewards and punishments. So the teachers started ignoring Ann when she approached them, but gave her immediate attention and praise whenever she approached or played with another child at the nursery school. Within two days, Ann was playing with the other children about 70 percent of the time, and interacting with the teachers only about 20 percent of the time. As soon as Ann began spending more time with the other children, they began rewarding her by becoming more friendly and attentive to her. Ann came to like the other four-year-olds so much that the teachers no longer had to give her deliberate praise for playing with her agemates. Some two months later, long after the experiment had ended, Ann was still spending about 70 percent of her time at the school playing with the other children.

DEVELOPMENT OF THE "SELF"

Freud saw us as being prisoners of our genes; some behaviorists and social learning theorists see us as being prisoners of our cultures or of our past rewards and punishments. But there is a middle ground between these two extremes. **Humanistic psychologists** such as Abraham Maslow (see Chapter 5) admit that our personalities develop in part because of our genetic blueprints, and in part because of our past experiences. But Maslow sees genes and society as creating within each human being a **conscious self** that is capable of directing its own mental, moral, and behavioral growth and development.

According to Maslow, we all have basic needs. Some of these needs are biological, some are social. As we live and grow and meet our needs, we create within our minds a conscious awareness of who we are and what we might become. If we are fortunate enough to be able to satisfy our basic needs, we can then go on to the much more challenging task that Maslow calls **self-actualization.** That is, we can become whatever we ourselves wish to become.

Maslow believes that self-actualization will occur in almost anyone whose basic needs are satisfied. Therefore, self-actualization is a sort of final stage of development that is as biologically determined as is Piaget's stage of autonomous morality. However, we must not lose sight of the thousands of experiments performed by the social learning theorists suggesting that self-actualization is a skill that must be learned.

Is there a "self" that can "actualize" itself? The scientific or empirical evidence suggests strongly that people can set and achieve personal goals even when society tends to punish such behaviors. But this same evidence shows that self-directed growth and development tend to occur only in those individuals who are taught (through modeling, association of events, or punishments and rewards) to monitor or measure the consequences of their own actions. That is, self-actualization is a characteristic of those individuals who discover what environmental inputs influence them, and how their own behavioral and intellectual outputs influence others. People who believe themselves to be prisoners of their genes, or of society, usually maintain their "prisoner" roles all their lives—they become victims of their own learned helplessness (see Chapter 6). But people who learn how to look at themselves and other people objectively can usually acquire the skills needed to reach that final stage of personal development that Maslow calls self-actualization and that Kohlberg calls the level of postconventional morality.

Portnoy's Complaint

Portnoy's Complaint is a funny book but a sad story about how one individual's personality development went wrong. Alexander's genetic inheritance gave him the possibility to grow and adapt and to become a self-directed individual in charge of his own destiny. But his parents and his friends did not give him the models or the encouragement that he needed for self-actualization. Only when

Alex became desperate did he go to see a psychiatrist for help. There are many types of therapy, and all of them can help certain people in certain ways. For the most part, all forms of treatment involve helping the individual understand his or her past so that the person can learn those skills or habits or roles the person failed to acquire while young. The important thing to remember is that it's never too late to start getting better, and even a journey of a thousand miles begins with a single step.

Or as Portnoy's Viennese psychiatrist told him, "So. Now vee may perhaps to begin. Yes?"

► SUMMARY

1. Alexander Portnoy had a problem. He didn't like the type of individual he had become. He was dissatisfied with his personality, and he wanted to change. How did Portnoy become what he was? How do any of us become what we are? As we have seen in this chapter, our personal development is determined to a large extent by how our biological, cognitive, and social needs have been met and by the degree of balance we achieve in fulfilling these needs.

2. Theories of how we develop our unique ways of dealing with our needs tend to emphasize either biological, cognitive, or social and environmental factors. One of the best-known theoretical approaches to personality development is that of Sigmund Freud, who emphasized biological and emotional needs.

3. According to Freud, we pass through five major stages of personality development—the **oral, anal, phallic, latent,** and **genital stages.** A child whose needs are not adequately met may become **fixated** at one of the early stages of development and may carry some childish habits and problems into his or her adult years.

4. Freud divided the human personality into three components—**the Id, Ego, and Superego,** which represent our biological, cognitive, and social needs. But because Freud emphasized biological needs over the other needs, some of his followers have expanded his theories in attempts to fully account for our other needs.

5. Unlike Freud, Erik Erikson believes that the Ego (our cognitive awareness of ourselves) is more important than the Id in influencing personal development. According to Erikson, the Ego's interactions with the environment and society are more important than the Ego's interactions with our unconscious sexual desires (the Id).

6. Erikson says that personality development does not stop at adolescence (Freud's genital stage) but goes through eight **psychosocial stages** into late adulthood. During each stage, individuals are faced with a particular type of crisis or conflict that must be resolved if they are to move successfully to the next stage of personal development.

7. Moral development, our changing perception of right and wrong, can also be explained as a progression through stages. Jean Piaget, who stresses biologi-

cal influences, describes three stages of moral development—the **premoral stage, the stage of moral realism** and the **stage of autonomous morality.**

8. Lawrence Kohlberg has expanded Piaget's explanation of moral development by taking into account the strong influences of social factors on human development. Kohlberg describes three levels of moral development, with each level having two specific stages. Kohlberg's levels are **the preconventional level, the level of conventional morality,** and **the level of postconventional morality.**

9. As important as our genes and other biological factors are to our personal development, it is the environment we are reared in that determines much of what we will become. Or as philosopher John Locke put it, the human mind at birth is a **tabula rasa,** a blank tablet that will be written on by what we experience and what we are taught. Social learning theorists examine how our experiences (including the effects of family and culture) influence personal development.

10. According to social learning theorist Albert Bandura, one of the major reasons we become what we are is that we tend to imitate the behaviors of people we live with, such as our parents who often serve as models. **Modeling** (learning by imitation) can account for many of our behaviors. Bandura and others have also shown that **modeling therapy** can be an effective way of changing some of our unwanted behavior patterns.

11. In addition to learning by imitation, many of our social behaviors, including stereotypical sex roles, are influenced by rewards and punishments. We tend to repeat actions that are reinforced either fairly or unfairly by society. But undesirable behaviors can be changed by wise application of rewards and punishments, as in the case of Ann.

12. Humanistic theories of personal development usually admit the importance of biological and social-environmental influences, but the humanists suggest there is more to human development. Abraham Maslow, for instance, says that genetic and social influences combine to create within us a conscious self that is capable of directing its own mental, moral, and behavioral development. When all of our basic needs are being adequately met, we go on and attempt to reach the final stage of personal development, or what Maslow calls **self-actualization.** In other words, we can become whatever we ourselves wish to become.

Suggested Readings

Bandura, Albert and Richard H. Walters. *Social learning and personality development.* New York: Holt, Rinehart and Winston, 1963.

Erikson, Erik. *Identity: Youth and crisis.* New York: Norton, 1968.

Maslow, Abraham. *Toward a psychology of being.* Princeton, N. J.: Van Nostrand, 1962.

Roth, Philip. *Portnoy's complaint.* New York: Bantam, 1972.

Sheehy, Gail. *Passages.* New York: Dutton, 1974.

Wolfe, Linda. The dynamics of personal growth. *House and Garden,* May 1976.

► STUDY GUIDE

A.   RECALL

Sentence Completion

1. Portnoy turned to _____ because it was the only thing (he would say) that he had to himself.

[p. 290]

2. We all tend to satisfy our needs by seeking out _____, _____ and _____ inputs from our environment.

[p. 291]

3. As a physiologist, Freud believed that our personalities are determined primarily by our _____.

[p. 292]

4. According to Freud, we pass through four stages of personality development, the _____, _____, _____, latent, and genital stages.

[p. 292]

5. The Freudian genital period is said to begin when the individual reaches _____.

[p. 292]

6. Freud divided the personality into three components, the _____, the _____, and the _____.

[p. 293]

7. For Freud, the conscious, cognitive component of the personality is the _____.

[p. 293]

8. Erikson's view of personality deals with _____ stages, the first of which is called _____ vs. _____.

[p. 294]

9. Erikson's _____ vs. _____ stage is like Freud's phallic stage during which the child becomes more assertive and outgoing.

[p. 295]

10. Unlike Erikson, Freud and Piaget feel that personality development ends by the time the individual reaches _____.

[p. 295]

11. Those people who have been successful in solving all of life's crises or conflicts reach what Erikson calls _____ _____.

[p. 298]

12. For Piaget, people pass through four stages of development rigidly determined by their _____ blueprints.

[p. 299]

13. Piaget's final stage of moral development is called the stage of _____ _____.

[p. 299]

14. Kohlberg sees moral development as composed of _____ levels, each including _____ stages.

[p. 300]

15. Most children begin to walk between the _____ and _____ month after birth.

[p. 302]

16. Locke's view is that a person is born with a mind that is a _____ _____, or blank tablet.

[p. 303]

17. Social learning theorists tend to concentrate on how _____ people are, not how similar they are.

[p. 304]

18. Bandura suggests that our parents often serve as _____ whose actions and beliefs we tend to adopt.

[p. 305]

[p. 305]
19. To overcome a phobia, Bandura would tend to use _____ therapy.

20. Child-abusers probably had parents who were _____-_____.

[p. 307]

21. Becoming masculine or feminine involves learning _____ _____.

[p. 307]

[p. 309]

22. _____-_____ is, for Maslow, the process of becoming whatever type of person we ourselves wish to become.

B.   REVIEW

Multiple Choice: Circle the letter identifying the alternative that most correctly completes the statement or answers the question.

1. Although there were many, the major source behind Portnoy's complaint was that:
   A. his psychiatrist failed to appreciate his true problems.
   B. he had too strong a self-image.
   C. his mother was overbearing.
   D. he found masturbation to be such fun.

2. Freud's stages of personality development:
   A. are rooted in genetics.
   B. emphasize cognitive or intellectual influences.
   C. take place within the first four years of life.
   D. end up with self-actualization.

3. For Freud, which of the following constantly seeks biological gratification?
   A. Id
   B. Ego
   C. Superego
   D. all of these

4. Erikson's stages of personality development:
   A. last until puberty or adolescence.
   B. are referred to as psychosocial.
   C. are most closely related to sexual, physical development.
   D. were the basis of Freud's stages of development.

5. Which of the following of Erikson's stages is one of latent development, characterized by the learning of social and intellectual skills?
   A. initiative vs. guilt
   B. trust vs. mistrust
   C. intimacy vs. isolation
   D. industry vs. inferiority

6. The last of Erikson's stages of development:
   A. involves the formation of basic trust.
   B. is reached when an individual goes through an identity crisis.
   C. is generally over by late adolescence.
   D. involves establishing Ego integrity.

7. According to Kohlberg, children behaving in an orderly fashion because they are forced to (for example, to avoid punishment) are in which stage of moral development?
   A. premoral stage

B. stage of moral realism

C. stage of autonomous morality

D. social justice stage

8. Which pairing is most reasonable?

A. Freud — social learning theory

B. Piaget — psychosocial levels

C. Kohlberg — moral development

D. Locke — innate influences

9. Bandura suggests that modeling therapy for phobias is useful _____ percent of the time.

A. zero

B. 25

C. 50

D. 100

10. Bandura would follow which line of reasoning concerning phobias?

A. They are symbolic representations of sexual traumas.

B. The are essentially incurable.

C. The are innate.

D. They are learned.

CONUNDRUM

I was 3 or perhaps 4 years old when I realized that I had been born into the wrong body, and should really be a girl. I remember that moment well, and it is the earliest memory of my life.

And please, God, let me be a girl. Amen.

It was also worrying me, for though my body often yearned to give, to yield, to open itself, the machine was wrong.

Sometimes I considered suicide, or to be more accurate, hoped that some unforeseen and painless accident would do it for me, gently wiping the slate clean.

It was a marriage that had no right to work, yet it worked like a dream, living testimony, one might say, to the power of mind over matter — or of love in its purest sense over everything else.

We produced five children, three boys, two girls, but by the nature of things sex was subsidiary in our marriage. It was a friendship and a union of equals, for in our house there could be no dominant male or female place. If we divided our responsibilities, we did it along no sex lines, but simply according to need or capacity.

My quandary was becoming obsessive, however hard I tried to concentrate upon my work, however comforting the consolations of family and friendship. The strain was telling on me—not only the strain of playing a part, but the strain too of living in a male world.

But it could not work forever. The instinct to keep moving played itself out, as I grew older, and as a cat expecting kittens prepares herself a nest in barn or chimney, so there came a time for me when the wandering had to stop. My time was approaching. My manhood was meaningless. With Elizabeth's loving help I abandoned the attempt to live as a male, and took the first step towards a physical change of sex . . . a slow-motion Jekyll and Hyde.

But I do not for a moment regret the act of change. I could see no other way, and it has made me happy . . . I would search the earth for surgeons, I would bribe barbers or abortionists, I would take a knife and do it myself, without fear, without qualms, without a second thought.

If society had allowed me to live in the gender I preferred, would I have bothered to change sex? . . . I hope so . . . But I think not, because I believe the transsexual urge, at least as I have experienced it, to be far more than a social compulsion, but biological, imaginative, and essentially spiritual, too.

These are the words of Jan Morris, a well-known British journalist who was born a male but who remembers always wanting to be female. In her biography, *Conundrum*, which means riddle or unanswerable question, Morris tells the story of her confusing life. As a young man named James Morris, he served in the army and then began a successful career as a foreign correspondent. In 1953, at the age of 26, he achieved world-wide fame as a reporter on an expedition up Mt. Everest. James Morris married, fathered five children, and lived as a male. Throughout all of this Morris was convinced that he should really be a woman, and he decided to do something about that conviction.

In 1964 Morris began eight years of hormone treatments. Hormones are the body chemicals that help control sexual development. During this time Morris took about 12,000 hormone pills that gradually changed his body chemistry and gave him the outward appearance of a woman. He began dressing like a woman, and in 1972 went to Casablanca in Morocco to have a sex-change operation. Since that time Jan Morris has been living as a woman in all ways.

C. NEWS STORY QUESTIONS

1. What does Jan Morris offer as an explanation for her wanting to give up the maleness she was born with to become a woman? _____

_____

2. What steps did Morris take to complete the change that she remembers realizing as important for her at the age of 3 or 4? _____

_____

Eldridge Cleaver, author of *Soul on Ice*.

Who are you? The study of human personality can help answer this question. And as we shall see, once you understand your personality, it becomes possible to make meaningful changes in your personality. In this chapter we will look at some of the major theories of personality and at some methods of assessing the human personality.

Personality: Theories and Testing

10 chapter

When you have completed your study of this chapter, you should be able to:

- ►Define "personality"
- ►Describe the three types in Sheldon's type theory of personality
- ►Summarize Allport's trait theory of personality
- ►Explain how libido operates in Freudian theory
- ►List and give examples of seven defense mechanisms
- ►Describe Rogers' and Maslow's view of the development of the self
- ►Compare and contrast objective and subjective measures of personality, giving examples

Cardinal trait. A cardinal trait is a very important or primary trait. According to Allport, most people have only one cardinal trait.

Catharsis (ka-THAR-sis). From the Greek word meaning "to purge" or to "clean out." Freud believed that psychotherapy could act as a psychological catharsis to cleanse the mind of bottled-up emotions.

Central traits. Although, according to Allport, each individual has only one cardinal trait, each of us presumably has up to 10 central or "main traits" that determine our personality make-up.

Common traits. Minor or secondary traits that are displayed in very specific situations.

Defense mechanisms. The various techniques that the Ego uses, according to Freud, to defend itself—particularly against the impulsive Id.

Displacement. A Freudian defense mechanism in which emotion that cannot be displayed toward one individual is displaced to a second individual (or thing).

Ectomorph (ECK-toh-morf). A person with a tall, thin body.

Ego. In Freudian theory, the conscious self.

Endomorph (EN-doh-morf). A person with a soft, rounded body and a big stomach.

Externalizers. Individuals who believe their lives are determined primarily by "fate."

Fixation. A Freudian defense mechanism in which the individual's psychosexual development remains fixed at a low level (such as the oral stage).

Heterosexual. Having a strong and abiding interest in individuals of the opposite sex. Opposed to homosexual, which is an interest in individuals of the same sex.

Hierarchy of needs (HIGH-er-ark-kee). Abraham Maslow believed that human needs could be listed in order, running from basic (biological) needs up to meta-needs, such as self-actualization.

Hormones. Complex chemicals released by various glands that control growth and sexual development.

Humanists. Psychologists, such as Carl Rogers and Abraham Maslow, who believe that people have an innate urge to better themselves and to become as healthy as possible.

Id. Freud's term for the unconscious, instinctual portion of one's personality.

Identification. A Freudian defense mechanism in which the Ego takes on values or behaviors similar to those of someone the Ego fears or admires.

Internalizers. People who believe that what happens to them is chiefly due to their own actions.

Libido (lib-BEE-doe). From the Latin word meaning "desire" or "lust." According to Freud, the libido is the life force, the instinctual drive to satisfy one's biological urges.

Locus of Personal Control Scale. A test developed by U. S. psychologist Julian Rotter (ROE-turr). Divides people into "externalizers" and "internalizers."

Mesomorph. (MEE-zo-morf). Someone with a hard, square, bony, athletic body.

Metabolism (mett-TAB-boh-liz-em). All the biological processes involved in building up your cells, organ, and whole body.

Meta-needs. According to Maslow, meta-needs are those instinctual urges that we try to satisfy once our basic or biological needs have been satisfied. Self-actualization is the highest meta-need.

Minnesota Multiphasic Personality Inventory (mull-tee-FAY-zick). Also called MMPI. A personality test made up of several hundred questions that the individual must answer "yes," "no," or "cannot say."

Morphology (morf-OLL-oh-gee). The study of biological forms, shapes, or body types. Ernst Kretschmer and W. H. Sheldon believed that a person's basic body type strongly influences what kind of personality the person is likely to have as an adult.

Objective tests. Tests that have right and wrong answers, which can be scored objectively.

Personality. From the Greek words meaning "to wear a mask." Your personality is the sum total of your thoughts, feelings, and actions—your characteristic way of living.

Phrenology (fren-NOLL-oh-gee). Reading the bumps or depressions on a person's skull in order to make guesses about the person's psychological abilities.

Pleasure principle. Freud's notion that we are all driven to satisfy our needs. The Id operates to reduce a drive and give us pleasure.

Projection. A Freudian defense mechanism in which the person projects onto someone else the person's own unacceptable desires or emotions.

Projective tests. Tests, such as the ink-blot test, which are so ambiguous in form that the individual taking the test presumably projects his or her own personality structure onto the test.

Psychoanalysis. As developed by Freud, psychoanalysis is a therapy for getting patients to relax sufficiently so that they open up and discuss the roots of their present problems. From listening to his patients, Freud developed the *theory* of psychoanalysis, which involves psychosexual stages of development and defense mechanisms.

Psychodynamic theories. Personality theories, such as Freud's, based on the belief that your personality is a balance among various powerful forces or sources of energy.

Reaction formation. A Freudian defense mechanism in which the person acts exactly opposite to the way he or she feels.

Reality principle. Freud felt that we have to learn that the world has a reality of its own, separate from what we wish it to be. The Ego operates to delay gratification when the consequences of immediate need reduction would be destructive.

Regression. A Freudian defense mechanism involving the return to a lower stage of psychosexual adjustment.

Repression. A Freudian defense mechanism involving denial of unpleasant truths.

Rorschach test (ROAR-shock). The ink-blot test. A projective personality test developed by Swiss psychiatrist Hermann Rorschach.

Social learning theories. Behavioral theories in which it is assumed that most actions and values are learned, chiefly through imitation and reinforcement.

Stereotype. A fixed or unconscious attitude or perception—a way of responding to some person or object solely in terms of the person's or object's class membership.

Subjective tests. Tests without firmly established right and wrong answers; must be "interpreted" by the psychologist giving the test.

Sublimation (sub-blih-MAY-shun). The most mature of the Freudian defense mechanisms. The use of sexual (libidinal) energy for creative or social purposes.

Superego. The Freudian term for conscience.

Thematic Apperception Test (thee-MATT-tick app-purr-CEP-shun). A personality test developed by Henry Murray. Consists of some 20 rather ambiguous stimulus pictures about which the subject responds by making up stories.

Trait theories. Trait theorists assume that your personality is determined primarily by the sum of the traits or general behavioral tendencies that you have.

Type theories. Theories based on the belief that all human personalities are a mixture of two or three basic inherited tendencies.

INTRODUCTION: SOUL ON ICE

Who am I?

Eldridge Cleaver, a full-time revolutionary in the struggle for black liberation.

Where did I come from?

I was born in Little Rock, Arkansas, raised in the ghettos of Los Angeles, and educated in prison.

Where am I now?

In prison for rape.

Where am I going?

I am going to get out of prison and work to make the world a better place for myself, for all blacks, and for everyone.

At one time or another, all of us ask ourselves the same sorts of questions. The answers that each person finds for these questions are likely to be different — the answers help define our personalities, and each of us is a unique individual. Yet there are certain regularities or similarities to our answers which suggest that psychologists should be able to study the human personality in an objective or scientific way. So let us look at these questions in a bit more detail.

Who am I?

If you look at your driver's license or any one of a number of similar documents, you will see that you are a name, a number, a member of a specific race and sex, and a collection of physical statistics — height, weight, color of hair, and color of eyes. Eldrige Cleaver was prisoner number A-29498 when he described himself in *Soul on Ice.*

But no one is just a number or set of statistics. Each person is a unique physical, intellectual, and social human being.

Where did I come from?

A birth certificate or a passport will tell you where you come from geographically. But that information is not enough. Each person comes from a unique physical, economic, intellectual, and social environment. Cleaver came from an environment in which money and education were hard to come by. He came from a social environment that regarded him as something worse than a second-class citizen.

Where am I now?

Everyone is someplace physically, whether it be at school, at home, on the job, or in prison. But everyone is also someplace on a scale of physical, intellectual, and social *development.*

In *Soul on Ice,* Eldridge Cleaver told the world where he was. He had been sent to prison at the age of 18 for possession of marijuana. Cleaver knew that he was a black man living in a white world, and that many whites discriminated against blacks. In prison, he and some other prisoners began to realize that they and their race were being treated unjustly. Cleaver, like many other blacks, began to hate and curse the society that acted as if it hated him. "We cursed everything American," he says, "including baseball and hot dogs." Cleaver cursed especially what he called the white race of devils created by their maker to do evil and to make evil appear as good. He preached that the white race is the natural, unchangeable enemy of the black race.

Cleaver was released on parole, but his hatred got him into trouble again. He was soon back in prison for rape.

Again in prison, Cleaver asked himself: Who am I? He did not like the answer. He admitted that he had gone wrong somewhere. He did not approve of rape, and he realized that his hatred of society included hatred of himself. He began a process of self-analysis and self-education to find out who he was, where he had come from, where he was now, and where he was going.

Where am I going?

The answers to the first three questions—who am I, where did I come from, where am I now—tell you that you are a unique individual with past achievements and failures and present values and responsibilities. The knowledge of values and responsibilities give you specific physical, intellectual, and social needs or goals that direct your life.

During nine years in prison, Cleaver had plenty of time to think about who he was and where he was going. "I had to find out who I am," he explains, "and what I want to be, what type of man I should be, and what I could do to become the best of which I was capable. I understood that what had happened to me had also happened to countless other blacks and it would happen to many, many more." Cleaver set some goals for himself. He decided to work to change the system. He realized that if he could change, others could change.

A hundred years ago, your answer to the question, "Where am I going?" would have been simple to give. A century ago, most people thought that your heredity and your early experiences would pretty well have determined your future for you. But modern psychologists realize that almost anyone can change, grow, become a different person. Your genes and your environment surely influence your choice of goals. But just as surely you have your own special way of selecting some of your goals and attaining them.

Simply put, your **personality** is your own unique way of adapting to your environment. We all have physical, cognitive, and social inputs that our brains and minds process in certain unique ways. Some of these internal processes or "programs" are determined by our genetic blueprints, some by our past experiences. The purpose of these internal "programs" is to turn inputs into outputs—thus, we all have characteristic ways of thinking about and responding to our inputs. If we have to change our outputs (thoughts and behaviors) in order to achieve our goals, then we must somehow change the internal programs that connect our inputs to our outputs. Human beings seem to be the only living creatures capable of deliberately reprogramming their inner processes in order to achieve new goals. Thus, the study of personality is to a great extent the study of how people learn who they are, where they come from, where they want to go, and how they may set about reprogramming themselves so that they can achieve new and more satisfying goals.

PERSONALITY THEORIES

Change and growth are very important parts of anyone's personality. Eldridge Cleaver, for instance, didn't like what he was—a hateful racist and a convicted rapist. He wanted to change. He wanted to change the way he thought, and he wanted to change the way he behaved. But just wanting to change usually isn't enough. Reprogramming yourself takes specific skills and specific knowledge. Cleaver first had to find out what it was he was doing that he didn't like, and what it was that he wanted to become. Next, he had to discover what he was actually doing now—how his thoughts and behaviors affected others and his own self-image. Then he had to find out what kinds of inputs his present environment was giving him—that is, how the people around him responded to his thoughts and actions. With this knowledge, he could decide which of his "internal programs" had to be changed and how those changes might be accomplished. He had to know himself in order to know how to become someone different than he presently was.

What Cleaver actually did was to develop his own private theory of personality growth and change. Almost everyone who has ever tried to explain personality has come up with a different theory of what personality is and how (or if) it can be altered.

The most important or most popular theories of personality in the field of psychology can roughly be divided into three categories, depending on what kinds of internal programs they emphasize. Theories that view physiological or biological processes as being most important are often called **type theories.** The second group of theories emphasizes cognitive or mental programs and is generally called the **trait theories.** The third type of personality theory focuses on social programs and is usually called the behavioral **social learning theories.** You will remember that we talked about social learning theories in Chapter 9. In this chapter we will discuss social learning theory from a humanistic viewpoint.

But each individual is a complex living system made up of biological, cognitive, and social input–output relationships (internal programs). So any theory that does not adequately consider or explain all three types of internal processes is incomplete. So far, psychologists have not developed any one theory that is completely adequate. Therefore, if you wish to get a well-rounded picture of what personality is all about, it will be necessary for you to look at all three categories or types of personality theories.

Type Theories

The type of body a person has has often been thought to be related to personality. Fat people are supposed to be jolly. People whose eyes are very close together are supposed to be criminal types. But such statements have never been found to be particularly true. Some fat people may be jolly, but many are quite sad—especially if they can't lose weight. The position of the eyes has no relationship at all to criminality. Even so, folklore about the relationship between body types and personality has been around for a long time. Palm-readers say they can see personality and future behavior in the palms of people's hands. **Phrenology** is the pseudoscience (or fake science) of reading the bumps or depressions on peoples' skulls. During the nineteenth century many phrenologists claimed that they could interpret personality by the shape of people's heads. Neither palm reading nor phrenology proved to be useful in describing a personality.

Not just outward appearances but more subtle genetic traits have sometimes been associated with personality characteristics. For centuries, the politics of Europe was based on genetics. Kings and queens were supposed to have the genetic qualities of leadership. They were supposed to pass those qualities on from generation to generation. The common people, with less royal genes,

A person's body type has often been thought to be related to personality. People who are overweight are often said to be jolly; obviously this is not always true.

weren't supposed to be able to do anything but work, fight wars, and pay taxes. Genetic politics made it easy to decide who would be the next ruler, but, in actuality, royal genes produced as many bad as good leaders.

Type theories are also responsible in part for a good many racial stereotypes. A **stereotype** is a simplified belief or set of characteristics supposed to apply to all members of a group. Depending on whom you listen to, almost every ethnic or racial group on the face of the earth has a negative stereotype. Blacks are shiftless and stupid. American Indians are lazy drunkards. Jews are pushy. Orientals are sneaky. Germans are cold and distant. The Irish are drunkards and fighters. Italians and Latin Americans are greasy sex-maniacs. WASPs—white, Anglo-Saxon Protestants—are cold, calculating conservatives. Honkies are white people with no feeling and no "soul." Such stereotypes make it seem easy to deal with and to predict how certain types or groups of people will behave, but stereotypes are almost always wrong. Stereotypes do not take into account individual differences, and the differences between any two individuals are almost always greater than the differences between groups or races.

A stereotype was responsible for Hitler's attempt to murder all of the Jews in Europe. A stereotype was and is responsible for many of the problems faced by Eldridge Cleaver and other blacks in the United States and elsewhere.

Biology and genes may not produce whole races or groups of personality types, but biology is an important factor in personality. **Hormones,** for instance, are chemicals secreted by various glands in the body. Hormones can affect such things as body size, sexual activity, and **metabolism** (the overall rate of the body's physical activities). These things, in turn, help determine personality. A person with a large body, extra amounts of sex hormones, and a high rate of metabolism may be aggressive and overactive. The same type of person, with a low rate of metabolism, may be overweight, sluggish, and dull.

Kretschmer's Theory

Ernst Kretschmer, a German psychiatrist, believed that hormones influence body shape and personality. After working with mental patients, Kretschmer developed a personality theory based on **morphology,** or body type. He measured the shapes and sizes of many patients and attempted to fit all humans into three basic body types. For each type, said Kretschmer, there are specific personality characteristics.

Kretschmer's theory did not work out very well. There are just too many people who don't fit exactly into any one of the morphological categories he described. Even those people who do fit a specific body type don't always have the personality characteristics Kretschmer said they should have.

Sheldon's Theory

W. H. Sheldon of Harvard University updated Kretschmer's theory in the 1940s and 1950s. Sheldon "typed" people more scientifically than Kretschmer did. With 4000 photographs of male college students, Sheldon, like Kretschmer, identified three basic body types:

Type theories also have been responsible for many racial stereotypes. Fortunately, there are exemplary exceptions to stereotypes such as farm labor-organizer Cesar Chavez.

1. **Endomorph:** A soft, round person who tends toward being fat, and whose muscles are often underdeveloped.
2. **Mesomorph:** A hard, rectangularly shaped person with strong muscles and bones; the "jock" type, whether male or female.
3. **Ectomorph:** A thin, often tall person with a well-developed brain and sensory receptors; the "intellectual" type.

Sheldon didn't stop with only three body types. There are seven degrees of each type, he said. And there are combinations of all the types and degrees. The result is 343 possible body types.

Sheldon next selected a number of personality characteristics that seemed to represent most human characteristics. By observing a group of young men for one year, Sheldon was able to relate combinations of personality characteristics with certain body types. And many of Sheldon's predictions seem to be at least partially correct. Some people who are highly mesomorphic (hard, muscular) do tend to be athletic, aggressive, and dominant, as Sheldon predicted. Some endomorphs (soft, round) do tend to be jolly and sociable, and some ectomorphs (thin, tall) do tend to be quiet and intellectual.

Genes could account for some of the relationships Sheldon found, but cognitive and social inputs can also explain why body type and personality are sometimes related. The way people view themselves—their cognitive awareness of themselves—might make them want to behave in certain ways. Fat or over-

Following the body-type theory of Kretschmer and Sheldon, you could probably classify these men as ectomorph, mesomorph, and endomorph.

weight people, for instance, might not like to take part in physical activities. In order to feel accepted in a group, some overweight people might try to be especially sociable and jolly. Society might reinforce this trait by always expecting fat people to tell jokes and be life-of-the-party types.

Ectomorphs (thin people), on the other hand, might see themselves as physical weaklings. To make up for what they see as a physical deficiency, they might concentrate on brain power. If such people avoid physical activities and stick to the books, society might respond by avoiding them. The result is a quiet, intellectual loner.

Mesomorphs (muscular and physically well built) may see themselves as physically competent or able. Because they know they are good at physical contests (whether it be wrestling or tennis), they are among the first to go in for such activities. Society sometimes sees this aggressiveness as bravery or courageousness and often turns to such people for leadership.

Sheldon's theory is much more useful and accurate than Kretschmer's, but like all personality theories, it is incomplete. There are always individuals who just don't fit in where the theory says they should.

Type theories have another drawback. They are limited as far as change is concerned. They suggest few therapies for changing the personality. Type theories say that leopards can't change their spots and people can't change their genes. People are, type theories suggest, what they were born to be. Children of royalty will be royal. Children of commoners will be common.

Hormone treatments and certain physical therapies are available that can change some physical conditions, but for the most part, type theories do not allow for much personality change after adolescence or after physical growth has stopped.

Eldridge Cleaver was born black, and he could not change that genetic trait.

He did, however, change the way he thought, the way he behaved, and, therefore, he changed his personality. Type theories cannot usually explain the changes Eldridge Cleaver went through.

Trait Theories

Before and after Eldridge Cleaver went through any changes, he had certain personality characteristics or traits that remained the same. All people have some traits that seem to be persistent and stable throughout life—no matter what happens to them. For example, students who are quiet, intelligent, or hard-working tend to be quiet, intelligent, or hard-working throughout their lives. People who are aggressive when young usually remain aggressive—though the aggression may take different forms. Young Cleaver was physically aggressive in his hatred of whites. Later he became intellectually aggressive in his fight for human rights.

An individual's particular set of personality traits is not always obvious. Physical traits (like size or weight) can be measured readily; but psychological traits such as intelligence, love, and hatred cannot be seen or directly measured. All we can do is observe the person's behavior or give the person various tests (standardized inputs) and then guess about what internal trait or program caused the person to respond as the person did. Despite the difficulty that we have in measuring psychological traits directly, whole theories of personality have been based on the belief that what we do is determined primarily by a limited number of mental traits.

Allport's Trait Theory

The first trait theories of any importance—most notably the one developed by the Greek physician Hippocrates 400 years before the birth of Christ—mentioned only a few basic human traits. But traits, like types, are numerous. In the 1930s, Gordon Allport of Harvard University and Henry S. Odbert compiled a list of traits from a dictionary. They came up with 17,953 traits or words like kind, loving, mean, stingy, brave, and bold.

Some traits, Allport found, are shared by many people. Similar biological, cognitive, and social inputs may call forth very similar behavioral outputs in many individuals. Allport called such widely shared internal programs **common traits.** But no two people are ever exactly alike, and Allport was interested in individual personalities. Therefore, he concentrated on what he called *individual traits.*

Some individuals, said Allport, are guided throughout their lives by one major or **cardinal trait.** Some people, for instance, seem to direct all or a good part of their thinking and behavior toward only one goal. The drives for money or power or religious holiness can be seen as cardinal traits in some individuals. Most people, however, are guided by a group of less powerful, more common traits. These Allport called **central traits.** Almost everyone, said Allport, has between 2 and 10 central traits that are important. Such things as a strong interest in music, education, or sex might be central traits. And, finally, says Allport,

Cardinal traits are major drives that nearly dominate an individual's total behavior. St. Francis was characterized by his striving for religious holiness.

Secondary traits — or preferences in clothes, mannerisms, or certain foods — are part of everyone's personality. Politician Bella Abzug almost always appears in wide-brimmed hats.

each personality is rounded out by a number of secondary or less important traits. Preferences for certain foods or clothes, certain mannerisms and habits, are secondary traits.

All of a person's unique personality traits or structures are important, Allport believed, because traits determine not only what a person has been but what that person will be. To Allport, a trait was a characteristic way of responding to stimuli in the environment. If we could somehow identify a particular trait in a given individual, then we ought to be able to predict how a person with that trait would react to future situations. Allport's theory, therefore, looks to the future and attempts to determine how a personality will grow, develop, and change.

Traits are obviously important parts of a personality, and they can sometimes be used to predict an individual's behavior. But traits are not as stable as some psychologists once considered them to be. Honesty, for instance, was once considered by some people to be a basic, lasting, and unchanging trait. Hugh Hartshorne and Mark A. May of Columbia University, in a set of experiments conducted between 1928 and 1930, showed that there is probably no such thing as consistently honest or dishonest behavior. Thousands of children were given tests as part of the experiment. After the tests were completed, the teachers collected the test papers and copied down each student's answers without the students' knowledge. The test papers were then handed back, and the students were allowed to correct their own exams. Almost everyone cheated or changed some wrong answers when they had the chance.

Hartshorne and May concluded that the trait of honesty, like most traits, seemed to depend on the situation. When there was little chance of getting caught (when the teacher wasn't paying close attention), when it was easy to

Throughout their lives, some people follow less powerful or central traits. Interest in drama has been a central trait in the life of Orson Welles, actor, director, producer, writer, storyteller.

change the answers, and when everyone else seemed to be changing answers, most students cheated.

In 1974, psychologists D. J. Bem and A. Allen pointed out another problem with trait theory—most of the traits that we talk about in everyday speech are really too broad to be meaningful. For example, many people would assume that "neatness" is a fairly specific trait that should be expressed in almost everything that the "neat" person does. But in a large study of college students, Bem and Allen found that "neatness" isn't really a general trait at all. Many of the students Bem and Allen interviewed almost always turned in neat, beautifully typed term papers to their teachers—but usually wore sloppy clothes and didn't comb their hair very often. Other students were almost always neatly dressed in public, but their dormitory rooms were usually a mess. According to Bem and Allen, we might be better off if we dealt with highly specific behaviors rather than attempting to describe personality in terms of very general traits.

Psychodynamic Theories

Many psychological experiments—as well as personal experiences such as Eldridge Cleaver's—suggest that traits are not always stable, and that personalities can change in dramatic and important ways. A good many theories have been developed during the past 50 years that attempt to account for changes of personality and personality traits. These theories, often called the **psychodynamic theories,** do not focus merely on the *structure* of personality; rather, they focus on the *functions* or internal processes that occur during personality development and change.

When newborn babies cry, they are said to be releasing libidinal energy, which brings them sensual gratification. According to Freud, the Id is obeying the pleasure principle. A child learns that it cannot always do what it wants, however. The child on the right would prefer to be playing rather than getting a haircut. The Ego develops to help control the Id and to help the child adjust to the demands of reality. Freud called this the reality principle.

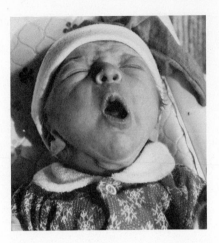 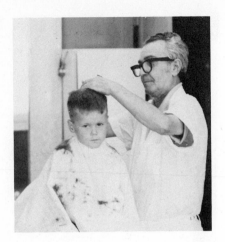

You will probably remember that *psycho* comes from the name of the Greek goddess Psyche and means "soul" (see Chapter 1.). The term *dynamic* comes from the Greek word for "power" or "force." Psychodynamic theories typically attempt to explain personality in terms of the interplay of various psychological forces within the individual.

Freud is the father of psychodynamic theory. His description of the three main dynamic systems of the personality (Id, Ego, and Superego; see Chapter 9) and his explanation of the stages of personality development (oral, anal, phallic, latent, and genital; see Chapter 9) represented a revolution in psychological thinking. Before Freud's time, only genetic and spiritual factors were thought to have anything to do with individuality or personality. It was Sigmund Freud who first attempted to explain the emotional or cognitive processes that might be involved in the growth of the human personality. The things that Freud talked about were so unheard of that he had to invent many of his own explanatory terms—and many of these terms are still in use today.

The Libido

Freud explained personality in terms of *tension*—the building up, the blocking, and the release of psychological energy. According to Freud, the **libido** is the psychic dynamo that creates the life force or "fuel" that keeps the mind running. The libido constantly creates new energy; this energy must be discharged or released (in thoughts, dreams, and behaviors), however, or the individual's mind will "explode" just like a balloon into which you've blown too much air.

When you are born, only your **Id** can discharge libidinal energy—because that's the way your genetic blueprint planned for things to be. In releasing this energy, the Id tends to seek pleasure and avoid pain. Thus, the Id obeys what Freud called the **pleasure principle**—it lets off steam by engaging in behaviors that bring it sensual gratification. During the oral stage of development, the Id releases libidinal energy through the mouth. Eating and drinking and other oral activities such as sucking and crying are the primary sources of pleasure and of releasing libidinal energy. But the child must live with others, and these other

According to Freud, a child develops a natural attachment to the parent of the opposite sex during the phallic stage. This little boy seems to be exhibiting the expected behavior for his age.

people (primarily the parents) force the child to learn about the realities of life. Most children soon learn that they cannot always have what they want when they want it. This imposition of reality on the child brings about the development of the **Ego,** which tends to obey what Freud called the **reality principle.** As the Ego develops, it begins to gain control over some of the energy that the libido is creating. The Ego brings the Id under control by blocking off or inhibiting the usual methods the Id has for discharging its libidinal energy. As the individual matures, the Id learns to release its energy and find pleasure in more socially approved ways. Thus, during the anal stage, the infant learns to control its bodily functions because of parental demands. Toilet training then becomes another battle between the Id and the Ego. And, as the child learns personal control, its Ego becomes stronger and better able to impose its own reality principle on the pleasure-seeking Id.

During the phallic stage of development, a new force enters the picture — the **Superego.** At about age four, the child (according to Freud) develops a natural attachment to the parent of the opposite sex — the girl for her father, the boy for his mother. This sensual love of the child for its parent is unacceptable to the Ego — and usually to the parent. The child resolves this conflict by identifying with — or taking on the values and behaviors of — the parent of the same sex. This process of **identification** creates the Superego — the representation of society within the child's mind. The Superego gains control over a limited amount of libidinal energy and attempts to discharge this energy by forcing the child to behave in socially approved ways no matter how painful the results may be both to the Ego and the Id.

For a period of time — which Freud called the latent period (five years to puberty) — the Superego manages to repress or inhibit most sexual behaviors. But when adolescence begins, the sudden increase in the amount of sex hormones in the young person's body increases the libidinal energy available to the Id and Ego. The well-adjusted adolescent resolves the conflict among Superego, Ego, and Id by learning to release sexual energies in enduring **heterosexual** relationships. For example, the young man no longer desires his mother, but substitutes a love for women of his own age instead. At this time too the Ego typically gains the upper hand again and helps discharge some libidinal energy through such Superego-approved behaviors as work, art, and studying.

Young adults usually have learned to resolve the conflicts among Superego, Ego, and Id and to release their energies in socially approved relationships.

Freud believed that each individual's personality is determined by the outcome of the battle among the Id, Ego, and Superego. And since each of us has had different personal experiences and differing amounts of libidinal energy, we all turn out to be different people.

Defense Mechanisms

Freud never saw an Id or an Ego, and he never invented a machine that could directly measure libidinal energy. He just saw his patients and heard how they reacted to certain situations. All of the terms that Freud invented were just his way of describing what he thought was going on in each personality — that is, the terms were just Freud's way of giving names to the internal programs that each of us have.

Freud found that his patients had various ways of coping with or reacting to personality conflicts. These characteristic behaviors, which can be seen as expressions of personality traits, usually took the form of some sort of defense against anxiety. Some of his patients feared that their physical urges were too strong and might cause them to do something bad. Freud said that such people were anxious because they feared their Ids would overpower their Egos. Other patients were discouraged and upset because they seemed too influenced by the people around them. Freud said that these patients were anxious because they feared their Superegos were overwhelming their Ids and Egos. According to Freud, the attempts these patients made to avoid or reduce their anxieties were actually psychological defenses that their Egos created to discharge tension. Freud called these anxiety-reproducing behaviors **defense mechanisms.**

Repression, said Freud, is the most common defense mechanism. A strong Ego keeps the desires of the Id repressed or pushed down into the unconscious part of the mind. As long as the Ego has enough strength or energy, anxiety-causing desires from the Id can be kept out of the conscious mind. If the Ego is not strong enough or if the libidinal energy of the Id builds up, unconscious or repressed desires may begin to become conscious. Repressed desires may begin to show up in dreams or in slips of the tongue and other seemingly unconscious behaviors.

Cleaver, like many blacks, managed to keep his hatred of the white race repressed for many years. "We lived in an atmosphere of novocain," he says, not feeling or thinking about the problem. "Negroes found it necessary in order to maintain whatever sanity they could, to remain somewhat aloof and detached from the problem." But Cleaver could not keep his feelings bottled up or repressed forever. The horrors of life in the ghetto and the indignities forced on him by white people caused an explosion of repressed energy.

For Cleaver the result was nine years of prison during which he had time to think about who he was, where he had been, and where he was going. He learned not to bottle up or repress his libidinal energy but to channel it into more socially acceptable, productive, and creative activities. "That is why I started to write," he explains, "to save myself."

A second form of defense mechanism is called **fixation.** Some children

Children may sometimes resent the attention given a younger sibling. Because the child cannot express this negative feeling openly, it may use a defense mechanism known as reaction formation. In such cases the child may show a lot of love and affection for the sibling it actually resents.

remain fixated or stuck at an immature level of psychosexual or personality development. Children in the oral stage who do not learn to cope easily with the problems of growing up may not develop a very strong Ego. Such people may prefer (unconsciously) to stay fixated at an immature stage of personality development because they are afraid to face the challenges of the next stages (see Chapter 9).

Regression, a third kind of defense mechanism, is like fixation in that it results from anxiety about coping with the problems of growing up. Children who have reached the phallic stage, for instance, may feel that they are unable to cope with their increased feelings of sexuality. If the Ego feels threatened by such problems, it may slip back or regress to an earlier stage—a stage whose problems have already been solved.

A fourth defense mechanism is **reaction formation,** which people sometimes use to cope with feelings or desires that they do not like or that cause anxiety. Love, for instance, is a very strong feeling that some people are afraid to show or display openly. People who feel anxiety about strong emotions sometimes react by hiding their true feelings and by displaying the opposite emotions. Lovers may sometimes unconsciously be cruel to each other. Enemies may force themselves to be excessively kind and loving to each other.

Projection is a fifth mechanism for getting rid of unwanted feelings. A teacher who hates children, for instance, might unconsciously try to deny the feeling of hate by saying that it is the children who are doing the hating.

Displacement is a sixth defense mechanism that results in numerous personality traits. Since the Id cannot always have what it wants, the Ego learns to shift or displace some of the Id's excess libidinal energy to more acceptable behaviors. Many people who quit smoking soon find that they are eating more. Freudian theory suggests that the Id's desire for oral pleasure is satisfied by the release of libidinal energy while sucking on a cigarette. If cigarettes are no longer available, the Ego may shift or displace libidinal energy to another oral habit. Some people may chew gum; others may eat more or talk more. Freud suggests that a good many habits and personality traits are the result of people's learning to displace libidinal energy.

A seventh mechanism is **sublimation,** a more mature form of displacement that is controlled by the Superego. Instead of displacing libidinal energy from one activity to any other adequate activity, the Superego channels some psychic energy into socially acceptable activities. Being in prison, Cleaver had a lot of excess sexual energy to use up. Some of it he displaced by lifting weights and doing exercises. But some of the excess energy he sublimated into the creative activity of writing. All artistic, creative, and culturally productive people, said Freud, are sublimating libidinal energy into socially worthwhile activities.

Catharsis

In working with his patients in therapy, Freud tried to cure emotional problems or change strange thoughts or behaviors by helping his patients release stored-up energy. He called the release of stored up energy **catharsis.** Catharsis means to clean out or purge. Freud tried to clean out or purge his patients of their blocked libidinal energy.

Freud believed that if he could find out what emotionally upsetting experience was causing the blockage of energy, he could get a patient to understand the problem and release energy by reliving the experience. Reliving an emotional experience and the subsequent release of energy is called catharsis.

At first, Freud used hypnosis to achieve catharsis. He found that some people under hypnosis can reach back into their memories and recreate the circumstances of the experience that is at the root of their problem. Hypnosis didn't always work, so Freud found another method. He discovered that if he could build up a strong personal relationship with his patients, if he could get his patients to trust him, he could sometimes get them to talk openly about their problems and whatever past experiences might be causing the problems. By discussing such experiences with patients, Freud was often able to bring about a catharsis. The system of examining past experiences and present problems is called **psychoanalysis.** (We will discuss psychoanalysis in more detail in Chapter 13.) By analyzing a great many people (all disturbed, remember), Freud was able to develop the first theory of personality that was not based entirely on genetic programming.

THE HUMANISTS

One of the differences between humans and animals is that we ask ourselves questions such as who we are, where we came from, and where we are going. When a dog is born, its genes dictate that it will grow up to be a dog. Society and the environment can teach a dog a few tricks, but the dog will always be a dog. That is, it will respond to its environmental inputs rather automatically without ever stopping to ask itself who it is and what it would have to do to become a better dog.

When Eldridge Cleaver was born, his genes dictated that he would grow up to be a human being. He too learned many tricks. But because he was born human instead of canine, he was capable of looking at himself objectively and deliberately changing what he was. Most humans strive to better themselves physically, cognitively, and socially. This desire to become something better is called the desire for *self-actualization.* Psychologists who are interested in the process of self-actualization are often called **humanists.**

Humanistic theories of personality tend to stress individuality and the conscious development of the self. Carl Rogers and Abraham Maslow helped develop the two most popular theories of humanistic psychology.

TABLE 10-1   **Personality Theories**

Theory	Description	Major Theorists
Type (Biological)	Belief that a person's body type (morphology) is associated with personality. While a person's body type may affect the way others react to an individual, strict adherence to this theory leads to stereotypes.	Ernst Kretschmer W. H. Sheldon
Trait (Cognitive)	Belief that an individual's personality is determined by psychological traits; identifying a particular trait can help predict how a person would behave in future settings, but traits can change and are often too broad to be meaningful.	Gordon Allport
Psychodynamic (Cognitive and Emotional)	Belief that personality can be explained in terms of the interplay of various psychological forces within the individual; focuses on the internal processes that occur during personality development and change.	Sigmund Freud
Humanistic (Cognitive)	Belief that personality can be consciously changed through stress on individuality and development of self; encourages achievement of self-actualization.	Carl Rogers Abraham Maslow

Carl Rogers

Psychodynamic theories suggest that much human behavior is the result of unconscious desires. Rogers does not deny the unconscious, but he says that the conscious self is more important. Rogers began to develop his theory of the self after listening to many clients who came to him with emotional problems. These people may have had unconscious problems, says Rogers, but they always seemed to talk in terms of self—"I feel I'm not being my real self." "I wonder who I really am." "I wouldn't want anyone to know the real me." "I never had a chance to be myself." It seemed clear to Rogers that the self was an important part of each person's experience, and that people with problems were having trouble becoming their "real selves" or achieving self-actualization.

Society ⟶ **REAL SELF**

Ideal Self ⟵

FIG. 10–1.
When society pushes an individual to develop in one direction and when personal feelings push the person toward another "ideal" self, the real self may become confused.

People become confused, says Rogers, when they are forced too often to deny their own true feelings and accept the values of others. The self begins to develop into something different from the real or ideal self. In other words, society tells a person to become one thing, while personal experience and true feelings tell the person to become something else—the ideal self. If the self is continually forced in two different directions, self-actualization stops. The self begins to feel uncomfortable and threatened. When Cleaver began to feel threatened, he fought back against society. Other people may react by becoming emotionally disturbed and by adopting unrealistic thoughts and behaviors.

But people need not lose touch with reality, says Rogers. Young children can be taught to express their true feelings in ways that do not conflict with society. If a child's values are similar to the values of its parents and society, the parents will rarely have to tell the child that it is being bad. The self will not become confused. And throughout life, says Rogers, people must keep re-examining their values and behaviors. People must be flexible and able to change if they are to maintain a realistic view of themselves and of society. In Cleaver's case, however, it was society that had the unrealistic view. It was society that had to change.

And change is possible, according to Rogers. People shape their own personality, he says, by finding out who they are and who they want to be. Once these questions are answered realistically, people can select the values and behaviors that will help them toward self-actualization.

Abraham Maslow

The term "self-actualization" is best defined by Abraham Maslow's list of self-actualizing people — Abraham Lincoln, Thomas Jefferson, Walt Whitman, Beethoven, Eleanor Roosevelt, and Albert Einstein.

Maslow — unlike Freud, Rogers, and many others — developed a theory of personality based on psychologically healthy and creative people. If you study sick or disturbed people, he said, you get a sick or disturbed view of personality. A true theory of personality, he said, must contain a description of the good as well as the bad. Maslow, therefore, set out to find out what makes some people live up to their fullest potential — or what makes some people self-actualizing.

You will recall from our discussion in Chapter 5 that Maslow has suggested a specific order or **hierarchy of needs** that each person must fulfill on the road to self-actualization. First there are the basic needs — such as food, water, shelter, sex, and security. If the social and physical environments can fulfill these basic physical and psychological needs, says Maslow, an individual has the chance to go on to satisfy the person's **meta-needs.** Meta-needs are such things as the desire for justice, beauty, order, and unity. The basic needs lead to physical growth; the meta-needs lead to psychological growth and self-actualization.

Few societies are perfect, however, so few people ever reach their full potential. But there are times in each person's life, says Maslow, when the full potential for a particular moment is reached. Maslow calls these "peak experiences." Peaks of perfect self-actualization may come through such things as religious experience, music, sex, natural childbirth, or almost any fulfilling experience.

MEASURING PERSONALITY

As the various personality theories came into being, psychologists developed specific way of trying to measure or assess those internal programs that we call personality. As you might suspect, each of the various theories called for different measuring instruments.

Generally speaking, the dynamic and developmental theories call for **subjective measures** — tests that allow the individual to express his or her thoughts, feelings, and emotions. These tests are *subjective* since inner experiences such as thinking and feeling cannot be observed directly. The psychologist must give the test and then *interpret* the subject's responses in terms of what kind of person the psychologist perceives the subject to be.

The social learning theorists, on the other hand, have tended to rely on **objective measures** — the recording of visible behaviors (including speech), or the use of tests, such as the IQ, that have "norms" or standards." The psychologist usually judges a subject's responses on an objective test by comparing them to the responses made by some group of presumably normal people.

Subjective Tests

The Rorschach

FIG. 10–2.
Although this is not an actual Rorschach ink-blot, it is typical of those used in testing. What do you see in this ink-blot?

Dynamic theories of personality (such as Freud's) are often based on the unconscious aspects of human experience. Dynamic theorists, therefore, have designed several tests whose aim is to get people to *project* part of their unconscious thoughts and feelings into the test answers. These subjective measures are often called **projective tests,** the best-known of which is the Rorschach.

The **Rorschach** or **ink-blot test** was devised by a Swiss psychiatrist named Hermann Rorschach (1884–1922). The test is based on the assumption that people tend to perceive and react to ambiguous shapes by projecting their own needs into the shapes. Specific reactions to these oddly shaped ink-blots, for instance, are supposed to reveal some of the more hidden or unconscious aspects of an individual's personality.

Rorschach tested many ink-blots on many people for 10 years. He finally selected the 10 specific ink-blots that seemed to get the most emotional responses from people.

The ink-blots, some of which are black and gray and others of which contain areas of color, are printed on cards. People being tested are asked to look at each card and decide what the irregular shape looks like. The person giving the test writes down the responses (three or four to each card) and then interprets the answers according to one of several methods.

The Rorschach does seem to give a good deal of information about someone's personality, especially if it is used together with other tests. The Rorschach, however, is not a completely valid or reliable test (see Chapter 8). Since there are no specific or correct answers to the Rorschach, each examiner might score the results differently.

Thematic Apperception Test (TAT)

Henry Murray developed a projective test in which subjects are supposed to reveal their personality characteristics by making up stories about a set of pictures. Like the ink-blot test, the **Thematic Apperception Test** (**TAT**) has no correct answers (see Chapter 5).

People taking the TAT are asked to explain what action led up to a scene in one of the pictures, what is going on in the picture now, and what will happen. The stories are recorded, studied, and interpreted. Specific themes in the stories people tell are supposed to reveal needs and emotions and personality characteristics.

Studies of the TAT have shown that it is useful in detecting aggressive feelings, the needs for achievement and affiliation, and feelings of hostility in minority groups from ghetto areas. But even if it is accurate in some cases, the TAT, like other projective tests, is a very subjective measure of personality. The way such tests are scored often tells as much about the tester as the testee.

Objective Tests

Objective tests, unlike subjective and projective tests, tend to have right and wrong answers—or at least to have answers that can be compared to some norm or reference group's responses. Thus, the scores that someone gets on an objective test are not likely to change very much merely because the tester likes or dislikes the person. The IQ test is a good example of a fairly objective type of measuring device. Other objective tests include the following:

The Minnesota Multiphasic Personality Inventory (MMPI)

The **MMPI** consists of 550 statements that are to be answered as "true," "false," or "cannot say." The statements cover 26 areas, including family life, marriage problems, sex-life, religion, and social activities. By comparing the subject's responses to those of a "normal" group, the psychologist is often able to discover in which of the 26 areas the subject might be having difficulties.

The MMPI was developed by J. C. McKinley and Starke R. Hathaway of the University of Minnesota School of Medicine. They designed the test for use in mental institutions. It was originally supposed to tell the difference between well-adjusted people and those with certain personality problems. The test was so successful in separating such individuals that it has now become a widely used test for assessing the personalities of individuals not in mental institutions. Students, employees, and people in the armed forces, for instance, are often given the MMPI. It is supposed to tell what kind of students they will be, what type of jobs they are suited for, or if they might need psychiatric help.

When used on certain types of people, the MMPI has been found to be a reliable tool for personality assessment. The MMPI, however, was standardized on a group of people in Minnesota. The standard or normal responses, therefore, are not necessarily valid for other groups of people. Even so, the MMPI is used hundreds of times a day in cities across the country by educators, employers, and psychologists to assess the personalities of people from all walks of life. Many people object to this widespread use of a test that was standardized on only a few people in one city.

Locus of Personal Control Scale (LOC)

Psychologist Julian Rotter believes that people can be categorized according to how much personal control they think they have over their own destinies. Those people whom Rotter calls **externalizers** tend to see their lives as being controlled by external forces, such as God or Nature or Chance. Those people whom Rotter calls **internalizers** tend to perceive their locus of personal control as being inside themselves. That is, internalizers believe that they themselves can have an effect on what happens to them, that they can achieve self-actualization if they try hard enough. Rotter has developed a test, the **Locus of Personal Control Scale (LOC),** which consists of 20 or more questions such as "Do you believe that your life is strongly influenced by forces over which you have no control?" According to the person's answers, Rotter can place the individual towards either the externalizer or the internalizer end of the Locus of Personal Control Scale.

Although Rotter at first believed that one's locus of personal control was a rather general trait, recent research suggests that it is not. Some people are internalizers when it comes to their own personal lives, but are externalizers while on the job. These people know how to get along with others in social settings, but feel that they have little or no influence on what happens to them in the organizations for which they work.

In a recent study at the University of Michigan, psychologist Carolyn Mills found that individuals who are externalizers on the job do not seem to benefit as much from job training as do people who are internalizers. However, when Mills gave special training to the externalizers by teaching them how to have more effect on the organization for which they worked, many of the subjects moved toward the internalizer end of Mills's Organizational Locus of Control Scale.

THE ETHICS OF TESTING

There are many ethical objections that can be raised concerning personality tests. To begin with, personality tests are—generally speaking—even less reliable and valid than are intelligence tests (see Chapter 8). Thus, no test has yet been designed that can give a true picture of any individual's personality.

Although personality tests are frequently administered in schools and businesses, they may constitute what some people consider an invasion of privacy. These tests often ask subjects questions about their sexual practices, religious and political beliefs, and about many other private thoughts and behaviors. Many people believe that educators and employers have no right to such personal information.

In addition, when personality tests are improperly used, they can become tools of discrimination. Most tests in widespread use—such as the MMPI—are standardized on white, middle-class attitudes, values, and beliefs in the United States. Such tests cannot therefore accurately assess the true personalities and potentials of most blacks and other minority-group members. Therefore, when blacks and whites are tested, the whites will almost always get more favorable scores. If the test is used as a job-screening device, the whites will usually have a better chance than the blacks of being hired.

A completely valid and reliable personality test may some day be designed. Until then, such tests should be used cautiously, and they should be administered and interpreted only by experts who realize the limitations of the tests.

SOUL ON ICE

Eldridge Cleaver was a hopeful internalizer. He assessed his own personality, decided who he was, and decided that he had some control over who he would become. Using his own theory of personality, he set out to make some changes. He began changing one after another of his internal programs, and then started

TABLE 10-2   **Personality Tests**

Type of Test	Specific Test	Description
Subjective Test inner experiences; must be interpreted by a psychologist; appropriate for psychodynamic and developmental theories of personality.	1. Rorschach	Developed by Hermann Rorschach. Subjects look at ink-blots and describe what they see in them; not completely reliable or valid.
	2. Thematic Apperception Test (TAT)	Developed by Henry Murray. Subjects look at set of pictures and make up stories about them; very subjective test; interpretation relies heavily on the person giving the test.
Objective Record visible behaviors; must be compared to standard or normal group; appropriate for social learning theories of personality.	1. Minnesota Multiphasic Personality Inventory (MMPI)	Developed by J. C. McKinley and S. R. Hathaway. Consists of 550 statements to be answered "true," "false," or "cannot say"; separates well-adjusted individuals from people with personality problems; not entirely reliable because it was standardized on group of people in Minnesota.
	2. Locus of Personal Control Scale (LOC)	Developed by Julian Rotter. Consists of 20 or more questions to determine how much personal control subjects feel they have over their own destinies; locus of control is not a general trait; some people are externalizers in certain situations and internalizers in others.

off full of hope on the road to self-actualization. But the road was a long one. Wanted by the police, Cleaver fled the country in 1968. After stays in Cuba, Algeria, and France, he finally gave up and returned to the United States in 1975. By then Cleaver was a changed person in many ways. He now calls himself a born-again Christian. In 1977 he was making television commercials for Christ.

Change for the better and self-actualization are not restricted to a few people like Eldridge Cleaver. While sitting in prison, Cleaver began to notice that a good many young whites were joining in the black struggle for human rights. Young whites were marching and sitting in with blacks in demonstrations across the country. If I can change, said Cleaver, and if young whites can change, then there is hope for America.

And hope and change begin with the answers to the questions:
Who am I?
Where did I come from?
Where am I now?
Where am I going?

► SUMMARY

1. Who am I? Where did I come from? Where am I now? Where am I going? Eldridge Cleaver asked these questions, decided he didn't like the answers, and set out to make some changes. In other words, he decided to change his personality, the record of which is *Soul on Ice*. As we have seen in this chapter, personality change is possible, but we must know ourselves — understand our personalities — in order to become someone different.

2. The most popular theories of personality can be divided into three categories — **type theories, trait theories,** and **social learning theories** — with each emphasizing (respectively) either biological, cognitive, or social inputs and outputs. But each human personality is the result of a complex mix of all three types of inputs. Therefore, if we are to understand our personalities we will have to look at all three types of personality theory.

3. The type of body a person has has often been said to be related to personality. Kretschmer believed that the hormones influence body shape and personality, and he developed a theory of **morphology** based on three body types. Sheldon expanded on this, identified three basic body types — **endomorph, mesomorph,** and **ectomorph** — and identified seven degrees of each type. An attempt was then made to relate combinations of personality characteristics with certain body types. Biology and genes do play important roles in personality development, but type theories are incomplete. There are many people who don't fit into any of the categories described, and even those people who do fit a specific category type don't always have the personality characteristics the type theories predict they should have.

4. Despite the difficulties we have in measuring psychological or cognitive traits, whole theories of personality have been based on the belief that the human personality is determined by a limited number of mental traits. The traits described in these theories are important, and knowledge of them can help predict how an individual will respond to a given stimulus. But cognitive traits have been found to be much less stable than they were once thought to be.

5. Because traits are not always stable and because personalities can change in dramatic ways, theories have been proposed that attempt to account for changes in personality. These **psychodynamic theories** focus on the functions or internal processes that occur during personality development and change. The most famous dynamic theory is that of Sigmund Freud.

6. Freud explained personality in terms of tension — the build-up, blocking, and release of psychological energy created by the **libido.** As the personality develops, said Freud, libidinal energy is released through the activity of the **Id, Ego,** and **Superego,** what Freud called the three components of the human personality. At first, the organism is guided by the **pleasure principle,** and eventually comes to follow the **reality principle.**

7. Freud described many of the characteristic behaviors or personality traits that he saw in his patients as defenses against anxiety over how libidinal energy should be released. **Defense mechanisms** include **repression, fixation,**

regression, reaction formation, projection, displacement, and **subli-mation.**

8. Freud tried to cure emotional problems or change strange thoughts and be-haviors by helping his patients release stored up energy. The release of stored up energy is called **catharsis.** By getting patients to talk about their problems and past experiences that might be causing problems, Freud was often able to bring about catharsis. The system of examining past experiences and present prob-lems is called **psychoanalysis.**

9. According to social learning theory, most humans can better themselves physically, cognitively, and socially. The desire to become something better is called a desire for **self-actualization.** Psychologists interested in self-actualiza-tion are called **humanists.** Humanists, like Carl Rogers and Abraham Maslow, stress the importance of understanding the real self. Maslow has suggested a **hi-erarchy of needs** starting with the basic needs and ascending to the **meta-needs.**

10. There are two basic ways to measure or assess personality — subjective and objective measures. **Subjective tests,** also called **projective tests,** such as the **Rorschach** and the **Thematic Apperception Test** (**TAT**), allow individu-als to express their thoughts, feelings, and emotions. Psychologists then interpret the subject's responses. **Objective tests,** such as the **Minnesota Mul-tiphasic Personality Inventory** (**MMPI**) and the **Locus of Personal Con-trol Scale** (**LOC**) tend to have right or wrong answers that can be compared to the answers given by a reference group. Because none of these tests is com-pletely valid, or reliable, such tests and the information they provide should probably be used only by experts who realize the limitations of the tests.

Suggested Readings

Cleaver, Eldridge. *Soul on ice.* New York: Dell, 1970.

Hall, Calvin S. and Gardner Lindzey. *Theories of personality.* 2d ed. New York: Wiley, 1970.

Maddi, Salvatore R. *Personality theories: A comparative analysis.* Homewood, Ill.: Dor-sey, 1968.

Rogers, Carl. *On becoming a person.* Boston: Houghton Mifflin, 1961.

► STUDY GUIDE

A.   RECALL

Sentence Completion

[p. 321]

1. Perhaps the greatest insight that Eldridge Cleaver had was that personality could _____.

[p. 321]

2. Your personality is your own _____ way of _____ to your environment.

[p. 322]

3. Personality theories that view biological processes as being most important are often called _____ theories.

[p. 323]

4. _____ is the pseudoscience of "reading" the bumps or depressions on people's skulls.

[p. 324]

5. A _____ is a simplified belief or set of characteristics that is supposed to be true for all members of the same group.

[p. 324]

6. The first serious theory of body types was devised by _____ and did not work out very well at all.

[p. 325]

7. Sheldon's body type of _____ is characterized by a soft, round, fat appearance, with underdeveloped muscles.

[p. 325]

8. Each of Sheldon's body types has _____ degrees of variation.

[p. 325]

9. _____ and _____ inputs, in addition to genes, could explain why there is sometimes a relationship between personality and body types.

[p. 327]

10. Consistent and unique personality characteristics are sometimes called _____.

[p. 327]

11. Allport called widely shared personality characteristics _____ traits.

[p. 327]

12. The one single most powerful trait that influences a person is what Allport called a _____ trait.

[p. 328]

13. The presence or absence of most traits often depends upon the _____.

[p. 329]

14. Rather than focusing on the structure of personality, dynamic theories focus on the _____ of personality.

[p. 330]

15. For Freud, it is the _____ that creates life force or energy that keeps the mind running.

[p. 330]

16. The Id follows the _____ principle, while the Ego follows the _____ principle.

[p. 331]

17. The Superego is thought to arise during the _____ stage of personal development.

[p. 331]

18. Most sexual behaviors are repressed or inhibited during the _____ period of development.

[p. 332]

19. Anxiety-reducing ways of coping are what Freud called _____.

[p. 333]

20. _____ is characterized by a slipping back to an earlier or more primitive stage of development.

[p. 334]

21. Reliving an emotional experience and releasing pent-up libidinal energy is called _____.

[p. 335]

22. Freud's technique of therapy is called _____.

[p. 335]
23. The desire to become something better is called the desire for _____-
_____.

[p. 335]
24. The two psychologists associated with humanistic psychology are Carl _____ and Abraham _____.

[p. 336]
25. The self that a person wants to become is what Rogers calls the _____ self.

[p. 338]
26. The _____ test and the _____ are examples of subjective measures of personality.

[p. 338]
27. Subjective personality tests are often called _____ tests.

[p. 338]
28. The TAT was developed by _____ _____.

[p. 339]
29. The MMPI consists of _____ statements covering _____ different areas.

[p. 339]
30. The LOC characterizes people as being either _____ or _____.

[p. 340]
31. According to Rotter, Eldridge Cleaver would be classified as an _____.

B.   REVIEW

Multiple Choice: Circle the letter identifying the alternative that most correctly completes the statement or answers the question.

  1. Eldridge Cleaver:
     A. blamed his genes for his problems.
     B. developed a personality theory for blacks.
     C. was an internalizer.
     D. all of the above.

  2. Personality theories that attempt to relate physical characteristics to personality are the _____ theories.
     A. type
     B. trait
     C. social learning
     D. humanistic

  3. Sheldon would call an athletic type with strong muscles and bones a(n):
     A. endomorph.
     B. ectomorph.
     C. mesomorph.
     D. psychomorph.

  4. Allport called the one major trait that guides a person throughout his or her life a(n) _____ trait.
     A. common
     B. cardinal
     C. individual
     D. central

5. Which of the following is the proper order of Freud's stages of personality development?

A. oral, anal, phallic, genital
B. anal, phallic, genital, oral
C. phallic, genital, anal, oral
D. genital, oral, phallic, anal

6. The release of psychic energy that may accompany the reliving of an emotional experience is what Freud called:

A. the pleasure principle.
B. the reality principle.
C. libido.
D. catharsis.

7. Which of the following defense mechanisms is characterized by a person's staying at one level of development for fear of moving to the next?

A. repression
B. fixation
C. reaction formation
D. displacement

8. When we see others as having characteristics that we do not like in ourselves, we are:

A. regressing.
B. projecting.
C. displacing.
D. sublimating.

9. Which of the following would view personality change as being under the individual's control?

A. Sheldon
B. Allport
C. Kretschmer
D. Rogers

10. Which of the following involves having subjects tell stories about ambiguous pictures?

A. the TAT
B. the MMPI
C. the AGCT
D. the LOC

PSYCHOLOGICAL TESTING: MMPI UNDER FIRE

In 1937 insulin therapy was becoming a widespread method of treatment for certain forms of mental illness. Some clinics, however, were reporting that the treatment was ineffective. J. C. McKinley and Starke R. Hathaway of the University of Minnesota School of Medicine thought the variation in effectiveness could be due to the fact that the patients treated with insulin in one clinic were not like those treated in another clinic. Estimations of a person's mental illness and of its severity were based on professional judgment that could vary with the training and background of the examining psychiatrist. To avoid this problem a personality test, the Minnesota Multiphasic Personality Inventory, was designed.

A list of items (verbal statements) was taken from case studies in text books on psychiatry and clinical psychology. The persons' responses of either "true" or "false" to these items were then used as an indication of symptoms and severity of mental illness. Once the items were selected, the test was standardized on a cross section of normal adults in Minnesota. They represented all socioeconomic and educational levels present there.

The test was originally intended as a diagnostic tool for use on mentally ill patients. But because of its simplicity and its ability to indicate personality types, the MMPI has developed into a 550-item test that is in use around the world. It has been administered to applicants to graduate schools, to high school students,

and to persons being considered for jobs. If the test indicates that the personality of an applicant is not appropriate to the job, both employer and employe can be protected.

But ten years ago Congressional hearings exposed the Federal Government's widespread use of the MMPI as a selective instrument for employment. As a result, the Civil Service Commission issued a revision of policy prohibiting tests like the MMPI except under medical supervision. The Department of Labor and the State Department acted similarly, and the Peace Corps ordered all personality answer sheets on its files destroyed. The Peace Corps continued to use the test but changed the instructions to permit omission of responses to any questions that the candidate might find offensive. The committees charged invasion of privacy because the questions on the tests delve into political and religious views without the informed and voluntary consent of the testee.

Ralph M. Dreger, a psychologist at Louisiana State University in Baton Rouge, insisted then that the Government and government agencies do not have the right to ask such questions whether or not the individual gives informed and voluntary consent. "This is one of the reasons, apart from technical considerations entirely (those having to do with utterly unqualified persons administering the test which has been the case in many instances) that I objected to the use of the MMPI in government selection procedures since before the matter became an issue in the Congress and courts," he says.

But Dreger does not stop there. He believes that even outside the government a person does not necessarily have the right to assess another's personality. Physicians not trained in psychology can administer the test and get a computer readout of the results. Dreger contends that this approach is useless in the hands of an unqualified person.

To be qualified, Dreger says, a personality assessor must be familiar with several dozen variables. Among them are societal and cultural goals, including ideologies; community structure and goals; geographical locale; socioeconomic status; child-rearing attitudes and practices; family structure, positions, roles and role expectancy; gene patterns; self concepts and attitudes, particularly self esteem; levels of aspiration, real and expressed; expressive opportunities, including vocational opportunities; peer relations; and cognitive styles.

He considers all these things necessary when assessing any personality and particularly when assessing the personalities of any minority. Dreger is especially interested in the use of personality tests on minority populations. "The research findings in which blacks are compared with the white Minnesota sample would lead us to believe that the majority of Negroes are manic-depressive schizophrenics," he says.

In *Comparative Studies of Blacks and Whites in the United States* (Seminar Press, 1972)

Dreger and Kent S. Miller of Florida State University evaluate much of the recent research on race. In a section on the MMPI, Dreger cites the work of Malcolm Gynther at St. Louis University and agrees with his suggestion that parts of the MMPI be restandardized on blacks in the same manner it was originally standardized on whites. Dreger says even clinicians who are otherwise qualified do not always understand the cultural biases built into the MMPI.

The Psychological Corp. of New York City is the publisher of the MMPI. James H. Ricks of the corporation's test division acknowledges that restandardization of the test for blacks is a legitimate suggestion. But, he says, the test could also be standardized for almost any particular group in the country. "The whole thing could be started over from scratch for special applications," he says, "but one of the things that is good about the MMPI is that it is a robust or sturdy instrument that has been useful in treatment of different groups and over time." In his view, this is because it is an empirical tool that does not depend on anyone's armchair opinion. The primary use of the test is to help the individual. If that person happens to be a member of a minority group, his particular situation and background would have to be allowed for, says Ricks. As for invasion of privacy, Ricks points out that a person is not required to answer every question.

Even so there is a philosophical qualification that Dreger makes. In his view, no one has the right to assess another's personality. But he does believe that if the assessor sees the person he is testing as a person and not as a case, and if the assessor is reasonably qualified, he may have the privilege—but still not the right —to attempt to assess another's personality.

C. NEWS STORY QUESTIONS

1. Although the MMPI has been used for many many purposes, why was it constructed originally? _____

2. Aside from the issue of invasion of privacy, what is Dreger's major objection to the indiscriminate use of the MMPI? _____

3. Why might the MMPI be inappropriate for blacks, and what could be done about it? __

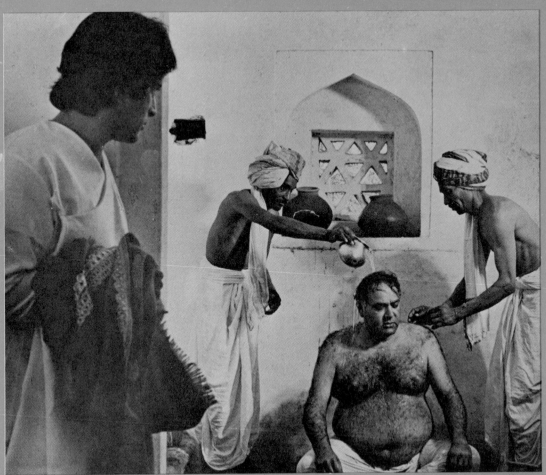

Movie still from *Siddhartha*.

The world is constantly changing, and we must learn to adjust to differing conditions. We must face up to and adjust to changes in the physical environment, the social world, and our own inner processes. Well-adjusted individuals are those who are best able to adjust to these three changing realities—the physical, the social, and the cognitive.

Personal Adjustment

chapter 11

When you have completed your study of this chapter, you should be able to:

▶ Discuss how the physical environment affects personal adjustment, and describe internalizers and externalizers
▶ Define biofeedback and contrast these techniques with meditation
▶ Define mirroring and present an example
▶ Describe Asch's experiments on group pressure and conformity
▶ Explain the relationship between conflict and stress; describing Lewin's four types of conflict and summarizing Selye's three stages of reaction to stress
▶ List and give examples of methods for coping with stressful situations, including "direct coping"

Aggression. A first or unprovoked attack, or any other form of hostile behavior.

Alarm reaction. The first of Selye's three stages of response to stress, during which the organism mobilizes its resources to meet an attack of some kind.

Antennae (ann-TENN-eye). From the Latin word meaning "feeler" or "sail." An antenna (ann-TENN-uh) is something that sticks up or out from an organism, or from a piece of electrical equipment. The purpose of the antenna is usually to gather in stimulus inputs of some kind.

Anxiety. A mild form of fear, often without a specific focus.

Biofeedback. The word *feedback* means "an informational input that tells you about your own performance." *Biofeedback* is "an informational input that tells you about the performance of your own bodily processes." Once you have this information (often from an EEG or "brain wave" machine), you can often gain voluntary control over the bodily processes that you're measuring.

Conflict. A fight, a battle, or a struggle between two or more forces. Also means a mental or moral struggle brought about by incompatible desires or goals. In an *approach-approach conflict,* you are torn between two pleasant or rewarding goals. In an *approach-avoidance conflict,* you cannot achieve a rewarding goal without risking unpleasant consequences that you would like to avoid. In an *avoidance-avoidance conflict,* you are forced to choose between two unpleasant goals or courses of action. Most forms of conflict are of the *"double approach-avoidance,"* in that no matter which goal you may choose, you will experience both rewards and punishments.

Coping (KOH-ping). From the Greek word meaning "to strike" or "to break." In modern English, to cope is to achieve or maintain success in the battle of life.

Curare (cure-RAR-ree). A paralyzing drug that occurs naturally in many plants native to South America.

Defensive coping. To adjust to the world or to your own problems chiefly by denying that you have problems, or by refusing to face real-life issues in the hope that they will eventually go away.

Depression. The opposite of arousal; to be "down" rather than to be "up." A depression is often accompanied by feelings of sadness or unhappiness, a loss of hope or faith, a turning inward, and by a considerable reduction in activity.

Direct coping. To adjust to the world by facing its challenges head-on. To change one's goals, feelings, or behaviors as reality demands.

Displacement. One of the Freudian defense mechanisms. If your boss criticizes you, you may not be able to express your anger without losing your job. So you go home and kick the cat instead. Your anger has been displaced from your boss to the cat.

Electrodes (ee-LEK-trodes). A device (usually a piece of metal placed either on the skin or directly within a nerve cell) to detect electrical activity, usually in the brain.

Exhaustion stage. The third of Selye's three stages of response to stress. During this stage, the organism is often so tired and without further energy resources that it becomes very depressed and often just gives up the battle.

Externalizers (EX-turr-nuh-lie-zers). People who—according to psychologist Julian Rotter—see their lives as being under the control of external forces over which the people have little or no influence.

Fixation (fix-AY-shun). One of the many Freudian defense mechanisms. According to Freud, if a child's needs are not met, the child's personality development may become arrested or fixed before its maturation is complete.

Frustration (fruss-TRAY-shun). From the Latin term meaning "to do something in vain." Anything that prevents you from achieving a goal is likely to give you strong feelings of frustration and conflict.

Hysterical blindness (hiss-TARE-uh-cal). Blindness due to psychological rather than physical causes. To prevent yourself from seeing a frightening or terribly unpleasant sight, your mind may "block off" all incoming visual inputs so that you see nothing at all.

Internalizers (in-TURR-nuh-lie-zers). According to psychologist Julian Rotter, people who believe their actions are under their own internal control.

Learned helplessness. A type of behavior—studied extensively by Martin Seligman—in which an organism reacts to frustration or pain by refusing to cope with its problems except by sitting quietly and doing nothing.

Mantras (MAN-trahs). Sounds that are repeated over and over again in one's mind during meditation.

Migraine (MY-grain). From the Greek words meaning "half the skull." A migraine is a periodic headache that is often extremely painful, but that usually is confined to one side of the head.

Modeling. A model is an idealized person or thing. When you act the way that you want others to act, you are serving as a model for their behavior. Most types of social modeling can be summed up in the Golden Rule: "Do unto others as you would have them do unto you."

Nirvana (near-VAHN-ah). From an ancient Indian word meaning "blowing out." In modern usage, Nirvana means a state of freedom characterized by the extinction of desire, passion, illusion, and the attainment of rest, truth, and unchanging being.

Projection. One of the many types of Freudian defense mechanisms. If you have desires or feelings that are unacceptable to you, you may project these feelings onto other people.

Reaction formation. A Freudian defense mechanism, similar to projection, in which the person acts exactly opposite the way he or she feels. Hate becomes love, and vice-versa.

Regression. A Freudian defense mechanism in which an individual who has reached a higher level of psychosexual adjustment may return to a more primitive or childish way of thinking and acting.

Resistance stage. The second of Selye's three stages of stress response, during which the body tries to repair itself while continuing to act in an aroused manner.

Stooge. A slang term coming from vaudeville. In psychological research, a stooge is someone paid to pretend that he or she is a "real" subject. In fact, the stooge simply responds to the experimenter as the stooge has been told to respond.

Stress. An abbreviated form of the word "distress." To be stressed is to be subjected to strong external forces that push you or strain you against your will.

Traumatized (TRAW-muh-tized). From the Greek word meaning "injury." To traumatize someone is to wound or injure that person—either physically or psychologically.

Yoga (YOH-guh). A type of mental discipline—found chiefly among the Hindus of India—that involves directing one's attention upon an object so that one can identify one's consciousness with that object. In some instances, the "object" is a part of one's body; in other instances, the "object" is God.

Yogi (YOH-gey; rhymes with "bogey"). Someone who practices yoga.

INTRODUCTION: SIDDHARTHA

He was a gambler, a drunkard, a ruthless merchant, and for 20 years he spent part of almost every day with a famous courtesan or prostitute. At times he was selfish and greedy, vain and lazy, stingy and cruel, arrogant and snobbish. And yet, he became one of the most respected men to ever walk the face of the earth. They called him The Enlightened One, The Illustrious One, The All Perfect, The Master, The Buddha. He was Gautama Siddhartha, the Indian philosopher who founded Buddhism almost 500 years before the time of Christ.

The story of the Buddha's successful search for human perfection is told in *Siddhartha*, the novel by the German author Hermann Hesse. As a child Siddhartha was the perfect son. He was bright, intelligent, obedient, and physically healthy. He could have followed his parents' wishes to become a priest, but Siddhartha had his own wishes. He did not know what he wanted, but he knew that his parents' desires were not the same as his. Siddhartha left home, gave away his clothes and possessions, and followed a group of mystics. For three years he lived in the desert, begged for his food, and practiced fasting and meditation. He denied all of his physical needs and emotions in an attempt to find some sort of spiritual reality for himself.

Siddhartha learned much in the desert, but he did not learn everything that he wanted to know. He felt that there was a special place in the world for him, but it was not in the desert. Siddhartha's search next took him to a city, where he became a merchant and grew rich and powerful. He had fine clothes and servants. Doing the opposite of what he had done in the desert, Siddhartha fulfilled all his physical and emotional needs — even to excess. He enjoyed the pleasures of the flesh and allowed himself to experience every human emotional sensation. For 20 years Siddhartha searched for himself in physical and social experiences and pleasures. But he was still unhappy. There was still something missing from his life.

At the age of 40, Siddhartha left town and walked until he came to a river. There he sat down in despair and began to think about suicide. He had been searching since he left his parents' home and still he hadn't found what he wanted. He had experienced everything from the desert to the city. There just didn't seem to be a place or a reason in life for him.

As Siddhartha leaned over into the river seeking death, a word came to him — Om — the sacred word he had repeated to himself over and over during meditation. Om means Perfection. And it dawned on Siddhartha that the meaning of life is perfection. His religion had taught him that people who do not achieve perfection will be reborn. They will have to go through another life seeking perfection. They will have to do this over and over. Only when they achieve human perfection will they die and achieve **Nirvana,** or absolute happiness. So suicide made no sense. Siddhartha would have to achieve perfection.

He sat by that river for 20 years thinking about the meaning of his life and true perfection. Siddhartha earned his living during this time by rowing people back and forth across the river, but mostly he just sat and thought and listened to the river. And the river taught him something. It taught him that life is not just a collection of experiences. Life, like the river, is one continuous, flowing, and unified experience. Life, he thought, is timeless. It is not just past experiences or future plans. Life flows and flows, and yet it is always there. It is always the same, and yet every moment it is new. Only the present exists for the river, but the present contains all of the past and all of the future. In order to understand himself, he would have to understand and accept all parts of his past life as well as whatever his future might be. Only when he understood the good and the bad, the young and the old, the spiritual and the physical, the desert and the city within himself and the world, would he be in harmony with the flow of life. Then would he reach perfection. Then would he be the Buddha.

PERSONAL ADJUSTMENT

Words like "unity," "timelessness," and "harmony with life" sound good, but those terms are very hard to define. What Siddhartha called unity and perfection, humanistic psychologists would call self-actualization. Other psychologists would speak of being "mature" or being "well-adjusted." But no matter what label we give the experience, most of us realize that we must come to some sort of understanding of the changing reality of the world. We must face and adjust to the physical environment, to the social world of other people, and we must find some understanding of our own personal inner processes. If and only if we can adjust to three separate realities—the physical, the social, and the cognitive—can we call ourselves well-adjusted.

Physical Reality

The law of gravity doesn't care whether you believe in it or not. It exists, and adjustments must be made for it. Astronauts who leave earth's gravity and fly to the moon must make several adjustments. First they leave the earth's gravity. In space there is little or no gravity, and on the moon there is a weaker gravitational pull than on earth. If they make the necessary adjustments, the astronauts get around quite well. If they don't adjust, their soup may float away from them in space, or they may fall all over themselves on the moon.

Winter and summer exist in most parts of the world. Birds adapt to cold weather by flying south. Bears adapt by crawling into a cave and staying there until spring. People adapt or adjust by going south, putting on more clothes, turning up the heat, or by doing whatever they can to keep from freezing. Those who can make the best adaptations or adjustments protect themselves from the environment.

Floods, fires, and earthquakes exist. Accidents happen. People have to adjust to these realities also. Adjustment, however, depends to a great extent on each individual's personal philosophy or view of reality. **Externalizers,** as Rotter explained (see Chapter 10), tend to view reality as something that is controlled by outside forces. They often believe in such things as astrology and mysterious external forces that rule their lives. **Internalizers,** on the other hand, believe that they themselves have some internal and conscious control over their own destiny. There are no pure externalizers or internalizers, but most people tend to lean in one direction or the other. Those who lean more toward the external-control position sometimes do not even attempt to adjust to reality. Such people may not make any sensible precautions even in the face of such realities as a flood, a fire, or a tornado. The internalizers who feel that they have some control of their own fate will usually attempt to adjust to reality. They will try to fight a fire or run away from a flood or tornado. Such people are usually better adjusted than those who let themselves become victims of the environment. They also tend to live longer.

Richter's Rats

Experiments conducted by psychiatrist Curt Richter suggest that even rats can learn some of the behaviors of human internalizers. And rats that have the hopeful outlook of internalizers are usually better able to adjust to reality and are better equipped psychologically to survive.

Richter was studying the effects of a hostile environment on rats. He would drop rats into a tub of water and let them swim until they were exhausted. He found that most rats would swim for about 80 hours if the water was kept at room temperature. These rats met the challenge of drowning and adjusted by swimming until their bodies gave out. If the water was too hot or too cold, or if Richter blew a stream of air into the rats' faces, the animals did not adjust as well. They became exhausted after only 20 to 40 hours and gave up.

While Richter was conducting these experiments, he noticed that some rats always swam in a clockwise direction while others always swam in a counter-clockwise direction. Such behavior was puzzling, but Richter knew that some insects showed similar circling behavior if one of their feelers or **antennae** was cut off. An ant that has lost its right antenna, for instance, will circle to the right. Richter wondered if the length of his rats' whiskers had anything to do with their circling tendencies. He asked his assistants to cut the whiskers off one side of a rat's face and then drop the rat into the water. When the assistants brought in a half-shaved rat and put it in the water, the animal did not swim for 80, 40, or even 20 hours. It swam wildly for about two minutes and then gave up all hope and sank to the bottom of the tub.

Richter knew that rats didn't swim with their whiskers, so he had to find another explanation for this strange behavior. He asked his assistants how they had prepared the rat for the experiment. The assistants explained that they had let the rat crawl out of its cage into a black bag. This procedure protected the experimenters from the rat's sharp teeth. While the rat was held tightly in the bag, part of the bag was pulled back until the rat's head stuck out. Large, noisy clippers were then used to chop the whiskers off one side of the rat's face. Once this clipping was completed, the bag was opened over the tub of water, and the rat was dropped. The animal, probably scared half to death by its experience in the black bag, did not seem to be ready to put up with another environmental disaster. When dropped into the water it quickly gave up and prepared to die.

But Richter found out something else about his rats. If a rat without whiskers was rescued before it gave up, it had a better chance of survival the next time it was put in the water. When Richter took the scared rats out of the water and allowed them a few minutes to recover from the shocks of the black bag and the water, the animals were then able to swim for at least 80 hours when they were put back in the water. These animals seemed to have regained hope and the desire to live.

Richter's experiments suggest that experience has a great deal to do with adjustment. People who meet challenges and adjust successfully usually begin to feel that they have some control over their own lives. They will stay afloat long enough to meet other challenges and make other adjustments. People who continually fail to make the proper adjustments may develop the externalizer's view of life and begin to feel that adjustment is not worth the effort.

You have no control over natural disasters such as earthquakes. However, when these events occur you must learn to adjust to physical reality.

Inner Reality: Emotional Awareness, Feedback, and Self-Control

As we noted in Chapter 5, our emotions are among the most powerful inner experiences that we must learn about and adjust to. Those emotional states we call love, hate, joy, grief, fear, and anger affect much of what we do. We have no choice about experiencing emotions—these feelings are part and parcel of life. But we do have a choice about how our emotions affect our adjustment to the world. We can either allow them to run our lives, or we can try to bring them under some kind of voluntary control when they keep us from coping. Either way, we adjust to our emotions. But to control them, we must learn to become aware of what our emotions really are, why they come about, and how we may influence them.

Human beings seem to be the only living systems capable of voluntarily developing any real measure of self-control. But "control" always implies some

FIG. 11–1.
The feedback you receive from your environment, your mind, and your own body helps you to develop self-awareness and emotional control.

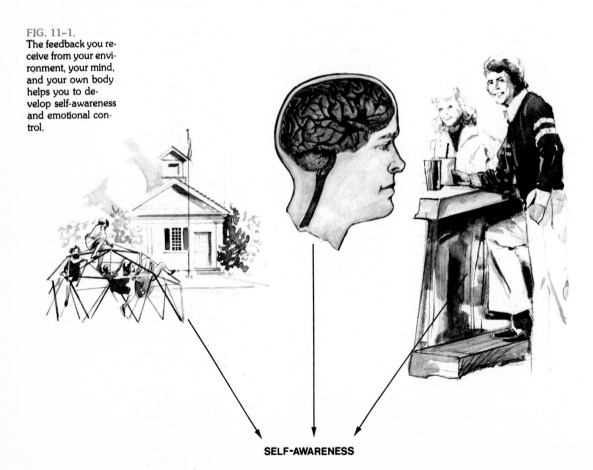

SELF-AWARENESS

measure of self-awareness, and self-awareness is dependent on feedback. If you are not aware of your bodily reactions during anger, for instance, you cannot hope to do a very good job of learning to control your temper. If you never take the time to spell out your own personal goals—if you never try to figure out who you presently are and what you would like to become—then you may not become much of anything at all. And if you never learn to notice the tremendous effect that other people have on your emotional development, you may never understand why you react so emotionally to what other people say and do.

There are, then, three main types of feedback that we must pay attention to if we wish to develop self-awareness and emotional control: feedback from our bodies, feedback from our minds, and feedback from our social environments.

Meditation and Biofeedback

For centuries, oriental religions have taught that meditation can lead to complete mental and spiritual development. When Siddhartha went to the desert, he began to practice one particular type of meditation—**yoga.** Yoga means "union." The various types of yoga stress physical training, such as learning to control one's breathing and one's body posture. While sitting and breathing properly, practicers of yoga concentrate on or repeat a specific word, question, or sound over and over. Siddhartha used the word Om. Other meditators use different sounds or **mantras.** Both meditation and concentration can help people become more aware of themselves—of what their bodies are doing, and how their minds are responding.

Meditation has long been used by followers of oriental religions to help their mental and spiritual development. These men are practicing Zen meditation before engaging in a Kung Fu exercise. Meditation provides feedback that leads to better control of the body.

After years of practice, many **yogis** gain such control over their bodily processes that they can voluntarily slow their heartbeat, decrease their intake of oxygen, slow down certain types of electrical activity in their brains, and reduce the type of sweating measured by polygraphs or lie detectors. These physiological reactions are those involved in emotional arousal. So Siddhartha, who became a master meditator, learned through experience to control almost completely his physical and cognitive reactions to emotional situations.

Meditation and the practice of yoga are not easy things to master. It typically takes years of practice to learn control over the functions of one's autonomic nervous system. But Western science has, in recent years, developed a technology that can accomplish the same ends rather rapidly. This technology is called **biofeedback,** because it involves using electronic devices to measure and to feed back to people's minds exactly what reactions are occurring in the people's bodies.

Among the pioneers in developing biofeedback technology were psychologists Neal E. Miller and Leo DiCara. They began by implanting **electrodes** in the brains of rats so that the psychologists could give the animals occasional but extremely pleasant electrical stimulation. The rats were then given a drug called **curare,** which paralyzed many of the muscles in the animals' bodies. The rats remained conscious, but they could not move their voluntary muscles.

Next, Miller and DiCara attached the paralyzed animals to a polygraph and began to record heart rates. The aim of the experiment was to teach the animals to decrease or increase their heart rates. The rats could learn this task only if they used the pleasurable stimulation as feedback to allow the rats to gain voluntary control over their autonomic nervous systems.

Once the rats were hooked up to the polygraph, Miller and DiCara watched their heartbeats as recorded on the polygraph. Every time an animal's heart rate increased a little, the psychologists gave the rat a brief burst of pleasurable stimulation. After a time, the rats seemed to learn how to speed up their heart rate voluntarily—presumably just to get another rewarding stimulation.

Miller and DiCara next reversed their procedure. They began rewarding the rats for slowing down their heart rate. The animals learned that control too—just as long as they were being rewarded for doing so.

The Miller and DiCara research produced considerable controversy at first because the scientists were not always able to duplicate their early results. Other scientists, however, have recently reported success in teaching animals to control blood pressure, sweating, salivation, urine formation, and stomach contractions.

More important, perhaps, is the fact that biofeedback has now been used to teach humans with heart problems to control their blood pressure. The patients watch a machine that tells them whether their blood pressure is going up, down, or staying the same. The machine provides *visual feedback* of the patient's blood-pressure level. When the machine indicates that their blood pressure is going up, the subjects try to think relaxing or less emotional thoughts. If their blood pressure then goes down, the patients try to repeat whatever thought or emotion they were experiencing when it went down. After considerable training,

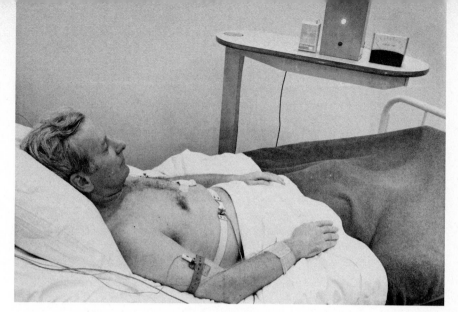

Electronic devices can help provide visual records of bodily functions. When made aware of the reactions occurring in your body, you can learn to control them. This man is learning to control his heart rhythm.

some patients can learn to control whatever emotions and thoughts might be affecting their high blood pressure.

Biofeedback can also be used to help people learn to control their brain waves, their skin temperature, and certain types of muscle tension. Research suggests that some **migraine headaches** are associated with increased skin temperature. Patients who have learned to reduce their skin temperature using biofeedback devices report having fewer migraine headaches.

"Mirroring" Thoughts and Behaviors

Students who have been treated with counterconditioning to help them lose "test anxiety" (see Chapter 5) report that they not only react differently in the classroom, they also perceive tests and examinations differently after treatment. More than this, they perceive themselves as being in greater control of what happens to them. Thus, counterconditioning affects their "self-image" as well as their "body image."

Humanist Carl Rogers (see Chapter 10) developed rather an unusual method of giving people feedback on their self-images. Rogers noted that many of the people who came to him for help had rather idealized notions of what they *should* be like, and that some of them had rather low opinions of what they were *presently* like. Because Rogers doesn't believe that the therapist should in any way direct the course of therapy, Rogers couldn't simply tell these people how to get better. But he could reflect back to them what they were doing and saying so that they could see for themselves what they were like. Rogers hoped that giving them this type of objective feedback would aid the people in changing themselves.

Many of Rogers's patients began treatment by answering a questionnaire designed to measure their self-images. Then Rogers worked with the patients for several months—faithfully reflecting back or *mirroring* to them the substance of what they said and did during therapy. At the end of treatment, the patients again took the self-image questionnaire. The majority of Rogers's clients apparently were able to use the cognitive feedback he gave them and hence achieved a greater degree of self-actualization (discussed in Chapter 5.) Most of them not only reported feeling better, but achieved better "self-image" scores on the questionnaire as well.

Seeing Yourself

Most of us are vaguely aware that other people praise and punish us, and thereby affect the way that we feel about certain things (including ourselves). But few of us appreciate two related facts. First, you influence others as much as they influence you. And second, people around you generally feel toward you and respond to you in much the same way that you feel and respond toward them.

Psychologists at the University of Michigan recently treated a patient using a novel type of affective feedback to help the man gain greater control over his emotions. This patient, whom the psychologists refer to as John R., had a number of physical and mental complaints. His marriage was failing because he could no longer perform the sex act with his wife. He described his wife as being a cold and unresponsive woman who "turned him off." His stomach was continually upset, he was constipated, and he had difficulty in sleeping. John R. was a very well-paid and successful sales executive who brought his company millions of dollars in business. Yet he was desperately afraid that he would be fired. He said his bosses were critical of him and didn't like him. The employees who worked under him were suspicious of him and very jealous of his success—according to John R. He could not relate warmly to anybody, and he couldn't understand why so many people around him seemed to hate him so.

Shortly after therapy began, John R. told the psychologists about a traumatic event that had occurred to him when he was 11 years old. He and his parents had been out driving when they got caught in a terrible thunderstorm. As the lightning crashed about them and the wind almost blew them off the road, John R. became so frightened that he broke down and cried. Once the storm was over, his father ridiculed the boy for "acting like a sissy." For years afterward, even though John R. behaved bravely from then on, his father criticized John R. for acting like a coward. Nothing the boy did ever seemed to evoke a smile or a pat on the back from his father.

From their initial observations of John R.'s behavior during therapy, the psychologists soon became convinced that as an adult, John R. was behaving toward others as his father had behaved toward him. He seldom smiled; he seldom was polite; he almost never thanked people no matter what they did for him. More than this, when the psychologists raised the issue of how he acted toward others, John R. criticized the psychologists for daring to suggest that his problems might even in part be his fault.

As part of John R.'s treatment, the psychologists made videotape recordings of him while he was talking to and interacting with several other people. Then they played the tapes back, asking John to record the number of times he smiled, the number of times that he praised people, and the number of times that he was negative, critical, and punitive. After watching the tapes for more than an hour, John had recorded not one instance in which he acted positively toward anyone else; but he had criticized or punished the others more than 50 times. And John was in something of a state of shock.

When people tell you how you're acting, you may reject their comments and claim that the people are biased against you. But tape recorders give objective evidence. John R. couldn't reject the evidence he saw on the video screen because he knew that the recorder neither liked him nor disliked him. So he decided to try to learn a different way of responding to the people around him.

The psychologists continued treatment by **modeling** (discussed in Chapter 6) or demonstrating how to give people positive feedback. John imitated what they had done while the psychologists again recorded his actions on video tape. The therapists pointed out every bit of improvement he was making. This feedback (and what he saw on the screen) gave John the information that he needed in order to learn how to respond affectionately and positively toward others. His physical complaints soon began to clear up and, as he began to reward the important people in his life, they began reacting more warmly toward him. He no longer feared for his job, and his relations with his wife improved considerably.

Social Feedback

As Carl Rogers pointed out, we all need objective "mirrors" to reflect back to us how we feel, perceive, and act. Since we can't usually make a videotape recording of our actions, we are forced to rely on the behavior of others to give us information about our own actions. We seek out and use this information even when we are not conscious of doing so.

One way that we have of getting feedback about our own behaviors is by associating ourselves with various groups of people with whom we share a common viewpoint or goal. But once we have joined a group, we are usually expected to conform to whatever standards the majority of the members of the group believe in. The groups you belong to encourage you to conform both by setting a model for you to imitate, and by giving you rewarding and punishing feedback as you attempt to behave "the group's way."

The behaviors that groups engage in to pressure their members to behave in a uniform way are sometimes called group pressures toward conformity. One of the first psychologists to study *group pressures* in the laboratory was Solomon Asch, who wanted to see if people would stick to their judgments even if they were pressured to give false reports. Asch's experiment was simple. He showed his subjects a white card with a black line on it, 20-cm (8 in) long. Then he showed them three more cards with lines on them. One line was about 25 cm long (10 in.), the second was about 22 cm (8.75 in.), while the third matched the standard 20-cm line. The subjects were asked to pick out (from memory) the standard line. As Asch had expected, almost all of the subjects could remember which of the three lines on the card matched the standard.

Then Asch changed the experiment. He seated three subjects together at a table and asked each one of them to select the standard line. Two of the sub-

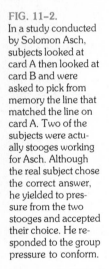

Standard line, 8"

A

$8\frac{3}{4}$"   10"   Standard
line   line   line, 8"

B

FIG. 11-2.
In a study conducted by Solomon Asch, subjects looked at card A then looked at card B and were asked to pick from memory the line that matched the line on card A. Two of the subjects were actually stooges working for Asch. Although the real subject chose the correct answer, he yielded to pressure from the two stooges and accepted their choice. He responded to the group pressure to conform.

jects, however, were **"stooges,"** who were working for Asch. Asch told the stooges ahead of time to give wrong answers at certain times while they were making the line comparisons. The third person at the table—the only true "subject" in the experiment—knew nothing of these arrangements and was told to answer last. The first time Asch asked the group to pick the standard line, the two stooges correctly identifed the 20-cm line. The experimental subject agreed and also picked the correct line. On the third trial, however, the first stooge picked the 25-cm line. So did the second stooge. To Asch's surprise, almost a third of the experimental subjects whom he tested "yielded" to the pressures of the stooges and picked the 25-cm line as matching the 20-cm line.

In further experiments, other psychologists found that they could get "yielding behavior" about two-thirds of the time if they had as many as four stooges judge first, and if they made the judgmental tasks more difficult or more confusing.

About half the subjects who "yield" in these sorts of experiments will readily admit that they knew they were making the wrong judgment and hence conformed because they "just didn't want to rock the boat." Phrased more precisely, these subjects accepted the social model set by the group of stooges and adjusted to it because the subjects feared punitive feedback.

The other half of the subjects who "yield" often insist that they were giving accurate judgments and were not influenced at all by what the stooges said or did! These subjects too accepted the social model and conformed. But since they apparently believed that conforming was a "bad thing," the only way they could keep their emotions in check was by denying that they had conformed.

Perhaps the most surprising thing about the group pressures experiments is not that so many subjects "yielded," but rather that so many of the yielders could not consciously handle the emotions associated with the act of conforming.

We all adjust to reality—to the ways our bodies feel and to the ways our minds perceive. Some of us—like Siddhartha—also learn to adjust to the realities of the society into which we are born. Others of us spend much of our lives torn in conflict between the natural demands made by our minds and bodies, and the learned requirements of the culture we live in.

SOCIAL ADJUSTMENT: CONFLICT AND STRESS

Sometimes people are forced to conform to society's expectations, while they also want to conform to group standards.

When Siddhartha was a young man and could no longer stand the stress and strain of living with his family, he fled to the desert. There he learned to control the functions of his body and to adjust to physical reality. But even the joys of meditation were not enough to satisfy him. He needed people. So he returned to the city, where he spent many years pursuing a life of sensual and social delights. After a while, Siddhartha found that the intense emotionality of his experiences was draining him of his health and will power. So once more he escaped—to sit by the side of the river, helping people by rowing them back and forth when they wanted to cross the stream.

In his early life, whenever Siddhartha found himself in conflict or under great stress, he adjusted by escaping. Later, when the stress was reduced, he tried to analyze the situation and then gain voluntary control over what was bothering him.

From time to time, we all face conflicts and experience stress. Most of these conflicts involve our relationships with people—past, present, and future. Therefore, it is likely that most of us worry more about social adjustment than we do about adjusting to physical or cognitive reality. Yet the three elements are so intertwined that it is often difficult for us to separate the social from the physical or cognitive. But only if we attempt to do so can we see how our lack of social adjustment, for example, can lead to such physical symptoms as ulcers or high blood pressure or to those cognitive quirks associated with mental illness.

Conflict

Siddhartha wanted to leave home and pursue his own cognitive goals. He also wanted to stay home and fulfill his social obligations by keeping his parents happy. There was a **conflict.** A student who wants to study but also wants to go to a party has a conflict. Someone who wants to be a doctor but can't stand the sight of blood has a conflict.

These children, faced with several appealing choices, are finding it difficult to choose. They are experiencing an approach-approach conflict.

Conflict occurs whenever two or more goals or needs are present and only one can be fulfilled. Siddhartha couldn't stay at home and still leave home. Students can't usually study at a party. Doctors can't always avoid the sight of blood. In order to adjust to the situation, people in conflict often have to give up one or both goals.

In the 1930s Kurt Lewin described three basic types of conflict. People, he said, are drawn toward certain people, places, and things (including thoughts and emotions.) Or, people are repelled by people, places, and things. The result is one of two kinds of behavior—approach or avoidance.

Approach-approach conflict occurs when people are drawn toward two positive but incompatible goals. Trying to decide between a number of good meals offered on a menu is an approach-approach conflict. A big eater might decide to order everything on the menu, but most people resolve the conflict by ordering only one thing and saving the others for later. But all approach-approach conflicts are not resolved so easily. A young woman in love with two men cannot usually marry one with the understanding that she will divorce him and marry the second man whenever she feels like it.

Avoidance-avoidance conflict occurs when we must make a choice between two or more undesirable goals. When all of the food on the menu is bad, the choice is between hunger and bad food—both undesirable. A student who doesn't want to study and who doesn't want to flunk out of school has a similar

The young man in this picture is experiencing a double approach-avoidance conflict. He would prefer to talk to his friend rather than study. However, he also wants to pass his literature exam, which requires that he study.

problem. People sometimes try to put off making a decision in an avoidance-avoidance conflict, but indecision sometimes may just bring on more problems.

The third type of conflict described by Lewin is *approach-avoidance conflict*. Many times one goal has both good and bad aspects. We are tempted by the good food on the menu, but we fear it may be too fattening or too expensive. The result is an approach-avoidance conflict.

Life doesn't always fall into the simple approach and avoidance patterns we have just described. Rather, as Lewin pointed out, most conflicts are complex, and many are what Lewin called *double approach-avoidance conflicts*. In such cases, the person is faced with two or more goals all of which have both good and bad aspects. A young woman might desire to study medicine because her parents want her to do so and because it offers a fine career. But perhaps the

Sometimes we must make a choice among only undesirable possibilities. A menu offering only unappetizing food presents an avoidance-avoidance conflict.

FIG. 11–3.
Approach drives gain strength slowly as you get closer to the goal. Avoidance drives gain strength more rapidly as you get closer to the goal. In an approach-avoidance conflict, you are attracted to the positive goal from some distance away, but as you get closer to it, the avoidance drive becomes strong so quickly that you turn away. But as soon as you move away, the approach drive becomes stronger, so you turn around again. Thus, you are caught in conflict at the point where the two drives overlap.

young woman really wants to be an artist. If she studies art, however, her parents have told her they will no longer give her financial support. In making her career choice, this young woman faces a double approach-avoidance conflict. If she makes a decision she can live with, she will have adjusted to her problems. But it is just as likely that, whatever choice she makes, she will feel some stress and anxiety because she has not been able to satisfy all her goals at once.

Stress

When you bend a stick in your hands, you put tremendous pressure on some of the cells inside the piece of wood. The farther you bend the stick, the more you squeeze these cells together. If you then bend the stick in the opposite direction, these cells are now stressed by being pulled apart rather than by being squeezed together. If you twist the stick back and forth enough times, the cells may collapse, and the stick will break. Even if you bend the stick but once, the cells may never recover fully, and the stick may remain bent.

Generally speaking, whenever you are threatened or pressured or put into a conflict situation, your body and your mind will undergo **stress.** The threat or pressure may be physical, cognitive, or social—or a mixture of all three. But if the pressure or conflict is great enough to cause you to expend more biological, mental, emotional, or behavioral energy than you normally would, then you will experience stress.

Canadian scientist Hans Selye has described three steps the body goes through while reacting to stress. The first stage is the **alarm reaction.** Generally speaking, the alarm reaction involves an arousal response similar to that you might experience during a strong emotion. The physiological changes that occur in your body during the alarm reaction prepare you either to face the challenge before you, to defend yourself, or to run away.

If the stress lasts long enough, you may go through the second step in the stress response—the **stage of resistance.** During this stage, your body not only expends energy on arousal, but also tries to repair whatever damage has occurred and to replenish its energy store as best it can. But if all your body's available energy is used up during the stressful experience, your body may enter the third stage—the **stage of exhaustion.** During this stage, most of the activity in your body is abnormally slowed down as you try to regain your physical and mental strength. But if the stress still continues while you are in the exhaustion stage, your body and your brain may begin to deteriorate. The result may be insanity or death.

Your cognitive reactions to stress follow much the same pattern described by Selye. During the alarm stage, you usually become alert and anxious as you begin to think of ways to handle the stressful situation. If the stress continues, however, you may become less and less able to think clearly and to make logical decisions. Eventually, in the stage of exhaustion, you may lose all hope of handling the situation and may simply give up.

Mental exhaustion and "giving up" may occur even when the body still has physical energy to meet the challenge. Because Richter's rats were **traumatized** just before they were dumped into the tub of water, they "gave up" and sank to the bottom. However, as Richter proved, their bodies still had sufficient strength to swim for at least 80 hours. Once he pulled them out for a few minutes, they learned that survival was possible. When he returned them to the water, they no longer "gave up," but rather began to swim effectively.

A stressful experience, such as a race, arouses your bodily responses and may even exhaust your available energy.

FIG. 11–4.
Life is full of stressful
situations that can
contribute to illness if
you can not cope
with them. Score
yourself in this
checklist. Record the
number of times an
event occurred dur-
ing the past twelve
months and multiply
it by the life-change
unit value. One sam-
ple of college fresh-
men scored between
42 and 3890, with a
median of 767 (half
the students scored
above and half below
this value). (Marx et
al., 1975)

College Schedule of Recent Experiences

		Life-Change Units
Indicate the number of times during the last 12 months that you:		
1.	Entered college	50
2.	Married.	77
3.	Had either a lot more or a lot less trouble with your boss.	38
4.	Held a job while attending school.	43
5.	Experienced the death of a spouse.	87
6.	Experienced a major change in sleeping habits (sleeping a lot more or a lot less, or changing the part of the day in which you sleep).	34
7.	Experienced the death of a close family member.	77
8.	Experienced a major change in eating habits (a lot more or a lot less food intake, or very different meal hours or surroundings).	30
9.	Made a change in or choice of a major field of study.	41
10.	Revised your personal habits (friends, dress, manners, associations).	45
11.	Experienced the death of a close friend.	68
12.	Were found guilty of minor violation of the law (such as traffic tickets and jay-walking).	22
13.	Had an outstanding personal achievement.	40
14.	Experienced pregnancy, or fathered a pregnancy.	68
15.	Had a major change in the health or behavior of a family member.	56
16.	Had sexual difficulties.	58
17.	Had trouble with in-laws.	42
18.	Had a major change in the number of family get-togethers (a lot more or a lot less).	26
19.	Had a major change in financial state (a lot worse off or a lot better off than usual).	33
20.	Gained a new family member (through birth, adoption, older person moving in).	50
21.	Changed your residence or living conditions.	42
22.	Had a major conflict in or change in values.	50
23.	Had a major change in church activities (a lot more or a lot less than usual).	36
24.	Had a marital reconciliation with your mate.	58
25.	Were fired from work.	62
26.	Were divorced.	76
27.	Changed to a different line of work.	50
28.	Had a major change in the number of arguments with spouse (either a lot more or a lot less than usual).	50
29.	Had a major change in responsibilities at work (promotion, demotion, lateral transfer).	47
30.	Had your spouse begin or cease work outside the home.	41
31.	Had a major change in working hours or conditions.	42
32.	Had a marital separation from your mate.	74
33.	Had a major change in usual type and/or amount of recreation.	37
34.	Had a major change in the use of drugs (a lot more or a lot less).	52
35.	Took a mortgage or loan *less* than $10,000 (as for purchase of a car, TV, or school loan).	52
36.	Had a major personal injury or illness.	65
37.	Had a major change in the use of alcohol (a lot more or a lot less).	46
38.	Had a major change in social activities.	43

College Schedule of Recent Experiences (Cont.)

Indicate the number of times during the last 12 months that you:	Life-Change Units
39. Had a major change in the amount of participation in school activities.	38
40. Had a major change in the amount of independence and responsibility (for example, for budgeting time).	49
41. Took a trip or a vacation.	33
42. Were engaged to be married.	54
43. Changed to a new school.	50
44. Changed dating habits.	41
45. Had trouble with school administration (instructors, advisors, class scheduling, and so on).	44
46. Broke or had broken a marital engagement or steady relationship.	60
47. Had a major change in self-concept or self-awareness.	57

Adapted from Anderson (1972) by Marx et al. (1975). Copyright 1975 by Pergamon Press Ltd. and reprinted with permission.

Anxiety and Frustration

Stress comes in many forms. Two of the most common are frustration and anxiety. **Anxiety** is a feeling of dread or fear that occurs for no apparent reason. Stress is associated with a specific threatening situation. Anxiety is the same type of feeling, but an anxious person does not know where the threat is coming from. Freud explained anxiety as a reaction to unconscious conflicts or threats. He used psychoanalysis to help people understand their unconscious conflicts so that they could make the proper adjustments. Just talking about feelings of anxiety to a friend is sometimes enough to lessen the anxiety. But even if the unconscious reasons for anxiety cannot be discovered, people can learn to control anxiety. Anxiety, as a form of stress, contains all of the biological changes associated with stress. People who learn to understand or control anxious feelings can usually avoid the physical and mental breakdown that anxiety sometimes causes.

Frustration is a form of conflict that leads to stress. If repeated attempts to approach a desired goal or avoid an unpleasant situation do not lead to success, the result may be frustration. A young child learning to ride a bicycle may get frustrated after falling off several times. A student trying to study in a noisy room may get frustrated if too much noise keeps interfering with concentration. The doctor who wants to save every patient may get frustrated when some people die.

Frustration is a form of stress caused by failure to reach a goal. The man receiving the speeding ticket may have been rushing to an important appointment. Being stopped and given a ticket would certainly frustrate him.

The "try, try again" attitude is often useful in overcoming frustration. Most young children keep trying and eventually learn to ride their bicycles. In some cases, the method of achieving a goal might have to be changed. The student in the noisy room will avoid frustration by going to a quiet spot for studying. In other cases, goals might have to be changed. Some goals are impractical or impossible to achieve. The ambitious doctor who wants to save everyone will have to accept the fact that some patients will not survive. Most people learn to pick realistic goals and to tolerate some failures. Too many failures and frustrations, however, can lead to stress and breakdown.

COPING

During your lifetime you have met many challenges, experienced many stress-inducing situations, resolved many conflicts, and worked your way through many emotional experiences. Which is to say that you have learned to adjust to the problems we all face in life. Psychologists often speak of learning to adjust as **coping** with the world.

Our problems typically come to us as inputs, which we must process some way and then react to. There are many different ways of *coping*—some ways involve changing, controlling, or even avoiding certain inputs. Other ways involve changing the way that we process or think about problem-related inputs. Still other ways involve altering our outputs—that is, changing the ways that we respond or behave when the problem occurs.

Some methods of coping with life's problems involve protecting ourselves as best we can. These methods are often called **defensive coping.** Other ways of handling stress, conflict, and emotionality involve meeting the challenge head-on. These methods are often called **direct coping.**

Defensive Coping

Most forms of defensive coping involve either mental or physical *escape* from the traumatic situation. The person either flees from the problem and in the future avoids going near the stress-inducing situation. Or the person blocks out the threatening inputs or denies that the inputs are stressful.

Many of the Freudian defense mechanisms (see Chapter 10) are types of defensive coping. If you are threatened by sexual stimuli, you may *repress* these inputs by simply ignoring them or by not paying attention to them until they become incredibly strong. **Hysterical blindness** is a similar form of defensive coping. During battles, soldiers who see their best friends shot down may become psychologically blind. Their eyes still work—but their minds refuse to process any incoming visual stimuli. By refusing to see anything at all, these men defend against having to witness (or even to think in visual terms about) more deaths.

Reaction formation, projection, and **displacement** are also forms of defensive coping. The mother who hates her child, but finds this hatred stress-inducing, may cope with this situation by repressing the hatred and reacting to the child with too much love. Or she may project her feelings onto the child by telling herself that she loves the child, but the child hates her. Or she may displace her feelings by kicking the cat when she really wants to kick the child.

Fixation and **regression** are forms of defensive coping that involve going back to old ways of behaving or refusing to learn new ways (see Chapter 10).

At first glance, it may seem that **aggression** should always be considered a direct or active form of coping (see Chapter 2). Sometimes it is. But more often, aggression is defensive, in that it terminates the stressful inputs without really solving the aggressor's basic conflicts. For example, suppose a father becomes angry or frustrated by the values and behaviors of his 13-year-old son. The man might cope with his anger directly by sitting down and talking the situation over with the young man. That way they both might try to adjust to each other's needs. But if the father is unable to face the fact that he might have to do as much adjusting as the son, the father may criticize or even beat up the youth "to teach him a lesson." To avoid further punishment, the son may yield to the father's demand—at least temporarily. But the boy may also become so severely depressed that he either runs away or attempts suicide. In any of these cases, the father's aggression will remove the stressful stimulus—the son—from the father's life. But because his actions were negatively reinforced (see Chapter 6), the father may not learn more effective ways of dealing with future conflicts.

Depression is one of the most common types of defensive coping. Most stressful or emotion-inducing situations involve arousal, or increased excitation of the sympathetic nervous system. This arousal can be blocked or countered by increased excitation of the parasympathetic system. Mild parasympathetic excitation can lead to relaxation; overstimulation of the parasympathetic system, however, can lead to depression and feelings of absolute helplessness.

Learned Helplessness

We all resort to defensive coping at one time or another. Defensive strategies "work" because they often get us out of the stressful situation for a while — they buy us time to find more effective ways of adjusting. But therein lies their danger. For defensive methods of coping may be so negatively reinforcing that we may continue to use them without bothering to seek more direct ways of dealing with our conflicts.

An example of the problems associated with defensive coping comes from experiments performed by Martin Seligman. A group of dogs in his experiment "learned to be helpless" because their escape route was blocked at the beginning of their training. So they simply sat and waited passively for the shock to end — even when the barrier in the shuttle box was lowered and the dogs could have jumped to safety before the shock occurred.

Seligman analyzed the situation as follows: "Sitting helplessly" was a response the dogs made naturally to the onset of the shock. The shock itself was punishing; but *termination* of the shock was negatively reinforcing! And eventually the shock always did terminate. Therefore, each time Seligman shocked this

FIG. 11–5.
Martin Seligman studied defensive coping in dogs and discovered that they could learn to be helpless. Here we see the dog confronting the problem but failing to learn coping behavior.

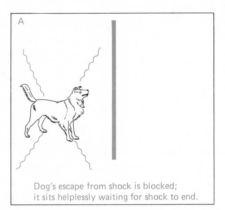

Dog's escape from shock is blocked; it sits helplessly waiting for shock to end.

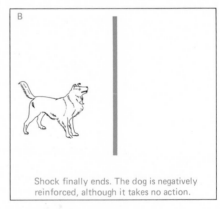

Shock finally ends. The dog is negatively reinforced, although it takes no action.

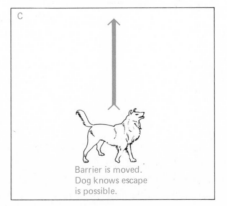

Barrier is moved. Dog knows escape is possible.

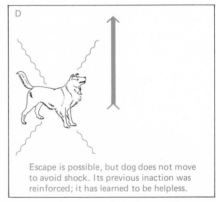

Escape is possible, but dog does not move to avoid shock. Its previous inaction was reinforced; it has learned to be helpless.

group of dogs, he was actually *rewarding* the "helpless" response rather than punishing it. Furthermore, the more painful he made the shock, the stronger was the reward when he turned off the electric current. So instead of forcing the dogs to cope with the situation directly by making the shock (apparently) more punishing, Seligman was actually making them more helpless.

At this point, Seligman decided to try other ways to teach the dogs to cope with the shock directly. First he tried putting food in the "safe" compartment and coaxing the dogs to jump the barrier. But the animals refused to be persuaded. Then Seligman put each dog on a leash and tried pulling it over the barrier to show it that it could escape the shock directly if it tried. This training technique worked—but some of the dogs had to be dragged to safety 50 times or more before they overcame their depressive reaction to the shock and learned a direct and active way of coping with the situation.

Direct Coping

Most forms of *direct coping* involve at least three steps:
1. An *objective analysis* of what the problem is, how it came into being, and how the person is presently responding.
2. A clear statement of how things might be better—that is, a precise description of what the *ultimate goal* or adjustment would be.
3. A *psychological road map,* or list of new approaches to life that the person might engage in to reach the goal.

Direct coping is not always easy, and it is often time-consuming. But usually the benefits outweigh the costs involved. Siddhartha had to learn how to cope to handle his sexual needs. When he first saw Kamala, she was the most desirable woman he had ever seen. When Kamala first saw Siddhartha, he was probably one of the most repulsive-looking young men she had ever laid eyes on. He was an undernourished beggar in rags who had just spent three years in the desert.

But Siddhartha knew how to cope with his problems and needs directly. Rather than becoming depressed or running away, he analyzed his situation and found that his physical appearance needed changing. So he went to the city, got a haircut and a shave, and even took a bath. The next day he visited Kamala and let her know that he wanted to become her friend and learn the art of love from her. Kamala laughed at the young man dressed in rags. But she appreciated his direct manner and gave him the "psychological roadmap" he needed to achieve his goal. She told him that he would have to be wealthy, and that he would have to bring her expensive gifts.

The direct approach does not always work, but Kamala was so impressed by Siddhartha's self-confidence that she even helped him to get a job. Siddhartha, with confidence in his abilities, got the job, got rich, and got Kamala. He did not regress, deny, or become hostile and aggressive. He made the necessary adjustments in his behaviors and thoughts and went directly to his goal.

One of life's most important adjustments is the acceptance of death — the death of parents, friends, loved ones. Ultimately, you must accept the idea of your own mortality.

THE FINAL ADJUSTMENT

Siddhartha made many adjustments during his life. He went to the desert to learn to adjust to physical reality and to learn how to control his own emotions. He went to the city to learn to adjust to social reality. He even learned to cope with other peoples' needs to adjust.

But the adjustment that Siddhartha considered the most important — adjustment to himself — took the longest. At the age of 60, he realized that everything in life was in a constant state of change, and in order to become adjusted to life he too would have to be in a constant state of change. Siddhartha realized that there was no one perfect spot in the world where he would be able to sit and be in perfect harmony with life. He realized that there was no one single answer or solution to the problems of life. Siddhartha had to adjust to the fact that he had to adjust to life constantly. When he finally adjusted to adjustment, he was adjusted both to life and to himself. Only then did he achieve the unity and harmony that he had been searching for.

► SUMMARY

1. Siddhartha, the Buddha, is a good example of how humans attempt to achieve some sort of comfortable adjustment to the realities of life. In his search for personal adjustment, Siddhartha had to come to terms with physical reality, with his own inner or cognitive reality, and with social reality.

2. Research suggests there are two basic ways of adjusting to physical reality. **Externalizers** are people who tend to view reality as something controlled by outside forces. **Internalizers** tend to believe that they themselves have some conscious control over their destiny.

3. In attempts to adjust to our inner or cognitive reality (including our emotions) it is sometimes necessary to learn to control our inner selves. There are three types of feedback that we must pay attention to if we wish to develop self-awareness and emotional control — feedback from our bodies, from out minds, and from our social environments.

4. Meditation and **biofeedback** are among the methods available for helping us learn to control our bodies and our inner environment. Carl Rogers' "mirroring" of thoughts and behaviors and other therapies (including the use of videotape, which lets us see ourselves objectively) have been developed that help us to be better able to control our own reality.

5. Group membership helps us learn about ourselves by providing us with feedback. Adjusting to social reality, however, puts various pressures on us, such as the pressure to conform.

6. Because adjustment to social reality involves our relationships with other people, most of us probably worry more about social adjustment than we do about physical or cognitive adjustment. From time to time our attempts to adjust to the social world may result in **conflict** and **stress.**

7. Conflict occurs when two or more goals are present but only one can be reached. Kurt Lewin has described three basic types of conflict — approach-approach, avoidance-avoidance, and approach-avoidance.

8. Conflict situations often lead to stress. According to Hans Selye the three steps the body goes through while reacting to stress are the **alarm reaction, the stage of resistance,** and **the stage of exhaustion.**

9. Two of the most common forms of stress are anxiety and fear. **Anxiety** is a feeling of dread or fear that occurs for no apparent reason. Anxiety contains all the biological changes associated with stress. **Frustration** is a form of conflict that leads to stress. If repeated attempts to approach a desired goal or to avoid an unpleasant situation do not lead to success the result may be frustration.

10. Learning to adjust to the physical, cognitive, and social aspects of life is sometimes called **coping.** Defensive coping usually involves mental or physical escape from a traumatic situation. Direct coping consists of objectively analyzing the problem, deciding on a goal or way of adjusting, and then finding the way to that goal.

Suggested Readings

Brown, Barbara. *Stress and the art of biofeedback.* New York: Harper & Row, 1976.

Fast, Julius. *The body language of sex, power and aggression.* New York: M. Evans, 1976.

Hesse, Hermann. *Siddhartha.* (Hilda Rosner, Tr.) New York: New Directions, 1951.

Selye, Hans. *The stress of life.* New York: McGraw-Hill, 1976.

► STUDY GUIDE

A.   RECALL

Sentence Completion

[p. 354]   1. We more commonly refer to the hero of Hesse's *Siddhartha* as _____.

2. The important insight that Siddhartha had, while repeating his Om, was that the
[p. 355]   meaning of life is _____.

[p. 355]   3. _____-_____ is the modern term in humanistic psychology
roughly comparable to Siddhartha's unity or perfection.

4. To be truly well-adjusted involves adjusting to three separate realities — the
[p. 355]   _____, _____, and _____.

5. _____ often believe in such things as astrology and mysterious outside
[p. 356]   forces that rule their lives.

6. _____ believe that they themselves have some degree of conscious con-
[p. 356]   trol over their own destiny.

7. The psychologist Curt _____ studied rats' reactions to very hostile envi-
[p. 356]   ronments.

8. Richter's experiments suggest that _____ has a great deal to do with ad-
[p. 357]   justment.

9. People who continually fail to make proper adjustments may develop the
[p. 357]   _____'s view of life and feel that adjusting is not worth the effort.

10. Self-awareness is dependent upon _____ which may come from a num-
[p. 359]   ber of different sources.
[p. 359]   11. _____ feedback refers to feedback from our own minds.
[p. 359]   12. Siddhartha meditated by practicing _____.

13. Using electronic devices to let your mind know exactly what your body is doing is
[p. 360]   called using _____.

14. A significant process in Carl Roger's therapy is _____ or faithfully
[p. 361]   providing feedback to the patient of what was said or done during the therapy session.

15. What Rogers is interested in changing through therapy is the patient's
[p. 361]   _____-_____.

16. Once we have joined a group, we often find that we are expected to
[p. 363]   _____ to the standards of that group.

17. Solomon Asch did one of the first experiments on the effects of _____
[p. 363]   _____ on conformity.

18. The Asch technique can be used to get as many as _____ of the subjects
[p. 364]   to "yield."

19. Whenever two or more goals or needs are present and only one can be fulfilled, we
[p. 366]   are in a _____ situation.

20. An _____-_____ conflict occurs when we must make a
[p. 366]   choice between two or more undesirable goals.

21. Most of the conflicts that we tend to encounter are those that Lewin called
[p. 367]   _____ _____-_____ conflicts.

22. _____ is the result of being threatened, pressured, or put into a conflict
[p. 368]   situation.

[p. 369]   23. The last stage of Selye's description of reactions to stress is _____.
[p. 370]   24. _____ is a feeling of dread or fear that occurs for no apparent reason.
[p. 370]   25. Freud explained anxiety by referring to _____ conflicts or threats.
[p. 372]   26. Psychologists speak of learning to adjust as _____ with the world.
[p. 372]   27. In addition to direct coping, we often handle stress by _____ coping.
           28. _____ and _____ are forms of defensive coping that in-
[p. 373]   volve going back to old or earlier ways of behaving, or refusing to learn new ways.
[p. 373]   29. Depression is a common form of _____ coping.
           30. The first step in direct coping is to make an _____ _____ of
[p. 375]   what the problem is, how it came about, and how one is presently responding.

B.   **REVIEW**

Multiple Choice: Circle the letter identifying the alternative that most correctly completes the statement or answers the question.

1. Hermann Hesse characterizes Siddhartha as:
   A. a perfect son, bright, obedient, and healthy.
   B. the founder of Buddhism.
   C. a gambler, drunkard, and ruthless merchant.
   D. all of the above.

2. People who believe that they have no real conscious control over their life situations
are classified by Rotter as _____.
   A. externalizers
   B. well-adjusted
   C. self-actualizers
   D. internalizers

3. Biofeedback:
   A. is a type of meditation.
   B. can help us learn to control some involuntary physiological functions.
   C. was pioneered by B. F. Skinner and Carl Rogers.
   D. involves the use of curare for controlling mental activity.

4. Carl Rogers may be classified as a _____ psychologist.
   A. behavioristic
   B. psychoanalytic
   C. humanistic
   D. cognitive

5. Early experiments on social pressure and conformity were performed by:
   A. Carl Rogers.
   B. Neal Miller.
   C. a group of psychologists at the University of Michigan.
   D. Solomon Asch.

6. Being faced with two positive goals, and being able to choose just one of them would put you in a(n) _____ conflict.

    A. approach-approach

    B. approach-avoidance

    C. avoidance-avoidance

    D. double approach-avoidance

7. Which of the following is the correct order of events in Selye's stages of stress reaction?

    A. alarm, exhaustion, resistance

    B. resistance, alarm, exhaustion

    C. exhaustion, alarm, resistance

    D. none of the above

8. Putting anxiety-producing thoughts out of your mind is an example of which of the following techniques of defensive coping?

    A. repression

    B. regression

    C. displacement

    D. projection

REALITY ORIENTATION

Quoting a World War I British Army war song, Douglas MacArthur said, "Old soldiers never die; they just fade away." How right he was. During fiscal year 1972 the Veterans Administration treated 108,500 aged persons. Many of these, says Lars P. Peterson of the VA Hospital in Tuscaloosa, Ala., were suffering from anxieties, depressions, hostilities, confusions, disorientations, lack of concentration and withdrawal from reality. In other words, they were fading away.

The problem is not limited to veterans. In 1970 there were 20 million aged persons (defined as over 65) in the United States. By the year 2000 there will be at least another 8 million. At present, 5 percent of these individuals are in institutions, 5 percent are living a borderline existence outside institutions and another 15 percent need extended care. Many of these older patients are classified as senile (confused and disoriented). Their situation is seen as hopeless and the process as irreversible. Peterson, however, says this need not be the case. At the VA Hospital in Tuscaloosa senescence is handled as more psychological than biological. "What we describe as senescence," he says, "may be more a coping mechanism of age and less the consequences of organic factors."

This reasoning, he says, is based on the typical sequence that brings aged patients to the hospital in the first place. The problem usually begins with a biomedical crisis (stroke, heart attack, pneumonia, etc.) or a psychosocial crisis (economic, social or emotional stress). This situation makes the person dependent on family care and the family reacts by giving extended care even in areas where the patient can function. This, in turn, makes the patient feel and act more helpless and the family begins to see the situation as hopeless. The end result is permanent institutionalization and a gradual fading away.

While the physical disabilities are obvious, says Peterson, we cannot neglect the consequences of the economic and social losses on the behavior of the aged person. It is the interaction of these factors that tend to increase the patients' confusion, disorientation and withdrawal from reality.

This situation need not be progressive, Peterson said. The process can be reversed or at least stabilized by a rehabilitation program known as reality orientation.

The program, explained Peterson, is a two-part treatment specifically designed for the elderly, confused patient. Part one is an around the clock orientation to the surrounding environment with emphasis on time, place and person. When the patient begins to ramble, is forgetful or disoriented, he is returned to reality in a matter-of-fact way.

Part two of the treatment consists of 30-minute class periods, five days a week. The basic classes involve a structured orientation to time, place and person. Various reality activities, with concrete objects and, in the advanced classes, more abstract concepts and ideas are brought into play.

The emphasis of the program is rehabilitation but Peterson suggests it be used as a preventive program in nursing homes and in general medical or surgical situations. While reality orientation is definitely not a cure for senility or the aging process, it is at least a method of keeping the brain from atrophying and for slowing down or even reversing some of the psychological effects of age. So perhaps the old folks' home need not be a last resting place and perhaps old soldiers need not fade away.

C.   NEWS STORY QUESTIONS

1. What is the typical sequence of events leading to the institutionalization of the aged, according to Peterson? _____

_____

2. What is the basic thrust of "reality orientation"? _____

_____

unit FOUR

ABNORMAL PSYCHOLOGY

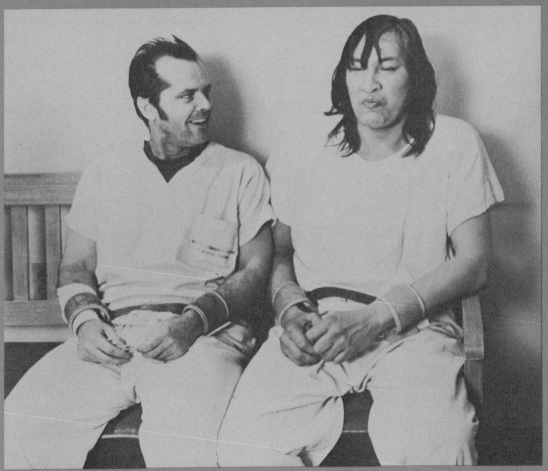

Movie still from *One Flew over the Cuckoo's Nest.*

Normal and abnormal are difficult terms to define as far as human behavior is concerned, but biological, psychological, and social problems appear to be involved in most forms of abnormal human behavior. The classification of abnormal behaviors by their major causes helps us better to understand and possibly to treat abnormal behaviors.

Normal versus Abnormal

12 chapter

When you have completed your study of this chapter, you should be able to:

- ▶ Discuss what is meant by "abnormal" and list Goldenson's standards for normal behavior
- ▶ Summarize at least five causes of abnormal behavior that are biological in origin
- ▶ Define "neurosis" and list the major symptoms associated with six neurotic disorders
- ▶ Define "functional psychosis" and describe five varieties of the disorder
- ▶ Describe the sociopathic personality
- ▶ Discuss sexual deviations in the context of abnormal behavior
- ▶ Discuss the implications of psychiatric labeling

Affective psychosis (aff-FECK-tive sigh-KOH-sis). A severe type of mental disturbance involving the person's emotional responses.

Amnesia (am-KNEE-see-uh or am-KNEE-zha). From the Greek word meaning "forgetfulness." Amnesia is a loss of memory. It may be temporary or permanent. It may also be highly specific, or very general.

Anxiety neurosis (new-ROH-sis). A relatively mild type of mental disturbance in which the person is continually anxious or nervously upset, usually for reasons of which the person is not aware.

Compulsion. From the Latin word meaning "to compel." A compulsion is a strong urge to act or perform in a certain way. One may feel compelled to behave in a particular manner "because society expects it," or because one's conscience (or unconscious) demands it.

Delirium tremens (duh-LEER-ee-um TREE-mens). A type of temporary mental unbalance characterized by hallucinations, confusion, and indistinct or strange speech patterns—and by trembling. Usually brought on by excessive and prolonged use of alcohol. Also called "the DTs."

General paresis (puh-REE-sis). A form of organic mental illness caused by the destructive action of the syphilitic germ on the brain. There is usually a lengthy incubation period in general paresis, the initial symptoms appearing between 5 and 30 years after the primary infection.

Genius. From the Latin word meaning "talent." Thus a person with great talent, ability, or mental powers.

Hypochondriacal neurosis (high-poh-kon-DRY-uh-cal). A relatively mild type of mental disturbance in which the person suffers from (mostly) imaginary physical complaints. A hypochondriac (high-poh-KON-dree-ack) is someone who seems to enjoy running to the physician for every little ache.

Hysterical neurosis (hiss-TARE-uh-cal). From the Greek word meaning "wandering womb." A type of mental disturbance marked by unrestrained emotionality—wild laughter or giggling that can change in a moment to outbursts of anger or tears. Hysteria was originally thought to be a neurosis found only in women experiencing some displacement or "wandering" of the womb.

Insane. A term meaning someone legally incapable of handling his or her own affairs, of making normal judgments, or of telling right from wrong. A legal term referring to psychological or behavioral disturbances as judged or defined by a court of law.

Manic-depressive psychosis. Two types of severe mental disturbances often lumped together and called an "affective psychosis." Most patients show either a manic reaction or a depressive reaction—but not both. Manic reactions are characterized by elation and hyperactivity, and range in degree from the mild through the acute to the delirious form. In a simple depression, the patient shows loss of interest in the world, becomes dejected, thinks of suicide, and refuses to work or eat. The patient suffering from depressive stupor often must be force-fed to be kept alive.

Masturbation (mass-turr-BAY-shun). The act of playing with one's sexual organs or of bringing one's organs to sexual climax. Self-stimulation; often called "self-abuse."

Medical model. The theoretical view that abnormal behaviors are only a "symptom" of an underlying mental disturbance. Hence "curing" the behaviors will not cure the underlying problem, any more than curing the headache associated with a brain tumor by giving the patient aspirin will get rid of the tumor. Opposite of the "social learning theory," which holds that the real problem is the abnormal behavior, which, being learned, can be unlearned.

Mental retardation. General term used to refer to individuals who score below 75 or so on an IQ test. Defined by *Webster's* as "a failure in intellectual development resulting in social incompetence that is considered to be the result of a defect in the central nervous system and (hence) incurable." However, we now suspect that many forms of mental retardation are "helpable," if not yet entirely "curable."

Multiple personality. In some cases, people act as if some part or parts of their basic personality had "split off" and had assumed a life or lives of their own. Thus a woman patient may behave normally under many conditions while calling herself "Mrs. White." However, at times, her body seems to be taken over by another side of her personality. She then misbehaves and calls herself "Miss Black."

Neurosis (new-ROH-sis). From the Latin word meaning "disease of the nerves." A mild yet persistent form of mental illness in which the patient can still adjust enough to his or her social environment so that hospitalization typically isn't required.

Normal behavior. The term has two meanings that must be kept distinct. The first means, "What most people do in a particular situation." The second means, "What most people *ought to do* in a particular situation according to some theory or religious principle."

Norms. Normal or expected behaviors.

Obsession (obb-SESS-shun). A thought or feeling or desire that recurs again and again, usually against the will of the person.

Organic abnormalities. Unusual behaviors or physical conditions that have (or seem to have) a purely physical cause. Color blindness is (usually) an organic abnormality since it is mostly inherited.

Organic psychosis. A type of severe mental disturbance that has (or seems to have) a known biological cause. As opposed to the *functional psychosis,* which is an equally severe mental disturbance that has no known biological cause.

Psychopath (SIGH-koh-path). Also called *sociopath* (SO-see-oh-path). A type of personality disorder marked primarily by failure to adapt to prevailing ethical and social standards and by lack of social responsibility. Both terms have been replaced by "antisocial personality."

Psychosis (sigh-KOH-sis). From Greek and Latin words meaning "disease of the mind." A severe form of mental illness that typically requires intensive treatment, often including hospitalization. The two major types are the organic and the functional psychoses.

Remission. From the Latin word meaning "to send back." When patients in a hospital are released back to society, they undergo "remission."

Schizophrenia (skits-zo-FREE-knee-uh). A psychological label that we apply to personality disturbances characterized by shyness, introversion, and a tendency to avoid social contact and close relationships. Distorted thought patterns, delusions, emotional impulsivity, and unusual body movements are often a part of the symptoms of the schizophrenic (skits-zo-FREN-ick). The four main types of schizophrenia are simple, hebephrenic (hee-buh-FREN-ick), catatonic (kat-tah-TAHN-ick), and paranoid (PAIR-uh-noid).

Senility (suh-NILL-ih-tee). Senile means "old" or relating to the weaknesses of old age. A severe form of mental disturbance associated with aging or old age. Often involves forgetfulness or amnesia, particularly a forgetting of recent events.

Thyroxin (thigh-ROX-in). A growth hormone secreted by the thyroid gland.

Tumor (TOO-mur). From the Latin word meaning "a swollen or distended part." Hence, an abnormal growth of some kind.

INTRODUCTION: ONE FLEW OVER THE CUCKOO'S NEST

For 20 years Chief Bromden played deaf and mute. He never said a word and pretended that he couldn't hear. He just pushed his broom around the ward and minded his own business. The Chief—whose father was chief of a tribe of Indians who lived along the Columbia River—hadn't always acted this way. His act began when other people seemed to quit listening to him. When the Chief was a child, a group of people came to his village and attempted to force the Indians to sell their land. Young Bromden was the only person there when the white people came, so he tried to talk to them and tell them where his father was. But the white people didn't listen to the young Indian. They acted as if he wasn't there and even made fun of him and called him names. In school, things were about the same. Some of the white teachers wouldn't listen to what the young Indian had to say. In the Army, people who outranked Bromden—and that was just about everyone—refused to listen to him. Eventually, Chief Bromden just decided to stop trying to talk to people. He began to play deaf and mute. But his act didn't work out very well. It got him thrown into "the cuckoo's nest." People thought the Chief was crazy, so they had him sent to a mental institution.

In the institution, the Chief kept up his game for 20 years. Because his act was convincing, he was allowed to move around freely and to overhear almost everything that was going on in his ward. One of the most interesting things the Chief heard was how one man, Randle Patrick McMurphy, got himself committed to the cuckoo's nest on purpose. The story of Chief Bromden and McMurphy is told in *One Flew over the Cuckoo's Nest*, a novel by Ken Kesey.

McMurphy was a big, loud, friendly Irishman with long, red hair and a shiny scar across his nose. When McMurphy came to the normally quiet ward, he made things happen. With his loud laugh, funny stories, and friendly handshakes, McMurphy got the other men interested in something besides their jigsaw puzzles. He told everyone how he came to be in the institution and how he planned to take over.

McMurphy was in jail on a work farm when he decided that life in a mental institution might not be too bad. All he had to do was pick a few fights, and before long the prison authorities were convinced that McMurphy was **insane.** He was diagnosed as a **psychopath** or **sociopath**—a person who lacks social responsibility and who is unable to live within the laws of society.

The staff of the mental institution read McMurphy's record, believed him to be a sociopath, and treated him like one. But McMurphy didn't care. He had what he wanted—a soft bed, three meals a day, and a lot of new suckers to gamble with. Everything went well for a while. The Irishman was having a good time. He won a lot of money, and even managed to sneak some of his women friends into the ward at night for a wild party. But there was one drawback. McMurphy found out that he was legally committed to the institution. This meant that he couldn't get out until he proved to the staff that he was not insane. McMurphy died in the cuckoo's nest.

One Flew over the Cuckoo's Nest is fiction. It isn't true. Real people don't get locked up in mental institutions the way McMurphy did—or do they? D. L. Rosenhan of Stanford University thinks they do. He thinks that mental health professionals can't always tell the difference between sane and insane people. Rosenhan set up an experiment to prove his point. Rosenhan and seven other people got themselves admitted to a number of different psychiatric hospitals in the United States. These people became pseudopatients or fake patients and didn't tell anyone on the staffs of the hospitals about the experiment. The object of the experiment was to determine whether or not the hospital staffs would discover that the pseudopatients were actually faking insanity.

Among the pseudopatients were three psychologists, a pediatrician, a psychiatrist, a painter, and a homemaker. Three of the pseudopatients were women, five were men. All were considered to be normal, and none had ever shown signs of serious psychological problems. Each of the pseudopatients called a psychiatric hospital for an appointment and was admitted after complaining of "hearing voices." The pseudopatients gave false information about their names, jobs, and places of employment, but everything else they told the hospital staffs was true. The significant events of the pseudopatients' life-histories were told as they had actually occurred. Frustrations and emotional upsets were described along with joys and satisfactions. If anything, says Rosenhan, these facts should have shown that the pseudopatients were sane since none of their histories of current behaviors were unusual.

Rosenhan published the results of his experiment in *Science* in January of 1973. In all cases, the pseudopatients were judged as being "mentally ill" or "insane" and were admitted to the hospitals. In 11 cases out of 12, the pseudopatients were diagnosed as being **schizophrenic**—that is, as having severely disturbed personalities.

The day after they were admitted, the pseudopatients stopped saying that they heard voices and tried to convince the hospital staffs that they were sane. But despite their public show of sanity, the pseudopatients were never once detected as fakers by the hospital staffs. Furthermore, the staff members were very slow to realize that these so-called crazy patients were suddenly much improved. About 30 percent of the other patients did detect the pseudopatients' sanity. The "real" patients told Rosenhan's people, "You're not crazy. You're a journalist or a professor. You're just checking up on the hospital, aren't you?"

On the average, it took the pseudopatients about 19 days to convince the staff members to release them. One pseudopatient was kept for 52 days, and finally had to run away because he could not convince the hospital doctors that he was sane. In most other cases, Rosenhan's people were eventually discharged, but were given the diagnosis of "schizophrenia in **remission**." In other words, the patients were still considered to be mentally ill, but their schizophrenia was supposedly "in remission" or not as bad as when the patients were admitted. "Once labeled a schizophrenic," explains Rosenhan, "the pseudopatient was stuck with the label."

Rosenhan's findings were shocking. Sane people could actually be declared insane by professionals who were supposed to know the difference!

Rosenhan next conducted an experiment to see if the supposedly insane people could be diagnosed as sane. Rosenhan told the staff of a hospital the results of his first experiment. Then he told the staff that one or more of his pseudopatients would try to get admitted to the hospital. The staff members were asked to rate each incoming patient to try to detect the pseudopatients. Ratings were obtained on 193 patients who were admitted for psychiatric treatment. Of them, 41 were thought to be pseudopatients by at least one member of the staff. Twenty-three were considered suspect by at least one psychiatrist. Nineteen were suspected by one psychiatrist and one other staff member. Actually, admits Rosenhan, no genuine pseudopatient (at least from his group) tried to get into the hospital.

Rosenhan's pseudopatients, just like McMurphy, had trouble proving they were sane. But Rosenhan's experiment is not fiction. It is a true story. And it took place just recently, not back in the Middle Ages. If sophisticated, modern psychiatric and psychological professionals can't tell sane people from insane, who can? Who is to decide what is normal and what is abnormal?

WHAT IS NORMAL?

Society and statistics usually decide what is normal and what is *abnormal* (or away from the norm). If most members of a society hear and speak, then hearing and speaking are considered to be normal behaviors. People who can't hear or speak because of a physical problem are considered to be physically abnormal. People who decide not to speak and pretend not to hear, like Chief Bromden, might be considered mentally abnormal by society's standards. Since most members of society don't hear strange voices, those people who do (or who *claim* they do) are sometimes considered abnormal and diagnosed as schizophrenic, like Rosenhan's pseudopatients.

Not all behaviors, however, are as easy to classify as hearing and speaking. What, for instance, is a normal score on an IQ test? If most of the people in a certain group score around 100 on an IQ test, 100 is considered to be a normal or average score. And, in fact, many IQ tests are constructed so that most people for whom the test was designed will score close to 100. Using the bell-shaped or normal curve of distribution, about 68 percent of the people taking the test should score close to the average 100 (see Fig. 12-1). People scoring outside (above or below) this median, or average range, might then be considered statistically abnormal to some extent. (See Statistical Appendix.)

Unfortunately for the people who are trying to decide who is normal and who is abnormal, life is more complicated than a simple set of statistics or

Behavior that is considered normal in some circumstances may be considered abnormal in other circumstances. (*Left*) Soldiers are expected to follow orders to shoot people in combat. (*Right*) Nazi Adolph Eichmann was tried as a war criminal for ordering the killing of Jews during World War II.

averages. People who get average scores on an intelligence test are considered to be normal. People who score high above the average are called geniuses. So, statistically speaking, a *genius* is abnormal. If 80 percent of the voting public elect a Democratic president, the other 20 percent of the voters might be considered politically abnormal. Very few people who take a psychological test ever get scores which indicate perfect adjustment on all scales of the test. People who do get such scores are not average individuals and, therefore, are statistically abnormal.

Statistics can be used to define average behavior, but behavior that is above or below average is not always what most people view as abnormal. Geniuses, Republicans, and perfectly adjusted people are not usually considered abnormal.

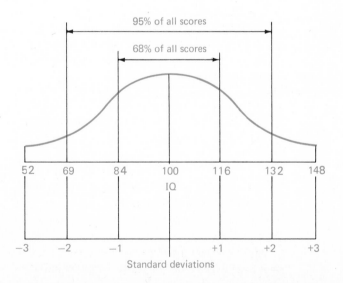

FIG. 12–1.
If 68 percent of the people score between 84 and 118 on an IQ test, people who score 52 would be considered abnormal.

391

One reason that statistics don't always correctly define normality is that there are subsocieties and cultures within each society. Each society, culture, or group of people has a different set of **norms.** And what is normal or average for one group might not be considered normal by another group. McMurphy's fighting, for instance, was considered quite normal, and it even won him respect in the rough logging camps of the Northwest. McMurphy's fighting spirit won him a medal after he fought and led a group of men out of a prisoner-of-war camp. That same fighting spirit won McMurphy a dishonorable discharge when he fought with his Army superiors. And finally, fighting helped get McMurphy locked away for good in a mental institution.

So what is considered normal can change from place to place, from time to time, and from society to society. Many societies, for instance, consider homosexuality abnormal. In 1972, however, the American Psychological Association removed homosexuality from its abnormal psychology category. In 1973, the American Psychiatric Association removed homosexuality from its manual of mental disorders. The statistics on homosexuality haven't changed much, but attitudes have changed somewhat with time.

When statistics don't adequately define normality, psychologists sometimes define **normal behavior** as "adaptive behavior." Any behavior, in other words, that helps an individual *or a society* adapt or adjust better to the environment is supposed to be normal. Any behavior that does not foster the well-being of an individual or a society is considered abnormal. Such things as alcoholism, unethical political and business practices, prejudice, and laziness might be considered maladaptive or abnormal — even in societies where such behaviors are statistically normal.

Obviously, there are problems in defining normal and abnormal behavior. There are too many societies, cultures, subcultures, and individuals for whom "normal" has different meanings. No ideal standard or perfect model of normalcy has yet been described that can satisfy the needs of every individual and of every culture. Keeping all these problems in mind, psychologists have made valiant attempts to define what they are talking about when they use such terms as "normal" and "abnormal." People whose behavior is considered normal, according to psychologist Robert M. Goldenson, usually meet certain flexible standards. The most important are as follows:

1. The ability to think, feel, and act in a coordinated way.
2. The ability to meet the demands of a socially acceptable (noncriminal or nondeviant) environment in a relatively mature, realistic, and nondefensive manner.
3. Freedom from extreme emotional distress (unhappiness, upset, apprehensiveness, and so forth) without going to the opposite extremes of apathy or unwarranted euphoria.
4. The absence of clear-cut symptoms of mental disorder.

Goldenson and other psychologists and psychiatrists have also attempted to classify abnormal behavior or "clear-cut symptoms of mental disorder."

CLASSIFICATION OF MENTAL DISORDERS

The clear-cut symptoms of mental disorders mentioned by Goldenson have been noticeable since history was first recorded. Ancient Chinese and Egyptian texts describe disturbed individuals. The Old Testament contains the story of King Saul who seems to have had what is now called a manic-depressive disorder. One time, Saul ran through a public place naked. Another time, he tried to kill his son Jonathan. Centuries before Saul, Greek mythology contained numerous stories of apparently mentally disturbed people. And the history and literature of almost all ages and cultures contains references to strange and abnormal behavior.

Of the various attempts down through history to describe abnormal behavior, perhaps the most successful has been the classification of abnormalities in terms of their causes. Biological, cognitive or psychological, and social problems all contribute to specific types of abnormal behavior patterns. Once we understand the causes of these abnormalities, we can often find ways to correct or cure the problems and thereby help the disturbed people.

BIOLOGICAL PROBLEMS

On the ward with Bromden and McMurphy was a man named Pete, whose head had two big dents, one on each side. The doctor who delivered Pete had pinched Pete's soft infant skull while trying to pull him out of his mother's womb.

FIG. 12-2.
King Saul's actions, described in the Old Testament, would probably be classified as manic-depressive today.

Parts of Pete's brain were damaged during this delivery accident, and Pete was never able to concentrate or to learn very much. Only with an exceptional effort and a lot of help was Pete able to learn enough to hold down a simple job and to take care of himself. And only with continued effort was Pete able to do the things that most six-year-old children could do with ease. After about 50 years of constant trying, Pete finally got tired and gave up. He was put in the institution where he sat around most of the time saying ''I'm tired.'' Pete was tired of trying to overcome a severe biological abnormality.

Because the brain and nervous system are responsible for almost all human thoughts and behaviors, damage to the brain or nervous system can be responsible for abnormal thoughts and behaviors. Head injuries, infectious diseases, poisons, hormone or body-chemical imbalances, genetic defects, brain tumors, and problems of blood circulation are among the biological problems that can sometimes lead to thoughts and behaviors that might be considered abnormal by society's standards. Because biological problems can cause obvious abnormalities of body chemistry, body tissues, or organs, such problems are often called **organic abnormalities.**

Mental Retardation

Mental retardation is usually defined as subnormal intellectual functioning that originates sometime during a child's development. Because mental retardation often is the result of an organic abnormality, it could actually be called organic or physiological retardation. Such retardation usually causes problems of learning, social adjustment, and maturation. Mental retardation is not always associated with mental disturbances, however. For 50 years Pete was mentally retarded, but he was not mentally or emotionally disturbed. Pete knew what his problem was, and he tried to adjust to it. Only when the frustrations of life became too great for him to handle did he seem to become mentally disturbed.

In the past, mentally retarded people were often put in homes where they could be cared for. Little was done to try to help such people. In recent years special educational and treatment programs have shown that many mentally retarded people can be trained and can lead happy, productive lives.

Old Age

On the ward with Bromden and McMurphy were a number of very old men who were confined to wheelchairs or beds. Many of these men couldn't care for or clean themselves and needed constant attention. Many of them couldn't talk, and those that did talk didn't make much sense. These men seemed to have little interest in each other or in life in general. Most of them just sat and stared and did little else. They didn't even seem to notice that a loud-mouth like McMurphy was running around and causing all sorts of excitement on the ward.

As the human body grows old, it usually begins to function less and less well. Some problems of physical or biological breakdown lead to mental abnormali-

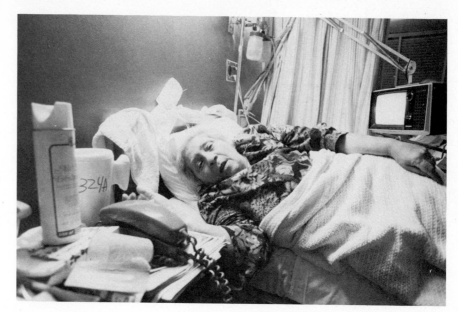

Some mental disorders, such as senile psychosis, have biological origins. As the human body grows older, blood supply to the brain is slowed or blocked, and tissue begins to die. This mental deterioration may cause forgetfulness and childish or confused behavior.

ties like those seen in the older men on McMurphy's ward. **Senility** and the more serious senile psychosis are the terms often used to describe the mental, emotional, and social deterioration sometimes seen in older people.

Senile psychosis occurs when the blood supply to the brain is blocked off or slowed down. Hardening of the arteries and a continuous buildup of materials inside the arteries characterize a condition that usually slows down the supply of blood needed by the brain. Gradually, with less blood, brain tissue begins to die, other biological changes take place in the brain, and senile psychosis sets in. The average age for people admitted to mental institutions for senile psychosis is 75. Such patients are often childish, confused, and forgetful. They may have hallucinations and show all the signs of mental deterioration.

Senile psychosis comes on gradually, but it can be hastened by physical illness and psychological stress. Older people who have friends, emotional security, affection, and an interest in life can sometimes postpone or reduce the effects of old age.

Infection

Syphilis is an infectious disease that has been known for many years to be a cause of biological abnormalities that lead to mental disorders. Germs associated with syphilis can be transmitted from person to person through sexual intercourse, and from pregnant women to their unborn children. Once the germs enter the body they can spread to the nervous system and to the brain, where they destroy tissues. The result is a type of physical and mental deterioration called **general paresis** (or juvenile paresis in cases where unborn children received the disease from their mothers).

Only about 3 percent of the untreated cases of syphilis actually result in general paresis, and many of these cases can be cured. A blood test—the Wassermann test—is administered to most people in the United States before they are allowed to get married. When the blood tests detect syphilis, the infection can be treated with penicillin and other drugs. If syphilis is detected early enough, complete recovery is almost always possible. But even with detection and treatment, syphilis (like other venereal diseases) remains a serious problem in many parts of the world. Untreated general paresis can result in personality deterioration, loss of good judgment and comprehension, severe emotional reactions, speech and writing disturbances, convulsive seizures, and eventual death.

Drugs

Alcoholism is one of the most common causes of abnormal behavior in the United States. Alcohol produces biochemical changes that can sometimes lead to hallucinations, confusion, and extremely violent behavior. The abnormal mental reaction most often associated with alcoholism is **delirium tremens.**

FIG. 12–3.
Overuse of drugs is a common cause of abnormal behavior. Addiction to alcohol can cause delirium tremens or agitated behavior, including trembling and hallucinations.

People who drink excessively for a long time often become excited and agitated. Their hands, tongues, and lips may begin to tremble. Other symptoms of delirium tremens, or DTs, may be disorientation in time and space; vivid hallucinations, often of small, fast-moving creatures like rats, roaches, and snakes; acute fear of hallucinated animals; and perspiration, fever, and rapid heartbeat.

Other commonly available drugs—heroin, barbiturates, amphetamines, LSD, and marijuana can, like alcohol, be psychologically addictive. Overuse or overdoses, as with alcohol, can sometimes cause physical as well as psychological deterioration.

Tumors

Abnormal growth or enlargements of body tissue are called **tumors.** Some tumors, like those caused by cancer, are malignant—they destroy the normal body tissue in which they grow. Nonmalignant tumors can be dangerous if they exert damaging pressure on the organs around them. Tumors of the brain and nervous system are relatively rare, but they can sometimes cause abnormal thought and behavior patterns if they damage surrounding organs or tissues of the nervous system or brain.

Many brain tumors can be removed by surgery. The degree of recovery depends on the size and location of the tumor and on the amount of brain tissue destroyed by the tumor or during the operation.

Hormones

For various reasons the body sometimes produces too much or too little of certain chemicals. The thyroid gland, for instance, controls the body's rate of metabolism. Too much **thyroxin** (the hormone produced by the thyroid gland) can cause a person to be tense, agitated, and emotional. Too little thyroxin can result in physical and mental sluggishness, loss of memory, and depression. The adrenal glands secrete or produce the hormones associated with emotions and stress. If the adrenal glands are overactive (see Chapter 11) the result can be physical and mental breakdown. Underactive adrenal glands can result in a lack of ambition, lowered sexual drive, and irritability.

The obvious effects of organic problems on mental functioning have caused some researchers to suggest that every form of mental disorder or abnormality may be due to organic causes. The effects of hormones and other body chemicals, for instance, prompted Ralph Gerard, an expert on the brain and nervous system, to say that there is "no twisted thought without a twisted molecule." Gerard was suggesting that abnormal body chemicals may be responsible for all abnormal thoughts and behaviors. In many ways he was correct. Alcohol, LSD, vitamins, hormones, and poisons can affect thoughts and behaviors. At present many researchers are searching for more chemicals that might be responsible for abnormal behavior. The hope is that all mental disturbances can eventually be

Drugs can also be used to help correct hormonal imbalances that cause abnormal behavior. Many mental patients can control their problems with carefully prescribed drugs.

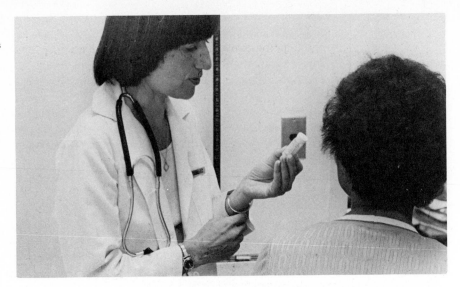

linked to certain chemicals. Then, abnormal behavior or mental disturbances could be corrected by simply adding or subtracting the necessary chemicals in the disturbed person's brain.

Unfortunately, mental problems are probably not as simple as chemical problems. Too much adrenalin can cause a breakdown of mental processes or "twisted thoughts," but twisted thoughts might also be the cause of the overproduction of adrenalin ("the twisted molecule") in the first place. Extreme fear of school, for instance, might be a twisted thought—especially if the fear causes anxiety and stress, and interferes with all normal thoughts and behaviors. In such a case, it is the twisted thought that is producing the molecule. The twisted thought causes stress, which causes overproduction of adrenalin, which, in turn, can lead to a breakdown. When this is the case, it is probably necessary to change the twisted thought in order to change or eliminate the molecule.

PSYCHOLOGICAL PROBLEMS

Twisted thoughts are believed to be involved in two specific types of abnormal behavior—neuroses (or psychoneuroses) and psychoses. Neuroses and functional psychoses are considered to be more the result of cognitive or psychological problems than of organic or biological problems. In general, a **neurosis** is a personality disorder consisting of emotional disturbances. A **psychosis** is a much more severe form of disorder consisting of extreme personality disorganization and loss of contact with reality. It is not known whether a psychosis is just a severe form of neurosis, or whether psychoses and neuroses are two unrelated and different types of cognitive problems.

The Neuroses

Neurotic symptoms usually consist of what appear to be exaggerated defense mechanisms (see Chapter 10). Most people use defense mechanisms consciously from time to time in attempts to cope with or adjust to reality. People diagnosed as having neurotic personalities seem to overuse defense mechanisms, usually unconsciously. For such people, defense mechanisms seem to become almost habitual and automatic methods of dealing with all of the problems and conflicts of life. But defense mechanisms sometimes distort or deny reality and lead to unrealistic, inappropriate, or abnormal thoughts and behaviors. Such thoughts and behaviors often cause disturbed people to see themselves, their work, their play, and other people in unrealistic terms.

Most people with neurotic symptoms know that they have problems and want to get well. Many even know some of the causes of their problems. Very few people with neurotic problems become psychotic, and many people with neurotic symptoms can hold a job and get along in society. A neurosis is not usually a cause for committing a person to an institution, though neuroses can cause severe psychological pain, in which case some sort of treatment or help is usually called for.

Patterns of neurotic behavior fall into several categories.

Anxiety Neurosis

Anxiety, a vague fear of danger from unknown sources, can sometimes become so severe that a person remains in a constant state of fear for no apparent reason. **Anxiety neurosis,** which is the most common form of neurosis, usually consists of constant apprehensiveness, inability to concentrate, and many of the physiological symptoms of stress. Neurotic anxiety is thought to be the result of failure to learn successful coping behavior.

Phobic Neurosis

A phobia is an extreme, unrealistic fear of specific people, places, thoughts, or things. Phobic neurosis can be the result of faulty behavior patterns learned through imitation or conditioning—like the child who is frightened by a horse and develops a long-lasting unrealistic fear of horses.

Obsessive-Compulsive Neurosis

One of the men in *One Flew over the Cuckoo's Nest* had been a fisherman for 25 years. One day he decided that everything was too dirty. He wouldn't go on his boat because it was too dirty. He wouldn't touch fish because they were too dirty. This strange behavior cost the fisherman his job and completely disrupted his life. He ended up in a mental institution where the staff members called him "Old rub-a-dub" because all he did all day long was clean himself and try to wash some invisible dirt off his clean hands. This fisherman was suffering from an obsessive-compulsive type of neurosis.

Obsessions have to do with thoughts; **compulsions** have to do with behaviors that are repeated over and over. Rub-a-dub was obsessed with cleanliness; thoughts of how dirty the world was crowded out all the normal things he might have thought of. In response to these obsessive thoughts, he compulsively washed his hands.

Hysterical Neurosis

Many of the people Freud worked with exhibited what is called **hysterical neurosis.** Two forms of hysterical neurosis—conversion and dissociative—have been described by Freud.

Conversion neurosis involves symptoms of physical illness that appear with no organic cause. These organic or physical symptoms are considered to be a form of defense. In time of war, soldiers have been known to develop paralyzed legs and other physical symptoms as an apparently unconscious attempt to avoid the stress of going into combat. Conversion reactions are rare, but people have been known to go blind or deaf as a form of defensive coping (see Chapter 11).

The dissociative type of hysterical neurosis is thought to be a method of avoiding stress or responsibility while still achieving certain goals. **Amnesia** (forgetfulness) and multiple personality are sometimes considered to be results of a dissociative reaction. A parent, for instance, who is tired of the stress and responsibility of raising a family might leave home and be gone for days or for months and then suddenly show up and not be able to remember the events of the recent past. Leaving home helps avoid the stress, and the amnesia helps avoid the guilt associated with leaving home and responsibilities.

To dissociate means to separate. Amnesia is a method of dissociating or completely separating one part of life from another. Multiple personality is another form of dissociation. A child who is accused of stealing something might invent another person to put the blame on. If this form of defensive behavior becomes habitual, the child may actually begin to believe that there is another person who steals and commits bad acts. If the made-up person becomes real enough, the child might develop a multiple personality—a good person and a bad person. The good child might fade out or seem to disappear psychologically and reawaken several hours or even days later to find out that the bad personality has been involved in many acts that the good child wouldn't consciously think of doing. If the good child is then to be punished, a third personality might even be created to take the punishment. True cases of multiple personality are rare, but some cases have been reported in which two or more dissociated personalities are involved.

Hypochondriacal Neurosis

People who are constantly worried about their physical health are sometimes thought to be suffering from what is **hypochondriacal neurosis.** Most people are interested in their physical health, but people who show an exaggerated interest and who constantly complain of nonexistent or minor physical problems

Hypochondriacal neuroses, or exaggerations of physical illness, are sometimes used as excuses to avoid stressful situations.

are sometimes thought to be exhibiting neurotic behavior. Exaggerations of physical illness are sometimes used as excuses to avoid stressful situations.

Depressive Neurosis

Most people get depressed or feel sad when something terrible happens, such as a death in the family. Depressive behavior is thought to be neurotic when people exaggerate their depression or do not return to a normal emotional state after a reasonable amount of time. The "learned helplessness" described by Seligman is probably a type of depressive neurosis (see Chapter 11).

The Functional Psychoses

Chief Bromden had a serious problem in addition to his refusal to speak. Bromden explained his problem simply. He said that the hospital had a fog machine that was used to punish the patients or to keep them quiet. Whenever the staff turned on the fog machine, a thick blanket of fog would roll across the ward. While the fog machine was on, Chief Bromden lost contact with all of the people in the ward and he saw and heard strange things. Sometimes the fog would turn into clear, hard plastic and nothing seemed to move. Time seemed to stand still. There was no fog machine, but that was how the Chief explained what sometimes seemed to be going on in his mind.

Chief Bromden thought that while things were fogged over, the staff would open him up and put in nuts and bolts and other pieces of strange machinery that would control him. When the fog cleared, things would get back to normal, but sometimes the Chief would find himself strapped to a bed or covered with bruises. He would hear people accusing him of being uncontrollable and of performing strange acts.

Some of Chief Bromden's behavior might have been considered neurotic, but the staff at the hospital decided that the Chief's behavior was psychotic. The term psychosis, unlike neurosis, usually implies complete personality disorganization and loss of contact with reality. People are said to be suffering from a psychosis if their thoughts are completely unrealistic and if their behavior keeps them from taking part effectively in society. Such people don't always understand that they have a problem. In severe cases they may be dangerous to themselves or to others.

Psychotic behavior is divided into two categories—organic and functional. **Organic psychosis,** such as senile psychosis, is primarily due to temporary or permanent brain damage. Functional psychosis is thought to have psychological or cognitive causes. There is growing evidence, however, that some forms of functional psychosis may have a hereditary or genetic component. This does not mean that psychosis runs in families. It only means that people who have inherited certain genes might, under some circumstances, be more likely than other people to show what is called psychotic behavior. Functional psychotic behavior usually falls into two major categories—schizophrenia and affective psychosis.

Schizophrenia

The word **schizophrenia** comes from the Latin for "splitting of the mind." Schizophrenia is not, however, a split personality or **multiple personality.** The condition called schizophrenia is usually characterized by a breakdown of personality functioning, withdrawal from reality, emotional upset, and disturbances of thought and behavior. Schizophrenia does not mean a split mind but rather a severely disorganized mind or personality.

According to most classification systems there are four types of schizophrenia: simple, hebephrenic, catatonic, and paranoid.

Simple Schizophrenia. Simple schizophrenia is often characterized by a withdrawal from social reality. People classified as simple schizophrenics often sit and stare at the wall or the floor. They have as little to do as possible with life and with other people. Such people can usually feed and care for themselves at a minimal level, but they seem to have no interest in coping.

Hebephrenic Schizophrenia. Simple schizophrenia usually implies a partial breakdown or weakening of the personality. A complete disorganization of personality is sometimes called hebephrenic schizophrenia. When most people think of "crazy," they are thinking of hebephrenic schizophrenia. A person diagnosed as a hebephrenic schizophrenic will seem to have a severely disorganized personality. The person may think and behave like another person—Napoleon, Queen Elizabeth, Sherlock Holmes, and so on. The individual's speech, thought, behavior, and emotions sometimes change to fit this new personality.

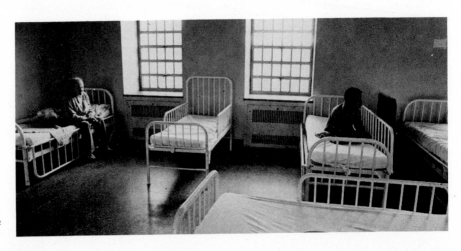

People diagnosed as catatonic schizophrenic are completely withdrawn from reality. They often sit frozen in one position for hours.

Catatonic Schizophrenia. One man on the ward with Bromden stood all day every day against the wall with his arms outstretched. This man never said or did anything. He just stood there. People who seem to be frozen into one position and who seem to be completely withdrawn are victims of catatonic schizophrenia.

Paranoid Schizophrenia. People who are suspicious and show mistrust of everyone are sometimes thought to be affected by paranoid schizophrenia. Such people not only tend to fear everyone but often have hallucinations or hear voices which tell them that someone is out to get them. They may feel, for instance, that people from outer space or from some political organization are trying to control their lives.

Affective Psychosis

The term "affect" has to do with the feeling or the arousal associated with an emotion (see Chapter 11). People who show extremely exaggerated emotional states are sometimes thought to be suffering from an **affective psychosis.** The person with this type of mental disturbance or abnormality may experience overactive or manic emotional states, underactive or depressed emotional states, or may swing back and forth from manic to depressive.

People exhibiting manic psychotic reactions sometimes act as if they have been taking uppers. Their thoughts and behaviors are speeded up. People exhibiting depressive psychotic reactions act as if they have been taking downers. Their thoughts and behaviors are slowed down or depressed. A person suffering from what is called **manic-depressive psychosis** may appear for a time to be hilarious, overactive, and silly in almost all situations. Then, after several months of this manic behavior, the same person will go into the depressive stage of the disorder and become withdrawn, quiet, and usually sad. During this stage, such a person may feel too depressed to eat or get out of bed.

SOCIAL PROBLEMS

Most forms of mental disturbance have biological, psychological, and social aspects. A child who is brain-damaged, for instance, may have only an organic problem to begin with. But society, including parents, teachers, and caretakers, may neglect or ridicule a mentally retarded child. These negative social inputs can then cause emotional or psychological problems, such as feelings of insecurity and anxiety. People with psychological problems also sometimes have problems with society, which can make the original psychological problem worse. Psychological problems can also lead to biological disturbances such as the physiological symptoms of stress. So most forms of mental disturbance seem to have biological, psychological, and social aspects that all work together.

There are certain types of abnormal behavior patterns, however, that usually cause problems for society and for other people rather than for the person exhibiting the behavior. Antisocial behaviors such as drug addiction and sexual deviations are among the abnormal behaviors that can cause social problems.

The Sociopathic Personality

Criminals such as executed murderer Gary Gilmore are often thought of as sociopathic personalities. They seem to have no sense of guilt and little or no conscience.

No matter how normality is defined, social standards must always be part of the definition. People who fail to accept any of the standards of their society are often classified as **sociopaths, psychopaths,** or as having antisocial personalities. Such people are frequently in trouble with the law. They seem to have few loyalties, little or no conscience, no sense of guilt, and little social control over their behavior. They usually see nothing wrong with their behavior and see no reason to change. Prisons are full of people who could possibly be diagnosed as sociopaths—habitual criminals, delinquents, con artists, embezzlers, rapists, racketeers, and alcoholics.

Many of the behaviors exhibited by McMurphy fit the description of a sociopath. He was always fighting and getting into trouble with authority. Sometimes he was unable to control his aggressive behavior. He felt no guilt about gambling and taking money from his friends. He told his friends (and himself) that they were getting their money's worth out of all the fun and excitement he was providing. McMurphy did have loyalty, however. He stayed in the cuckoo's nest in order to help his friends, even though it cost him his freedom and eventually his life.

Many things—including organic, psychological, and social problems—might be responsible for sociopathic behavior. Sociopathic behavior is not, however, usually classified as neurotic or psychotic. The antisocial person does not usually seem to have a conscience or guilt feelings that could cause emotional or neurotic problems. The condition described as sociopathic, unlike that described as psychotic, does not usually involve loss of contact with reality.

Drug Addiction

In addition to the organic and personal problems sometimes caused by alcohol and drugs, addiction often causes problems for society. Therefore, addictive behavior can be called antisocial. Addicts often are forced to steal to support their habits, and they often cannot take on any serious social responsibilities. Drunkenness is responsible for about 25,000 deaths per year due to automobile accidents and for 15 percent of the murders committed in the United States. Alcoholism costs business more than one billion dollars per year due to lost time and accidents on the job. And we spend an additional one billion dollars a year just trying to take care of alcoholics.

Sexual Behavior

Societies have usually attempted to decide which types of sexual behavior are normal and which are abnormal. Heterosexual contact within marriage has often been considered the only moral, legal, and normal form of sexual behavior. But societies, attitudes, and behaviors change — sometimes more rapidly than moral and legal codes change. In the 1940s and 1950s Dr. Alfred Kinsey's surveys of sexual behavior pointed out that many types of sexual behavior were being practiced in the United States with little regard for religious or legal restrictions.

Kinsey's surveys and more recent investigations have helped to redefine sexual behavior on a statistical level. But many of the people whose sexual behavior deviates from the statistical norm do not consider themselves to be abnormal. So deviations from the statistical norm are as limited as religious or legal codes in defining normal sexual behavior.

Another way of defining normal sexual behavior has to do with adaptation. Any behavior that is biologically, psychologically, or socially harmful to the people involved might be considered maladaptive or abnormal. According to such a definition, sexual behavior would have to be examined both on a personal or individual and a societal basis before any decision as to normality or abnormality could be made. What is harmful or maladaptive for one person may not be harmful for another person. What is harmful at one time or in one place may not be harmful at another time or place. Depending on the person, place, and time, for instance, **masturbation** can be either adaptive or maladaptive — biologically, psychologically, or socially. According to Kinsey, 62 percent of the females and 92 percent of the males in the United States masturbate at some time in their lives. Usually such behavior is considered to be a normal form of sexual behavior or release. Masturbation might, however, be physically harmful if it is engaged in continuously to the point of exhaustion. Masturbation might be psychologically harmful if it brings on excessive feelings of guilt and anxiety. Masturbation might be socially harmful if it keeps people from joining in social activities or if it is practiced in public.

What is considered abnormal sexual behavior depends on time, place, and circumstances, and whether or not the practices are harmful to the people involved. Do you think the patrons of this establishment engage in abnormal behavior?

The normality or abnormality of all forms of sexual behavior must be considered with respect to person, place, and time and with respect to possible physical, psychological, or social harm.

A GLOSSARY OF SEXUAL DEVIATIONS

At various times, in various societies the following behaviors have been considered deviant or abnormal.

Impotence: Inability of a male to achieve or sustain erection.

Frigidity: Inability of a female to achieve orgasm or sexual satisfaction. Not to be confused with occasional inability to perform the sex act satisfactorily, which happens to most people; it is often a temporary condition caused by psychological or physical problems.

Satyriasis and Nymphomania: Satyrs and nymphs are characters in ancient Greek mythology who displayed an almost continuous desire for sex. Satyriasis and nymphomania are the terms used to describe males and females, respectively, who suffer from a condition in which the person is driven to promiscuity due to inability to achieve satisfaction.

Sodomy: Any form of sexual intercourse that is termed "unnatural"; oral–genital contacts and anal intercourse were often considered to be "unnatural."

Voyeurism: Sexual gratification derived from watching other people engage in the sex act.

Exhibitionism: Sexual pleasure obtained from displaying one's genitals in public.

Sadism: Sexual gratification derived from inflicting physical pain on sex partner.

Masochism: The need to feel pain inflicted by the partner in order to achieve sexual gratification.

Bestiality: Humans engaging in sex with animals.

Fetishism: Sexual attraction for things not usually considered to be sex objects, such as undergarments or shoes.

Prostitution: Form of sexual behavior in which males or females are paid for sexual services.

Incest: Sexual relations between close relatives such as father and daughter.

Pedophilia: Use of a child as a sex object by an adult.

Rape: Sexual behavior with an unwilling partner.

Homosexuality: Sex between members of the same sex; female homosexuals are also called *lesbians*. While many people still consider this practice abnormal, both the American Psychiatric Association and the American Psychological Association have removed homosexuality from the "abnormal psychology" category.

Transvestitism: Sexual pleasure derived from wearing clothes of the opposite sex; both heterosexuals and homosexuals engage in this practice.

Transsexualism: Feeling that one was born with a body of the wrong sex (for example, deep psychological conviction of being a female but having a male body); hormone treatments and operations have helped such people to change their sex.

TABLE 12-1
Types of Abnormal Behavior Problems

Biological (or Organic)	Psychological	Social

1. *Mental Retardation*
Physiological abnormalities can cause problems in learning, social adjustment, and maturation.
 	
2. *Senile Psychosis*
In old age, brain tissues begin to die, resulting in mental, social, and emotional deterioration.
 	
3. *Infection*
Venereal diseases such as syphilis cause physical and mental deterioration: loss of good judgment and comprehension, severe emotional reactions, speech and writing disturbances, and convulsive seizures.
 	
4. *Tumors*
Abnormal growths or enlargements of body tissue may damage or interfere with functions of brain or nervous system.
 	
5. *Hormones*
Imbalance of certain body chemicals can cause agitated and emotional behavior.
	1. *Neuroses*
	Personality disorder consisting of emotional disturbances
	  A. Anxiety Neurosis
	  B. Phobic Neurosis
	  C. Obsessive-Compulsive Neurosis
	  D. Hysterical Neurosis
	  E. Hypochondriacal Neurosis
	  F. Depressive Neurosis
	
	2. *Functional Psychoses*
	More severe form of disorder consisting of extreme personality disorganization and loss of contact with reality
	  A. Schizophrenia (loss of contact with reality resulting in completely unrealistic thought and behavior)
	    (1) Simple
	    (2) Hebephrenic
	    (3) Catatonic
	    (4) Paranoic
	  B. Affective Psychoses (extremely exaggerated emotional states)
	    (1) Manic-depressive
		1. *Sociopathic Personality*
		Person who fails to accept any of the standards of society; has few loyalties, little conscience, no sense of guilt; sees nothing wrong with own behavior.
		
		2. *Drug Addiction*
		Because of dependence on alcohol or other drugs, addicts cannot take on any serious social responsibility and often engage in antisocial behavior.
		
		3. *Sexual Behavior*
		What is considered normal sexual behavior depends on the people involved, the time, and the place. Any behavior that is biologically, psychologically, or socially harmful to the participants may be considered abnormal.

407

FIG. 12–4.
Psychiatric labels are often attached to the person instead of certain behaviors exhibited by the person. As a result, labels sometimes prevent us from seeing normal behavior.

LABELING

McMurphy was diagnosed as psychotic by a prison psychiatrist. The term or label "psychotic" was picked up and used by the staff members at the mental institution where McMurphy wound up. The psychotic label stuck with him until he died. But what good is a label? A label on a person doesn't tell you what is inside that person—it just describes certain patterns of behavior that may have nothing to do with what the person is really like.

The main reason for classifying and studying mental disorders is to understand and help the people who are troubled by such disorders. Labeling—calling people psychiatric names—has done little to help disturbed people. In fact, labeling often adds to the problem. McMurphy's label, for instance, kept the people in the mental institution from really examining McMurphy's problem. The staff members thought he was psychotic or a sociopath. Therefore, when they looked at him, they only looked for and took note of those behaviors that seemed to fit the psychotic label. Even though only a few of his behaviors fit the pattern, those behaviors were enough to convince the staff that the label was correct. Rosenhan's pseudopatients ran into the same problem. Once they ended up on a ward labeled schizophrenic, they had trouble convincing the staff members that they were sane.

Psychiatric labeling not only tends to hide normal behavior, but labeling can make abnormal behavior worse as well. Many people treated Chief Bromden as if he didn't exist. They were, in effect, labeling him as "a nothing." After the Chief had been treated as a nothing enough times, he began to fit the label. He began to act like "a nothing." We often tend to behave as others expect us to behave. People who are constantly labeled as criminals or neurotics may eventually begin to behave like criminals or neurotics. A person who has a slight problem with overeating, for instance, might be labeled as a compulsively neurotic eater. The overeater might take advantage of the label and use it as an excuse to eat even more. In such cases, labeling creates what is called a "self-fulfilling prophecy."

Psychiatric labeling causes other problems. Many psychiatric labels originally had medical meanings. "Neurosis," for instance, comes from the Latin word for "nerve." Neuroses were once thought to be physical problems of the nerves. For many years, all mental disturbances were thought to be organic or medical problems. This is known as the medical model. Because of such thinking, the term "mental illness" came into being and is still used, but Freud and his followers showed that mental problems need not have medical causes. They can have psychological causes.

More recently, research has shown how social and learning problems can be the cause of "mental" disturbances and abnormal behavior. Even so, the old medical labels are still used to a great extent. The use of medical labels has often resulted in biological treatments being used in attempts to solve people's psychological or social problems. Medicines, surgery, and other medical treatments can often be used to help organic problems, but they are usually of little use in changing abnormal behavior caused by psychological or social problems.

ABNORMAL BEHAVIOR: CAUSES AND CURES

For thousands of years, people who behaved abnormally were thought to have been touched in some way by the gods. If good gods were involved, the people with strange behavior were sometimes honored by members of their society. If bad gods were involved, the people with abnormal behavior patterns were sometimes burned as witches or tortured as devils. So long as the gods were thought to be responsible, however, most people saw no hope for curing or changing abnormal thoughts and behaviors.

Some 200 years ago, our viewpoint about the causes of insanity changed. Rather than blaming abnormal behavior entirely on the gods, we began locking troubled and disturbed individuals away in large insane asylums where they could cause little trouble, and where they would be out of the way of the other members of society.

The medical model of mental illness came into prominence less than a century ago. Once we decided that people were "mentally ill" rather than "insane," the asylums became mental hospitals, and medical treatments were tried out on almost every type of mental disorder. Many medical treatments, such as powerful drugs and some forms of brain surgery, did manage to keep patients quiet and calm but actually did little to solve the social and psychological problems that were the cause of some disturbances.

In recent years the medical model of mental illness has come under attack. New York psychiatrist Thomas Szasz, for instance, says that mental illness is a myth. He says that mentally disturbed people just have more problems with living than do normal people. Calling or labeling such people "sick," says Szasz, just makes them feel that they are not responsible for their problems and gives them an excuse to act sick. Washington psychiatrist E. Fuller Torrey says much the same thing. There are some organic illnesses, he says, but many disturbed people have nothing biologically wrong with them. They just have problems and need help learning how to cope with them. Another psychiatrist, R. D. Laing, goes even further. He says that society is crazy. It is society, he says, that needs to change. Laing even suggests that schizophrenics might be the normal members of society. Their behavior just seems abnormal because everyone else in society is crazy.

Not everyone would agree with Laing, with Torrey, or with Szasz. But most psychologists probably would admit that human problems are really much more complex than we once thought they were. Our descriptions of abnormal functioning are often simplistic and inadequate; our ideas about the causes of these conditions are poorly formulated and incomplete; and our notions about how to cure psychological abnormalities are often sadly lacking in scientific proof. What we *can* say, however, is that most human problems involve biological, psychological, and social factors. We surely do people an injustice when we attempt either to diagnose or to treat their difficulties at *just* a biological level, or at *just* a psychological level, or at *just* a social level.

Although Chief Bromden was diagnosed as being psychotic, he really had a wide range of difficulties that stemmed from many causes and experiences. His autonomic nervous system did not react to stress the way a "normal" person's would. His emotional responses were strange and complex. He did not speak or relate to others as most of us would. These social problems came in no small part from many years of ill treatment by whites and by members of the hospital staff — but his early experiences with his family surely added to his difficulties. His cognitive or psychological problems resulted in his losing touch with reality when the imaginary fog machine was turned on — but possibly his genetic blueprint made him a prime candidate for this sort of mental problem. Thus, labeling him a psychotic or a schizophrenic neither told the staff what he was really like nor showed them how best to treat him.

During the course of *One Flew over the Cuckoo's Nest,* Chief Bromden changed remarkably. His behavioral outputs changed — as did his internal processes — because his inputs changed. When people stopped labeling him as psychotic and began treating him like a normal human being, he began to hear and speak again. When McMurphy made friends with him and showed him respect, the fog machine first faded into the background and finally turned off for good.

Abnormal physical, cognitive, and social inputs — all working together — had caused the Chief's problems in the first place. When these inputs changed for the better, his outputs became normal.

So, we have our choice. When we encounter people whose thoughts and behaviors seem abnormal to us, we can either hang what may be inappropriate labels on them, or we can try to understand them in all of their marvelous complexity. If we give them labels, we may end up blaming them for their problems and store them away in asylums or mental hospitals. But if we try to appreciate who they are and how they got that way, we may end up hunting for the physical, cognitive, and social influences that will help them get better. That way, we may help them fly over the cuckoo's nest rather than land in it.

► *SUMMARY*

1. People in mental institutions are not always **insane** or abnormal. Some of the fictional characters in *One Flew over the Cuckoo's Nest* were there because they thought life in an institution would be easier than trying to adapt to life in society. The participants in the Rosenhan study were in mental institutions because they had convinced hospital officials that they were insane. What is frightening is the difficulty the participants then had in convincing the officials that they were, indeed, normal or sane.

2. What is normal human behavior? Statistics and societies are usually involved in deciding what is normal and what is abnormal, but statistical norms and social codes change from time to time and from place to place. As a general definition, **normal behavior** can be described as "adaptive behavior."

3. What is abnormal human behavior? One of the common ways of describing abnormal behavior has been the classification of abnormalities in terms of their apparent causes — biological, cognitive or psychological, and social.

4. Biological problems resulting in abnormal behavior are often the result of damage to the brain or nervous system. Because biological damage affects the body and its organs, biological abnormalities are often called **organic abnormalities.**

5. Mental retardation, which is often the result of an organic abnormality, should probably be called organic or physiological retardation. Such retardation usually causes problems of learning, social adjustment, and maturation, but mental retardation is not always associated with mental disturbance.

6. As the body grows older, it begins to function less and less well. **Senility** and senile psychosis are the terms used to describe the mental, emotional, and social deterioration sometimes seen in people as they grow older.

7. Infections, various drugs, tumors, and over- or underproduction of certain hormones, or body chemicals, are also among the biological conditions that can lead to abnormal behavior.

8. Neuroses and functional psychoses are terms used to describe abnormal behavior patterns that are thought to be more the result of cognitive or psychological problems than of biological problems. A neurosis is a personality disorder consisting of emotional disturbances. A psychosis is a more severe form of disorder, consisting of extreme personality disorganization and loss of contact with reality.

9. Neuroses can cause severe psychological pain. The six types include **anxiety, phobic, obsessive-compulsive, hysterical, hypochondriacal,** and **depressive** neuroses.

10. Schizophrenia, a form of functional psychosis, is characterized by a breakdown of personality functioning, withdrawal from reality, emotional upset, and disturbances of thoughts and behaviors.

11. The term "affect" has to do with the feeling tone or the arousal associated with an emotion. People who show extremely exaggerated emotional states are sometimes said to be suffering from an **affective psychosis.**

12. Although biological, psychological, and social problems are involved in most forms of abnormal behavior, there are certain types of abnormal behavior that cause problems for society and for other people, rather than for the individual exhibiting the abnormal behavior. Failure to accept the standards of society, drug addiction, and sexual deviations are among the abnormal behaviors that can cause social problems.

13. Even though psychiatric classifications are still in use, psychiatric labeling — calling people psychiatric names — can lead to several serious problems. Labeling, by focusing on only certain aspects of a person's behavior, sometimes obscures or hides the more normal aspects of that person's behavior. Labeling can also make abnormal behaviors worse by creating what is known as a self-fulfilling prophecy.

14. Human problems are much more complex than we once believed them to be. Descriptions of abnormal behavior are often simplistic and inadequate. We can say, however, that most problems of abnormal human behavior involve biological, psychological, and social inputs. All three factors should probably be considered when attempts are made to understand and treat problems of abnormal behavior.

Suggested Readings

Kesey, Ken. *One flew over the cuckoo's nest.* New York: NAL, 1975.
Laing, R. D. *The politics of experience.* Middlesex, England: Penguin Books, 1967.
Postman, Neil. *Crazy talk, stupid talk.* New York: Delacorte, 1976.
Schreiber, Flora R. *Sybil.* New York: Warner Books, 1974.
Szasz, Thomas. *The myth of mental illness.* New York: Harper & Row, 1961.

▶ STUDY GUIDE

A. RECALL

Sentence Completion

1. In *One Flew over the Cuckoo's Nest,* Chief Bromden played _____ and
[p. 388]   _____ because no one ever paid him any attention.
2. Although he probably was not one, McMurphy was diagnosed as a
[p. 388]   _____.
3. D. L. Rosenhan of Stanford had fake patients, or _____, admitted to
[p. 389]   psychiatric hospitals.
4. Of the 12 fake patients that Rosenhan had admitted to psychiatric hospitals,
[p. 389]   _____ of them were diagnosed as _____.
5. The only people who realized that Rosenhan's fake patients were really fake were
[p. 389]   _____ _____.
6. Every subsociety has its own set of rules, expectations, or _____ to
[p. 392]   define what is normal or abnormal.
7. Mental disorders have been written about for a long time. In fact, King Saul seems to
[p. 393]   have been what we would now call _____-_____.
[p. 394]   8. Biologically based difficulties are often called _____ abnormalities.
9. The difficulties and deterioration that occasionally accompany old age lead to what is
[p. 395]   called _____ psychosis.
10. A type of physical and mental deterioration that may result from syphilis infection is
[p. 395]   _____ _____.
[p. 396]   11. The _____ test is used to detect the presence of syphilis.
12. The abnormal mental reaction most often associated with alcoholism is
[p. 396]   _____.
[p. 397]   13. Abnormal growths or enlargements of body tissue are called _____.
14. The _____ glands secrete hormones associated with emotions and
[p. 397]   stress.

[p. 399]
15. Neurotic symptoms usually consist of what appear to be exaggerated _____ _____.

[p. 399]
16. _____ is a vague fear of danger from unknown sources.

[p. 399]
17. _____ _____ is the most common form of neurosis.

18. A _____ is an extreme, unrealistic fear of specific people, places,
[p. 399]
thoughts, or things.

19. _____ have to do with thoughts, while _____ have to do
[p. 400]
with behaviors that are repeated over and over.

20. Amnesia and multiple personality are sometimes considered to be the result of a
[p. 400]
_____ reaction.

21. Someone who is constantly worried about his or her physical health may be a
[p. 400]
_____.

22. As opposed to organic psychosis, _____ psychosis is thought to have
[p. 401]
psychological or cognitive causes.

23. Severely disorganized, broken-down personalities characterize _____
[p. 402]
schizophrenia.

24. Suspicion and mistrust, accompanied by hallucinations, are typical of
[p. 403]
_____ schizophrenics.

25. A manic-depressive reaction psychosis can be thought of as a form of
[p. 403]
_____ psychosis.

26. _____ tend toward ways of crime — they often become habitual crimi-
[p. 404]
nals, rapists, delinquents, and the like.

27. Alcohol abuse may be responsible for as many as _____ deaths per year
[p. 404]
through automobile accidents.

28. Included among sexual deviations are _____, or engaging in sex with
[p. 406]
animals, and _____, or the use of a child as a sex object by an adult.

29. When people come to act in a way that is consistent with the way they have been
labeled, they may be following what is called a _____-_____
[p. 409]
prophecy.

30. Szasz says that mental illness is a _____, and R. D. Laing goes ever far-
[p. 410]
ther, saying that it is _____ that is crazy.

B. REVIEW

Multiple Choice: Circle the letter identifying the alternative that most correctly completes the statement or answers the question.

1. In *One Flew over the Cuckoo's Nest,* Chief Bromden's problem stemmed from the
fact that:

    A. no one ever paid any attention to him.

    B. he was mentally ill and no one knew it.

    C. he was a sociopath, but diagnosed schizophrenic.

    D. he was deaf and could not hear the questions he was asked.

2. When Rosenhan told the staff of a psychiatric hospital that he was going to send
them fake patients:

A. the staff failed to identify them.

B. he never followed up by doing so.

C. the staffs did not believe him.

D. only fake patients who were particularly good actors were not detected by the staff.

3. The definition of normality:

A. is a statistical term.

B. changes from time to time.

C. depends upon the subsociety to which one belongs.

D. all of the above.

4. Mental retardation:

A. really has nothing to do with abnormal behavior.

B. is a form of neurotic disorder.

C. can cause adjustment problems.

D. is essentially uncurable.

5. General paresis is associated with:

A. delerium tremens.

B. syphilis infection.

C. senility.

D. hormone deficiency.

6. Neurosis can be characterized by:

A. the inappropriate use of defense mechanisms.

B. institutionalization.

C. hallucinations and delusions.

D. persons who often have prison records.

7. A thought or idea that keeps constantly intruding into one's awareness is a(n):

A. phobia.

B. compulsion.

C. dissociation.

D. obsession.

8. Amnesia and multiple personality are generally associated with:

A. psychotic reactions.

B. dissociative reactions.

C. hypochondriacal neurosis.

D. depressive neurosis.

9. Total withdrawal and statuelike postures may be found in the _____ schizophrenic.

A. simple

B. hebephrenic
C. catatonic
D. paranoid

10. Homosexuality is:
A. a sexual deviation.
B. symptomatic of neurosis.
C. a biologically based behavior disorder.
D. none of the above.

SCHIZOPHRENIA

The nature-nurture controversy has been brought to bear on almost every facet of the human condition. Alcoholism, criminality, homosexuality, I.Q. and an array of psychoses and neuroses have all been ascribed, at one time or another, to either genetic or environmental factors. But arguments on both sides have been attacked as inconclusive and, like the chicken and the egg, no one has yet proved which came first. In the case of schizophrenia, however, the genetic hypothesis may be losing ground or at least heading for a compromise.

The idea that schizophrenia could be genetically caused took hold as statistics made it obvious that the disease ran in families. David Rosenthal of the National Institute of Mental Health explained the thinking behind this theory: "With a few rare exceptions," he says, "the incidence of schizophrenia in first-degree relatives of schizophrenic probands [subjects] is appreciably higher than the incidence of the disorder in control groups or in the population at large."

Studies of twins, by Rosenthal and many others, reflect similar findings. Identical twins, with identical genes, should develop the same genetic disease more often than non-identical twins. If this were true in even a small percentage of the cases, it would bolster the genetic thesis. A review of such studies, says Rosenthal, shows that this is the case approximately 50 percent of the time. Likewise, children of schizophrenic parents should have a higher incidence of the disorder, even when they are adopted and reared by non-schizophrenic parents. This also has been shown. "Thus," says Rosenthal, "all the major evidence points to the implication of genetic factors in this disorder, and this conclusion now finds common acceptance."

But common acceptance is not universal acceptance. For one thing, the disease has not been found in the chromosomes of a schizophrenic's parents.

Fifty years ago the thalidomide disaster would probably have been seen as genetic. Now it is known that the human fetus can learn or can be conditioned. So, schizophrenia could also be the result of prenatal trauma (especially during the last trimester), perinatal or immediate postnatal trauma. According to Virginia Johnson, Los Angeles clinical psychologist, nutritional deficiency, anoxia, microcirculatory collapse, drugs or even damage by forceps could be responsible for the disease. If this were the case, schizophrenia would be congenital but not genetic. Sarnof Mednick, working along these lines, studied the hospital records of 20 mentally ill children in Denmark. He found that 14 of them had suffered serious prenatal or birth complications. Findings based on such studies, and her own observations of perinatal effects prompt Johnson to argue that there is every reason to explore early conditional factors for schizophrenia in greater depth.

In fact, no specific genetic theory in regard to schizophrenia has been established and the results of these and thousands of studies have been conflicting and could be used to bolster either side of the hereditary-environment argument. Or, they could lead to a multivariable conclusion. Says Rosenthal, "Genetic influences are an important factor, perhaps a necessary one, in the development of schizophrenia, but environmental influences are also important." In other words, a person might have to have the genetic predisposition to develop the illness which could be precipitated by various kinds of stress.

Genetically minded scientists will continue to look for the schizophrenia chromosome and psychodynamically minded investigators will continue to try to elucidate the psychological and biodynamic factors responsible for the illness. But at least, research cannot be restricted solely to the gene theory.

C.   NEWS STORY QUESTIONS

1. What data does Rosenthal cite to support the notion that schizophrenia is genetic in origin? _____

2. What evidence does Johnson cite to support the notion that schizophrenia is congenital, not genetic in origin? _____

3. Can *both* Rosenthal and Johnson be right? _____

_____

Esther Greenwood, central character in *The Bell Jar*.

Therapies designed to correct or change abnormal thought or behavior patterns fall into three major categories— biological, cognitive or insight, and social/behavioral. In this chapter we will examine and evaluate examples of each type of therapy. But because almost all human behaviors have biological, cognitive, and social influences, we will see that the most successful forms of therapy are usually those that attempt to treat all aspects of the problem.

Therapy

13 chapter

When you have completed your study of this chapter, you should be able to:

- ► Compare, contrast, and evaluate various forms of biological, cognitive, and socio-behavioral therapies
- ► Trace the history of the mental health movement from the Greeks to the present
- ► Define and give an example of the "placebo effect"
- ► Summarize the essential processes of insight therapies, including psychoanalysis and client-centered therapy
- ► Outline the purposes and techniques of various group therapies
- ► Discuss environmental therapy and describe Meyer's holistic approach to psychotherapy

Client-centered therapy. A type of psychological treatment developed by humanist Carl Rogers, who believes that most therapy is directed toward solving the needs of the therapist rather than reaching the goals of the client. In client-centered therapy, the therapist is nondirective and positively accepting of the client. The therapist helps the client achieve self-understanding and personal growth.

Coma (KOH-muh). A deep sleep or state of unconsciousness, usually brought on by disease or injury.

Electroconvulsive therapy. A type of treatment first used by Cerletti and Bini in which electrical stimulation to the brain is used to induce convulsions. The belief is that shocking the brain may cause selective forgetting. There is little evidence that shock therapy (or ECT) is of much value to patients suffering from any disturbance other than massive depression.

Encounter group. A group therapy technique that involves bringing strangers together for brief periods of time and getting them to develop awareness and learn new communication skills.

Environmental (milieu) therapy (mill-YOU). The French word for "social environment" is *milieu*. Milieu therapy involves changing the patient's environment in order to induce changes in the patient indirectly.

Exorcism (EX-or-siz-em). A religious term meaning "to deliver a person or place from an evil spirit, usually by prayer or magic."

Free association. Sigmund Freud's method of getting people to remember the traumatic events of their childhoods. The patient usually lies on a couch and is encouraged to say whatever comes into his or her mind—that is, to freely give whatever mental associations occur to the patient.

Gestalt therapy (guess-TALT). The German word *gestalt* means "good form." According to the Gestalt pyschologists, we tend to perceive the world in wholes, which are the "best possible forms." Anyone whose perceptions are "incomplete" or "broken in bits" may well suffer from some form of mental illness.

Group therapies. Forms of treatment in which several patients are treated at a time—in a group rather than individually.

Heretic (HAIR-ruh-tick). Anyone opposed to the prevailing view or theory held by authority.

Historical approach. The belief that human problems can be understood (and cured) only when they are traced to their roots, usually in early childhood. Freud took an historical approach in developing psychoanalysis.

Holistic approach. From the word "whole." Holistic therapy is that which aims at treating the patient as a whole individual rather than as a collection of symptoms.

Humanistic therapy. A form of treatment in which the client is encouraged to direct and participate directly in his or her therapy. Helping people grow and experience and become what they wish to become, rather than imposing goals or values on them.

Insight therapy. Psychoanalysis—a form of insight therapy—was developed by Freud to give patients understanding, or insight, of what early experiences led them to think and feel and act as they presently do. Freud believed that once the patient had insight into his or her problems, the patient was usually capable of self-cure.

Insulin shock (INN-sue-linn). People with diabetes (die-uh-BEET-eez) don't secrete enough insulin to allow the body to digest sugar and usually must take daily injections of insulin. However, too large an injection of insulin will put the person into shock or cause convulsions. Insulin injections have been used as an alternative to electroconvulsive therapy, but typically have had little measurable success in helping mentally disturbed individuals.

Interpretation. In Freudian treatment, the analyst often helps the patient achieve insight by interpreting what the patient has said. Interpretation usually involves pointing out connections between events or feelings that the patient has not yet seen — that is, helping the patient achieve insight.

Lobotomy (low-BOTT-uh-mee). The Greek word *otomy* means "to cut," while the word *ectomy* means "to remove." A lobotomy is an operation in which nerve tracks running to the frontal lobes of the brain are cut, theoretically in order to prevent highly emotional messages from reaching the brain. A lobectomy is a similar operation, but involves removing portions of the frontal lobes.

Placebo (pluh-SEE-bo). From a Latin phrase meaning "to please." A harmless drug given for its psychological effect especially to satisfy the patient or to act as a control in an experiment. A sugar pill.

Psychoactive drugs. Drugs or chemicals that affect a person's moods, perceptions, thoughts, or behaviors. Most particularly, drugs that cause hallucinations or that badly affect a person's mental capacities.

Psychodrama. A theatrical therapy developed by J. L. Moreno. Some part of the patient's life is usually acted out on a stage, often by professional actors. The patient may play one of the roles, or may simply observe.

Psychosurgery. Removal of or deliberate damage to some part of the patient's brain in order to create a psychological cure. A lobotomy is a type of psychosurgery. The vast majority of mentally ill patients do not seem to have damaged brains and do not benefit from this sort of treatment.

Reserpine (ree-SIR-peen). From the word "serpent." So named because this powerful tranquilizer was first discovered in the snake root plant in India.

Role playing. Acting, or playing a part — either on stage or in real life. Role playing is often used in therapy to help patients act out (in a supportive environment) problems that they sometimes cannot readily face.

Sham. A trick or a hoax. A sham doctor is someone who knows little about medicine, but who pretends to have a medical degree.

Symptomatic (simm-toe-MATT-tick). A symptom is the visible evidence of a disease. Having a high fever and a yellow-colored skin is "symptomatic" of a disease called yellow fever.

Therapeutic community. A type of environmental or milieu therapy in which a small community is built with the deliberate purpose that everything in the community will help a certain type of patient get better.

Token economies. Artificial economies set up in an institution to help staff members and patients focus on what the patients are doing right, rather than focusing on what the patients are doing wrong. The patients are rewarded for positive (socially approved) behaviors by being given "tokens," which may be exchanged for various types of rewards.

Transactional analysis (trans-ACT-shun-al). Psychiatrist Eric Berne believed that people "play games" with each other without realizing what they are doing. Transactional analysis (or T.A., as it is often called) is Berne's therapeutic technique in which clients learn to analyze their interpersonal "games" or "transactions."

Transference (trans-FURR-ents). In psychoanalysis, the patient is encouraged to transfer to the analyst the emotions and attitudes the patient has concerning the "power figures" in the patient's life — chiefly his or her mother and father.

Trephining (TREFF-inn-ing). Using a special saw to cut open a patient's skull. In ancient times, trephines (or trepans) were saws used to cut holes in the skull in order to "let evil spirits escape from the brain."

INTRODUCTION: THE BELL JAR

Esther Greenwood needed help. Her college days were not as carefree and as fun-loving as she thought they would be. During the summer of her junior year, when Esther was 19 years old, things began to fall apart.

Esther had always been a model child and a good student. She was so good, in fact, that she won a sort of scholarship that awarded her one free month in New York City. Esther, along with a group of other young women from around the country, was invited to New York at the expense of a publishing company. During the days, the young women were supposed to learn something about the publishing business. During the evenings, they were wined and dined and escorted about the city. This was exactly what Esther wanted. The trip to New York fit her plans perfectly. She thought she wanted to be a writer, so the experience in publishing would be helpful. And she had never done much traveling, so the trip to the big city would be exciting.

After the trip to New York, Esther planned to go home to the suburbs of Boston and take a special writing course in summer school. Then, after her senior year and possibly graduate school, Esther planned to come back to New York as a writer. But something went wrong during the New York summer.

Esther had problems in several areas. *Physically,* she was strong and healthy; but she felt that she had two slight problems—she was somewhat flat-chested, and she was ashamed of her height. Esther was five feet ten, and whenever she was with short men, she would slouch over and try to make herself smaller. This behavior only gave her bad posture and made her feel worse about herself. During the New York summer Esther experienced another physical problem—a severe case of food poisoning.

Esther's *cognitive* or mental problems were somewhat more complex. She had worked hard for many years, but now she felt like dropping out. She met many successful people in New York, and because of their success she began to feel inadequate. She had always wanted to be a writer, but now she began to have some doubts about her future. Life, to Esther, was like a fig tree with many different juicy fruits to choose from. One fig, for instance, was a famous poet. Another was a teacher, and another was a rich magazine editor. One fig meant she would be a mother and a wife. Another meant she would travel around the world and have many interesting lovers. Another meant she would be an Olympic champion. Esther wanted all of the figs, but choosing one meant losing the rest. If she didn't make a decision, she would starve. But all summer long, making decisions became more and more difficult. As she sat there, unable to decide between the various figs, the fruits began to get rotten and fall to the ground.

Like many college students, Esther was having trouble deciding what she wanted to be. She wanted to be everything, and yet she didn't want to be anything.

Esther's *social* problems were complicated by the confused sexual attitudes of society. Esther's mother sent Esther an article from a popular magazine. The article, written by a woman, explained how men and women are born to be different both emotionally and sexually. Women, the article implied, must remain pure and virginal for their husbands. Men, on the other hand, are allowed to fool around a little bit and should not be expected to be sexually inexperienced on their wedding night. Esther's boyfriend had recently confessed to having had an affair, but he expected Esther to be pure. Esther was confused. She couldn't stand the idea of having to lead a single, pure life, while men were allowed to do whatever they wanted. To further confuse Esther's ideas about sex, marriage, and men, a man she was with as a blind date on her last night in New York tried to rape her.

Esther began to lose control of her thoughts, emotions, and behavior. By the time Esther got home she was physically weakened by the food poisoning. She was emotionally unable to react to anything. She was cognitively confused about herself and her future. The attempted rape had added to her sexual confusion and upset her ideas about herself as a female member of society. Then Esther's mother gave her the bad news. Esther had not been accepted for the special summer-school writing course. This was the last straw. As long as Esther had something to do, some activity to keep her busy, she might have kept going. But now, without summer school to keep her busy, things began to close in on her. She couldn't sleep at night, but she didn't want to get out of bed. She didn't want to wash or get dressed. She didn't want to do anything. She didn't want to live. Esther needed help. She felt as if she were suffocating inside a glass container.

A bell jar is a round, glass jar with a flat, closed top and an open bottom. When fragile objects are put on display, bell jars are sometimes put over them for protection. Bell jars are also used to keep the objects they are covering in a controlled atmosphere or environment. No stale air can get out and no fresh air can get in. Esther felt like she was suffocating under a bell jar—stewing in her own sour air. Esther could not make contact with the world through the glass of the bell jar, and what she saw of the world was distorted by the curved glass of the bell jar. Esther needed help.

The Bell Jar, a novel by Sylvia Plath, tells of Esther Greenwood's problems and of her successful search for help. It tells how the bell jar was finally lifted and how Esther found fresh air and a new life.

Esther's problems, looked at one at a time, were not too serious. Many people experience the same doubts and frustrations that troubled Esther. College students, for instance, sometimes have trouble deciding about the future and may feel confused about their sexual and social roles. But Esther's problems came to a head all at once, and she needed help. Other people, even those whose problems may be less numerous or less severe, may also need help from time to time. So where does one find help?

OLD AND NEW HELP

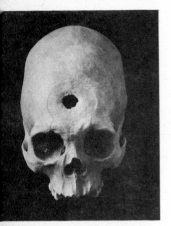

This is an ancient trephined skull. Primitive societies believed they could cure people of abnormal behavior by cutting holes in their skulls to allow the evil spirits to escape.

Theories about the causes of abnormal behavior usually dictate therapies for the treatment of such actions. In primitive societies, when people exhibited strange behavior, witch doctors were often called in to rid the troubled person of evil spirits. If prayers and magic spells didn't chase the evil spirits away, the witch doctor would sometimes cut a hole in the affected person's skull to let out the bad spirits. This primitive operation, now called **trephining,** sometimes worked. Some ancient skulls that show evidence of the trephining operation also show signs of healing around the edges of the hole. This evidence suggests that some patients may have survived such operations. Trephining probably would not have been the best solution to Esther's problems. But in certain parts of the world today, Esther could still get help or therapy from a witch doctor.

Hippocrates, the famous Greek doctor who lived about 2300 years ago, believed that mental problems and abnormal behavior were due to physical brain damage or to an imbalance of body chemicals. According to how he viewed each case, Hippocrates prescribed rest, a vegetarian diet, or bleeding.

The Romans, who conquered the Greeks, kept and expanded upon many of the Greek theories of abnormal behavior. The Romans believed abnormal behavior to be a sign of mental illness. They set up rest homes where mentally disturbed people could be treated. The rest homes provided pleasant surroundings

FIG. 13-1.
The Romans provided rest homes with pleasant surroundings for mentally disturbed people. This drawing shows such a temple, where patients slept on an open porch.

for disturbed people and kept such people busy with simple jobs and entertainments. Dieting, light exercise, massage, and a type of hypnotism were the therapies often prescribed.

The Greek and Roman therapies, except for blood letting, might have helped Esther. They would have kept her occupied and protected in pleasant surroundings while she had time to think about her problems. In some places around the world today, Esther might still get similar treatment.

When the Roman empire was overthrown, the results of centuries of education and training were lost. Greek and Roman theories and therapies were discarded, and devil or "bad spirit" theories became popular again in Europe during the Middle Ages.

At first, during medieval times, prayers, holy water, special oils, and holy objects were used in an attempt to force devils out of possessed people. Then **exorcism** became popular. A priest or exorcist would talk to the devil through the disturbed person and try to force the devil to leave the disturbed person alone. If that didn't work, stronger methods were tried. Beatings, starvation, immersion in

FIG. 13–2.
During medieval times, priests tried to treat disturbed people by exorcism or casting out the devils.

By the 1700s, the mentally ill were confined to asylums, where conditions were often deplorable.

hot water, and various forms of torture were used to make disturbed people so physically uncomfortable that no devil would want to stay in their bodies. If that treatment didn't work, the only thing left to do was get rid of the body altogether. Many disturbed people were condemned as witches and burned at the stake.

Life might have been made very uncomfortable for Esther if she had lived in Europe during the Middle Ages. Her strange behavior might have been reason enough for her to be tortured or burned. Even if she disagreed with religious or political authorities, she might have been declared a witch or labeled as crazy or a **heretic.** The few people who dared to speak up against the possession theories were quickly labeled as heretics and were sometimes subjected to torture and burning.

In the sixteenth and seventeenth centuries, as scientific investigation became popular, scientific theories and therapies began to appear. Disturbed people were not mistreated on purpose but were sent off to asylums where they could be cared for. But even in asylums, conditions were not always good. Disturbed people were sometimes chained down or kept in very small cells. The asylums attempted to offer care and protection, but little therapy was offered. The disturbed people were thought to be ill, but no one knew how to cure them. People often became worse, instead of better, in asylums.

In the nineteenth and twentieth centuries, with the rapid growth of medical science, physicians were put in charge of mental patients, and asylums became mental hospitals. In the past 100 years, various types of medical theories and therapies have been developed. As a result, hundreds of medicines and other forms of medical treatment have been used. Freud and his followers developed psychoanalytic theories and therapies. The humanists, behaviorists, and social psychologists developed their own types of theories and therapies. By the time Esther had her breakdown, there were (and still are) hundreds of therapies from which to choose.

Choosing a Therapy

Esther's breakdown was the result of a combination of physical, emotional, cognitive, and social problems. Her cognitive or psychological problems, however, were perhaps the most severe. She didn't understand herself well enough to know what she wanted to do with her life. She needed help, and many psychologists faced with a client such as Esther would probably have recommended some form of therapy that would give her *insight* into her mental difficulties. These psychologists would assume that at some point in her mental development, something had gone wrong. Perhaps Esther hadn't met and solved all the crises that Erikson, Freud, Piaget, and Kohlberg described (see Chapter 9). These psychologists would have suggested that she work through her early life until she found those experiences or conflicts that were still bothering her. Once she understood (or had insight into) the nature of her problems, she would then be able to do something about solving them.

Other psychologists—particularly the humanists—might focus more on Esther's present needs than on her past problems. By helping Esther determine who she presently was, these psychologists would hope to give her the intellectual and emotional tools to become whatever she wished.

Still other psychologists—the social learning theorists and behaviorists— would usually be more intrigued by Esther's future goals than by her past problems or present state of being. These psychologists would assume that most of Esther's present thoughts and actions were the result of improper or inappropriate learning. They would hope to help Esther set specific goals for the future, and then help her acquire the specific skills needed to reach these goals.

Yet another group of therapists—the medically oriented psychiatrists—would surely emphasize the biological aspects of her difficulties. These medical doctors might assume that Esther's mental problems were caused primarily by some malfunctioning of her brain or body. Therefore, the psychiatrists might prescribe medical treatment, such as specific pills, drugs, or even surgery of some kind.

Insight therapies are historical in approach—they deal with the past in order to cure present problems. Humanistic therapies, on the other hand, focus on the present in order to build a better future for the patient. Social learning therapists and behaviorists take an ahistorical approach. Because these psychologists emphasize the importance of learning and social environment, they believe it is not necessary for patients to "work through" their pasts. Rather, it is necessary for the patients to learn new and more effective ways of achieving future success. In marked contrast to these purely psychological approaches, the psychiatrists would assume that one cures the body in order to cure the mind.

Which type of therapy should Esther have chosen? There is no easy answer to this question. All types of therapy can achieve success with certain types of problems and with certain types of patients. But whenever a disturbed person such as Esther considers psychological or psychiatric treatment, there are certain specific questions the person should ask about the therapy:

1. Has the therapy been scientifically proven as a valid cure for the types of problems the patient has? In other words, does the therapy bring about the changes in thoughts and behaviors that the patient desires? When the desired changes *do* occur, are they long-lasting or do they tend to disappear when the treatment stops? In brief, what is the therapy's proven "cure rate" for a particular kind of psychological disturbance?

2. Has the therapy been proven a reliable form of treatment? Does the therapy work for all people who have similar problems, or is the therapy successful only in a few cases? Therapies often tend to be reliable only when applied to people of a particular background and education.

3. What are the side effects of the therapy? Some forms of therapy seem to be valid and reliable but bring with them undesirable side effects. Some medicines can calm highly excited people but might also make the excited people too passive to take part in normal activities. The potentially dangerous side effects of any form of therapy must be carefully weighed against the possible good results of that therapy.

4. What sort of changes does the therapy produce? Does a shy person want to become loud and obnoxious? Societies and therapists sometimes decide what is abnormal and may attempt to impose their views and values on people who do not agree with them. The particular changes that a therapy is designed to produce must always be considered before a therapy is selected.

In the United States today, there are hundreds of therapies and thousands of therapists—including friends, parents, teachers, counselors, and religious leaders. Each therapy and therapist has certain degrees of success and reliability. Each treatment has certain side effects. And each attempts to produce certain types of changes. The trick is to find a therapy and therapist that fit the problem, the person, and the circumstances. Therapies generally fall into three categories —biological, cognitive or psychological, and social.

BIOLOGICAL THERAPIES

Some mental problems are clearly related to biological difficulties. Alcoholism, drug addiction, senile psychosis, some types of mental retardation, strokes, tumors, and disease can all cause cognitive, emotional, and social difficulties (see

Chapter 12). When psychological problems are clearly related to physiological causes, then medical treatment is usually the therapy of choice. However, psychiatrists — almost all of whom have medical degrees — often assume that *all* mental disturbances must have a biological basis. Therefore, psychiatrists often prescribe medical treatment for problems even when there is no clear evidence that the patient's difficulties stem from some malfunctioning of the patient's body.

Insulin Shock Therapy

Esther was eventually sent to a mental hospital where, for several weeks, she received an injection every morning. Suddenly one day she passed out and went into a **coma,** or prolonged period of unconsciousness. Esther was experiencing an **insulin shock** coma. Insulin is a chemical that burns up the body's supply of glucose, or sugar. When people are given large amounts of insulin, as Esther was every morning, the sugar that fuels the brain is used up. Eventually, the lack of sugar slows the brain down, and a coma results. When Esther came out of her coma, she felt calm and relaxed.

The shock to the brain and the coma caused by insulin are sometimes useful in quieting anxious or excitable patients, but insulin shock therapy, which was popular 30 or 40 years ago, is rarely used today. The treatment was not found to be highly valid or reliable. Statistical studies showed that insulin therapy only worked with about half the people half the time. Even when it did work, the undesirable behaviors often returned after a short time. Insulin shock can also produce dangerous side effects. People who are not physically strong could be seriously injured by insulin shock.

Electroconvulsive Therapy

A Hungarian psychiatrist, Ladislaus J. Meduna, noticed in 1935 that very few people who suffer from epilepsy also suffer from schizophrenia. He decided that the convulsions produced by epilepsy might keep schizophrenia from appearing. Meduna decided to induce convulsions in patients diagnosed as schizophrenic. He produced the convulsions by injecting various drugs. The drugs, however, turned out to be very dangerous, and some of his patients died.

Later research showed that many schizophrenic patients do, in fact, suffer from epilepsy, so Meduna's original theory about convulsions and schizophrenia does not seem to be valid. Nonetheless, because *some* of Meduna's patients did show improvement, many doctors continued to study and to use convulsive therapy with mentally disturbed individuals.

In 1938, two researchers working in Italy — Ugo Cerletti and L. Bini — found that electricity was a less dangerous method of producing convulsions than was drugs. For a period of time thereafter, electroshock, or **electroconvulsive therapy (ECT)** became popular as a means of treating mental disorders.

There is little evidence that ECT has any positive effect on most types of men-

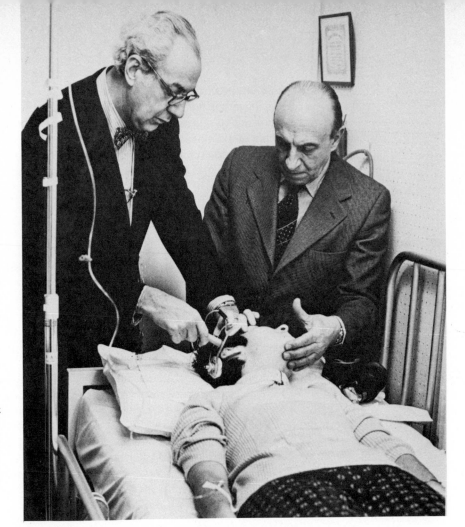

These doctors are administering electroconvulsive-shock therapy to a patient suffering severe depression. While this type of therapy has potentially dangerous side effects, it is often effective in cases of severe depression.

tal disturbances. However, it is often effective in bringing severely depressed patients out of their depressions for a brief period of time (see Seligman's research on learned helplessness and depression in Chapter 11). The possible side effects of shock therapy, however, have produced considerable controversy over its continued use even with depressed patients. Temporary and sometimes long-term loss of memory, and possible damage to the brain, heart, and lungs are reasons many scientists give for not using ECT except as a last resort.

Psychosurgery

One of the women Esther met at the mental hospital was Valerie, a large, healthy-looking girl who was very pleasant and calm, and who had scars on each side of her forehead. Valerie's scars and her calmness were the result of a **lobotomy.**

Since behavior is always affected by the functioning of the brain, surgeons occasionally have attempted to change behavior by physically changing the brain. Portions of the frontal lobes of the brain, for instance, are known to be involved in emotional and sometimes in aggressive behavior. In 1936, the Portuguese psychiatrist Egas Moniz operated on the frontal lobes of patients who were considered to be too emotional or too aggressive. In some patients, the desired result was produced. The destruction of areas of the frontal lobes sometimes produced a sort of perpetual calmness. In 1942, Walter Freeman introduced the frontal-lobe operation, or lobotomy, into the United States, where it became popular for a while.

After hundreds and even thousands of lobotomies had been performed, some researchers began to realize that lobotomy was not as effective or reliable as was first thought. Some patients were not helped at all. Some became worse and a few even died. Even in the patients who were helped, there was an unfortunate side effect. The parts of the brain destroyed by lobotomy are associated with aggression and emotional behavior, but the same areas of the brain are also associated with ambition, imagination, and other aspects of the personality that are usually highly valued in human individuality. The lobotomy not only destroyed the aggressiveness but also destroyed important positive aspects of the patient's personality. Valerie was no longer overly aggressive after her operation, but she had no will to lead a useful life. She wanted to do nothing but remain in the mental hospital. She would not have been able to function in society.

Lobotomy has another drawback. It is irreversible. Once a lobotomy has been performed, it cannot be undone. The brain tissue that is destroyed by lobotomy cannot be replaced and does not grow back. Some of the people who were operated on in the 1940s and 1950s were actually turned into human vegetables with no ambition and no will. These people never recovered from the side effects of a lobotomy.

Psychosurgery does, however, help certain types of patients. In 1976, a National Academy of Sciences committee studied all the available evidence on brain operations. The committee reported that surgery is occasionally a valid and reliable cure for some specific types of mental disorders. However, because of the dangers associated with psychosurgery—the already mentioned destruction of irreplaceable brain tissue and possible loss of healthy aspects of personality—psychosurgery is usually reserved only for the most severe cases.

Drug Therapy

Insulin therapy, ECT, and lobotomy were thought to be especially effective when they were able to calm down excited patients. These therapies, however, lost much of their popularity in the 1950s, when less drastic methods of controlling and changing behavior were found. Certain **psychoactive drugs** were discovered that seemed to have success in changing behavior. Drug therapy became and remains today one of the most widely used forms of therapy for mental disorders.

Two types of drugs have been found to be especially effective in the treatment of people with mental problems—tranquilizers and energizers. Tranquil-

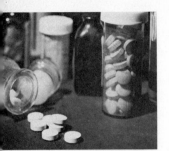

Certain drugs have been successful in controlling abnormal or dangerous behavior and have helped many people avoid hospitalization.

izers are drugs that help make highly agitated or excited people more tranquil or calm. Energizers help make depressed people more energetic or active, both physically and cognitively. By controlling what might be dangerous or abnormal behavior, drugs have helped many people avoid hospitalization or control their behavior well enough to get out of hospitals.

There are many different types of tranquilizers, energizers, and other drugs that combine the effects of both tranquilizers and energizers. Some of the drugs are thought to work by correcting a chemical imbalance in your body. Other drugs seem to work by changing a person's behavior long enough for that person to learn new and more acceptable behaviors. In the case of energizers, it is felt that they might give depressed people enough energy to think about their problems or to take part in some form of cognitive or social therapy.

Drugs, unlike lobotomy, are usually reversible. If one drug doesn't work or if it produces undesirable side effects, it can be withdrawn and another drug can be used. But psychoactive drugs, the drugs used in psychotherapy, can be dangerous and are almost always given only under a physician's directions. For each person, a drug must be carefully selected. The person's reaction to the drug must be watched. If there are dangerous or undesirable side effects, the drug can be changed or the dosage can be altered.

Psychoactive drugs sometimes present another problem. The drugs can hide the symptoms of a problem so well that a more effective and possibly necessary therapy is not searched for. Highly emotional behavior due to a brain tumor, for instance, can sometimes be controlled by psychoactive drugs. The symptoms of the problem might go away, but the tumor remains. In such cases, a dangerous tumor might go undetected and untreated. By causing temporary changes in a patient's behavior, psychoactive drugs might also hide cognitive or social problems that might need to be treated.

The Placebo Effect

St. Elizabeth's Hospital in Washington, D.C., is one of the largest government facilities for the treatment of people with mental disorders. Werner Mendel, Professor of Psychiatry at the University of Southern California School of Medicine, received some of his psychiatric training at St. Elizabeth's. While there, he was put in charge of a ward of Spanish-speaking people who were considered to be hostile and aggressive. Some of the patients were even considered to be homicidal and had to be kept in straitjackets. The patients seemed so dangerous that Mendel usually took two large attendants along as bodyguards whenever he visited the ward. The fact that Mendel couldn't speak Spanish only tended to make matters worse.

In 1954, a tranquilizer called **reserpine** was just being introduced into psychiatric use in the United States. The staff of St. Elizabeth's had heard good reports about the drug and decided to test it on some of their patients. A double-blind experiment was set up (see Chapter 1). The patients on certain wards were selected to receive the drug, while patients on other wards received a **placebo,** or fake drug. The experiment was *double-blind* because neither the patients nor their doctors knew who received the real drug and who received the placebo. Once the experiment was completed and the reactions of all the patients observed, the doctors checked to see who had the real drug and who had the placebo. In this way, the effects of the drug are compared to the effects of taking something that only looks like a drug. Any changes in behavior experienced by patients taking the drug and not by the patients taking the placebo were credited to the drug.

Mendel asked that the violent patients on his ward be included in the experiment. Almost as soon as the experiment began, he noticed changes in his patients. He was sure that his ward was one of the wards selected to receive the reserpine instead of the placebo. Mendel's patients became so tranquil that he no longer needed his bodyguards. Most of the patients in straitjackets no longer needed to be restrained.

But Mendel was wrong in assuming that simply because his patients took pills and got much better, they must have received reserpine. In fact, his patients were all in the control group that received sugar pills. When he found out the truth, Mendel did some serious thinking about his own attitudes and behaviors. If his patients hadn't received the reserpine, what could have caused the dramatic change in the way the patients acted? Perhaps, thought Mendel, his *expectations* about the patients had changed. When they began taking the pills, Mendel thought the patients would become more peaceful, so he started treating them as if they were more peaceful. The patients, in turn, met his expectations and *did* become more calm. It appeared to Mendel that his patients improved because of the way he responded to them, not because their bodies were changed by a drug.

Some years later, when Mendel was in charge of a large mental hospital on the West Coast, he found that 80 percent of the patients were put on drugs as soon as they were admitted to the hospital. Because Mendel believed that his doctors were often prescribing drugs because they thought it was expected of them, Mendel issued orders forbidding the doctors to give drugs to any patient who had not been in the hospital for at least 12 hours. The medication rate immediately dropped to less than 20 percent, and more patients showed signs of improvement than ever before.

Do Placebos Work?

Drug therapy has produced great changes in the treatment of mentally disturbed people, but the placebo effect must always be taken into account. In 1955, H. K. Beecher reported in the Journal of the American Medical Association on an experiment conducted with placebos. More than 1000 patients with a variety of problems were given placebos when they thought they were getting medicine. One third of the patients reported that they were getting better. Some of the patients even reported that the medication (which they did not realize was fake) was making them sick. So placebos can make some people sick, can have no effect on others, or make still other people well.

Placebos don't always have to be sugar pills. Injections of harmless substances or even "useless" or **sham** surgery might do the trick. One of the experiments that forced scientists to re-evaluate the effects of lobotomies involved a type of placebo or sham operation. Tulane psychiatrist R. G. Heath divided a group of severely disturbed mental patients into two groups. The first group received lobotomies; the second, or control group, received a sham operation in which Heath didn't damage even a single nerve-cell. Since the patients' wounds looked the same no matter which group they were in, the staff members could not tell which patient had received which type of operation. Heath then insisted that all patients be given the best possible *psychological* care once they had recovered from the physical effect of the surgery. In fact, almost all of the patients showed signs of recovery, and many were able to return to their homes. Heath concluded that it was the expectations of the staff members and of the patients—coupled with the fine psychological care—that brought about the improvement in the patients. The surgery itself seemed neither to help nor to hinder the patients in any provable way.

From all of these studies, we may conclude that *no matter what the therapy is,* the chances for success seem better when both the therapist and the patient feel confident that the treatment will work.

COGNITIVE OR INSIGHT THERAPY

When Esther began to have problems in New York, the first thing she did was take a hot bath and try to forget about her problems. That didn't work so she tried to get her mind off her problems by becoming more interested in both work and play. Her problems still didn't go away, so she began to look for someone to talk to. Her friends, however, were too interested in their own problems to take time to try to understand Esther's situation. And Esther had only known the other girls in New York for a few weeks, so she didn't really want to tell them all of her personal problems. Next, Esther turned to the woman she was working for at the publishing company. This woman seemed to understand some of Esther's worries but did not take them too seriously. She just suggested more work.

When Esther got home, she tried to talk to her mother. But Esther's mother was even less helpful. She just suggested shorthand lessons—something Esther knew she didn't want to do. Eventually, Esther wound up talking to a psychiatrist.

Since talking about a problem with someone often makes the problem easier for us to accept and handle, many of us turn to close friends and members of our families when we are troubled. Or if we are too embarrassed to discuss a personal problem with someone close to us, we may turn to strangers—including therapists—for help. The person who listens may give us advice, sympathy, or may simply reflect our thoughts and feelings back to us so that we can see ourselves more clearly. What we are usually hoping for when we talk to people about our difficulties is some intellectual or emotional insight into what is troubling us. For that reason, "talk therapy" is often called **insight therapy.**

Insight therapy has probably been around since humans first chatted with each other. Sigmund Freud, however, was one of the first to attempt an explanation of how insight or talk therapy works. Freud made his own form of insight therapy—*psychoanalysis*—into an accepted form of treatment for cognitive or psychological disturbances. Freud suggested that most mental and emotional disturbances are the result of unconscious conflicts that produce anxieties, fears, and abnormal behavior patterns. Biological therapies—shock, surgery, drugs— might change some behaviors, Freud suggested, but do not get at the real cause of the problem. For this reason, psychoanalysis is an attempt to help the person understand unconscious conflicts that are rooted deep within the individual's personality. Freud believed that through psychological analysis, a troubled person might gain an understanding or acceptance of how the problem began. Freud further believed that once the individual had achieved insight into the problem, the **symptomatic** or abnormal behaviors would gradually disappear.

Psychoanalytic Therapy

Psychoanalysis is a very personal and subjective form of therapy that varies from patient to patient and from therapist to therapist. The course of most psychoanalytic therapies, however, follows several basic steps. The patient is encouraged to build up a strong emotional relationship with the analyst. Once confidence and trust are established, the patient is encouraged to talk freely about past problems, feelings, emotions, and experiences. The analyst then attempts to interpret the experiences (including dreams) and to help the patient figure out what past cognitive or developmental problems may be causing the present distress.

A psychoanalyst encourages his patient to make free associations and talk about anything that comes to mind.

Psychoanalytic therapy may take place in clinics, mental hospitals, or in private offices. In most cases, the treatment setting is a private place where the patient feels secure, comfortable, and free to express all thoughts and emotions. If a couch is used, the therapist generally sits behind the patient in a position from which the patient's facial expressions and bodily reactions can be observed. In many cases, however, patient and analyst sit and face each other as they talk.

Transference

The first step in analysis is usually what is known as **transference.** The patient is encouraged to engage in **free association** — that is, to talk about anything that comes to mind. But because psychoanalysis emphasizes the past, patients are sometimes encouraged to talk out or make mental associations about memories from childhood. The patient's feelings about parents and other important individuals or experiences from childhood are thought to be especially important. The transference takes place when the patient begins to project or *transfer* these feelings about people from the patient's past onto the analyst.

Transference is thought to be an important step in analysis because it helps to release unconscious emotional feelings. Once such feelings are out in the open, the patient can examine them. Irrational fears, hatreds, feelings of guilt, and associated behaviors can sometimes be understood and coped with once the cause for such feelings is discovered and discussed during analysis.

Interpretation

The first job of a psychoanalyst is to get a patient to talk. Once the person begins to talk about thoughts, feelings, dreams, and behaviors, the analyst must attempt to interpret the talk in terms of psychoanalytic theory. Because the unconscious is thought to be the home of many cognitive problems, the analyst must search the patient's conscious talk for clues to the unconscious. Slips of the tongue, some of the apparently meaningless talk that comes out during free association, and the content of dreams and fantasies often contain clues to the unconscious. Some psychoanalysts also use hypnosis and special drugs to get people to unlock unconscious thoughts. As the clues to the unconscious are assembled, the therapist attempts to interpret the sometimes symbolic clues and to discover rational explanations of the past that will explain the person's present irrational thoughts and behaviors.

Finding the clues and making the right interpretations is not easy, and that is why psychoanalysts need many years of training. Ninety percent of the psychoanalysts in the United States are psychiatrists. They have gone through college and medical school and many have gone through four years of psychiatric training; they all have been analyzed themselves. The other 10 percent of the psychoanalysts are clinical psychologists. They usually earn a Ph.D. in clinical psychology, and then study at a psychoanalytic institute and are analyzed.

Psychoanalysis usually takes from two to five years, although some patients may remain in analysis for 20 years or more. Fifty-minute sessions with the therapist are held as often as five times a week. The treatment is very expensive, and a full analysis may cost $30,000 or more.

Evaluating Psychoanalysis

Is psychoanalysis a valid and reliable therapy? The answer to that question depends on one's definition of valid and reliable. As psychologists Seymour Fisher and Roger Greenberg point out in their book *The Scientific Credibility of Freud's Theories and Therapy*, there is precious little scientific evidence that psychoanalysis is better than any other form of treatment. They also note that long treatment is no better than short treatment. However, it is true that analysis seems to be successful with some of the people some of the time. The patients who seem to have the most success in analysis are usually between 15 and 50 years of age, are intelligent enough to understand their problems and the process of analysis, want to solve their problems, and are willing to cooperate with the therapist. Analysis is more successful in treating people with neurotic problems than in treating people with psychotic problems. People who have lost all touch with reality, for instance, usually can't form the transference relationship, and often can't make sense of what the therapist is saying about their unconscious problems.

Fisher and Greenberg note that Freud was exceptionally accurate in his descriptions of certain personality types and problems — the oral person, for instance, does seem to have an unusual need to find security through dependence on others. And the so-called anal characters are often mean, compulsive, and stubborn. Unfortunately, as Fisher and Greenberg point out, there is little evidence that these personality types are associated with developmental problems that occurred during the oral and anal stages of development. Furthermore, there are no hard data supporting Freud's basic notion that once the patient gains insight into the cause of the problem, the patient's present abnormal behaviors will simply "fade away." In fact, the analyst's own insights, interpretations, and behaviors toward the patient are much more responsible for "cures" than are the patient's understanding of early developmental difficulties.

Last, but surely not least, Fisher and Greenberg state that Freudian theory is much more applicable to men than it is to women. Freud believed that all women suffer from an innate sense of inferiority because they do not possess male sex organs. This feeling of inferiority supposedly makes it difficult for women to develop a sense of sexual identify and makes them uncomfortable with their bodies. In fact, as Fisher and Greenberg point out, "Consistent evidence suggests that the female exceeds the male in general body awareness, sense of body security, adaptability to changes in body sensations, and appearance."

Fisher and Greenberg criticize Freud strongly for trying to impose his own masculine values on women. But this type of criticism can often be leveled against any type of talk or insight therapy. Esther and her mother, for instance, disagreed about the value of shorthand. Esther was able to reject her mother's values, but Esther might not have been able to reject as easily the views of a psychoanalyst who thought that all women should learn shorthand. So psychoanalysis with a male analyst who tried to impose his masculine values on Esther might not have been the most suitable form of treatment for her.

Humanistic Therapy

Some psychoanalysts play a very active and direct role in therapy. They give directions, advice, guidance, and suggestions. Humanistic therapies emphasize the client's conscious awareness of the present situation and of future goals rather than unconscious problems or conflicts from the past. Humanistic therapists, therefore, try in a nondirective manner to help clients become aware of what they are and of how other people see them. Once clients have stated their goals, humanistic therapists attempt to give their clients objective feedback on the road to self-actualization.

Client-centered Therapy

One of the most popular of the humanistic therapies was developed by Carl Rogers. It is called Rogerian or **client-centered therapy.** According to Rogers, psychotherapy should be centered around the goals and needs of the client rather than on what the therapist believes should be the goals of the client.

Each person or client, according to the humanists, has a unique personality with unique problems, abilities, and goals. Therefore, clients rather than therapists must set the speed and direction of the therapy, and the clients themselves must decide which thoughts or behaviors should be changed. The therapist helps clients through this process by providing what is called "unconditional positive regard." The therapist establishes a permissive atmosphere in which clients feel free to do or say whatever they please. The unconditional positive attitude of the therapist is supposed to help clients open up to say what they really feel and think.

Once clients begin to open up, the therapist attempts to help them understand themselves by reflecting or mirroring the clients' behavior. Therapists provide this "mirror" feedback by repeating in an understanding manner the major points of whatever the clients are saying. With the therapist's reflection and clarification, clients should begin to understand themselves by seeing how they appear to other people. Clients who can see themselves clearly can begin to see what changes might be necessary. Once changes are made, clients can reflect their new images off the therapist. When clients begin to like what they see, they no longer need the reflection and can end the therapy to become independent or fully functional.

Few therapists are pure Freudians or pure Rogerians. Most use some of each technique. Some clients, for instance, need a more directive approach, while others are more comfortable in a nondirective situation. Many therapists, therefore, attempt to mold the therapy to fit the needs of the client.

In humanistic therapy, the therapist establishes a permissive atmosphere in which clients feel free to express any emotion.

Are Insight Therapies Successful?

"Neurotics get better regardless of treatment," says British psychologist H. J. Eysenck in *Psychology Is About People* (The Library Press, 1972). Eysenck believes that psychoanalysts have not proved that they can help anyone. As evidence, Eysenck points to studies showing that people who seem to have neurotic problems often get rid of their problems with no help. In one study of 500 people who had neurotic problems so severe that they could not work, two out of every three recovered within two years. These people were receiving pensions so they were not really pressed to go back to work. After five years, almost 90 percent of the patients appeared to be completely recovered. All of these people saw their family physicians and had their physical problems treated, but they received no specific form of psychotherapy.

More recent studies—conducted in the United States by psychoanalysts—suggest that Eysenck's results may not be entirely applicable to patients in the United States. Psychiatrist R. Bruce Sloane and his associates at the Temple University School of Medicine in Philadelphia compared the results of giving patients three types of treatment—insight therapy, behavioral therapy, and no therapy at all. Sloane and his group report that insight and behavioral therapy both achieved significant results in terms of long-lasting personality changes, but that behavioral therapy was better at helping people who had specific problems involving their work or getting along with others. Many of the individuals in the no-treatment control group showed objective signs of getting better as well. But the important point about these patients is that they did not *perceive* themselves as having improved until they were given therapy after the study had ended. If the no-treatment patients were dissatisfied with their own progress, can we legitimately say (as Eysenck does) that they had "gotten rid of their problems with no help?"

Insight therapies deal with subjective or internal changes in perceptions, emotions, attitudes, and internal processes that simply cannot be measured objectively. Therefore, it is almost impossible to prove scientifically that insight or cognitive therapies actually "work."

Psychoanalysts and their clients, however, often do report that significant changes take place in the client's basic personality patterns during therapy. Sloane and his colleagues report about an 80 percent success rate in their study for both insight therapy and behavioral therapy patients. Clients who have gone through humanistic therapies report similar success rates. However, the measure of success in most cases involves the feelings and insights that the patients experience during treatment. If we demand more objective or scientific measures of success, then we are forced to conclude that insight or cognitive therapies are not as successful as they once were thought to be.

SOCIAL/BEHAVIORAL THERAPIES

After closely examining her own life situation, Esther decided that she had a cognitive problem and needed some insights. She sought insight therapy and afterward believed that she had achieved successful changes in her personality. But if she had suffered from what were clearly social rather than cognitive difficulties, she might have been better off if she had sought some form of social or behavioral therapy. Abnormal emotions or behavior patterns that, at first, appear to be the result of cognitive problems may actually turn out to be due to poor learning caused by a bad social environment. The stresses of the world around us—the weather, a nagging or hostile family, a bad work situation, anxieties induced by thoughtless teachers, and so forth—may become more than we can cope with and hence bring on abnormal thoughts and actions. In fact, almost every abnormal behavior is strongly influenced by the world the person grew up in or is presently living in. Social therapies have been designed to change such thoughts and behaviors. Therapies that concentrate on changing the way an individual responds to society are called **group therapies.** Treatment that concentrates on changing the way society responds to an individual is called environmental or milieu therapy.

Group Therapy

Group therapy is any form of therapy that attempts to treat two or more individuals at the same time. Like talk therapy, group therapy has been around for centuries. Religious and political leaders have often attempted to change the thoughts and behaviors of their followers. Only in the past century, however, has group therapy become an accepted form of psychotherapy. In 1905, a Boston physician, J. H. Pratt, brought together a group of patients suffering from tuberculosis. He gave the patients lectures on good health practices and attempted to help them overcome their feelings of discouragement. But the patients gained in other ways. The group meetings provided friendship and emotional support for patients who found out that they were not alone in their suffering.

With the success of Pratt's treatment, therapists began to use the group approach to treat people with other problems. Neurotic behavior, alcoholism, and sexual problems were discussed in group sessions. Therapists soon began to see that group therapy might be a good way to provide treatment for more people than could be helped by individual therapy. During World War II, when many people were having problems and there weren't enough individual therapists to go around, group therapy became one of the most popular forms of treatment. At present there are almost as many types of group therapy as there are human problems to be treated.

Traditional Group Therapy

The earliest form of group therapy, similar to that used by Pratt, is often used in institutions, clinics, and hospitals. This traditional form of group therapy is usually highly structured. That is, group sessions or meetings follow a set pattern or

Group therapy is often used to treat people with similar problems. This photo shows a group therapy session at a drug rehabilitation center.

structure in which a professional group leader actively guides the session like a teacher in a classroom. The therapist usually leads a group discussion after lectures, printed materials, or films have been presented on the topic to be discussed. The materials selected are supposed to help the group members begin to examine their problems. During the discussion that follows, the therapist and members of the group discuss individual problems. A film on alcoholism might be shown to a group of alcoholics. The discussion following the film might focus on individual or group reaction to the film. This directive form of group therapy is thought to be especially effective with severely disturbed people who have trouble understanding and expressing their own problems. In situations where group members are less disturbed, a less directive approach is sometimes used. The members of the group might decide what problems will be discussed. The therapist then helps lead the discussion along the line chosen by the group.

Because human problems are so complex and because therapists and groups are always different, group therapy may take many forms. But, according to psychologist J. D. Frank, group therapies are usually based on the principle "that intimate sharing of feelings, ideas, experiences in an atmosphere of mutual respect and understanding enhances self-respect, deepens self-understanding, and helps the person live with others."

Psychodrama

Most talking therapies rely on free association to get patients to reveal their problems. But there is more to life (and problems) than just talking. In 1910, J. L. Moreno began using a type of group therapy that encourages patients to act out troublesome situations. The therapy, called **psychodrama,** consists of **role-playing.** The patient or the therapist will set up a particular situation. The patient and other members of the group then play the necessary roles in the drama. When the members of the group really get into the role-playing, troublesome emotions often come into the open and tension is often released. In psychodrama, patients are free to say and do things that they want to do but might be afraid of doing in a real-life situation. Many behavior patterns are displayed that might not come out during free association, and patients are often able to see themselves and their problems more clearly. Also role reversals help patients view situations more objectively.

Transactional Analysis

"All the world's a stage," said Shakespeare, and psychiatrist Eric Berne believes that people go through life playing parts. This role-playing, says Berne, can often be confusing and can lead to troublesome transactions between people. Berne developed a type of group therapy that attempts to analyze the transactions that go on between people. The therapy, called **transactional analysis** or T.A., is supposed to help make people more aware of their social interactions.

The role-playing that goes on between people and the "games people play" not only lead to confusion but can be psychologically destructive, says Berne. He has found that people play three typical roles—parent, child, and adult.

Someone playing the parent role tends to treat other adults as children. Adults who are treated as children may then take up the child role and react in a childish manner. This type of transaction, says Berne, is often the cause of misunderstandings in marriages, in social situations, and at work.

During T.A. group sessions, the therapist watches members of the group interact freely. The roles and the games that people play with each other are then analyzed, and unconscious reasons for the games are sometimes found. A person playing the child role, for instance, may feel insecure in any other role. As unconscious and conscious problems are worked out through T.A., patients are supposed to learn to rely less on roles and games and learn to treat each other as adults.

Gestalt Therapy

The German word for "whole" is **gestalt.** Frederick (Fritz) Perls developed a type of therapy based on the theory that troubled people are not whole. That is, they are not in touch with all of their thoughts and feelings. People who exhibit neurotic symptoms, for instance, may be repressing or denying certain troublesome thoughts or feelings. Gestalt therapy was designed to help troubled people get in touch with and understand all of their thoughts and behaviors, including dreams, emotions, tone of voice, and gestures. In a Gestalt group session people may be asked to talk about themselves and to describe every emotion and behavior. They may be asked to act out dreams or to look at certain behaviors and bodily sensations that are often ignored. When people are "whole" they are supposed to be able to accept every situation and be flexible enough to accept and understand every aspect of every social or personal situation.

Encounter Groups

Groups provide settings in which people can meet or encounter each other on physical, cognitive, and social levels. Gestalt psychologist Kurt Lewin found that group discussions can help to change people's attitudes toward themselves and each other — especially if the group meeting helps people to become sensitive to the feelings and problems of other members of the group. In a type of group therapy called sensitivity training or T-group training, people are taught to understand and become sensitive to their own feelings as well as to the feelings of other members of the group.

Sensitivity training therapy began more than 20 years ago at the National Training Laboratory in Bethel, Maine. Since then, sensitivity training and encounter groups have become one of the most popular forms of therapy in the United States. Hundreds of different types of encounter groups have received wide publicity. There are leaderless groups and closely controlled groups, directive and nondirective groups. There are groups that meet on a regular basis, and marathon groups that meet only once for 24, 36, or even 48 nonstop hours. There are outdoor meetings, indoor meetings, and meetings in heated swimming pools. There are fully clothed encounter groups and nude encounter groups that are supposed to help people really get to know and become sensitive to each other. Groups of friends, groups of enemies, groups of strangers, and groups of people with similar problems may encounter and attempt to understand each other better.

The goals of an encounter group usually depend on the specific problems of the group. In most cases, however, attempts are made to achieve the goals through complete honesty, openness, and frankness. Various techniques are used to get encounters started and to encourage frank communication.

Encounter groups usually consist of from 6 to 12 people. One or more group leaders may take part in the encounter or may just watch over the group and try to provide an atmosphere of freedom, security, and emotional or psychological safety so that group interactions are frank but not destructive.

Evaluating Group Therapy

Is group therapy a valid and reliable form of therapy? Does group therapy have undesirable side effects? Does group therapy produce the changes that it is supposed to produce? Many group leaders and people who have had beneficial experiences in group therapy say yes. In some cases group therapy does seem to help people learn to understand each other and learn to interact in a trusting and truthful manner. Group therapy is supposed to help people continue this type of behavior outside of the group. Some people report, however, that group therapy produces no real or long-lasting changes. Some experts even suggest that group therapy can be harmful to certain people.

Morton A. Lieberman, Irvin D. Yalom, and Matthew B. Miles have attempted to answer in a scientific manner some of the questions about group therapy. In their book *Encounter Groups: First Facts* (1973) Lieberman, Yalom, and Miles describe a study conducted with 206 Stanford University student volunteers who wanted to take part in group therapy. The students were evaluated before the experiment began, and then they were assigned to one of 17 different groups. Traditional psychoanalytic groups, psychodrama, T.A., T-groups, and Gestalt therapy were among the types of group therapies the students were assigned to. In addition to the students who took part in group therapy, 69 students who applied but who could not be fitted in were used as untreated control subjects.

The subjects were re-evaluated one or two weeks after group therapy began and again six to eight months later. The students reported whatever changes the therapy might have caused in their own thoughts and behaviors and the changes they noticed in other members of the groups they were in. Group leaders and close friends of the students also reported the changes they saw. Objective measures of symptom removal or measurable changes in behavior were reported as well as subjectively felt changes.

The results of the experiment suggest that, when scientifically evaluated, group therapy is not particularly valid or reliable. Immediately after the group therapy, 65 percent of the students reported positive changes. Six months later, only one third of the students showed or reported any positive changes. Another one third showed and reported no changes at all. The final one third had negative reactions to group therapy. In fact, 8 percent of the students in group therapy were listed as "casualties." They showed signs of serious psychological difficulties that were most probably the result of the group experience. In the control group that had no therapy, 77 percent of the students reported no change or some positive change. Only 23 percent reported negative changes, and there were no "casualties." Of the various types of group therapies tested, there seemed to be little difference in effectiveness.

It appears that group therapy is neither completely valid nor reliable. It does not work for all of the people all of the time, and any changes that may be produced are not always long-lasting. In addition, group therapy presents the possibility of dangerous side effects. Some emotionally disturbed people may find that their problems are made worse by the group experience. Lieberman, Yalom, and Miles conclude that group therapy does offer a way for humans to explore and express themselves, but that group therapy is not the solution for all disturbed people or for all problems.

Environmental Therapy

When the bell jar came down on Esther Greenwood's life, everything changed. Her cognitive problems began to interfere with all aspects of her life, including her social life. Esther, looking through the curved glass of the bell jar, could not see her environment clearly and, therefore, could not relate effectively to the people around her. Esther had problems with her mother, her friends, strangers, and even with the various therapists she eventually had to see.

One of the easiest ways to change the way people react to their environment is to change the environment. Overworked or depressed people may try to "get away from it all" by taking a walk or going on a vacation. If the problems don't go away, the troubled person might have to escape by changing jobs, changing schools or friends, or by leaving home. Even the ancient Romans took disturbed people out of one environment and put them into the healthier milieu of a special sanitorium. And today, one type of environmental therapy consists of taking disturbed people out of society and putting them into mental hospitals.

When Esther's cognitive problems became too serious for her to manage by herself, she sought help. Unsuccessfully she tried a nondirective psychoanalyst, shock therapy, and a dreary, overcrowded mental institution. Finally with assistance from a wealthy friend, Esther was moved to what is sometimes called a **therapeutic community.**

Social and behavioral theories suggest that mental disturbances are often the result of unhealthy living conditions. The best form of therapy, therefore, is to put the disturbed patient into an environment or therapeutic community that is especially designed to promote mental health. In a therapeutic community everything that goes on, 24 hours a day, is supposed to be part of the treatment. Therefore, everything—including the paint on the walls, the type of meals, the social interactions, and the attitudes of the staff members—is designed to help patients develop new thoughts, behaviors, and social reactions. Meanwhile, other physical, psychological, and social therapies may be used whenever they seem to be called for.

At the therapeutic community to which Esther was sent, there were several dormitorylike buildings. Each was set aside for certain types of patients, depending on the severity of their problem. As patients showed signs of improvement they were moved up to the next building. In each succeeding building patients were allowed more privileges, privacy, and freedom. The privileges included social events, music, and art therapy, private rooms, and — in the highest or best building — passes that allowed patients to go on short trips outside of the institution. Esther, like most of the other patients, worked to get better and move into the best building. From there, the next step was into the outside world and back into society. Getting patients back into society should be the ultimate goal of any form of environmental or institutional therapy.

Token Economies

Not all institutions have different buildings into which patients can be transferred as they become better. All institutions do, however, have privileges that can be given to patients. In recent years, a type of therapy based on earnings privileges has been put to work in many institutions. In order to encourage patients to change their behavior patterns, **token economies** have been set up. In a token economy, every approved or healthy behavior is rewarded with a sign of approval such as a token. Unhealthy or inappropriate behaviors are not rewarded and are usually ignored. The patients cash in the tokens to purchase whatever privileges they prefer. Token economies are designed to make patients feel they are responsible for their own improvement, and to give patients instantaneous feedback whenever they show signs of getting better. Token economies also prepare patients for reentry into society, where they will have to work to earn a living just as they work to earn tokens in the institution.

Token economies and other behavioral therapies have been proven to be very effective with specific types of disturbances. For instance, token economies seem to be especially good for depressed, withdrawn, and antisocial patients and for teaching simple social skills and preventing the loss of interest in life that many people seem to suffer when they are confined to an institution.

Evaluating Environmental Therapies

Behavioral and environmental therapies, like all treatments, are not entirely valid or reliable. Behavioral therapies seem to be highly effective with many types of behaviors, but they do not work for all of the people all of the time. Environmental therapy, however, does have the advantage of being a much more humane form of treatment than just locking up disturbed people.

The undesirable side effects of most behavioral therapies are minimal. In most cases, patients are even allowed to choose not to take part in the therapy. They don't have to work for the tokens, and the institution will still provide whatever care and other forms of therapy seem to be called for.

Does behavioral therapy really bring about the desired changes? The

At Walter Reed Army Medical Center a token economy program was devised initially for soldiers with severe personality disorders and later was extended to the treatment of schizophrenics and drug addicts. On the left is shown a general planning meeting where soldiers earn points for attendance and additional points for brief, relevant speech. The soldier on the right is "spending" some of the points he has earned to play pool.

problem of who is to decide what is normal is not so serious in behavioral therapy because the patient is usually allowed to decide exactly which behaviors are to be changed. But even when the desired changes are brought about, there is some argument as to the real effectiveness of behavior therapy. Some therapists claim, for instance, that changing a particular behavior does not really change the underlying or unconscious cause of that behavior.

Some therapists say that another symptom or disturbing behavior may take the place of the behavior that has been changed if the problem causing the behavior is not solved. Someone who uses behavior therapy to learn to give up cigarettes, for instance, might begin to eat or drink too much. A Freudian therapist may say that the underlying problem causing the oral behavior has not been solved. Therefore, another oral symptom replaced the one that was eliminated.

Such arguments may be valid, but it is difficult to measure unconscious causes or to tell when unconscious problems have been solved. The only thing that can be objectively measured is the outward behavior, and very few therapists have reported cases of symptoms replacing each other. In fact, just the opposite usually occurs. R. Bruce Sloane and his group at Temple University report that when one type of symptomatic behavior improved in their patients, many other types of related problems also began to clear up.

COMPLETE THERAPY

Not too many years ago, psychotherapy was thought to be something reserved for "crazy" people. People were looked down upon if they had to seek help from an analyst or if they had to spend some time in a mental institution. Many people were (and some still are) ashamed to admit that they or a member of their family needed psychiatric help. Retarded children were often sent off to homes or kept hidden. Emotional and personality problems were sometimes ignored. People with social problems were often sent to prison. If Esther had been ashamed to seek help, she might have eventually succeeded in her attempts to commit suicide. The bell jar might have come down over her life for good.

Fortunately, attitudes are changing. Some people even seek psychotherapy when they have no specific problem. Encounter groups and psychoanalysis are especially popular for people who just want to learn more about themselves or who want to find ways of making their lives more fulfilling and enjoyable than

TABLE 13-1
Types of Therapies

Biological	Cognitive or Insight	Social/Behavioral

Insulin Shock
  Produces dangerous side effects. Rarely used today.
 	
Electroconvulsive Shock (ECT)
  Positive, temporary effect on depressed patient; can cause physical damage. Used as last resort.
 	
Psychosurgery
  Irreversible; can unexpectedly affect other behaviors. Used for some specific types of disorders.
 	
Drug Therapy
  Can help control dangerous behaviors if carefully monitored. Can hide the causes of problems, which unfortunately will then go untreated.
	Psychoanalytic Therapy
	  Originated with Sigmund Freud; therapist attempts to help patient understand unconscious conflicts by getting patients to talk about past experiences and by then interpreting those thoughts. It is often a long and expensive process; works better with neuroses than psychoses; Freudian theory is more applicable to men than women.
	
	Humanistic Therapy
	  Nondirective therapy based on patient's conscious awareness of present situations and future goals. As developed by Carl Rogers, therapy is centered around goals set by client. Therapist provides a mirror feedback of client's behavior.
		Group Therapy
		  Concentrates on changing the way an individual responds to society. Attempts to treat two or more individuals at the same time; provides friendship and emotional support. Various forms include:
		  a. Traditional group—developed by J. H. Pratt
		  b. Psychodrama—developed by J. L. Moreno
		  c. Transactional Analysis (T.A.)—developed by Eric Berne
		  d. Gestalt Therapy—developed by Fritz Perls
		  e. Encounter group—associated with Kurt Lewin
		Group therapy does not work for all of the people all of the time; changes produced may not be long-lasting; there is a possibility of dangerous side effects.
		
		Environmental (Milieu) Therapy
		  Concentrates on changing the way society responds to the individual by removing patient from society to a therapeutic community. As therapy progresses, patient gradually prepares for re-entry into society.
		
		Token Economies—are often used to encourage patients to change their behavior patterns.
		
		Environmental therapy does not work for all of the people all of the time; a more humane form of treatment, it has undesirable side effects that are minimal.

they already are. People who do have psychological difficulties are beginning to realize that problems are something to be solved, not something to be ashamed of. With increased scientific knowledge about human problems, and with a growing number of therapies available, there is more hope than ever before that people who need it will be able to get effective help.

Adolf Meyer was one of the most influential forces in the field of mental health. He began his research by looking for the biological causes of mental disorders. He got such poor results that he began to investigate cognitive and social or environmental causes. Finally, Meyer came up with what is known as the **holistic approach.** The whole individual, he said, must be treated because almost every human behavior is the result of biological, psychological, and social influences. Any therapy that attempts to treat only one part of a problem, therefore, will probably fail.

Meyer's holistic approach has had a great impact on the field of mental health. More and more, therapists are adopting the holistic approach to individual human problems. In some hospitals, for instance, a team of therapists is available to treat each patient. One therapist looks at biological problems and applies specific biological therapies. Another therapist attempts to find out what type of cognitive or insight therapy might be most helpful in a particular case. Other therapists work on changing specific behavior patterns, and still other therapists attempt to determine which environmental and social factors may be contributing to an individual problem. As much or little of each type of therapy can then be applied according to each individual's specific needs.

Human problems are probably much too complex ever to be completely understood. And without complete understanding, there will never be one form of therapy that works for all of the people all of the time. But for the moment, the holistic approach proposed by Adolf Meyer is probably the best type of therapy available. It worked for Esther Greenwood and allowed her to rejoin society and

This is a staff meeting of a mental health team, including psychologists, psychiatrists, physicians, social workers, and medical attendants. The holistic approach to therapy involves biological, psychological, and social influences on the patients.

to fulfill many of her dreams. The holistic approach can be applied to all human problems, and if it is properly applied, we can almost always help people like Esther lift the bell jar and let in some fresh air.

► SUMMARY

1. In Sylvia Plath's *The Bell Jar,* the problems that led to Esther Greenwood's breakdown stemmed from several sources, and, therefore, she had difficulty finding the correct therapy.

2. Theories about the causes of abnormal behavior usually dictate the type of therapy that will be used for the treatment of such behavior. In general, therapies fall into three major categories—biological, cognitive or insight, and social/behavioral.

3. When mental problems are clearly related to biological difficulties, biological therapies are usually called for. **Electroconvulsive therapy (ECT)** and **psychosurgery** are two such therapies; but since the 1950s, drug therapy has become the most widely used form of biological therapy. Tranquilizers and energizers are the psychoactive drugs that have been found to be especially effective.

4. Talking about a problem with someone often makes the problem easier for us to accept or handle. Talk therapy can also provide intellectual or emotional insight into what is troubling us. Talk therapy is often called **insight therapy.**

5. Sigmund Freud made his own form of insight therapy—psychoanalysis—into an accepted treatment for cognitive or psychological problems. Freud believed that once a person had achieved insight into a problem, the abnormal thoughts and behaviors associated with the problem would gradually disappear. **Transference** and **interpretation** are two major stages of psychoanalytic therapy.

6. **Humanistic therapy,** which emphasizes self-actualization, is another form of cognitive or insight therapy. Client-centered humanistic therapy focuses on the needs of the client rather than on what the therapist believes the client needs.

7. When people suffer from what are clearly social rather than biological or cognitive problems, they may be in need of some form of social or behavioral therapy. Social/behavioral therapies that attempt to change the way an individual responds to society are called group therapies. Treatment that concentrates on changing the way society (or the environment) responds to an individual is called **environmental or milieu therapy.**

8. Group therapies are based on the principle that the intimate sharing of feelings, ideas, and experiences in an atmosphere of mutual respect and understanding enhances self-respect, deepens self-understanding, and helps us live with others. **Psychodrama, transactional analysis, Gestalt therapy,** and **encounter group therapy** are among the most popular forms of group therapy.

9. One of the easiest ways to change people's behavior is to change their environment. This is what environmental therapies attempt to do. Therapeutic com-

munities have been designed in which everything that goes on, 24 hours a day, is supposed to promote mental health.

10. Token economies, in which approved or healthy behaviors are rewarded, are often used in environmental therapies to encourage and help patients change their behavior.

11. Of the many therapies currently available (biological, cognitive, and social), none has proved to be completely valid or reliable. That is, no one therapy seems to work for all the people all of the time. Each, however, has its special uses; and no matter which therapy is applied (including placebos), the chances for success seem better when both the therapist and the patient feel confident that the treatment will work.

12. With the growing number of therapies available, there is more hope than ever that people who need help will be able to get effective help. But because almost every human behavior is the result of biological, psychological, and social influences, any therapy that attempts to treat only one aspect of a problem behavior will probably fail. The holistic approach, in which all aspects of a problem are examined and treated, is probably the best form of therapy available.

Suggested Readings

Berne, Eric. *Games people play*. New York: Ballantine, 1976.

Janov, Arthur. *The primal scream*. New York: Putnam, 1970.

Lieberman, M. A., I. D. Yalom, and M. B. Miles. *Encounter groups: First facts*. New York: Basic Books, 1973.

Plath, Sylvia, *The bell jar*. New York: Bantam, 1975.

► STUDY GUIDE

A. RECALL

Sentence Completion

1. Esther, the major character in Plath's *The Bell Jar*, went to New York thinking that
[p. 422]   she wanted to be a _____.

2. Esther's cognitive or mental problem was essentially that she was unable to
[p. 423]   _____ what to do with her life.

3. In primitive, ancient societies, strange behaviors were often attributed to
[p. 424]   _____ _____.

4. _____ is the term used to describe the process of boring a hole in the
[p. 424]   skull to let out evil spirits.

5. During the _____ _____, Greek and Roman therapies
[p. 425]   were discarded in favor of devil or "bad spirit" theories.

6. _____ is the process of having a priest force the devil out of a disturbed
[p. 425]   person by talking to it.

[p. 426]   7. Institutions to care for disturbed people, called _____, were popular in the sixteenth and seventeenth centuries.

[p. 427]   8. In treating mental problems some psychologists, particularly the _____, prefer to focus more on the patient's present needs than on their past problems.

[p. 427]   9. Medical aspects of treating the mentally ill are generally handled by _____ rather than by psychologists.

[p. 428]   10. In the United States today there are _____ of therapies to choose from, and thousands of therapists.

[p. 429]   11. The apparently critical stage of insulin shock therapy is when the patient goes into a _____.

[p. 429]   12. Convulsive therapy had its beginnings when Meduna mistakenly concluded that _____ are seldom also schizophrenic.

[p. 430]   13. ECT can be useful for some _____ patients.

[p. 431]   14. To cut nerve tracks leading to the frontal lobes is a technique known as _____.

[p. 431]   15. One of the major drawbacks of psychosurgery is that it is _____.

[p. 431]   16. _____ and _____ are two types of drugs that have been found to be particularly useful in treating people with mental problems.

[p. 432]   17. When people think that they are being given a drug when in fact they are not, they may get "better" anyway, suggesting a _____ effect.

[p. 434]   18. Very much like placebo medication is the use of _____ or "useless" surgery.

[p. 435]   19. Asking people to talk through their problems in hopes that they can find out something about themselves is often called _____ therapy.

[p. 436]   20. _____ _____ is a Freudian technique used to get the patient to say whatever comes to mind.

[p. 436]   21. Clues to the unconscious can often be found in slips of the tongue, _____, and _____.

[p. 437]   22. Psychoanalysis seems to be more successful for people with _____ problems than for people with _____ problems.

[p. 438]   23. A popular humanistic therapy, _____-_____ therapy, was developed by Carl Rogers.

[p. 439]   24. _____ claims that neurotics get better regardless of treatment.

[p. 440]   25. _____ therapy concentrates on changing the way society responds to an individual.

[p. 441]   26. The group approach, originated by Pratt, began as an attempt to help patients who had _____.

[p. 442]   27. Moreno's type of group therapy where patients act out their problems is called _____.

[p. 442]   28. The phrase "the games people play" is associated with Berne's _____.

[p. 443]   29. The therapy that tries to reach the "whole person" is _____ therapy.

[p. 443]   30. Sensitivity training therapy can be viewed as a form of _____ group exercise.

31. In an institution where virtually all positive behavioral changes are rewarded, a

[p. 446]
_____ _____ may be in use.

32. Meyer's approach to mental health can be referred to as an _____

[p. 449]
approach.

B.   REVIEW

Multiple Choice: Circle the letter identifying the alternative that most correctly completes the statement or answers the question.

1. In *The Bell Jar,* Esther's problems stemmed from the fact that she:
   A. was not very bright.
   B. was forced to go to New York when she did not really want to go.
   C. could not handle all of the popularity she had in school.
   D. was physically and emotionally weakened by her experiences.

2. A common treatment of mental illness used by the Romans was:
   A. sending people to rest homes.
   B. trephining.
   C. exorcism.
   D. imprisonment in asylums.

3. Which of the following takes primarily an historical approach of dealing with the past in order to cure present problems?
   A. insight therapies
   B. social learning therapies
   C. humanistic therapies
   D. behavioristic therapies

4. When we ask about the "cure rate" for a particular therapy, we are asking about its:
   A. reliability.
   B. side effects.
   C. validity.
   D. standardization.

5. Electroconvulsive Therapy (ECT):
   A. was discovered by accident.
   B. is sometimes useful for treating massive depression.
   C. should only be used with senile psychotics.
   D. is an established form of treatment for neurotics.

6. A drug that has no real biological effect, but which may produce psychological changes is:
   A. a psychoactive drug.
   B. a placebo.

C. reserpine.

D. insulin.

7. The use of free association is found in:

A. client-centered therapy.

B. Rogerian therapy.

C. Gestalt therapy.

D. psychoanalysis.

8. A patient who stands the best chance of success in psychoanalysis would be all but one of the following.

A. between 15 and 50 years old.

B. well motivated.

C. female.

D. of at least average intelligence.

9. Group therapy:

A. first began in the early 1900s.

B. became most popular during and after World War II.

C. is neither very reliable nor valid.

D. all of the above.

10. The man credited with advancing the notion of an holistic or complete program of treatment for the mentally ill is:

A. Meyer.

B. Rogers.

C. Lieberman.

D. Berne.

SYBIL

Sybil was perplexed. She sat there in what she knew to be the fifth-grade classroom, but couldn't understand why she was there instead of in the third grade where she belonged. When the teacher asked Sybil to work a multiplication problem, she was at a loss. She had learned to add and subtract in the third grade but knew nothing of multiplication. Another thing Sybil knew nothing of was her own multiple personality.

The last thing Sybil remembered was attending her grandmother's funeral two years earlier. But gradually, as she looked around and began to recognize her classmates, it dawned on her that she must have been having another one of her memory lapses, or memory blackouts. What she didn't realize was that these seeming losses of memory were much more than that. While Sybil was "gone," or blacked out, for two years, several totally different personalities had been doing things and had been in complete control of her mind and body.

Sybil is a real person, and this is only one of the many bizarre incidents that make up her life story, the story of a woman with 16 complete and totally different personalities. The book *Sybil* reads like fiction, but according to the author, the only facts that have been changed are those that would identify the woman called Sybil. The real Sybil helped supply information for the book, as did Cornelia Wilbur, the psychiatrist who treated Sybil for 11 years.

Sybil began seeing the psychiatrist in 1954. She realized that she had a problem—in the form of blackouts that lasted anywhere from minutes to years—but felt guilty about it and could not bring herself to tell the analyst. Then one day Sybil went through a change in the psychiatrist's office. The usually shy, timid young woman flew into a rage, ran across the office, and broke a window. She began speaking like a young girl, pronounced words differently, moved differently, and called herself Peggy. A few minutes later she returned to her chair, seemed to calm down, and asked about the broken window. Sybil had returned and knew nothing of what Peggy had been up to. She did not even know that Peggy existed, but under questioning she admitted that she had been experiencing time lapses for as long as she could remember.

This was Dr. Wilbur's first indication of what Sybil's problem might be. She thought that perhaps Sybil was two people, a dual personality. Before the psychiatrist could confront Sybil with this, she was shocked to meet a third and completely different person in Sybil's body. This third woman, who called herself Vicky, was sophisticated, warm, and friendly. She knew all about Sybil and Peggy and was willing to talk about them. During the next several years and with the help of Vicky, the psychiatrist met and got to know all of the 16 personalities who were taking turns using Sybil's body.

Each self, when in control of

Sybil, was a whole person. These personalities came in various ages and sexes — infants, adolescent boys, and mature women — and each had a distinct voice and vocabulary. Each carried herself (or himself) in a distinct manner and had a different body perception. Some saw themselves as thin, others as plump; some were tall, others short; some said they were blond, others brunette. Each had a personal philosophy and life-style, but all shared a rather strict morality.

Using hypnosis, Dr. Wilbur was able to speak to all of Sybil's selves. The conversations while Sybil was under hypnosis were extraordinary. Two, three, or more of Sybil's selves would emerge to talk with the analyst or with each other. The details of these conversations helped the psychiatrist piece together the details of Sybil's harsh childhood.

Sybil's mother had been an extremely disturbed woman who sexually abused and tortured her. Sybil was regularly beaten, locked in closets, and almost killed by her mother on several occasions. Sybil's father was a stern man who kept himself emotionally distant from Sybil and never questioned her bruises or broken bones.

While it is difficult to know what was actually going on in the mind of young Sybil, Dr. Wilbur offers a theory to explain how the numerous personalities came to be. By the time Sybil was 3 years old she realized, at least unconsciously, that she was not loved by her parents. This discovery was so emotionally shocking to the child that it forced her first dissociation, or personality separation. According to the theory, what Sybil did — even though she was not conscious of doing so — was create another person, a person who would suffer abuse and punishment in her place. Whenever there was trouble Sybil would let this other person take over. In this way she was protecting her basic self from her parents. The tactic worked so well as a defense mechanism that it was used over and over, and 16 personalities were born.

Under hypnosis each personality told what experience was responsible for his or her existence. Each was the instrument for coping with a specific emotion, while Sybil herself remained free of all emotions. Peggy, for instance, was assertive and enthusiastic. She came out whenever Sybil was angry and needed those characteristics. Mary was thoughtful and home-loving. Sid and Mike, patterned after Sybil's father and grandfather, were carpenters and handy around the house. Nancy and Clara were religious. Vicky — who knew everything about all of the others — was the self-assured type of woman Sybil seemed to want to be.

Eventually, after years of sessions with her psychiatrist, Sybil began to understand the conditions associated with her problem. She finally became a seventeenth personality — a completely new Sybil with all the emotions, memories, and feelings of her former selves. She remembers the cruelty of her mother, the multiplication tables someone else learned, and the piano lessons someone else took. Sybil has become a whole person and is now a respected artist and teacher at a Midwestern university.

C. NEWS STORY QUESTIONS

1. How many "personalities" did Sybil have, and how did her psychiatrist find out about them? _____

_____

2. What is Dr. Wilbur's explanation for why Sybil started developing multiple personalities? _____

_____

unit FIVE

SOCIAL PSYCHOLOGY

Philip Nolan, central character in "The Man without a Country."

Social behavior — the interaction of two or more individuals — is one of the most important influences on human beings and is necessary for the survival of the individual and the species. Social psychology, as we will see in this chapter, examines how society affects us and how we affect society. But in most cases it is the relationships among people or groups that social psychology attempts to explain.

Social Behavior

14 chapter

When you have completed your study of this chapter, you should be able to:

- ▶ Define "territoriality" and "pecking orders," and give examples
- ▶ Summarize Harlow's experiments on social isolation with monkeys, and cite cases of human social isolation
- ▶ Summarize the essential characteristics of a general systems theory
- ▶ Define "social role," "conformity," and "bystander apathy" in the context of group structure
- ▶ Compare and contrast task specialists and social—emotional specialists as leaders
- ▶ Discuss the effects of territoriality and crowding on human behavior

Bystander apathy. The tendency for people in a crowd not to respond to the needs of hurt or threatened individuals. Not offering to help a stranger in need because you assume that others will do so.

Conformity. From the Latin word meaning "to make or be like." To conform is to become what you expect others want you to be, or to behave in the way that you believe others want you to behave.

Ecological factors. Ecological factors are those things that have to do with how living systems relate to each other and to their environments. Plants give us food and oxygen, and help retain rainwater in the soil. When we destroy plants, we destroy part of the complicated ecological system that sustains our very existence.

General systems theory. According to general systems theory, human beings can be viewed as living systems. A living system is a set of related components or subsystems which have a common goal, are self-motivated and self-regulating, and are controlled by feedback. Your brain is a living system; so are you; so is a football team.

Group. A living or social system comprised of a few individuals who almost always have direct physical or psychological contact with each other. A Girl Scout troop is a group; so is a family.

Instinct. A set of inherited goals or motivations; an innately determined series of reflexes.

Interaction groups. Groups composed of individuals who are generally in some kind of direct, face-to-face physical or psychological contact with each other. Field hockey teams are almost always interaction groups. All the students enrolled in a large lecture course might be considered a group, but seldom would be considered an interaction group since most of the students would not know

and interact with all other members of the class.

Leadership. The ability to set goals for a group or larger social unit, or the ability to influence the actions of others. According to Bales, there are two types of leaders: Task-oriented individuals who keep groups moving toward group goals, and socially oriented individuals who influence group performance by giving personal feedback to group members.

Mammals. The word *mammary* means "breast." Mammals are those higher animals whose mothers breast-feed their young.

Mutations (mu-TAY-shuns). To *mutate* is to change, particularly in physical form. In biological or genetic terms, a mutation is a sudden and unexpected change in shape or form brought about (presumably) by accident.

Organ. An organized set of cells which, functioning together, do things that no single cell can do. Your heart is an organ made up chiefly of thousands of tiny muscle cells. Your heart can pump blood; no single muscle cell in your heart is capable of that.

Organism (ORR-gann-izem). A single plant or animal. Thus an organized set of cells and organs that is capable of functioning on its own (and usually of reproducing). Cells, organs, and organisms are all "living systems."

Overcrowding. Putting too many organisms together so that they can no longer function as freely as they might wish to function.

Pecking order. The hens in a barnyard soon establish a hierarchy based on strength and quickness. The dominant hen can peck at all other hens, but none of them will peck at her. The second-most dominant hen can peck at all the hens except the dominant hen, and so forth.

Peers. From the Latin word meaning "equals." Your peers are people of the same rank or quality as you. According to United

States law, if you are tried for a crime, the jury must be made up of your peers—that is, people who are similar to you in background, education, race, and social station.

Personal space. According to many psychologists, each of us has around us an invisible "bubble" of space that we consider our own, and which we don't like to have violated by strangers (or sometimes even by close friends). Overcrowding may cause stress because it forces organisms to intrude on each other's personal space.

Primates (PRY-mates). From the Latin word *primus*, meaning "best" or "of the top rank." The primates are those animals at the top of the animal kingdom that are human-like in shape—the monkeys and apes, and human beings.

Procreation (pro-cree-AY-shun). The act of creating new life.

Roles. A set of behaviors, attitudes, or feelings —a set of social expectancies. We expect all mothers to care for and to love their children; therefore, in our society we have a "maternal role" that includes these behaviors and attitudes.

Rules. A set of formal guides intended to regulate social behaviors. Our laws are, for the most part, sets of social rules. The word actually comes from a Latin term meaning "to guide" or "to lead straight."

Social–emotional specialists. Bales's second type of leader who guides group behavior by responding (giving feedback) to the social and emotional needs of the group members.

Social behavior. Observable behaviors, usually actions that take place in the presence of other individuals. What you do in the privacy of your own room is not generally a social behavior—unless you choose to tell other people about your actions.

Social psychology. The scientific study of the interactions among members of groups, organizations, and even society. In social psychology, the focus is not on individuals, but on relationships among individuals or groups.

Socialization. The process by which individuals (or groups) learn social behavior or attitudes. Social development (as opposed to cognitive or emotional or biological development).

Society. A living (or social) system made up of organisms, groups, and organizations—just as your body is a living system made up of cells and organs.

Surrogate (SURR-oh-gate, or SURR-oh-gatt). From the Latin word meaning "to substitute." A surrogate is a substitute or stand-in. A surrogate mother is an artificial or substitute mother that "stands in" for the organism's real mother.

Task specialists. Bales's first type of leader who guides group behavior by setting goals and guiding activity.

Territoriality (tare-ih-tor-ee-AL-ih-tee). Territory selection that contributes to survival and successful reproduction by ensuring protection and solidarity among group members.

INTRODUCTION: THE MAN WITHOUT A COUNTRY

"Damn the United States! I wish I may never hear of the United States again!"

Philip Nolan made that statement in 1807, and his wish was immediately granted. For the next 56 years, until 1863, Nolan was kept at sea where he was never allowed to see or hear of the United States again. He became known as "The Man without a Country."

Philip Nolan's loss of home, country, and friends came about as a result of the part he played in a political intrigue known as the Spanish Conspiracy. The conspiracy, or plot, was hatched by ex-Vice President Aaron Burr and several other highly placed government and military officials. Their plan was to start a war between the United States and Spain. Once a war broke out, the conspirators thought it would be possible to liberate Mexico from Spain and set Burr up as emperor of Mexico. But things went wrong. The war never came about, and President Thomas Jefferson discovered the plot and had those involved arrested and tried for treason. Burr and some of the other high-ranking officers were acquitted, but the young officer, Philip Nolan, was found guilty.

It was at the end of the trial that Nolan made his angry statement damning the United States. The patriotic members of the court-martial were shocked. They decided that such a statement—on top of treason—deserved a fitting punishment. Nolan was taken from the court and placed on an outward-bound Navy ship. He was to be kept onboard ship, always at least 100 miles from the United States, for the rest of his life. Whenever a ship he was on headed for home, prisoner Nolan was transferred to another outward-bound vessel. This procedure continued throughout Nolan's 56 years of captivity. He died at the age of 80.

Life for Philip Nolan was not physically hard. On each ship he was given a private stateroom plus adequate food and clothing. Nolan's social life, however, was restricted. Because he was never to hear of the United States, he had to be kept away from the ships' crews who often spoke of "home." Nolan ended up spending most of his time alone. He was not only a man without a country—he was a man without a home, without friends, and without a place in society.

Philip Nolan's story, "The Man Without a Country," is fiction. It was written in 1863 by Edward Everett Hale. On the surface, the story of Philip Nolan is a piece of political propaganda. And that is just what it was meant to be. Hale wrote the story to encourage nationalism, patriotism, and love of country in the northern states during the Civil War. But while most propaganda is forgotten soon after it is written, "The Man Without a Country" has lived on. In recent years it has been made into an opera, a movie, a play, and a television drama, and has become almost a part of the folklore of the United States. The story has not survived simply because patriotism is an especially powerful force in the United States. Philip Nolan's story has probably remained popular because it is about a human need much more basic than love of country. It is about the human need to belong, to be part of a group, or to be a member of society. Philip Nolan was cut off from society, and his predicament is one that most individuals can understand and relate to. Human beings are social animals, and to be cut off from home, family, friends, and institutions is a serious problem.

Why is **society** such an important and necessary part of the human condition? Studies of animal societies provide part of the answer.

ANIMAL SOCIETIES

Animals are basically selfish. That is, each species or type of animal has developed a set of behaviors that will provide the best possible chance for the survival of that species (often at the expense of other species). If allowed to, each species would probably grow in numbers until it overran the earth. In most cases, however, environmental factors keep animal populations in check. Therefore, during millions of years of evolution and adaptation, each species has had to develop a life style or set of behaviors that would make survival and reproduction possible in a specific environment. And among most species, the chances of successful survival and **procreation** are increased by a specific type of behavior—social behavior.

Social behavior is the interaction of two or more animals. Even the most selfish animals, for at least a part of their lifetime, are members of some sort of social structure. In *Biology: The Behavioral View*, Roderick A. Suthers and Roy A. Gallant describe some of the factors that have made social behavior an important part of almost all forms of animal life.

One of the best known examples of social behavior is the highly organized social system of the honeybee, in which each organism has its place and in which individual survival depends on the actions of the society as a whole. When the hive is attacked, social action is called for. One bee-sting would hardly scare away a hungry bear looking for honey. But when a swarm of worker bees rushes out to defend the colony, a bear might be forced to look elsewhere for food.

Territoriality

Territory selection, or **territoriality,** has become an important form of social behavior for many species because a well-defined and protected territory gives an animal a secure place in which to feed, mate, and rear its young. Male song sparrows, for instance, establish a territory and fly from branch to branch around the edge of their staked-out area. At certain branches, or song posts, the male sparrow will sing for several minutes. Other males of the same species recognize

Birds have established social hierarchy. When they move from one place to another to find food, birds fly in formation following the leader of the flock.

the song, understand that the territory has been claimed, and usually fly elsewhere to establish their own territory.

This selection of a territory limits the freedom of individual animals but provides several benefits that are important to the survival of individuals and the species as a whole. Self-imposed limits allow a bird to get to know its own territory very well. This gives the bird the opportunity to discover the best food and hiding places in its own territory. In most species, including humans, stress and tension inhibit the ability to perform sexually. A secure territory helps to reduce tension. Mates confined to a territory get to know each other well, learn to cooperate, and are usually better prepared to care for their young. Territories, by keeping other birds out, also limit competition and aggression among members of the same species.

In addition, territories help to strengthen a species in another way. Song sparrows in a populated area will usually stake out about an acre of territory. If the number of sparrows in a particular area becomes too great, however, the size of territories will have to be decreased — some birds will even be squeezed out of their territories. As the birds are forced out of their territories or into smaller territories (with less food), the weaker members of the species will begin to die off. When this happens, the stronger members will be able to increase the size of their territories again. The physically weaker members of the society will have been weeded out, and the species as a whole will usually be better able to survive and reproduce successfully.

Pecking Order

Songs are not the only method birds have of claiming a territory. The strongest or most dominant hen in a barnyard usually has the run of the whole yard. Less dominant birds have a smaller area in which they are free to scratch and feed. Dominance among hens is determined by a form of social organization known as **pecking order.** When hens are confined in a territory they will usually squabble and peck at each other until one bird gradually emerges as the strongest of the flock. This hen becomes the socially dominant hen and has the right to peck every other hen in the yard. The second strongest hen will not peck the dominant hen, but she can peck everyone else. This type of pecking order continues on down the line to the weakest or least dominant bird who is allowed to peck no one, but who is pecked by everyone.

This hierarchy is a "ladder" of social dominance that helps to keep aggression and competition to a minimum among the hens. The bird at the top of the pecking order can go wherever she pleases in the yard without fear of being attacked. Birds lower down the social ladder learn and accept their position in the social hierarchy and will usually stay out of the way of the more dominant birds. The strict social positions imposed by the pecking order are often for the good of the species. The strongest members of the society are thus assured of the necessary territory and food.

Social Mammals

Mammals, in general, are more highly developed and more intelligent than are insects, fish, or birds. Because of their greater intelligence, mammals do not have to rely on social systems as much as do the lower species. A worker honeybee, for instance, will not survive long if she is cut off from the hive. Because of their small, relatively unsophisticated brains, honeybees survive best when they only have to perform a limited number of behaviors. The workers have certain things to do, the drones have other functions or duties, and the queen has her own set of behaviors. Each organism, in other words, has its own special role to perform. But none of the bees, not even the queen, could survive without social inputs from the other members of the hive.

Most mammals, on the other hand, have the ability to perform almost all of the behaviors or roles necessary for survival. In many cases, mammals only need to come together socially for the purpose of reproduction. Some mammals do live socially (packs of wolves, flocks of sheep, herds of whales, and so forth), but for the most part mammals are solitary and have relatively simple social patterns. Most mammals do not even form long-lasting pair relationships for breeding. During much of the year individual males and females live alone in their own widely spaced territories. During the mating season males leave their territories and enter the territories of the females. Even then, males and females usually come together only for the brief period of time it takes to mate. Because female mammals breast-feed their offspring, males are not usually needed to care for and feed the infants. In many species, the males are chased away by the females soon after mating.

When mammals do form social units, it is usually for the same reasons that the more social species live together: There is safety in numbers. A flock of sheep has hundreds of eyes, ears, and noses that are a great help in detecting a hungry wolf. Even if a few sheep (usually the slowest and weakest) are caught by the wolf, the stronger members of the flock might escape and survive.

Social Primates — A Special Case

Honeybees are born with a set of behavior patterns that allow them to survive in the hive. Without these inborn behaviors or instincts, the bees would not know which behaviors are expected of them, and their society would fall apart. For bees (and for most forms of animal life), instincts are a necessary part of survival (see Chapter 6). But instincts also limit the life-styles of animals. Instincts don't usually change overnight. If environmental or **ecological factors** change, an animal may be left with a set of inappropriate instinctual behaviors.

Primates — the group of mammals to which monkeys, apes, and humans belong — have a special ability that helps them to change their environment. Because of their relatively large brains, primates can learn new behavior patterns and don't have to rely entirely on instincts. But learned behavior, just like instinct, has limitations. In order to acquire the behaviors necessary for survival, primates have to be social animals and have to rely on other members of their species. Most primates, therefore, go through a long juvenile period during which they learn the cultural patterns and behaviors that will be necessary for their survival as adults.

Harlow's Experiments

Just how important is **socialization** to primates? The work of Harry Harlow and others at the University of Wisconsin suggests that early social experiences are extremely important if monkeys are to have any chance of successful survival as adults.

Harlow began his work with an attempt to investigate how organisms learn. For his studies he decided to use young monkeys. To get the animals, Harlow and his wife Margaret started a monkey breeding program. They soon found out, however, that the program was in danger because the infant monkeys often caught diseases from their parents. To avoid this problem, the Harlows began taking the infants away from their mothers at birth and rearing them by hand. The infants were individually caged with a type of artificial or **surrogate** mother that seemed to provide some of the comfort, warmth, and security the infants needed. The surrogates were wire frames fitted with a nipple to provide milk. The surrogates had doll-like heads and were covered over with soft terry cloth to provide comfort.

At first, the artificial mothers seemed to be just what the infants needed. The young monkeys appeared to be growing and developing normally, and they appeared to have behavioral patterns similar to monkeys reared under more normal conditions. But when the surrogate-reared monkeys, who had never seen other monkeys, were put together in a cage, they displayed abnormal amounts

Monkeys reared alone with a surrogate or artificial mother were very aggressive when put into a cage with other monkeys. Being isolated, they had not learned proper social behavior.

of aggression. Not only were they overly aggressive, they seemed not to have developed any of the social behaviors seen in most monkeys. Some of the surrogate-reared animals, for instance, became paralyzed with fear whenever they were approached by another monkey. Others showed strange stereotyped behavior. That is, they would make oddly repetitive movements that seemed to have no function. They would sometimes freeze into bizarre postures, or they would just sit and stare at nothing for hours on end. Apparently, the surrogate-reared monkeys did not learn the normal social behaviors that a real mother would have taught them.

These monkeys were socially isolated. Not only had they been deprived of mothers, they had not been reared with other young monkeys. Play among **peers,** or animals of the same age, seems to be another important learning ground for social behavior. Young monkeys at play, for instance, often engage in what appear to be sex games. Young males, long before they are mature enough to perform sexually, will chase young females around and mount them as a sort of practice for the real thing. Monkeys who are reared alone, without peers to play with, don't get any sexual practice. When they are old enough to mate, as the Harlows found out, such animals don't usually know the first thing about sex. Even when peer-deprived animals were placed with sexually experienced animals, nothing happened. Those monkeys that had not learned any sexual behaviors just would not cooperate.

Rats and other lower animals reared in similar isolation do not seem to have many problems with sex. If they are released from isolation when they are mature enough, they will know instinctively how to reproduce. Primates, with weaker instincts, need time to learn social behaviors such as the sex act.

The Harlows conducted many other isolation studies, including rearing infant monkeys in isolation from parents, peers, and from all contact with living organisms. All of these studies suggest that for primates, the social learning process is extremely important. Without it, primate species would not survive.

HUMAN SOCIETIES

Humans are primates, but they are much more intelligent than monkeys or apes. With this increased intelligence, humans rely even less on instincts and more on learning than do monkeys. Instead of fitting into an environment with a particular set of genetically imposed, instinctive behaviors, humans have a brain capable of devising behaviors appropriate for a great many environments. Not only do humans change their behaviors to fit different environments, they can also use their intelligence to change the environment. But even with the ability to manipulate the environment, humans (like all primates) are dependent on society. During their long childhood, humans can learn the skills and develop the behaviors necessary to reproduce and survive successfully. In addition, almost all human learning comes through various forms of society—family, friends, religions, schools, and hundreds of social institutions.

Because of their more complex brains, humans can develop more compli-

Hiroo Onoda, a Japanese soldier during World War II, lived alone on an island in the Philippines for thirty years. When discovered in 1974, he did not know his country had surrendered. Onoda was able to survive because he was fully socialized before he became isolated.

cated social patterns than other animals can. For instance humans can adopt many of the social patterns seen in the lower species. Humans can live in hivelike societies or colonies. They can live and travel in flocks or packs, and then break off from the pack in pairs for mating. Humans establish territories, dominance hierarchies, and pecking orders. Among the lower animals, social patterns evolved as methods of coping with the environment and as efficient methods of reproduction. With their ability to change and control the environment, humans are free to form an extremely wide variety of social institutions that are not seen in any other species.

Socialization

If humans can live alone, how necessary is society? First of all, humans must still come together for reproduction. But even beyond that, society is necessary. The Japanese officer Hiroo Onoda (seen in the photo on this page) had to be physically and intellectually developed (through socialization) to a certain extent before he was able to survive on his own.

Total isolation experiments, like the Harlows', might demonstrate just how necessary socialization is to humans, but such experiments would be too dangerous with human subjects. There are, however, cases on record that show the disastrous effects of rearing a child in isolation from other humans.

The Wild Boy of Aveyron

In 1799, in the forests of southern France near Aveyron, hunters captured a young boy who had apparently been living alone in the woods. The "wild boy," about 11 years old, was exhibited in a cage for about a year until a French physician, Jean Itard, took over his care.

The wild child, as might be expected, was not like most humans — physically or psychologically. He walked and ran more like an animal than a human. He seemed to have highly developed senses of hearing and smell. He could roam around unclothed in freezing weather without getting sick. He could grab food out of boiling water or out of a fire with no sign of pain or no damage to his skin tissue. The child, who was given the name Victor, showed no evidence of social training. He made no attempts to communicate, except to grunt once in a while, and he seemed to look on other human beings as nothing more than obstacles to his needs.

Philippe Pinel, a prominent French psychiatrist, examined Victor and concluded that the child was an incurable idiot. It was even suggested that mental retardation may have been why the boy was abandoned in the first place. Itard took a different position. He thought that Victor's behavior was the result of early and lengthy social isolation. Itard also thought that he might be able to educate Victor.

For more than five years Itard worked with Victor. He taught the boy to read, write, and understand several words, but Itard could not teach the boy much more than that. When Victor died, at about the age of 40, he was still undeveloped socially. He never learned to play or to behave socially, and he never learned to respond sexually.

The Wild Boy of Aveyron was 11 years old when he was found in the forests of southern France. He behaved more like an animal than a human. He lived to age 40 but never completely developed socially.

The Wild Boy of Salvador

In 1932, in South America, police captured a five-year-old boy who had apparently been living in the jungle with animals. Because of his ability to swing through the trees, the boy was nicknamed "Tarzancito," or "Little Tarzan." Unlike Victor, Tarzancito was able to readjust to society. He was put in the care of psychologist Jorge Ramirez Chulo, and within three years he was wearing clothes, taking baths, and using the normal vocabulary of a child his age. Apparently, because the child was captured at an early enough age, the effects of social deprivation could be overcome.

SOCIAL PSYCHOLOGY

When Philip Nolan first heard his strange sentence, he may have chuckled to himself. After all, he could have been hanged for treason. Instead, he was just being sent on a long ocean voyage, more like a vacation than a punishment. It didn't take long, however, for Nolan to realize that his sentence was a serious one and that being a man without a country was no joke. After several months at sea, Nolan realized that by being cut off from society he had been deprived of almost everything that makes life worth living.

Like Nolan, psychologists have learned that society is one of the most important factors in every human life. Traditionally, psychology has attempted to understand and predict the behavior of individual human beings. More recently, psychologists have come to realize that almost every human behavior has in some way been influenced by society. Philip Nolan's behavior, for instance, could have greatly affected the society to which he belonged had he and Burr been successful in starting an international war. And, of course, the society to which Nolan belonged greatly influenced his behavior. The United States government, speaking through the court-martial board, changed Nolan's life forever.

It is such relationships—the interactions among members of a society or among various societies—that are the subject matter of **social psychology.** Social psychology may examine how a society affects an individual's behavior or how an individual can change a society. But, in almost every case, it is the *relationships among people or groups,* rather than the *individual person,* that social psychology attempts to understand.

General Systems Theory

One method scientists have of examining the workings of a society is through what is known as the **general systems theory.** A living system is a group of related parts or units that interact for the purpose of achieving a common goal—to keep on living. According to general systems theory, all living systems, from the simplest one-celled animals to the most complex societies, operate along the lines of three general principles:

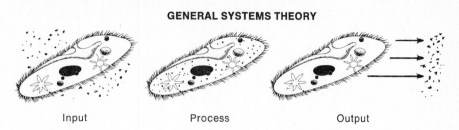

GENERAL SYSTEMS THEORY

Input   Process   Output

FIG. 14–1.
The paramecium, one of the lowest forms of life, exhibits the general systems theory. The paramecium takes in food, processes it, and moves on to find more food.

1. Living systems have inputs. Food and information from the environment are the inputs that the one-celled paramecium needs if it is to survive.
2. Living systems process their inputs. The paramecium digests its food and makes decisions about incoming information.
3. Living systems have outputs. Paramecia digest their food and release wastes. Other outputs may be in the form of behavior. An environmental input, for instance, might let a paramecium know that a certain area is too cold. The paramecium processes this information and then attempts to act (output) by moving into a warmer area.

When the inputs, processes, and outputs of a living system like the paramecium are explained, the behavior of that system often becomes understandable and predictable. According to general systems theory, the behavior of all living systems should be understandable and predictable once their inputs, processes, and outputs are fully explained.

But paramecia and other individual cells are relatively simple systems compared to an **organ** like the human heart. In order to understand the behavior of the heart, it is necessary to examine the inputs, processes, and outputs of the whole organ as well as of the individual cells that make up the heart. A single cell in the heart does not pump blood to the rest of the body. It is the behavior of all the cells working together that pushes the blood through your body. It is the input–output relationships among the cells that produce the distinct behavior of the organ.

A more complex system, the **organism,** is a group of organs working together. You are an organism, but you are much more than just a collection of the inputs, processes, and outputs of your individual organs. In some way we still don't entirely understand, the outputs of all your organs combine to produce the complex internal processes and complicated behavior patterns that are seen only at the level of the organism. Consciousness or self-awareness, for instance, is a type of internal process that occurs in organisms but not in organs. Simply by thinking about it, you can change your own behavioral outputs; as far as we know, no organ is capable of this sort of "self-change."

The next most complicated living system is the **group,** which is made up of organisms that are somehow related to or in communication with each other. Groups have internal processes and behavioral outputs that are far more complex than the actions of any of the individual organisms or people who

A group consists of two or more people who are in some way related or dependent on each other for a period of time. Groups can be based on common religious, political, cultural, or musical interests.

belong to a group. Sexual reproduction, for instance, is a *group process* in that it typically involves two or more individual organisms that relate to each other in a specific manner.

You are an organism, and you surely think of yourself as being a unique individual. Because you have consciousness and self-awareness, it may be difficult at first for you to see how many of your own outputs are actually part of a *group process*—just as many of the actions of your individual organs are also part of a group process. When you are out walking at night alone and become frightened, your brain "communicates" with your adrenal glands so that the rest of your organs become aroused for possible fight or flight. The same sort of *group arousal* occurs when a next-door neighbor rushes over to warn your family that the place is on fire. The response of your family group to this external threat would surely be more complex than your own individual response would be—just as your "organism" response to being frightened while out walking would be more complex than the responses of your adrenals, heart, and lungs. Similarly, the responses of your adrenal glands are themselves more complicated than the reactions of any individual cell in those glands.

Cells make up organs, organs make up organisms, and organisms make up groups. According to general systems theory, the reactions of all the cells in a

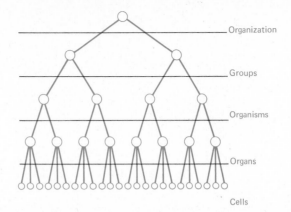

Organization

Groups

Organisms

Organs

Cells

FIG. 14–2.
In the social struc-
ture, individual parts
combine to form
larger units, building
up into an organiza-
tion.

given organ make up the internal processes of that organ. The responses of all
your own organs go together to make up your own internal processes. And the
activities of all the individual members of a group make up the internal processes
of that group. But the outputs of the group are something more than the sum
total of the behaviors of all the group members, just as your own behaviors are
something more than the sum total of the outputs of all the organs in your body.

Groups combine to form organizations, and organizations work together to
form societies. Societies form nations, and nations can form even more complex
systems like the United Nations. It is the task of the social psychologist—sometimes with the help of general systems theory—to attempt to make
the behaviors of groups, organizations, and even societies more understandable.

THE GROUP

The social system with which we are most familiar is the group—two or more
people considered as a single unit. The groups that have the most influence on
human behavior are usually those that remain together for a long time and in
which individual members are in some way related to or psychologically dependent on each other. Ethnic groups, family groups, business, religious or political
groups, friends, and lovers are often responsible for some of the most important
influences on human behavior. **Interaction groups,** those in which individuals
have frequent face-to-face encounters, are probably among the most important
factors in any human life. In order to understand how groups affect human behavior, we must look at the structure and function of groups—including individual and group inputs, processes, and outputs.

Group Structure and Function

Humans, like animals, band together and form groups for two basic reasons:
survival and procreation. These goals are most easily achieved when individual
behavior can be predicted and controlled. Successful societies, therefore, usually

All societies are guided by rules and regulations.

make behavior predictable by providing a pattern or model set of behaviors for individuals to follow. When a particular group is not in immediate danger and when survival is fairly certain, the group activities often make survival not only possible, but pleasant and rewarding as well. In order for groups to function properly, however, the structure of the group must be maintained. In other words, individual members of a group must accept and follow certain rules, or play certain **roles** — just as the individual organs of your body must play certain roles if the physical structure of your body is to be maintained intact.

The social structure of a beehive is usually easily maintained, because the roles the bees play are pretty much determined by their genes. All the worker bees in a hive, for instance, process informational inputs in a similar manner. Their genetically determined outputs are almost always the behaviors that are best-suited to insure the survival of the hive.

Information processing in human groups does not always produce behavior that is best for group survival, however. Because humans do not behave rigidly in accordance with predetermined genetic patterns, groups must set up rules and regulations to govern the actions of their members. In informal groups the **rules** are not always spelled out. But members of such groups usually know what sort of behavior is expected of them. People at a party usually know better than to destroy furniture, spill drinks, or insult other people. People who do not obey such unwritten rules may lose their place in the group. An obnoxious party-goer might not be asked to return for the next party.

In more formal and highly structured organizations, rules and regulations are often spelled out. The legal code of the United States, the Ten Commandments, and the directives of employers for their employees are formal rules intended to maintain the structures of various societies or organizations. People who obey the rules keep their place in the group and remain eligible for whatever pleasures or benefits group membership might provide. Philip Nolan did not follow the rules, and he lost his place in society.

Conformity

Rules and regulations are set up to insure that the smooth functioning and proper structure of groups and societies are maintained. If one individual disobeys the rules, the order of a group might be upset. If a group disobeys regulations, the order of an organization might be upset. If many of its organizations disobey the rules, a society might be in real danger. Therefore, societies have developed methods of restricting individuality and making their members conform (*conformare* in Latin means "to have the same form").

Conformity is obvious in a beehive. All of the drones look alike, more or less, and all of the workers do more or less the same things. This conformity or similarity among individual bees is due primarily to the fact that most of the bees are children of the same mother, the queen bee. Genetic similarity not only makes the bees look alike, it makes them act alike—for the good of the hive. Few bees ever step outside the laws of the hive.

In more complex societies, conformity is often imposed on individuals by external methods. An army, for instance, forces all of its members to wear similar uniforms, to eat the same food, to get up and go to bed at about the same time, and to follow a strict set of rules. By taking away or restricting individuality, armies attempt to get their members to perform in accordance with army standards rather than individual standards. In this way, conformity becomes one of the major factors that often makes group behavior quite different from individual

Conformity is demanded by all social groups. Some groups require a stricter code of conformity than others.

behavior. Soldiers, with the protection and security provided by the group, will often perform actions they would never dream of committing as individuals.

Conformity is not always the result of something as obvious as a uniform or a strict set of well-enforced rules. Other external forces can compel individuals to conform and behave as a social unit. Strangers stuck in an elevator, for instance, will usually give up their individuality in order to work together for the common goal of escaping. The members of a basketball team or a political organization become similarly dependent on each other and conform to group rules once they realize that group behavior is more likely to be succcessful than individual behavior. Members of a group yield or conform to group standards because such actions usually promote survival for all concerned.

There are times, however, when conformity does not function for the good of society. Several years ago, in New York City, a young woman named Kitty Genovese was brutally stabbed to death outside her home. The murder took place at 3:00 A.M., and her screams brought 38 of her neighbors to their windows. For 30 minutes, while Kitty Genovese unsuccessfully fought off her attacker, the neighbors watched in horror. They watched, but not one of them called the police or attempted to help. They refused to get involved.

The Kitty Genovese case is a vivid example of **bystander apathy.** Why were the bystanders apathetic? Why did they refuse to get involved and help their neighbor? John Darley, Bibb Latané, and their colleagues interviewed the witnesses to the Genovese murder and conducted several experiments in an attempt to understand bystander apathy. Their research suggests that the more witnesses there are, the less likely it is that a victim will get help.

When one individual witnesses a crime, the odds are excellent that the person will become involved or summon help. But as Darley and Latané have shown, when there are several witnesses, each person tends to think before acting. Most witnesses apparently perceive themselves as being part of a group. It is the *group's* responsibility to respond to the emergency, not the individual's

In modern urban society, many people don't want to get involved in helping strangers or neighbors. Like the man pictured above, they become apathetic bystanders.

alone. If no one in the group of witnesses perceives his or her role to be that of leader or decision-maker, then all of the witnesses may watch passively because they perceive passivity as being their role until some leader summons them to action. To act independently might be to go against group expectations. However, as Darley and Latané also demonstrated, if just one witness gets involved and begins to help, the entire group of witnesses may "follow the leader" and spring into action. Unfortunately, in the Genovese case, none of the bystanders was willing to take on the leadership role.

Leadership

Conformity, by making individuals more alike, usually brings group members closer together and helps the group to function as a unit. But conformity is not the only social process that helps groups to function smoothly. Most groups rely on a dominance hierarchy and various forms of **leadership** to determine group behavior. The success of a group often depends upon the success of its leaders.

Among the lower animals, success usually means surviving in the environment and producing offspring. The leaders of most animal societies, therefore, are those individuals who have proved themselves to be the best survivors.

The qualities of leadership in human societies are not as clear-cut and easy to see as they are in animal societies. Most people, for instance, have certain qualities that allow them to be leaders at one time or another, or in one situation or another. Some people become leaders of large, important groups or societies, while other individuals, farther down in the pecking order or dominance hierarchy, prove their leadership abilities in smaller groups. Even in the smallest groups, such as a husband-and-wife team, a leader is necessary if the team is to function efficiently. In some situations the qualities of the husband will make him the obvious leader. In other situations, the wife, because of her particular qualities, will be called upon to take the lead.

What are the qualities that make a leader? Experiments conducted by sociologist Robert Bales and his colleagues at Harvard University suggest that human leadership might consist of at least two basic qualities. For the experiments, college students served as subjects. The students were asked to work as groups on solving certain problems. While the students were working, their verbal behaviors were measured. After the problem-solving session, the subjects were asked to rate the other individuals in the group. They were asked especially to indicate which people they liked the best, which person seemed to have the best ideas, and which individual seemed to be a leader.

Once all the information was collected and examined, Bales and his associates were able to pick out two types of leaders. The individuals in the problem-solving groups who received the highest ratings from their fellow workers were either "task specialists" or "social–emotional specialists."

The **task specialists** were those individuals who, during the working session, came up with the most ideas, suggestions, and opinions. They kept reminding the group of its goals and wouldn't let the group get sidetracked into

The qualities of leadership may vary with time and place. U. S. Ambassador to the United Nations Andrew Young is an appropriate leader to address a conference in support of independence for the peoples of Zimbabwe and Namibia in southern Africa.

other areas. These task specialists directed the cognitive or intellectual resources of the group and were *respected* for "modeling" their knowledge and expertise.

The **social–emotional specialists** were those individuals who asked for rather than gave suggestions. They patted other people on the back for good performances, smoothed over arguments, and attempted to keep the group working together as a unit. These people used feedback to direct the emotional resources of the group. They were *liked* for their ability to hold the group together as a social unit.

The perfect social unit should be structured so that it functions smoothly and moves toward its goals. The perfect leader, therefore, is probably someone who both acts as a task-oriented model, and who also gives social–emotional feedback to other group members to let them know how close they are coming to achieving the task at hand. In other words, a successful leader is usually someone who is both respected for setting a good example and well-liked for using positive feedback.

SOCIAL COSTS

The human race would not have survived if its earliest members had not formed groups and societies. The family group and larger societies were necessary for the creation and rearing of children as well as for protection from the environment, including protection from other groups of humans. In the modern, industrialized world, society is still necessary, and the benefits of belonging to a society are many. Protection, education, and stimulation (intellectual, social, sexual, recreational) make life possible and even worthwhile. But societies don't just give, they take. Members of a society usually must pay for what they get. And some of the costs are high.

Human Territoriality

One of the most useful but costly mechanisms societies have for protecting their members is territoriality. Nations, states, cities, neighborhoods, and homes are all territories that have been staked out by the members of various societies. These territories are supposed to provide protection, security, and a certain amount of freedom for their inhabitants. But territories are expensive. By limiting a group's space, territoriality leads to crowding as the group grows. Crowding increases pollution and limits the resources within a territory for individual members. When resources become limited, groups often attempt to extend their territories, and this behavior often leads to aggression and conflict with other groups. Philip Nolan's punishment was the result of an attempt he and Aaron Burr made to take over someone else's territory.

Crowding

Pollution is one of the costs we have been made to pay for an industrialized society.

One of the most dramatic demonstrations of the effects of **overcrowding** came from an experiment conducted by John B. Calhoun of the National Institute of Mental Health. In July 1968, Calhoun put four pairs of healthy white mice in an eight-foot-square territory that he called a "mouse universe." The mice were given everything they needed and were protected from environmental factors. In this almost perfect universe, the animals had plenty of food and water and did not have to fight diseases, the weather, or predator animals. The mice took advantage of their comfortable surroundings. They prospered and multiplied, and by February 1970, there were 2200 mice in the cage. By then, the effects of overcrowding were beginning to show. Not another mouse was born in the colony after March 1970. In January 1973, the last mouse died.

While the experiment was under way, a variety of abnormal activities occurred that Calhoun attributed to overcrowding. Once the population reached 620, strange things began to happen. Normally peaceful animals became aggressive and began to attack other mice. Some of the adults turned to cannibalism and began to eat the younger mice. Mothers deserted their young, and sexual activity became perverted. Some males tried to mate with females who were too young or not in heat. Other males made no sexual advances at all.

Under more natural circumstances, the mouse population probably would not have risen much above 600. Some animals would have been killed by predators or other environmental factors, and some would have been forced to migrate to other territories. But when the population went past 620, there was

Humans are usually able to adapt to over-crowded conditions although the result may be strain in personal relationships and physiological stress.

no more room for the mice to establish new territories. The adults had separated in 14 distinct social groups, and they refused to let the newer, younger members join the groups. The younger members then became frustrated, and many turned to aggression and abnormal behaviors. Others, about 400 of them, became apathetic and inactive and just huddled in a mass in the center of the cage.

The effects of overcrowding on humans may not be as disastrous as on mice. There are indications, for instance, that humans are better able to adapt than are animals to overcrowded conditions. The residents of Tokyo (Japan) and Hong Kong seem to be able to accept their crowded conditions fairly well. Members of one African tribe — the !Kung — even choose to live under extremely crowded conditions.

Anthropologist Patricia Draper of the University of New Mexico has studied and reported on the living conditions of the !Kung tribe. (The ! represents a clicking sound which is a part of their language.) The !Kung have enough territory to give each individual 10 square miles of space. Even so, the !Kung deliberately build very small camps in which family groups are crowded together. They live, says Draper, in conditions equal to about 30 people in a single room. In fact, !Kung individuals are almost always in physical contact with one or more other members of the group. In the October 19, 1973, issue of *Science,* Draper reports that the !Kung do not appear to show most of the physical signs normally attributed to overcrowding — stress and high blood pressure.

People can and do live successfully in small, overcrowded territories. But this fact does not mean that crowding is the best way to live. Many studies suggest that crowding can produce some undesirable psychological effects.

Personal Space

Robert Sommer of the University of California at Davis has been studying individual territories for many years. Each person, it seems, has a certain psychological territory or **personal space.** This personal space, like an invisible bubble, surrounds the individual, and is protected by that individual in the same way that a bird or fish will protect its territory.

The size of an individual's personal space is influenced by many factors, such as personality, status, age, and culture. When this personal space is violated or entered, the person may become aroused or anxious. In the United States, personal space usually extends about two feet from an individual. In Scandinavian countries, personal space is even larger, but in Middle Eastern countries it seems to be much smaller. The interactions of Arab people, for example, usually involve more physical closeness and touching than do the interactions of Scandinavians. People with a great deal of status, such as presidents, usually have exceptionally large personal spaces and are approached only with caution. Infants and young children usually have little status and very small personal spaces. They may be aproached, picked up, or patted by almost all other members of a society.

In some instances the violation of personal space is acceptable. People usually do not mind being touched by their doctors, barbers, or hairdressers. A caress from a lover is usually pleasantly accepted. But when a stranger unexpectedly grabs at you, you might feel threatened. And threatening situations can lead to stress, frustration, and aggression (see Chapter 11). The constant violation of

Personal space is like an invisible bubble that surrounds and protects an individual from intrusion. In Arabic cultures, personal space is much smaller than in other cultures.

personal space, as in overcrowded cities, is thought to be responsible for the type of stress that may lead to high blood pressure and even to heart attacks in some people.

INDIVIDUALITY

Individual cells within an organ all have a certain place and function. As long as the cells cooperate and work with each other, the organ should be able to function. But if one cell does not function properly, the result can sometimes be deadly.

Disease, physical damage, and genetic **mutations** (changes) are among the factors that can cause a cell to lose its ability to function properly. In most cases, nonfunctioning cells just die off. But when they don't die, they must be destroyed or cut out. The same is true of organs that don't function for the good of the organism. A burst appendix, swollen tonsils, or a cancerous kidney can and must be removed for the good of the organism.

Within societies, individuals who don't function properly will sometimes die off. But if the behavior of an individual becomes dangerous to other members of the society or to the society as a whole, the individual might have to be removed —as in the case of Philip Nolan. His behavior, if allowed to continue, might have won him fame and fortune. But that same behavior might have destroyed the society that had fed and clothed him. Therefore, he had to be cut off for the good of society.

An extreme example of the dangers of too much individuality and too little cooperation has been reported by anthropologist Colin M. Turnbull, who lived with a group of people who destroyed their society and themselves. In *The Mountain People* (Simon and Schuster, 1972), Turnbull describes the terrifying results of human individuality among an East African tribe known as the Ik.

For years, the Ik people roamed through their territory as hunters and gatherers. But gradually, as African nations redrew their boundaries and as game preserves were established, the Ik were forced into a small territory that was unable to support their needs. Life became so difficult that people of the tribe soon forgot about each other's needs, and the simple social concept of sharing was replaced by individual selfishness. One man sold all of the medicine Turnbull gave him for his sick wife. The wife died, but the man kept taking and selling the medicine until Turnbull found out. Husbands and wives hid food from each other, and parents were no better. They refused to feed their children and forced them out of the home at the age of three. The children, if they were lucky, survived for a while on partially eaten fruits left over by baboons. Old people were abandoned and allowed to die. The children would sit calmly by and watch their starving parents perish rather than help them.

Like Calhoun's mice, the Ik showed signs of both extreme withdrawal and aggression. On one occasion Turnbull sat for three days with a group of Ik men. The men had withdrawn into themselves and spoke not a word to each other for the entire three days. The men just seemed to be sitting waiting for food that never came. Aggression usually showed up when someone died. Then the other

Some people are just as protective of their property as they are of personal space. These neighbors are exchanging harsh words over a trespassing dog.

members of the tribe would fight over the corpse and strip from it whatever rags or possessions might be of value.

Individuality, like a cancer, grew among the Ik until they were doomed as a society. But individuality is not always dangerous. In many instances it is even necessary for survival. Bees, with their inherited behavior patterns, are at the mercy of the environment. If the environment changes permanently, the unchanging bees may be doomed. And many animals species have died out because they could not adapt to or change with the environment. In the species that have survived, it is individuality (usually in the form of genetic changes or mutations) that has helped them to survive.

In humans, individuality often shows up in the form of thoughts and behaviors that are different from the thoughts and behaviors of the rest of the members of society. Christopher Columbus had an idea with which many members of his society probably disagreed. Because Columbus's mutant idea was not harmful to the rest of society, Columbus was allowed to carry on. If he had fallen off the edge of the world, his mutant idea would probably have died with him. But Columbus's individuality paid off — for him as well as for his society. He gave his civilization new territory into which it could expand.

Billions of individual mutations in the animal world have produced millions of successfully surviving species. Billions of individual thoughts and behaviors have produced the hundreds of successfully surviving human societies. But all along the way, harmful mutations have had to be weeded out. Individuality that was harmful to other members of society or to the society as a whole has had to be restricted (as Philip Nolan found out) so that society could continue to survive. If society does not survive, individuals do not survive, and all forms of individuality become impossible.

► SUMMARY

1. In "The Man Without a Country," Philip Nolan was sentenced to spend the rest of his life isolated from home, family, friends, and society. Why would Nolan's punishment be such a difficult one for any of us to accept? The answer, as we have seen in this chapter, is that humans are social animals. The inputs that society provides are important and necessary to human survival.

2. Social behavior, the interaction of two or more individuals, has had a long evolutionary history. We can gain some understanding of the importance of human social behavior by examining how social behavior has evolved in the lower species. In most cases, social behavior increases the chances for successful procreation and survival of the species.

3. **Territoriality,** the selection and holding of a territory, is an important form of behavior for many species because a well-defined and protected territory gives an individual a secure place in which to feed, mate, and rear its young.

4. Social dominance hierarchies, as seen in the **pecking orders** of some species of birds, ensures that the strongest members of a group have first choice of territories and food. Dominance hierarchies that give each individual a place within the group help to limit competition and aggression within the group.

5. **Primates,** the group of mammals to which monkeys, apes, and humans belong, have to learn many of the behaviors that will be necessary if they are to survive as adults. Much of what primates learn comes through social interactions. Harlow's experiments with isolated monkeys help demonstrate the necessity of social learning and social behavior among primates.

6. Humans, like all primates, are dependent on society. During a long childhood human infants begin to learn many of the skills and develop many of the behavior patterns that will be necessary if they are to reproduce and survive successfully. Social psychology examines how individual behavior affects society and how society affects individuals. But in most cases it is the relationships among people or groups, rather than the individual person, that social psychology attempts to understand. **Socialization** has been found to be important to survival, and Harry Harlow has worked with monkeys to show the effect of isolation and early nurturing on monkeys.

7. **General systems theory** is one method by which scientists have attempted to examine the workings of a society. When the inputs, internal processes, and outputs of a living system (such as an **organ, organism, individual,** or **group**) are explained, the behavior of that system becomes understandable and predictable.

8. Social goals can be most easily met when individual behavior can be predicted and controlled. Successful societies have often attempted to make behavior predictable by providing a pattern or model set of behaviors for individuals to follow. Social **rules** and regulations are among the methods societies have developed for restricting individuality and making group members conform.

9. **Conformity,** by making individuals more alike, helps a group to function as a unit, but most groups rely on a dominance hierarchy and various forms of leadership to determine group behavior. Social experiments suggest that there are two kinds of leaders—**task specialists** and **social–emotional specialists.** A successful leader combines both of these qualities and is both respected for setting a good example and well-liked for using positive feedback.

10. The human race would not have survived if it had not been for the benefits provided by social behavior. Social behavior, however, does have its costs. **Territoriality,** for instance, sometimes leads to increased pollution, reduced resources, aggression, and conflict. Social behavior also puts limits on individuality.

11. Individuality, whether in the form of a mutant gene or a mutant idea, is sometimes necessary for survival, but mutations that are harmful to society sometimes have to be eliminated for the good of society. If society does not survive, individuals do not survive.

Suggested Readings

Adams, Richard. *Watership down.* New York: Aron, 1976.
Ardrey, Robert. *Territorial imperative.* New York: Dell, 1971.

Calley, William L. *Lieutenant Calley: His own story.* (As told to John Sack.) New York: Grosset & Dunlap, 1974.

Hale, Edward Everett. *The Man without a Country and Other Stories.* New York: Airmont, 1968.

Morris, Desmond. *Naked ape.* New York: Dell, 1969.

Suthers, R. A. and Roy A. Gallant. *Biology: The behavioral view.* New York: Wiley, 1973.

Turnbull, Colin M. *The mountain people.* New York: Simon & Schuster, 1974.

► STUDY GUIDE

A.   RECALL

Sentence Completion

1. Philip Nolan became "a man without a country" after he was convicted of
[p. 464] _____ in 1807.

[p. 465] 2. Your text claims that animals are basically _____.

[p. 465] 3. _____ _____ is the interaction of two or more animals.

4. Male song sparrows, securing a place in which to feed, mate, and raise their young,
[p. 465] are evidencing _____.

5. Territories help to reduce tension, force cooperation, and limit _____
[p. 466] and _____ among members of the same species.

6. Social   orders   based   on   dominance   are   called   _____
[p. 467] _____.

7. To say that an animal may have certain things to do, functions or duties to perform
[p. 467] within its society, is to say that it has a _____ _____.

8. The work of _____ suggests that early social experiences are very im-
[p. 468] portant in the development of monkeys.

9. One of the first signs of trouble with monkeys raised with surrogate mothers is that
[p. 469] they appear overly _____ when later placed with other monkeys.

10. Socially isolated monkeys show problems related to a lack of contact with their
[p. 469] _____, or other monkeys of their own age.

11. The wild boy of _____ apparently lived alone in the woods until he was
[p. 470] about 11 years old.

12. "Tarzancito" was able to readjust to society because he was only _____
[p. 471] years old when he was captured.

13. According to general systems theory, living systems have _____, they
[p. 473] _____ their inputs, and then they have _____.

14. In terms of complexity, _____ fit in between organisms and organiza-
[p. 473] tions.

15. _____ groups are characterized as having frequent face-to-face en-
[p. 475] counters and being among the most important factors in human life.

16. In _____ groups, the rules or roles are not always well structured or
[p. 476] spelled out.

17. When members of a group all follow the same rules and exhibit similar behaviors, for
[p. 477] whatever reason, we can say that they are _____.

[p. 478]
18. The Kitty Genovese case is a vivid example of _____ _____.

[p. 479]
19. In most animal societies the leader is the member of the group who has demonstrated the best ability for _____.

[p. 479]
20. Bales found two types or styles of leadership, _____ specialists and _____-_____ specialists.

[p. 480]
21. Of the two types of leadership identified by Bales, the _____-_____ specialists were liked more than the other.

[p. 481]
22. John B. Calhoun is best known for his studies of _____.

[p. 483]
23. When personal space is violated, an individual may become aroused or _____.

B. REVIEW

Multiple Choice: Circle the letter identifying the alternative that most correctly completes the statement or answers the question.

1. Philip Nolan was banned from his country because of his participation in a plot to:
    A. kill Aaron Burr.
    B. get South Carolina to leave the Union.
    C. start a war with Spain.
    D. have Thomas Jefferson arrested.

2. Territoriality:
    A. can be found in some animals, but not in humans.
    B. may limit the freedom of individuals.
    C. works against the forces of evolution.
    D. none of the above.

3. Pecking orders:
    A. assure security for the weaker members of the society.
    B. tend to increase levels of competition and aggression.
    C. are generally associated only with the primates.
    D. are essentially dominance hierarchies.

4. As opposed to "lower" levels of animals, mammals:
    A. spend less time off by themselves.
    B. rely more on their brains than their instincts.
    C. do not have social roles.
    D. come together in groups only to mate and raise their young.

5. Harlow found that socially isolated monkeys:
    A. grow and physically develop normally.
    B. display abnormal amounts of aggression when put with others.
    C. often show strange "stereotyped" behaviors.
    D. all of the above.

6. As opposed to other mammals, humans generally seem unable to:
   A. live in hivelike societies or colonies.
   B. travel around in flocks or packs.
   C. establish territories or pecking orders.
   D. none of the above.

7. Of the following who never became fully socialized?
   A. the wild boy of Aveyron
   B. Hiroo Onoda
   C. Philippe Pinel
   D. the wild boy of Salvador

8. Social psychology generally focuses on:
   A. relationships among people or groups.
   B. the impact of one society on another.
   C. how groups affect organizations.
   D. the individual.

9. In general systems theory, which is the most complex?
   A. organizations
   B. societies
   C. groups
   D. organisms

10. Conformity:
   A. is seldom voluntary.
   B. is a uniquely human phenomenon.
   C. does not always function for the good of society.
   D. is not present in bystander apathy.

CITIES, CROWDING & CRIME

Sexual perversion, irrational and excessive aggression, increased mortality rates, lowered fertility rates, maternal neglect of young, withdrawal and other psychotic behavior — these are among the reactions of rats, monkeys, hares, shrews and fish that have been experimentally forced to live in overcrowded conditions. Are overcrowded human populations subject to this type of psychological and physiological dis-integration? Can such reactions, for instance, explain or in part account for crime in the crowded cities?

Recently, psychologists reported results of studies on the effects of crowding on humans. One study was conducted in the Netherlands, one of the most densely populated countries in the world (323 persons per square kilometer). Leo Levy and Allen N. Herzog of the University of Illinois Medical Center in

Chicago compared high-density areas to low-density areas and found that higher density appeared to be positively related to such things as deaths due to heart disease, admissions to hospitals and mental hospitals, juvenile delinquency, illegitimacy, divorce and infant mortality. In Honolulu density was related to adult and infant death rates, TB, VD and prison rates. In Chicago one measure of density, the number of people per room, was correlated with various types of social disintegration (*Science News,* 4/15/72, p. 247). All of these findings tend to support some of the results of animal studies and suggest that human crowding is related to social disintegration and crime.

Arousal, stress, anxiety and frustration seem to be among the important results of crowding that can lead to personal and social degeneration. One thing that can sometimes lead to stress or anxiety, for instance, is infringement on personal space. Personal space or interpersonal physical distance (IPD) is defined as the area surrounding a person's body into which intruders may not come. Gay H. Price and James M. Dabbs Jr. of Georgia State University investigated the effects of age and sex on IPD. They found that personal space requirements become larger as children grow older. First grade boys and girls allowed another child to approach until a comfortable conversational distance was reported. Both boys and girls showed an IPD of 0.30 meters— about 12 inches. As children grow older, however, they need more personal space. Females in the 12th grade needed 0.45 meters and males at the same age needed 0.60 meters.

Other studies have shown cultural and racial differences in desired interaction distances. British and Germanic people prefer to interact at a greater distance than do Middle Eastern or Latin American people. Blacks tend to interact at greater distances than do whites. Maintaining this personal space is not always easy in a crowded city, and overly close contact with strangers can sometimes lead to psychological discomfort and may even be perceived as threatening. This, in turn, can lead to arousal, anxiety and stress that can be physically harmful and that can sometimes lead to antisocial activity.

Yokov M. Epstein and John R. Aiello of Rutgers University have made physiological measures of arousal caused by crowding. Skin conductance levels were used as a measure of arousal. The subjects were monitored as they sat quietly in either a crowded or noncrowded room. Arousal increased over time in both conditions, but arousal increased significantly under the crowded conditions. And arousal was higher under all conditions for men.

In another set of experiments Epstein and Robert A. Karlin examined some of the social and behavioral effects of crowding. According to their definition, social crowding exists when the distance between individuals is less than the expected appropriate distance for a particular setting. What is appropriate in the bedroom, for instance, is not appropriate in the subway. Whenever the appropriate distance is not maintained, say Epstein and Karlin, stress reaction can result. Such things as heat, odors, noise and bodily contact add to the perception of crowding.

What happens socially when crowding is perceived? Groups of men and women were subjected to crowded and noncrowded conditions. They were given various tests and tasks to complete while their reactions and interactions were monitored. In general, report Epstein and Karlin, crowded men concealed their distress from each other, became competitive and developed attitudes of distrust and hostility—all of which can lead to aggression, stress and crime. Women, in contrast, have usually been subjected to social norms and training that allow them to react quite differently. They tend to share their distress. In a number of crowding experiments women reacted as if they were in the same boat rather than becoming competitive. They formed cooperative groups. There were usually positive sentiments between individuals. When asked to evaluate other members of the group, the crowded women gave more positive evaluations than did the noncrowded women or any of the men's groups.

One reason for criminal activity and social breakdown, therefore, may be that when crowded, men feel more negatively about each other, become more competitive, fight with each other and even become more disposed to engage in criminal activity to achieve their own ends at each other's expense.

With good evidence that crowding does contribute to social problems and increased criminal activity, is there any hope that crime rates can be lowered in the already overcrowded cities? Hong Kong is the most densely populated area in the world (3,912 persons per square kilometer) yet its crime rate is only half that of the United States (22 persons per square kilometer). So crowding need not always be a great contributing factor to criminal activity. Cultural attitudes are involved. The people of Hong Kong react differently to crowding than do the people of the United States. Similarly, women react differently to crowding than do men. But changing the cultural patterns, even if possible, would be only a long-range solution to the problems caused by crowding. It will be as difficult to achieve as eliminating poverty.

C.   NEWS STORY QUESTIONS

1. List some of the results that seem to be associated with humans living in high-density areas. _____

_____

2. What are some of the initial reactions to invasion of personal space that may ultimately lead to those results listed above? _____

_____

3. What sex differences have been observed in overcrowding experiments? _____

_____

Still from the animated *Animal Farm*.

Attitudes are the basis of much human behavior, and, therefore, it is necessary to have an understanding of what attitudes are, how they are formed, and how they can be changed. In this chapter we will look at how attitudes affect our behavior, and we will see that attitudes play a special role in politics and advertising.

Attitudes

When you have completed your study of this chapter, you should be able to:

- ► List the characteristics associated with the "authoritarian personality"
- ► Summarize Milgram's experiments on obedience
- ► Explain Allport's processes of attitude formation
- ► Summarize Newcomb's Bennington College study
- ► Discuss Helson's adaptation-level theory in the context of attitude change
- ► Discuss how communication may be used in changing attitudes
- ► Define "counterpropaganda" and give an example of its use
- ► Describe how role playing may be used to bring about attitude change

Adaptation-level theory. According to Harry Helson, a person's perceptions, judgments, and attitudes are strongly influenced by three factors—the physical and social dimensions of the stimulus input, the background in which the input appears, and the personality structure (traits, attitudes, past experience) of the perceiver. Often called A-L theory.

Advertising. Any form of public communication that is intended to benefit the communicator is generally considered to be advertising.

Attitude. A relatively consistent way of thinking about, feeling toward, or responding to some environmental stimulus or input. Made up of cognitive, emotional, and behavioral components.

Attitude formation. The process by which attitudes are formed or created. Most members of the Nazi Party have a strongly negative attitude toward Jews. Since the individual Nazis were not born with an innate hatred of Jews, the Nazis must have acquired their negative viewpoint by learning — or by imitating the thoughts and behaviors of others. The process by which anyone acquires a viewpoint toward or set of social expectancies about some person or thing can rightfully be called "attitude formation."

Authoritarian (aw-thor-ih-TAIR-ee-un). A dictatorship is a perfect example of an authoritarian system — one in which the person on top rules with an iron fist.

Authoritarian personality. In 1950, several social scientists identified a group of traits or behavior patterns that make up what they call "the authoritarian personality." These traits include a high degree of conformity, overcontrol of feelings and impulses, rigidity of thinking, and prejudice toward other races and religions. Individuals possessing these traits are said to have highly conventional values, are preoccupied with gaining power and status, and try to think and act like their political or social leaders. The authoritarian personality is said to develop in people who were subjected to very strict parental control early in their lives, and who learned to bury their resentments and adopt an attitude of giving in to authority in order to survive.

Communication. From a Latin word meaning "to impart" or "to convey." Literally, to communicate is to pass a message (input) from one living system to another. In psychology, the communication process is often broken into four parts: the communicator, the message, the receiver or audience, and feedback from the audience to the communicator.

Counterpropaganda. Communications designed primarily to overcome or to cancel the effectiveness of propaganda issued by someone else.

Credibility (kred-uh-BILL-it-tee). From the Latin words meaning "worthy of lending money to." Literally, the power or ability to inspire belief.

Ethnocentrism (eth-no-CENN-trizem). The Greek word *ethnos* means "nation." Ethnocentrism is the act of placing your nation or your people at the center of things — that is, the belief that you and your people are the most important of all.

Fascism (FASH-izem). The Fascist Party was to Italy in the 1930s and 1940s what the Nazi Party was to Germany. The Fascists were an authoritarian, ethnocentric political party which believed that the law should be blindly obeyed, and that Italians were the best people in the world.

Media (MEE-dee-uh). From a Latin word meaning "that which lies in the middle" or "the substance through which a force acts." The singular is "medium." Money is a "medium of exchange." Newspapers are a medium "by which information is spread or communicated." In the United States, the news media—radio, TV, magazines, and newspapers—are very influential in swaying public opinion, particularly about political matters.

Obedience experiments. A series of experiments conducted by Stanley Milgram. Milgram asked his subjects to give an increasingly strong electric shock to "learners" who, in fact, never received shock at all but who pretended to feel great pain. Despite the fact that the subjects usually protested to Milgram that the experiment should stop, the majority of them continued to give shock in obedience to Milgram's orders. One of the most disturbing aspects of Milgram's research is that most people similar to Milgram's subjects will insist that they personally would not blindly obey orders such as Milgram gave—yet many studies by Milgram and other psychologists suggest that most people would in fact blindly obey if put to a real-life test.

Persuasion (purr-SWAY-zhun). From the Latin words meaning "to urge" or "to advise." To persuade is to induce someone to adopt a cerain attitude by argument or pleading, or to win someone over to your way of thinking.

Propaganda (prop-uh-GANN-duh). From a Latin source meaning "to enlarge" or "to extend." When you have children, you propagate the human race by extending or enlarging the number of humans on earth. Technically speaking, propaganda is the spreading of doctrines, ideas, arguments, facts, or rumors through any communication medium in a deliberate effort to further a cause.

Reference group. A group that sets social norms we are expected to live up to. Reference groups typically give us goals that we should attain if we are group members, as well as giving us rewarding or punishing feedback as we move toward or away from these goals.

Role playing. A role is a more or less stereotyped set of responses that a person makes to related or similar situations. To play a role is to take on or act out a set of stereotyped reactions.

Socialist. Socialism is a political and economic theory of social organization in which there is collective or governmental ownership of all resources. A socialist is someone who believes that the government should take over and run all businesses, and should own all or most private property.

Totalitarian (toe-tal-ih-TARE-ee-an). Someone who believes in a one-party system of government, or a type of government in which no dissent or freedom of opinion is allowed. The Nazi and Fascist Parties both were totalitarian, as are most Communist parties.

INTRODUCTION: ANIMAL FARM

When the pigs took over the farm, almost everyone was pleased. The animals believed that life on the farm would be much easier with the pigs in charge rather than a human being. And, in fact, things did run much more smoothly for a while. But almost anything would have been better than the old system. For years the farm had been owned and mismanaged by an incompetent drunkard named Jones, who overworked, underfed, and cruelly beat the animals. Then came the revolution.

It happened on a weekend. Jones had gone off on a two-day drunk without feeding the animals. When he came home, he passed out but was soon awakened by the noise of the hungry animals who had broken into the storeroom. Jones rushed out with his whip, intending to beat the animals back to their proper places. Instead of running, the animals fought back and ran Jones off the farm. The animals' revolution was a success.

The pigs, because they were more intelligent than the other animals, took over management of the farm. They set up a **socialist** system in which every member of the society was to do a fair share of the work and get a fair share of whatever was produced. No longer would the animals have to work for a greedy farmer who kept all of the profits. The name of the farm was changed from Manor Farm to Animal Farm. The slogan of the revolution was: ALL ANIMALS ARE EQUAL.

Napoleon and Snowball, the two pigs who had led the revolution, ran the farm, but they never seemed to agree on anything. So, after a brief power struggle, Napoleon, with a pack of vicious dogs, chased Snowball off the farm.

Napoleon and the other pigs did not take part in the actual farm labor; they were the managers. However, the pigs got fatter and fatter from the efforts of the working animals. Eventually Napoleon gained complete control of Animal Farm and could do as he pleased. He became a **totalitarian** leader, and everyone obeyed him.

Napoleon and the other pigs took advantage of their authority and power. They began to make changes in the way Animal Farm was run. The pigs moved into Jones's house, slept in his beds, drank his liquor, wore his clothes, and even carried his whips. To make the change complete, the pigs learned to walk on their hind legs, just like humans. It was as if the revolution had never taken place. Finally, Animal Farm was renamed Manor Farm, and the slogan of the revolution was changed to: ALL ANIMALS ARE EQUAL, BUT SOME ANIMALS ARE MORE EQUAL THAN OTHERS.

Animal Farm has been called a fairy tale by its author George Orwell, but it is more than just a children's story about talking animals. *Animal Farm,* published in 1945, was Orwell's way of describing the social system in Russia under Joseph Stalin (Napoleon the pig). Orwell, a Socialist, was not against the Socialist or Communist form of government, but he was against totalitarianism. What was supposed to be a dictatorship by all the people had turned into a dictatorship by one ruthless individual. Thousands of Russians were murdered at Stalin's command so that he could remain in control.

What happened in *Animal Farm* and in the U.S.S.R., however, was not just a takeover by an **authoritanian** ruler (one who believes in absolute obedience to authority). There was something about society itself that made the takeover possible. Most of the people had a deep respect for authority and tended to obey whoever took command.

An **attitude** refers to a consistent way of thinking about, feeling toward, or responding to an object, idea, person, or situation. Unlike consciously held beliefs and opinions, attitudes often operate at an unconscious level and produce thoughts, feelings, and behaviors that cannot always be easily explained. For the most part, attitudes are learned through experience.

OBEDIENCE TO AUTHORITY

An attitude of strict obedience to authority can obviously be one of the most powerful forces in any society. The disastrous effects of such attitudes were quite evident after World War II, and psychologists began to investigate possible reasons why people would do things under orders that they might not ordinarily do. Researchers started by examining some of the most obvious traits of Hitler's Germany. The German government was a form of **fascism** — an extremely authoritarian and conservative dictatorship based on aggressive nationalism and **ethnocentrism** (belief in the superiority of one's own race or ethnic group). German ethnocentrism consisted of an intense hatred of Jews, blacks, and most other ethnic groups except white Germanic types. Because racial hatred and prejudice seemed to be important aspects of what had happened in Germany, researchers at the University of California in Berkeley developed a set of questions that were supposed to give a scale or measure of a person's ethnocentrism. The scale was designed by T. W. Adorno, E. Frenkel-Brunswik, and their colleagues.

The ethnocentrism scale was based on a number of questions about attitudes toward minority groups. The people who scored high on the scale were those who seemed to see the world in terms of a few special in-groups, and who were intolerant of all other groups. The in-groups were to be wholeheartedly supported, and the other groups were to be ignored, repressed, or even attacked if aggression became necessary.

The people with the highest ethnocentric attitudes were singled out for further study. Interviews, various personality tests, and three more scales of attitudes were used. People who scored high on the ethnocentrism scale also tended to score high on scales of anti-Semitism, economic and political conservatism, and fascism. Anyone who scored high on all four scales was identified by the researchers as an **authoritarian personality.**

The Authoritarian Personality

The authoritarian personality is said to consist of a group of traits including a high degree of conformity, dependence on authority, overcontrol of feelings and emotions, rigidity of thinking, and ethnocentrism. People with these traits usually adhere to conventional values, are preoccupied with power and status, identify with authority figures, and are generally hostile to members of minority groups. (E. R. Jaensch, a German psychologist and member of Hitler's Nazi party, described the ideal Nazi in many of the same terms used to describe the authoritarian personality.)

Authoritarianism is a learned or acquired attitude. Interviews with and personal histories of people who scored high on the California test suggest that such people tend to have had rigid, punitive parents who subjected their children to strict parental control. Because their parents were so powerful and punishing, the children may have learned to cope with stress by being overly obedient, by following parental orders blindly, and by overcontrolling their feelings and impulses. Given the parental model they grew up under, it is not surprising that the children themselves developed authoritarian attitudes early in life and tended to show the same behavior patterns as adults. They then treat their own children

More recently, United States soldiers in Vietnam said they were following orders when they shot civilians and buried the bodies in mass graves.

Parents who are harsh and punitive sometimes cause children to be overly obedient to authority. Such children, may follow orders blindly in order to avoid punishment and to please the parent.

as they were treated, and the authoritarianism is passed along to yet another generation.

The people described as authoritarian by the California test bear a striking resemblance in personality to those people described as externalizers by Julian Rotter (see Chapter 10). They tend to see their lives as being controlled by external or outside forces rather than by their own internal resources.

As interesting as the California study is, it has many flaws. To begin with, few things in life (especially personalities) are either completely good or completely bad. Thus, few people are authoritarians all of the time, just as few people are externalizers in all of life's complex situations. Furthermore, there is always the problem of the difference between a person's answers on a questionnaire and the person's behavior in real life. The study also tended to focus on politically conservative or right-wing individuals and did not point out that liberals and radical, left-wing types can also be rigid and authoritarian. Stalin was certainly not a political conservative in the usual sense.

But even with its drawbacks, the California study made some important discoveries. It pointed out that early childhood experiences can result in strict, rigid adult behaviors and thinking patterns. It also suggested how such personality patterns might even be rewarding to some individuals. People with rigid, authoritarian attitudes are usually free of doubts about how to behave. As long as they have an authority figure to identify with and to take orders from, they do not have to form their own opinions or make independent judgments. For some people, in certain situations, such freedom from responsibility comes as a blessing.

Animal Farm inhabitants grew up under the strict discipline of Jones and learned to obey without thinking. It was only under a set of severe circumstances that the animals rebelled and threw Jones out. Then before long, with the pigs in charge, the animals were back in the same condition. With little or no protest, the animals accepted Napoleon's authority after he had a few of them executed. Similarly, the people of Germany may have been ripe for a takeover by an authoritarian like Hitler because they had learned strict obedience much earlier in life. Little protest was heard when Hitler took over and ordered the extermination of millions of Jews. Just how far will people go before they abandon their attitudes toward obedience and begin to protest?

Milgram's Experiments

In the 1960s, **obedience experiments** were conducted by social psychologist Stanley Milgram at Yale University. Milgram's studies suggest that under certain circumstances a good many people will obey authority even to the point of inflicting severe pain on helpless individuals. Milgram told the subjects of his experiments that he was studying the effects of punishment on learning. The subjects were instructed by the experimenter to ask a set of questions to another subject (the "learner"). Whenever the "learner" gave a wrong answer, the subjects were told to push a button that would give the learner an electric shock. If the learner still gave a wrong answer, the subjects were told to increase the strength of the shock. The subjects were constantly reminded by Milgram that the shocks were part of the experiment, and that the experiment would not be successful if his orders to shock were not followed.

The subjects were all given a sample shock at 45 volts. The controls they used to administer the shocks, however, were clearly marked and could be turned from 15 volts up to 450 volts — severe shock — which can inflict great pain and even physical damage.

The learner was strapped into something that looked like an electric chair. The subject, in another room, could hear the learner's responses over an intercom system. At first, the learner gave the correct responses almost every time, and few shocks had to be administered. As the experiment proceeded, however, the learner gave more and more wrongs answers, and the voltage had to be turned up. At 75 volts the learner began to moan. At 150 volts the moans were replaced by demands to be released from the experiment. But even when the learner began to complain, Milgram insisted that the shocks must continue. The subject giving the shocks was told, "You have no other choice, you must go on!" At 300 volts the learner began to scream in pain. As the voltage reached the danger level, the screams stopped and the learner was deadly silent as if injured. But even then, the experimenter ordered the subject to continue administering shocks.

In Milgram's obedience experiments no one was really shocked. The electric controls were fake, and the learner was really a ''stooge'' who was part of the experiment. The learner gave the wrong answers on purpose and only pretended to be shocked.

Many of the subjects in the experiment were ''shocked,'' however. They were *psychologically* shocked to realize that they actually had the capacity to follow orders to the point of inflicting severe pain on a helpless, strapped-down individual.

Most of the subjects in the experiments followed orders and gave at least a few painful shocks. Some of the subjects, when ordered to do so, actually turned the voltage all the way up and gave what they thought to be dangerous shocks. Only 35 percent of the people who took part in the experiments refused to follow orders. The others, many of whom probably thought of themselves as kind or gentle individuals, found out that under certain circumstances they were not as kind as they thought they were. Some even found out that they might have a streak of cruelty in their personalities.

In another set of experiments, Milgram reversed the procedure. The experimenter changed places with the learner. Under these circumstances, it was the experimenter — the person in authority — who would be getting shocked on the orders of the learner who was supposed to be just another subject in the experiment. The subjects' attitudes toward authority became evident quite soon. The subjects all stopped following orders and stopped giving shocks as soon as the experimenter began to protest at 150 volts.

This is a scene from *The Tenth Level*, a television drama based on obedience experiments conducted be Stanley Milgram. Many subjects continued to follow the experimenter's order to continue administering shocks even when the ''learner'' began to scream out in pain.

(Milgram's experiments and others like them do not inflict physical harm, but they might be responsible for psychological damage to the subjects. The people who gave what they thought were severe shocks will have to live for many years with the guilty knowledge of what they did. Because of the potential psychological harm such guilt can cause, the American Psychological Association's code of ethics now prohibits experiments like Milgram's.)

Milgram's studies are sometimes called "the Eichmann experiments." They have been named after Adolf Eichmann, the Nazi war criminal who, like many of Hitler's followers, claimed he was "only following orders." But the capacity to follow antisocial or even criminal orders is not restricted to Nazis or even to a certain type of personality. Milgram, in fact, could find no strong personality differences between those subjects who followed orders and those who refused to give shocks. Even though Milgram's experiments took place under rather unnatural conditions in a laboratory, there are many examples of people performing inhumane acts and committing crimes in the name of authority.

ATTITUDE FORMATION AND STABILITY

Certain attitudes may lead to unpleasant situations, but life would be much more complicated than it already is if people didn't have attitudes or predetermined ways of responding to the world. Attitudes allow people to make fairly accurate predictions about other people, places, and things. Attitudes about food allow people to avoid foods they dislike. Attitudes about certain people suggest ways of behaving when with those people. Attitudes that correctly predict future events or responses are usually rewarding or help people to avoid punishment. With an established pattern of attitudes, each individual decides what to eat for breakfast, what radio station to listen to, what clothes to wear, how to behave at a party, and how to vote in an election. Those attitudes that are most often rewarding tend to stick with people for a long time and often become basic parts of an individual's personality.

Because attitudes have such an important influence on human behavior, psychologists have attempted to discover how attitudes are acquired and maintained. One explanation of the development of attitudes was put forward in 1935 by Gordon Allport. He suggests four basic processes in **attitude formation:**

1. *Individuals gradually assimilate or absorb the ideas and reactions of the people around them with whom they closely identify.* A child who grows up in a family of classical musicians and artists will often develop favorable attitudes towards classical music and art. Someone whose friends are all interested in astrology may soon develop an interest in the stars.
2. *Attitudes may be the result of dramatic experiences.* A terrible hangover resulting from someone's first experience with beer may lead to a life-long dislike or unfavorable attitude toward beer. That attitude toward beer might even become "generalized" and lead to a dislike of alcohol in general.

A profound religious experience can change one's attitude toward other humans and the way one lives.

3. *Everyday experiences can shape certain attitudes.* People in different parts of the world have different attitudes about food. These attitudes can be the result of constant exposure to the foods available in a certain area. A teacher's constant mentioning of a specific theory can encourage students to develop favorable (or unfavorable) attitudes about that theory. Repeated exposure (such as through advertising) can help establish attitudes about everything from toothpaste to politicians.

4. *Attitudes can also be adopted or selected on purpose.* Children might assimilate the religious attitudes of their parents, but people can also make a conscious decision to join a religious group and then adopt the already existing attitudes of that group.

The Bennington Women

Once people have established a set of attitudes, those attitudes may be long-lasting. Studies have shown, however, that many students tend to change some attitudes and to become more politically liberal during their college years. Even students who previously held the attitudes of their highly conservative parents often change their political views while at college. This change of attitude may be due to the fact that liberal arts colleges are often populated by teachers and students who are politically liberal. A student from a conservative background may be bombarded by liberal ideas in such a situation and may gradually assimilate those attitudes or adopt them in order to become a socially acceptable member of the campus group. But do such attitudes hold up when the student returns home to a more conservative social atmosphere?

Social psychologist Theodore Newcomb investigated the stability or permanence of political attitudes on the campus of a women's college in the 1930s. Newcomb was teaching at Bennington, a respected liberal arts college in Vermont. Most of the 600 students were from wealthy, conservative families. Most of the faculty were quite liberal, and they felt it their duty to impress their political and social attitudes on the students. Since the school was rather isolated and because the students rarely left the campus, the liberal teachers had a captive audience for their views.

Newcomb's research showed that the more conservative women at Bennington were often looked down upon by the liberal students. The women who had the most prestige and status on campus were those who held the most liberal attitudes. Newcomb also found that the longer students stayed at Bennington, the more likely they were to assimilate or adopt the views of the liberal majority. Seniors, on the average, were much more liberal than first-year students. In the 1936 presidential election, 62 percent of the first-year women supported the Republican candidate, and only 9 percent were for the Socialist or Communist candidates. Among the seniors, only 14 percent supported the Republican, while 30 percent were in favor of the Socialist or Communist candidates.

Newcomb explained that the Bennington student body served as a sort of **reference group** — a group that individuals can refer to on matters of social behavior and attitudes. The Bennington reference group rewarded liberal attitudes with acceptance and punished conservative attitudes with disapproval. As one woman put it, "What I wanted here was intellectual approval of teachers and the more advanced students. Then I found out you can't be reactionary [ultraconservative] and be intellectually respectable."

Newcomb measured the women's attitude changes during their college years. Then he attempted to discover what would happen to their liberal ideas once they left college. He followed the lives of 150 Bennington women for 25 years. Many of the women returned to their conservative social surroundings, but most of them did not give up their liberal attitudes as Newcomb thought they might.

During the 1960s the anti-war movement became the reference group for many college students. Jerry Rubin, a leader of the movement, is shown at one of the anti-war demonstrations.

Newcomb reports that the women had several methods of maintaining their liberalism. They tended to marry liberal men who would reinforce their political views. They got involved in socially oriented projects that would bring them into contact with other liberal thinkers, and they kept in close contact with their Bennington classmates.

Newcomb's findings suggest that if a particular set of attitudes has been important or rewarding, people will (consciously or unconsciously) seek environments that will maintain and support those attitudes.

ATTITUDE CHANGE

Maintaining an attitude is not as simple as it may seem. Sometimes it is almost impossible to avoid the thousands of environmental inputs that might affect our personal attitudes. In the United States, for instance, most people encounter about 1500 advertisements every day. All such **advertising** is an attempt to persuade or to change our attitudes.

Attitude *stability* is difficult to measure because, as Newcomb found out, the subjects have to be studied for many years. Attitude *change,* however, can take place almost instantly, and many experiments have been used to investigate the factors involved in attitude change.

Helson's Adaptation-Level Theory

Group pressure, as in the Bennington study, can play an important role in attitude change. Asch and many others (Chapter 11) showed that group pressure, when applied by "stooges" in an experiment, can even influence such things as perception. Robert R. Blake, Harry Helson, and their colleagues at the University of Texas carried the perception experiments several steps further. These scientists showed that group pressures can sometimes force people to conform and change their attitudes toward such things as war, violence, and violating social rules.

Before Harry Helson teamed up with Blake to study social perceptions, he had spent years investigating visual perception in individuals. During this time Helson had developed what he called the **adaptation-level theory** to explain such things as why a white rose appears to be pure white when viewed against a black background, but looks reddish when seen on a background of blue-green

Which of these numerous roadside signs would be most prominent to a driver? Different people may have different answers. The sign (or stimulus) most readily seen may be the "Dean" sign because it blinks off and on, making it stand out from the background. Or it may be liquor signs because the driver is ready for a drink.

velvet. According to Helson's adaptation-level theory, perception is influenced by three things: stimulus, background, and personality factors.

Stimulus factors usually have to do with the physical properties of what is perceived. Advertisers often use large, brightly lit billboards to make sure that their message is easily seen.

Background factors have to do with the situation in which the stimulus is presented. One billboard standing alone on the side of a road might be very noticeable to passersby. The same sign, seen in a landscape (background) littered with advertisements will be much less perceptible.

Personality factors that influence perception include genetically determined responses, individual traits, and past experiences.

When Helson began working with Blake on studies of social perception, it became obvious to him that these three factors influencing physical perception were also involved in such things as social perceptions, personal judgments, and attitudes.

Stimulus Factors

In general, the more vague a stimulus is, the easier it is to get people to change their attitudes about that stimulus. For instance, it is often possible to get people to change their minds about the effectiveness of a brand of toothpaste because there are many brands, and the differences between them are usually minimal or vague. It is much more difficult to get people to change their judgments about concrete facts such as the difference in length between eight- and ten-inch lines.

In Milgram's experiments on attitudes toward authority and obedience, the commands of the experimenter acted as a stimulus. The weaker the stimulus, the less likely the subjects were to administer painful shocks. When Milgram stood right over the subjects and told them that they must give the shocks, 65 percent obeyed. When Milgram left the room and gave his orders by phone, only 22 percent of the subjects followed orders. When Milgram, the authority figure, was not right there as a vivid stimulus, many of the subjects seemed to change their attitudes about obeying authority.

FIG. 15-1. According to Helson's adaptation-level theory, our social perception (and therefore our behavior is influenced by background and personality as well as by stimulus. When asked to contribute to a charity, your response often depends on the generosity of others as well as your own.

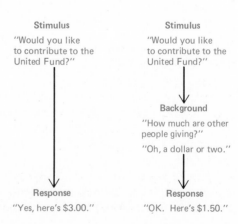

Background Factors

In social situations a group often acts as a background that can affect individual perceptions and attitudes. The Bennington study and experiments on conformity and group pressure show how social backgrounds or situations often influence personal attitudes and cause people to make judgments they might not make if they were alone.

In several experiments, Milgram examined the effects of a social background on the responses of his subjects. Three people were put in a room and instructed to give the shocks to the learner. Two of the people, however, were "stooges." When the two stooges refused to give anything more than mild shocks, the real subject had to decide between following the lead provided by the group or the orders of the experimenter. The social background was usually more influential than the authority figure stimulus. More than 90 percent of the subjects refused to complete the experiment.

Personality Factors and Past Experience

Personality tests are not yet valid or reliable enough to tell us what factors influence attitudes in all situations. In general, however, a number of personality characteristics seem to be linked to an individual's tendency to yield, obey, or conform—especially under group pressures. Yielders tend to have lower IQ scores and less complex personalities than do nonyielders. People who conform most readily tend to be conventional, inconsistent, anxious, and group-oriented.

Attitudes are consistent ways of perceiving, feeling, thinking about, or behaving toward an object, idea, person, or group of people. As such, certain attitudes may be influenced by our genetic blueprints. But for the most part, attitudes are learned through experience. Previous experience with authority or with inflicting pain probably had a great deal to do with the attitudes displayed by the subjects in Milgram's experiments. Previous experience with psychological experiments could also have been important. Anyone who knew that Milgram was up to might have reacted quite differently to the experimenter's authority.

COMMUNICATION

Persuasion is a deliberate attempt by a person or group to change someone else's attitudes or behaviors. Milgram's experiment was set up to persuade his subjects to give shock to the "learner." Political leaders often try to persuade people to vote one way or another. Advertisers continually attempt to persuade us to buy their products. In all these instances, the act of persuasion consists of getting sensory information to the individual whose attitude is to be changed. In other words, **communication** is one of the most important aspects of persuasion.

Advertising is based completely on communication. The most successful communicators persuade the most people and sell the most products. Political persuasion also relies heavily on communication. Any dictator who wants to

Communication with voters is the major factor in getting politicians elected. Candidates for public office carefully plan the information they include in handbill, posters, and advertisements.

remain in authority usually begins by taking control of all forms of public communication. When Napoleon the pig took over Animal Farm, he used a pig named Squealer as his press agent or communications expert. Squealer was a brilliant talker who could convince the animals of almost anything. "He could turn black into white," the animals said. When Napoleon cut the workers' rations, Squealer called the reduction a "readjustment" and convinced the animals that it was for their own good. Hitler and Stalin both took complete control of communications and set up vast propaganda machines — organizations designed to give out **propaganda** or information that would influence public opinion and attitudes.

Because of the persuasive power of the **media** on human behavior, psychologists have attempted to determine how communication functions in the formation of attitudes. There are four basic factors in the communications process—the communicator, the message, the audience, and the response of the audience.

The Communicator

The communicator is the person (or group) trying to bring about a change in attitude. Obviously, the most important trait a communicator can have is believability, or **credibility.** Because few people will pay much attention to a known liar, an untrustworthy person often has trouble getting a message across.

Some of the first scientific investigations of persuasion and credibility were conducted in the 1940s and 1950s at Yale University by Carl I. Hovland, Irving L. Janis, and their colleagues. In one experiment on credibility, Hovland and H. C. Kelman had a speaker give a talk strongly in favor of leniency to juvenile delinquents. Three audiences of high-school students heard the same speech, but the speaker was introduced differently to each group—once as an authority (judge of a juvenile court), then as an unidentified member of the audience, and finally as a dope dealer out on bail. As expected, the people who thought they had been addressed by a judge were the most influenced by the speech. The dope dealer was by far the least credible and persuasive of the three, even though he spoke exactly the same words as did the judge.

Hovland, Janis, and their colleagues identified a number of factors that influenced credibility. People who are well-liked and who seem to be acting naturally rather than "playing roles" are usually the most trusted. People who are in some way similar to their audience tend to be believed. Status also affects credibility. Since doctors, scientists, and church leaders tend to be more believable than are people with obvious low social status, people dressed as doctors, scientists, or priests often appear in advertisements.

The Message

The message is the informational input that a communicator sends or transmits to an audience. The content of a message is obviously important, but the way in which a message is presented has been found to be an especially important factor in attitude change. The two most common ways of presenting a message are the "emotional" appeal and the "logical" appeal.

The relative effectiveness of the emotional versus the logical appeal was investigated by G. W. Hartmann during the 1936 presidential campaign. Hartmann prepared two leaflets urging people to vote for the Socialist party candidate. One leaflet used highly sentimental and flowery language to describe the wonderful political changes the Socialist party could bring about. The "logical" leaflet presented a series of highly rational arguments, facts, and figures that pointed out the goals of the Socialist party. The leaflets were distributed in two

A communicator must establish credibility if his message is to be accepted by the intended audience. When President Jimmy Carter was trying to convince the nation to accept his energy conservation policy, he often appeared in a heavy sweater.

different parts of a test city. A third section of the city received no leaflets and served as a "control" or comparison population for the experiment.

In 1936, because of the severity of the great economic depression, many people were looking for a new form of government and were willing to give the Socialists a chance. In the control section of the test city, where none of Hartmann's propaganda leaflets were passed out, there was a 24 percent increase in support for the Socialist party as compared to the 1932 election. In the parts of the city where the logical leaflets were handed out, Socialist support was up 35 percent. Where the emotional leaflets were used, however, there was a 50 percent increase in support of the Socialist party.

In an attempt to find out why the emotional appeal was more effective than the logical appeal, Hartmann interviewed many voters after the election. He found out that more voters remembered (and possibly read) the highly emotional leaflet than remembered the rather dry rational leaflet. Emotionality, it seems, like credibility, helps the communicator get the attention of the audience. Once the audience's attention is captured, the logical facts of the message can do their part in attitude change or formation. Presumably, if Hartmann had been able to get all of the test subjects to read the propaganda, the increase in Socialist support would have been the same among both groups.

Advertisers realize the importance of the emotional appeal in getting people to pay attention to their message. Sex is one of the most often used emotional stimulants in advertising. Fear is another emotion that advertisers and propagandists often resort to as an attention getter. Television campaigns against smoking and drinking cite cancer statistics and show horrible scenes of automobile accidents. Such emotional tactics do get some people to pay attention and do scare some people into changing their attitudes and behavior. Experimental evidence, however, suggests that fear-arousing messages may be less effective in the long run than they appear to be at first glance.

In 1953, Irving Janis and Seymour Feshback investigated the effects of fear-arousing messages on high-school students. For the experiment the researchers wrote three different 15-minute lectures on tooth decay. The "high fear" lecture contained 71 reference to pain, cancer, paralysis, blindness, mouth infections, inflamed gums, ugly or discolored teeth, and dental drills. The second lecture ("moderate fear") discussed pain and disease but only made 46 such references. The third ("minimal fear") lecture did not mention pain or disease. Instead, it suggested how to avoid cavities and tooth decay through proper dental care.

Each lecture was delivered to a group of 50 students. Attitudes toward dental care were tested one week before, immediately after, and one week after the lectures were given. When questioned immediately after the lecture, the high-fear group reported that they thought the lecture impressive, excellent, interesting, and important. Most admitted that the lecture got them very worried about their own teeth. The minimal fear lecture was not found to be so impressive, and few of the students who heard it reported that they became worried about their teeth. The moderate fear lecture produced a mixed reaction about halfway between the results of the other two groups.

Some advertisements attempt to change attitudes and actions by using logic, such as this public service ad from the United States Department of Transportation. It says young people are for life and against killing, therefore, they should do what they can to stop killing on the highways.

THE NUMBER ONE KILLER OF YOUNG AMERICANS IS YOUNG AMERICANS.

You march against war. You fight for clean air and clean water. You eat natural foods. You practice yoga. You are so much for life. And you are so much against killing.

It would be unthinkable for you to kill another human being on purpose.

So then, why is this happening?

You don't mean to be. But

DRUNK DRIVER

At first, the fear tactic appeared to be working. But one week later, when the students were asked how the lecture had affected their tooth-care *behavior*, the real results of the fear-arousing message became apparent. Only 28 percent of the high fear group reported taking better care of their teeth, while 20 percent actually reported doing worse. In the minimal fear group, 50 percent were doing better while only 14 percent said they were doing worse. The high fear tactics had backfired. When it came to long-term attitude change, as measured by actual behavior, fear had produced just the opposite of what the communicator had in mind.

Counterpropaganda

Successful propaganda must withstand the test of time, but it also has to stand up against the claims of other propagandists. **Counterpropaganda** consists of messages designed to cancel out the effects of previous propaganda messages. After the one-week follow-up of the students who had received the dental lectures, Janis and Feshback exposed the students to some counterpropaganda. The students were then asked whether or not they believed the information that contradicted the original lectures. Twice as many students from the high-fear group were affected by the counterpropaganda, as compared to subjects from the minimal fear group. Janis and Feshback concluded that "under conditions where people will be exposed to competing communications dealing with the same issues, the use of a strong fear appeal will tend to be less effective than a minimal fear appeal in producing stable and persistent attitude changes."

Counterpropaganda seeks to reverse the effects of previous propaganda. Korean evangelist Sun Myung Moon was successful in changing the attitudes of hundreds of young people and converting them to his fundamentalist sect. When the new converts renounced their parents, a counterpropaganda campaign was launched by the unhappy parents to stop the work of Reverend Moon.

The work of Janis and Feshback suggests two reasons why fear and threats often fail to bring about effective attitude or behavior changes. For one thing, many people cope with frightening or stress-inducing information by repressing or denying the facts. For another, our emotions can arouse us and prepare us for action, but our perceptions are what guide our behaviors (see Chapter 5). A fear-arousing lecture, for instance, focuses attention on the *problems* of tooth decay, but does not give us the facts about *solutions to the problems* so that we can perceive what we must do to avoid getting decay. The high-fear subjects reported being worried about their teeth, but they didn't seem to know what to do about handling the problem. In such a situation, people may be receptive to counterpropaganda, especially if it offers them a useful solution to their difficulties.

The most successful propaganda messages, therefore, are usually those that are constructed with just the right amount of emotional content—enough to arouse audience attention, but not enough to detract from the message itself.

The Audience

The people whose attitudes are to be shaped make up the communicator's audience. In terms of Helson's adaptation-level theory, the communicator and the message are stimulus factors. The audience contains the background and personality factors that determine the effect a message will have on attitudes. Therefore, a good communicator usually attempts to find out as much as possible about the social background in which a message will appear and about the past experiences and personality characteristics of an audience. Advertising agencies and their clients spend millions of dollars each year in market research to gather this kind of imformation. The persuasive message is then shaped to fit a particular audience.

The inhabitants of Animal Farm hated and feared their previous human master. Napoleon, knowing the personality and past experiences of the animals, had little trouble convincing his audience to work harder. His messages always suggested that Jones would come back if the animals didn't follow orders. Germany, like most nations just prior to World War II, was in the midst of an economic depression. Hitler, knowing the psychological state of his audience, was able to create a warlike attitude among a great many German people. He just promised them that their economic problems would be solved once some new territories were acquired.

Whenever communicators fail to learn as much as possible about their audiences, the communicators' attempts to get their messages across are likely to fail. A group of social scientists working in Cincinnati, Ohio, inadvertently proved that fact shortly after World War II, when they attempted to change people's attitudes toward the United Nations. A large-scale advertising and publicity campaign was directed at the citizens of Cincinnati. During six months of intensive "mass education," the audience was bombarded with propaganda favorable to the U.N. Millions of dollars worth of free time and space were donated to the effort by the owners of billboards, newspapers, and radio and television stations.

Sociologists Shirley Star and Helen Hughes took surveys of attitudes in Cin-

FIG. 15–2.
Advertisers repeat their message often so that the audience remembers the product. If this man hadn't seen the Clean-O television commercial, he may not have chosen the product from the supermarket shelf.

cinnati before and after the six-month campaign. They reported that the massive effort to mold public opinion had failed. Only those people who were already interested in and in favor of the U.N. paid attention to the propaganda. The people who knew little about the U.N. and who were uninterested in it were supposed to be the audience, but they turned out to be the least likely to be affected by the propaganda. The multimillion dollar effort at communication had reached the wrong audience.

Actually, as Star and Hughes report, the greatest attitude changes took place in the people who were taking an active part in running the campaign. Their attitudes became even more favorable toward the U.N.

Audience Response

Why did the wrong people respond to the Cincinnati study? Because the propagandists failed to take into account a critical factor in the communication process — audience response.

If a communicator doesn't know how the audience is responding to a particular message, the effort at communication might be a complete failure. Successful communicators set up a link or feedback loop that constantly monitors audience response. Then if the feedback indicates that the audience is not responding, the communicator knows to change the message.

FIG. 15–3.
Successful communication depends on feedback from the audience to the communicator.

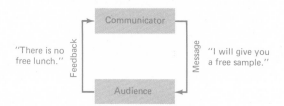

In the Cincinnati study, a target population was identified. Surveys had suggested that the poor, the uneducated, and the elderly knew the least about and were the least interested in the U.N. But among this particular audience at the time of the study (the late 1940s), few people could afford television sets, and few read the newspapers. The message, therefore, had little chance of getting through to them. Because they failed to monitor the actual response of their intended audience, the propagandists did not know that their message was not reaching the right people.

Role Playing and Attitude Change

One good way to make sure that members of an audience are getting the message is to have them act out or "play the role" represented by the attitudes the communicator wants them to acquire. Numerous studies have shown that the greatest attitude changes of all come about when the audience can be convinced to take part in **"role playing."** One such study was conducted in 1957 by W. A. Scott, who measured undergraduates' attitudes toward college football. Some students wanted bigger and better teams, while others wanted to do away with football on their campus.

Two weeks after the students' attitudes were first measured, Scott asked 58 of the undergraduates to take part in debates on the importance of football. The debates were set up so that all the students would have to argue against the positions they had taken during the attitude test. In this manner, Scott arranged for the students to "play a role" opposite to what their scores suggested their attitudes really were.

The debates were held in front of a class of students who voted afterwards to decide who had won. Scott, however, did not use the real results of the vote. Half the students were told they had won and half were told they had lost the debate. Later, Scott remeasured the debaters' attitudes. Those who thought they won the debate had shifted toward the position they took during the debate — even though this was against their previous attitude. Those who had lost shifted in the opposite direction — they became more convinced that their previous position was correct. The rewards of winning the debate apparently helped shift attitudes in favor of the position taken during role playing.

In a similar experiment, Irving Janis and B. T. King measured attitudes toward military service and then asked students to debate against their own opinions. For this experiment, half the students were given a prepared script to read in the debate, and half were asked to make up their own arguments. The people who read the prepared script showed little change in attitude after the debate. Those who had made up their own arguments showed a significant shift away from their original attitude. People, it seems, will tend to resist the ideas of others (prepared scripts) but might accept their own arguments if they can be made to express those arguments during role playing.

Highly successful selling campaigns often use some form of role playing in an attempt to shape a buyer's attitudes. A prospective buyer, for instance, might be asked to help demonstrate a vacuum cleaner or some other product. People who agree to take part in this sort of role playing are putting themselves in a position where they will have to argue in favor of the product. And in order to argue, they must pay attention to the product (the message). While arguing, they tend to express their needs in their own terms rather than in the "prepared script" terms of the seller. This sort of role playing establishes a direct feedback loop between buyer and seller, and even allows the seller to reward the buyer by agreeing with the arguments. In this manner, role playing has helped change the attitudes and break down the sales resistance of many people who neither wanted nor needed a new vacuum cleaner.

ATTITUDES AND THEORIES

For a period of twenty years or so — from 1945 to about 1965 — the major thrust in the field of attitude research had to do with how attitudes are formed, maintained, and changed. Hovland, Janis, and their associates at Yale studied persuasion and propaganda. Sherif, Asch, Helson, and Blake investigated the many pressures that groups put on their members to conform. A group of psychologists in California measured the attitudes of so-called authoritarian personalities, and Milgram showed how people with authoritarian attitudes could be induced to obey commands.

But around 1965, the field of attitude research took on a new and perhaps more challenging direction. For about this time, many psychologists began to question the usefulness of the very concept of *attitude*. The term had usually been defined as "an enduring way of thinking about, feeling about, or acting toward an object, idea, person, or situation." Attitudes were thus thought to be mental representations of people's cognitions, emotions, and behavioral tendencies. But attitudes were almost always *measured* by giving the subjects a pen-and-paper test of some kind — the belief being that the answers that people gave reflected how the people really felt about or behaved toward the objects of their attitudes.

By 1965, there was a growing body of experimental evidence showing a strange and unexpected difference between what people *said* about themselves and their attitudes on questionnaires, and how these same people acted in real life (see Chapter 16). Few people who answered the questionnaires saw themselves as being authoritarian or conforming, yet a great many of them behaved in an authoritarian or conformist manner. Furthermore, many people apparently have very inconsistent or conflicting attitudes. They might state on one questionnaire that they were in favor of better schools, yet state on another test that they were firmly opposed to increased school taxes.

According to most social psychologists, whenever you state an attitude, you are making a prediction about your future thoughts, feelings, and behaviors. Sometimes attitudes result in prejudice or highly emotional negative response to certain groups. But what does the psychologist do when it turns out that your attitudinal statement doesn't predict very well at all what you actually think, feel, and do at some future time?

Chinese and Blacks Keep Out!

The research study that first opened up this problem was reported by R. T. La Piere in 1934. La Piere had spent considerable time driving across the United States with a Chinese couple. Although at the time, there was a very strong "anti-Chinese" prejudice to be found among many Americans, La Piere and his friends had been refused service only once by hotels and restaurants during 10,000 miles of travel. Later, when they were safely home, La Piere sent questionnaires to all the hotels and cafes where they had stopped. One item on the questionnaire asked, "Will you accept members of the Chinese race as guests in your establishment?" More than 90 percent of the places responded with a very firm "no." Yet all but one of these hundreds of establishments actually had accepted the Chinese couple without question or comment. The hotels and restaurants obviously had (at that time) the expected anti-Chinese attitude — yet this attitude seldom was translated into real-life rejection of Chinese guests.

There is often a difference between what people say and their actions. These patriotic demonstrators are trying to disrupt an anti-war rally. Yet when asked if they believe in the right to free speech, they would probably answer yes.

In a similar study reported in 1952, Kutner, Wilkins, and Yarrow had three young women visit various restaurants in a fashionable suburban community in the Northeastern part of the United States. Two of the women were white; the third woman was black. All were well-dressed and well-mannered, according to the authors of the report. The two white women always arrived at the restaurant first, asked for a table for three, and were seated. Shortly thereafter, the black woman entered, informed the head waiter or hostess that she was with friends who were already seated, found the table, sat down with the two white women, and was served without question.

Two weeks after each visit, Kutner, Wilkins, and Yarrow wrote a letter to the manager of each establishment asking if they would serve blacks. Not one of the restaurants replied. Each establishment was then called on the phone. The experimenters report that the caller was treated in a very cool and distant manner that suggested the restaurant managers held a highly prejudiced attitude toward blacks. Yet, as in the La Piere study, this attitude simply was not translated into action when the managers were faced with actually seating a black person.

Since 1965, there have been dozens of other experiments, all of which suggest that attitudes (as measured by questionnaires) are very poor indicators of what people actually do, think, and feel in many real-life situations. Furthermore, there is often little relationship between attitude *change* and a subsequent change in the way a person *behaves*. Just as important, the reverse is also frequently true—that is, people often change their behaviors without changing those attitudes related to the behaviors.

Attitudes toward Attitudes

In their classic 1956 book *Opinions and Personality,* M. Brewster Smith, Jerome Bruner, and Robert W. White ask a most important question—Of what use to a person are his or her opinions? The answer to that question is not an easy one to find. Smith, Bruner, and White believe that attitudes or opinions *serve needs.* According to these theorists, whenever we express an attitude, we are really describing some need or goal that we are "driven" to fulfill. When we express

517

TABLE 15-1   **Attitude Theories**

	Theory
Pre-1965	1. Psychologists believed attitudes to be *mental representations* of people's cognitions, emotions, and behavioral tendencies.
Post-1965	1. Social psychologists believe attitudes are *internal processes* that guide our behaviors.
	2. Behavioral psychologists believe attitudes are simply *verbal statements* about our behaviors, which are under the control of external stimuli.

our attitudes to the people around us, therefore, we are often hunting for others with similar needs who might somehow assist us in achieving mutual goals. Like most social psychologists, Smith, Bruner, and White believe that attitudes are *internal processes* that somehow guide or direct our behaviors.

A radically different approach to the subject, however, was stated in the late 1960s by D. J. Bem. According to Bem, attitudes are simply verbal statements about our own behaviors. Bem—like B. F. Skinner—is a behaviorist. Bem believes that most of what we do is under the control of external stimulus inputs, not under the influence of internal or mental processes. Therefore, says Bem, our beliefs and opinions are really controlled by external stimuli that we often aren't aware of. Bem points out that studies such as the one by La Piere are really measuring two quite different responses that occur in markedly different environments. La Piere's questionnaire, for example, seems designed to elicit a negative response from the hotel and innkeepers to whom it was sent. But when La Piere presented himself and a well-dressed Chinese couple at the desk of a hotel, the stimulus situation was so different that the behavioral response of the innkeeper was bound to be different as well.

Bem believes that there really are no such things as "attitudes," unless you wish to consider them as verbal explanations of why we do what we do. Attitudinal statements then don't predict well at all—they merely give a rational picture of what we've already done. One might summarize Bem's position as follows: "How do I know what I think until I see what I've done?"

Are attitudes internal processes or external behaviors? The problem posed by these two highly different attitudes toward attitudes is much like the old question, "Which came first, the chicken or the egg?" Do we form attitudes (that is, internal processes) first, and then act in accordance with our opinions and beliefs? Or do we learn to behave in a certain way in the presence of certain environmental inputs, and then justify our behaviors later on by expressing verbal attitudes toward what we have done? Or do we do both things simultaneously?

At the moment, there is no agreed-upon solution to the puzzling differences we find between attitudes and behaviors—just as their is no agreed-upon solution to most of the basic problems in the field of psychology. We can measure attitudes, and we do know a great deal about how to change or maintain them. And we can measure behaviors, and we likewise know a great amount about how to train people to behave in different ways. Given this knowledge of how to create and change both attitudes and behaviors, perhaps the most important issue of all concerns who has the right to use these powerful techniques of personal change.

ATTITUDES AND ETHICS

Is it right to talk someone into buying a vacuum cleaner? Is it ethical to convince a nation that aggressive warfare is the solution to economic problems? Is it a morally responsible act to persuade people to commit criminal acts? Is it ethical to teach children religion or economic theories? Shouldn't all individuals be free to make up their own minds without interference from persuasive sources?

The ethical questions involved in persuasion and attitude formation are numerous and complex. Such questions become even more difficult to answer in cases of unintentional persuasion, like the influence parents have on their children or the subtle and indirect propaganda found in many textbooks and newspapers.

Psychology, as an objective science, is not in a position to answer ethical questions. Psychology can, however, attempt to provide some of the information and facts that are necessary in ethical decision making. One important point that psychology makes about attitude formation is that no one is free of the influence of others or free of the responsibility of influencing others. Every member of society is involved in attitude formation as both communicator and audience. Whenever two or more people get together, the outputs (messages) of one individual become the inputs of others. And this exchange of outputs can result in behavior or attitude change.

If every human behavior is, at least, potentially a persuader, then the only way people can hope to judge the ethical value of their actions is to have an understanding of how their behavior affects others and of how their own attitudes were shaped in the first place. Only when we know the full facts of how people communicate with and influence each other can we hope to make good ethical decisions about human attitudes and behaviors.

Psychology does more than explain how your behavior may be influencing others. The same information helps explain how others are influencing you. A scientific knowledge of how persuasion (on a conscious or unconscious level) takes place can help you to protect your own attitudes and allow you to evaluate objectively the stimuli you receive from the many persuasive forces within our society. Do you think, for instance, that the German people are likely to let another Hitler take over in the near future? If the inhabitants of Animal Farm had realized what was happening, would they have allowed the pigs to manipulate them in such a way?

► *SUMMARY*

1. In George Orwell's "fairy tale," the animals took over Animal Farm, but they then allowed themselves to be cruelly treated and controlled by an **authoritarian** pig. Why did the animals allow themselves to be so treated? As we have seen in this chapter, it was the animals' attitude toward authority that got them into trouble.

2. An **attitude** is a consistent way of thinking about, feeling toward, or responding to an object, idea, person, or situation. Experimental studies suggest that attitudes, such as the tendency to respect authority, can be learned as a result of early childhood experiences. The **authoritarian personality** was probably formed by authoritarian parents. Milgram's experiments further suggest that under certain circumstances a good many people will obey authority even to the point of inflicting severe pain on helpless individuals.

3. Certain attitudes may lead to unpleasant situations, but life would be much more complicated if we didn't have some predetermined ways of responding to the world. Because attitudes have such an important influence on human behavior, it is necessary that we have some understanding of how attitudes are formed. Such an awareness will help us deal with such phenomena as **fascism, ethnocentrism,** and the events in Hitler's Germany.

4. It has been suggested that there are four basic processes in **attitude formation:** (1) Attitudes can be assimilated or absorbed from individuals with whom one closely identifies; (2) attitudes can be formed as a result of a dramatic experience; (3) attitudes can be shaped by everyday experiences; and (4) attitudes can be selected on purpose.

5. Research by Newcomb (the Bennington women) and others suggest that if a particular attitude has been important or rewarding, people will attempt to maintain and support it. The attitudes and approval of the **reference group** become very important. Attitudes can, however, be changed. Attitude change is the main objective of most **advertising.**

6. According to Helson's **adaptation-level theory,** stimulus factors, background factors, and personality factors are especially important in influencing social perceptions, personal judgments, and attitudes.

7. Persuasion is a deliberate attempt by a person or group to change someone else's attitudes or behaviors. Because the act of persuasion consists of getting sensory information to the individual whose attitude is to be changed, **communication** is one of the most important aspects of persuasion or attitude change.

8. The four basic factors that must be considered if the communication process is to be successful are the communicator, the message, the audience, and the response of the audience. If feedback indicates the audience is not responding, the message can be changed. **Counterpropaganda** may also be used to cancel out the effects of previous **propaganda.**

9. About 1965, several studies revealed that there is often a difference between what people say about their attitudes and the way they behave in real-life situations. This discovery caused psychologists to look for a new definition of attitude. Social psychologists say that attitudes are internal processes that guide our behavior; behavioral psychologists say that attitudes are merely verbal explanations of why we do what we do.

10. However we define attitudes, they play an important role in human behavior. But most attitudes are learned, and there are many factors in our environment that can affect our attitudes. Knowledge of how persuasion and attitude formation take place can help us to understand not only how our own behavior affects others, but how others affect us and our behaviors. Attitudes and ethics are inseparable.

Suggested Readings

Ibsen, Henrik. A doll's house. In *Ghosts and three other plays by Henrik Ibsen.* (Michael Meyer, Tr.) New York: Doubleday, 1966.
Orwell, George. *Animal farm.* New York: NAL, 1974.
Selznick, Gertrude J. and Stephen Steinberg. *The tenacity of prejudice: Anti-Semitism in contemporary America.* New York: Harper & Row, 1969.
Terkel, Studs. *Working.* New York: Pantheon, 1974.

► STUDY GUIDE

A. RECALL

Sentence Completion

1. In Orwell's *Animal Farm,* when the pigs first took control of the farm, they set up a
[p. 496] _____ system.

[p. 497] 2. *Animal Farm* is really about _____ under _____ rule.

[p. 497] 3. For the most part, attitudes are _____ through experience.

[p. 497] 4. _____ is the belief in the superiority of one's own race or ethnic group.

5. Individuals who scored high on all four of Adorno's scales were said to have
[p. 498] _____ personalities.

6. The authoritarian personality is characterized by someone who adheres to _____ values and who is generally _____ to minority group
[p. 498] members, among other attributes.

[p. 498] 7. Parents of people with authoritarian personalities tend to be _____ and
[p. 498] _____.

[p. 499] 8. Julian Rotter would describe an authoritarian individual as an _____.

9. Milgram's experiments studied the extent to which people will _____
[p. 500] authority.

10. In Milgram's experiment, when "learners" made an error, the subjects gave them
[p. 500] what seemed to be an _____ _____.

11. Milgram's experiments violate the American Psychological Association's present
[p. 502] _____ of _____.

[p. 502]   12. Allport suggests that we assimilate or absorb ideas and/or attitudes of the people with whom we closely _____.

[p. 503]   13. Many students tend to move away from parental attitudes and to become more politically _____ during their college years.

[p. 504]   14. _____ _____ did a classic study of the affect of a liberal college environment on girls from conservative families in the 1930s.

[p. 504]   15. A _____ group is one that individuals can refer to on matters of social behavior and attitudes.

[p. 505]   16. _____ devised his adaptation-level theory while working on problems of visual perception.

[p. 506]   17. According to adaptation-level theory, perception is influenced by the factors of _____, _____, and _____.

[p. 506]   18. For Helson, the more _____ a stimulus is, the easier it is to get people to change their attitude about that stimulus.

[p. 507]   19. Conformers, or yielders, tend to have less _____ personalities than do nonyielders.

[p. 507]   20. _____ is a deliberate attempt to change someone else's attitudes or behaviors.

[p. 507]   21. Advertising is based on the _____ process.

[p. 509]   22. The four basic factors in the communication process are the communicator, the _____, the _____, and the response of the audience.

[p. 509]   23. The most important trait of the communicator in changing attitudes is that he or she have believability, or _____.

[p. 509]   24. Communication messages can have either _____ appeal or _____ appeal.

[p. 510]   25. Emotional arguments may have a greater effect than logical ones because they get the _____ of the audience.

[p. 510]   26. In the Janis and Feshback study on tooth decay, the "_____ fear" group showed the least amount of long-term attitude change.

[p. 511]   27. _____ consists of messages designed to cancel out the effects of previous messages.

[p. 514]   28. Successful communicators set up a link or _____ loop that constantly monitors audience response.

[p. 515]   29. In Scott's study of attitude change involving debates about football on campus, those students who thought that they had _____ the debate showed the greatest amount of change.

[p. 516]   30. When La Piere asked hotels and cafes if they would accept Chinese as guests in their establishments, _____ percent said "no."

[p. 517]   31. Smith, Bruner, and White feel that a person's attitudes or opinions serve his _____.

[p. 518]   32. _____ believes that there are no such things as "attitudes."

B. REVIEW

Multiple Choice: Circle the letter identifying the alternative that most correctly completes the statement or answers the question.

1. In Orwell's *Animal Farm,* the animals' revolutionary slogan was:
   A. DOWN WITH JONES.
   B. ALL ANIMALS ARE EQUAL.
   C. WE SHALL OVERCOME.
   D. ANIMALS ARE BETTER THAN PEOPLE.

2. Joseph Stalin in the U.S.S.R. and the pigs in *Animal Farm* were able to gain control because their "subjects":
   A. were not intelligent enough to realize what was going on.
   B. had a long history of respecting anyone in authority.
   C. elected them before they became authoritarian.
   D. had never tried dictatorships before and thought it would be worth a try.

3. Which of the following is *not* generally listed as a characteristic of someone with an authoritarian personality?
   A. rigidity of thinking
   B. creativity
   C. ethnocentricity
   D. proneness to conformity

4. People with authoritarian personalities:
   A. tend to be internalizers, seeing themselves as being in control of their own destinies.
   B. are almost always politically conservative.
   C. are usually free of doubts about how to behave.
   D. are very often members of minority groups.

5. In Milgram's first experiment on obedience, _____ percent of the subjects refused to follow orders to shock another subject.
   A. 15
   B. 35
   C. 60
   D. 85

6. Newcomb's study at Bennington College demonstrated that:
   A. seniors were more liberal than freshmen.
   B. the faculty at the college was more conservative than the students.
   C. when graduates went back home their attitudes always reversed to their previous position.
   D. authoritarians do not make good students.

7. Adaptation-level theory:
   A. was devised by Harry Helson.
   B. originally dealt with perceptual phenomena.
   C. talks about stimulus, background, and personality factors.
   D. all of the above.

8. Hovland and Kelman found which of the following communicators to be most effective in changing attitudes about juvenile delinquency?
   A. a juvenile court judge
   B. a student from the audience
   C. a real juvenile delinquent
   D. a dope dealer out on bail

9. Using high fear appeals to influence attitudes:
   A. may backfire and result in less change.
   B. is much better than using low fear messages.
   C. can be referred to as a message with "logical appeal."
   D. is more effective in the long run than it is at first.

10. Studies like those of La Piere and Kutner, Wilkins, and Yarrow demonstrate that:
   A. people are probably less prejudiced than they think they are.
   B. anti-Chinese attitudes are stronger than antiblack attitudes.
   C. attitude scales are both reliable and valid.
   D. there may be little relationship between what a person says and what a person does.

WATERGATE: A PSYCHOLOGICAL PERSPECTIVE

One year of Watergate is enough! Two years of Watergate is too much! But no matter what anyone says or does, it will be quite a few years before we really get Watergate behind us. A variety of novelists and movie makers will have their say as will psychologists and social scientists. Watergate has given them much on which to speculate.

One of the most intriguing questions about the Watergate affair is: What made it happen? Bertram H. Raven of the University of California at Los Angeles has attempted to analyze Watergate in terms of group dynamics. His conclusions are based in part on a review of the transcripts of the President's tapes and testimony given before the Sen-

ate Select Committee and the House Judiciary Committee.

Conformity was once believed to be the major factor in making group decisions. People do tend to go along with the crowd. In recent years, however, social psychologists have reported on another phenomenon of "group-think." "Risky shift" is the term used to describe the tendency of certain groups to become more extreme or to take riskier positions in their judgments. The risky-shift phenomenon is explained by the pressure of an individual within a group to at least equal or preferably exceed the group average. The trend, therefore, is not to keep up with the Joneses but to surpass them. When this begins to happen within a group, says Raven, the effect is a movable or runaway norm that leads to more and more extreme positions.

In the Nixon Group the norm was to be tough and strong, take risks and be uninhibited in dealing with the enemies — the press, the intellectuals, etc. Those who went the farthest in this respect rose the fastest in the group.

Various falls from power were equally educational. Robert Finch and Herbert Klein, for instance, had reputations for being too soft. The lessons were clear for all to see, says Raven. "To be a rising member of the team you had to be loyal to the chief, steadfast, strong, hard-hitting, merciless to your enemies and not get wound up worrying about the methods which you used." It is not hard to see how such attitudes could be behind the actions of Watergate.

The actions of people in the White House, however, are only part of Watergate. The reactions to what was going on in the White House provide psychologists with another area of inquiry. James B. Garrett and Benjamin Wallace of Western Illinois College have been investigating the great diversity of public opinion that existed during the unfolding of Watergate.

Garrett and Wallace feel that the theory of cognitive dissonance can help explain some human behavior and motivation in a situation such as Watergate. The theory of cognitive dissonance suggests that after making a choice (between cars, presidents or whatever) people are subsequently motivated to believe that they have made the right choice and will commit themselves to that selection.

The cognitive dissonance theory was applied to Watergate. College students were polled. Nixon voters, compared to McGovern voters, were less likely to believe that Nixon had prior knowledge of the Watergate bugging or of the cover-up. And they were less likely to believe that he should be impeached even if he did know of them. Such people maintained cognitive consonance by defending their previous decision.

"The potential determinants of attitudes on Watergate were, of course, not nearly exhausted," say Garrett and Wallace. "However," they go on, "of the ones that were tapped, it is clear that many psychological processes operate in determining opinions and establishing and even swaying attitudes toward such politically potent events as Watergate."

C.   NEWS STORY QUESTIONS

1. What is meant by the "risky shift" phenomenon in group dynamics? _____
_____

2. How can cognitive dissonance theory be applied to Watergate? _____
_____

Orlando and Rosalind in "As You Like It."

Love, liking, and interpersonal relationships play important roles in our social, psychological, and emotional lives. In this chapter we will look at some of the ways in which psychologists have attempted to make human interpersonal relationships more understandable and more predictable.

16 chapter

Interpersonal Relationships

When you have completed your study of this chapter, you should be able to:

- ▶ Summarize the research on the importance of making a good first impression
- ▶ Define "stereotype" and show how stereotypes and reputations affect impression formation
- ▶ Define the "attribution process"
- ▶ Define "altruism" and give an example of an experiment demonstrating altruistic behaviors
- ▶ Explain how "cognitive dissonance" operates
- ▶ Describe the pattern of behaviors associated with motherhood and summarize the effects on children of being raised in fatherless homes
- ▶ Show how social play influences the socialization process

Affection. From the Latin word meaning "to apply oneself to" or "to do." An affection for something is a feeling or emotion, usually a moderately positive liking for that thing or person.

Altruistic (al-true-ISS-tic). From the Latin word meaning "other people." Altruism is having regard for, and devotion to, the interests of other individuals. Generally speaking, a behavior is altruistic if it benefits someone else much more than it does you. Altruistic is thus unselfish.

Attribution process (att-trih-BYEW-shun). The act of projecting personality traits or motives onto others so that we can explain their past or present behavior, hence predict what they may do in the future. The attribution process was first described (and named) by social psychologist Fritz Heider.

Body language. Essentially, nonverbal communication. Getting your message across without speaking. We all have characteristic ways of dressing, of combing our hair, of moving our arms and legs, of looking toward or away from people as we speak or listen, of smiling, and of frowning. All of these reactions make up our own unique pattern of "body language."

Cognitive dissonance (KOG-nih-tiv DISS-oh-nance). The feeling we get when our behaviors differ markedly from our intrapsychic values. According to Leon Festinger, we are strongly motivated to reduce this dissonance; we do so either by changing our values or attitudes, or by changing our behaviors. According to Festinger, most of us seem to prefer to change our attitudes rather than changing the way we behave.

Dilation (die-LAY-shun). When you look at something that you like, or are interested in, your pupils will open wider—or *dilate*. Dilation is thus the act of opening up, or getting wider.

Father figure. Someone who represents your father, or who takes the place of your father. Some older person—usually a man—who is accorded deep respect or even reverence. George Washington—"the Father of our country"—is a perfect example of a "father figure" in politics. In Freudian therapy, the analyst (whether male or female) is often referred to as being a "father figure," in that he or she takes on many of the rewarding and punitive aspects of a male parent.

Interpersonal attraction. The process by which one person becomes attracted to, or develops affection for, another individual. Two people deeply in love with each other typically show strong and mutual interpersonal attraction, in part because they tend to be pulled to each other physically much as iron is attracted to a magnet.

Manipulators (mann-NIPP-you-lay-ters). The Latin word *manus* means "hand." To manipulate something is to move it by hand. Technically speaking, you manipulate someone whether you push them into a pond, or pull them out to save them from drowning. In everyday speech, however, the word "manipulate" has a strongly negative feeling to it, for it typically means "to push people around for one's own gain." Manipulators are thus people who attempt to move other individuals, or to sway their opinions.

Peers. Equals. People of the same rank, age, or station in life.

Person perception. That part of social psychology which has to do with discovering the stimulus inputs that influence one individual's perception of or attitude toward another individual. Many of the rules concerning the perception of objects also hold for person perception.

Promiscuous (pro-MISS-cue-us). From the

Latin word meaning "to mix things or people indiscriminately." Thus a promiscuous man or woman is someone who "mixes things up with" lots of people and engages in sexual acts with just about anybody.

Rationalization (rash-uh-null-ih-ZAY-shun). From the Latin word meaning "to find a reason." To rationalize is to find a logical explanation for one's actions—or to give a nice, acceptable reason for one's emotional behaviors.

Respect. From the Latin word meaning "to look back." If you have respect for someone, you view them as worthy of esteem or look up to them.

Role playing. To act out a social role. To behave in a way designed to get what you want, rather than acting as perhaps you'd like to.

Self-fulfilling prophecy. If you keep telling yourself that you're going to enjoy a particular rock concert, you're more likely to enjoy it than if you've told yourself beforehand that you probably won't like it. To prophesy (PROF-uh-sigh) is to make a prediction about what will happen in the future. A self-fulfilling prophecy is one that is likely to come true simply because you've made the prophecy.

Social roles. A set of standard responses to certain social situations. A set of behavior patterns appropriate to a given environment.

Stereotyped (STAIR-ee-oh-typed). A stereotype is a fixed or unconscious attitude or perception—a way of responding to some person or object solely in terms of that person's or object's class membership. A stereotyped response is thus a rather rigid and impersonal way of reacting to something or somebody.

INTRODUCTION: AS YOU LIKE IT

It was love at first sight. Rosalind and her cousin Celia had been invited to a wrestling match to watch Charles, the mightiest wrestler in the land, fight Orlando, a handsome young gentleman. When Rosalind saw Orlando, she immediately felt sorry for him. He seemed to be no match for the powerful Charles. But Orlando fooled everyone and won the match without even working up a good sweat.

Rosalind and Orlando had never met before, but they exchanged a few glances and a few words at the wrestling match. By the time they parted, each was madly in love with the other.

Rosalind and Orlando are the main characters in "As You Like It," one of William Shakespeare's most popular comic plays. Shakespeare, probably the greatest playwright of all time, was an extremely talented observer and recorder of human behavior. Even when the plots of his plays seem confusing and improbable, the thoughts and behaviors of his characters almost always reveal something about human nature. In "As You Like It," the main theme is love, and Shakespeare uses the play to examine various aspects of love. In addition to Rosalind and Orlando's romance, the play contains three other love stories.

Shakespeare was fascinated by love, and theater audiences have responded to his love stories for almost 400 years. Most people, it seems, are interested in love, and there is little doubt that love, liking, and interpersonal relationships are important parts of our social and emotional lives. But what is love, and how does one gain the love of others? Shakespeare attempted to answer these questions through the words and deeds of his characters. In this chapter we will see some of the ways in which psychologists have attempted to explore human interpersonal relationships.

If you want to be liked or loved, you must decide, first of all, how you want to be liked. As Bales pointed out (see Chapter 14), some leaders are warmly liked for the social and emotional feedback they give us. Others are coolly respected as intellectual models. Harvard psychologist Zick Rubin suggests in his book *Liking and Loving* that these same two factors—affection and respect—are important in all forms of personal attraction. **Affection** is a tender feeling of warmth and closeness. **Respect** is a cooler, more intellectual, and less emotional feeling of esteem or honor.

People usually want both affection and respect. Depending on the situation, however, they may emphasize one over the other. An employer or a teacher may be more interested in respect than affection. Lovers and friends usually want warm, affectionate relationships. Once people decide which type of liking or loving they want, they usually attempt to behave in a manner that will earn them either affection or respect—or perhaps both. They try, in other words, to make the desired impression on other people.

FIRST IMPRESSIONS

Some people work long and hard to earn respect and affection. Other people seem to be liked almost immediately because they make a good first impression. As soon as Rosalind saw Orlando, she was impressed. When Orlando won the wrestling match, Rosalind was further impressed. In other words, Orlando had won a certain amount of respect. By the end of the play he had also earned Rosalind's affection. Their love, however, did begin with a first impression. In the 1940s, psychologist Solomon Asch demonstrated the importance of first impressions. He gave a group of subjects a list of adjectives describing a man they might meet. Half of the subjects were told that the person was "intelligent, industrious, impulsive, critical, stubborn, and envious." The other half of the subjects were given the same list in the opposite order: "envious, stubborn, critical, impulsive, industrious, and intelligent." All of the subjects were then asked to write a brief description of what they thought the unknown person might be like. The responses made by two of Asch's subjects are good examples of the importance of first impressions.

When the first adjective on the list was "intelligent" one subject wrote, "The person is intelligent and fortunately he puts his intelligence to work. That he is stubborn and impulsive may be due to the fact that he knows what he is saying and what he means and will not therefore give in easily to someone else's idea which he disagrees with."

When the first adjective on the list was "envious," another subject wrote, "This person's good qualities such as industry and intelligence are bound to be restricted by jealousy and stubbornness. The person is emotional. He is unsuccessful because he is weak and allows his bad points to cover up his good ones."

Obviously, the first word on the list was of critical importance in determining the subjects' attitudes toward the unknown person. The second, third, and fourth words only added to and filled out the initial impression.

In another experiment, Edward Jones and his colleagues asked a group of subjects to watch a college student attempt to solve 30 difficult problems. Later, the subjects were asked if they remembered how many problems the student had solved correctly and how well they thought the student would do in a second test.

The subjects were divided into two groups. One group saw the student, who was actually a "stooge" in the experiment, solve most of the first problems correctly and then do more and more poorly toward the end of the test. When the second group was watching, the student performed poorly at the start and then began to get more correct answers toward the end. In both situations the stooge answered 15 of the 30 questions correctly.

The subjects who saw the student go from good to bad seemed to be most favorably impressed by the performance. Their estimate of the number of correct answers was very high, and they expected that the student would do better in the future. The other subjects, who had seen the student start off on the wrong foot, were not favorably impressed. They remembered the mistakes and thought that the student would do poorly on future tests.

Experiments like those performed by Asch, Jones, and many others suggest that anyone who wants to be liked should attempt to make a good first impression. Unfortunately, people don't always get to make their own impressions on others. Sometimes, their reputations precede them.

Reputations and Stereotypes

The reputation of Orlando's family had a great deal to do with Rosalind's attitude toward Orlando. The reputation (a general impression held by a great many people) of Orlando's family was good. In fact, Orlando's father and Rosalind's father had been close friends. Rosalind had always heard good things about Orlando's family from her father, and her attitude toward Orlando was affected by what she had heard. If Orlando and his family had not had a good reputation, Rosalind's attitude toward him might have been different. Wrestlers, for instance, are not always thought of as romantic figures. There is even a **stereotyped** image which suggests that wrestlers are not very intelligent or socially acceptable. If Rosalind had held or believed such a stereotyped attitude about wrestlers, she might not have given Orlando a second glance after she found out he was going to be involved in a wrestling match.

Reputations and stereotypes, good or bad, deprive people of the chance to make a first impression. Experiments conducted by Harold Kelley of the Massachusetts Institute of Technology have shown how important reputations are. Kelley told a group of students that they would have a visiting lecturer and that they would have to evaluate the visitor's performance. Then Kelley handed out some biographical information about the visitor. The lecturer was described as a "rather warm individual" in half of the biographies and as a "rather cold individual" in the other half. The students didn't know that two descriptions had been used.

The visiting instructor led a class discussion, and Kelley recorded how many times each student asked questions or made comments. Afterward, the students were asked to write a brief description and to rate the lecturer on a set of attitude scales. All of the students witnessed the same performance at the same time, but those who had been told the lecturer was a warm individual were more likely than the others to use words like informal, sociable, good-natured, and humorous in their descriptions and ratings. Also, 56 percent of the students given the "warm" description interacted with the lecturer. Only 32 percent of those who were told the visitor had a "cold" reputation entered the discussion. Apparently, those students who did not like the visitor's reputation figured they would not like the visitor in person. They attempted to avoid contact with a person they thought they wouldn't like. This tendency to avoid people who have bad reputa-

How accurate are first impressions? This man has been described as mild-mannered, dedicated, bookish, shy, lonely. He is David Berkowitz, convicted murderer of six young people in New York City.

Impressions formed on physical appearances alone can lead to stereotypes and deprive people of the chance to form unbiased attitudes. Do you think these two people are likely to become friends?

tions or who make poor first impressions makes it difficult for such people to even get a chance at making a second impression.

How do people communicate or send impressions to each other? The most obvious method is verbal communication. People talk to each other. When it comes to first impressions, however, it seems that verbal language is not the most influential form of communication. People are often more impressed at first by nonverbal communication or **body language** — the way you look or dress or move.

Nonverbal Communication

When a new teacher walks into a classroom, students immediately go through the important process (consciously or unconsciously) of forming attitudes about the teacher. The process of attitude formation is part of an attempt to make sense of the social environment, and it is important because it suggests to us ways of responding to any new stimulus or person. Therefore, even before the teacher says a word, the students form attitudes about the teacher based on nonverbal clues. The new teacher, for instance, is male or female, young or old, and has a certain body shape, way of moving, and style of dress. These physical factors influence each student's attitude toward the teacher — whether the students realize it or not. Generally speaking, these attitudes will be favorable if the teacher somehow meets the students' expectations of what a teacher should be like, or if the students perceive the teacher as a positive, warm, rewarding person.

Cultural expectations in the United States suggest that young people will be more energetic, enthusiastic, idealistic, and liberal than old people. A student who has had rewarding experiences with young, liberal teachers might immediately form a positive impression when a young-looking teacher enters the class. The impression, of course, may turn out to be false, but it is not easy to erase previous experiences; the student may even continue to have favorable first impressions of all young teachers.

First impressions based on sex are similarly hard to erase. In the United States, as well as in many other cultures, women have traditionally been assigned the role of homemaker and sex object. Some men and women continue to form attitudes based on these stereotypes even though many women and men are no longer content to fill all the roles assigned to them by society.

Size, shape, skin color, and physical beauty also play an important part in the impressions people make on each other. Sheldon's entire theory of personality was based on such factors (see Chapter 10). As long as attitudes based on physical types are correct (rewarding) at least some of the time, we will probably continue to hold them. But even when physical traits do not correctly predict behavior, one particular trait—physical beauty—will probably always make a good first impression on most of us.

Beauty's Rewards

Those people who fit society's standards of beauty, such as fashion models, often have a certain advantage in their social relationships.

In every age and in every culture, there have been standards of physical beauty for men and for women. The people who come closest to those standards have a certain advantage in their social relationships because beauty, itself, is usually rewarding enough to make a good first impression. People, realizing this fact, spend billions of dollars on cosmetics and clothes designed to make them look beautiful.

People who are successful in achieving beauty may have all sorts of good characteristics attributed to them. In *The Social Animal*, psychologist Elliot Aronson mentions several experiments which all suggest that it pays to be beautiful.

In one of these experiments Elaine Walster and her associates used a computer to match students at the University of Minnesota for blind dates. The students had all been given personality tests, and the computer should have been able to match people according to their likes and dislikes. The most important factor determining whether or not the students liked each other, however, turned out to be physical attractiveness. The people most likely to want to repeat their dates were those who had been matched with an attractive partner.

In another study, Karen Dion and her colleagues asked students to view three photographs of college-age people. One was physically attractive, one was average, while the third was unattractive (as judged by college students). The students were asked to rate the people pictured according to 27 personality traits and to make predictions about the future happiness of the people in the photos. The attractive people were almost always assigned the most desirable traits and were predicted to have a bright, happy, successful future. (Studies by Stanford psychologist L. M. Terman do, in fact, suggest that people with high IQs do tend to be slightly larger, healthier, and better looking than average. So there might be some truth to the idea that good-looking people are likely to be bright.)

Dion and Ellen Berscheid have found that physical attractiveness is even important among nursery-school children. When these scientists asked young children about their schoolmates, unattractive boys were often considered to be more aggressive and "scary" than the attractive boys.

In another experiment, Dion found that physical beauty affects adults' attitudes toward children. Women were asked to read reports of a severe classroom disturbance committed by a young girl. When a photograph of an attractive girl was attached to the report, the women tended to excuse the bad behavior. In describing the child, one woman said, "She plays well with everyone, but like anyone else, a bad day can occur. Her cruelty . . . need not be taken too seriously." When the same behavior was described and a picture of an unattractive girl was shown, another woman said, "I think the child would be quite bratty and would probably be a problem to teachers. She would probably try to pick a fight with other children her own age." Beautiful people, it seems, are given the benefit of the doubt and are probably given more favorable treatment than are less attractive individuals.

Considering these and other experiments, Aronson says, "It appears to be true that physical beauty is more than skin-deep. We are more affected by physically attractive people than by physically unattractive people, and, unless we are specifically abused by them, we tend to like them better."

Even children's stories help to develop the attitude that beauty is a desirable trait to be rewarded in social relationships while ugliness is something frightening which should be avoided. This is a scene from the movie *Beauty and the Beast.*

Body Movements

People can't do much about their size, shape, or skin color. Indeed, some people may never succeed in making themselves really attractive. There are, however, other ways of making a favorable impression. People are sometimes judged by whether their handshake is firm, limp, or clammy. People who walk with a firm, steady gait are sometimes seen as being dedicated, aggressive, or proud. People who slouch often give us the impression of being lazy or sloppy.

All of the possible unconscious messages that might be contained in body language have not been identified, but several studies suggest that people do use their bodies to indicate their attitudes toward each other. Albert Mehrabian, for instance, asked men and women to act out the ways in which they would sit when talking to someone they liked or disliked. He reports that both men and women leaned forward to express liking. And men (more so than women) leaned back and became more tense when addressing someone they disliked.

Another study had similar findings. Psychologist Donn Byrne and his associates used the computer dating technique to match couples for blind dates. After the couples got to know each other, Byrne asked them to come to his office together. While the couples stood in front of his desk, Byrne explained to them that they were to fill out a questionnaire. The questionnaire asked about the couple's attitudes toward each other. The results of the questionnaires were then compared to the couple's behavior in Byrne's office. The people who liked each other had stood much closer together than did the couples who didn't care much for each other.

Eye Contact

Eye contact is a very important aspect in interpersonal relationships. Lovers often spend intense moments staring into each other's eyes.

Among the various forms of nonverbal communication, facial expressions are probably the most important. Smiles and frowns usually give a very clear indication of the type of impression a person is trying to make. But another aspect of facial expression, eye contact, is also very important. A prolonged gaze can, depending on the circumstances, indicate either aggression, love, attraction, or interest.

In the United States, middle-class whites learn certain eye messages at a very young age. People tend to stare at someone who is talking or lecturing. Such staring indicates attention and encourages the speaker to continue. When people shift their eyes away from a speaker, they may be indicating boredom or a desire to speak themselves. A speaker who doesn't want to be interrupted may look away from the audience or listener in order to avoid eye contact and to avoid the other person's signal to stop talking. As long as people know and obey the hints provided by eye contact, conversation shifts smoothly from person to person. People who avoid these social rules may be thought of as rude, pushy, immature, or overly aggressive.

Eye contact does more than help regulate conversation. People who avoid eye contact in certain situations are sometimes thought of as being guilty or afraid about something. R. V. Exline and his colleagues have examined this theory. First they gave their subjects a type of personality test that indicated whether the subjects were **manipulators** or not. Some of the subjects turned out to be real "people-pushers" or social manipulators. Then all of the subjects were given another experimental test to take. During this test, the subjects were subtly encouraged to cheat.

After the test, the subjects were interviewed. Those who had not cheated engaged in normal eye contact during the discussion. Those who had cheated did one of two things. Some cheaters avoided eye contact as if they were guilty about their performance. Others, those who had high manipulator scores, did not seem to feel guilty at all. They stared directly into the experimenter's eyes. Apparently, manipulators or people-pushers do not have the same guilt reactions as less manipulative individuals do.

In another set of experiments, E. H. Hess demonstrated that even very subtle and almost unnoticeable eye language can have an important effect on attitudes. Hess was studying pupil **dilation** or enlargement as an indication of arousal or interest. Magicians sometimes watch for pupil dilation as an indication that the proper card has been turned up. Knowing this, Hess asked subjects (20 men) to look at a series of slides through an apparatus that allowed him to measure the

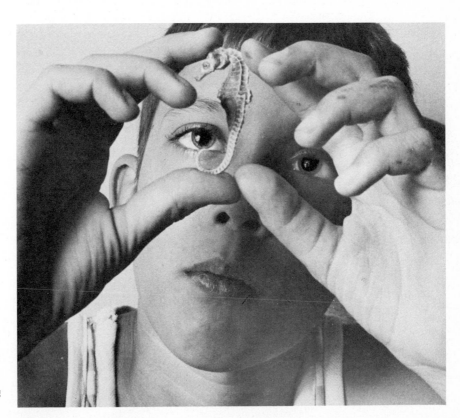

Studies have shown that pupil dilation or enlargement is an indication of arousal or interest. This boy seems to be very interested in examining the sea horse.

subject's pupil response (dilation) to the slides. During the presentation, a slide of an attractive woman was shown two times. The two slides were the same except for one subtle change. On one of them, the woman's pupils had been retouched so that they appeared to be very small. On the other, the woman's pupils were extra large. After the slide show, the men reported that the two slides of the woman were identical. None had noticed the difference in pupil size. During the presentation, however, there was a great difference as measured by the men's pupil dilation. The men responded more than twice as strongly to the woman with the large pupils.

PERSON PERCEPTION

Suppose a teacher asked you to read up on the topic of schizophrenia, and then to demonstrate to your class "what a person suffering from schizophrenia might act like." Suppose too that you then visited a mental hospital, watched patients classified as schizophrenic, and successfully imitated many of their behaviors subsequently in class. The question is, would your performance affect in any significant way the impressions your classmates have of you?

Before you answer, you might consider some facts and some research. The attitudes and impressions that other people have of you—and that you have of others—are part of what Harold Kelley calls **person perception.** Whenever people who don't know you too well watch you for a while, they usually try to "psych you out." That is, they often try to perceive what you are like, why you act and dress as you do, and what you might do next. Thus, when people perceive you, part of the impression they get includes the guesses they may have made (right or wrong) about your own personality.

Attribution Process

We know from Helson's theory that perceptions of people are influenced by stimulus, background, and personality factors (see Chapter 14). You are the stimulus in class, of course. But your classmates' perceptions of you will be influenced not merely by how you look and act, but by situational or background factors and by their own emotional and cognitve biases. The trouble is, many of your classmates may not be able to separate the stimulus (you) from your background and from their own attitudes. Thus, they may try to explain what you say and do solely in terms of your own personality, rather than taking into account the situation you are in and their own state of mind. Your classmates may even *attribute* false or improper motives and psychological traits to you in order to make your actions more understandable and hence predictable. We call this sort of perceptual distortion the **attribution process.**

The attribution process has been studied by many psychologists since Fritz Heider first called it to our attention in 1958. For instance, in an experiment by E. E. Jones and V. A. Harris, subjects were asked to give a speech either strongly favoring or strongly opposing racial integration. The subjects had no choice in the position they took, or in the arguments they used. It didn't matter what the subjects really believed – their job was to say what Jones and Harris told them to say. A group of students listened to the arguments, then rated the speakers in terms of what the students thought the speaker's *real* attitudes toward integration were. Although the students knew perfectly well that the speakers were simply role-playing, most of the students reported that "deep down inside" the speakers surely believed much of what they were saying. Thus, the students *attributed* to the speakers beliefs the speakers didn't really hold – because the students' emotional reactions to the arguments distorted their perceptions of the speakers.

To return to the question we asked earlier, if you acted liked a schizophrenic in class, would your performance affect in any significant way the impressions your classmates have of you? If your actions evoked much emotionality in the other students, the answer probably would be *yes*. For under these circumstances, your classmates might perceive you differently. They might even attribute some mental problems to you – even though they realized intellectually that you had been told to "act crazy" by the teacher.

Altruism

We not only attribute personality traits and motives to others, we attribute them to ourselves as well. Unfortunately, the way that we see ourselves is often just as distorted as the manner in which we view others. For instance, after Stanley Milgram had completed his first experiment on "obedience" (see Chapter 15), he asked a great many college students how they thought they would react if told to give dangerous shock to someone in an experiment. Almost all of the students stated that neither they nor other college students would "obey" Milgram by shocking a defenseless subject. More than this, many students were surprised and annoyed that Milgram would ask them such a question, since almost all of the students perceived themselves as being too **altruistic** (or concerned for the welfare of other people) to do such a thing. Yet when Milgram actually tested students in the obedience situation, almost two-thirds of them followed his instructions and gave the stooge what the students thought was dangerous shock.

Altruism appears to be a personality trait or motive that is so approved by society that we all presume we have lots of it to spare – or at least we tend to answer psychological questionnaires as if we perceived ourselves as being highly altruistic. In real-life situations, however, our behaviors may not quite match our prior perceptions. As an illustration of this fact, consider an experiment reported in 1977 by Alexander Tolor, Bryan B. Kelly, and Charles A. Stebbins of Fairfield University in Connecticut. These psychologists first gave a pen-and-paper test of altruism to a group of college students and to a group of severely disturbed psychiatric patients at a mental hospital. As expected, the college students showed a high level of altruism by responding positively to such statements as "Every person should give some of his or her time for the good of the town or city the person lives in." Quite unexpectedly, however, the psychiatric

Most people consider themselves to be altruistic. If questioned in a survey, the majority of people would say that they would certainly help a hungry man. But how many people would be willing to aid this man if they met him in the street?

patients showed the same high level of altruism—at least as measured by the questionnaire.

Then Tolor, Kelly, and Stebbins put the matter to a real-life test. First they arranged to have 25 of the students and 25 of the patients (one at a time) wait in a small room. Then they had a stooge hobble into the room on crutches, stumble, and cry out in pain as the stooge fell to the floor.

Now, the important question is—who will come to the help of the stooge, and what kind of help will the person give?

To the surprise of almost everyone connected with the experiment, all 25 of the patients immediately came to the aid of the fallen stooge, while only 72 percent of the students expressed a willingness to help. But compared to the patients, the students really didn't do much to be of assistance. Some 72 percent of the patients physically assisted the stooge, while only 32 percent of the students actually touched or attempted to lift the stooge to his feet. Some 60 percent of the supposedly psychotic patients helped the stooge with his crutches, while only 28 percent of the students offered this kind of aid.

To summarize, 100 percent of the severely disturbed mental patients rendered the stooge practical aid of some kind. About 75 percent of the students offered to help *verbally*, but only one in three actually did so.

Tolor, Kelly, and Stebbins conclude, "When faced with a life-like situation, the psychiatric patients behaved significantly more altruistically than did normal people." The Fairfield University psychologists also conclude that "the extreme idealism often attributed to college students and other youthful groups may not always find expression in actual deeds, and may even have been greatly exaggerated by observers of the social scene."

Cognitive Dissonance

Suppose that you had been one of the 25 students in the Fairfield experiment. When asked about altruism on a pen-and-paper test, you respond that you are very altruistic. But when faced with a real-life situation demanding altruistic behavior on your part, you fail to act as you had earlier presumed you would do when you answered the test. How would you explain this great difference or *dissonance* between your perception of yourself and your actual behavior?

Chances are—if you are like most people—you will engage in what Freud called **rationalization.** That is, you may insist that you *meant* to help the fallen stooge, but that you really didn't perceive the stooge as needing much assistance. Or you may tell yourself that "you knew all along that it was a trick," and that you didn't respond because you wisely saw through the game the psychologists were trying to play.

Stanford psychologist Leon Festinger has for many years studied situations in which people's perceptions of their motives differed greatly from what they actually did. Festinger believes that in these circumstances we are very likely to experience **cognitive dissonance.** That is, whenever we do something we think we shouldn't or fail to do something that we think we should have done— we face psychological conflict. This conflict involves the fact that our actions are in dissonance with (or different from) our mental expectations of what we're really like. According to Festinger, cognitive dissonance creates a painful drive that we are strongly motivated to reduce—just as we are motivated to reduce a hunger drive when we go without food for many hours (see Chapter 5). Generally speaking, we tend to reduce the drive of cognitive dissonance by changing our beliefs or attitudes or perceptions. Festinger reports that we seldom attempt to reduce cognitive dissonance by actually changing the way that we act or behave.

Cognitive dissonance occurs in many situations—in the Milgram obedience studies, for instance, in which students perceived themselves as being altruistic but behaved in an authoritarian or nonaltruistic fashion. Cognitive dissonance also tends to explain why so many of the subjects in the "group pressures towards conformity" studies changed their *perceptions* of what they had seen rather than changing their *behaviors* (see Chapter 11).

Putting the matter another way, most of us are taught from birth that altruism is good but that conformity is bad. Once we accept these social values as being "acceptable," we tend to see ourselves as possessing the behaviors that go along with the values. But, in truth, altruistic behaviors are often punished, while

FIG. 16–1.
Cognitive dissonance occurs when your behavior conflicts with your professed belief. The conflict is usually solved by changing your perception of what you believe.

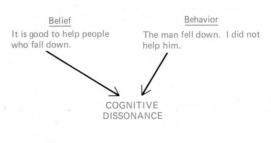

Belief
It is good to help people who fall down.

Behavior
The man fell down. I did not help him.

COGNITIVE DISSONANCE

Solution
The man only pretended to fall down. He did not really need help. Therefore, I did not help him.

conforming behaviors are rewarded. We may therefore behave in a conforming way a great deal more often than perhaps we realize. Rationalization is one way we can reduce the cognitive dissonance we experience whenever our actions are not in accord with the rather idealized *social roles* that we are taught from birth.

SOCIAL ROLES

"All the world's a stage and all the men and women merely players: They have their exits and their entrances; and one man in his time plays many parts . . ." These famous lines are spoken by Jaques, one of the few characters in "As You Like It" who doesn't fall in love. Jaques's lines suggest that we all spend a lot of time play-acting in our daily lives and in our interpersonal relationships, and there seems to be some truth in this. During our lives we play many **social roles** — those of child, parent, student, teacher, friend, lover, and so forth. Some roles may last only a few minutes — such as the mask that we might put on while being interviewed for a job. Other roles, like that of being a parent, may last for years. But in every social situation, no matter how informal or how short-lived, we tend to play a role and thereby attempt to impress the people around us.

Role playing, however, is not restricted to our public appearances. Social roles also influence our private thoughts and behaviors by helping to create our attitudes toward ourselves. Most roles are designed to win the approval or the positive attitudes of other people. If an individual's role is successful and if people react to it positively, the individual is likely to develop a positive self-concept. Because successful roles are rewarding, they are usually repeated and may eventually become a lasting part of an individual's personality. Unsuccessful roles tend to have the opposite effect. People who are never rewarded for their social behavior may begin to dislike themselves. This dislike may then influence their future public and private behavior. The unattractive children in Karen Dion's studies, for instance, were more likely than the attractive children to be blamed for misconduct. We know, explains Elliot Aronson, that if people are treated poorly, it affects the way they come to think of themselves. They may begin to think of themselves as bad or unlovable. Ultimately, they may begin to behave in a way that is consistent with this self-concept, a way that is consistent with how they were treated to begin with — an example of **self-fulfilling prophecy.**

Role Development

The roles played by Shakespeare's characters were written for them, but in real life we don't always have a script to follow. How then do we learn our various roles? Some theories (such as Sheldon's trait theory, see Chapter 10) suggest that biological and genetic factors are responsible for the development of personalities and social roles. Most studies, however, suggest that experience is primarily responsible for social roles. Society teaches, and people learn their roles.

Biological factors also play a part in determining social roles, but even those roles that seem almost completely dependent on biology—motherhood and sex roles—are, to a great extent, the result of learning.

Harry Harlow's experiment with monkeys isolated from their parents, peers, and from normal monkey society suggest the importance of role learning (see Chapter 14). When the isolated monkeys were put back into the monkey colony, they refused to take part in any form of social activity. They had not learned their social roles and, therefore, did not know how to behave. They didn't know how to join in sexual activities, and the females didn't know how to be mothers.

Motherhood

Because the formerly isolated monkeys did not know much about sex, Harlow and his associates had a difficult time getting the females pregnant. Finally, with the aid of a special apparatus, several of the females were impregnated by experienced males. When these females gave birth, they turned out to be what Harlow called "monster mothers." Because they had not learned the maternal role from their own mothers, the formerly isolated animals did not know what motherhood was all about, and they did not know how to respond to their infants. In some instances, the motherless mothers just ignored their children. In more extreme cases, they stepped on their babies, crushed their infants' faces into the floor of the cage, and on several occasions they chewed off their babies' feet or fingers before they could be stopped.

In some instances, when the infants persisted, the mothers did eventually attempt to provide some warmth and comfort. Once the mothers learned how to handle the infants, they did do a better job of mothering. When they were again impregnated, they were more competent at taking care of the second infant.

Motherhood is usually thought of as a natural instinct that makes females want to have and take care of infants. But as Harlow's studies show, the maternal instinct only provides females with a tendency to be interested in their offspring. This tendency cannot be fully expressed if the female has not learned something about the proper role of a mother from past experiences.

Because instincts and innate tendencies seem to be much weaker in humans than in other animals, humans have to rely even more heavily on learning. The

In our interpersonal relationships we all play various roles at different times. The man here is shown as (A) worker with his supervisor; (B) husband with his wife; and (C) friend at a birthday celebration.

Harlow found that female monkeys reared without mothers did not know anything about motherhood because they had no model for learning the maternal role. They became "monster mothers."

failure to learn correct social roles can sometimes be disastrous. In 1971, Serapio R. Zalba, writing in the magazine *Transaction*, estimated that there may be as many as 250,000 cases of child abuse per year in the United States. Of these, 40,000 may result in serious injury, and thousands of children may actually be killed by their parents. Cases have been reported in which parents locked their children in cages, raised them in dark closets, burned them with cigarettes, slashed them with knives, boiled them, starved them, shot them, and broke their bones.

Harlow's "monster mothers" had been socially deprived and neglected as children. Zalba states that most abusive human parents who have been studied also suffered from neglect and abuse as children. Since the grandparents were poor models, the parents did not acquire the social skills necessary for bringing up their own children.

Fatherhood

Hitler's father was a brutal tyrant and a drunkard who unmercifully beat his wife and children. He not only attacked his family, he attacked every social institution including education, religion, morality, and the government. Benjamin Franklin's father was kind, understanding, and sensible. He devoted a lot of time to young Franklin and introduced him to the exciting worlds of society and intellectual accomplishment. It is possible that these two kinds of fathering produced two drastically different kinds of children. Hitler was a brutal man who had no respect for humans or their social institutions. Franklin was a loving, hard-working man who played important roles in the intellectual, scientific, social, and political worlds of his time.

For years, psychologists have been aware of the important effects a father can have on his children. Even so, most psychological studies have concentrated almost entirely on the mother–child relationship. This is a serious mistake, say psychologist Henry Biller and his associate Dennis Meredith. In their book *Father Power,* they suggest that modern society, which places almost the entire burden and responsibility for child-care on women, may be depriving children of adequate masculine models.

Several studies have shown that some boys reared without fathers tend to be less aggressive, more dependent, and to have more "feminine" interests than do boys who are reared with a mother and a father. Many of these behavior patterns may decrease when the young boys are old enough to go to school and can learn masculine roles from males outside the home. In other cases, fatherless boys tend to develop extreme masculine behaviors as if to compensate for the loss of their fathers. During the first six years of life, at least, it seems that young boys need a man around the house if they are to learn their masculine roles. By watching their parents interact, boys learn how to act around women. They might learn, as Hitler seems to have, that it is proper for a man to beat a woman. Under certain circumstances, boys can learn to treat women as equals.

Not only boys, but young girls as well seem to need a **father figure** to learn from. Girls, by watching and by interacting with their fathers, learn how to react to males and how males will react to their sexuality. A study reported in 1973 by Mavis Heatherington examined some of the effects of father deprivation on young girls. Heatherington studied the behavior of 72 teen-age girls with three different types of family background. In one group of 24, the girls had been deprived of a father because of divorce. Girls in the second group had been reared by their widowed mothers. Those in the third group were from normal families with both a mother and a father. None of the girls had brothers. Few of the young women had any noticeable behavior problems, and all were doing reasonably well in school; but there were definite differences in the way girls from each group reacted to males.

As part of the study, each girl was shown into an office where she was interviewed by a man. There were three chairs in the office for the girls to use. Girls reared by divorced mothers tended to sit in the chair closest to the interviewer and to adopt an open and sprawling posture. They leaned forward toward the man, looked into his eyes often, smiled often, and were talkative. Heatherington reports that the girls whose fathers had died acted quite differently. They sat stiffly upright in the chair farthest from the male interviewer, tended to turn their shoulders away from him, and did not smile, establish eye contact, or talk as much as the other girls did. Girls from normal two-parent homes were in between these two extremes but were much more at ease with the man than were

By watching the same-sex parent, children learn appropriate sex roles. This little boy is learning to shave by observing his father.

the father-absent girls, who tended to pluck at their clothes, pull at their fingers, and twirl their hair. When the girls were interviewed by females, however, the differences between the three groups tended to disappear.

Heatherington found that the attitudes displayed by the girls during the interviews also showed up in the girls' social relationships with males. Girls from divorced families sought more attention and praise from males than did girls of the other two groups. These girls were also more likely to spend much of their time hanging around places where young men could be found — gymnasiums, carpentry and machine shops, and in the stag line at community or school dances. In their search for attention, these girls tended to use their bodies to attract boys. They dated more often, tended to be sexually **promiscuous,** and engaged in sexual intercourse more often and at an earlier age than did girls of the other two groups. Girls whose fathers had died tended to avoid males. They started dating much later than usual and seemed to be sexually inhibited. At one dance observed by the psychologists, these girls avoided the male areas of the dance floor, and two even hid in the ladies' room for the entire evening. These differences were not due to popularity, says Heatherington, because the girls received equal numbers of invitations to dance when they were in the dance hall.

Heatherington's study suggests that a girl's sexual behavior can be related to the father's absence or neglect. It also shows that a child's attitude toward males is influenced by the reason the father is gone. Interviews of the girls indicate that the daughters of divorced parents tended to dislike their fathers — perhaps

Studies suggest that children in single-parent homes may suffer psychological damage. The possible damage sometimes can be avoided by providing a substitute for the missing parent. Organizations such as Big Brother help provide a father figure for fatherless boys.

because of the mother's negative attitude toward her ex-husband, and perhaps because the girls felt that their fathers had abandoned them. Girls whose fathers had died were more likely to remember their fathers as idealized images or models of masculinity, which no other male could live up to. Though they expressed it differently, both groups of father-absent girls were insecure in their dealings with men. And insecurity in relating to men was greatest in the girls who lost their fathers before the age of five.

Heatherington's studies, like Harlow's, suggest that children who do not have the opportunity to learn social roles from their parents may suffer psychological damage. But for many reasons — death, war, prison, divorce, desertion — the loss of one or both parents does occur frequently. The possible damage caused by such a loss, however, need not always be permanent. Harlow has found that some socially isolated monkeys can be rehabilitated if the proper therapy is applied soon enough.

Isolated monkeys who had been deprived of social contact for at least six months were the subjects of a special type of therapy. The isolated monkeys were put into a cage for two hours every day with a monkey "therapist." The therapist was an infant monkey, three or four months old, who had been reared by a normal mother. Harlow figured that the isolates had been deprived of physical and social contact, and that the infants, who were still in the clinging stage, could provide such contact. Older monkeys either ignored or were aggressive toward the isolates. The infants, however, would attempt to cling to whatever monkey they were caged with.

The isolate monkeys, who usually sat huddled up in a ball, did their best to ignore the infant therapists. But the infants did not seem to realize that they were being ignored. They needed to have someone to cling to, and they kept on trying to cling no matter how many times the isolates pushed them away. Gradually, the isolates became less and less afraid of the clinging infants. Eventually, the isolates even began clinging to the infants. They seemed to be satisfying a need for something they had missed as children. Within a few weeks, the isolates and the infants were playing enthusiastically together. After six months of therapy, most of the isolates lost their abnormal behavior patterns, and many recovered completely from the effects of isolation. The infant therapists, it seems, were able to supply the contact and love that parents had not provided.

Peer Relationships

What Harlow's isolates didn't get from their parents, they apparently got from their infant playmates. And in most societies, children learn a lot about social behavior and social roles from their **peers** and playmates. Among the Muria people of the jungles of Central India, for instance, almost all social education is left up to the children. Only infants live with their parents. The rest of the Muria children, from the age of 6 to about 17, live in a "ghotul" or children's house at the edge of the adult's village.

The ghotuls are built and supervised by the children. There, they work and

Social play is an important part of the socialization process. Rough-and-tumble play is to be expected among children of a certain age.

play as they please with no parental supervision. The parents—mostly farmers, hunters, and fishers—do provide meals, in return for which the children do a large part of the farm work. But every evening at six o'clock, the children return to the ghotul to play among themselves and to plan the next day's activities.

The Muria children learn about sex from each other as soon as they move into the ghotul. Every night the boys and girls pair off as sleeping partners. To avoid jealousy and competition, the children never sleep with the same partner more than three nights in a row. In the ghotuls, the Muria children learn to share everything, including each other. An account of the Murias in the German magazine *Stern* (August 1972) suggests that the Muria children learn healthy attitudes toward sex and are not afraid or ashamed of their sexuality. And their other social attitudes seem to be equally healthy. According to statistics gathered by the Indian government, there is no prostitution, homosexuality, or criminality—even petty theft—among the Muria. The roles that they teach each other as children seem to prepare them for a harmonious social life as adults.

Few societies give children the amount of freedom (or responsibility) that the Muria have, but play and peer relationships among children do seem to be important factors in teaching social roles in almost every society.

Social Play

One of the most common types of play seen among children is the rough-and-tumble, physical "free play" that worries many parents who are afraid the children might hurt themselves or each other. This type of play, says Harlow, is critically important to the socialization process. Young monkeys begin to learn sex roles while engaging in rough-house activities. But they also learn other social behaviors. Most young animals respond to frustration and pain by striking out at the nearest object, even other animals. During physical free play, however, the young monkeys soon learn that there are certain animals that they had better not hit. Gradually, during play, the monkeys learn their place in the social order, and they learn to limit and control their aggressive impulses.

Psychologist N. G. B. Jones observed rough-and-tumble play in British children and found that it begins as early as 18 months and may continue until the fourth or fifth year. Both boys and girls engage in such activities, but as the children grow older, sex differences begin to appear. A three-year-old boy may spend twice as much time engaged in physical-contact play as does a girl of the same age. Since the same sex differences are seen in young monkeys, Harlow believes that hormones are responsible for the different amounts and types of activity.

In human societies, cultural patterns are often used to reinforce the natural or biological differences between boys and girls. Young girls are often encouraged to play house and to cook and sew. Boys are often encouraged to continue their more physical play in such games as football or cops and robbers. Children's toys are also important. The Greek philosophers Plato and Aristotle both suggested that children should be given toy tools to play with, to shape their minds for future activities as adults. In Western societies, girls are often given dolls to play with, while boys are given erector sets and chemistry sets. In this manner, societies, rather than hormones, reinforce sex differences and help to determine sex-roles.

At first, size and physical ability are important in setting the social order among playing children. But as children develop speech, verbal cleverness becomes important in determining their social roles. With the addition of speech,

Children learn the society's sex roles in play. Boys engage in contact sports such as football while girls play with dolls and baby carriages.

children's games become more complex and more formal. Free play is replaced by games in which the children must obey rules so the youngsters begin to learn how rules control society. As children develop and gain experience, they acquire more and more roles that they will use (consciously or unconsciously) throughout life. Eventually, the games of childhood are put aside for school and work roles. The dating role may be replaced by marriage and parenthood. Some roles, like sexual identity, may be relatively permanent and unchanging. But many roles, like masks, can be put on and taken off as the situation demands.

REWARDING ROLES

Why do we wear masks? In the most obvious cases, people play roles in order to get such things as money, good grades, power, or position. More often, however, roles are used to gain such things as respect, recognition, warmth, affection, intellectual stimulation, or good companionship. In the most obvious cases, role playing can be seen as an insincere, selfish attempt to manipulate other people. More often, however, people play their roles quite naturally and unconsciously, especially after they have played the same parts for many years. For the most part, we play roles because we have been taught to do so, because we are following the models set by others, because role playing makes our behaviors more predictable and acceptable to the people around us, and because the groups to which we belong pressure us to do so. In some cases, however, people take on certain behaviors or roles in order either to get something from someone, or to give something to someone.

Getting, of course, implies that the other person is giving. People who take without giving are usually disliked, ignored, or socially isolated. The most valuable and lasting relationships seem to be those in which people are satisfied with what they get for what they give.

Similar Roles

Shortly after Rosalind and Orlando met and fell in love, they were separated. Orlando was forced to leave town because someone was trying to kill him. The wrestling match was actually part of a plot to get rid of Orlando. Rosalind was forced to flee because her father was a poltical enemy of their country's present ruler. Orlando and Rosalind (disguised as a man) escaped separately into the forest where, after much confusion, they were reunited. When they did finally get together they decided that they wanted to get married and stay together. Many factors enter into such a decision, but one of the most important reasons for Rosalind and Orlando was that they were similar in many ways and they agreed on many things. Rosalind and Orlando came from similar backgrounds, and they shared many likes, dislikes, and attitudes. A great many psychological studies, many of them conducted by Donn Byrne, do indicate that similarity of attitudes is almost always an important factor in determining who likes whom.

In one study, Byrne asked hundreds of subjects to fill out questionnaires about their attitudes on a number of topics. Each subject was then shown a second questionnaire supposedly filled out by a complete stranger. The second questionnaire was a fake. It had been filled out so that the stranger appeared to have attitudes either very similar to or very dissimilar from the subject. The subjects were then asked whether they thought they would like or dislike the stranger. In almost every case, similarity of attitudes determined who was liked. Byrne found this to be true of people of all ages, nationalities, educational levels, and social and economic status.

There are many reasons why people with similar attitudes tend to like each other. For one thing, people usually feel rewarded when others agree with them. The more alike people are in basic attitudes, the more likely it is that they will be able to agree with and reward each other without having to suffer the stress and anxiety of playing an insincere role. Predictability is another important factor. The more alike people are, the more easily they can predict each other's behavior. Knowing how to behave around another person helps to increase our rewards and decrease our punishments.

Opposite Roles

The work of Byrne and many others suggests that husbands and wives tend to be significantly similar to each other not only in attitudes but also with respect to age, race, religion, education, social status, height, weight, eye color, and intelligence. If similarities are so important, why then do opposites sometimes attract? Can such attraction lead to a long-term relationship? Answers to these questions might be provided by the investigation that E. Lowell Kelly started more than 30 years ago.

Kelly selected several hundred engaged couples for his study. He measured their attitudes, backgrounds, IQs, personalities, and even such things as their heights and weights. He then kept track of the individuals for 20 years to see if they stayed together. Some broke off the engagements. Others got married and then divorced. Still others got married and stayed married. Kelly thought that by comparing the outcomes of the engagements with personality and physical factors, he might be able to come up with a simple explanation for long-term, **interpersonal attraction.** The results, however, have not been as simple and straight-forward as Kelly expected. Many of his findings are still being reviewed. But even though unfinished, Kelly's work offers some interesting findings.

Physically, Kelly's couples could be divided into three types: Some couples consisted of men and women who were quite similar (both fat, both tall, and so forth). The second group was made up of men and women who were very dissimilar (a fat man with a thin woman, a tall woman with a short man, and so on). The third type fell in between the two extremes. They had some differences and some similarities, but they were somewhat more alike than if they had been paired off at random.

When Kelly followed up on the engaged couples he found out that opposites do sometimes attract—but not for long. Most of the people who were physically dissimilar broke off their engagements. Apparently, these people became inter-

A study by E. Lowell Kelly suggests that couples who stayed together longest were similar enough to be attractive to each other but different enough to remain interesting. Do you think the couple on the left will stay together as long as the couple on the right?

ested in each other in part because of some exciting but superficial physical qualities. Once the initial stimulation wore off, the couples tended to drift apart.

The couples who were very similar also tended to drift apart, but after a longer time. Many of them got married and then divorced. Possibly these people, too, were only attracted by superficial qualities. Their physical similarities drew them together, but these similarities may have grown boring after awhile. Superficial similarities, it seems, are not usually enough to make a relationship last.

In Kelly's opinion, the people who stayed together were those who were interested in each other for "deep" rather than superficial reasons. They were similar enough in important ways (including height and weight) to be pleasing and rewarding to each other, but they were different enough to be stimulating and challenging to each other. As Kelly explains, the people who stayed together apparently found ways of balancing their needs for the "security of being similar" with their needs for the "novelty of being different." Such needs, of course, differ from person to person and can change during the years of a marriage. Kelly found that people who stayed together seemed to have found ways of maintaining both their similarities and their differences. That is, they did not grow more and more alike, and they did not grow apart. For instance, if the wife gradually changed her political attitudes, the husband tended to shift his opinions just enough to keep up the original difference. These people seemed to respect each other's right to change and to grow, and they seemed to place more value on maintaining their psychological compatibility than on such surface attractions as height and weight.

CONCLUSION: AS YOU LIKE IT

We do not know whether or not Rosalind and Orlando lived together happily ever after, but we do know that many couples find happiness and fulfillment in their interpersonal relationships. While there is no definite way of predicting whether or not two people will fall in love or remain in love, much of the psychological research discussed in this chapter does shed light on the workings of human relationships. With the knowledge gained from such research, we are all in a position to better understand and perhaps even predict how our interpersonal relationships will work out. The more you understand and the better able you are to predict, the more likely it is that things will work out happily—or, AS YOU LIKE IT.

► SUMMARY

1. Poets and playwrights have devoted much time and effort to descriptions and discussions of love. The best of their attempts, such as Shakespeare's "As You Like It," do help us to understand some of the thoughts, feelings, and behaviors involved in human love. Psychologists, as we have seen in this chapter, have also investigated interpersonal relationships. The results of their work not only describe but help predict the course of human relationships.

2. Two factors—**affection** and **respect**—are important in all forms of interpersonal relationships. Affection is a tender feeling of warmth and closeness. Respect is a cooler, more intellectual, and less emotional feeling of esteem or honor.

3. Numerous experiments have shown that first impressions are important in earning the respect and affection of others. In many cases, however, reputations and stereotyped attitudes prevent us from forming our own unbiased first impression.

4. Age, sex, size, shape, skin color, body movements, eye contact, and physical beauty are among the nonverbal factors that often enter into the formation of a first impression, or **person perception.** Although physical factors do not always accurately predict what a person will be like, we will probably continue to form attitudes about others based on their physical appearance as long as those attitudes are correct more often than they are incorrect.

5. People's perceptions of us will be influenced not only by how we look and act but by situational and background factors and by their own emotional and cognitive biases. This process is known as the **attribution process.**

6. We not only attribute personality traits and motives to others, we attribute them to ourselves as well. But the way we see ourselves is often as distorted as the way in which we view others. Most of us, for instance, tend to believe that we are more **altruistic** than we actually are, a finding based in part on Milgram's work with students in a shock situation.

7. When there is a difference between our perceptions of ourselves and our actual behavior, we are likely to experience **cognitive dissonance.** In general, we tend to reduce cognitive dissonance by changing our beliefs, attitudes, or perceptions rather than by changing our behavior. We may also rely on **rationalization** to deceive ourselves.

8. During our lives we play many **social roles.** Biological factors play a part in determining social roles, but most of our roles are learned. Even our feminine and masculine sex roles and such things as the so-called maternal instinct, which seem to be biologically determined, are greatly influenced by our social

and environmental experience. We learn many of our roles from our parents and peers.

9. We engage in role playing for many reasons, but in some cases we take on certain behaviors in order to either get something from someone or to give something to someone. The strongest and most lasting interpersonal relationships are usually those in which the people involved are satisfied with what they get for what they give.

10. Similarity of attitudes is important in determining who likes whom because the more alike people are the more likely it is that they will be rewarding to each other. Research suggests that lasting relationships are those in which individuals are similar enough to be pleasing and rewarding to each other but different enough to be stimulating and challenging to each other.

Suggested Readings

Aronson, Elliot. *The social animal.* 2d ed. New York: Viking Press, 1976.
Biller, Henry and Dennis Meredith. *Father power.* New York: Doubleday, 1975.
Fast, Julius. *Body language.* New York: M. Evans, 1970.
Rubin, Zick. *Liking and loving: An invitation to social psychology.* New York: Holt Rinehart & Winston, 1973.

► STUDY GUIDE

A.   RECALL

Sentence Completion

1. Shakespeare's "As You Like It" is basically a play about the _____ between Rosalind and Orlando. [p. 530]

2. _____ may be defined as a tender feeling of warmth and closeness, while _____ is a cooler, more intellectual, and less emotional feeling. [p. 530]

3. In Asch's experiment, it was reported that _____ impressions are the most important. [p. 531]

4. In Jones' experiment on impression formation, subjects were asked to predict students' ability to _____ _____. [p. 531]

5. A person's _____ is essentially a general impression about that person held by a great many people. [p. 532]

6. When we attribute to an individual characteristics we assume he will have because of his group membership, we are using a _____. [p. 532]

7. Techniques of nonverbal communication are sometimes referred to as _____ _____. [p. 533]

8. One trait that almost always leads to a good first impression is physical _____. [p. 534]

9. Walster determined that blind dates who were most preferred tended simply to be _____. [p. 534]

10. Mehrabian reports that when talking to someone they _____ people tend to sit leaning forward. [p. 536]

[p. 536]   11. Of the various forms of nonverbal communication, _____ expressions are probably the most important.

[p. 537]   12. Among other things, R. V. Exline demonstrated that _____ tend to avoid eye contact if they were not manipulators.

[p. 538]   13. The process of distorting the perception of a person on the basis of one's own attitudes is part of the _____ process.

[p. 539]   14. To be concerned for the welfare of others is to be _____.

15. In Tolor, Kelly, and Stebbin's experiment, all of the _____ _____ who acted as subjects made an attempt to help a person who was obviously in trouble.

[p. 539]

[p. 541]   16. When there is a discrepancy between what a person says and what he or she does, the person may be in a state of _____.

[p. 541]   17. One of the most common ways of reducing cognitive dissonance is the process that Freud called _____.

[p. 541]   18. Festinger claims that to reduce cognitive dissonance we seldom change the way we actually _____.

[p. 542]   19. It is quite common that people play many _____ _____ in order to impress those around them.

[p. 542]   20. Most social roles develop through learning or _____.

[p. 543]   21. Harlow demonstrated that the so-called "_____ instinct" needs to be supported by experience and learning.

[p. 544]   22. Supporting the notion that good parenting behavior is not innate is the fact that there are approximately _____ cases of child abuse every year.

[p. 545]   23. During the first _____ years of life, it seems that young boys need a man around the house if they are to develop normal masculine roles.

[p. 546]   24. Hetherington's studies suggest that girls whose fathers were divorced from their mothers were _____ promiscuous than girls from normal homes.

[p. 547]   25. What Harlow's monkeys could not get from their parents, they could often get from their _____.

[p. 548]   26. Muria children learn most of their social and sexual roles from _____.

[p. 549]   27. Harlow believes that _____ are responsible for the observable differences between boys and girls in "free play."

[p. 550]   28. A number of studies indicate that _____ of attitudes is almost always an important factor in determining who likes whom.

[p. 552]   29. It is Kelly's opinion that couples who stay together tend to do so for "_____" rather than superficial reasons.

B.   **REVIEW**

Multiple Choice: Circle the letter identifying the alternative that most correctly completes the statement or answers the question.

1. Shakespeare's "As You Like It" is basically a play about:
   A. loving and liking.
   B. a psychotic king.
   C. a group of transvestites.
   D. violence and aggression.

2. In terms of impressing other people, it is generally true that:
   A. most recent impressions are the most lasting.
   B. positive traits are more influential than negative ones.
   C. many interactions are needed to form an impression.
   D. none of the above.

3. In Jones' study of impression formation, students were perceived as being able to solve a new set of problems if they were:
   A. initially perceived as being bright.
   B. just "acting" lazy.
   C. males.
   D. perceived as being poor problem solvers at first, but did better later on.

4. Which of the following may be defined as a general impression held by a great number of people?
   A. a stereotype
   B. an attribution
   C. a reputation
   D. a social role

5. Nonverbal cues:
   A. include mode of dress.
   B. may have their effect unconsciously.
   C. may be more important than verbal cues.
   D. all of the above.

6. In studies of students computer-matched for blind dates, preferred partners tended to be:
   A. intelligent.
   B. unintelligent.
   C. attractive.
   D. unattractive.

7. When a listener wants a speaker to continue he or she may:
   A. constrict his or her pupils.
   B. lean back and look relaxed.
   C. stare at the speaker.
   D. shift their eyes from the speaker.

8. When asked about their own altruism, college students tend to:
   A. overestimate their altruistic tendencies.
   B. underestimate their altruistic tendencies.
   C. estimate their altruistic tendencies accurately.
   D. be unable to make an estimate of their altruistic tendencies.

9. The name most commonly associated with "cognitive dissonance" is:
   A. Stanley Milgram.

B. Leon Festinger.
C. Harry Helson.
D. Harry Harlow.

10. Monkeys who were raised in social isolation in Harlow's experiments:
   A. quickly adapt to other monkeys once they reach adulthood.
   B. could be rehabilitated with the help of therapist monkeys.
   C. never recovered from the damage they suffered.
   D. seldom lived to adulthood.

DIVORCE: THE FIRST TWO YEARS ARE THE WORST

Divorce American Style
Divorce for the Unbroken Marriage
Creative Divorce
Divorce in the Progressive Era
Divorce: Chance of a New Lifetime
Divorce: The Gateway to Self-Realization
Divorce: The New Freedom

As these current book titles suggest, divorce is becoming increasingly popular in the United States. They also suggest that divorce can be an exciting and fun thing and that it can open the door to liberation and new possibilities. The first suggestion is true. In fact, if the 1974 trend continues (about one million divorces per year) 40 percent of all new marriages will ultimately end in divorce. The second suggestion is more difficult to evaluate. Divorce can be a positive and liberating solution to certain family problems, but it can also be a time of crisis that results in stress, conflict and trauma for the divorcees and for their children. Some of the problems that follow in the wake of divorce have been described by E. Mavis Hetherington of the University of Virginia.

Most divorce research in the past has focused on mothers and children and has been largely descriptive. The characteristics of divorced mothers and their children have been described and compared to those of mothers and children in intact homes. Hetherington's research, conducted with Martha Cox and Roger Cox, is one of the first studies to concentrate on the entire family system. It makes an in-depth analysis of changes in family interaction and functioning in the two years following divorce.

A total of 96 white, middle-class families took part in the study. They consisted of 24 boys and 24 girls and their divorced parents and the same number of children and parents from intact families. The children were all about four years of age at the start of the study. In all divorced families custody of the children had been granted to the mothers (as is the case in more than 90 percent of divorces involving children). A multimethod, multimeasure approach was used in the investigation of family interactions. The measures used included interviews of and diaries kept by the parents, observations of parents and children interacting in a laboratory setting and at home, checklists and parent ratings of children's behavior and a battery of personality tests of the parents. In addition, observations of the children were made in nursery schools, and ratings of the children were obtained from their peers and teachers. Parents and children were evaluated by these measures two months, one year and two years after the divorce.

As would be expected, some of the first problems faced by divorced parents were those related to household maintenance and economic and occupational difficulties. Many of the men, particularly those from marriages in which conventional sex roles had been maintained and in which the wife was not employed, experienced considerable difficulty in running a household and reported a "chaotic life style." Although the men had more problems, the households of both divorced men and women were more disorganized than those of intact families, especially in the first year following divorce. Divorced men slept less, had more erratic sleep patterns and had more difficulty with shopping, cooking, laundry and cleaning. These problems sometimes interfered with job performance and were further complicated by the economic stress associated with maintaining two households.

Divorce also led to changes in self concept and emotional adjustment. Two months after the divorce about one third of the fathers and one fourth of the mothers reported an ebullient sense of freedom, but by one year this had largely been replaced by depression, anxiety or apathy. One of the most obvious changes in divorced parents in the first year following divorce was a decline in feelings of competence. They felt they had failed as parents and spouses and expressed doubts about their ability to adjust well in any future marriages. They reported that they functioned less well in social situations and were less competent in heterosexual relations. Nine of the divorced fathers reported an increased rate of sexual dysfunction.

Social life and the establishment of meaningful, intimate interpersonal relationships also present problems for divorced parents. Almost all complained that socializing is organized around couples and that being a single adult, especially a single woman with children, limits recreational opportunities. Divorced mothers reported having significantly less contact with adults and often commented on the sense of being locked into a child's world. This was less true, however, of working women who had social contacts through their co-workers. Divorced men had a restricted social life two months after divorce, followed by a surge of activity at one year and a decline in activity to the wife's level by two years. In contrast with the women, divorced men complained of feeling shut out, rootless and at loose ends and of a need to engage in social activities even if they were not pleasurable. Both men and women spoke of intense feelings of loneliness.

Happiness, self-esteem and feelings of competence in heterosexual behavior increased steadily during the two years following divorce for males and females, but they were not as high even in the second year as those of married couples. The stereotyped image of the happy, swinging single life was not altogether accurate. Many males, but few of the females, were pleased with the increased opportunity for sexual experiences with a variety of partners, but by the end of the first year both men and women were expressing a need for intimacy and a lack of satisfaction in casual sexual encounters.

Poor parenting on the part of divorced parents was apparent in most cases during the two years following divorce. The researchers found that divorced parents make fewer maturity demands of their children, communicate less well with their children, tend to be less affectionate and show marked inconsistency in discipline and a lack of control over their children when compared with parents in intact families.

The interviews and observations showed that the lack of control divorced parents have over their children was associated with different patterns of relating to the child for mothers and fathers. The mother tries to control the child by being more restrictive and giving more commands that the child often ignores or resists. The father wants his contacts with his children to be as happy as possible. He begins by being extremely permissive and indulgent with his children but becomes increasingly restrictive during the two-year period, although never as restrictive as fathers in intact homes.

These findings, of course, represent averages. There were wide variations in coping and parenting within intact and divorced families. However, of the families studied, there were none in which at least one family member did not report distress or exhibit disrupted behavior, particularly during the first year following divorce. Previous research has shown that a conflict-ridden intact family may be more harmful than divorce for family members, but this does not mean that divorce itself does not represent a crisis.

"We did not encounter a victimless divorce," says Hetherington. Since this seems to be the rule rather than the exception and since statistical evidence suggests that the rate of divorce is likely to increase, Hetherington concludes that "it is important that parents and children be realistically prepared for problems associated with divorce that they may encounter."

C. NEWS STORY QUESTIONS

1. What were some of the problems faced by divorced men in Hetherington's study? ____
_____

2. In this same study, how did men and women react to their new swinging life styles? ____
_____

3. What changes occurred in parenting methods after divorce?
_____
_____

CONCLUSION

Michael Valentine Smith, central character in *Stranger in a Strange Land*.

People who understand the present are in a position to make reasonable predictions about the future. People who understand the future are in a position to do something about shaping the future. In this final chapter we will look at some of the ways in which psychology, the human science, may contribute to the shaping of a better world for all of us.

The Future

17 chapter

When you have completed your study of this chapter, you should be able to:

- ► Place the "Psychological Revolution" in historical perspective
- ► Summarize the changes in biological psychology suggested by Smith's poll
- ► Define "biofeedback" and comment on its future use
- ► Trace the history of child-rearing practices over the past 35 years
- ► Discuss the likelihood for changes in the future of education
- ► Discuss the future use of behavior modification and changes in community mental health

Behavioral engineering. A construction engineer takes various building materials and links them together to form a house, or a school, or an office building. The same construction materials can be tied together to make many different types of structures. A behavioral engineer takes the various behaviors produced by a person (or animal) and links these behaviors together to help the organism acquire new behavioral "structures." Using modeling techniques and reinforcement, the behavioral engineer "shapes" the responses of the organism into a new form or pattern. Behavioral engineering is thus the set of techniques someone uses to engineer or shape new action patterns.

Eidetic memory (eye-DETT-ick). A photographic memory. The ability to look at a printed page or visual scene for a brief period of time, and then reproduce that visual input in considerable detail.

Electrodes. Devices, usually made of metal, for detecting electrical activity in one or more nerve cells. The two main types of electrodes are disk and needle. Disk electrodes are flat metal sensors that are placed on the scalp to detect brain waves (that is, the firing patterns of large numbers of neurons). Needle electrodes are typically thin slivers of metal that are inserted into the brain to detect the firing patterns of a small number of neurons. Needle electrodes can also be used to stimulate nerve cells.

Extraterrestrial. Our word *terrestrial* comes from the Latin word for "earth." An extraterrestrial is anything that comes from outside earth. A "man from Mars" would be an extraterrestrial.

Genetic engineering. A genetic engineer is someone who takes genes and reshapes them so that they produce a different sort of offspring. So far, genetic engineering has been practiced primarily with tiny organisms such as bacteria and viruses. Theoretically, it should be possible in the future for parents to have a genetic engineer reshape their genes so that the children the parents have would be stronger, healthier, more intelligent, or different-looking than the children their genes would normally have produced. The limits of human genetic engineering are not known, but the ethical considerations are considerable and hotly debated.

Industrial Revolution. Prior to the mid-1700s, almost all objects in the world were produced by people working singly or in small groups. Beginning about 1750, however, people learned how to work together in large organizations, each person performing a separate job. Because of this division of labor, material objects could be produced much faster and cheaper. However, the Industrial Revolution could not have occurred unless the physical sciences had already developed the manufacturing tools that the industrials put to practical use. Similarly, the physical sciences did not emerge from the ages of ignorance until a few brave souls began to insist—about 1600—that material objects obeyed physical laws, hence could be studied in an objective and scientific manner. The Industrial Revolution was thus based on our taking a new and, at the time, radically different view of the objects in our physical environment.

Mass communications. Persuasive efforts aimed at large groups of people. Television is a medium for mass communications because one person can (and has) spoken to hundreds of millions of viewers simultaneously.

Medical Revolution. The Industrial Revolution was based on the new viewpoint toward, and new findings about, the physical world that chemists and physicists began coming up with in the 1600s. Biology began developing in the late 1700s and 1800s, when innovative thinkers began to insist that our bodies obey physiological laws, and hence we can look at our bodily processes scientifically and objectively. The practice of medicine (which is a form of applied biology) entered a revolutionary time of great advancement in the late 1800s, when physicians began to apply the new viewpoints and findings of the biologists.

Pleasure centers. In the brains of most higher organisms there are clusters of neurons—or nerve centers—that appear to give the organism intense pleasure when these neurons are stimulated electrically. Most rats act as if they prefer direct brain stimulation of their "pleasure centers" to such needs as food, water, or sex.

Psychological pollution. The word "pollution" means to poison or degrade. Environmental pollution is a result of the introduction of chemical or other poisons into our air, food, or water. Psychological pollution results whenever psychological poisons are introduced into the social environment. Among the most potent forms of psychological pollutions are punishment, destructive criticism, ridicule, and rejection.

Psychological Revolution. The Industrial Revolution occurred when we learned to look objectively at the behavior of physical objects. The Medical Revolution occurred when we learned to look objectively at the functioning of our bodies. The Psychological Revolution—which seems just to be starting—is the next step toward understanding what we can do when we learn to look objectively at the functioning of our minds and at the ways in which our behaviors are influenced or controlled.

Sheltered environments. Patients in mental hospitals usually have little or no real contact with the everyday world that most normal people live in. But not everyone with psychological problems needs to be so severely separated from social reality. Many individuals profit most from living or working in an environment that allows them frequent contact with the normal world, but which shelters them from many of the usual demands the normal world places on people. Residents in these sheltered environments usually find rejoining normal society an easier task than do patients released to society straight from a mental hospital.

Synthesized. To synthesize is to form a whole from a bunch of parts. In you analyze a diamond, you tear it apart to see what it is made of. If you want to synthesize a diamond, you would take the elements found in the diamond (chiefly carbon or coal) and press these elements together to make the parts into a new whole. Psychoanalysis typically involves tearing apart a patient's early experiences to see what they are. Once the analysis is complete, the patient should be able to synthesize these experiences into a new and healthier personality structure. What we call "insight" is actually a form of mental synthesis.

INTRODUCTION: STRANGER IN A STRANGE LAND

Valentine Michael Smith—human by ancestry, Martian by environment—was only an infant when his pioneering parents perished. Conceived in space and born on Mars, Smith was the sole surviving member of an expedition of interplanetary space travelers who attempted to establish the first earthling colony on Mars. Young Smith survived only because some inquisitive Martians wanted to experiment with a member of the human species.

Like psychologists trying to teach chimpanzees to communicate, the Martians investigated human capabilities by seeing how much they could teach Smith. Being a good student, Smith learned much from the Martians. He learned things that no one on Earth could have taught him, and he mastered powers that made him unlike any earthling.

For 25 years Smith lived and learned with the Martians. Then, when another expedition from Earth landed on Mars, his teachers gave him back to his people. Again Smith became the subject of an experiment. He was taken "home" to Earth so that human scientists could examine the so-called man from Mars. But Earth was hardly home to Smith. He was a stranger there. *Stranger in a Strange Land* is Robert A. Heinlein's science-fiction novel that tells of Valentine Michael Smith's strange adventures and eventual death on Earth.

Smith had learned near perfect control of his body, of his mental processes, and even of the physical world around him. Because of low gravity and an inactive life on Mars, Smith's muscles had not developed. When he got to Earth, he simply "taught his muscles to grow" by directing his body in the production of muscle tissue. He also knew how to slow his heart beat and oxygen consumption and could sit under water for hours meditating.

Smith could read an encyclopedia, a dictionary, or an entire library as fast as he could turn pages. Then, with total recall (**eidetic memory**) of what he had read, he would go into a meditative trance and stretch his sense of time until seconds seemed like hours. He used this time to concentrate on and attempt to understand all that he had read and stored in his memory.

Smith's powers included the ability to move objects without touching them, and the ability to make things (including people) disappear. He could also communicate with plants and animals; he could even read people's minds.

Like most science fiction, Heinlein's novel is set in the future. And like most good science fiction, its imaginary future is at least partially possible or believable because it is based on a precise knowledge of the present. Much of what Smith learned from the Martians, for instance, gave him "superhuman" powers by today's standards. But many of these same fictional powers are presently under investigation in scientific laboratories around the world. Some of them may prove to be "factual" rather than "fictional" in the future. Thus, Heinlein reminds us that a knowledge of what the future might be like is becoming increasingly important as the rate of change in our technologiclal world continues to speed up.

For people who lived 300 years ago, the future was not something with which they had to be greatly concerned. They believed that their children and their children's children would come into a world that was little changed by time. Since then, the Industrial and Medical Revolutions have changed the world rapidly and drastically. Today the future is more than a vague dream. It is a reality over which we are gaining some control. The world is changing so rapidly that it presents a wide range of ever-differing possibilities and environments for each new generation. Even within a single lifetime, people are presented with choices and changes that can affect their whole way of living. People alive today used to wait weeks for a letter from Europe. Now, messages from Mars arrive only minutes after they are sent.

The changes that are bringing the future rapidly into the present offer exciting possibilities, but they also present us with problems. In a slow-moving world, people had time to adapt to change. Today there is less time in which to face more changes. Adaptation is more difficult, and failure to adapt might result in what Alvin Toffler calls future shock — stress and disorientation caused by a rapidly changing world. In his book *Future Shock,* Toffler suggests that one method of avoiding the stress of change is to be prepared for whatever the future may bring.

THE PSYCHOLOGICAL REVOLUTION

In the 1600s, physics, astronomy, and eventually chemistry, began to develop as scientific disciplines. Through objective observation, scientists gained knowledge of the physical environment. With an increasing understanding of the behavior of physical objects, scientists soon learned to predict and to control the future behavior of certain objects. In the 1700s, the application of scientific knowledge about the physical world led to the rise of technology and to the **Industrial Revolution.**

In the 1800s, biology became a true science as researchers began to observe our bodies more closely and to understand certain physiological processes. It became possible to predict and control certain biological behaviors. The application of biological technology led to the **Medical Revolution.**

In the 1900s, psychology and the social sciences began their revolution. In the past 50 years, objective methods of observing human behavior have become possible. As human behavior becomes more understandable, methods of predicting and controlling future human behaviors become possible. The application of such psychological technology is bringing about a **Psychological Revolution.**

The Industrial Revolution replaced the horse and buggy and handwritten books with supersonic jets and high-speed communications and computers.

We of the twentieth century have had to adapt to drastic change of a technological and social nature. Films such as "Logan's Run" reflect our interest in a future filled with amazing possibilities.

Before the Medical Revolution, surgery meant sawing off limbs. Today a surgeon can transplant human organs. What sort of changes will the Psychological Revolution bring with it? It is important for us to ask this question because only if we know what the future might be like can we hope to avoid "future shock."

Science fiction, suggests Toffler, might be one useful method of helping us prepare for the future — because science-fiction writers often explore the political, social, psychological, and ethical issues we may face in the years to come. But even the most creative writer cannot accurately predict the future without knowledge of the present. Today's scientists, says Toffler, are the people best prepared to provide the knowledge upon which tomorrow will be based. Today's psychologists are best able to predict what tomorrow's behaviors will be like.

Forty experts in the field of psychology were recently polled and asked to make predictions about the future of psychology. The poll was conducted by Mike Smith of the Department of Applied Psychology at the University of Wales Institute of Science and Technology. The psychologists' predictions about the future of their field were published in the October 10, 1974, *New Scientist*. Their predictions fall into the three major areas of psychology: biological, cognitive, and behavioral or social psychology.

THE FUTURE OF BIOLOGICAL PSYCHOLOGY

With inputs from the Medical Revolution and biological technology, psychologists are learning more and more about the biological basis of behavior. In 1973, scientists at the University of Wisconsin reported that they had **synthesized** a gene in a test tube. Other researchers have transplanted genes from one type of organism to another. These developments bring with them the possibility of eventually making and replacing human genes. With this ability, we might someday change those behaviors caused by genetic defects. Long before such **genetic engineering** becomes possible, however, psychologists will be using other methods of biologically controlling human behavior.

Future Drugs

Toward the end of this century, the Smith poll predicts, there will be a breakthrough in understanding the biological and chemical processes involved in specific thoughts and behaviors. This development is predicted to begin in the 1990s with a practical capability of using drugs to control specific behaviors. Techniques will evolve that will allow for much more selective and specific control than is presently possible. We may be able someday to lower the sexual impulses of a sex offender, for instance, without interfering with that person's life in other ways. This would be quite different from the fate of Alex in *Clockwork Orange*. Drug control, rather than prison control, might be possible in some cases.

In the late 1900s, drug technology will be advanced to the point where it is possible to speed up or slow down learning processes. Knowledge of the physiological processes of learning and memory will be so complete that biological methods will be available for selectively erasing memories. People who have emotional problems caused by unhappy memories will simply have the unfortunate memories erased. Support for the present psychoanalytic and clinical techniques of treating emotionally troubled people will collapse, the Smith poll predicts, "and the ideas of Freud will be relegated to the psychological museum." This will happen by the year 2038. (The rather precise dates attached to the predictions are averages of the inputs from all 40 psychologists who took part in the poll.)

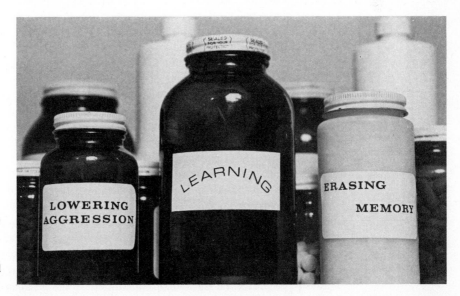

The drug technology of the future will permit us to influence learning processes, memory, and aggression.

Biological Feedback

Drugs offer only one method of controlling the human body. Valentine Michael Smith, the man from Mars, didn't use drugs to control his heart beat, his oxygen consumption, or his other biological processes. He controlled them with his mind, and today many people are learning similar types of control with the help of biofeedback machines (see Chapter 5). Numerous experiments have shown that many physiological processes can be voluntarily controlled. With the use of an EEG machine, for instance, an epileptic patient can sometimes see the signs of an oncoming epileptic seizure. If the patient can learn to relax and think calm thoughts when the first sign of a seizure shows up on the EEG, the patient can often avoid the epileptic attack.

With biofeedback methods, people can learn to control not only their brainwaves, but heart rate, blood pressure, appetite, kidney functioning, and muscle tension as well. It may even be possible to use biofeedback techniques to influence the production of human sperm and eggs. Thus, a form of voluntary control could replace the present methods of birth control.

The Senses and the Brain

While it's hardly likely that any of us will ever encounter space travel or extraterrestrial life-forms, many of us still find the idea entertaining.

Valentine Michael Smith had such acute senses that he could see quite well in almost total darkness. As we learn more about the sense receptors and the human brain, it might be possible to enhance sensory perception. More importantly, we might someday be able to build electronic eyes and ears that would be connected directly to the brains of blind and deaf people. Perhaps we can build artificial arms and legs that could be connected directly to motor output areas in the brain. Such mechanical limbs would respond to orders from the brain almost as well as natural limbs do.

Brain specialists have already implanted **electrodes** in the so-called pleasure centers of the human brain and delivered highly pleasant electrical impulses to implanted patients. Smith, after polling psychologists, says, "It is not inconceivable that our knowledge of the anatomy of the human brain, and our surgical techniques, will have advanced to a point where a device the size of a portable cassette tape recorder could deliver carefully controlled electrical impulses to the brain. Self-stimulation of pleasure centers," Smith suggests, "could well make sex, alcohol, gambling and eating obsolete as modes of human gratification." To date, however, research does not support this prediction. The so-called **pleasure centers** in humans do not operate like those in animals. Artificially stimulated pleasure in humans is probably not as intense as it is in animals, and the basic human pleasures will probably remain basic.

On the subjects of ESP and the ability to communicate with plants and animals, the psychologists in Smith's poll are skeptical. They do not expect within the next 100 years, if ever, "to see such things as a convincing demonstration of thought transference with animals or any reliable application of ESP. Furthermore . . . the psychology of space travel and **extraterrestrial** life forms is unlikely to become a major topic of concern [emphasis ours]."

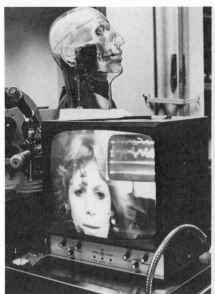

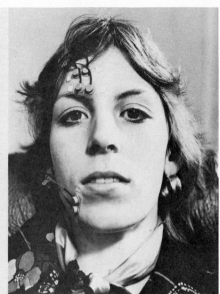

This woman's mood state is being tested by electrodes to see if the drug treatment she is getting is effective. Technological advances will aid the therapy of the future.

THE FUTURE OF COGNITIVE PSYCHOLOGY

While some claim that Uri Geller is a fraud, he has been able to develop his mental powers to the point that he can bend spoons and start watches just by concentrating. Try it with other members of the class and see what happens.

The biological sciences are understandable and, therefore, predictable because they are concerned with observable and measurable objects. The human mind, however, is not as easy to work with as are brain tissues and chemicals. For this reason, the future of cognitive psychology is more difficult to predict than other areas of the social and behavioral sciences. It is likely that continuing advances in the various areas of cognitive psychology will probably affect people's thoughts and behaviors as they have in the past.

For example, Toffler explains how radical changes in the image of the child in society and in theories of child rearing have caused future shock in the past several generations. At the turn of the century, scientific belief held that behavior was primarily the result of heredity. Bad children were thought to be the result of bad genes. Crime was thought to be hereditary. Child-rearing practices based on such ideas offered us few techniques for shaping or molding our children's personalities.

In the first decades of the twentieth century, the work of Watson and Pavlov suggested that environmental rather than hereditary factors were primarily responsible for shaping a child's personality. These ideas led to radically different child-rearing practices. For instance, parents learned to feed their infants on schedule and would refuse to pick them up when they cried. By the late 1930s, another change in child-rearing practices was brought about as Freud's ideas gained in popularity. Parents began to worry about "the rights of children," "oral gratification," and "Oedipal complexes." Permissiveness became popular in child care. In the 1960s, Freudian theory began to lose ground to advances in humanistic psychology, learning theory, and behavioral technology. With all of these changes, parents in the course of 30 years are faced with at least three different scientific theories of child rearing. As personality theorists gain still newer insights into "what makes people tick," it is likely that parents will have even better child-rearing techniques available to them.

Most advances in cognitive psychology will probably come from the work of the humanistic psychologists. Older theories of personality assumed that the human personality was relatively stable and unchangeable throughout life. The humanists emphasize the present and the individual's potential for "becoming." Personality and IQ tests, for instance, have attempted to measure what a person is. In the future, tests might be developed that will suggest what a person can become with training and encouragement. As the humanists discover more about human goals and values, applied psychology will be able to help direct people toward those goals.

Psychological Pollution

Among the future goals we may achieve will be the cleaning up of the *psychological* environment. The Industrial Revolution brought with it, among other things, atomic warfare and hundreds of forms of physical and biological pollution that are destroying the external environment and human health. Now ecologists are faced with the task of cleaning up the environment and preventing future pollution.

One of the most important goals of many psychologists is to clean up the psychological environment to prevent **psychological pollution.** Hatred, war, violence, threats, and punishment are forms of pollution that can ruin anyone's mental environment. If such pollution is allowed to continue, it may destroy the best parts of our personalities and eventually the world. As one psychologist puts it, "Criticism (justified or not) can kill a person's spirit as quickly as lead or mercury can poison a person's body. My own opinion is that most of the hang-ups and inhibitions that people have are a direct consequence of the punishment, ridicule, and hostility that we too often aim at each other." The future of psychology will have to be aimed at reducing this sort of pollution.

Future Education

When Valentine Michael Smith landed on Earth, he was like a 25-year-old infant. He knew nothing about the earth and had to be educated in all of its ways. The type of education Smith received bore little resemblance to anything that is found in today's schools. He didn't sit in an assigned seat in a classroom and learn what everyone else in his age group was learning. He had no schedule or time limit, and his course selection was not based on some age-old tradition. Through computers Smith had the knowledge of the world available to him at his fingertips. Whatever interested him, he studied. When he wanted more practical knowledge, he went out into the world and learned by doing and by watching others at their jobs.

Today's education system, Toffler explains, is a result of the Industrial Revolution. Schools, like factories, process students according to rigid regulations. Certain courses are available, and all students are supposed to learn them in the same manner and at the same time. Students are forced to fit into a prescribed slot in the education system and to follow the often authoritarian dictates of their teachers. Upon graduation, every student is supposedly prepared to fit into a certain slot in society. But society is changing, and the old slots are no longer always available. Schools, too, will have to change if they are to educate people for the future.

The results of Smith's poll of psychologists suggest that the students of the future will learn in much the same manner that the man from Mars did. By the year 2009, the standard educational techniques will be slide–tape packages and computer learning. Because programmed courses will be available to their students through teaching machines, teachers will be able to concentrate their efforts on tutoring small groups of pupils.

As the world continues to speed up and as the amount of knowledge available continues to pile up, learning will become a life-long necessity. People who were graduated from medical school 20 years ago, for instance, would probably not qualify as doctors today if they haven't kept up with the advances in their field. With the help of memory drugs, people may be able to unlearn what is no longer relevant. With advances in learning theory and the help of teaching machines we will be able to learn rapidly new information as it becomes available. Both schools and formal exams, as they now exist, will probably disappear within 35 years.

Not only will psychology have an impact on education, psychology itself, by the year 2000, will become a major school subject and will have replaced more

The child rearing of the future will be affected by the humanists' emphasis on the person's potential for "becoming."

traditional subjects. This trend is already well under way. One of the traditional aims of a liberal education, for instance, has been a better understanding of human behavior. But psychology, with its reliance on the scientific method, attempts to explain behavior in a more systematic way than do traditional liberal arts courses like English literature and history. In fact, says Samuel Feldman of New York University, "Psychology is fast replacing history and English as the basis for a liberal education."

THE FUTURE OF SOCIAL AND BEHAVIORAL PSYCHOLOGY

There are many factors responsible for the increased interest in psychology. But one of the most important, suggests Feldman, is the fact that our society is becoming more and more service-oriented. There are a growing number of drug treatment programs, halfway houses, and community mental health centers that provide a wide variety of social services. And to best help people, we must know and understand them. This fact necessarily makes the field of psychology an important one. The Smith poll predicts that this trend will continue, and that "the number of psychologists will have doubled by the year 2000. The areas of greatest growth will be in social psychology and occupational psychology. These developments," Smith explains, "will be the result of the need of other professions to use psychologists to help them carry out their jobs. In an increasingly complex and specialized world, experts, planners and designers will be forced to become more remote from 'ordinary' people and they will need to call on the techniques of psychology — opinion-polling techniques and some of the psychological techniques of communication — to bridge a widening gap." Psychologists, in other words, will be the experts who help the experts. They will provide a meeting ground for the planners and those who are being planned for. By the mid-1990s, it is predicted that psychologists will be actively involved in planning and designing cultures and social systems for ordinary living and for special purposes such as mental hospitals and prisons.

Community Mental Health

Mental hospitals, as they are presently known, will probably vanish by the year 2000. In their place will be clinics, re-education centers, halfway houses, group homes, therapeutic communities, and other forms of **sheltered environments** where people with mental or behavioral problems may go for short periods of time. Psychologists and other behavioral scientists will be available to help disturbed people find solutions to their problems. The patients will then be eased back into society gradually instead of being discharged abruptly with little after-care. Behavioral psychologists will also be involved in helping to change the social environment into which a patient must return. Family counselors will work to change a patient's family situation. Other specialized psychologists will work in businesses, schools, and industries to help ensure the mental health of employees, students, and customers. Community mental health centers are already playing an important role in attempting to clean up some of the psychological pollution of society.

Behavior Modification

One of the most important technologies psychologists will have for gaining control over the social environment is behavior modification. The Smith poll predicts that by 1987 the methods and techniques of controlling behavior — such as the type of conditioning described by Skinner (see Chapter 6) — will be reliable and sophisticated. Psychologists might develop a series of self-manipulative procedures or a battery of "experience packages" that could enormously expand the options of life styles open to all individuals.

Behavioral technology and conditioning in the form of token economies have already proved to be of great help in treating certain types of mentally disturbed patients. This type of **behavioral engineering** will not only help to empty mental hospitals, but may make the vast prison system obsolete as well. The token economies already in use in some prisons reward prisoners who demonstrate personal growth and impulse control. The same type of conditioning is used to teach prisoners the social and occupational skills they will need when they are released. Such rehabilitation (or re-education) has been found to be a much more effective method of dealing with law-breakers than is punishment. Preliminary figures suggest that prisoners released from rehabilitation prisons are much less likely to return to jail than are prisoners from traditional "punishment" prisons. This fact alone could help us decrease crime in society; and as we gain more control over our social environment, fewer people are likely to become law-breakers. The result will be an important step forward in social evolution.

Mass Communication

Advances in social evolution have always been noticed after the fact. Because the changes came about slowly, explains Toffler, society could adapt unconsciously. Today, unconscious adaptation is no longer adequate. Changes come too rapidly, so we must take an active part in planning our own social evolution, and we must make conscious decisions about what our future will be. We must decide about such things as warfare, economic inequality, mass starvation, racism, sexism, ecological problems, and energy concerns. Modern technology offers many ways of meeting these problems, but it is up to us to choose which solutions we use. Our decisions, however, must be based on the needs of all the people involved. In the past, the needs of minority groups were often overlooked. Today, in a delicately balanced technological society, even the smallest of minorities can completely disrupt the mechanism. The Arab nations, by raising the price of oil, threw the economic balance of the world out of order. A small band of dissatisfied rebels can effectively terrorize a whole city.

Future technology, however, will offer a means of letting minorities be heard. Through **mass communications,** all people will eventually be able to take part in making the decisions that will affect their future. A politician of the future will give a speech, and people around the world will be able to respond instantly. This immediate feedback will be made possible by cable television and other advances in mass communications media. Computers will tabulate the responses, and the politican, as well as the public, will be provided with instant feedback. In this manner, policy-makers will be able to measure accurately the rapidly changing psychological needs of society and will be able to make decisions based on those needs.

SHAPING THE FUTURE

With arms outstretched, Valentine Michael Smith stood calmly one evening while an angry mob of his fellow earthlings murdered him. Even with his futuristic powers, the man from Mars was unable to insure himself a long and fulfilling life. He had tried to share his powers and his secrets with a world that was not

Psychology,. "the human science," offers us the tools with which we can help create a long and fulfilling life.

ready to accept the future that he offered. The people who didn't understand Smith mistrusted and murdered him.

The people who killed the future were the ones who did not understand it. Yesterday, power plants and factories were the tools that shaped the Industrial Revolution. Today, that technology pollutes the world. If yesterday's planners had understood today's needs, they might have acted differently.

Today, psychology offers people the tools with which they can shape their bodies, their minds, and their social environments. People who understand the needs and the possbilities of tomorrow will use the tools of the Psychological Revolution to shape the future closer to their heart's desire.

► STUDY GUIDE

A.   RECALL

Sentence Completion

1. In Heinlein's novel, Valentine Michael Smith was born and raised on
[p. 566]   _____ for _____ years.

2. The _____ and _____ Revolutions of the past 300 years
[p. 567]   have rapidly and drastically changed the world.

3. Failure to adapt to the changes that the future might bring may result in what Alvin
[p. 567]   Toffler calls ''_____ _____.''

4. What we can all the ''Psychological Revolution'' began in the _____
[p. 567]   century.

[p. 568]   5. Accurate predictions of the future require a knowledge of the _____.

6. It is predicted that by the _____s we will have a practical capability to
[p. 569]   control specific behaviors with drugs.

7. _____ affords the control of biologically based behaviors without the
[p. 570]   use of drugs.

8. The Smith poll suggests that stimulation of the brain's _____
                _____ could make sex, alcohol, gambling,and the like, obsolete modes of
[p. 570]   human gratification.

9. Around 1900 it was widely believed that behavior was the result of
[p. 571]   _____.

10. Your text claims that most advances in cognitive psychology will probably come from
[p. 572]   the work of the _____ psychologists.

11. Toffler suggests that today's educational systems are a direct result of the
[p. 573]   _____ Revolution.

12. Both schools and formal exams, as they now exist, will probably disappear within
[p. 573]   the next _____ years.

[p. 574]

13. As we know them now, mental hospitals will probably vanish by the year _____.

[p. 576]

14. Through _____ _____ all people will eventually be able to take part in making decisions that will affect their future.

B.   REVIEW

Multiple Choice: Circle the letter identifying the alternative that most correctly completes the statement or answers the question.

1. In Heinlein's novel, Valentine Michael Smith:
   A. tried to bring an earthlike society to Martians.
   B. developed very strong muscles and bones while on Mars.
   C. found the adjustment to Earth an easy one to make.
   D. was murdered by earthlings who mistrusted him.

2. Biology became a true science in the:
   A. 1600s
   B. 1700s
   C. 1800s
   D. 1900s

3. The use of drugs to control specific behaviors:
   A. may reduce the need for prisons.
   B. does not seem feasible at this time.
   C. is called genetic engineering.
   D. may be referred to as biofeedback.

4. Self-stimulation of the "pleasure centers" of the brain:
   A. is already a powerful tool for many people.
   B. provides a good example of ESP.
   C. may be more useful for nonhuman animals than for humans.
   D. will be commonplace by the end of the twentieth century.

5. Accepted child-rearing practices:
   A. may have changed at least three times in the past thirty years.
   B. presently stress permissiveness.
   C. are largely based on Freudian principles today.
   D. are seldom influenced by professional psychologists.

6. Most advances in cognitive psychology:
   A. have already taken place.
   B. will probably come from the Skinnerians.
   C. will be produced by genetic changes.
   D. will probably come from the work of the humanistic psychologists.

7. Token economies:
   A. are already in use.
   B. are a form of behavior modification.
   C. can be used in prisons as well as mental hospitals.
   D. all of the above.

appendix

STATISTICS

by James V. McConnell

The Red Lady

I was sitting in the student union not long ago, talking with a friend of mine named Gersh, when these two young women came over to our table and challenged us to a game of bridge. The two women — Joan and Carol were their names — turned out to be undergraduates. They also turned out to be card sharks, and they beat the socks off Gersh and me. Joan was particularly clever at figuring out how the cards were distributed among the four bridge hands — and hence good at figuring out how to play her own cards to win the most tricks.

One hand I will never forget, not merely because Joan played it so well, but because of what she said afterwards. Joan had bid four spades, and whether she made the contract or not depended on whether she could figure out who had the Queen of Diamonds — Gersh or me. Joan thought about it for a while, then smiled sweetly at Gersh. "I think you've got the Red Lady," she said, and promptly captured Gersh's Queen of Diamonds with her King.

Gersh, who hates to lose, muttered something about "dumb luck."

"No luck to it, really," Joan replied. "I knew you had five diamonds, Gersh, while Doc here had only two. One of you had the Queen, but I didn't know which. But since you have five of the seven missing diamonds, Gersh, the odds were five to two that you had the Little Old Lady. Simple enough, when you stop to think about it."

While Gersh was dealing the next hand with noisy frustration, Joan turned to me. "I know you're a professor, but I don't know what you teach."

"Psychology," I said, picking up my cards for the next hand. The cards were rotten, as usual.

"Oh, you're a psych teacher! That's great. I really wanted to study psych, but they told me I had to take statistics. I hate math. I'm just no good at figuring out all those complicated equations. So I majored in history instead."

STATISTICS — A WAY OF THINKING

I shook my head in amazement at what Joan said. I don't know how many times students have told me much the same thing — they're rotten at mathematics, or they just can't figure out what statistics is all about. But these same students manage to play bridge superbly, or figure out the stock market, or they can tell you the batting averages of every major league baseball player, or how many miles or kilometers per gallon their car gets on unleaded gasoline.

Statistics is not just a weird bunch of mathematics — it's a way of thinking. If you can think well enough to figure out how to play cards, or who is likely to win the next election, or what "grading on the curve" is all about, then you're probably already pretty good at statistics. In fact, you surely use statistics unconsciously or intuitively every minute of your life. If you didn't, you'd be dead or in some institution by now.

Sure, a few of the equations that statisticians throw around get pretty fancy. But don't let that fact discourage you. I've been a psych prof for more than 20 years, I minored in mathematics, but even I don't understand all the equations I see in the statistical and psychological journals. But those "fancy formulas" are usually of interest only to specialists. Forget about them — unless you happen to be a nut about mathematics.

The truth is that you already know most of the principles involved in basic statistics — if, like Joan, you're willing to stop and think about them. Yet many psych students reject statistics with the same sort of emotionality that they show when somebody offers then fried worms and rattlesnake steak for dinner. Well, worms are rich in protein, and rattlesnake meat is delicious — and safe to eat — if you don't have to catch the snake first. But you may have to overcome some pretty strong emotional prejudices before you're willing to dig in and see what snake meat (or statistics) is all about.

Odds and Ends

I've been a gambler all my life, so maybe I didn't get conditioned to fear numbers and "odds" the way a lot of people do. But whether you realize it or not, you're a gambler too, and you (like Joan) are pretty good at figuring out all kinds of odds and *probabilities*. Every time you cross the street, you gamble that the odds are "safely" in your favor. Each time you drive a car and cruise through a green light without slowing down, you gamble that some "odd" driver won't run the red light and hit you broadside. Every time you study for a true–false exam, you're gambling that you can learn enough to do better than somebody who refuses to study and who just picks the answers randomly. And every time you go out with somebody on a date, you're gambling that you can predict that person's future behavior (on the date) from observing the things that the person has done in the past.

So you're a gambler, too, even if you don't think of yourself as being one. But if you're going to gamble, wouldn't it be helpful to know something about odds or probabilities? Because if you know what the odds are, you can often do a much better job of achieving whatever ends or goals you have in mind.

One way or another, almost everything in statistics is based on *probability theory*. And, as luck would have it, probability theory got its start some 300 years ago when some French gamblers got worried about what the pay-offs should be in a crap (dice) game. So the gamblers (who were no dummies) hired two brilliant French mathematicians to figure out the probabilities for them. From the work of these two French genuises came the theory that allows the casinos in Las Vegas to earn hundreds of millions of dollars every year, that lets the insurance companies earn even more by betting on how long people will live — and that lets psychologists and psychiatrists employ the mental tests that label some people as being "normal" and other people as being "abnormal."

The Odds in Favor

If you want to see why Joan was so good at playing bridge, go get a deck of cards and pull out the 2, 3, 4, 5, 6, 7, and Queen of Diamonds. Turn them face down on a table and shuffle them around so you won't know which card is which. Now try to pick out the Queen just by looking at the back of the cards. If the deck is "honest" (unmarked), what are the odds that you will pick the Red Lady instead of the 2, 3, 4, 5, 6, or 7? As you can see, the odds are exactly 1 in 7. If you want to be fancy about all this, you can write an equation (which is what Joan did in her mind) as follows:

The probability (p) of picking the Queen (Q) is 1 out of 7, therefore
$$pQ = 1/7$$

Now shuffle the cards again, place them face down on the table, and then randomly select two of the cards and put them on one side of the table, and put the remaining five face-down on the other side of the table. Now, what are the odds that the Queen is in the stack of five cards (Gersh's bridge hand), and what are the odds that the Queen is in the stack of two cards (my bridge hand)?

Well, you already know that the probability that any one card will be the Queen is 1/7. I have two cards, therefore, I have two chances at getting the Queen, and the equation reads:

$$pQ \text{ (Me)} = 1/7 + 1/7 = 2/7$$

Gersh had five cards, so his probability equation is:

$$pQ \text{ (Gersh)} = 1/7 + 1/7 + 1/7 + 1/7 + 1/7 = 5/7$$

So if you dealt out the seven cards randomly 70 times, Gersh would have the Queen about 50 times, and I would have the Queen about 20 times. No wonder Joan wins at bridge! When she assumed that Gersh had the Queen, she didn't have a sure thing, but the odds were surely in her favor.

Outcomes and Incomes

Now let's look at something familiar to everybody, the true–false examination. Suppose that you go to a history class one day, knowing there will be a test, but the teacher throws you a curve. For the exam you get is written in Chinese, or Greek, or some other language you simply can't read a word of. The test has 20 questions, and it's obviously of the true–false variety, but since you can't read it, all you can do is guess. What exam score do you think you'd most likely get — zero, 10, or 20?

Maybe you'd deserve a zero, since you couldn't read the exam, but I'm sure you realize intuitively that you'd most likely get a score of about 10. Why?

Well, what are the odds of your guessing any single question right, if it's a true–false exam?

If you said, "Fifty percent chance of being right," you're thinking clearly. (See what I said about statistics' being a way of thinking?)

The probability (p) of your getting the first question right (R_1) is 50 percent, or 1/2. So we write an equation that says:

$$pR_1 = 1/2$$

The probability of your getting the first question wrong (W_1) is also 50 percent, or 1/2. So we write another equation:

$$pW_1 = 1/2$$

Furthermore, we can now say that, on the first or any other question, the

$$pR + pW = 1/2 + 1/2 = 1$$

Which is a fancy way of saying that whenever you guess the answer on a true–false exam, you have to be either right or wrong — because those are the only two *outcomes* possible!

Now, suppose we look at the first two questions on the test. What is the probability that you will get both of them right, if you are just guessing at the answers?

Well, what outcomes are possible? You could miss both questions (W_1W_2), or you could get them both right (R_1R_2), or you could get the first answer right and the second answer wrong (R_1W_2), or you could get the first one wrong and the second right (W_1R_2).

Thus, there are four different outcomes, and since you would be guessing at the right answer on both questions, these four outcomes are *equally likely to occur*. Only one of the four outcomes (R_1R_2) is the one we're interested in, so the odds of your getting both questions right is 1/4.

$$pR_1R_2 = 1/4; \ pW_1W_2 = 1/4; \ pR_1W_2 = 1/4; \ pW_1R_2 = 1/4; \text{ and}$$
$$pR_1R_2 + pW_1W_2 + pR_1W_2 + pW_1R_2 = 1/4 + 1/4 + 1/4 + 1/4 = 1$$

In a sense, getting both questions right is like selecting the Queen of Diamonds when it is one of four cards face down on the table in front of you. In both cases, you have four equally likely outcomes, so your chances of getting the Queen (or being right on both answers) in one out of four, or 1/4.

As you can see, if you're taking an exam, playing bridge, or trying to add to your income by buying a lottery ticket, it will surely pay you to consider all the possible outcomes.

Actually, we can figure the odds of your answering the first two questions correctly in a much simpler way. We simply multiply the odds of your getting the first question right (pR_1) by the odds of your getting the second question right (pR_2):

$$pR_1R_2 = pR_1 \times pR_2 = 1/2 \times 1/2 = 1/4 = 25\%$$

Maybe you can see, too, that the odds of your getting both answers *wrong* would be exactly the same:

$$pW_1W_2 = pW_1 \times pW_2 = 1/2 \times 1/2 = 1/4 = 25\%$$

If the exam had just three questions to it, the odds of your getting all the answers right by chance alone (that is, by guessing) would be:

$$pR_1R_2R_3 = pR_1 \times pR_2 \times pR_3 = 1/2 \times 1/2 \times 1/2 = 1/8$$

To put the matter another way, on a 3-question exam, there are 8 different outcomes: $R_1R_2R_3$; $R_1R_2W_3$; $R_1W_2R_3$: $R_1W_2W_3$; $W_1R_2R_3$; $W_1R_2W_3$; $W_1W_2R_3$; and $W_1W_2W_3$. Since only one of these 8 possible outcomes is the one you want ($R_1R_2R_3$), the odds in your favor are only 1 in 8.

If the test had four true–false questions, there would be 16 different outcomes — twice as many as if the test had but three questions. These outcomes would range from $R_1R_2R_3R_4$, $R_1R_2R_3W_4$. . . all the way to $W_1W_2W_3R_4$ and $W_1W_2W_3W_4$. If there are 16 different outcomes, only one of which is "all answers right" or $R_1R_2R_3R_4$, what would be the odds of your guessing all the answers on a 4-question true–false test?

(If you said, "1 in 16," congratulations!)

Now, let's take a giant leap.

If the exam had 10 questions, the odds of your getting all 10 answers right by guessing would be:

$$pR_1R_2R_3R_4R_5R_6R_7R_8R_9R_{10} =$$
$$1/2 \times 1/2 \times 1/2 \times 1/2 \times 1/2 \times 1/2 \times 1/2 \times 1/2 \times 1/2 \times 1/2 =$$
$$1/1024$$

So if you took the exam 1024 times and guessed randomly at the answers each time, just *once* in 1024 times would you expect to get a score of zero, and just *once* in 1024 times would you expect to get a score of 10.

Now, at last, we can answer the question we asked a few paragraphs back: If you took a 20-question exam on which you had to guess at each answer, what exam score do you think you'd most likely get: zero, 10, or 20?

Well, what are the odds that you'd get a score of flat zero? In fact, the odds are astronomically against you, just as they are astronomically against your getting a score of 20 right. In either case, the probability would be:

$$pW_{1-20} = pR_{1-20} = 1/2 \times 1/2 \times 1/2 \ldots (20 \text{ times!}) =$$
$$1,048,576 \text{ to } 1!$$

So the odds are more than a million to one that you won't get all the answers right or all the answers wrong on a 20-question true–false exam just by guessing. Which might give you good reason to study for the next exam you have to take!

Bar Graphs and Normal Curves

Next, let's throw in some pictures just to liven things up a bit. Statisticians have a way of plotting or graphing probabilities that may make more sense to you than equations do.

Let's make a diagram of the *distribution* of outcomes when you take a 4-question true–false exam:

```
                6 |                      WRWR
                5 |                      WRRW
                4 |            WRRR    WWRR    RWWW
 Distribution   3 |            RWRR    RWRW    WRWW
     or           
 Frequency      2 |            RRWR    RWWR    WWRW
                  | RRRR + RRRW + RRWW + WWWR + WWWW
                1 |_____
                     4 right  3 right  2 right  1 right  0 right
```

There's just one outcome that will give you four right, but four outcomes that will give you three right (and one wrong). That is, you could guess the first three questions correctly, but miss the last one (RRRW), get the first two right, miss the third, and get the last one correct (RRWR), and so forth.

Now, looking at this diagram, can you tell what the odds are that you will get *exactly* two questions right and two questions wrong? Well, count up the number of different outcomes that involve two Rs and two Ws. There are six. And there are 16 possible outcomes. So the odds of your getting *exactly* two questions right (and two wrong) are 6/16.

We can draw a bar graph or *histogram* that shows the same possibilities:

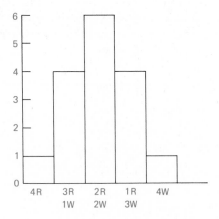

If the exam had eight questions on it, the histogram or bar graph would look something like this:

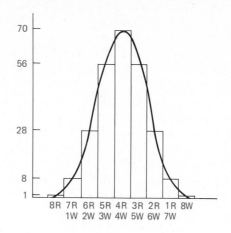

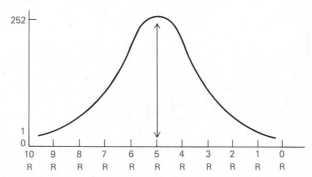

A bell-shaped curve showing the distribution of "right answers" expected when taking a 10-item true–false exam.

Notice that we've added a curve to connect up the bars. Once you get to eight or nine questions, curves are easier to handle than are bar graphs. So let's draw a curve for a 10-question exam:

As mentioned earlier, the number of possible outcomes in a 10-question exam is 1024. So the odds of getting all 10 questions right just by guessing ("by chance alone") would be 1 in 1024. Not very good odds. But the probabilities of your getting 5 questions right and 5 wrong would be 252 in 1024, or about 25 percent. And the odds of your getting 4, 5, or 6 questions right would be well over 60 percent! That makes sense, because just looking at the curve you can see that better than 60 percent of the possible outcomes are bunched up right in the middle of the curve.

DESCRIPTIVE STATISTICS

The curve we've just drawn is the world-famous, ever-popular "bell-shaped curve." In fact, the curve describes a *random distribution of scores* or outcomes. That is, the curve describes the outcomes you'd expect when students are forced to guess—more or less at random—which answers on a true–false exam are correct. Naturally, if the exam were written in clear English, and if the students knew most of the material they were being examined on, the curve or distribution of scores would look quite different.

There are many sorts of "outcomes" that fit the bell-shaped curve rather nicely. For example, if you randomly selected 1000 adult U.S. males and measured their heights, the results you'd get would come very close to matching the bell-shaped curve. Which is to say that there would be a few very short men, a few very tall men, but most would have heights around 5'10" (178 centimeters). The same bell-shaped curve would fit the distribution of heights of 1000 adult women selected at random—except that the "middle" or peak of the bell-shaped curve would be about 5'5" (166 centimeters).

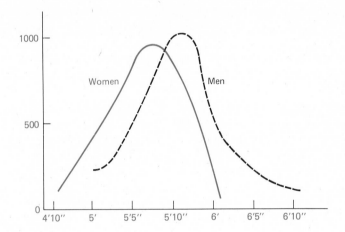

Measures of Central Tendency

As we noted in Chapter 8, IQ tests are constructed so that the scores for any age group will approximate a bell-shaped curve. In this case, the peak or "middle" of the distribution of IQ scores will be almost precisely at 100. A very few individuals would have IQ scores below 50, a very few would have scores above 150; some two-thirds of the scores would fall between 84 and 116.

Why this bulge in the middle as far as IQ scores are concerned? Well, think back for a moment to the true–false test we were discussing earlier that had 10 questions on it. There were 1024 possible outcomes. If you wanted to get all 10 questions right, there was only one way you could answer the 10 questions—all had to be correct. But there were 256 ways in which you could answer the questions to get a score of 5—right in the middle.

There is only one way you can earn a top score on an IQ test—you've got to answer all the questions rapidly and precisely the way the people who constructed the test say is "right." But there are thousands of different ways you can answer the questions on the usual IQ test to get a "middle score," namely an IQ between about 84 and 116.

In a similar vein, there are precious few ways in which you can earn a million from norm rather than making rough guesses. The psychologist tends to use and $15,000 a year. So if we selected 1000 adult U.S. citizens at random, asked them what their incomes were, and then "took an average," what kind of curve (distribution of incomes) do you think we'd get?

Whenever we measure people psychologically, biologically, socially, intellectually, or economically, we often generate a distribution of outcomes that looks very much like a bell-shaped curve. Each person in the world is unique, it's true. But it is equally true that, on any given *single* measuring scale (height, weight, grade-point average, income) most people's scores will be somewhere in the middle of the range of possible outcomes.

Psychologists have a variety of tools for measuring the "middle" of any curve or distribution of outcomes. These techniques are often called *measures of central tendency,* which is a fancy way of saying that these techniques allow us to measure the center or midpoint of any distribution of scores or outcomes.

Mean, Median, Mode

1. *The Mean.* The *mean* is simply the statistical "average" of all the scores or outcomes involved. When you figure your grade-point average for any semester, you usually multiply your grade in each course by the number of credit hours, add up the totals, and divide by the number of hours credit you are taking. Your grade-point average is actually the *mean* or mathematical average of all your grades.

Course	Hours Credit	Grade	Hours × Grade
History	3	A	$3 \times 4 = 12$
Psychology	4	A	$4 \times 4 = 16$
Mathematics	4	C	$4 \times 2 = 8$
Spanish	4	B	$4 \times 3 = 12$
TOTALS 15	15		48
GPA = 48/15 = 3.2			

2. *The Median.* Since the mean is a mathematical average, it sometimes gives very funny results. For example, according to recent government figures, the "average" U.S. family was made up of about 4.47 people. Have you ever known a family that had 4.47 people in it? For another example, if you got two As and two Cs one semester, your average or "mean" grade would be a B. Yet you didn't get a B in any of the courses you took.

There are times when it makes more sense to figure the exact midpoint *score* or outcome, rather than figuring out the *average* score. At such times, psychologists often use the *median,* which is the score that's in the precise middle of the distribution — just as the "median" of an expressway is the area right down the middle of the highway.

If some semester, you got two As, one B, and you flunked two courses completely, your *mean* grade (grade-point average) would be slightly better than a C. But your *median* or middle grade would be a B, because it is right smack in the middle of the five grades you got.

The median is particularly useful when you must deal with a distribution of outcomes that has a few extreme cases. For instance, there are a handful of people in the United States who earn millions of dollars each year — and millions of people who don't earn very much at all. These few millionaires pull the average up considerably because their incomes are so huge. The *mean* annual income per person in the U.S. is noticeably higher than is the *median* annual income.

If that last statement doesn't make much sense to you, consider yourself and 9 other people. Let's assume that you and 8 others earn $1000 a year each, but the tenth person earns a cool million bucks. The mean or average income for this group is about $100,000, but the median income is $1000. Which figure do you think is the better description of what the "average" income of the group really is?

3. The Mode. The word *mode* is defined in the dictionary as "the prevailing fashion or most popular custom or style." When we are talking about distributions of scores or outcomes, "mode" means the most popular score. That is, the mode is the highest point (or points) on the curve. If the distribution has two points that are equally high, then there are two scores that are *modal,* and we can call the curve *bi-modal* (having two modes).

Skewedness

If the distribution of scores is more or less bell-shaped, then the mean, median, and mode usually come out to be the same. But not all curves do us the favor of being so regular in shape. For example, suppose you were interested in whether a particular teacher — Dr. Johnson — started and ended her classes on time. To find out, you take a very accurate watch with you all semester long and make a scientific study of Dr. Johnson's behavior. During the term, let's say, there are supposed to be 50 lectures by Dr. Johnson. So the number of possible start-time scores or outcomes will be 50. For the most part, Dr. Johnson begins on time, but occasionally she starts a minute or two early, and sometimes she's a minute or two late. Now and again, she gets to class fairly late, and once she didn't show up at all. But she *never* begins a class more than two minutes early. If you put all of her starting times on a graph, it would look something like the curve on the left. If you plotted all her closing time scores on a similar graph, it would look like the curve on the right.

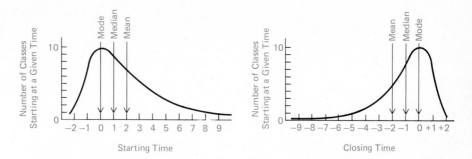

The term we use to describe such curves is *skewedness,* which means they are "slanted" or "pushed out of shape." In the starting-time example, the curve slants out far to the right-hand side, so we say that the curve is "skewed to the right." The other curve has a tail that slants out to the left, so the curve is "skewed to the left." As is the case in many distributions where the scores are measures of reaction times or beginning times, the mean, median, and mode are fairly different.

Range and Variation

There are two more important concepts we have to get out of the way before we can begin to make sense out of statistics. The first concept is the *range* of possible scores or outcomes; the second is the *variability* of the scores. The first concept is easy to understand, but the second will take some careful thought on your part.

What is the *range* of possible scores on a 10-item "fill in the blanks" test? From 0 to 10—and since you can't guess as easily on this type of test as on a true–false examination, you can't really tell ahead of time what the class average is likely to be. The range on a 100-item test would be from 0 to 100—and again, you have no way of knowing before you take the test what the "mean" or average score is likely to be. Let's suppose that you took a 10-item "fill in the blanks" examination and got a score of 8 right, which also turned out to be the mean or average score for the whole class. Then you took a 100-item "fill in the blanks" test and again you got a score of 8, which again turned out to be the class average. What does knowing the *range* of possible scores tell you about the level of difficulty of the two tests? Wouldn't you say that the 100-item test was considerably more difficult, even though the class average was the same on both tests?

Now, let's add one more dimension. Suppose that on the 10-item examination, *everybody in class* got a score of 8! There would be no *variation* at all in these scores, since none of the scores *deviated* (were different from) the mean. But suppose on the 100-item "fill in the blank" exam, about 95 percent of the class got scores of flat zero, you got an 8, and very few "aces" got scores above 85. Your score of 8 would still be the *mean* (but not the median or mode).

But the *deviation* of the rest of the scores would be tremendous. Even though you scored right at the mean on both tests, the fact that you were better than 95 percent of the class on the 100-item test might well be very pleasing to you.

The variation or variability of test scores is a very important item to know if you're going to evaluate how you perform in relation to anybody else who's taken the test.

The Standard Deviation

Statisticians have developed a "handy little gadget" that lets us measure variability of scores rather easily. The device (or gadget) is called the *standard deviation*. If you ever have to figure out the standard deviation of a distribution of scores, you'll find the mathematics involved fairly simple. But you don't need to know a thing about math in order to understand the concept itself.

Suppose we gave an IQ test to all the 16-year-olds in the U.S. and then plotted their scores on a graph. Since IQ tests are made to give a "normal distribution of scores" or bell-shaped curve, the results would look something like this:

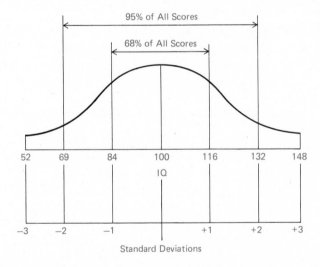

The mean, median, and mode of the distribution would be almost exactly 100 (if the test were built to yield those results, as most are). Furthermore, about 68 percent of all the scores would fall between 84 and 116. Which is to say that about one-third of the people would earn scores (101–116) that *deviated* slightly above the mean (100), while another one-third of the people would earn scores (84–99) that *deviated* slightly below the mean (100).

For very sound mathematical reasons, statisticians have decided that scores which fall between 84 and 116 are *within one standard deviation of the mean*. Since a score of 84 is *exactly* one standard deviation below the mean of 100, and 116 is *exactly* one standard deviation above the mean, you can see immediately that the *standard deviation* on this particular IQ test would be 16 IQ points.

Before you get too bored with this whole business, let's try to give the concept of the standard deviation some real-life meaning.

On any test or exam that you take,

1. If your performance on any measure is within one standard deviation of the mean or midpoint, you are technically considered perfectly normal.
2. If your performance on any measure is between one and two standard deviations from the mean, you have deviated somewhat from the average.
3. If your performance on any measure is more than two standard deviations from the norm, you are behaving differently from about 98 percent of the population. Therefore, your performance should be considered *significantly* abnormal. You may score higher than the rest of the people, or below the rest (if we're measuring things like income or IQ). But surely you are *measurably* different from the rest of the crowd.

If you don't understand all the mathematical complexities underlying the mean, median, mode, range, and standard deviation the first time you read about these terms, don't let it worry you. For our present purposes, it is much more important that you realize that you've been using these *concepts* all of your life. For instance, have you ever called somebody a "dumbbell" or an "idiot"? If so, you obviously have a notion of what an average IQ is, and you are implying that the "dummy" in question is more than two standard deviations below the norm. Have you ever laughed at some acquaintance for being a "kook" or a "nut"? Then you must have consciously or unconsciously determined what normal behavior is, drawn a mental bell-shaped curve representing normality, and placed the person at the extreme bottom-end of the distribution.

We make judgments about people all the time, and probably always will. Usually these judgments are based on values that we believe (or have been taught) are cultural norms or "means." As we learn more about people, our perceptions of them tend to change. Perhaps the major differences between your judgments and those a trained psychologist would make are as follows: The psychologist realizes that norms and values are arbitrary and may vary greatly from culture to culture. The psychologist tries to get exact measurements of deviations from norms rather than making rough guesses. The psychologist tends to use neutral descriptive terms such as "two standard deviations from the mean" rather than "kook" or "nut." Last but surely not least, the psychologist measures abnormality in terms of standard deviations from the actual or *measured* midpoint of the distribution of scores or outcomes or possible behaviors.

This last point is particularly important. I have a good friend who is so conservative politically that he thinks the Republican party is positively filled with radical, left-winger liberals. The Democrats—all of them!—are even worse. But this man believes that his political opinions are at the absolute midpoint (mean, median, *and* mode) of the distribution of opinions in the United States. He thus *perceives* himself (and a *very* few of his friends) as "representing the majority opinion" in the U.S. In fact, he *sees* almost everybody as being "politically abnormal," or three or four standard deviations away from his "perceived midpoint." I long ago stopped arguing with him, since he rejects any data or measurements which might suggest *he* is the abnormal one.

Before you stick an "abnormal" label on some person you know or hear about, wouldn't it be wise to make sure that you know exactly what the *measurable* mean, median, mode, and standard deviation are of the trait or behavior that led you to assume the person abnormal?

INFERENTIAL STATISTICS

If all that statistics were good for was to describe distributions of scores or outcomes, then stat would surely have a place in the psychological world. But we probably wouldn't mention it much in an introductory text such as this one. As we have already seen, however, statistics have yet another use — to help us make decisions about things.

Technically speaking, there are two kinds of statistics — *descriptive statistics* and *inferential statistics*. Those mathematical techniques (such as the mean and the standard deviation) which help us describe things are called descriptive statistics. Those mathematical techniques which help us make judgments, inferences, or guesses about things are called inferential. The inferential statistics are a bit more difficult to handle mathematically, but they are really a great deal more fun and more useful than are descriptive statistics.

Surprise!

My garage has five ceiling lights in it, so when I flip the light switch in the garage, the whole place really lights up as if it were high noon. At least, most of the time that's what happens. Unfortunately, the garage lights are on the same electrical circuit as my air-conditioning and heating system. And, sometimes, when it's very hot or very cold, the furnace or cooling system uses too much current and blows a fuse. So about three or four times a year, when I walk into the darkness of the garage and flip the switch, *absolutely nothing happens*. Except that I get a kind of sudden psychological shock.

Why should I be surprised when the lights don't go on? Well, I must flip that light switch three or four hundred times a year, and it works at least 99 percent of the time. Therefore, I expect that turning on the switch will always turn on the lights. If the switch worked only 50 percent of the time, I might be annoyed if it didn't work, but I certainly wouldn't be very surprised.

Much of inferential statistics is based on the element of surprise. If you took a 10-item true–false test in Chinese, and you got all 10 answers right, surely you'd be surprised. (Now that you know such an outcome would occur by chance only 1 time in 1024, perhaps you'd be even more surprised.) But think about it for a moment. If there were 1024 people in your class, none of whom spoke Chinese, and they all guessed randomly at the answers on the exam, wouldn't you expect that one person or so in the class would get a perfect score, another would get a flat zero, while about 256 would get exactly five items right and five items wrong?

Quite true. But if there were only two of you in the class, and one of you got all 10 right and the other person got all 10 wrong, you would have reason to be very surprised indeed—and perhaps even a little suspicious.

Generally speaking, scientists are surprised when the results of any study they run seem to violate what we might call "normal probabilities," or normal expectancies. But what do we mean by *normal*?

Back to our good friend, the standard deviation. On a 10-item true–false test, where you must guess at the answers, the average or mean number of correct items is 5. The standard deviation is about 1.1 items. Therefore, about two-thirds of the time, your "chance" score on such a test should be 4, 5, or 6 items right—because these are the scores that lie within one standard deviation of the mean.

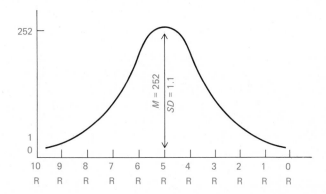

If you got seven items correct, you might be fairly surprised. A score of seven right is about two standard deviations above the mean and would occur by chance alone (if you were guessing at the answers) about 5 times in 100. A score of 10 right, of course, is more than four standard deviations above the mean and occurs less than one time in 1000. One time in 1000 is a very, very surprising outcome indeed.

But how surprised would you have to be in order to suspect that maybe something other than the laws of chance was affecting your results?

Over the years, scientists have learned that whenever they obtain results that should occur "by chance alone" about 5 percent of the time, then the scientists have a right to be mildly surprised. Psychologists write this as $p = .05$ (where p is probability). If their results should occur "by chance alone" less than 1 percent of the time, $(p = .01)$ then the scientists believe they have a right to be very surprised. And if their findings would occur by chance only one time in 1000 or more $(p = .001)$, then the scientists are usually very, very surprised (and often very, very pleased).

A score (or experimental result) that is two standard deviations above or below the mean is one that would happen "by chance alone" about 5 percent of the time. Therefore, scientists usually say that such a result or outcome is surprisingly (or *significantly*) different from their usual expectations. (When psychologists say that their results were "significant at the 5-percent level," they're merely saying that these results should occur by chance alone about 5 percent of the time— $p = .05$.)

A score (or experimental result) that is three or more standard deviations above or below the mean is one that would happen "by chance alone" about 1 percent of the time, or less. Therefore, scientists usually report that such a result is very surprisingly (or *very significantly*) different from their usual expectations. (When psychologists say that their results were "significant at the 1-percent level," they're really saying that these results should occur by chance alone less than 1 percent of the time.)

Significant Differences

The two major reasons we use statistics are to help us describe things accurately, and to help us draw inferences or conclusions that are meaningful and that will stand the test of time. Thus, when we talk about the relationship between "surprising" outcomes and standard deviations, we're really asking a very important question: Can we infer from the statistics we use that a given outcome or score is *significantly different* from that which we might have expected?

To phrase the matter a little differently, by understanding and using standard deviations (and other statistical techniques), we can often answer the important question: When does a difference *make* a difference?

Suppose you saw an ad on TV claiming that Brand X aspirin "had been proved scientifically to give people faster relief than Brand Y aspirin." The sponsor of the ad is obviously contending that Brand X is *significantly* superior to (or different from) Brand Y. But what are the data?

In many such experiments, people who have headaches are given one brand or another of aspirin and asked to tell the experimenter when they "get relief." The experimenter then records the amount of time it took for each subject to report that she or he had "gotten relief."

Suppose that you ran such an experiment, and when you added up the data, you found the following results: The average "relief time" for the 100 subjects who took Brand X was 19.00 minutes, while the average "relief time" for the 100 subjects who took Brand Y was 19.01 minutes. Would you be surprised at this "difference" between the two groups? Would you be willing to bet that Brand X *really* "gives people faster relief than Brand Y"? To make the matter clearer, if Brand X aspirin cost 10 times as much as Brand Y, which brand would you buy?

(You might also note another important fact: When you run a scientific study, *your statistics are never better than your experimental design.* There are dozens of different ways to "fudge" an experiment so that the results will turn out the way you want them to. In the aspirin study, for example, what sorts of things could you do to make sure that Brand X looked better than Brand Y? For example, could you select different sorts of people to take Brand X than take Brand Y? Would it matter how large the two types of aspirin tablets were, or what color or shape they were? Would it matter what you told the two groups of subjects, how much you smiled at them, or whether you knew which pill was Brand X and which was Brand Y? Generally speaking, unless your experimental design is clean and unbiased, your statistics are going to be meaningless no matter how large or "surprising" the differences among your groups turn out to be.)

Now let us suppose that you are hired to test the effectiveness of two types of therapy in curing acutely depressed patients in a mental hospital. Type-A therapy involves giving the patient a newly discovered antidepressant drug. Type-B therapy involves using a relearning technique similar to the one Martin Seligman used when he was studying "learned helplessness" (see Chapter 11). Let us further assume that you will measure "effectiveness" by having a number of highly trained psychologists interview the patients before and after treatment. These psychologists will report whatever changes they see in the patients in terms of a "scale score." The "improvement scale" they will use looks as follows:

0	1	2	3	4	5	6	7	8	9	10
Very Much Worse		Somewhat Worse			No Change		Somewhat Improved			Very much Improved

Thus, at the end of the study, each patient will have a "number" assigned by the psychologists. This number — from 0 to 10 — will tell how much improvement the psychologists have noticed in this particular patient.

Now, how many groups of subjects would you want to use? Well, obviously you would want at least two groups — patients who get the pill, and patients who get the relearning therapy. But wouldn't you want an untreated control group? How else would you know what changes you might expect in these patients if they hadn't received any therapy at all?

You might even consider a fourth group — patients that are given *both* the new drug (Type-A therapy) *and* the relearning treatment (Type-B therapy). Since there is no reason to suspect that the two types of therapy might work against each other, the use of a "combined" or AB-therapy group might give you most intriguing results.

Next, you randomly assign 100 patients to each of the four groups, and you make certain that the psychologists doing the interviewing don't know which patient has received which type of treatment. At the end of three months, you get the final evaluations from the psychologists and add up the data.

The results for the untreated control subjects look like this:

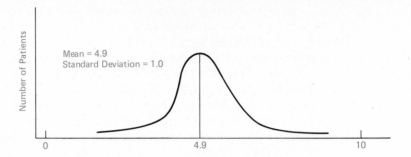

The results for the Type-A (drug) treatment group look like this:

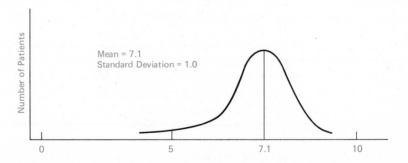

The results for the Type-B (relearning) treatment group look like this:

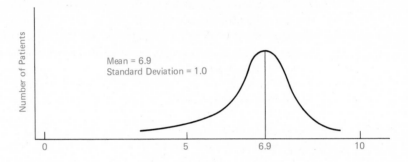

The results for the Combined AB-treatment group look like this:

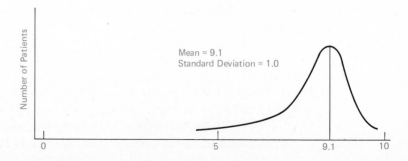

Now, what inferences or conclusions can you draw about the effectiveness of the various types of treatment?

The answer is "none"—until you make use of some statistical tools. The mean "improvement scale score" for the untreated control group patients was 4.9, while the standard deviation for this group was 1.0. These patients didn't get better, but really didn't get much worse.

The mean for the Type-A (drug) group is 6.9, and the standard deviation is 1.0. Since 6.9 is two standard deviations above the mean for the untreated control subjects, you are "surprised." The odds of this result's happening "by chance alone" are about 1 in 20, so you may conclude with some confidence that the drug treatment is *significantly* superior to no treatment at all.

The mean for the Type-B (relearning) group is 7.1, and the standard deviation is 1.0. Since 7.1 is slightly more than two standard deviations above the mean for the untreated control subjects, you are again "surprised." The odds of this result's occurring "by chance alone" are again about 1 in 20, so you may conclude with some confidence that the relearning therapy is *significantly* superior to no treatment at all.

You note with interest that the mean for the Type-B group is 0.2 scale units higher than the mean for the Type-A group. But does this difference *make* a difference? No, not as far as the data you gathered are concerned. Perhaps if you had used several other measures of improvement, you might have gotten different results. But since the differences you actually found between the mean scores for the two groups is much less than one standard deviation, the rules of science suggest that this difference probably occurred "by chance alone." Thus, you are forced to conclude that there was not a meaningful or *significant difference* between these two groups.

But what about the combined AB group? Their mean improvement score is 9.1, which is more than four standard deviations better than the untreated control group patients, and at least two standard deviations better than either the Type-A or the Type-B patients. Therefore, you may conclude that "combined" treatment is *very significantly* better than no treatment at all, since such a result would occur by chance less than one time in 1000. You may also conclude that "combined" treatment is *significantly* better than either the drug or the relearning therapy given by itself, since the odds are 1 in 20 that these differences would occur by chance alone.

To put the matter in more realistic terms, if a very good friend of yours were hospitalized for acute depression, what type of treatment would you suggest—based on the assumption that you (or someone else) had really run such an experiment?

Correlations

There are many different types of statistical tests, most of which you probably would encounter only if you took graduate work in psychology (or some other science). Should you ever need to read up on the subject, you might wish to look at William L. Hays's *Statistics for the Social Sciences*, the second edition of which was published by Holt, Rinehart and Winston in 1973.

There is one type of statistical test that everybody uses every day, however, that we haven't yet mentioned directly. Remember the law of association (see Chapter 6)? Briefly stated, the law of association says that whenever two events or stimulus inputs occur or appear closely together, we tend to form an association between the two. If, on several occasions, we ring a bell and then give a dog food, the dog will begin to salivate as soon as we ring the bell (before we give it food). Why does the dog salivate to the sound of the bell? Because the ringing of the bell and the presentation of the food become *correlated* or associated in its mind.

The word *correlation* simply means "connection" or "association." As an example of the sort of correlation you are likely to encounter in most schools, there is a very close connection or *correlation* between IQ test scores and grade-point averages. Thus, if we give an intelligence test to all incoming freshmen at a particular college, and we determine their grades at the end of their first collegiate year, we would expect to find a relationship something like the following between these two measures:

	Entrance Test IQ Score	Grade-Point Average (GPA)
Ann	152	3.91
Bill	145	3.46
Carol	133	2.77
Dick	128	2.35
Elmer	112	1.51
Mean	134	2.80
SD	15.54	0.94

We can find out how strong the relationship or correlation is in a number of different ways. One of the easiest is to assign "ranks" to each of the sets of scores. For instance, in the table above, Ann is Number 1 in both IQ score and GPA, Bill is Number 2, Carol is 3, Dick 4, and Elmer is 5 in both measures. The *correlation* between the two sets of scores is thus nearly perfect.

If we plotted these data on what is called a *scatter diagram,* we'd get pretty much a straight line. (A scatter diagram shows how the scores for each subject are *scattered,* or distributed, across the graph or diagram.)

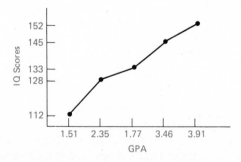

If we reversed the scores, so that Ann got an IQ score of 152 but a GPA of

1.51, Bill got an IQ score of 145 and a GPA of 2.35, and so forth, we'd get a scatter diagram that looked like this:

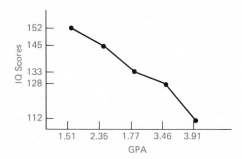

Generally speaking, the closer the scatter diagram comes to being a straight line tilted to the right or left — as these are — the higher the correlation between the two scores or measures.

Correlations run from -1 to $+1$. A correlation of $+1$ means that the two events or tests are perfectly correlated in a positive way. The scores plotted in the first scatter diagram above have a correlation of about $+0.99$, which means that they are almost perfectly correlated. Thus, if I told you that a student named Martin had an entrance test IQ score of 148, wouldn't you be willing to bet that Martin's GPA at the end of the first year would be between 3.46 and 3.91?

The scores plotted in the second scatter diagram have a correlation of about -0.99, which means that they are almost perfectly correlated too — in a *negative* way. That is, the students with *high* IQ scores tend to get very *low* GPAs, and the students with *low* IQ scores tend to get very *high* GPAs. Now, if I told you that Martin had a GPA of 2.02, wouldn't you be willing to bet that Martin's IQ score was between 145 and 152?

If two sets of scores or measures are unrelated (such as length of hair and IQ score), the correlation will be at or near zero.

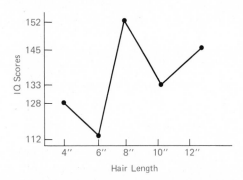

Correlations are important because they allow us to predict one set of scores if we know a second set of scores, provided that the two sets of scores are highly correlated (either positively or negatively).

(As it happens, IQ scores and GPAs *are* highly and positively correlated, for a very simple reason. IQ tests are *designed* so that IQ scores will correlate positively with GPAs! If a particular IQ test yields scores that don't correlate strongly with GPAs, the makers of the test usually rework the test until the two sets of scores do correlate positively!)

Uses and Abuses of Correlations

The ability to make quick correlations or associations is one of the most useful traits that your mind has available to it. Correlations allow you to profit from experience, because correlations allow you to predict (and adapt to) what may happen to you in the future. If one of your teachers gives you a "pop quiz" the first three Mondays of a semester — but never gives an unexpected exam on any other day of the week, don't you think you'd be likely to do some studying before the fourth Monday rolled around?

But there is a dark and dangerous side to correlations. The mere fact that two events or inputs are correlated doesn't mean that one event *causes* the other! No matter what Pavlov's dog might have thought, the bell doesn't *cause* the food to appear. (Pavlov caused both the bell to ring and the food to appear.) A lot of students with very high GPAs don't study very much, while many students with lower GPAs have to study frantically just to survive. So there might be a strong *negative* correlation between good grades and the amount of time a student studied. But does lack of studying *cause* students to get good grades?

At their very best, correlations can not only help us predict future stimulus inputs, but also give us clues as to what the underlying causal connections among these inputs or events might be. However, in daily life we too often misuse correlations. If you want to make your psychology teacher very happy indeed, say "Correlations don't determine causes" over and over again — until you're conditioned like Pavlov's dog to believe it!

CHOICE OR CHANCE?

To summarize, statistics simply give you a more precise and accurate way of doing the same things you've always been doing. You don't have to be a whiz-bang mathematician to comprehend statistics. Joan hated and feared stat so much that she changed her major to avoid taking statistics. And yet, she used statistics cleverly but intuitively every time she played bridge. And all the time she was whomping Gersh and me at the bridge table, I said a small prayer of thanks that she hadn't bothered to learn how easy stat really is. Had she done so, she would probably have played cards even better than she actually did.

Many students like Joan probably hate statistics because they believe that "people aren't numbers, and you can't measure the important things in life mathematically." Well, people aren't *just* numbers, that's true. It's likewise true that we can't yet and maybe never will be able to measure everything about human experience as precisely as psychologists might wish. But it's also a fact that everything you do—all your behaviors and most of your thoughts—can be measured and numbered. Your brain "guesses" at these numbers every time you move a muscle or think a thought.

So—you have a choice. You can either shy away from statistics—and from looking at yourself and other people as objectively as possible when the occasional demands it. You'll still do okay in life, if you work hard. You can still win bridge games or drive safely, but you'll be as handicapped as someone who puts a blindfold on his or her eyes much of the time. In brief, you can leave things to chance if you are willing to pay the price.

Or you can learn as much about statistics as seems sensible to you, as much about stat as interests you. In which case, you'll find life a little easier, and you'll discover that your own behavior and that of the people around you makes more sense and is much easier to understand. You'll probably get farther in life, win more battles, work more efficiently, achieve more of your own goals, and not have to be a slave to your own emotions and intuitions.

The choice is up to you.

As for me, I've been studying probabilities a lot lately, and so has Gersh. After we study just a little bit more, we're going back to the student union to see if we can't arrange a return match at the bridge table with Joan and Carol!

REFERENCES

Chapter 1   Kinsey, A. C., C. E. Martin, and W. B. Pomeroy. *Sexual behavior in the human male.* Philadelphia: Saunders, 1948.

Kinsey, A. C., W. B. Pomeroy, C. E. Martin, and R. H. Gebhard. *Sexual behavior in the human female.* Philadelphia: Saunders, 1953.

Chapter 2   Azrin, N. H., R. R. Hutchinson, and R. McLaughlin. "The opportunity for aggression as an operant reinforcer during aversive stimulation," *Journal of Experimental Analysis of Behavior,* 1965, *7,* 223–227.

Lorenz, K. Der Kumpan in der Umwelt des Vogels. *Jour. Ornith.,* 1935, *83,* 137–213, 324–331.

Lorenz, K. Vergleichende Verhaltensforschung. *Zool. Anz. Suppl.,* 1939, *12,* 69–102.

Sperry, R. W., "Left-brain, right brain." *Saturday Review,* August 9, 1975, 30–33.

Chapter 3   Gibson, E. J. and R. D. Walk. The "visual cliff." *Scientific American,* 1960, *202,* 67–71.

Heron, W., W. H. Bexton, and D. O. Hebb. "Cognitive effects of a decreased variation in the sensory environment." *American Psychologist, 8,* 366 (abstract), 1953.

Magoun, H. W. The waking brain (2d ed). 2/e Springfield, Ill.: Charles C Thomas, 1963.

Chapter 4   Heber, Rick. Cited in R. J. Trotter, "The Milwaukee Project." *APA Monitor,* Sept., 1976.

Hess, E. H. "Shadows and depth perception." *Scientific American,* 1961, *204,* 138–148.

McGinnies, E. "Emotionality and perceptual defense." *Psychological Review,* 1949, *56,* 244–251.

Skeels, H. M. "Adult status of children with contrasting earlylife experiences." *Monographs of the Society for Research in Child Development,* 1966, *31*(3), 1–65.

Chapter 5   McClelland, D. C. "Testing for competence rather than for 'intelligence.'" *American Psychologist,* 1973, *28,* 1–14.

Maslow, A. H. Motivation and personality (2d ed.). New York: Harper & Row, 1970.

Udry, J. R. and N. M. Morris. "Distribution of coitus in the menstrual cycle." *Nature,* 1968, *220,* 593–596.

Wolpe, J. *The practice of behavior therapy.* New York: Pergamon Press, 1969.

Chapter 6   Pavlov, I. P. *Conditioned reflexes.* New York: Oxford University Press, 1927.

Stuart, Richard B. Cited in R. J. Trotter, "Obesity and behavior." *Science News, 76,* Aug. 3, 1974.

Watson, J. B. and R. Rayner. "Conditioned emotional reaction." *Journal of Experimental Psychology,* 1920, *3,* 1–14.

Chapter 7   Piaget, J. *The origins of intelligence in children.* New York: International Universities Press, 1952.

REFERENCES

Chapter 8

Terman, L. M. *The measurement of intelligence.* Boston: Houghton Mifflin, 1916.
Zajonc, R. B. "Family configuration and intelligence." *Science,* 1976, *192* (4236), 227–235.

Chapter 9

Bandura, A., E. B. Blanchard, and B. Ritter. "The relative efficacy of desensitization and modeling approaches for inducing behavioral, affective, and attitudinal changes." *Journal of Personality and Social Psychology,* 1969, *13,* 173–199.

Chapter 10

Hartshorne, H. and M. A. May. *Studies in the nature of character.* Vols. I–III. New York: Macmillan, 1928–1930.
Kretschmer, E. Cited in Robert N. Goldenson, *Encyclopedia of human behavior.* Garden City, N.Y.: Doubleday, 1970.
McKinley and Hathaway. Cited in R. J. Trotter, "Psychological Testing." *Science News,* 189, Sept. 16, 1972.
Maslow, A. H. *Toward a psychology of being.* New York: Van Nostrand Reinhold, 1962.
Murray, H. Cited in Robert N. Goldenson, *Encyclopedia of human behavior.* Garden City, N.Y.: Doubleday, 1970.
Rorschach, H. *Psychodiagnostics.* Berne, Switzerland: Hans Huber, 1942.
Sheldon, W. H. *The varieties of temperament.* New York: Harper & Row, 1942.

Chapter 11

Asch, S. E. "Effects of group pressure upon modification and distortion of judgments." In E. E. Maccoby, T. M. Newcomb, and E. L. Hartley (Eds.), *Readings in social psychology* (3d ed.). New York: Holt, Rinehart and Winston, 1958.
Miller, N. E. and L. V. Di Cara. *Instrumental training of visceral functions.* Mental Health Program Reports, No. 6 (DHEW), Publication No. (HSM) 73-9139. Chevy Chase, Md.: National Institute of Mental Health, 1973.
Richter, C. P. "On the phenomenon of sudden death in animals and man." *Psychosomatic Medicine,* 1957, *19,* 191–198.
Rogers, C. Cited in Robert N. Goldenson, *Encyclopedia of human behavior.* Garden City, N.Y.: Doubleday, 1970.
Seligman, M. E. P. "Depression and learned helplessness." In R. J. Friedman and M. M. Katz (Eds.), *The psychology of depression: Contemporary theory and research.* Washington, D.C.: V. H. Winston, 1974.

Chapter 12

Rosenhan, D. L. "On being sane in insane places." *Science,* 1973, *179,* 250–258.

Chapter 13

Eysenck, H. J. *Psychology is about people.* London: Allen Lane, Penguin Press, 1972.
Heath, R. B. "Electrical self-stimulation of the brain in man." *The American Journal of Psychiatry,* 1963, *120*(6), 571–577.
Moreno, J. L. Cited in Robert N. Goldenson, *Encyclopedia of human behavior.* Garden City, N.Y.: Doubleday, 1970.

Chapter 14

Bales, R. F. *Personality and interpersonal behavior.* New York: Holt, Rinehart and Winston, 1960.

REFERENCES

Calhoun, J. B. How the social organization of animal communities can lead to a population crisis which destroys them. Reported by M. Pines, Mental Health Program Reports, No. 5 (DHEW), Publication No. (HSM) 72-9040. Chevy Chase, Md.: National Institute of Mental Health, Ced. 1971.

Harlow, H. F. *Learning to love.* San Francisco: Albion, 1971.

Sommer, R. *Personal space: The behavioral basis of design.* Englewood Cliffs, N.J.: Prentice-Hall, 1969.

Turnbull, C. M. Some observations regarding the experiences and behavior of the Ba Mbuti pygmies. *American Journal of Psychology,* 1961, *74,* 304–308.

Chapter 15

Adorno, T. W., E. Frenkel-Brunswick, D. J. Levinson, and R. N. Sanford. *The authoritarian personality.* New York: Harper & Row, 1950.

Helson, H. Adaptation level theory. In S. Koch (Ed.), *Psychology: A study of a science.* Vol. 1. New York: McGraw-Hill, 1959.

Helson, H. *Adaptation-level theory.* New York: Harper & Row, 1964.

Janis, I. L. and S. Feshbach. *"Effects of fear-arousing communications."* Journal of Abnormal and Social Psychology, 1953, *48,* 78–92.

Milgram, S. "Behavioral study of obedience." *Journal of Abnormal and Social Psychology,* 1963, *67,* 371–378.

Newcomb, T. M. "Attitude development as a function of reference groups: The Bennington study." In H. Proshansky and B. Seidenberg (Eds.), *Basic studies in social psychology.* New York: Holt, Rinehart and Winston, 1965.

Chapter 16

Aronson, E. *The social animal.* San Francisco: Freeman, 1972.

Biller and Meredith. *Father power.* New York: David McKay, 1974.

Byrne, D. *The attraction paradigm.* New York: Academic Press, 1971.

Byrne, D. "Attitudes and attraction." In L. Berkowitz (Ed.), *Advances in experimental social psychology.* Vol. 4. New York: Academic Press, 1969.

Exline, R. V. and L. Winters. "Affective relations and mutual glances in dyads." In S. Tomkins and C. Izard (Eds.), *Affect, cognition, and personality.* New York: Springer, 1965.

Festinger, L. *A theory of cognitive dissonance.* Stanford, Ca.: Stanford University Press, 1957.

Harlow, H. F. and R. R. Zimmerman. "The development of affectional responses in infant monkeys." *Proceedings of the American Philosophical Society,* 1958, *102,* 501–509.

Hess, E. H. "Pupillometrics: A method of studying mental, emotional and sonsory processes." In N. E. Greenfield & R. A. Steinbach (Eds.), *Handbook of psychophysiology.* New York: Holt, Rinehart and Winston, 1972.

Jones, E. E. and V. A. Harris. "The attribution of attitudes." *Journal of Experimental Social Psychology.* 1967, *3,* 1–24.

Kelley, H. H. "The warm-cold variable in the first impressions of persons." *Journal of Personality,* 1950, *18,* 431–439.

Chapter 17

Smith, M. *New Scientist,* October 10, 1975.

NAME INDEX

NAME INDEX

SUBJECT INDEX

---

* Boldface numbers indicate pages on which the definition of the term may be found.

ANSWER KEY

CHAPTER ONE

A. Recall

1. 3000
2. actions, or behaviors; mind
3. objective
4. astrology
5. explain
6. soul
7. measure
8. consciousness, or the mind
9. empiricism
10. hypothesis
11. recognize and/or define
12. Wundt
13. functionalism
14. mental matter
15. introspection
16. adaptive
17. behaviorism; John B. Watson
18. more than
19. perception
20. psychoanalysis
21. cognitive
22. eclectic
23. surveys; questionnaires
24. sexual practices
25. naturalistic observation
26. right/wrong
27. control
28. dependent
29. blind
30. engineering

B. Review

1. A
2. B
3. D
4. D
5. D
6. A
7. B
8. C
9. A
10. D

CHAPTER TWO

A. Recall

1. learned
2. nature–nurture
3. survive
4. 1859
5. internal processes
6. natural selection
7. reflexes
8. instinct
9. ethology
10. imprinting
11. innate releasing mechanism
12. neuron
13. dendrite(s); cell body; axon(s)
14. nerve net
15. 3000; 10,000,000,000
16. brainstem
17. cerebrum, or cortex
18. left
19. left
20. left
21. corpus callosum
22. electroencephalogram, or EEG
23. mirror focus
24. internal, or mutual
25. past; future
26. cortex
27. innate releasing mechanism
28. pain; frustration
29. Tasaday

B. Review		
	1. C	6. C
	2. D	7. D
	3. A	8. C
	4. B	9. A
	5. B	10. B

C. News Story

1. Although originally very quiet, he became very emotional, irreverent, profane, and stubborn.
2. Just before answering a question, a brief glance to the left indicates activity of the right hemisphere of the brain, and a quick glance to the right is associated with "right brain" activity.
3. The most important function is language and verbal behavior. Nonemotional questions are also processed in the left hemisphere.

CHAPTER THREE

A. Recall

1. drugs
2. McGill
3. hallucinates
4. sensory inputs
5. reticular activating system
6. coma
7. deprivation
8. reflexes
9. taste; smell
10. taste buds
11. sweet, sour, bitter, salt
12. skin
13. nerve; conduction
14. cornea; retina
15. rods; cones
16. fovea
17. rods
18. Vitamin A
19. inherited; men
20. stereoscopic
21. visual cliff
22. EEG
23. REM
24. cigarettes, coffee, alcohol
25. neurotransmitters
26. depressant
27. uppers, or stimulants
28. barbiturates, sleeping pills, tranquilizers
29. analgesics
30. hallucinogens
31. marijuana
32. THC

B. Review		
	1. A	6. C
	2. D	7. D
	3. B	8. A
	4. C	9. C
	5. B	10. B

C. News Story

1. Probably much more like the Leboyer method — more quiet, darker, and basically "natural," although, no doubt, more physically dangerous.
2. While doing everything to protect the health and safety of both mother and child, make the process as "natural," quiet, and protective of the newborn's senses as possible.
3. Yes, children born with this method seem to have an accelerated rate of physical

development—walking, using their hands, toilet-training, feeding themselves, and the like.

CHAPTER FOUR

A. Recall

1. brain
2. coded messages
3. Perception
4. senses
5. constant
6. Input overload
7. reticular activating system
8. limited
9. adaptation
10. changes
11. personal interests
12. McGinnis
13. overestimated
14. past experience
15. colors; figures from backgrounds
16. unusual
17. orphans
18. familiar
19. blind spot
20. illusion
21. blind spots
22. test

B. Review

1. D	6. A
2. A	7. B
3. A	8. D
4. C	9. B
5. B	10. B

C. News Story

1. S. B.'s darkened corneas, which did not allow light to pass into the eye, were surgically replaced with healthy ones.
2. No, although there was considerable, obvious benefit, he now saw a good deal of the real ugliness that exists, which he really had not experienced before.

CHAPTER FIVE

A. Recall

1. Holland
2. move
3. inner force, or spirit
4. drive
5. primary
6. drive
7. drive state
8. homeostasis
9. secondary
10. learned, or acquired
11. primary drives
12. arousal
13. sensory deprivation
14. emotions
15. physiological
16. cognitive awareness
17. feedback
18. autonomic nervous system
19. sympathetic; parasympathetic
20. hormones
21. adrenal
22. free-floating
23. run
24. strength
25. polygraph
26. emotional reactions, or responses
27. feedback
28. emotional conditioning
29. Wolpe
30. Thematic Apperception Test (TAT)
31. Maslow; self-actualize

B. Review   1. D   6. C
                  2. C   7. C
                  3. A   8. D
                  4. B   9. B
                  5. B

C. News Story   1. The EMG, or electromyograph; happiness, sadness, anger, fear, surprise, and disgust.
2. When asked to think about a specific emotion a subject also pushes a button. *How* the button is pushed is computer analyzed and shows differences among the emotional reactions.

CHAPTER SIX

A. Recall

1. violent, antisocial, and/or sexual
2. rewards or reinforcement
3. learning
4. learn
5. association
6. classical conditioning; Pavlov
7. food; salivation
8. conditioned response
9. strength
10. conditioned; unconditioned
11. extinction
12. operant
13. B. F. Skinner
14. voluntary or emitted
15. modeling
16. reinforce
17. negative
18. decrease
19. immediately
20. feedback
21. behavior therapy
22. extinguished
23. attention
24. successive approximations
25. generalization
26. discrimination
27. overweight; husbands
28. 70

B. Review   1. C   6. B
                  2. A   7. D
                  3. C   8. C
                  4. B   9. A
                  5. B   10. C

C. News Story   1. They are thought to be beyond parental control, and it does keep them off the streets.
2. By providing immediate reinforcement (points) for appropriate behaviors that can be exchanged for meaningful rewards (privileges).
3. Yes. Not only is school attendance way up, but number of offenses committed and recidivism (return to the institution) are way down.

CHAPTER SEVEN

A. Recall

1. language; thinking; remembering
2. signs; symbols
3. symbol
4. Herodotus
5. babbling
6. action
7. linguistics
8. tool making
9. visual–gestural
10. four
11. imitate
12. innate
13. John B. Watson
14. cognitive
15. adaptation
16. assimilation; accommodation
17. sensory-motor
18. pre-operational
19. formal operations
20. sensory-information
21. five; nine
22. rehearse
23. chunking
24. mnemonics
25. long-term
26. coded, or encoded
27. associations
28. into; out of
29. eidetic imagery
30. STM; LTM
31. repression
32. RNA or protein
33. try out, or test
34. anxiety
35. mental set
36. functional fixedness

B. Review

1. B
2. A
3. D
4. D
5. B
6. A
7. C
8. C
9. A
10. B

C. News Story

1. The way we are asked about it, *and* answers we have previously given.
2. Whether or not a stop sign happened to be a part of an accident scene, if subjects are first asked a question involving a stop sign they will tend to "remember" the sign as having been there.

CHAPTER EIGHT

A. Recall

1. phonetics
2. personality, or outlook on life
3. mental
4. survive
5. behaviors
6. reaction time
7. slowly
8. mental age
9. 75
10. L. M. Terman
11. bell
12. primary mental abilities
13. genes, or inheritance
14. WAIS
15. U.S. Army
16. psychometricians
17. reliable
18. valid
19. white, middle-class
20. well; poorly, or less well
21. enzyme
22. 47
23. retardation
24. Montessori
25. 20; 30
26. nature; nurture
27. process; interaction

B. Review

1. D		6. D	
2. B		7. A	
3. B		8. B	
4. C		9. A	
5. B		10. C	

C. News Story 1. (a) Machines can be built (and programmed) to approximate intelligent behaviors and to perform tasks that humans cannot do. (b) By trying to approximate human intelligence, we find out more about what intelligence really is, e.g. teaching language to a computer may tell us a great deal about language learning in humans.

CHAPTER NINE

A. Recall

1. masturbation	12. genetic
2. biological; cognitive; social	13. autonomous morality
3. genes	14. three; two
4. oral, anal, phallic	15. twelfth; eighteenth
5. puberty	16. tabula rasa
6. Id; Ego; Superego	17. different
7. Ego	18. models
8. psychosocial; trust; mistrust	19. modeling
9. initiative; guilt	20. child-abusers
10. adolescence	21. sex roles
11. Ego integrity	22. self-actualization

B. Review

1. C		6. D	
2. A		7. A	
3. A		8. C	
4. B		9. D	
5. D		10. D	

C. News Story 1. Not a "social compulsion" but a biological, imaginative, spiritual urge.
2. For eight years she took hormone treatments (about 12,000 pills) to change body chemistry and give the outward appearance of a woman, and in 1972 had a sex-change operation in Morocco.

CHAPTER TEN

A. Recall

1. change	4. phrenology
2. unique; adapting	5. stereotype
3. type	6. Kretschmer

7. endomorph
8. seven
9. cognitive; social
10. traits
11. common
12. cardinal
13. situation, or environment
14. functions
15. libido
16. pleasure; reality
17. phallic
18. latent
19. defense mechanisms

20. regression
21. catharsis
22. psychoanalysis
23. self-actualization
24. Rogers; Maslow
25. ideal
26. Rorschach; TAT
27. projective
28. Henry Murray
29. 550; 26
30. externalizers; internalizers
31. internalizer

B. Review

1. C
2. A
3. C
4. B
5. A
6. D
7. B
8. B
9. D
10. A

C. News Story

1. It was developed as a clinical instrument used to refine diagnoses of mental illness and was constructed for persons with psychiatric histories (although it was standardized on a normal population).
2. The interpretation of the results of the test requires a qualified examiner with considerable training.
3. At best the test was originally standardized on a population of whites in Minnesota. It could be standardized again on a large black population.

CHAPTER ELEVEN

A. Recall

1. Buddha
2. perfection
3. self-actualization
4. physical; social; mental
5. externalizers
6. internalizers
7. Richter
8. experience
9. externalizer
10. feedback
11. cognitive
12. yoga
13. biofeedback
14. mirroring
15. self-image

16. conform
17. group pressures
18. two-thirds
19. conflict
20. avoidance-avoidance
21. double approach-avoidance
22. stress
23. exhaustion
24. anxiety
25. unconscious
26. coping
27. defensive
28. regression; fixation
29. defensive
30. objective analysis

B. Review
1. D   5. D
2. A   6. A
3. B   7. D
4. C   8. A

C. News Story
1. There is first a biomedical or psychosocial crisis making the patient dependent upon family care, which makes the patient feel more and more helpless. As the patient deteriorates, the family sees the situation as hopeless.
2. Part One calls for around the clock orientation to the surrounding environment with emphasis on time, place, and person. Part Two consists of 30-minute classes five times per week focusing on real, concrete objects and activities.

CHAPTER TWELVE

A. Recall
1. deaf; mute
2. sociopath, or psychopath
3. pseudopatients
4. 11; schizophrenic
5. other patients
6. norms
7. manic-depressive
8. organic
9. senile
10. general paresis
11. Wassermann
12. delerium tremens
13. tumors
14. adrenal
15. defense mechanisms
16. anxiety
17. anxiety neurosis
18. phobia
19. obsessions; compulsions
20. dissociative
21. hypochondriac
22. functional
23. hebephrenic
24. paranoid
25. affective
26. sociopaths
27. 25,000
28. bestiality; pedophilia
29. self-fulfilling
30. myth; society

B. Review
1. A   6. A
2. B   7. D
3. D   8. B
4. C   9. C
5. B   10. D

C. News Story
1. The fact that it seems to "run in families." Approximately 50 percent of identical twins both suffer from schizophrenia if one does, for example.
2. Mednick's data, for example, which reports that of 20 mentally ill children 14 had suffered serious prenatal or birth complications.
3. Of course. Our genes may provide a predisposition toward schizophrenia, but the disorder may require some action from the environment before it appears.

CHAPTER THIRTEEN

A. Recall

1. writer
2. decide
3. evil spirits
4. trephining
5. Middle Ages
6. exorcism
7. asylums
8. humanists
9. psychiatrists, or doctors
10. hundreds
11. coma
12. epileptics
13. depressed
14. lobotomy
15. irreversible
16. tranquilizers; energizers
17. placebo
18. sham
19. insight
20. free associations
21. dreams; fantasies
22. neurotic; psychotic
23. client-centered
24. Eysenck
25. milieu
26. tuberculosis
27. psychodrama
28. transactional analysis
29. gestalt
30. encounter
31. token economy
32. holistic

B. Review

1. D
2. A
3. A
4. C
5. B
6. B
7. D
8. C
9. D
10. A

C. News Story

1. 16; Sybil changed (into Peggy) during a regular session. One of her personalities (Vicky) told the psychiatrist about other personalities. Hypnosis was also very helpful.
2. Raised by a cold, aloof father and a mother who sexually abused and tortured her, Sybil unconsciously "created" another person to take the abuse and punishment in her place.

CHAPTER FOURTEEN

A. Recall

1. treason
2. selfish
3. social behavior
4. territoriality
5. aggression; competition
6. pecking orders
7. social role
8. Harlow
9. aggressive
10. peers
11. Aveyron
12. five
13. inputs; process; outputs
14. groups
15. interaction
16. informal
17. conforming
18. bystander apathy
19. survival
20. task; social–emotional
21. social–emotional
22. crowding
23. anxious

B. Review

1. C	6. D
2. B	7. A
3. D	8. A
4. B	9. B
5. D	10. C

C. News Story

1. Deaths due to heart disease, hospital admissions, juvenile delinquency, illegitimacy, divorce, infant mortality, TB, VD, prison rates, and social disintegration.
2. Arousal, stress, anxiety, and frustration.
3. Men concealed their distress, became competitive, and developed attitudes of distrust and hostility, while women tended to share their distress and formed cooperative groups.

CHAPTER FIFTEEN

A. Recall

1. socialist
2. Russia; Stalin's
3. learned, or acquired
4. ethnocentrism
5. authoritarian
6. conventional; hostile
7. powerful; punishing
8. externalizer
9. obey
10. electrical shock
11. code; ethics
12. identify
13. liberal
14. Theodore Newcomb
15. reference
16. Helson
17. stimulus; background; personality
18. vague
19. complex
20. persuasion
21. communication
22. message; audience
23. credibility
24. emotional; logical
25. attention
26. high
27. counterpropaganda
28. feedback
29. won
30. 90
31. needs
32. Bem

B. Review

1. B	6. A
2. B	7. D
3. B	8. A
4. C	9. A
5. B	10. D

C. News Story

1. Unlike conformity, it is the tendency to be more extreme, to take riskier positions in judgment; not to keep up, but to surpass.
2. Students who voted for Nixon reduced dissonance by being less likely to believe that Nixon was really and truly implicated in the goings-on. They were also less likely to believe that he should be impeached.

CHAPTER SIXTEEN

A. Recall

1. love
2. affection; respect
3. first
4. solve problems
5. reputation
6. stereotype
7. body language
8. beauty
9. attractive
10. like
11. facial
12. cheaters
13. attribution
14. altruistic
15. psychiatric patients
16. dissonance
17. rationalization
18. act, or behave
19. social roles
20. experience
21. maternal
22. 250,000
23. six
24. more
25. peers, or playmates
26. each other
27. hormones
28. similarity
29. deep

B. Review

1. A
2. D
3. A
4. C
5. D
6. C
7. C
8. A
9. B
10. B

C. News Story

1. Basically they reported a "chaotic life style" — sleeping less, and having difficulties with household tasks, some of which interfered with job performance. Many felt depressed, anxious, or apathetic after one year.
2. At first the males, but few females, expressed pleasure with the increased opportunities, but by the end of the first year, both expressed needs for intimacy and a lack of satisfaction in casual sexual encounters.
3. Parents made fewer maturity demands, communicated less well, tended to be less affectionate, showed less control, and were more inconsistent in discipline.

CHAPTER SEVENTEEN

A. Recall

1. Mars; 25
2. industrial; medical
3. future shock
4. twentieth
5. present
6. 1990
7. biofeedback
8. pleasure centers
9. heredity, or genes
10. humanistic
11. industrial
12. 35
13. 2000
14. mass communications

B. Review

1. D	5. A
2. C	6. D
3. A	7. D
4. C	